"This book is wonderfully refreshing and very inspiring. It is vital reading for any of us who have felt we are invisible, on the margins or do not comfortably belong in the academy. Reading this book assures me I am not alone in how I have experienced my academic life and it inspires me to authentically own my professional path."

Hannah Rumble, *Centre for Death and Society, University of Bath, UK*

"Academic careers have a long-lasting history with very deep roots. Over the last fifteen years, academic careers have changed immensely, and few of us have discussed these changes. That is why this is a welcomed book analyzing different sides, dimensions and contexts of academic careers. It brings a collection of very thought-provoking and inspiring chapters written by some outstanding academics. This is a must-read book for new and experienced academics. More importantly, it inspires new futures."

Rafael Alcadipani, *FGV-EAESP, Brazil*

"*Doing Academic Careers Differently* challenges linear accounts of the academic career and it rebukes the hegemonic moves that push academics into impossible, unsustainable, unhealthy conduct, values, and practices. By collaborating, theorizing, and writing differently 82 academics from 21 countries tell stories with images, poetry, prose, interviews, and essays on contemporary academic lives. The stories thrive on complexity, difference, dialogue, creativity, divergence, and ambiguity. Robinson, Bristow, and Ratle beautifully curate the emerging richness in this book that becomes an enthralling and contemplative new archive of academics' lives where finally alternative voices, knowledges, and experiences can be heard over the conformism and pain of career as individual/ individualizing competition and instrumentality. The book offers a refreshing, powerful, and life-affirming read."

Alessia Contu, *UMass Boston, USA*

"Many academics lose their sense of direction in a university environment that prioritises journal rankings and other forms of 'excellence'. It is easy to end up believing that there is only one kind of academic career – the type that is laid out by performance management systems. The enthralling stories of struggle, hope, and leap of faiths shared in this timely book demonstrate the narrowness of this perspective and offer a powerful reminder of the many different ways in which one can be an academic. *Doing Academic Careers Differently* is essential reading for anyone pursuing or considering an academic career today."

Sverre Spoelstra, *Associate Professor in Leadership and Strategy, Copenhagen Business School, Denmark*

"A courageous book that inspires, surprises, awes, and eventually heals. Creatively and thoughtfully written and curated, this book restores hope in academics despite the brute corporatization contemporary academia has subjected them to. I felt such longing to walk through such a place as I read through this beautiful manuscript."

Ghazal M. Zulfiqar, *Lahore University of Management Sciences, Pakistan*

"The most creative inspiring enjoyable exhilarating academic work of art on academia I have ever come across. These playful, sardonic, ironic and heartful stories are in a garden of delights that will provide a wonderful learning experience as well as a rigorous piece of research."

Damian Ruth, *Massey Business School, New Zealand*

DOING ACADEMIC CAREERS DIFFERENTLY

Should academic careers always unfold in exactly the same way? Is there one best way of being an academic? This book says no. Assumptions about who academics are and what they should do are becoming increasingly narrow and focused on achieving so-called 'excellence' in teaching and research above anything else. This book problematises this and explores the scope for doing academic careers differently.

Authors paint individual or group portraits of their academic careers, working with metaphors which challenge the dominant discourses of how academic careers should be led. From rejecting the pressure to focus on 'one big thing', to prioritising nurture and care, transcending disciplinary boundaries, reshaping own daily practice, connecting with communities, and being academics outside academia, the chapters in this book offer those considering, starting, or developing an academic career a treasure trove of many alternative possibilities.

Presented as a portrait gallery through which readers are encouraged to meander at will, this compilation of insights into alternative academic lives will help to inspire and encourage current academics to re-think and take ownership of their careers in their own terms, according to their own strengths, weaknesses, and circumstances.

Sarah Robinson is Professor of Management and Organisation Studies at Rennes School of Business, France.

Alexandra Bristow is Senior Lecturer in Organisational Behaviour at the Open University, UK.

Olivier Ratle is Senior Lecturer in Organisation Studies at the University of the West of England, UK.

DOING ACADEMIC CAREERS DIFFERENTLY

Portraits of Academic Life

Edited by
Sarah Robinson, Alexandra Bristow, and Olivier Ratle

LONDON AND NEW YORK

Designed cover image: © Getty Images / syolacan

First published 2024
by Routledge
4 Park Square, Milton Park, Abingdon, Oxon OX14 4RN

and by Routledge
605 Third Avenue, New York, NY 10158

Routledge is an imprint of the Taylor & Francis Group, an informa business

© 2024 selection and editorial matter, Sarah Robinson, Alexandra Bristow, and Olivier Ratle; individual chapters, the contributors

The right of Sarah Robinson, Alexandra Bristow, and Olivier Ratle to be identified as the authors of the editorial material, and of the authors for their individual chapters, has been asserted in accordance with sections 77 and 78 of the Copyright, Designs and Patents Act 1988.

All rights reserved. No part of this book may be reprinted or reproduced or utilised in any form or by any electronic, mechanical, or other means, now known or hereafter invented, including photocopying and recording, or in any information storage or retrieval system, without permission in writing from the publishers.

Trademark notice: Product or corporate names may be trademarks or registered trademarks, and are used only for identification and explanation without intent to infringe.

British Library Cataloguing-in-Publication Data
A catalogue record for this book is available from the British Library

Library of Congress Cataloging-in-Publication Data
Names: Robinson, Sarah, 1964– editor. | Bristow, Alexandra, 1979– editor. | Ratle, Olivier, 1975– editor.
Title: Doing academic careers differently : portraits of academic life / Edited by Sarah Robinson, Alexandra Bristow and Olivier Ratle.
Description: Abingdon, Oxon ; New York, NY : Routledge, 2023. | Includes bibliographical references and index.
Subjects: LCSH: College teachers. | Career development.
Classification: LCC LB1778 .D57 2023 (print) | LCC LB1778 (ebook) | DDC 378.1/2—dc23/eng/20230331
LC record available at https://lccn.loc.gov/2022060870
LC ebook record available at https://lccn.loc.gov/2022060871

ISBN: 978-1-032-21260-9 (hbk)
ISBN: 978-1-032-21261-6 (pbk)
ISBN: 978-1-003-26755-3 (ebk)

DOI: 10.4324/9781003267553

Typeset in Bembo
by codeMantra

Sarah dedicates this book, in loving memory, to Mark Easterby-Smith who staunchly led his career *his way* and who supported her in becoming the academic *she* wanted to be.

Alex dedicates this book to Karen Legge, the most brilliant teacher who inspired her journey into academia, and a much-loved friend.

Olivier wishes to acknowledge the labour, love, and sacrifices of Caroline. Without her unwavering care for their children, he would not have been able to work on this book, and he would find it much harder to be *doing academic careers differently*. Now that this book is done, he hopes to dedicate himself to enabling her hopes, just as he dedicates this work to her.

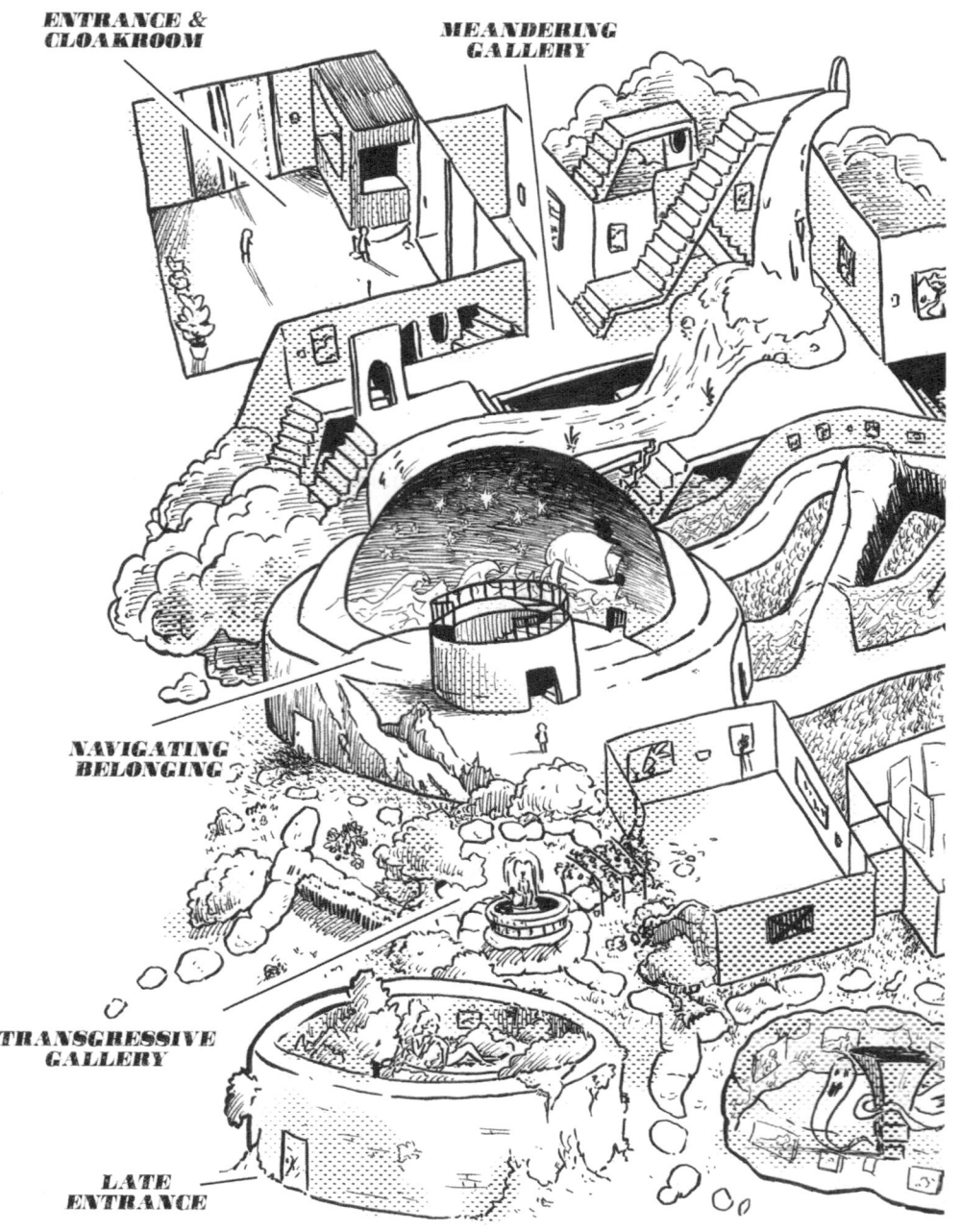

FIGURE P.1 Exhibition map by Joe Latham

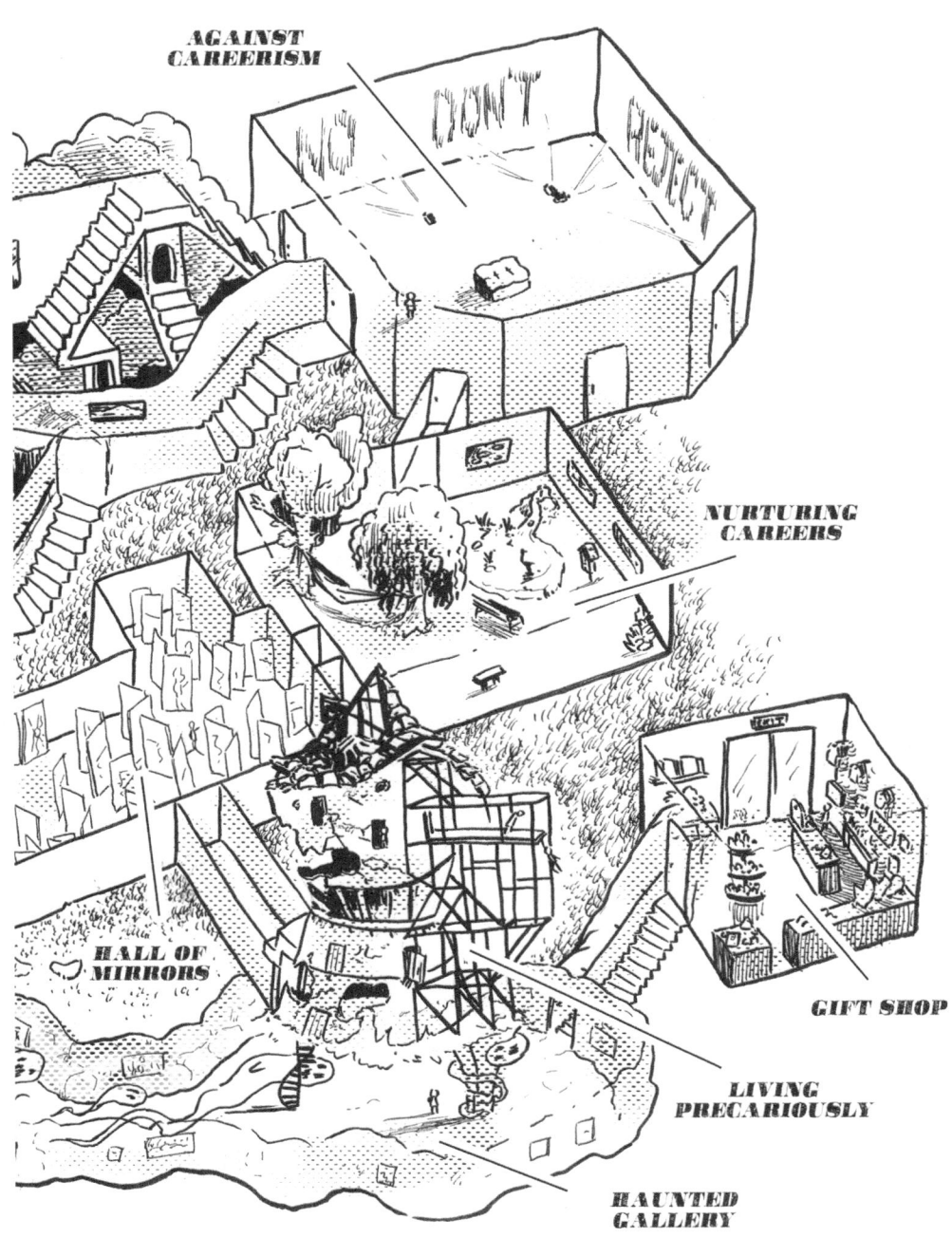

CONTENTS

Notes on contributors   *xvii*
Foreword   *xxvii*
Gibson Burrell
Acknowledgements   *xxix*

Introduction: entrance hall and cloakroom   1
Alexandra Bristow, Olivier Ratle, and Sarah Robinson

I
The meandering gallery   7
Curated by Alexandra Bristow

I hope your journey is a long one: meandering careers   9
Alexandra Bristow

Meandering academics   13
Linda M. Sama, Mark Egan, Victor J. Friedman, David R. Jones,
Nicholas D. Rhew, and Sarah Robinson

The all-over-the-place academic: how to fit in an academic niche but
also be free to pursue new and exciting research ideas   23
Lucas Amaral Lauriano

A pebble skipper's tale   29
Mark N.K. Saunders

The general academic   40
Rweyemamu Alphonce Ndibalema, Essa Bah, and Sophia Kokugonza Ndibalema

II
Against careerism   47
Curated by Sarah Robinson

On ducks and vocations: notes against careerism   49
Sarah Robinson

Careering through my career: how I failed to become a business school Dean   52
Mark Learmonth

Ducks at the university? Two connected biographies in seven images   61
Jesús Rodríguez-Pomeda and Fernando Casani

Excellence and disruption: a mid-career dialogue   70
Eugenie Hunsicker and Clare Hutton

Collectively creating conditions that nurture: the bushland as metaphor for the academic ecosystem   75
Sumati Ahuja, Mihajla Gavin, Simone Grabowski, Najmeh Hassanli, Anja Hergesell, Walter Jarvis, Pavlina Jasovska, Ece Kaya, Alice Klettner, Helena Liu, Jennie Small, Christopher N. Walker, and Ruth Weatherall

III
Navigating belonging   91
Curated by Sarah Robinson

Across hostile waters to brave new lands? Notes on navigating academic belonging   93
Sarah Robinson

The collective academic: a conversation across worlds   96
Jurdene A. Coleman, Mac T. Benavides, Aliah Mestrovich Seay, and Tess Hobson

Before you decolonize, let me into the game: virtue, a key to unbridling the shackles of oppression   107
Armand Bam

How to become an academic, and alienate people: the working-class academic   116
Suzanne Albary

The back-door academic   120
Sarah Stookey

The ingenuous communitarian *Emma Newport*	128
The journey of a surprised academic *Laurie N. DiPadova-Stocks*	133
The self-made academic: from business to a business school *Adrián Zicari*	137

IV
Nurturing careers
Curated by Olivier Ratle

141

Nurturing careers: on the importance of care and relationships *Olivier Ratle*	143
The permaculture academic *Maribel Blasco*	146
A room for three: living academic, feminist lives (or the unfinished reading of *A room of one's own*) *Jenny Helin, Nina Kivinen, and Alison Pullen*	158
The non-conformist academic: professor, parent, provider *Mary Godwyn*	167
The mom academic (fragmentation) *Elizabeth Siler*	177

V
The hall of mirrors
Curated by Sarah Robinson

187

Mirroring academia: reflections from a hall of mirrors *Sarah Robinson*	189
Reflections, distortions – the mirrored academic *Victoria Pagan*	192
Academic misfits *Magnus Hoppe, Steffi Siegert, Serdar Temiz, Fatemeh Seifan, and Anton Hasselgren*	196

Becoming a (never) good enough critical scholar? On precarious academic subjectification processes — 205
Mie Plotnikof

The art of being a reflexive academic: painting a never-complete self-portrait — 210
Russ Vince

The poetic academic — 219
Friederike Landau-Donnelly

I am you, as you are me: academic lives as a mirror of ourselves — 224
Oscar Javier Montiel Méndez, Duncan M. Pelly, and Araceli Almaraz

VI
The transgressive gallery — 235
Curated by Alexandra Bristow

In the garden of dreams: transgressive careers — 237
Alexandra Bristow

Seek & destroy – From transgression to contestation. *And back* — 241
Sophie Del Fa

Meeting the threads that pull: a feminist declaration of consequence towards academia — 247
Camila Fredes

The absurd academic — 257
Jaime Andrés Bayona

Crafting a career in 'academic journalism' — 266
Todd Bridgman

Blinds and bananas: Metaphor in the margins — 275
Stephen Linstead

A clown's tale — 284
Ralf Wetzel

VII
The late entrance — 295
Curated by Olivier Ratle

The late entrance: muddy water and dry grass? — 297
Olivier Ratle

Late portrait arrival 300
Catherine Heggerud

Disturbing bodies? Prospective and retrospective second-careering
within the doctoral candidature 303
Margaret Ying Wei Lee, Olivia Davies, and Kathleen Riach

Better late than never: the 'up the hill backwards' academic 313
Mark Stringer

VIII
The living precariously gallery 319
Curated by Olivier Ratle

Living precariously and overcoming the odds 321
Olivier Ratle

The happy and smiling, but inwardly crumbling gig academic: reflections
on early career precarity and anxiety 324
Emily Yarrow

The "sack-race" academic: a post-socialist portrait of a single mother
facing social expectations and the trade-offs of an academic career path 329
Gabriella Kiss

Re-imagining the dialectic of work and motherhood in academia 338
Chrysavgi Sklaveniti

Waiting for Godot: the impaired academic 347
Garance Maréchal

Some counsel to doctoral students from a naïve and shell-shocked academic 358
Ann Armstrong

"Why even bother?" The defiant practice of the independent scholar 362
Molly Hand

IX
The haunted gallery 367
Curated by Alexandra Bristow

Haunting careers: the realm of academic ghosts 369
Alexandra Bristow

Higher education in India: the *academic outsider* and the lived
experiences of a reclusive rebel 374
Subir Rana

Morals of the demoralised: the non-collaborative academic 383
Alexia Cameron

Doing philosophy differently: learning to fight gender-bias by giving up
on stereotypical academic norms 387
Tone Grosen Dandanell

Being an academic ghostwriter: be(com)ing me(thodology) 390
Martha Emilie Ehrich

Unwaged and repurposed: transitions from accidental to
non-institutionalised academic 401
Ruth Elizabeth Slater

The redundant academic: am I academic, or am I still an academic? 408
Mark Hughes

Exit via the gift shop 417
Olivier Ratle, Sarah Robinson, and Alexandra Bristow

Index *423*

CONTRIBUTORS

Sumati Ahuja is Senior Lecturer in Management at the University of Technology Sydney. Her research combines multidisciplinary perspectives from management, design, and innovation. She has published in a range of leading International Management and Design journals, including *Human Relations*, *Management Learning*, and *Journal of Product Innovation Management*.

Suzanne Albary, Royal Holloway, University of London, is an Art Historian turned careers educator turned learning developer who works as a Senior Lecturer in a Business School. Her research and writing meander through student partnership, co-production of learning, employer interventions employability, and academic identities. She is interested in aesthetics and performativity.

Araceli Almaraz is Professor at COLEF. Her research focusses on Mexico's northern border dimension (Business History). Her contributions within COLEF have been in the preparation of two new graduate programmes. She is one of the two women from Baja California who belong to the Mexican Academy of History.

Ann Armstrong, PhD, is a Lecturer at the University of Toronto. She enjoys teaching and conducting research on the design and impact of social enterprises. As well, she has just designed a Commerce course that highlights diverse economies, which may be the first such course in Canada.

Essa Bah is an international trade economist with a research focus on regional trade, institutions, and economic development. Essa is currently a Teaching Fellow at the University of Birmingham, Dubai where he teaches multiple modules in economics and business, mathematical economics, and statistics.

Armand Bam holds a PhD in Business Administration. He is Head of Social Impact and The Small Business Academy at Stellenbosch University Business School, South Africa. As a Senior Lecturer his research and teaching interests are focussed on disability, diversity, and inclusion. As a practitioner he still runs non-profit organizations.

Jaime Andrés Bayona is Associate Professor in Human Resource Management at Pontificia Universidad Javeriana, Colombia. His research and teaching interests include internal corporate social responsibility and the relationship between philosophy and organizational behaviour / human resource management.

Mac T. Benavides is Assistant Professor in the Staley School of Leadership at Kansas State University, where he earned his PhD in leadership communication. His research and practice centre around global and domestic intercultural learning, community-based learning, leadership education, and creating inclusive and equitable learning environments at HEIs.

Maribel Blasco is Associate Professor at Copenhagen Business School, Denmark. She teaches cultural awareness and conducts research into management education, which has been widely published across a range of outlets. Maribel is a keen gardener and animal lover, and holds a Permaculture Design Certificate from the Nordic Permaculture Institute.

Todd Bridgman is Professor in the School of Management at Victoria University of Wellington, New Zealand. Todd's research and teaching explores the origins of management theories and challenges their representation in best-selling textbooks. He is Emeritus Editor of the SAGE journal *Management Learning*.

Alexandra Bristow is Senior Lecturer (Associate Professor) at the Open University, UK. She has been researching and writing about academic careers for many years. A former academic ghost, a migrant, and a committed meanderer, she is deeply invested in showcasing and nurturing alternative career pathways and meanings of career success.

Alexia Cameron is based in Melbourne, Australia, practising independent sociology. Her work situates affect within realms of immaterial labour, work, and production. She focusses on ecosystems of feeling that feed cultural capitalism yet exist irrespectively of it, forming affective architectures that house atmospheres, personhood, and economies of desire.

Fernando Casani is Associate Professor of the Department of Business Organization of the Autonomous University of Madrid, and Director of the Research Institute for Higher Education and Science (INAECU), which is an intercollegiate institute of the Autonomous University of Madrid and the Carlos III University of Madrid, Spain.

Jurdene A. Coleman is Director of Therapy and Recovery Services at Pawnee Mental Health Services and doctoral student at Kansas State University Staley School of Leadership. She researches the intersection of public service and race, specifically how Black community leaders understand and experience leadership in predominately white civic spaces.

Tone Grosen Dandanell (1987) teaches philosophy and gender theory at the folk high school Testrup Højskole in Denmark. She holds a MA in philosophy and is a book reviewer for the national Danish newspaper Dagbladet Information.

Olivia Davies works in research, production, and editorial roles across non-fiction film and television, reflecting her interest in audio-visual data collection, analysis, and publication methods. She is pursuing her passion for documentary filmmaking after completing her PhD, which focussed on the entanglement of humans and other species that work together.

Sophie Del Fa is Assistant Professor at the University of Louvain's School of Communication, Belgium. Her research focusses on social movements and alternatives in resistance to neoliberal capitalism, with a communicative perspective. She is part of several grassroots projects, and she militates for education as a practice of freedom.

Laurie N. DiPadova-Stocks is Professor of public administration at Park University Missouri. She earned her undergraduate degree in sociology from the University of Virginia, her Master of Science degree in sociology from the University of Utah, and PhD degree in public policy and administration from the State University of New York.

Mark Egan is a Lecturer in Organizational Psychology at The University of York Management School, UK. His areas of interest include technology, emotion, and culture. Recent work has investigated the socio-material relations of academic well-being.

Martha Emilie Ehrich is an interdisciplinary scholar, working as a postdoc at the Film University Babelsberg and conducting research on gender inequality in the film (festival) industry. Their research bridges organizational sociology, critical political economy and gender studies, drawing on multiple methodologies including network analysis and visualization, historization, and autoethnography.

Victor J. Friedman lives in Israel with his wife, children, and grandchildren. He is an action researcher, combining a Jewish life with an open, reflective approach. For 40 years, he worked in academia, making contributions to inclusive education, intercultural communication, conflict resolution, and social entrepreneurship.

Mihajla Gavin is Senior Lecturer at UTS Business School. Her PhD at the University of Sydney was on how teacher trade unions have responded to neoliberal education reform. Her current research includes: restructuring of teachers' work and conditions of work in the public sector, worker voice, and gender and employment relations.

Mary Godwyn is a Professor of Sociology in the History and Society Division at Babson College (USA). She holds a BA in Philosophy from Wellesley College and a PhD in Sociology from Brandeis University. Her work focusses on issues of inequality in formal and informal organizations.

Simone Grabowski is a Senior Lecturer in Management and International Business at the University of Technology Sydney. She has a PhD and first-class honours degree in

Tourism Management and a BA (International Studies). Her research spans volunteerism, sustainability, mobility, cross-cultural psychology, community, disability, and diversity management.

Molly Hand is an Associate Lecturer in English at Florida State University, USA. She co-edited the volume *Animals, Animality, and Literature* (Cambridge University Press, 2018), and her work appears in various journals and collections. Her current research focusses on animals and the occult in early modern England.

Najmeh Hassanli is Senior Lecturer at UTS Business School. Underpinned by her commitment to deliver practical benefits to individuals, organizations, and society, her research focusses on social sustainability and ethical practices in small-micro businesses, and the role of leisure for socially disadvantaged and under-represented groups in society.

Anton Hasselgren is an Assistant Professor in finance and economics at Jönköping University in Sweden. Anton's research interests include behavioural finance, international finance, and market efficiency and information. He is currently researching the effects of social connections and behavioural traits of top CEOs.

Catherine Heggerud has been at the University of Calgary, Canada, since 2013. Working originally in IT management roles, Catherine found her home at the Haskayne School of Business, where she is an Associate Professor (Teaching). In addition to teaching and holding administrative roles, she is currently completing her DBA.

Jenny Helin is Associate Professor in Organisation at Uppsala University, Finland. She is involved in two research projects: one about organizing for generosity and another about non-digital organizing. Besides, Jenny holds a great interest in collaborative research methods and academic writing.

Anja Hergesell is a Lecturer in Event Management at UTS Business School. Before this appointment, Anja worked at UTS in various other positions, including as a Postdoctoral Research Fellow, and taught and researched at universities in Austria and Denmark. Anja's research interests include sustainability, mobility, and tourist behaviour.

Tess Hobson earned a PhD in Student Affairs in Higher Education from Kansas State University, where she instructed in leadership. Utilizing a Critical Whiteness lens, her research revolves around the power of storytelling as a pedagogy in developing students' capacity to disrupt whiteness and practise inclusive leadership for social change.

Magnus Hoppe is an Associate Professor in business administration at Mälardalen University in Sweden. His research concerns both private and public organizations and spans intelligence, entrepreneurship and innovation. Of particular interest is the questioning of dominating perspectives and dogmatic academic positions.

Mark Hughes is a former university Reader in Organizational Change. Author of organizational change journal papers, monographs, and textbooks. Since exiting institutional academic employment, further academic ramblings, publications, and contact details can be accessed at woodlanddecay.com.

Eugenie Hunsicker is a Reader in Mathematics at Loughborough University, UK. Her research is in data science, analytical chemistry, and metrology. She holds a national role as the Honorary Officer for Equality, Diversity and Inclusion at the Royal Statistical Society.

Clare Hutton is a Reader in English and Digital Humanities at Loughborough University, UK. Building on her monograph, *Serial Encounters: Ulysses and the Little Review* (OUP 2019), she is curator of *Women and the Making of Joyce's Ulysses*, a major exhibition at the Harry Ransom Center, University of Texas.

Walter Jarvis is Director of the UTS Master of Management and Senior Lecturer in ethical-moral stewardship, economic-ethics and corporate governance. His research investigates decision-making and judgement, foregrounding pedagogical aims which cultivate moral-relational accountability of leaders to regain public trust in enterprise management.

Pavlina Jasovska is a Lecturer in International Business & Strategy at UTS Business School. Her research interests are: internationalization of firms that face severe resource constraints and possess limited power, such as craft and emerging market firms. She applies the theories of institutional embeddedness, cultural entrepreneurship, and firm internationalization.

David R. Jones is Professor of Sustainability & Management Learning at Newcastle Business School, Northumbria University, England. He is passionate about changing the landscape of HE to improve academic working lives. His research explores alternative meandering spaces to underpin well-being, collegiality, and interdisciplinarity.

Ece Kaya is a Lecturer in the Management Department at the UTS Business School. She completed her PhD in heritage and tourism studies. Her research and teaching interests include revitalization of industrial spaces, urban tourism, placemaking, creative problem solving, research skills, and new applications in teaching and learning practices.

Gabriella Kiss is an Associate Professor at the Corvinus University of Budapest, Hungary, where she teaches decision sciences and ecological economics. Her research interests revolve around participatory approaches to environmental decision-making and sustainable behaviour, as well as participatory learning processes in relation to sustainability in higher education.

Nina Kivinen has recently moved from a business school in Finland to industrial engineering and management at Uppsala University, Sweden. Her research is on gender creative labour and particularly questions of materiality, space, and affect. Nina has a keen interest in art-based methods in teaching and research.

Alice Klettner is a Senior Lecturer at the UTS Business School. Her research examines corporate governance from both a legal and management perspective, particularly the impact of soft law on organizational behaviour. Research interests include the responsibilities of company directors, regulation of corporate sustainability, and gender diversity in leadership.

Friederike Landau-Donnelly is an urban sociologist, political theorist, and cultural geographer. She currently works as Assistant Professor of Cultural Geography at Radboud Universiteit in Nijmegen, The Netherlands. Her empirically grounded research interweaves political theories of conflict and urban space with literatures on artistic activism, social movements, civic self-organization, and care.

Lucas Amaral Lauriano is an Assistant Professor at IESEG School of Management – Paris, France. He got his PhD from King's Business School – King's College London. His research interests are broadly at the intersection of organizational behaviour and sustainability strategy.

Mark Learmonth is a Professor of Organization Studies at Nottingham Trent University, UK, having previously worked at Durham University and the Universities of Nottingham and York. Before becoming an academic, Mark worked as a health services administrator.

Margaret Ying Wei Lee' research is focussed on the social experience of health and illness at work, with a particular interest in traumatic health events in organizational and online work settings. Margie is currently completing a doctoral thesis at Monash University, Australia, exploring how people experience life after workplace burnout.

Stephen Linstead is Professor of Management Humanities at the School of Business and Society, University of York. His work has been blurring professional and scholarly boundaries for 40 years. Passions include filmmaking and poetry, and he sang at the Edinburgh Fringe for the first time at the age of 66.

Helena Liu is an Associate Professor of Management at Bond Business School located on the unceded land of the Kombumerri families of the Yugambeh language region. Her research critiques the way power sustains our enduring romance with leadership and imagines the possibilities for organizing through justice, solidarity, and love.

Garance Maréchal is Senior Lecturer in Strategic Management at the University of Liverpool, UK. She has interests in gender, autoethnography, sensuous methodologies, and photography. She has published in *Qualitative Inquiry*, *Organization Studies*, and *Human Relations*, and served as Representative at Large for the Academy of Management's Critical Management Studies Division.

Aliah Mestrovich Seay, LCMFT, ABD is the Executive Director for UFM Community Learning Center at Kansas State University. With over 20 years of experience in higher education and the not-for-profit sectors, Aliah's research interests involve intercultural communication, critical whiteness studies, critical empathy, and intercultural listening for racial healing and reconciliation.

Oscar Javier Montiel Méndez is Professor of management at Universidad Autónoma de Ciudad Juárez (UACJ), Mexico. He has published in international journals as well as being an editor of several books (published by Emerald).

Rweyemamu Alphonce Ndibalema is a Lecturer at the University of Birmingham, UK. His research focusses on understanding how to unleash the human potential through the psychological state of employee engagement. He teaches multiple subjects in the area of business and management.

Sophia Kokugonza Ndibalema is an Assistant Lecturer at the University of Dar es Salaam, Tanzania. She is currently undertaking her PhD at the University of Bath, UK. Her research focusses on corporate social responsibilities, power, and local communities.

Emma Newport is a Senior Lecturer in English Literature at the University of Sussex, UK. Emma is the director of the student-led initiative Sussex Writes and the creator of a conference series called Women, Money and Markets. She is also a Sussex Sustainability Research Fellow.

Camila Fredes Ortiz is a social psychologist with a master's on women, gender, and citizenship studies. She is currently working as Gender Expert at Universidad de Chile, while teaching social psychology and gender studies. She is a descolonial feminist activist, incipient writer and friend of textile practices.

Victoria Pagan is Senior Lecturer in strategic management at Newcastle University Business School, UK. Her research interests are structured around the intersecting themes of knowledge (its generation, uses, and violations), the expression/suppression of moral emotions, and social justice. She is currently researching the use and impact of non-disclosure agreements.

Duncan M. Pelly is an Associate Professor of Entrepreneurship, Director of the Center for Free Enterprise and Entrepreneurship, and Director of International Business Programs at McMurry University, USA. His interests include entrepreneurial opportunity, adhocracies, autoethnography, and philosophical foundations of entrepreneurship.

Mie Plotnikof is Associate Professor at Aarhus University, Denmark. Her research questions the constitutive dynamics of discourse, subjectivity, dis/organization and power/resistance – often in the context of education. She has published in: *Gender, Work & Organization*; *Organization Studies*, and *ephemera* (among others), and in international and Danish books.

Alison Pullen is Co-Editor of the journal *Gender, Work and Organization*. As a feminist qualitative researcher, she has been interested in exploring the boundaries of academic writing, feminine knowledge, and seeing where this embodied/writing will take her. Alison has just published Organizing Corporeal Ethics (2022, with Carl Rhodes).

Subir Rana has a PhD in Sociology from the Jawaharlal Nehru University, Delhi, and a Postdoc from the NIAS Bengaluru, India. Besides his research which grapples with understanding societies and cultures, he also loves to travel, sketch, paint, and write poetry. He is a committed philatelist and a numismatist.

Olivier Ratle is a Senior Lecturer in Organisation Studies at the University of the West of England. He has been preoccupied for a long time by the issue of diversity in research, which has led him to study the politics of methodology in management, and the predicament of early-career academics.

Nicholas D. Rhew is an Assistant Professor of Management at the Romain College of Business, University of Southern Indiana, located in Evansville, Indiana, USA. He is passionate about improving management education. For restoration, he plays golf, travels, and plays keyboards in church *and* rock and roll bands.

Kathleen Riach is based at the Adam Smith Business School, University of Glasgow, UK. Her research focusses on the experience of growing up and older in and around the workplace, with a particular interest in intersections surrounding gender, identity, and the body.

Sarah Robinson is Professor of Management and Organisation Studies at Rennes School of Business, France. She has a long-standing interest in academic careers, well-being, and restoration. Other interests include organizational and individual learning; issues of power, resistance, identity and socialization within professions often drawing on Bourdieu's sociology.

Jesús Rodríguez-Pomeda is Associate Professor of the Department of Business Organization of the Autonomous University of Madrid, and Member of the Research Institute for Higher Education and Science (INAECU), which is an intercollegiate institute of the Autonomous University of Madrid and the Carlos III University of Madrid, in Spain.

Linda M. Sama is the Joseph F. Adams Professor of Management and Associate Dean at the Peter J. Tobin College of Business, St. John's University, NY, USA. Her research spans business ethics, CSR, micro-lending practices, and well-being. For restoration, she sings with her choir and meanders with colleagues.

Mark N.K. Saunders is Professor of Business Research Methods and Director of Global Engagement at Birmingham Business School, University of Birmingham, UK. He was awarded a Fellowship of the Academy of Social Sciences in 2019 recognizing his contribution to methods and human resource management research and social science researcher development.

Fatemeh Seifan is a Data Scientist at Paradox Interactive. Before joining industry, she was a researcher at the Department of Informatics at the University of Erlangen, and before that she did her PhD studies in theoretical computer science at the University of Amsterdam, where her research was focussed on logic, automata, and games.

Steffi Siegert is a Senior Lecturer in Organisation and Leadership at Linnaeus University in Sweden. Her research interests center digitalization, sustainability, and academic work.

She is particularly interested in how digitalization influences the changing nature of work. Steffi's fascination with academic work is driven by a perception of misfitting.

Elizabeth Siler is Professor, Business Administration and Economics Department, at Worcester State University in Massachusetts, USA, where she teaches a wide range of management courses and is an advocate for Open Educational Resources. She studies pregnancy loss and work.

Chrysavgi Sklaveniti is *living precariously* since her principal work occupation lies outside of academia. She is a catalyst, consultant, and project manager at LIVEsciences where she is valued for her professional skills. She maintains links to academia as adjunct Lecturer in Organisational Psychology in the University of Basel, Switzerland.

Ruth Elizabeth Slater is an academic and early on in her career an HR practitioner. Formerly Senior Lecturer and Course Leader in HRM at the University of Central Lancashire (UCLan), Ruth is affiliated with several UK institutions supervising dissertation and doctoral students.

Jennie Small is an Honorary Associate in the Management Discipline Group at UTS. Taking a Critical Tourism approach, her specific interests are gender, age, embodiment, body image, disability (vision impairment), mobility, and experience of air travel, drawing on the feminist research method, memory-work in much of her work.

Sarah Stookey is Associate Professor of management and organization in the School of Business at Central Connecticut State University. She has done community-based research and education in Nicaragua and other countries. She has a PhD in organization studies from the University of Massachusetts, Amherst. She studies and teaches about capitalism.

Mark Stringer works at Birkbeck College, University of London as a Lecturer and as Head of Department for Organizational Psychology, and is nearing the completion of his PhD. He is also a musician and a creator of soundscapes as part of the Fractured Strings collective.

Serdar Temiz is an Associate Professor at the Department of Civil and Industrial Engineering at Uppsala University. His PhD is from the KTH-Royal Institute of Technology. He researches business model innovation, new product development with emerging technologies, open data, blockchain, and open innovation. He goes by #DrZero at his performances.

Russ Vince is Professor Emeritus at the School of Management, University of Bath, UK, and Honorary Professor of Management at the University of St Andrews, UK. He is an academic with artistic tendencies who hopes to become an artist with academic tendencies.

Christopher N. Walker is a doctoral researcher based in Dharawal country in Sydney, Australia. His work strives towards freer, fairer, and more prosperous social structures, focussing in particular upon opportunities for contranormative ways of being and doing to inform and facilitate more effective, inclusive, and liveable organizing and organizational practices.

Ruth Weatherall is a Lecturer in Not-for-Profit Management at the UTS Business School. Her research takes a range of perspectives including feminist, decolonizing, queer, and the ghostly. No matter which perspective, her focus is on how people organize to create social change, particularly in relation to gendered violence.

Ralf Wetzel is Professor of Applied Arts at Vlerick Business School, Belgium. He is an awarded business educator and an acknowledged theatre performer (Edinburgh Fringe Festival 2019, Zagreb Clown Festival 2020, Financial Times 2019). He co-founded the Global Play Brigade New York/US and the Institute of Performative Inquiry Brussels/Belgium.

Emily Yarrow is a Senior Lecturer in Management and Organisations at Newcastle University Business School, UK. Emily's scholarly work contributes to contemporary understandings of gendered organizational behaviour, women's experiences of organizational life, governance in higher education, and the future of work.

Adrián Zicari is Professor of Accounting at ESSEC Business School, Paris. Before academia, he was a practitioner in Argentina. His research interest is measurement systems in sustainability. His work appears in several academic journals: *Journal of Business Ethics*, *Journal of Cleaner Production*, among others.

FOREWORD

Gibson Burrell

This is an important book about how the academic career might be, and has been, done differently. Through the metaphor of the curation of exhibits, a large number of academics are invited to reflect upon their 'careers' in a non-linear way, suggesting meanders, nurturing, disruption, careering (as out of control), the mirror, narcissism and the portrait, transgression (a particularly powerful gallery), haunting, demoralization, and even a garden. But even in this more positively oriented framing, the roots of academia appear rotten and all that looks lovely in our gardens is covered in thick, vicious thorns. It is an absurd profession with failure only a whisker away. Indeed, it appears that failure is our constant companion.

As part of this context, there is some powerful stuff in the pages of this book where colleagues open up about what has happened to them in their academic lives. Much of it is uncomfortable because identity relies so heavily upon occupation and problems in one's work life create problems in one's core identity. And all academics face problems that are threats to our core. I once worked with an eminent sociologist who walked into a campus bar many a lunch time and proclaimed that for another day he had not been found out and 'had got away with it'. Many of us think like that at whatever stage in our careers we are. 'Career', historically, is a term that has always paralleled the lives of university academics. It is a concept that parallels the lives of the vast majority of bureaucrats and professionals over the centuries as they lived out their organizational lives, sometimes within guild-like systems. But we must note that each generation faces new and different occupational challenges. Changes in organizational numbers, entry criteria, reward systems, forms of control and surveillance, and in pressures on autonomy all create different working lives from previous career expectations. For example, the generation in the UK taking their first academic posts in the 1970s saw the university sector was fissiparous with 'new universities' being dismissed by those who worked in venerable institutions and inhabited Senior Common Rooms. PhDs were certainly not essential for a career. There were no members of the precariat on campus. The faces of staff you met in the corridors were most often bearded and white.

Some 50 years later the landscape in Britain and many other countries is somewhat different. Diverse students in very large numbers and diverse staff are to be found on campus. Many more women are part of the academic profession. University administrators rule the roost. The *sine qua non* of getting an appointment is a PhD and maybe some publications. Both are fraught with painful power dynamics. The American system of ejection from the profession is seen as superior and worth mimicking. Many young staff are on precarious contracts. In the face of this, the aims of the book are to bring hope and courage to those who do, or would like to do, their academic careers differently. This is illustrated through many of the accounts on offer. It is clear that there is still room and scope to undertake a meaningful career in some academic contexts and although this may take intense struggle, and require tenacity and courage, the authors individually and/or collectively find creative and interesting ways of reflecting on and practising their careers. Of course, key to this hope of achieving meaningful professional lives is insight about resisting creeping normative pressures found throughout the university sector.

What all the authors say in a variety of ways is diverse and international, suggesting that the career normally associated with straight line progress in a very direct, upwardly orientated way is not as usual as we might expect. The careerist does exist, of course, as we all know, and they seem to understand the path which they must follow to climb ever upwards and onwards. But they do not appear on these pages. The writers here are beset by their academic contexts in which career is problematic. But all is not angst. Far from it. **Doing Academic Careers Differently** faithfully reflects this Brave New World of University life, where in 2023, the fundamental absurdity of what we do is so obvious; yet we struggle to comprehend it – *for that is what we do*. This book is academically insightful and full of professionally driven emotion – *for that is what we need*. For all who enter the exhibits contained within, here true hope is not abandoned!

ACKNOWLEDGEMENTS

We sincerely thank all our contributors for their moving, creative, and thought-provoking accounts which have made this book so special and unique. We are also very grateful to Gibson Burrell for the thoughtful and generous foreword. Additionally, we would like to thank the editorial team at Routledge/Taylor & Francis for their support throughout the process. In particular, we would like to say a special thank you to Terry Clague, the Senior Editor who indulged our wish to write and present this book differently and came up with creative solutions for making it possible. Our warmest gratitude also goes to Joe Latham for working so closely with us on the illustrated table of contents and taking on board all our comments and suggestions to bring to life the vision of this book as a portrait gallery. Finally, we are indebted to colleagues (too many to name here) whose academic practice and friendships over the years have inspired us to think of academic careers differently. This includes the participants of our research programme into the predicament of early-career academics. Your spirit inhabits these pages and makes academic lives vibrant and worth living. Thank you.

INTRODUCTION

Entrance hall and cloakroom

Alexandra Bristow, Olivier Ratle, and Sarah Robinson

This book is an outcome of more than a decade of research, conversations, and writing about contemporary academia. Equally importantly, it is an outcome of our own and our authors' many collective years of experiences of being academics, of raging against academia's many challenges and injustices, and of trying to do things differently. It contains and shares collective wisdom acquired by going against the grain of the suffocating linearity and normativity that is so often presumed necessary to achieve what narrowly counts as academic career success. This book is part of our project to give voice, space, and hope to visions of an alternative, more nurturing, diverse, and inclusive academia.

Academic career trajectories have long been normative and prescribed and are arguably becoming more so since the advent of the neoliberal 'New Higher Education' (Jary and Parker, 1998) and its audit culture of academic performance measurement and management (Strathern, 2000). Ideals of what makes a good or successful academic are increasingly seen through the achievement of various institutionally set targets such as publications in top journals and high teaching scores, and through performance management systems which routinely review individuals across a considerable number of pre-determined criteria. Academics are encouraged to carefully cultivate their 'research profiles' and digital presence, displaying their 'H index' scores, high-level publications and esteem factors, publicly showing allegiance to such externally set manifestations of 'excellence' (Butler and Spoelstra, 2012, 2014). In this book we problematise such trends and explore the scope for doing academic careers differently.

To do this, we subvert the emphasis on academics' official public profiles and delve beyond them to probe the tensions and contradictions behind such limited measures of academic success, exploring and demonstrating alternative ways of building and leading fulfilling academic careers. Our book therefore develops critical academic career studies by challenging orthodoxies and power relations in academic career trajectories. In so doing we build on critical career studies (for example, Gowler and Legge, 1989; Ibarra and Obodaru, 2016; Prasad et al., 2007; Reis and Baruch, 2013) and on an increasing body of literature critiquing the neoliberal emphasis on academic 'excellence' (Hazelkorn, 2011; Saunders, 2015),

DOI: 10.4324/9781003267553-1

performance (Jones et al., 2020), and excesses of managerialism and control mechanisms (Huzzard et al., 2017; Kallio et al., 2016; Ratle et al., 2020). In addition, we build on related work demonstrating how academia has become fundamentally physically and mentally unhealthy (Bristow et al., 2019; Morrish, 2019), with widespread academic anxiety and insecurity (Bristow et al., 2017; Knights and Clarke, 2014; Smith and Ulus, 2019).

In the spirit of the medium reflecting the message, we wanted this book about doing academic careers differently to also be a different kind of book, edited and presented differently. We started by crafting an open call for contributions, considering this essential to ensuring diverse voices and career trajectories are included. In the call, we asked potential authors to use the analogy of 'portraits' to paint individual or group, full or miniature portraits of their academic careers, working with metaphors which challenge the dominant discourses of how academic careers should be led. In particular, we asked authors to consider the following questions:

1. Are there more inclusive and less prescriptive ways of being an academic which play to individual strengths, motivations, and vocations?
2. What lies behind the homogenised institutionalised masks (profiles) we show to the world? What issues, tensions, and contradictions have individual academics struggled with? What paths have not been taken or what stories lie (up to now) hidden or untold?
3. What alternative academic trajectories have been taken that others can learn and take inspiration from?
4. And (as we were writing the call amidst the lockdowns while witnessing the manifold changes wrought by the pandemic) how has the Covid-19 pandemic informed our understanding of academic careers, and how might ways of doing academia differently develop in the post-pandemic world?

Following the call, we were both delighted and overwhelmed to receive over 80 abstract submissions, and after a great deal of discussion and difficult decision-making we were able to accept 50, which eventually became the 46 contributions in this book. Together, these contributions address the questions we posed in our call through the stories of 82 academic authors at different stages of their careers (from PhD to post-retirement), in different fields (mostly in business and management but some in sociology, psychology, philosophy, English, and maths) and from different parts of the world (representing 21 countries across all inhabited continents) who, through choice and/or circumstance, do not (fully) play the game or conform to academic career norms, thus challenging orthodoxies and inspiring readers to consider ways of doing academic work differently. Our authors come out from behind their official 'profiles' and instead paint individual or group self-portraits which reflect individual and/or shared struggles, contradictions, and hidden stories. Provocatively, many authors use metaphors for their portraits to challenge current assumptions of the neoliberal academic.

In working with our authors' contributions, we soon realised that we had something even more special and precious in our hands than what we had initially hoped for. We were moved, shocked, provoked, awed, and inspired by the candid and eye-opening experiences authors have shared in their portraits and by the sheer diversity of creative ways in which they have carved out their unique paths through and around academia. Our concept of the book developed accordingly, and particularly the need to edit and present this book differently. Starting from an aspiration to produce an updated and alternative version of

Frost and Taylor (1996) that compiled personal accounts of academic life, we moved to unfold our idea of 'portraits' more fully and develop the book into a 'portrait exhibition'. In a process that could be considered inductive data analysis, we spent much time discussing the accepted abstracts and categorising them into individual 'galleries' or rooms (aka book sections) based on how authors do their academic careers differently. We then developed the initial floorplan (table of contents) and ideas for what each gallery could look and feel like. We shared these with our authors together with their proposed allocation to galleries and encouraged them to respond with reactions and suggestions for further development of the galleries. We also emphasised our openness to chapters being written differently, in ways that felt authentic and meaningful to authors. The responses we received were affirming and inspiring, and one of the suggestions was to hold collective online meetings so that we (authors and editors) could share experiences, ideas, and struggles while working on full chapters. We subsequently held four Zoom sessions, alternating between time zones to include authors from different geographies. Through these meetings, a sense of community started to emerge (particularly uplifting in pandemic times), as well as many ideas (for example, that of the gift shop – see below).

The result is a book that is the product of our collective labour of love. From rejecting the pressure to focus on 'one big thing', to prioritising nurture and care, transcending disciplinary boundaries, reshaping own daily practice, connecting with communities, and being academics outside academia, the contributions in this book offer those considering, starting, or developing an academic career a treasure trove of many alternative possibilities to inspire and encourage others to forge their own career paths through re-thinking and taking ownership of their careers. It is not a 'how to do it' book offering prescriptive advice but is rather an immersive experience in which you, the reader, are invited to explore a portrait exhibition through which you can meander at will in the spirit of discovery, adventure, and reflection.

The book aims to give you choice and freedom in your reading. Of course, readers are free to read books in whichever order they choose to anyway, regardless of what authors or editors intended. However, taking inspiration from Burrell's (1997) *Pandemonium*, we wanted to explicitly challenge the assumptions of linearity that underpin academic writing, just like they underpin the norms of academic career trajectories. Although we do not go as far as to run the text of the book in both directions, the nine galleries in this portrait exhibition and the portraits within them have been intentionally arranged to be visitable in any order. Joe Latham's[1] beautifully illustrated table of contents is key to this, acting as the exhibition floorplan and a visual representation of what is to come to facilitate your meandering and exploring. Capturing a non-Euclidean maze, a hall of mirrors, an observatory, a garden, a dilapidated tower, and a haunted basement (among other spaces), it communicates the spirit of each gallery as well as that of the overall exhibition.

You currently find yourself in the *Entrance Hall and Cloakroom*. It is a simple but spacious room, where you can store your coat and bag, pick up this guide and a copy of Joe's map, and start orienting yourself in the exhibition. Many choices, routes, and directions beckon from here. Which of the nine galleries calls to you first? Whichever you choose, each gallery is 'curated' by one of the three editors who provide 'curators' notes' (gallery introductions). The curators set the scene for you in order to facilitate an immersive experience in their gallery by describing its physical environment, colours and smells as well as its aims and intentions, and introduce individual exhibits. Contributions are arranged into galleries based on how the authors do their academic careers differently. Yet there are many possible links and connections between the galleries, as well as inevitably, due to the complexity of our authors' career trajectories, overlaps. Many portraits could belong in multiple galleries, and some acknowledge as much explicitly. We encourage you to draw out such connections and tensions for yourself, and to take away your own key themes and inspirations. However, the distinct career difference for each gallery is as follows:

Meandering Gallery – authors in this gallery resist the pressure to specialise and to stick to 'straight and narrow' academic trajectories. Instead, they choose to 'meander' and follow their multiple interests: as such, this gallery sets the tone for the entire book.

Against Careerism – authors in this gallery resist careerism itself and the neoliberal expectations of an 'excellent' and 'ideal' academic.

Navigating Belonging – authors in this gallery prioritise searching for belonging in their careers. They reflect on how their careers are shaped differently by their different backgrounds and by connecting with and shaping different communities.

Nurturing Careers – the careers of authors in this gallery are shaped differently by various kinds of nurturing and caring, including motherhood, care for the environment and broader communities, care for each other as colleagues, and care and nurture of self.

Hall of Mirrors – this gallery is a reflexive place in which doing academic careers differently arises through the authors' reflections on their own daily practices and different ways of approaching these.

Transgressive Gallery – arguably the place of most radical career differences, this gallery displays portraits of authors who transcend disciplinary and academic boundaries, and engage in philosophy, activism, journalism, performing arts, and film making.

The Late Entrance – for authors in this gallery, academia is a second or a third career. The portraits here reflect how this 'late entrance' has shaped different kinds of academic careers.

Living Precariously – authors in this gallery reflect on how different kinds of precarity, danger, and suffering have made their careers different.

The Haunted Gallery – authors in this gallery are 'academic ghosts', who have left formal academic employment but carry on doing academic work.

The book concludes with an *Exit via the Gift Shop*, filled with a fitting assortment of artefacts, knick-knacks, and curiosities, where you are encouraged to select your own take-aways, souvenirs, and gifts (or not). You can avoid the gift shop by escaping via a fire exit.

We hope this compilation of insights into alternative academic lives moves, provokes, and inspires you as much as it has us. We hope it will help to encourage and support future and current academics to re-think and take ownership of their careers in their own terms, according to their own strengths, weaknesses, and circumstances. We hope you enjoy your meandering through this portrait exhibition of academic lives, among many ideas for doing academic careers differently.

Note

1 Lookhappy Design, Bristol, UK. See joelathamillustration.co.uk.

References

Bristow, A., Robinson, S. and Ratle, O. (2017). Being an early-career CMS academic in the context of insecurity and excellence: The dialectics of resistance and compliance. *Organization Studies* 38(9): 1185–1207.

Bristow, A., Robinson, S. and Ratle, O. (2019). Academic arrhythmia: disruption, dissonance and conflict in the early career rhythms of CMS academics. *Academy of Management Learning and Education* 18(2): 241–260.

Burrell, G. (1997). *Pandemonium: Towards a Retro-Organization Theory.* London: Sage.

Butler, N. and Spoelstra, S. (2012). Your excellency. *Organization* 19(6): 891–903.

Butler, N. and Spoelstra, S. (2014). The regime of excellence and the erosion of ethos in Critical Management Studies. *British Journal of Management* 25(3): 538–550.

Frost, P. J. and Taylor, M. S. (Eds.) (1996). *Rhythms of academic life: Personal accounts of careers in academia.* Thousand Oaks, CA: Sage.

Gowler, D. and Legge, K. (1989). Rhetoric in bureaucratic careers: Managing the meaning of management success. Chapter 21 in Arthur, M.B., Hall, D.T. and Lawrence, B.S. (Eds.) *Handbook of Career Theory.* Cambridge: Cambridge University Press, 437–453.

Hazelkorn, E. (2011). Measuring world-class excellence and the global obsession with rankings. Chapter 29 in King, R., Marginson, S., and Naidoo, R. (Eds.) *Handbook on Globalization and Higher Education.* Cheltenham: Edward Elgar, 497–516.

Huzzard, T., Benner, M. and Kärreman, D. (Eds.) (2017). *The Corporatization of the Business School: Minerva Meets the Market.* London: Routledge.

Ibarra, H. and Obodaru, O. (2016). Betwixt and between identities: Liminal experience in contemporary careers. *Research in Organizational Behavior*, 36: 47–64.

Jary, D. and M. Parker (Eds.) (1998). *The new Higher Education: Dilemmas and directions for the post-Dearing university.* Stoke-on-Trent: Staffordshire University Press.

Jones, D. R. et al. (2020). The performative University: 'Targets', 'Terror' and 'Taking Back Freedom' in Academia. *Management Learning* 51(4): 363–377.

Kallio, KM., Kallio, TJ., Tienari, J., et al. (2016). Ethos at stake: Performance management and academic work in universities. *Human Relations* 69(3): 685–709.

Knights, D. and Clarke, CA. (2014). It's a bittersweet symphony, this life: Fragile academic selves and insecure identities at work. *Organization Studies* 35(3): 335–357.

Morrish, L. (2019). *Pressure Vessels: The epidemic of poor mental health among higher education staff,* HEPI Occasional Paper 20. London: Higher Education Policy Institute. Available at: www.hepi.ac.uk/wp-content/uploads/2019/05/HEPI-Pressure-Vessels-Occasional-Paper-20.pdf

Prasad, P., D'Abate, C. and Prasad, A. (2007). Organizational challenges at the periphery: Career issues for the socially marginalized. Chapter 10 in Gunz, H. and M. Peiperl (Eds.) Handbook of Career Studies. London: Sage, 169–187.

Ratle, O., Robinson, S., Bristow, A. and Kerr, R. (2020). Mechanisms of micro-terror? Early career CMS academics' experiences of 'targets and terror' in contemporary business schools., *Management Learning* 51(4): 452–471.

Reis, C. and Baruch, Y. (Eds.) (2013). *Careers without Borders: Critical Perspectives.* London: Routledge.

Saunders, D.B. (2015). Resisting excellence: Challenging neoliberal ideology in postsecondary education. *Journal for Critical Education Policy Studies* 13(2): 391–413.

Smith, C. and Ulus, E. (2019). Who cares for academics? We need to talk about emotional wellbeing including what we avoid and intellectualize through macro-discourses. *Organization* 27(6): 840–857.

Strathern, M. (Ed.). (2000). *Audit cultures: Anthropological studies in accountability, ethics and the academy.* London and New York: Routledge.

I
The meandering gallery
Curated by Alexandra Bristow

I HOPE YOUR JOURNEY IS A LONG ONE

Meandering careers

Alexandra Bristow

Step into the Meandering Gallery, visitor. Welcome. Have you just come from the Entrance Hall, having left your coat in the cloakroom? Perhaps you have walked in here briskly, full of excitement to explore and discover. Or have you made your way from the Late Entrance, through the wild seas of Navigating Belonging, or stepped through a glass, darkly, in the Hall of Mirrors, or through a portrait in the Haunted Gallery? Is it the smell of fresh air in your hair, pollution, or the smoke of burnt manuscripts? There are many ways of arriving in this gallery…

There are many ways through this gallery. It adjusts itself to you, enabling you to forge a path that is uniquely yours, giving you what you need. It will not disappoint your sense of adventure, but it *will* slow you down. Look around and you will understand why. This space is non-Euclidean, with distinctly M.C. Escher-esque vibes. On the one hand, the room feels endlessly spacious, walls rising to cavernous heights lost in unfathomable darkness above, bending at impossible angles. On the other, its perspectives confuse the senses, making it maze-like, mysterious. Passages run through it in all directions and along all planes. As you turn towards them, they acquire more clarity and solidity, and as you turn away, they fade or even disappear entirely.

There are three passages in front of you that seem reassuringly solid. A sign stands before each, marking them 'Teaching', 'Research', and 'Academic Service'. The central one, 'Research', seems particularly inviting – it is wide and well-lit, its smooth marble floor padded with a lush red carpet. Gilded portraits of the great and the good line up neatly on its walls. Everything about it exudes prestige. 'Only the brightest and the best', the subtitle on its entrance sign proclaims seductively. You cannot resist – surely this is where you are meant to go? But soon after you start down that path, the light dims, beginning to play diabolical tricks with the gilded portraits. Before you know it, the passage narrows dramatically, pressing down on you until you can hardly crawl or breathe. A disembodied voice accompanies you, measuring how fast you move and relentlessly counting down. It is unclear what will happen when it reaches zero, but it fills you with existential dread. Desperate, you persevere and squeeze through a narrow opening at the end of the passage, just in time, only to find yourself emerging into an arena lit by gigantic floodlights that illuminate every detail below. Inside the arena, you see academics fighting like gladiators, inflicting pain on each other without hesitation or remorse. Some seem to be enjoying it. Horrified, you turn around and flee the way you came.

Back at the three signs, you read the annotation that has appeared under 'Teaching' and 'Academic Service': 'If you have failed as a Researcher, try us instead'. You head towards the one marked 'Teaching', which looks somewhat less glamorous than 'Research' but nevertheless comfortingly respectable. Here, too, portraits of academics neatly line the walls, though the frames are much more modest. You do not recognize any of the faces. You are more careful this time, stopping at the entrance and listening intently. As you do, you detect repetitive, mechanical sounds in the distance, accompanied by a robotic rendition of Pink Floyd's *Another brick in the wall*. You are no longer deceived. You walk away, not even giving 'Academic Service' a glance. A strong whiff of managerialism wafts over you as you pass it, however. You pinch closed your nose.

You veer off to the left, moving widdershins, going deeper into the maze, picking a path through and around its impossible angles. From time to time, you come across doorways and tunnels, but you are more attuned to your own wishes now, and none feel right until you stumble across a spiral staircase winding its way upwards. You know this is yours. As you start to climb, it feels endless, but slowly your perspective begins to change. The darkness above you fills with stars. An ocean of mist rolls over the maze, and where it clears in places you can see wondrous landscapes below. Or is it above? The world flips and the misty landscapes are now the sky, with the starry abyss below.

You step off the staircase onto a platform that marks the start of a network of ephemeral bridges interconnecting this and other platforms. Clocks of various kinds and sizes float in mid-air, stand or lie broken on the floor. Each shows a different time. In a corner, one of Dali's melting clocks slowly drips mercury into the eyes of a reclining statue of Loki. In another stands a large, airport-like perplex box with a deposit slot in its lid, full of watches. 'Abandon Time All Ye Who Enter Here', reads the notice above it.

In the middle of the platform, I am waiting for you at a bistro table with a freshly brewed pot of tea and a generous slice of cake. Come, join me. In a world of endless possibilities, sometimes there is nothing as grounding as chocolate.

Let me tell you a bit about the images in the sky. They are portraits of an entirely different kind to the bombastic abominations that have temporarily misled you in the maze. The academics you will meet here have in common a desire to do academic careers differently by refusing to be pressured into specializing in a particular sphere of academic work, which is often advocated as the most effective – and fastest – way of progressing an academic career. The stories they write in the clouds epitomize the spirit of this book because they take joy in meandering freely to find one's own, alternative career pathways.

Let us cloud spot together. Can you see flashes of silver – a river meandering through verdant lands? If you explore its twists and turns, its many tributaries, you will encounter Linda Sama and colleagues, individually and together on a 'quest for experimentation and knowledge creation outside of the norm, however unique their circumstances'. They are master river-farers and joyful nomads, filled with 'wanderlust for learning and alterity', following and crossing rivers of their own and others' making, along trajectories that are solely their own. Though their journeys stem from troubled waters, their 'stories of wander and wonder' tell of courage, rebelliousness, and will to agency and self-determination.

Non-conformism drives them: as they put it, 'none of [them] had "mentors" – or at least not acceptable ones – who paved the way for [them]. None of [them] wanted, or were willing, to be shaped in the image of someone else'. On their journeys, they willingly oscillate between order and chaos, as they seek and give up safe anchorage in academic institutions, navigate rapids, and go for purposefully slow swims in the swirling currents. Each moves at their own pace, to a rhythm that makes sense to them. The collage of their adventures is a good starting point for exploring this gallery and, indeed, this book, as their aim is to legitimize 'meandering pathways in the context of the scholarly life – that is, to recognize the impact that a digression from what is an established, sequential trajectory can ultimately have in fostering innovation and creativity'.

On a high bank overlooking the treacherous waters, you will see a billboard portrait that will momentarily take you back into the maze, before 'the brightest and the best' research passage. It is a portrait of a rising star academic, fresh out of a PhD, pursuing a specialized and well-defined research agenda. You might wonder what it is doing here, in the Meandering Gallery. But as you move along the river, your perspective will shift, and you will realize that the portrait is a façade. Behind the façade is Lucas Lauriano, the all-over-the-place academic, brooding over the changing reflections in the restless currents. Lucas' façade is a decoy, a pragmatic response to the tension that is particularly acute for early-career academics: how to do meaningful research that enables the researcher to follow open-ended and diverse, empirically driven interests while becoming established, which requires positioning themselves clearly and coherently within a recognizable niche. He argues that creating a coherent façade enables him to 'send a clear message' when introducing himself to new audiences, which simultaneously frees him 'to explore several exciting possibilities… in the background'. He asserts that 'Being "all over the place" is good, it shows our passion, complexities, and diversity', while giving him 'more career options, as well as continually motivating [him] to pursue what [he finds] interesting, and not what is in vogue in a specific subfield'.

Further along, not far from the endless flow of the river, fed perhaps by one of its streams, lie the still waters of a pond enveloped by a rocky shore. Here you will meet Mark Saunders, cheerfully skipping pebbles across the mirror-like surface. A geographer turned management academic, Mark knows his igneous from metamorphic and sedimentary rocks and appreciates their different and varied properties. So it is also with the academic pebbles, he tells us, which fall into the three main types of teaching, research, and service (where each can be further sub-divided), each skipping in different ways. His career story is of learning to skip a 'wide assortment of pebbles that comprise academic life' chosen from all three types of pebbles on the basis that they 'look interesting, appear exciting and fun, and… matter to [him]', while enabling him to work with people he likes. Despite these criteria, skipping pebbles is not always easy; it takes time to learn and even then, some are hard to handle, let alone skip. Some sink immediately without a trace, yet others skim far and wide across the surface, like Mark's research methods book that, originating in his teaching, unexpectedly became a leading international bestseller, causing ripples across the academic pond.

Last but not least (though your own path may well take you to them first), following a tributary of their own choosing are Rweyemamu Ndibalema and colleagues. They renew the critique of the systemic privileging of research over teaching, which, they say, pressures early-career academics into narrow specialisms. By contrast, they reassert and reimagine the value of teaching as a pathway for those they call 'general academics'. These are academics 'who are versatile, have a passion and mainly engage in teaching', and for whom research in multiple areas is a means of developing themselves as broad-minded, well-informed, and inspiring educators who can teach anything to students from diverse backgrounds and in diverse contexts. Arguing that general academics are less well-known than research-oriented academics 'because their stories have not been told', they point out that being an inspirational teacher can be at least as impactful as being a well-published researcher. They offer hope, connection, and optimism for general academics, concluding that their 'stories show that being a general academic can mean doing academia differently, but it does not mean doing academia wrong'.

Having introduced the portraits, I fall silent and let you gaze at the pictures in the sky. Do you see it now, I wonder? Your path, running like a bright, golden thread through the web of bridges? I cannot see it, for it is uniquely yours. Only you can.

As you set off from the platform, I 'hope your road is a long one, full of adventure, full of discovery'.[1] Your journey, like everyone's, transcends this gallery, transcends any narrative, breaking its banks, and flooding the constraints that are designed to channel it.

Where will you go next? There are many ways of leaving this gallery...

Note

1 C.P. Cavafy, *Ithaka* (translated by E. Keely).

MEANDERING ACADEMICS

Linda M. Sama, Mark Egan, Victor J. Friedman, David R. Jones, Nicholas D. Rhew, and Sarah Robinson

Introduction

In this chapter, we explore the multiple interpretations of, and avenues to academic career success as experienced by a group of scholars self-defined as "meandering academics". Bringing to the discussion our shared exploration of "meandering as method" (Friedman et al., 2020), we embark on a deeper understanding of the meandering metaphor as applied to our own career trajectories. We delve into our individual stories of wander and wonder to arrive at a collective appreciation of the ways in which we deviated from prescribed courses of action, conceived of pursuits and norms of behavior more consistent with our own personal values, and empowered ourselves to adapt our careers to our unique outlooks on the meaning of work and success. Our goal in presenting our individual narratives on meandering is twofold: (1) to demonstrate that while we represent fundamentally different disciplines, discrete phases in our careers, and diverse research emphases, we nonetheless arrive at a shared destination of fulfilled purpose; and (2) to legitimate meandering pathways in the context of the scholarly life—that is, to recognize the impact that a digression from what is an established, sequential trajectory can ultimately have in fostering innovation and creativity.

We began our exploration by applying the meandering metaphor to our individual treks through the academic panorama. We found that this metaphor is particularly relevant to a discussion of "doing academic careers differently" because it conjures up difference or deviance in its very articulation. Each narrative that slowly took shape to depict individual portraits of meandering in our collage evidenced themes specific to that journey—consonant themes that spoke to our shared experiences, and dissonant themes that created a bas-relief, projecting ever so slightly from the architecture of the whole. The portraits share themes of identity, insider-outsider dichotomy, self-care and collective care, notions of freedom against superimposed constraints, a love of knowledge and learning, resilience, and ultimately, seeking a "home"—a place of rest. Standing out from this background are foreground themes not always in harmony including concepts related to privilege, differing prioritization schemes with respect to the three-legged pillars of academic life

DOI: 10.4324/9781003267553-4

(that is, teaching, research and service), chaos or structure defining our protruding images, purposeful meanders and accidental meanders, the role of family, the role of dissent, and the very headwaters from which our meanders flowed.

Surveying these themes and stories, we arrive at some foundational concepts that undergird our meandering expeditions and how they have fortified our academic lives, identifying guideposts along the way that may encourage fellow meanderers setting their sights on an academic career to strike their own path at their own pace. We recognized lives of activism, of advancement and of retreat, of railing against convention in ways that slowly transformed the very environments in which we operated, and that could also cause transformations of ourselves, as we adjusted our flow to meet exigent, non-negotiable external demands. We beat against the barriers of obdurate stone walls, eroding their impact at times, and forcing us to take another path at others. We sometimes suffered snags and slowdowns, and went off into trajectories that would revive us, always keeping our eye on the river banks that anchored us. These were the very shapers of our flow as much as we shaped the shoreline—the institutions in which we flourished as academics. And ultimately, we traveled at different paces—some strolling, some rushing—always generating more energy to sustain our excursions. When all was said and done, we realized that with the meanders we fashioned, we carried with us elements for which we had a responsibility and on which we had an impact, and acknowledged our role as good stewards of our planet, of our institutions where we work, and of all who come into the fold after us.

In this gallery, we curate our meanders for the reader in short abstracts of the six meandering academics' experience. These are briefs of much longer narratives that were shared and transcribed over a period of six weeks, and serve as a sort of collection of ink drawings that led to the final, colorful collage we display—a revelatory exposé on the twists and turns of a meandering academic life. We conclude the exhibit with a codicil on the collage that emerged from our work, culminating in a poem in free verse that represents our collective meandering experience.

Our meanders

Nick: turn! turn! turn!

I never planned to be an academic. I just *knew* I was going to be a lawyer-turned-politician. I remember following the 2000 election, age 14, and debating with teachers thrice my age. This interest persisted in high school, but I had little interest in school itself. It is no small miracle that I graduated.

But I did graduate and was accepted to a university in my hometown. College was as interesting and stimulating as high school was disinteresting and depressing—I could not get enough. I spent a semester in England—my first international experience—and picked up a love for cross-national differences. That semester was instrumental in moving my worldview from insular and sure to tolerant and curious. But I still marched toward my original goal. I earned my degree and moved to Chicago to begin law school.

My first year of law school was dreadful. I spent most weekends at home for the worst reasons. Death and disease can spark reflection on life's big questions. I realized that the more I learned about the legal world, the less interested I was in it, and that held for politics.

Abandoning my lifelong dream was liberating; old dreams can exert much pressure. Having finally vocalized my desire to change course near the end of that first year of law school, I felt free to craft what I wanted out of my professional life, *happiness* first. Reflecting on my college experiences, I decided to pursue academia.

After earning my MBA, I applied to doctoral programs and opted for the University of Memphis, where I could work in their international business center. I again loved what I was studying, and I plotted my course to accomplish my own goals. This may not have been possible elsewhere, but it was at Memphis.

In my second year, I saw a flyer about scholarships for a doctoral student teaching boot camp. I wanted to be a master teacher like those who influenced my own learning, but little attention is paid to effective teaching in most doctoral programs. I applied for and received the scholarship. The conference opened my eyes to field of management education. There, I also met several Coastal Carolina University faculty members. These people were seemingly very *happy*. I made a mental note to keep an eye on whether they were hiring.

In my third year, I taught for the first time, and I *loved* it. Late in the year, I saw an ad for a position at CCU. I knew I could finish my dissertation in time to start the position if I put in the long hours needed; I had planned my dissertation work to eliminate many obstacles that prolong defense. I applied for the job, was offered the position, and gladly accepted it.

At CCU, I have been free to chart my own course. I can pursue research that piques my interest. I teach courses that I enjoy and can experiment in the classroom. I have been free to develop study abroad programs—paying forward experiences similar to those that were so transformational for me. I have meaningfully impacted the institution through my service work. I have been *happy*.

David: the wanderlust for learning and alterity

My meander has highlighted 3 tensions which seem to have been prevalent across my academic career and has roots from family, school, university and business life prior to becoming an academic:

1 The first tension is around my continual need for crafting the freedom of an outsider (alterity), with the need to contest unfair, inequitable internal practices within the HE institutions I have worked in.
2 The second tension is my continual need for crafting restorative spaces/places/communities of practice for self-care, whilst at the same time, wanting to support and offer a collective care for other academics.
3 The third tension is my continual need to craft a career around a love of learning and trust more broadly to balance out my anger and hatred of the lingering neo-liberal working environment, with a love of money, markets and mistrust.

These tensions emerged in my early career as a lecturer, when I set up an external leisure crafting initiative, called the Slow Swimming Club, with the aim of providing not only an individual respite to higher education managerialist practices, but a collective resilience and a resistance back in the academics' respective universities. This experience led me to understand the interrelationship between self-care, collective care and the confidence and courage to contest unjust and inequitable practices. It also highlighted the love of learning drawn from an aesthetic and emotional empathy forged between academics from different levels, faculties and universities.

This experience has been crucial in offering an alternative meander possibility in my middle career stage, as a Head of Department (HOD), and in my senior career stage, as a professor. What I realized was that to progress through these stages does not mean that you only play the academic game, but you also can play your own game, which I hope in future can be instrumental in changing the wider institutional game. For example, as HOD and professor I have setup core external research development initiatives, for departmental and faculty respectively, which engage with internal academics through dialog with external academics to foster an ethos around love of research, counter-performativity, interdisciplinary and collegiality. These initiatives are setup to offer critical perspectives around university futures with a view to opening up opportunities for people to not only to contest managerialist practices, but to assert alternatives which also assert an equality back on the system. This resistance is born out of an appreciation of freedom from physical and social space and place, including a bio-cultural connection—embodied practices of disconnection through an ecological connection, such as around an emotional affinity with water, e.g. connecting to river and coastal contexts.

The one crucial lesson I would offer an early career academic is that an alternative meander can be enacted not only by accident but by design as well. Individually and collectively crafting a meander in this proactive way is possible if you can begin to emotionally and aesthetically disconnect and connect back in a reflexive, critical manner at different times and spaces.

Sarah: on crossing and following rivers…

Back and forth, forth and back, swept between two slightly hostile, incompatible worlds: a neglectful, chaotic family life and a rigid, regimented convent school, not feeling at home in either. I try to bridge them and not fall into treacherous waters, to be engulfed in outbursts and chastisement. Silently, I observe, learn how to blend in—to be a chameleon, changing color according to whichever bank I'm washed up onto. Learning helps me to survive but not (yet) to thrive. My brain struggles to focus, to read and write. Instead, I imagine faraway worlds beyond the rigidity and chaos. At 18 my learning difficulties acquire a name, intriguing if unspellable and enable entry to a university far from home.

University provides both the stability and freedom I craved. Books, no longer impenetrable, are a revelation, they take me to the worlds of my dreams. I choose new rivers to follow rather than cross. Pleasantly overwhelmed, I randomly navigate Chinese and Soviet history—my first meander. I find a voice, and affirmation rather than chastisement. I start to participate as well as observe.

I didn't want this journey to stop but didn't have the means to continue formal study. I start to travel, work in Spain and France. Decide on a career in international development so I can keep moving and follow new courses. Do a Masters, join the British Council: four years, three cities in China, three years in Ukraine meandering the country by slow train. Then caught in the currents of politics and mind still racing, too many questions and puzzles. I need to (re)attend to my learning: I announce (rather to my own surprise) "I'm going to do a PhD".

Loved the idea of a whole department of (Management) Learning, where I'm awarded a scholarship, a bit of an outsider in a Business School but found like-minded folk within. I discover Bourdieu—another revelation. He helps me understand my past experiences to reconcile my outsiderness and to put it to use in helping others, and in understanding how chameleon tendencies can be useful for more than survival.

My subsequent academic career has meandered—move jobs every four years, or so… first following a teaching tributary then a research one and then an affective one. Not sure when I stopped trying to find the home I was desperately searching for, but rather have learned to make the most of whatever bank I have clambered onto.

My research has also meandered. Have worked on at least ten different themes in 15 years, my mind keeps moving. I become interested in what I encounter on my physical and intellectual meanders. Love the meanders with students but if honest, not always the subjects I teach—still searching for the right "niche" but perhaps I should stop looking and trust to the meander.

Victor: the not-so-accidental academic

My meander was shaped by a tension between academic knowledge and practical knowing. I always thought I was an "accidental" academic because I had never intended to become one, envisioning myself rather as a practitioner-change agent. In retrospect, I discovered that my meander through academia was not accidental but rather my response to a calling—a passion for learning that would enable me to make a difference in the world.

I started off with the dream of making peace in the Middle East. As an undergraduate, where I studied Arabic and Middle East Studies, I loved the freedom to learn that was so different from high school, but I also felt a gap between academic performance and really knowing. As a young inquirer into Arab-Jewish relations in Tunisia, I experienced "the best failure I ever had" because I learned that learning means engaging the chaos of reality and making enough sense of it to navigate in the world. Learning also requires going through a period of getting lost (not knowing, uncertainty).

In graduate school, in my early professional experiences, and during the first 15 years of my academic career, I felt like I was sailing in a fog, guided by a distant foghorn; I never knew exactly where I was headed, or even where I was, but something called me—emanating from God and resonating with an inner voice. I had wonderful teachers who challenged me, but never a mentor. Part of me longed for that, but perhaps it was fortunate because I learned to listen to that voice. I switched from Arabic to cross-cultural counseling to organizational consulting and action research. Opportunities presented themselves: consulting experiences, great partners, and institutions that provided me freedom to develop in my own way without having to conform. I also had a loving, supportive family.

I responded to the call even if I didn't know where it was leading me. It just felt like the right way to go. Usually it meant doing action research that responded the real needs of people and teaching in ways that meant listening to my students and colleagues, and responding to their needs for growth and development. I felt like I was making a difference even if only a little. I learned to "play the academic game" in a way that enabled me to thrive without losing my self and stopped feeling like an imposter when I could bring my full self to teaching and research. Eventually, through my meander, the fog cleared and I discovered where I am even if I still do not know where I am going.

Linda: an odyssey of reflection, self-discovery, and homecomings

The backdrop to my story of an academic life is marked by a duality—alternating between retreats from trauma and trouble, and forward-seeking movement *toward* an academic home. Ultimately a quest for purpose, I rode the tidal waves of change with both anxiety and anticipation.

I began with no intentions to become something defined in academic circles as "success"—rather, I sought to quell my thirst for knowing and to realize my vision of difference-making. I knew only that, for me, success would mean marrying the personal values I cherished with the professional markers of accomplishment and achievement. Weaving throughout this wandering meander were side explorations that probed different countries, languages and cultures—an important element of my academic life from undergraduate studies and continuing on through today.

Personal and professional loss and trauma propelled me into academe—an escape of sorts from a "borrowed" identity—and yet there also was an element of serendipity, and I broached this new adventure as one of my own making, running toward the prize. I bore visions of what greatness meant for me in this new context—a great teacher, a great scholar—and framed that vision in a panoply of freedoms—freedom of choice, freedom to set priorities, freedom to identify as I wish, and freedom to carve out my own agenda.

Although thwarted at most every turn, I persisted in my quest. Constraints came in the form of financial limitations that narrowed my choices, and from ill-intentioned figures of authority who soured my outlook. My doctoral program carried me up in surges of boundless energy and excitement, and at times drowned me in disappointment, yet I emerged victorious. Seeking escape again from these mournful experiences in New York City to the southwest US for my first post-doctoral faculty job, I landed exactly where I needed to be, and gained the independence and confidence I needed to create my own identity and pursue projects I cared about—all in a safe environment.

In time, my love of NYC propelled my return "home" and I found myself blocks away from the World Trade center in September of 2001 for my second faculty job, only to face another traumatic event that fully marked my return. Yet I persevered. Earning tenure and promotion by largely following conventional norms, I did buck trends and advice by taking on an administrative position several years before going up for tenure that may have spelled political suicide. But I was determined to follow my bliss! That led to another fulfilling administrative role in global programs as a full professor at a new institution in NYC. There, I finally feel free enough to truly engage in meaningful work with students as founder of a micro-lending program that has, for the last 12 years, satisfied my scholarly inclinations while allowing me to spread the message of business as a vehicle for positive social change. And I continue to meander…and continue on my quest.

Mark: recursive metamorphosis: the carnival comes and goes

A life story that is part of everyone's conversational repertoire is describing the worst job you have done. My early life was littered with crap jobs, and the day I decided to forge a career, I was 27 and stood selling balloons at a theme park, batting away kids who couldn't resist running at me and the surrounding mass of inflated foil. I'd simply had enough. Standing around the theme park gave me time to think and plan, I had no sense of academia and merely wanted a route out through education and the supportive structure of a career away from the carnivalesque.

Even from educationally necessitous beginnings, I harbored a passion for learning and felt furthering my education was a card I could play when ready to escape. After years of meandering from various dead end jobs, education became my transformative offshoot. Learning was an escape from the anti-intellectual surrounds of seaside life, of tabloid newspapers in the work canteen, and the dispiriting opinions and judgments that were the sediments of an academically antithetical place that repeatedly topped the national tables for signifiers of deprivation, and was the largest town in the UK without a university.

After studying at night school, I entered Higher Education at 28, and began a change, through many recursive metamorphic moments, not just of my career outlook, but many cultural identifications and embodiments of working class life. The town of my birth and upbringing, home to the tallest roller coaster in the world, was a place of adrenaline fixes, and dangerous rhythms. It had imbibed me with carnival intimidations, where aggressions of guttural sounds and harshness of fast talk attempt to occupy conversational space. University life readjusted the personifications of my upbringing, and shifted my posturing, intonations and hooligan aesthetics to subtler academic tonalities, where I learned to lilt and give people, ideas and thoughts room to ruminate and develop my understandings. More akin to gentle spinning teacups than thrills of the big dipper.

Once my academic career began, and I reached my desire for permanence, I never felt any urgency for career progression and chasing research stars. I have since rejected unhealthy obsessions with research careers and took on more teaching-centered work. My present goals in life have become divergent to the dominant logics and discourses of success aligned to the academic career. My focus has moved elsewhere, to my home, with family, and toward the local community.

When I gained university employment, and the nominal career I'd sought and meandered toward, the desire for furthering a career ceased. Perhaps the metamorphosis was a search for a stabilizing force that I have now found, that the heavy anchorage of institutions provide. It's certainly a more permanent setting than holding aloft a veritable cornucopia of strung out helium balloons.

Codicil: seeing the whole, and imparting experience

We wanted to share these stories of the meandering academic from diverse sources to embolden scholars who opt to amble off the beaten path in their quest for experimentation and knowledge creation outside of the norm, however unique their circumstances. Our meandering is, we affirm, a testament to intellectual curiosity and the fostering of creative solutions, as well as a pillar in forming faculty well-being.

Certain themes weave through our merged portraits:

Theme 1: Love of learning. Each of us was driven by a love of learning—perhaps also sharing that love with others. Certainly, it appears as more than a love of achievement, though learning means something different to each of us.

Theme 2: Tension between learning and orthodox academia. Perhaps each of us strove to integrate on-going learning into our lives but not necessarily as defined, and confined, by orthodox academia and careerism.

Theme 3: Nomadism. All of us emphasized a kind of intellectual, and sometimes physical, perpetual motion, or Nomadism, in our narratives, shaped by oscillation between order and chaos. On the one hand, looking for an intellectual-professional home (order?) and, yet, never wanting to be tied down (challenging, moving on, breaking boundaries). In some cases, this motion was understood as a moving forward and "towards", and in others, retreating or "escape".

Theme 4: Insider-Outsider duality and Self-determination. Being both insiders *and* outsiders was common to all of us, and being non-conformist. None of us had "mentors"—or at least not acceptable ones—who paved the way for us. None of us wanted, or were willing, to be shaped in the image of someone else.

Theme 5: Rhythms, and strolling intensities. Each of us "meandered" at a slightly different pace or with a different rhythm, and these paces and rhythms often shaped our journeys.

For our purposes, meandering allows us to relinquish conventional mores or patterns. Our careers are marked by instances of thinking differently about how to approach the profession, of interactions that cultivated our attitudes and behaviors in unique ways, and of movement into spaces—both physical and spiritual—that permitted restoration and reflection, transcending the accepted wisdom of how academic careers are fashioned. Interestingly, in sharing our stories, we all discover that meandering offers a highly sustainable means of navigating academic waters and of channeling our inner strength to challenge the status quo. This meandering allocates time and contemplative space, freeing us—if even momentarily—from the over-sized demands of urgent timetables; the perspective of students as customers rather than citizen-learners; the incessant, often pointless meetings; and a judgmental performance management agenda built around an insecure, risk-averse dash for accreditations and premier league table standing.

Rather than complying, game-playing or contributing to a nostalgic cynicism, our meanders seek new possibilities for growth and development. They avoid the pitfalls that accompany an overly stipulated progression from junior to senior faculty member—pitfalls borne of a corporatization of universities and a power dynamic that restricts choice and favors authority. To meander is to embrace change and flexibility, and to listen to the signs and signals that alert us to our own intentions—indicators that might have been lost to us without the courage to move off the main riverbed.

The work of Cunliffe (2018, p. 8) resonates with us, as she writes about making deliberate choices within our careers, and "struggling with" our "sense of self in relation to the wider academy". She captures our sense of stewardship and personal responsibility in her story-telling, which we acknowledge as our legacy in passing the baton to those just embarking on their academic careers, or seeking to re-design them. With that in mind, these are the emerging lessons we are eager to share: you *can* have wide-ranging research interests and still have a successful, even prodigious, academic career; you *need not* focus endlessly on one knowledge silo to "make a name for yourself"—rather, you *can* engage in unfettered learning that rejects orthodoxy and embraces diverse perspectives; you *can* enjoy teaching as much as researching and excel in both—understanding that institutional demands may not make it easy, but your resoluteness makes it possible; you *do* have more control over the arc of your career than you think, that is, you *can* take time off and come back to it, you *can* reject mentorship that is unsolicited and unhelpful, and seek mentorship in different disciplines or even professions that is grounding and useful; you *can* incorporate your personal loves into your professional lives in ways that restore you and permit reflection; you *can* refuse to accept unrealistic demands for excellence (often leading to mediocrity) and insist on honest aspiration embracing vulnerability, and by doing so, you *will* earn the respect of your peers—or at least those who count!

Gallery visitors—as you stand back from these individual sketches, you will see how our meandering expeditions coalesce into a collage of portraits that blur at the edges where interwoven themes intersect, yet feature distinct depictions, or bas-reliefs, that reflect stories of agency and self-determination. These are sparked by courage or even rebelliousness, and serve to overcome the barriers to creativity that are placed in the way of exploration outside of the boundaries of a linear and prescribed career path. The process of unveiling this collage is as important to our meandering endeavor as the very individual meanders themselves, as it was a process of deep sharing, uncovering of thematic elements that are at times in harmony, and at times dissonant, and a scratching away at the brushstrokes to find the underlying structure of the bends and curves of our wandering. Our collective meander is an exquisite expedition that came together from our individual journeys, and brought us to this:

Collage—collective meander

> Waters disturbed by troubles, swirling,
> Drive me downstream, eroding surfaces, and depositing unwanted debris,
> Multiple meandering to places unimagined.
> Hearing the language of the river's melodious currents, discovering the contours of my riverbed,
> The shadows of its recesses, the sediments carried in my surges and reversals,
> I rail against the confines obstructing freedom in journeying.
> Yet I have no quarrel with nature's truth shining its light on experience as knowing,
> Carrying me forward even as I digress,
> Showing me the path that honors my longings,
> Posing the storms that demarcate my isolation, urging me, uninhibited, to explore new tributaries.
> What identifies this flow that is my odyssey? Is it betrayal that thwarts forward movement,
> Ever forward, twisting, turning?
> Or is it my own adaptation to the snags and impediments that push me back, further back,
> Only to spin in an eddy of action, resolute, inquiring, unafraid.
> Ah, peaceful settling home, a confluence of experiences,
> Arriving, resting, intending to break away once more,
> A waiting world to explore…
> My strength is in this, my resolve to push away—to overcome the brutishness of unsavory waters,
> Disguised as placidity, I bear the cloak of conformity.
> Still, beneath this tranquil flow—unbounded energy, magically untangling me from webs of pretense,

Healing lacerations ragged and torn
Winding, looping in this meander, I meet my companion rivers, mates
And still the sea awaits.
I attend to its call—the siren's call—redemptive in its song.

References

Cunliffe, A.L. (2018). 'Alterity: The Passion, Politics, and Ethics of Self and Scholarship', *Management Learning*, 49(1), pp. 8–22. Available at: https://doi.org/10.1177/1350507617737454 (accessed 15 January 2021).

Friedman, V.J., Robinson, S., Egan, M., Jones, D.R., Rhew, N.D., and Sama, L.M. (2020). 'Meandering as Method for Conversational Learning and Collaborative Inquiry', *Journal of Management Education*, 44(5), pp. 635–650.

THE ALL-OVER-THE-PLACE ACADEMIC

How to fit in an academic niche but also be free to pursue new and exciting research ideas

Lucas Amaral Lauriano

Introduction

> It seems you're quite experimental in your research, with articles covering too many different topics and theoretical perspectives. You know, at some point, you will have to focus and stick to a specific stream if you want to be recognised by your research.

This conversation happened between a senior lecturer from a well-known business school in London and me. I had previously sent her an e-mail to discuss possible research partnerships and, hopefully, a post-doc position, when I finish my PhD in the upcoming year. Her speech puzzled me, as since the beginning of my studies I was told a researcher has to be flexible and open enough to visualise the mysteries of organisational practices (cf. Alvesson & Kärreman, 2007). However, she was telling me to do quite the opposite: to narrow my view to the point that I could be recognised as a specialist of one specific topic. *How can a junior scholar reconcile producing interesting research and finding only a narrow academic field interesting?* In this chapter, I will explore this question using experiences and reflections from my PhD journey.

Critically analysing the institutionalised practices in academia is essential, especially for junior scholars that struggle to understand how, why and whether they should fit the extremely competitive neoliberal system adopted by business schools (Bristow, Robinson, & Ratle, 2019). Publishing in top journals, having a PhD from a prestigious institution, a great relationship with your supervisors and peers, active participation in conferences, events and social media are some of the long list of norms that one is expected comply with to prosper in academia. The so-called "regime of excellence" (Butler & Spoelstra, 2014) puts pressure on academics at all levels, but is particularly overwhelming to junior scholars, who have to familiarise themselves with the rules rapidly so that they do not "waste time". In this productivity logic, the idea of narrowing down the scope of our research makes sense, as we specialise in one sub-field, direct our efforts to a specific audience, with words, concepts and theories that others researching similar topics (and maybe only them) will understand. However, once junior scholars start following "the rules of the game", and focussing only on one academic niche, frustration might arise. The world has complex and interesting problems, and following alternative theoretical explanations for these new topics that emerge along our academic journey may be tempting.

In retelling my PhD experience and how I navigated through some of these tensions, I adopt an analytic auto-ethnography style (Humphreys & Learmonth, 2012), which allows me to unfold some implications of these events. I broadly divide my narrative according to my studies' years. I argue that one way to reconcile the contradiction of producing interesting research and yet focussing on a narrow field is to create a coherent façade of ourselves to the world but, at the same time, explore different topics, in the background. In this way, we can infiltrate the system. After all, a "narrow academic field" is a construction, a representation of reality, a spectacle (Flyverbom & Reinecke, 2017) and, as such, can be moulded through discourses and narratives.

First year – trying to find a niche

I was a researcher before starting my PhD, so I already knew that I was deeply interested in how organisations implement sustainability. However, I was soon told that I needed to find a more specific and theoretical area, a topic to define my research in the next three years, at least. This sounded like a great responsibility, and it was a very individual and lonely moment that contrasted with some articles I read on the need to craft mysteries, and find different interesting topics to research (e.g. Alvesson & Kärreman, 2007; Davis, 1971). What if I picked a niche now, and later I found out it was not that interesting, or relevant? My supervisors were great and always gave me many suggestions of possible pathways, but the final decision was still mine to make.

After a few months of exploration, many reflections about my own experience and conversations with my supervisors, I decided not to follow a specific theoretical niche but a practical problem. I decided to focus on an empirical problem that I experienced in my previous employment. Before starting my PhD, I worked at a multinational car automaker's subsidiary in Brazil for several years. There, we had an acute problem of alignment and coordination of activities between departments. With limited communication, it was common to find out that other departments were conducting similar projects, that managers did not trust each other, and even competed for resources and prestige. I thus decided to explore how this internal disorganisation was harming their sustainability initiatives, which ultimately demand cross-functional integration. By defining at least a problem to explore, by the end of my first year I could answer the recurring question of "what is your PhD about?". I was not sure if this topic would work out, or the specific "niche" I would be contributing to, but still, just by having an answer to one of the most stressful questions I was asked gave me some momentarily peace of mind.

Second year – lost in possibilities

This was the worst part of my PhD journey. I was not a newbie anymore and could not play dumb when professors or peers asked me detailed questions about my research (e.g. Oh! I just started my PhD, don't know what I'm doing yet). Moreover, it seemed I was already moving towards the end of the PhD, without even having a specific theory to contribute to yet. Even though I was feeling optimistic about the idea of understanding a problem I experienced in my previous job, not knowing exactly how my thesis would turn out or how I would present myself in job interviews was particularly frustrating.

The situation worsened when I spent four months at my previous employer, conducting ethnographic observations, and came back to the UK with many ongoing ideas. Themes "emerged" from my data in a rather eclectic manner. My initial aim was to observe the sustainability activities that my previous employer conducted, and understand their main coordination problems. However, when I started talking to sustainability analysts, they told me about exciting projects to improve diversity in the organisation, and I felt this could be an excellent research opportunity.

I also interviewed many employees, and was very much surprised by a specific group: the participants of a biannual graduate programme the organisation conducted. They were extremely unsatisfied with the project and the company, and claimed they were promised an organisation that did not exist. This case was so fascinating that I knew I needed to explore it somehow. I had then many ideas that, initially, were not convergent. It did not bother me, until I had to explain to others what I was researching.

Third and fourth years – creating a façade

At the beginning of the third and what was at the time the last[1] year of my PhD, I started looking for post-docs and assistant professor positions. This was when I met the senior lecturer I mentioned at the beginning of the chapter. Although I had always felt that I was following a rather unconventional path in my studies, it was the first time that another person was struggling to understand exactly what I was doing and being quite normative about how I should develop my career.

In a way, she was correct because I was presenting myself in a, to some extent, confusing way. "Oh, I'm researching this group of trainees, and also why sustainability practices do not achieve their intended results. Also, I'm very much interested in how stigmatised employees deal with the growing demand for social media usage for work purposes". (This last topic came from the initial conversations on diversity with workers at the company.) In sum, my research was "all over the place". However, I could not stop thinking that she was wrong, that I would never limit myself by focussing only on one specific stream of theory. After all, that was the main reason I decided to quit my previous job, to follow this curiosity and hunger for learning new topics.

I then realised the main reason why this conversation was so shocking was that I had very open-minded academics surrounding me. For them, it was customary to pursue different research topics, but that was not the case in the broader mainstream academic world. Inspired by the many articles I read on façades, identities and discursive construction of reality (e.g. Abrahamson & Baumard, 2009; Cho, Laine, Roberts, & Rodrigue, 2015; Flyverbom & Reinecke, 2017), I then decided to create my own façade in response to the need of presenting my research in a constrained subfield. Sustainability implementation became my choice of "niche", as it was broad enough to incorporate the topics I was exploring (diversity and long-term HR perspectives could be part of a sustainability strategy, as they indeed were connected in the organisation I was studying). Additionally, sustainability implementation had the benefit of being specific enough so that I could build the argument of contribution to a theoretical stream. From then on, every time I am applying for a position or presenting myself to a new audience I reinforce that I am very much focussed on sustainability implementation. It is a simple answer that avoids many questions, and at the same time positions me within some of the necessary "boxes" of academic knowledge.

However, do not be fooled! This façade works to synthesise my research, to satisfy more conservative academics, but also allows me to pursue different research topics in the background. My research on stigma management, for example, is relatively far from what we traditionally understand as sustainability implementation. Such an "academic niche" is typically concerned with tools, approaches and tensions in organisations to deal with social and environmental aspects (e.g. Hahn, Figge, Pinkse, & Preuss, 2018; Hahn, Pinkse, Preuss, & Figge, 2015; Hengst, Jarzabkowski, Hoegl, & Muethel, 2019). In my study, however, I draw on identity work and social media studies (Bataille & Vough, 2020; Vitak, 2012; Vitak, Lampe, Gray, & Ellison, 2012), because after many iterations with colleagues, peers and reviewers, I concluded that those were the streams of theory that were most compelling to explain my case. Had I been tied to a specific theoretical niche, I would insist on applying the same perspectives over and over again, limiting myself considerably. I have seen many colleagues with this view about their research in conferences. Other peers made relevant and interesting suggestions with alternative theories to explore the articles being presented, only to be discarded by the authors, who claimed that "this is not my/our expertise field".

Therefore, by creating this coherent façade when I need to introduce my research to new audiences, I send a clear message that also frees me to explore several exciting possibilities to explain the world in the background.

The main takeaways

In this chapter, I was guided by the question: *how can a junior scholar reconcile the contradiction of producing interesting research and finding only a narrow academic field interesting?* I used my own experience to show how I moved from a broad research interest to many different research projects. Finally, I summarised such ideas into the academic niche of "sustainability implementation", even though, for each specific part of my studies I drew on streams of theory that divert considerably from what traditional studies on sustainability implementation would typically explore.

Critically analysing my own ideas, four main steps could help other junior scholars that, like me, are excited about the opportunity of studying virtually anything, but at the same time feel constrained by the current system:

1 *Start with the empirical.* Which are the phenomena that excite you? Focussing on cases gives us time to explore different theoretical explanations and serves as an answer to the frightening question "what is your PhD about?" in the first year, at least. It also gives us more confidence, as we can test the waters, see what others think about the topic, and peers may even suggest future theories to be explored.
2 *Let the themes emerge.* I acknowledge that themes do not just "pop up" from the data, as our perceptions and experiences very much direct our attention to specific topics. Still, exciting ideas can be developed when one does not limit themselves to a specific theoretical stream upfront. Let the ideas flow, work with assumptions, explanations, observations. Even the craziest ideas might be polished later to fit the "academic norms".
3 *Create a short explanation of your research.* Although the different themes may seem initially dispersed, it is highly likely that one could find an academic synthesis of the many

emerging topics. This is important to comply with the more mainstream idea that we have to tie ourselves to an academic niche, but do not worry, as this is only the façade you are creating. Also, it helps a great deal when looking for jobs, and you have to present yourself to the world in a coherent manner.
4 *Use the façade, and explore alternative possibilities in the background.* This is perhaps the most important step. Once you locate your main research interests into one "niche" to the "external world", you are free to explore endless possibilities, theories and explanations for your cases. You will be fine, as long as you are compelling in your arguments, methodologically robust, and, of course, refer back to the façade of the academic niche, when demanded.

The advantage of letting our ideas flow first, and only then trying to locate a niche to use as a façade is that, in this process, we become tied to our research interests, and not the academic field. Looking at the applications for jobs I am making, for example, beyond specific positions that deal directly with sustainability (or corporate social responsibility (CSR)), I can easily argue that I am working heavily on Organizational Behaviour, as many of my cases are on reactions and perceptions from employees. I can also argue I work with International Management, as my cases are from Brazil, and I often explain the institutional environment in my theory-building. In sum, being "all over the place" is giving me more career options, as well as continually motivating me to pursue what I find interesting, and not what is in vogue in a specific subfield.

How much does this approach change the current "rules of the game"?

One could argue that those who adopt such a façade are actually not changing anything, as they are mainly complying – at least partially – with current mainstream academic demands. This might be true, especially in the case of junior scholars like me, who are still trying to figure out how this each day weirder academic world works. I could not just get crazy and conduct completely different studies that would not translate into a thesis later. These are strongly traditional norms that I could not overcome during my PhD. I found a way through, a less painful alternative to rigid academic rules.

However, the exercise of sharing these ideas, by trying to persuade others also to be more flexible about their own research, can generate an impact. With this chapter, I hope that, whoever is reading it, can somehow identify with the challenges and dilemmas I went through. I am pretty sure I am not alone in this, and many others struggled, or are still struggling, with these institutional pressures that limit us. Being "all over the place" is good, it shows our passion, complexities, and diversity. Thus, change and normalisation of trying different approaches and theories do not come from what I did, but from what we can do, as academics, in the future. In my view, changes start with writing chapters and books like this, that make us stop and reflect on our own practices. These reflective moments show that there are multiple ways of reaching the same ends, and hopefully, will incentive us to accept such differences when we face them, be it in our conferences, supervisions, or academic research processes.

Note

1 Later I decided to extend it to a fourth year, Covid happened and we all know the rest.

References

Abrahamson, E., & Baumard, P. 2009. What Lies Behind Organizational Façades and How Organizational Façades Lie: An Untold Story of Organizational Decision Making. *The Oxford Handbook of Organizational Decision Making.* https://doi.org/10.1093/oxfordhb/9780199290468.003.0023.

Alvesson, M., & Kärreman, D. 2007. Constructing Mystery: Empirical Matters in Theory Development. *Academy of Management Review*, 32(4): 1265–1281.

Bataille, C. D., & Vough, H. C. 2020. More than the Sum of My Parts: An Intrapersonal Network Approach to Identity Work in Response to Identity Opportunities and Threats. *Academy of Management Review*, https://doi.org/10.5465/amr.2018.0026.

Bristow, A., Robinson, S., & Ratle, O. 2019. Academic Arrhythmia: Disruption, Dissonance, and Conflict in the Early-Career Rhythms of CMS Academics. *Academy of Management Learning and Education*, 18(2): 241–260.

Butler, N., & Spoelstra, S. 2014. The Regime of Excellence and the Erosion of Ethos in Critical Management Studies. *British Journal of Management*, 25(3): 538–550.

Cho, C. H., Laine, M., Roberts, R. W., & Rodrigue, M. 2015. Organized Hypocrisy, Organizational Façades, and Sustainability Reporting. *Accounting, Organizations and Society*, 40: 78–94.

Davis, M. S. 1971. That's Interesting! *Philosophy of the Social Sciences*, 1(2): 309–344.

Flyverbom, M., & Reinecke, J. 2017. The Spectacle and Organization Studies. *Organization Studies*, 38(11): 1625–1643.

Hahn, T., Figge, F., Pinkse, J., & Preuss, L. 2018. A Paradox Perspective on Corporate Sustainability: Descriptive, Instrumental, and Normative Aspects. *Journal of Business Ethics*, 148(2): 235–248.

Hahn, T., Pinkse, J., Preuss, L., & Figge, F. 2015. Tensions in Corporate Sustainability: Towards an Integrative Framework. *Journal of Business Ethics*, 127(2): 297–316.

Hengst, I.-A., Jarzabkowski, P., Hoegl, M., & Muethel, M. 2019. Toward a Process Theory of Making Sustainability Strategies Legitimate in Action. *Academy of Management Journal*, 63(1). https://doi.org/10.5465/amj.2016.0960.

Humphreys, M., & Learmonth, M. 2012. Autoethnography in Organizational Research: Two Tales of Two Cities. Chapter 18 in Symon, G. & Cassell, C. (Eds.) *Qualitative Organizational Research: Core Methods and Current Challenges*, 314–330.

Vitak, J. 2012. The Impact of Context Collapse and Privacy on Social Network Site Disclosures. *Journal of Broadcasting & Electronic Media*, 56(4): 451–470.

Vitak, J., Lampe, C., Gray, R., & Ellison, N. B. 2012. Why Won't You Be My Facebook Friend? *Proceedings of the 2012 IConference* (February 2015): 555–557.

A PEBBLE SKIPPER'S TALE

Mark N.K. Saunders

Introducing pebbles, skipping and the academic pond

Ever since I can remember I have 'skipped' rock pebbles over water, seeing how far each travels and counting the bounces off the surface (Figure 4.1). In this chapter I offer my story as an academic pebble skipper with the gift of hindsight and from a position of privilege. I am white, male, born and raised in rural south-east England. After school, my university education – including a master's degree, teaching qualification and doctorate in Geography – was free to me. Following five years working in 'research' jobs in planning and social care, I have spent three decades embracing all aspects of academic work. While working at a college and three universities, for over half the time as a full professor, I have selected from the wide assortment of pebbles that comprise academic life, those that look interesting, appear exciting and fun, and which matter to me. While trying to make each skip across the academic pond, I have worked with and continue to work with amazing people whose company I value and who both challenge and support. Inevitably there have been times when aspects of the work have been gruelling and I have doubted my own skipping abilities but, overall, I have been employed to do something I still enjoy.

For me the pebbles that are the foci of academic work, like rock pebbles, comprise three types. However, rather than being either an igneous, metamorphic or sedimentary rock, academic pebbles comprise research, service (citizenship), and (learning and) teaching. Just as each of the three types of rock can be further sub-divided, so can academic pebbles: basic or applied research, programme leadership or school management, specific subjects or groups of students, to name but a few. Each pebble has distinguishing characteristics which come to the fore when, engaging with others, we try to make it skip across the water that is the academic pond in which we work. Some are easy to skip, skimming across the pond. Others are more difficult, skipping one or two times before sinking beneath the surface. Some pebbles leave a trail of ripples, the associated energy moving outwards through waves and, when combined with others, further increasing their power. Others almost glide across the pond, curving perhaps left or right, leaving a wake-like trail behind them as their energy fades quickly.

DOI: 10.4324/9781003267553-6

FIGURE 4.1 Pebble skipping. Photograph by author.

Over the years I have improved my pebble skipping skills, learning with and from colleagues and students. Yet, I am nowhere near being an academic world record holder for skipping any type of pebble.[1] While I have a smattering of publications in top-ranked academic journals which are well cited, most are at best 'reasonable'; and my research income is mainly from industry rather than highly prized sources such as research councils or governments. Similarly, although I have undertaken a range of service roles in universities and for learned societies, I realised a fair few years ago I did not want to become a business school dean or chairperson. My teaching evaluations are usually good, although the perfect score remains elusive. I have however written a number of textbooks, including one which is considered a best-seller[2] selling far more copies than I ever dreamed possible.

In summary, I see myself as reasonably adept at research, teaching and service and, crucially, as someone who values and enjoys working with others to skip the variety of pebbles that can make up academic life.

In the following pages I offer a post hoc, reflective, quasi-chronological account of skipping pebbles on the academic pond. I start with my nascent skipping skills when I took my first academic post and my first decade at a teaching-focussed college (now a university). Here I explore my learning with others to skip a variety of pebbles, their subsequent trajectories, and reflect on the genesis of one particular pebble – my most successful skip yet. I next recount my evolving abilities for skipping teaching, research and service pebbles with colleagues, across what I have come to realise is a worldwide pond. Within this I offer first examples drawn from pebbles skipping at a research informed university where I was increasingly drawn into management. I then consider my refocussing on those pebbles that really matter to me while working at two research intensive (led) universities. Here I reveal how the energy from the pebbles (represented by ripples) appeared for a while to dissipate, causing me to question my skipping skills. I conclude with a postscript reframing my learning as a series of questions for other pebble skippers. These I derived from those aspects that continue to be important to my career path; one of embracing the variety of pebbles, doing what matters to me and crucially working with people.

Learning to skip

Five years after my doctorate I needed a career change. I had been working in local government first as a planner building demographic forecasting models and databases, and subsequently as a researcher in social services. I had been promoted, developed as a manager, lead 'research' projects, become a steering committee member for a national network of social care researchers organising their annual conference, co-authored and published practitioner focussed articles and written a pamphlet to support social workers researching their practice. Yet, while enjoyable, I missed academia, in particular bouncing ideas with colleagues and teaching students. The local college of higher education had just started offering business studies undergraduate degrees and advertised for a lecturer in business information technology and statistics. I thought this fitted my skills, and they wanted a person with work experience and a higher degree. I reckoned skills already gained through my teaching qualification and then developed while undertaking doctorate, although somewhat rusty, would help. My self-assessment of my academic business knowledge was 'zero', but the post looked interesting, so I crafted an application, submitted it and was invited for interview.

Teaching pebbles

A month later I had not heard the outcome so telephoned. I was told that although someone else had accepted the post, they would like me to teach information management, statistics and operations management. While I had some knowledge of the first two subjects, I had never heard of operations management. Their initial response: 'You talked about that in your interview' was unhelpful. Having established what operations management was, I accepted the job and returned to the academic pond. For the next year, my life was prepare, teach, sleep, repeat; culminating in marking numerous assignments, and it was fantastic! I was teaching mainly undergraduate and post-experience classes. Supported by my new colleagues, I experimented and discovered which pedagogic approaches worked well with different groups and, by the end of the year I could skip these teaching pebbles. For statistics and information management modules I felt on top of the practical aspects and now knew sufficient business academic literature. I worked with wonderful colleagues who supported me with advice, teaching materials and who encouraged me to try out ways of making the pebbles skip.

The only module where I was, literally, on my own was operations management for post-experience students. This pebble was difficult to grasp and in my early classes failed to skip, slipping from my hand and sinking with few ripples. I asked for help and was told 'you're doing fine, you can't be worse than the previous person'. I talked to the students about how we could work together to improve their learning experience, amended my delivery and the pebble began to skip, albeit bouncing only a few times. By the end of my first year in academia I had taught over 550 hours face-to-face, learnt a vast amount and, most importantly enjoyed teaching students and working with colleagues.

Research and service pebbles

With experience, preparation became less time consuming. A colleague and I started writing about our pedagogic practice, publishing a few articles; and I co-authored my first textbook on business statistics. Recognising what they considered 'expertise' in survey design and analysis, colleagues invited me to contribute to a range of consultancy projects within areas of human resources. These applied research 'pebbles' were concerned mainly with aspects of employee involvement and communication so, invariably I began to build my human resource management (HRM) knowledge; developing friendships as I co-authored research papers based on these projects and, increasingly, teaching on such modules. My previous employer invited me back as a consultant to undertake an employee satisfaction survey and, concerned about my lack of knowledge, I invited a colleague with HRM expertise to help. Our finished report was praised by the organisation who acted upon the recommendations, subsequently awarding us further work. Alongside these consultancies we developed journal articles, the applied ripples' 'energy' enabling our academic research through access to data and, crucially, funding for conferences.

Our Dean encouraged us to develop an applied research centre in HRM and, because of my research methods knowledge, I was asked to lead it. As a small team we developed a 'clever consultancy' strategy of working with organisations and, with their permission, using the data collected to inform our academic research; thereby ensuring the ripples from both pebbles were constructively reinforcing. Within the centre, we worked to develop members as researchers, ensuring we shared our skills and knowledge within each project, reading and commenting critically on each other's work; and working together on papers on aspects of change, in particular downsizing and employee communication. These we submitted to conferences and, subsequently, journals. This was exciting and meaningful; I was developing my knowledge of research methods and HR implications of change, as well as linking practice with academia.

Alongside co-authored HRM papers, I continued to write with colleagues about our pedagogic practice such as developing dissertation assessment criteria and issues associated with teaching focussed academics becoming researchers. Although there was no real pressure then to publish in particular journals I was, with the support of colleagues, honing my writing abilities and developing my academic knowledge. Among others I crafted what I now call my 'conversion paper', through which I moved mentally from being a geographer to a management academic. This single authored paper integrated the human resource management and migration literatures on vacancy notification and employee mobility, the subject of my doctorate, highlighting issues about how the topic was researched. Although this pebble skipped very few times, sinking almost without trace, it helped establish *me* as a management academic in my mind.

The genesis of my most successful pebble skip (yet)

The College was expanding its postgraduate programmes and, as one of the people considered research active, I was fortunate to be involved in these exciting developments; recruiting doctoral students and teaching research methods. For the research methods module we could not find one textbook covering everything, so recommended our students needed to purchase three. They felt a better option was for us to write the one book needed. I discussed this idea with the two colleagues with whom I co-taught the module, and, with persuasion, they offered to co-author if I lead the project. Having reviewed existing books, I used my pamphlet on research methods as the starting point of the proposal for what became *Research Methods for Business Students* (RMB). As co-authors we debated and refined the proposal over the next few months and I approached potential publishers. Responses were, without exception, negative. Despite having already published a textbook, this new teaching pebble appeared unlikely to be ever thrown, let alone skip.

By chance I mentioned RMB to a publisher's representative who, rather than dismissing, showed interest. She asked for a proposal and sample chapter and, following positive reviews, we had a contract; albeit with the warning that such books did not sell in large numbers, probably less than a thousand a year. We drafted RMB, trialling each chapter with our master's students and colleagues and incorporating their and each other's feedback. The book took over my life. I built a small table in the utility room and wrote at evenings and weekends, my young daughter often sitting next to me and 'writing' her book. In spite of the publishers' warning, the book skipped across the academic pond, selling over four thousand copies in its first year!

Since the first edition was published our RMB pebble has taken on a life of its own, selling nearly half a million copies. The ripples created and the subsequent impact of their energy on the amplitude of other pebbles' ripples have been considerable helping create and enhance my reputation.[3] We have incorporated some findings from my methods research with colleagues in subsequent editions, and these have also been amplified around the globe by translation into five other languages. One aspect, my conceptualisation of the research process as peeling layers from a 'research onion' has become a pebble in its own right creating its own ripples, this metaphor somehow sticking in people's minds. Yet the onion nearly did not make it into the book. A prototype diagram spent months on the whiteboard in my office, visitors being asked their opinions. Although I was enthusiastic, my co-authors were less so initially. However, as others found it helpful, it was included. RMB has continued to evolve, reflecting the growing body of knowledge and developments in research methods and methodology. In this we have been helped by numerous friends and colleagues who have given feedback, occasionally harsh but always fair, as well as contributing case studies from their disciplines. I continue to make copious notes on aspects potentially worthy of inclusion in the next edition, ensuring the book's skipping abilities are supported by being up to date, relevant and useful.

Trying for promotion

I now had co-authored textbooks, an applied research track record with associated income and journal articles, teaching experience from undergraduate to doctoral level (including doctoral summer schools) accompanied by good teaching scores, and was supervising three PhD students. I had been promoted a few years earlier, but felt I now met all the criteria for a readership (associate professor). I applied and was told I still needed a PhD completion. My next application for promotion was turned down because I needed a professional qualification. With my partner now unable to work for health reasons, developing my career had an urgency. I took the first year of the Diploma in Personnel Management course, being taught by colleagues, and became a member of the Chartered Institute of Personnel and Development via their 'portfolio route'. Applying now with this professional qualification, two PhD completions, additional co-authored journal articles and further textbooks, I was rejected because I needed more single authored publications. My self-confidence in my abilities was knocked but, eventually, I remembered I enjoyed my job and got on well with my colleagues; and my partner's health had begun to improve.

A few months later, I was chatting at a conference and was asked if would consider moving to another institution. I was flattered, but presumed it was just a conference conversation. A few weeks later I was invited for an informal chat about a possible job focussed on developing research capacity in a research informed university's business school. I met and liked the people, was excited by the job, applied, was interviewed and accepted the job offer.

Skipping research, teaching and, particularly, service pebbles

Perceived pebble skipping abilities

At the new university, others' perceptions of me seemed different. People assumed I knew how to skip research, teaching and service pebbles. I operationalised my service role as working with and enabling others to skip both research and (research methods) teaching pebbles. I also commenced my still ongoing involvement in the British Academy of Management's (BAM) Research Methodology Special Interest Group (SIG), presenting at their 'sharing our struggles' workshop on teaching research methods. At the university, we developed doctoral training which could be accessed by both full and part time students, establishing a summer school drawing on my learning from the College. We were successful in a bid to provide 25 doctoral students with a residential week of intensive research methods learning. The students developed as researchers forming a strong cohort identity; the summer school pebble continuing to skip for many years, for some jointly with another university.

I also picked up a new pebble which has evolved into an enduring interest in trust within and between organisations, researching and publishing both with colleagues at the new university and my previous college. Together we developed a bid for research council money to fund a seminar series and were successful. A contract for a book was signed and, alongside papers utilising data from ongoing clever consultancy, we began to expand our expertise.

We were excited believing this new pebble, while fundamental to organisations, posed as yet unanswered questions and offered a number of captivating methodological issues.

The lure of a service pebble

The business school's preparations for the next national research assessment exercise, in my view, needed a more strategic approach. Although not skipping this research management pebble, I voiced my concerns to the Research Director who agreed. We discussed ideas of how we might develop a fully costed inclusive strategy and invited all associate and full professors to an awayday to start to build a research strategy for the School. After much debate, we found a way forward and built the strategy, presenting it to the Dean and School Management Team.

Although asked to lead the implementation I refused arguing it would be disrespectful to the existing Research Director. An additional 'service' role to lead the strategy was created for which I applied and was appointed. I was also asked to apply for promotion to full professor (of research methods) but declined, feeling I could not deal with a potential rejection. Years later when more confident; with considerable support from the Dean, other colleagues and my external referees, I applied and was successful.

Crystalising which pebbles really matter

As a Research Director my responsibilities for operationalising the strategy and preparing the research assessment submission took a far greater proportion of my time. I was supported to attend the BAM and Chartered Association of Business School's (CABS) Development Programme for Directors of Research to learn about directing research. Here I met people who were to become lasting friends. Colleagues suggested subsequently I should consider my next promotion and think about becoming a dean. I attended a dean's development programme, and it remains one of the most useful courses I have ever taken. It revealed that I did not wish to even pick up, l°one skip, a business school dean pebble. I was finding it increasingly difficult to make time to keep both research and teaching pebbles skipping alongside the service pebble while ensuring also the RMB pebble was kept up to date. Initially I found that by working evenings and at weekends I could keep on top of everything, but soon even this did not create sufficient time; and the enjoyment was declining. I needed to do something, so spoke with my Dean. He was understanding, helping me reflect on what it was that really mattered to me and to think through potential scenarios for my future. With the School's submission for the research assessment exercise now complete, I would devote more time to skipping both teaching and research pebbles.

While at the new university I began to be asked to externally examine doctorates in HRM, often being asked to focus particularly on the methodology. These were fantastic opportunities as they nearly always allowed me to extend my knowledge, have a good 'research' discussion as well as get to know new researchers. Where the doctorate was an area where I had reasonable expertise I usually agreed. One such examination was at a research-intensive university where a former colleague was now working. I travelled the afternoon before so we could go out for supper and chat. Towards the end of the evening she dropped into the conversation that her Dean wanted to talk to me about a job vacancy!

The student provided an excellent defence of the PhD thesis and, afterwards, the Dean asked if I would be interested in moving to his School. I knew I was able to and enjoyed skipping teaching pebbles but, while wanting to develop further my skipping skills, was uncertain whether I could make research pebbles skip sufficiently for a research-intensive university. I needed time to think; although my family were supportive, taking such a job would mean a weekly commute or moving home. By chance I spent time with the research group I might be joining at a conference. They were warm and inspiring people, so I applied.

Refocussing on skipping pebbles that matter to *me*

Constructive and destructive ripples

I arrived at the research-intensive university on crutches with a knee injury, gave my presentation and waited for my interview! Interview questions were much as I had expected, but I was asked what I would say if invited to be the research director? To their very obvious surprise, I answered 'no' explaining I wished to focus on (skipping) research and teaching (pebbles). Despite, or perhaps because of, this I was offered the full professorship, leading master's level research methods teaching and having plenty of time for research. I found a small hotel and began my weekly commute.

My new normal at this research-intensive university was joyous. Whereas previously I had been chastised by some for saying research is fun and part of what we do, now research pebbles were everyday working life. I had numerous conversations with colleagues about research and taught with people who were also researching methods. Every week I was skipping both research and teaching pebbles and I knew I was developing. My new colleagues were awe-inspiring and willing to share. I discussed a reviewer's comment on an article with one and, in addition to answering my questions, we mapped out a new research project which we undertook. Discussion with another colleague about our parents, as patients, trusting clinicians even when they made errors, evolved into a project. Yet another asked for some help when meeting a potential applied research client. We won the contract and became good friends; undertaking a series of research projects and publishing together until his untimely death.

Opportunities to skip new service pebbles were also increasing. Alongside a continuing membership of the BAM's Research Methodology SIG, I had been elected onto BAM Council and was tasked with coordinating their annual doctoral symposium. I became a regular presenter at the First International Network for Trust (FINT) and the University Forum for Human Resource Development (UFHRD) conferences and, for a number of years, organised the latter's doctoral symposium. Invitations came to give master classes on research methods at different universities and present our trust research, both in the UK and overseas. The ripples from RMB and my research ripples were constructively reinforcing each other.

Teaching continued to be fun and I was contributing to research methods classes for all postgraduates. Masters' students' dissertations' quality improved and my feedback scores for the classes were good. A new Dean was appointed, and I became the Director of PhD programmes for the School. I was invited to apply to another research-intensive university, was interviewed and, despite being offered the job, declined. I was really enjoying working on doctoral programmes with colleagues and across the university. Our work seemed to be making a difference to students and their studies, and I was promised my first ever sabbatical at the end of my directorship term. We were also creating a new PhD with integrated doctoral training, adapting the North American model for the UK environment. However, although praised, adopted elsewhere in the university and recruiting well, our new PhD was not considered sufficiently American necessitating us developing a replacement.

My sabbatical was now especially welcome. I concentrated on my research and publications, revised RMB for the next edition and, thanks to a friend recommending me, spent a month as a visiting professor in Australia. I kept in touch with colleagues at the business school, but it no longer seemed a happy place. All staff had been told voluntary redundancy was available; one colleague in our subject group had already left, and others were looking to leave. Still on sabbatical I was told my research outputs were poor quality, an article which is still one of my favourites was particularly poor (my current university has a different opinion!), and I would no longer be responsible for research methods teaching. I was told I should skip pebbles with people who were better researchers, rather than my current collaborators. This had a destructive impact on my self-belief. I questioned whether I could skip service and, in particular research pebbles and my enjoyment dissipated. Colleagues were supportive but some, sadly, were receiving similar messages about their skipping skills. I needed to find another job; the only time I had actively searched since taking up my first academic post. Five people left our research group that year, four on the same day including me.

Returning to constructive ripples

My current University is also 'research intensive'. I am once again enjoying skipping all three types of pebbles with colleagues and, crucially, have regained some confidence in my abilities. I know that engaging with all three types of pebbles and the variety they offer is part of me. Although I am considered someone who can skip all these pebbles, I still have doubts about my abilities, especially with research pebbles. These research pebbles continue to focus on methods and trust. I am fortunate and enjoy working with friends, colleagues and doctoral students from previous and current institutions, addressing issues and questions we find relevant and exciting. Together we continue to skip methods and methodology pebbles, looking to better understand the implications of participant selection and sample size alongside different aspects of research reporting to try and enhance methodologically rigorous research. The ripples from these pebbles reinforce, and are reinforced by, RMB. I also continue to pick up and skip trust pebbles exploring trust (and distrust) in situations where a better understanding of how trust is formed and developed can make a real difference to people's lived experiences. These include relationships between patients and doctors, SMEs and universities, as well as within virtual teams and consultancy firms. The ripples each pebble makes are, invariably, amplified as their impact constructively reinforces our growing body of work.

My teaching pebbles continue to focus on enabling people to use research methods rigorously and ensuring the textbook is up to date and remains useful. There are clear synergies between these teaching and research pebbles and the service pebbles I skip. After I joined the university, I was Director of the Master's in Social Research Methods, which delivers methods training to all our social science doctoral students. Subsequently I have been Director of Postgraduate Research Programmes for the business school and am now Director of Global Engagement, developing both teaching and research relationships. I have also continued to skip service pebbles outside the university with BAM; and by delivering, principally, research methods seminars and workshops, as well as co-organising doctoral colloquiums such as for trust researchers through FINT. I still see other exciting pebbles to pick and try to skip as I continue my career path.

Postscript

An alternative interpretation of much of this tale could be a gradual consolidation of the three types of pebbles into a conglomerate comprising proficiency in research methods. Indeed, while meandering along my career path, I have been fortunate to witness the emergence of research methods as a legitimate field; now with its own academic experts, recognised journals and sections within journals, and a plethora of books.

However, in reflecting on the pebbles and the people with whom I skip them, certain aspects have been and continue to be important to *me*. My enjoyment and belief in the cruciality of rigorous research methods remains integral to much of my engagement with all three types of pebbles. A friend said recently that I always start by saying how much I enjoy everything, when I should start by saying how much I've accomplished. Yet for me, this enjoyment is essential. It comes from working and learning with people to skip the three types of pebble, and through enabling others. Pebbles that sank without a ripple or failed to skip have provided crucial learning. Throughout colleagues and friends have been companions, dispensing tough love when needed. These and other aspects have been outlined in my tale; they are part of and are fundamental to *me*. Consequently, rather than simply summarising I encourage you to reflect on possible choices for your own pebble skipping using, at least initially, the following questions:

- What matters to you most about skipping academic pebbles?
- How important is it that you really enjoy skipping the pebbles you pick up?
- How important is it to make a difference with the pebbles you skip?
- Is it more important to skip pebbles with people you like or people who will advance your career?
- Have you considered how the ripples from the different pebbles you skip can constructively reinforce each other?
- How important is it for you to have synergies between the pebbles you skip?
- Have you reflected on your learning from both pebbles that skipped well and those which sank, almost without a trace?
- Have you thought about how you will deal with future failures to skip pebbles?
- Will you focus on a few types of pebble or skip a wider variety?

My list is not exhaustive; different questions may be important, and over time answers may alter. But, as a friend reading an earlier draft commented, in the academic pond we have the opportunity to experiment skipping different pebbles, to sometimes get it wrong, and continue to learn. We are fortunate.

Acknowledgements

My pebble skipping would not have happened in this way without the caring criticism, love and warmth of colleagues, friends and family. Each of you has played an important part in my story and yet, sadly, together you become too many to namecheck. I hope you recognise my tale as one representation of heartfelt thanks for helping me learn and grow into *me*, and your part in co-creating this career path.

Notes

1. At the time of submission (January 2022) the Guinness World Record for skipping stones is 88 skips, achieved by Kurt Steiner in 2013. https://www.guinnessworldrecords.com/world-records/most-skips-of-a-skimming-stone/.
2. Saunders, M.N.K., Lewis, P. and Thornhill, A. (2019) *Research Methods for Business Students* (8th edition), Harlow: Pearson.
3. In June 2021, I discovered *Research Methods for Business Students* had been ranked 1st as the most influential business and economics textbook in the "FT (Financial Times) Teaching Power" worldwide league table [Jack, A. (2021) 'Harvard's teaching power puts business school in the lead for influence' *Financial Times* 31 May]. Thank you to all who recommend it on their reading lists and, crucially, to those who use and find the book useful.

THE GENERAL ACADEMIC

Rweyemamu Alphonce Ndibalema, Essa Bah, and Sophia Kokugonza Ndibalema

Introduction

The Oxford Dictionary defines an academic as a teacher or scholar in a university or other institution of Higher Education (HE). Arguably then, the identity of an academic is established through their role as a teacher, researcher, or both in a HE institution. In theory, teaching and research roles and, therefore, teaching and research staff have equal importance and status as academics. The average person on the street may consider us all as lecturers. However, this is a far cry from the current practices. For quite a while now, teaching and research have by no means been perceived to be equal in academic circles. More often, research appears to take centre stage, especially in universities that tend to top the international league tables. Conferences organised to prepare PhD students for an academic career tend to emphasise the need to develop expertise in a niche area of research as well as publishing multiple articles in high ranked journals. Thus, an academic's value and potential for career development appears to stem from and revolve around research portfolios and publications.

Teaching only, on the other hand, while a necessary function of a university, is rarely given as much recognition. For some academics, teaching only is not considered a symbol of prestige and does not appear to elevate one to an elite status in the academic community. From our experiences, it is very common to receive advice on career development and promotion revolving around 'publish or perish' culture.

Prestigious universities increasingly tend to hire early-career academics to teaching-only posts. These early-career academics tend to be conditioned to shift to research contracts to 'escape' the path of becoming an unsuccessful academic. But is this the reality? Does focusing on teaching only ultimately lead to an unsuccessful academic career? We think not. In fact, despite these concerns, there are other academics who solely base their career on their passion for teaching. They believe that teaching is just as important as research. If they do engage in research, it is in multiple areas to broaden their understanding and improve their teaching delivery. We introduce the term 'general academic' to represent a broad group of academics who fit this profile. Academics who are versatile, have a passion and mainly

FIGURE 5.1 Footsteps of an academic. Photograph by author.

engage in teaching. Why is it, though, that these academics do not tend to be as well-known as the more research-oriented academics? We believe that it is because their stories have not been told. In a sense, many academics who fall into this category rarely see themselves become recognised in the grand scheme of things as far as HE is concerned. This makes others feel like they are on their own with no one else to identify with their journey. Thus, this chapter shares three stories of 'general academics' who have done academia differently, to show others that they are not alone. We hope that these stories can spark others to venture into academia in a way that they see fit for them.

Ray's story: 'Following my father's footsteps'

Both of my parents were academics, so I did imagine working in a HE institution one day from a young age. Growing up, I never understood any of the work my parents did except teaching. In short, what I knew about being an academic was to become a teacher at a university. My passion for the profession did not drive my desire to be an academic at the time, but it was simply because it was what my parents did. When I started my bachelor's degree, I was beginning to question becoming an academic mainly because of the lecture sessions falling below my expectations. I had envisioned university to be a place to have fantastic interactive sessions, day in day out with my lecturers, but they were far from it on many occasions. Until this time, I had never seen or heard my parents teach. One day, I went to visit my Dad at work, and this was when everything changed. When I arrived, he was in the middle of delivering a lecture in a large lecture theatre. The students in attendance were so many that they exceeded the theatre's capacity, and some were listening in from outside. Throughout his lecture, all I heard was laughter, claps and massive excitement from students. I overheard several students saying that his lectures were the best and they would not miss them for the world. The reality was that my Dad was an enthusiastic, energetic, funny and truly inspirational person. He brought all of these qualities and his wealth of knowledge to his teaching. In his lectures, you could see how much he loved teaching. In his classes, he taught with every fibre of his being. This made me love teaching, and it sparked a desire to become not just an academic by title but an academic who would engage their classroom the way my Dad did. My reason for pursuing an academic career was now not because my parents were academics. However, a passion was ignited by observing an amazing lecturer who just happened to be my Dad.

But then, something kept bugging me. Why were other lecturers, some with even higher academic ranks than my Dad, not as enthusiastic and sometimes seemed not prepared when they were in class? It was when I overheard my Dad's colleague suggest that he should 'teach less and publish more' that I realised that there was more to academia than teaching. My Dad continued delivering excellent lectures, but his promotion took longer than some of his colleagues'. I listened to more of his lectures and noticed how much he relied on his knowledge of multiple concepts from different fields to entice students from different backgrounds. He would come up with impressive impromptu examples that were funny but to the point and explained rather complex questions with ease. During a conversation with my Dad, he told me he enjoys applying concepts from other areas to his own. He eventually got his promotion without compromising his excellent teaching. To me, he is the epitome of who an academic in any institution should be.

Fortunately, my academic journey began immediately after my Bachelor's degree, where I was offered a teaching-related job at a small college in Tanzania. The college offered UK-based diploma in business. Learning from how my Dad delivered his lectures, I made it my mission to teach all multiple subjects, even those not closely related to my bachelor's degree. Diving into these different subjects gave me a broader understanding of different areas in business, from management, marketing, finance and economics. Then I did an MBA, after which I applied for an assistant lecturer position in a Tanzanian university. My Dad said he was proud of the academic I was becoming. To thoroughly follow in his footsteps and be considered an academic, I applied for a PhD abroad.

Interestingly, I was not the only one inspired by my Dad to become an academic. I have met many of his students who are already academics and attribute him as their inspiration for choosing this career.

Now several years have passed. I have obtained my PhD, I have become a lecturer just like my Dad, and my passion for teaching has never wavered. I am confident in and enjoy teaching multiple subjects. I am occasionally introduced as the academic who can teach everything, and I am proud of it. In short, I followed in the footsteps of my Dad, an outstanding academic. Sadly, he never got to see me obtain a PhD; he never saw me leave Tanzania and become a lecturer in a Russell Group university in the UK. He never got to hear the stories of multiple students who told me that my lectures are some of the best they have ever heard. He died the year I applied for my PhD abroad.

But this is not meant to end as a sad story. This story shows how an academic who did things his way has become an inspiration to a generation of other academics. Interestingly, doing academia in his way has made him a perfect example for many. Years on after he passed, I still remember my Dad's lectures as though it was yesterday. His inspirational teaching is just as important as academic research. We need academics like my Dad. To me, he is 'the epitome of an academic'.

Sophia's story: 'I am a shoemaker; it is not one size fits all!'

I started my career as a humble teacher at a secondary school in Dar es Salaam. I say humble because it was a privilege to be in such a position, or at least it felt like a privilege at the time. Born a girl in a rural African village and going to school and becoming a teacher was no joke in my days. Not in particular that there were no other girls who had strived that far, but in my family, like many other families, boys went to school, and girls stayed home. Some may call it luck, others fate, but I think it might be both and added to my desire to be different and make a difference. I say luck and fate had something to do with it because I do not believe that I was the only girl with such aspirations in my village, but I was among the very few who were noticed. It was a young day-care teacher who passed through our house every morning going to work who took the courage to ask my father that I join her class. Despite being young and that none of my sisters were at school, I was allowed to go. Through that, not only did I begin going to the Nursery School to play and have some free porridge, it became a key to a world of possibilities.

My career progressed alongside my education. After my first degree, I moved from being a secondary teacher to teach in a college and later to the Ministry of Education after completing a master's degree from Toronto, Canada. My eagerness to learn would not leave me alone, so after a few years at the Ministry of Education, I started a PhD at the Massey University in New Zealand through a scholarship. This opened the doors to my academic career at a HE distance learning institution in Tanzania.

The humble beginning of my life and my career in academia is a backbone of who and how I am within the academic community. Although I have done a fair share of administrative work at the management level in the university, I am a teacher who aspires to transfer knowledge and create a great learning experience for students and myself. I believe that how knowledge is delivered affects how it is acquired. I think I can better describe myself as a shoemaker! I do not see one size fitting all in teaching. Creativity and flexibility of delivery ensure that knowledge is acquired and not only shared. It is central to my passion for teaching. I enjoy projects that allow creativity in knowledge delivery.

Not conforming to the conventional academic norms comes with the cost of being misunderstood or misplaced in a system where the promotion of academics is mainly dependent on refereed journal articles, which leaves little room for creativity. Anything out of this structure is questioned or somewhat confuses the panel. There was a particular time where I experienced a problem regarding my promotion. I remember a paper I wrote with some colleagues about guiding secondary teachers on how to deliver teachings in class to fit the context of their students. I submitted the publication for promotion but was rejected by the panel who appeared rather confused and suggested that this did not meet the criteria for promotion at their institution. The research was multidisciplinary and was therefore not specifically focused on my field. I challenged this, though it took some time, and the institution eventually agreed and made multidisciplinary research and teaching criteria for promotion. It is enlightening to see that more HE institutions are embracing creativity and thinking out of the box. There is a paradox, and the one-size-fits-all career development does not match the current composition of academics in HE.

Essa's story: 'Practising what you teach'

I had been working in the industry sector for over 20 years. Five years ago, I decided to move from the industry and teach in universities. I passionately believed that the experience I had amassed working in the industry would greatly benefit the younger generation. I felt that universities would be keen to have me, given that I could support students who intend to work in the industry after graduation. Surprisingly, that was not the case. In fact, on various occasions, my suitability for providing teaching to university students came into question. I had several Master's degrees, including an MBA, but did not have a PhD. This was seen as a significant weakness to teach in universities. I wanted a full-time teaching-only contract, but there was some resistance. Universities were willing to give me a part-time teaching contract, but not as permanent staff. This is similar to a common approach where universities request external speakers to add value to teaching and learning, but the university does not hire them. Thus, I began teaching in multiple universities but was not considered as a member of the academic staff at any of them.

Finally, a breakthrough came when I saw a teaching-focused lectureship advertised in a respected university. I applied for the post and got the job. I believed that the teaching experience acquired got me the job rather than the invaluable industry experience. I got the opportunity to be a recognised member of a university, and this was where I would make my mark. I was enthusiastic about teaching and always pointed out current practices in the industry, this being well received by students. However, I had some challenges. I applied for a promotion after a few years of experience, which was immediately rejected because I did not fulfil the university's criteria. Examining these, I realised that aspects given strong consideration are not remotely related to teaching. Apart from multiple administrative related roles, I was advised to get a PhD, which is a general expectation at universities, although I always wonder how and where it fits into my passion for teaching and disseminating my industry experience to students. Excellent student evaluations were not taken into account for promotion. I felt there was a conflict between my passion for teaching and my desire for promotion. I kept wondering why promotion should not also be focused on impactful teaching.

More seasoned academics suggested that I adapt to HE norms, which meant developing theories and giving these to students rather than concentrating on the experience from the industry. While I believed that industrial experience made students more employable, I began doing some research and enrolled on a PhD. While I have picked up some helpful research skills, I have found that I am slowly drifting away from what is happening in the industry. I am slowly getting more confident to talk about academic research than current industry practices. I am in a dilemma about balancing the HE norms and the teaching passion that led me there. I thought that I was facing these challenges alone. I now see more academics discussing these issues. I will have to strike a balance between adhering to university norms and preserving and updating my industry knowledge. After all, most university students do end up working in the industry, and I believe academics like me are well equipped to prepare them for that journey by practising what we teach.

Alternative career paths

The stories above point out something that has been at the heart of HE for a while. For far too long, research has been at the centre of academic progression. With the impact factor and journal ranking added to the mix, there is too little room for valuing any other work done by an academic. Thus, there is a lack of or limited career progression opportunities for non-research oriented academics. Being research oriented is not wrong, and it has an important role to play in universities and the world. However, it is not necessarily the best path for everyone. For various reasons, some academics may not have the means to conduct multiple 'world-beating' research projects that fit specific criteria to publish their work. Some academics may not be interested in focusing on a research area for the sake of being promoted. Others may not even desire to do research and instead have a passion for teaching and scholarship. All these are reasons for us to accept that being an academic is far broader than what the narrative of the existing HE structures appears to display. So, is it all doom and gloom for the general academics? If recent trends are anything to go by, then the answer is no. Research by the Higher Education Statistics Agency (HESA) shows that the proportion of academic staff on teaching-only contracts has increased from 10% in 2005 to 31% in 2019. This shows increased diversity in the composition of higher education academic staff. This may have triggered some universities to reconsider their promotion criteria and salary scales to reflect the contribution of all academics, which to a great extent removes ambiguity among general academics.

For example, the University of Birmingham has introduced a new system where through the completing of a structured course, a general academic can advance their teaching skills and contribution to the university and become promoted, hence making career progression for the general academic possible in a shorter time period. Moreover, some universities have introduced roles such as teaching-focused lectureships, which are on equal footing with any other lecturer at the university in terms of pay.

In some universities, teaching-focused professors now play important management roles and thus, cement the trend of acceptance and value of non-research oriented academics in HE. Moreover, there is an increasing number of students who are currently within industries in need of skills that will bring immediate change to their careers, businesses and organisations they work for. Universities are picking up on this by introducing executive programmes to cater for such industrial needs. Therefore, academics who have both bathed in the water of the industry and dressed in the theoretical wardrobe are indeed an asset in such programmes and should not feel less important.

Some universities have created career network groups such as teaching leadership networks, which discuss various issues, including establishing measures that provide a realistic career path for general academics. These can be an indication of greater recognition of the role of the general academic in HE.

Conclusion

We can now ask ourselves, can a general academic have a successful academic career in the current HE narrative, where research and publications are valued more than other aspects in academia? A reflection on the three stories offers a good point to start answering this question.

Reflecting on Ray's story, 'Following my father's footsteps', a takeaway relevant to current and aspiring academics can be based on the idea of success. The story depicts that being a successful academic transcends beyond promotion and recognition at work. If you are passionate about teaching and desire to make an impact, you should not be discouraged because others appear to favour research. If anything, this is another opportunity to cement the relevance of your work as an academic. Inspirational teaching is as impactful as research publications. The more inspired the students become from teaching, the more likely it becomes that the society and the HE industry will understand, appreciate and recognise the value of the general academic. Who knows, you may inspire others to follow in your footsteps, and that's a sign of success.

Sophia's story, 'I am a shoemaker, it is not one size fits all' provides another dimension of what it means to be a different academic. The story offers optimism, as it showed that resistance towards changing academic progression criteria could be broken over time. The young girl from a society that favoured boys going to school grew up and influenced an institution to re-examine what constitutes academic work. The one path of publishing in a specific area is not the path for everyone, and HE institutions are acknowledging and are beginning to embrace this. Like the shoemaker who makes shoes of different shapes and sizes, not all academics are the same. Therefore, no one size fits all.

Finally, Essa's story 'practicing what you teach' reminds us that academics can come from anywhere and begin this career at any time. It also highlights that coming from industry is one of the many paths people take to become an academic. Despite more academics being research-oriented, there has been an increase in demand for programmes that connect theory to real-world experience. This signals that HE is demanding institutions go beyond theoretical frameworks and 'practice what you teach'.

We conclude by saying that the short stories in this chapter are a reflection of the experiences of three general academics. They do not exhaust the experiences of all academics in HE and likely they have just scratched the surface of the different academics that exist today. However, we hope they provide some hope for those general academics who feel lost or have not quite found their way. The stories show that being a general academic can mean doing academia differently, but it does not mean doing academia wrong.

II
Against careerism

Curated by Sarah Robinson

ON DUCKS AND VOCATIONS

Notes against careerism

Sarah Robinson

You might be surprised on entering the Against Careerism gallery as it is quite different from the other galleries you may have already visited. It is a large, stark, white-walled gallery where Pop Art primary colours jar and jangle messages of resistance against the commercialisation and codification of the neoliberal university. Video installations loop and project defiant images: 'STOP', 'THINK', 'SAY NO', 'RESIST' on the white walls. Disembodied voices encouraging you to take on more and to career towards 'excellence', also on a loop, break the silence and reverberate around the empty room. This gallery is a wakeup call, a place to stop careering, to sit down on the red benches and reflect on why you entered academia, what it has become and what it could be. It is a place for hushed conversations plotting alternative futures leading to bolder collective action. It is a slightly disturbing and provocative space but one that nevertheless allows for lone and collective voices to assert themselves against the recorded scripts and to gather momentum. The authors bring their own images and metaphors to adorn the empty walls, to start to reclaim the space, make it their own place and to showcase what is important (to them).

I have chosen four complex and thought-provoking exhibits for this gallery. They speak of 'failure' to adhere to established, normative career scripts and what can be learnt from that. Rallying against received definitions of academic excellence, they illustrate how gaining power and research success are not the only ways to measure success in an academic career and illustrate that much personal satisfaction can be gained from devoting one's career to community engagement or teaching. The stories however tell of how easy it is to get taken in by the dominant onward and upward excellence discourses. Failure, illness or competing commitments lead to realisation that there are other ways to lead meaningful academic lives. Then consideration is given to how careers can be nurtured and developed individually or collectively. The exhibits in the gallery challenge you to stop trying to be good at everything and instead to follow what is important and rewarding *for you*. This involves stopping careering and doing some stocktaking, which may be an individual activity or done in conjunction which colleagues at similar career stages, as the two double portraits here beautifully illustrate.

Another important aspect of such slowing down is paying attention to the wider environment in which your career takes place, to your working space and wider wellbeing at work and beyond, to look around at who and what is important to you and inspires you in work and life more widely.

The only single portrait in this gallery, *Careering Through My Career: How I Failed to Become a Business School Dean* by Mark Learmonth, is an intriguing monologue about why the author tried and ultimately failed to become a Business School Dean. Although the story ends without success in the conventional sense in that Mark never did get a Dean's job, the portrait is full of learning from this career episode (let's not say failure). His narrative subtly develops both a critique of the governance and orientation of Business Schools. But it also speaks to the importance of finding one's own career strengths and preferences despite normative pressures to chart a straight and upwards career course, especially, as Mark points out, if one adheres in some way to what senior management might see as the ideal academic type/manager. The portrait is important for those wishing to become a Dean, challenging them to think about how taking and developing such a role thoughtfully could result in making a positive, critical difference to the world. But also, and equally importantly, it gives courage to those who do not really want to do this role but think they should or who are (just) tempted by material and status benefits, to walk on by.

In contrast, the following double portrait paints the linked career trajectories of two academics who have taken between them a cross-section of senior management roles. The evocatively titled: *Ducks at the University? Two Connected Biographies in Seven Images* by Jesús Rodríguez-Pomeda and Fernando Casani, is an interesting career mosaic which illustrates it is possible for the two authors to attain tenure by combining the fulfilment of individual academic requirements with a dedication to the common good. Neither have focussed on research but have developed careers integrating university administration and societal outreach. They illustrate a critical engagement with a socially responsive university, based on parrhesia as conscious ethical and political behaviour. Developing the concept of the *collective academic*, they paint how their cooperation, first in gaining tenure and secondly in developing roles in university administration as critical management scholars and thus in working towards becoming intellectuals, engaged with benefiting society as a whole. Their interlinked stories illustrate how it is possible to succeed in taking what appears to be mainstream trajectories, yet forging personal paths encompassing vocation, ethics, public service, adaptation to circumstances and cooperation. They (modestly) draw on the metaphor of ducks (capable of swimming, walking and flying without being a specialist in any of the three activities), to demonstrate how they have developed all the main 'professors' functions' and as such have (a) been able to survive in the neoliberal meritocracy an (b) make a difference in the wider world.

Sitting side by side with this double male portrait is a double female portrait: *Excellence and Disruption: A Mid-Career Dialogue* by Eugenie Hunsicker and Clare Hutton. Whereas the previous portrait is by business school academics, the subjects of this portrait are a Mathematics and English scholar respectively, yet with similarities in terms of career stage and some life experiences and as such they bring their own understandings to the meaning of academic 'excellence'. Their dialogue proceeds to challenge usage of excellence in the academic context and its link to an ideal academic trajectory, undeflected by "disruptions" such as raising children or illness. They consider how disruption in fact can lead to the discovery of excellence in previously uncharted territory.

The final exhibit, *Collectively Creating Conditions That Nurture: The Bushland as Metaphor for the Academic Ecosystem* by Sumati Ahuja, Mihajla Gavin, Simone Grabowski, Najmeh Hassanli, Anja Hergesell, Walter Jarvis, Pavlina Jasovska, Ece Kaya, Alice Klettner, Helena Liu, Jennie Small, Christopher N. Walker and Ruth Weatherall, is the largest portrait in the whole building and takes up an entire wall. Although (in its authorship) monumental it is yet also a delicately and intricately crafted colourful patchwork. Turning from careering to nurturing, this portrait uses the metaphor of the Bushland and arts-based methods to unpack how diverse academics make sense of their individual identity and the conditions necessary for them to flourish in their different ways. Like the Bushland, academia offers both possibility and beauty, as well as increasing threats from overuse and an unpredictable climate. Although these challenges and opportunities are universal, individual academics require unique conditions to thrive. We can appreciate how 13 Australian academics make sense of their individual identity and bring together soil, water, air and light in their own ways to support both the self and the collective. The arts-based methods work in parallel with the metaphor of the Bushland to create intimate and insightful portraits of academic identity and careers. In its entirety the work provokes the reader to step out of the gallery and examine their own Bushland of academia and how they might nurture supportive conditions with others.

The exhibitions in this gallery provoke and challenge you to engage with different career perspectives, and as per modern art this is done largely in the abstract rather than in directive ways. It is up to you to interpret what you see and to take away the inspiration you may currently need to resist, change and indeed to say 'no'. The exbibits here are both in your face and subtly contemplative. They encourage you to engage with wider societal, environmental forces. And running through all the exhibits is the power of individual, dual and collective dialogue, in combatting careerism and moving towards the essence of vocation and self. As you get up from the red bench perhaps start the conversation: what stops you careering to the next responsibility and helps you to stop, repair and find meaning?

CAREERING THROUGH MY CAREER

How I failed to become a business school Dean

Mark Learmonth

At my first Academy of Management (AOM) conference in Seattle USA, I bumped into a friendly professor who offered to take me under his wing. I was grateful he did – navigating around the huge conference on my own was overwhelming, and more than a bit intimidating. He suggested that we went to various drinks receptions that evening to introduce me to some of the people who I had cited in my PhD. Now that *really was* intimidating! I thanked him, but declined. "Well, okay" he said, "but if you don't go to these receptions it may be career limiting".

At the time, having my career limited sounded like a good idea. I had just escaped into academia from a career of some 17 years in health administration; a career that had often felt much more like careering – in the sense of being out of control – than an ordered progression through various levels of a profession. It was something of a relief then, that for the next few years my careering became somewhat limited, as I started to work my way "up" to full professor and began to imbibe the rules of a conventional academic career.

After my PhD, settling into a full-time academic post, it felt like my teaching and research were motivated by excitement with my new knowledge – allied to a genuine belief that it should be as widely promulgated as possible. What I did at this stage in my life can also be seen, however, as making the right moves in the academic career game (MacDonald and Kam, 2007). I published in "good" journals; got a grant; put enough effort into teaching that students generally said nice things about me; and while I carried out a range of administrative jobs, I was fortunate that no one asked me to do anything too time-consuming or stressful.

In any event, being a man (a white, tall, able-bodied, heterosexual, native English-speaking man, and privately educated to boot) helped enormously. Without really trying, I already fitted the received image of a professor. Predictably enough therefore, I got a chair at a research-intensive UK university business school within a few years. It was shortly after this appointment however, that my career started to career again, when the School's Deputy Dean (Research) left to go to a Dean's job at another School.

The pressure of taking the lead on REF2014 was on the horizon, so no one, me included, wanted his job. However, in one of the rare examples of when looking the part can be a disadvantage, colleagues apparently saw me as the best replacement. I eventually capitulated to (relatively gentle) emotional blackmail and mild bribery and agreed to do the job. So, between 2011 and 2016, I was Deputy Dean (Research). Counter to my expectations, I gradually grew to like certain elements of the role. Indeed, when I got emails from head-hunters telling me that I would be perfect as Dean at School X, I didn't necessarily press delete; sometimes, I applied. But though I had several interviews, I now realise that I was never likely to get a Dean's job (I am no longer trying).

This chapter is a story about my latest (and hopefully last) experience of careering through my career. Even though it ended unsuccessfully for me (at least in the conventional sense – I never did become a Dean) I hope that this account may still prove useful for those who want to do less careering and have more of a career as a Dean of a business school. Particularly to those whose aims in becoming a Dean include wanting to make something of a positive, critical difference to the world. (See also Brown, Lewis and Oliver, 2019; Burrell, 2009; Gjerde and Alvesson, 2020; King and Learmonth, 2015, Parker, 2004.)

Tasting the life of a Dean

As soon as I'd been appointed as Deputy Dean, I started to get insights into what being a Dean is like. One of the most noticeable – if mundane – things that happened was that the number of my emails went through the roof. Colleagues copied me in to all sorts of correspondence, presumably because they felt they should do so, or so that they could say the Deputy Dean had been informed. Initially this felt rather overwhelming, and a source of anxiety. Over time, I did learn (reasonably reliably) which emails could be ignored, which I'd better read and which demanded a quick response. Still, the form of (mild) anxiety I still associate with work emails seems a legacy from this time.

Another reasons I associate emails with anxiety is probably because it was often through emails that I got wind of difficult issues. They often kept me awake at night – particularly when they promised to involve nasty forms of interpersonal conflict – or when I was expected to handle them in ways I felt ambivalent about. Now, it's hard now to remember anything specific about these difficulties – most of them simply faded away without the conflict I expected; which isn't to say that I've learnt to stop worrying about such things.

Something else I didn't enjoy was having to read, comment on, and contribute to policy, accreditation, and similar documents. I found many beyond tedious – some were virtually unreadable for me. I soon gave up trying to give most more than a cursory flick-through, enough to pretend to have read them for the relevant meeting. I mostly seemed to get away with the façade; though perhaps I got away with it so regularly might have been because colleagues on the same committees were similarly pretending. Anyway, I ended up nodding through documents that were emblematic of things in the business school world that make me uncomfortable. For example, my School was triple accredited (holding EQUIS, AACSB, and AMBA), and this fact is important to the prestige, and income, of the School. As a Deputy Dean I became complicit in okaying (and sometimes writing parts of) our reaccreditation proposals. I sat in many a meeting biting my tongue about how we had decided to deal with many significant matters about the course the School was taking – decisions that appeared unchallengeable.

Talking of meetings, and in spite of their reputation as the apogee of bureaucracy, meetings turned out to be a relatively pleasant experience for me. Most of my meetings within the business school were friendly occasions. Naturally, this was not always the case, but if anything, people appeared to be perhaps slightly too deferential. The main exception to this however, was meetings with colleagues in other parts of the University, outside the Business School. Here, it quickly became evident that the Business School was widely held in low regard – sometimes verging on contempt, and occasionally even hostility – with negative views being voiced at Faculty committees. In this wider arena I was also made very conscious that being a (mere) departmental research director cut little ice with people in the Faculty hierarchy. Many were dismissive of the advice they occasionally sought from me – doubtless rightly so.

Still, I did get to influence and even change *some* things within the School. This opportunity to "make a difference" (something that Fournier and Grey (2000, p. 28) believe people in Critical Management Studies [CMS] usually fail to take) felt not just personally satisfying, but even perhaps actually important. Take influencing staff appointments. I couldn't make actual job offers (this was the Dean's job), but I was on interview panels for most professorial appointments, and my opinion about candidates did seem to count. In any event, quite a few "critical" scholars (broadly speaking) were appointed during my tenure. Not only could I personally encourage people to apply, colleagues perhaps might have been more likely to do so knowing that I was on the interview panel.

In other words, I was able to list things that I not only regarded as positive – the start of making a critical and progressive difference, however modest the difference might be – but I could also list these same things as "achievements" for my cv. Naturally enough, the fact that I could construct at least some of the things I did as "making a difference" was pleasing. In fact, I'd like to think that the possibilities for making a difference in the world of business schools was the most important reason for starting to consider becoming a Dean. Another factor was the personal challenge involved. I'd spent the last 15 years or so up to this point doing basically the same job – teaching and writing research papers. In that time I'd proved (at least to myself) that I could do the job of an academic relatively satisfactorily. But with retirement looming on the horizon, I began to wonder whether life at my particular career stage might be more satisfying if I did something with a relatively new challenge – such as running a business school. Not that I didn't have other, perhaps less worthy motives too.

For instance, I've always liked travelling. As Deputy Dean I got to do quite a lot more of it than I had ever done before. Indeed, after starting the role, I was soon upgraded to Silver on my favourite airline's loyalty programme. I never made Gold, but Silver still meant that the "standard plus" cabins, which university policy allowed me to book for official duties, were occasionally upgraded to business class. These upgrades were the source of a special kind of pleasure; a pleasure that somehow went beyond the complimentary champagne. Perhaps it was because travelling business class on expenses has always felt a little bit illicit. I was also entrusted with a corporate credit card, making it easier to go to nice restaurants while on official trips. And let's not forget salary. I got quite a significant rise as part of the deal when I became Deputy Dean. Further rises were to follow, in part because the role gave me a bargaining power that would probably been less available to an "ordinary" professor. In any event, it did not escape my attention that there'd be more travel and more money (rather a lot more of both) if I became a Dean. In other words, I was aware that becoming a Dean might entail the risk of having my critical (and personal) values compromised even further than they already were.

I say *even* further because I've felt similarly compromised – albeit the feeling had been more nebulous – throughout my time as an academic. Universities have long been caught up in the wider neoliberal project, such that simply accepting a salary arguably makes any employee complicit to a certain extent. Indeed, the relatively comfortable, secure, middle-class lifestyle that many academic posts allow means that it's not just Deans and their Deputies who get to do international travel, go to restaurants on expenses, etc. Furthermore, the ironies tied up with "being educated" as, in itself, a mark of entitlement – not to mention the paradoxes of getting promoted by being critical (e.g. by writing about other people's workplace resistance) – have never been entirely lost on me (see Learmonth and Humphreys, 2012).

Anyhow, by way of summary, here's an email I wrote back in 2015 to a small, friendly audience while we were conducting a wider discussion about making CMS practical. I wanted to see what they thought about the idea of applying to be a Dean; and I got broadly encouraging replies:

> The whole question of getting involved with more senior university roles is something that's coming on my radar. I've had a taste of them, acting as Deputy Dean for Research in my school, and am now regularly contacted by headhunters asking me to consider deans jobs. I'm starting to convince myself that were I not to put forward for such jobs it would be about keeping my relatively quiet and comfortable life once I step down as Deputy Dean. So I'm starting seriously to consider going for some dean jobs for the following kinds of reasons:
>
> - Personal challenge – spending the next (and last) 10 years of my career simply doing what I've done for the last 10–15 years seems relatively unattractive. Even if it were to be an entirely frustrating and personally damaging experience (getting turned into the archetypal bastard dean [in the original email, I'd named someone here]; helplessness in thrall to forces greater than me; or simply an inability to cope with the job) at least my experience would probably make a good participant-observation study.
> - "Politics" – it's just about plausible to believe that there's a higher probability of making some sort of positive difference (however modest) by doing a dean role than by just continuing to write and teach – even with the substantial risks of failure, the need to compromise on many issues, etc., that are involved.
>
> Also, compared to say the NHS (where I used to work) in which any kind of speaking out against top management practices is very risky indeed (and is therefore almost never done other than by whistle-blowers) universities seem a relatively good bet. There would be potential allies and resistant discourses circulating in other parts of the institution, so it seems possible, in principle at least, to do things in the name of academic freedom, work-life balance, diversity etc. which might have emancipatory potential. Furthermore, while becoming a dean might be seen to be siding with the forces of neo-liberalism, it's mere middle management in terms of university hierarchy. And anyway, aren't we all compromised in a similar way, just by taking our salary from such an institution?
>
> The bottom line, it seems to me, is that if no critters try then we are simply going to get even more over-run with neo-liberal zealots in the top business school

jobs. (Of course, I actually just want to improve my pension, travel the world in business-class, and "network" with powerful people at exclusive restaurants.)

Looking back, I'd particularly emphasise now that I think what I really wanted to do at the time was to find out more about myself. Would I, in fact, be able to deal with the personal demands of the job? Could I cope with what I assumed would be the high-pressure environment and the inevitable sleepless nights? Throughout my whole career I had rarely worked in the evenings or at weekends – would I have to start working at a very different pace as a Dean? What about the uncertainty around when to compromise and when to stick to my guns? Would I be able to remain true to my principles if only to some extent, or would I inevitably get entirely swallowed by neoliberalism? I had written papers speculating about the possibilities of making CMS practical (Griffin, Humphreys and Learmonth, 2015; Learmonth, 2007; King and Learmonth, 2015). Becoming a Dean represented an opportunity to replace speculation with action.

All that remained now was the small matter of actually getting a job.

We are particularly keen to connect with you

Here's the opening paragraph of the sort of email I kept getting from head-hunters:

> I am writing from ABC associates, executive search firm regarding our work with the University of XYZ on their appointment of a new Dean for their Business School, and we are particularly keen to connect with you about the role. I have attached the appointment details document to this email for reference....

Nothing unusual about the email itself; every job that the head-hunters handle presumably involves them dispatching hundreds of similar emails across the world. The accompanying "appointment details" were always extremely impressive though, at least in terms of their length, glossiness, and their upbeat accounts of the University and the School. What was really striking however, were the head-hunters' offices. I found myself gazing out on some of the most expensive views in London. St. Paul's Cathedral and Big Ben both come to mind.

Between 2015 and 2017, I put in six applications and got shortlisted on three occasions (all the jobs were in the UK). I can't be entirely sure why I got interviews in some places and not others. Interestingly enough though, one of the places I did *not* get an interview was at a School which had had a reputation for being critical (and where I'd received explicit support for my application from some of the staff). Perhaps I was an unattractive candidate because, as it turned out, the Vice Chancellor wanted the School to revert to the mainstream.

Generally however, I sensed an indifference to whether or not I was critical. As long as a candidate was credible as a business academic, that was all they seemed to be interested in. Not unreasonably perhaps, they were more concerned about things like having a vision for the School that was in line with the university's expectations. In fact, at one of the Schools where I got a final interview, I was asked to start proceedings with a presentation entitled "My vision for the XXX University Business School, in the context of the University's strategic intent with reference to relevant regional developments". (It's hard to imagine a more exciting title.) The head-hunters advised: "They will need to have absolute clarity on where you would like to take XXX, what success would look like. We are particularly interested in the areas of specialisation you would like to see XXX develop ('what XXX will be known for'), and how the Home/EU and also international student cohorts can be enhanced. The format will be a discussion, with no slides or handouts". So here's an anonymised version of the notes for my presentation:

> XXX will be increasingly internationally known, in academia and beyond, for important, agenda-setting, multi-disciplinary research and teaching across all main business disciplines. A great place to be an academic or a student – successful, supportive, interest(ed)ing colleagues who create a buzz for students & staff. Improvements in metrics (NSS REF) an outcome of success; not success itself. My approach would be to bring about an upward step change in performance by building on existing strengths in XXX and making sure the developments resonate strongly with some of the university's wider aims.
>
> **In terms of research,**
> The ABC Institute seems already successful with good potential for further growth and scope for impact, big EPSRC grants and short term demonstrable effects on the local economy. If it ain't broken don't fix it.
>   DEF research group has links to GHI research theme in wider university Already got some people in this area trained in wider social sciences and humanities so evident interdisciplinary potential and real world impact. Corporations have some pretty wicked ethical dilemmas that many people in industry concerned to understand and respond to better. Two examples of possible research (i) what constitutes a fair wage – especially in the Global South – neat links with the JKL Institute (modern slavery etc); (ii) why don't women get to the top of corporations? …
>   Focus on these 2 areas with major conferences here and guide our recruitment strategy – for staff and research students.
>
> **Enhancing teaching and learning.**
> There are 111 UK business schools and undergrads all doing pretty much the same thing. Students typically are instrumental with an eye v much on the job at the end. My own belief is that business would be better served by a broader business education at u/grad level – element of liberal arts and or science – as well as offering certain business modules to other departments. We clearly need a strong undergrad offering as backbone of the way the school is funded – 60% of funding from u/g teaching and I think a more diverse portfolio for students good be a good USP – if a little risky.
>   Masters can be focussed on business – biggest growth market is finance. On face of it scope to merge some of the degrees with a lot of core modules. Query about an academic-style dissertation. Effective marketing to overseas markets essential – problem should be capping numbers.
>   MBA Next few years emphasis on survival. Big reduction in market because of visa restrictions and fashion. Reinvent MBA with something much less standard and more creative. Key question about whether to continue with MBA.
>   Possible developments – DBA can be a lucrative "premium product" – and makes strong links with real business problems etc.

In conclusion, ABC is a major business school that is basically functioning well. I can see how it can develop in ways that resonate even better with the priorities of the wider university and the region while making a step change in its own performance. Ultimately, satisfying and worthwhile experienced for me – my colleagues, students and the wider university.

So why was I unsuccessful?

Clearly, I'm speculating here. I have rarely received useful (or even credible) feedback after most job interviews in general. With the benefit of hindsight though, some of my errors seem pretty plain.

I can readily see now that my approach often had a certain naïveté about it. For instance, I had assumed that when Vice Chancellors said things like "give me your honest appraisal of the realistic prospects for the Business School" they really did want my honest, realistic appraisal. What I suspect today, is that this kind of question is more likely to be a coded way to test candidates' political nous. The "correct" "honest" answer (it seems obvious now) is one that is as optimistic, upbeat, and ambitious as a generously stretched credibility would allow. Similarly, it now seems pretty clear that no one on interview panels for these kinds of jobs is interested in what a candidate actually plans to do; rather they are seeking reassurance that candidates understand what the university expects them to do. It's best to keep quiet about actual intentions until well after the job is in the bag.

While many of my failures were doubtless down to naïveté, perhaps certain failures had more complex roots. On some issues, I already knew what I should say, but simply couldn't say it with any kind of sincerity. I was aware that traces of a grin would inevitably appear on my face were I to say things I didn't really believe in, so I had little option but to say what I actually thought. This was certainly true of the question I dreaded most, but realised was inevitable: the "leadership" question. It is obvious that what I should have done is memorised a scripted answer to a question like "What is your leadership style?" Any response needed to *sound* authentic, with just the right mix of bullshit. I knew that then, just as much as I know it now. For reasons that Kevin Morrell and I explore in our book, *Critical Perspectives on Leadership* (Learmonth and Morrell, 2019) however, I just couldn't – in all conscience – bring myself to do it. And anyway, conscience aside, I'm not a good enough actor to pull off the required performance.

What all this implies is that I was never *really* committed to getting a Dean's job. The reason I started to apply was more from a sense of obligation – a feeling that I should – because it would give me the chance to make some kind of a difference to the way a business school is run. I wanted to take on board the challenges implicit in the observations of scholars such as du Gay (1998, p. 422), for whom CMS devotees 'practice a form of "secular holiness" characterized by an exemplary withdrawal from the governmentally administered world' (1998, p. 422). Or Burrell's comment that 'it is always easier to *write* something that is different, than it is to *do* something that is different' (2009, p. 555, emphasis in original). However, such challenges never got beyond an intellectual level for me. In Goffman's (1959) terms, perhaps my desire to be a Dean was surface acting; never the sort of deep acting that would be required to pull off a convincing performance at interview.

One of the Schools where I was interviewed required me to undergo a psychological profile and an interview with an occupational psychologist prior to the university interview.

Parts of the report (a copy of which I received after the interview) make interesting reading in terms of why I was unsuccessful:

> *Mark presented as a rather diffident interviewee, who was uncomfortable talking about him-self and did not over promote him-self and/or his achievements… with a propensity to more self deprecation than usually seen in a job related interview … Mark acknowledges that he himself seeks to avoid conflict, so seldom overtly criticises or challenges others. Additionally when seeking to persuade others Mark is not somebody who uses his social skills tactically to get their buy-in. He believes in being relatively straight talking, providing a rational argument on the lines of an academic paper, rather than customising his approach according to the needs of his audience. Within the senior management team he will be a follower rather than leader.*

Conclusion

All that said, if I had kept on trying, even I would probably have eventually secured a Dean's post – particularly if I had applied for everything available across the world – if only because there are so many jobs relative to the numbers of plausible candidates available. On balance though, it's probably just as well (for everyone concerned) that I never got a job offer. I somehow doubt whether I'd have been seen as particularly successful in the role – by anyone – not least by myself.[1]

In sharing a story of some of my own personal experiences however, I do not wish to imply that *no one* should try. At the time of writing, across the globe, there are people associated with CMS who are business school deans; there are even published examples of success, albeit of a limited and perhaps compromised nature. Such examples suggest nevertheless, that a critical project for a business school dean is not bound to end in failure. The most recent account I am aware of is from Kitchener and Delbridge (2020, p. 307) whose approach was "founded on a commitment to enhancing the public good of business schools". They emphasised the inescapability of "wrestling with … [a critical] dean's dilemma" (p. 312) and, citing Kay (2011:6) recognised "that what we want… has many elements. We will never succeed in specifying fully what they are, and to the extent we do, we discover that they are often inconsistent and incompatible" (p. 319). Still, they did make a difference: "Because so many colleagues 'bought into' the aspiration for … [the School] there emerged a participative process of shaping the nature of the change … across teaching, research, governance, and engagement" (p. 320).

In other words, one place where *some of us* could realistically start engaging critically in practice is by taking on significant management roles within our own workplaces – workplaces which for most people reading this chapter will, I presume, be universities. Taking on a position like a Dean (if only being in such a role temporarily) can represent a further way in which to resist the audit regimes, discriminatory practices, and other dysfunctional aspects of university life to which CMS has drawn attention.

Note

1 I do not think of my career as having come to an end because I failed to become a Dean – I'm now simply pursuing other opportunities for growth and learning – such as being the Editor-in-Chief of a journal.

References

Brown, A.D., Lewis, M.A. and Oliver, N. (2019) Identity work, loss and preferred identities: a study of UK business school deans. *Organization Studies*, doi.org/10.1177/0170840619857464.

Burrell, G. (2009) Handbooks, swarms and living dangerously. In: Alvesson, M., Bridgman, T., and Willmott, H. (eds) *The Oxford Handbook of Critical Management Studies*. Oxford: Oxford University Press, 551–562.

Du Gay, P. (1998) Alastair MacIntyre and the Christian genealogy of management critique. *Cultural Values*, 2: 421–444.

Fournier, V. and Grey, C. (2000) At the critical moment: conditions and prospects for critical management studies. *Human Relations*, 53: 7–32.

Gjerde, S. and Alvesson, M. (2020) Sandwiched: exploring role and identity of middle managers in the genuine middle. *Human Relations*, 73: 124–151.

Goffman, E. (1959) *The Presentation of Self in Everyday Life*. New York: Doubleday.

Griffin, M., Humphreys, M. and Learmonth, M. (2015) Doing Free Jazz and free organizations, "A certain experience of the impossible"? Ornette Coleman encounters Jacques Derrida. *Journal of Management Inquiry*, 24: 25–35.

Kay, J. (2011) *Obliquity: Why Our Goals Are Best Achieved Indirectly*. London: Profile Books.

King, D. and Learmonth, M. (2015) Can critical management studies ever be 'practical'? A case study in engaged scholarship. *Human Relations*, 68: 353–375.

Kitchener, M. and Delbridge, R. (2020) Lessons from creating a business school for public good: obliquity, waysetting and wayfinding in substantively rational change. *Academy of Management Learning & Education*, 19: 307–322.

Learmonth, M. (2007) Critical management education in action: personal tales of management unlearning. *Academy of Management Learning & Education*, 6: 109–113.

Learmonth, M. and Humphreys, M. (2012) Autoethnography and academic identity: glimpsing business school doppelgangers. *Organization*, 19: 99–117.

Learmonth M. and Morrell, K. (2019) *Critical Perspectives on Leadership: The Language of Corporate Power*. New York: Routledge.

MacDonald, S. and Kam, J. (2007) Ring a ring o' roses: quality journals and gamesmanship in management studies. *Journal of Management Studies*, 44: 640–655.

Parker, M. (2004) Becoming manager; or, the werewolf looks anxiously in the mirror, checking for unusual facial hair. *Management Learning*, 35: 45–59.

DUCKS AT THE UNIVERSITY? TWO CONNECTED BIOGRAPHIES IN SEVEN IMAGES

Jesús Rodríguez-Pomeda and Fernando Casani

Introduction

This chapter is composed of two connected careers in a Spanish university, explained in a seven-image framework. The images show some key points of our professional trajectories. Our two voices (Jesús Rodríguez-Pomeda, JRP, and Fernando Casani, FC) appear successively in each image.

Jesús has developed his 26-year career at the Universidad Autónoma de Madrid (Autonomous University of Madrid), after five years of professional work as economist and manager at several private-owned firms. From the beginning, collaboration and teamwork has characterized his academic career. The main colleague in that collaborative work is Fernando, who has also been at the university for nearly 30 years, and with whom he has shared during this time, the same vision of academic activity, characterized by cooperation and team action, in what we can call a collective academic model, as opposed to the individualist dominant paradigm, who seeks specialization and personal competitiveness as a form of professional advancement. For this reason, it seemed natural to us to show our interrelated academic trajectories together instead of highlighting each one on their own.

The neoliberal society considers that "selves are to be reconstructed as isolated and entrepreneurial", even when "the self is social" (Busch, 2017: 18, 21). We consider that academic roles arise from societal needs, and growth through collaboration. So, we have developed a long-standing partnership in different endeavours, together with a number of colleagues from several universities. As a result, our trajectories conform to the collective academic model. This political choice is opposed to the dominant view of the present-day neoliberal university: scholars are dehumanized by considering them as "human capital" (Sassower, 2019: 98). As a consequence, the political self is construed in economic terms and "the foundation vanishes for citizenship concerned with public things and the common good" (Brown, 2015: 39). Some consequences for our careers emerge from this opposition. The main one is a delay (related to some colleagues' careers) in our promotion from the tenured status that jeopardizes the attainment of the professor's position.

In this context, we try to reflect on this issue based on our own experiences in academia over the course of some three decades during the neoliberal era in Spain. Given that we have no exemplary intention whatsoever, the objective of this text is to provoke the reflection of young academics on whether an academic position (tenure) can be obtained in Spain at the first quarter of the twenty-first century following careers focussed on collective matters.

Indeed, our somewhat heterodox trajectory considering our professional field (Spanish academia, specifically the business/organization field) has been based on a cooperative and group approach (*the collective academic*) aimed at developing our activities regarding the issues that we deem to be of interest, regardless of the current academic fashion. We have carried out not only generic teaching and research activities (oriented to standard objectives, i.e., the good assessment of teaching and impactful publications) but also research applied to companies and other organizations (including professional experience prior to the start of our academic careers) and active participation in management and academic management, all of which has always been approached from our perspective of the social utility of knowledge and an integrating vision of the university. One of the authors (FC) has served as the head of administration of our university, and the other author (JRP) has held positions of vice-rector, vice-dean and the director of the department (as well as supervisor of various foundations linked to the university).

As ducks at the university, our careers have been developed without a sharp specialization in one of the main activities of any scholar: teaching, research, university administration and engagement. Instead, we have tried to serve the common good by working sequentially on those activities. Even when the allocation of the years devoted to each activity is uneven, we think that all of them are equally relevant. As management and organization scholars, we have learnt a lot about the realities of university management. Also, we were gifted with some prominent university appointments where theoretical analysis and managerial action were intertwined. So, as academics, now we are a little bit wiser.

Our critical commitment to the university can be understood from the Foucauldian elaboration of the concept of "parrhēsía" (παρρησία), which represents an ethical position that leads to taking a risk to tell the truth (Foucault, 1999). This concept consists of saying publicly that which the subject, i.e., the "parresiastés", thinks should be said and done and doing so in the way that he or she deems most appropriate. It is a practice in which ethics, politics and language come together, aiming to move others towards virtue (understood as a way of life subject to truth). Consider two professionals who live in the academic world, have two separate voices, share several similarities (and some contrasts) regarding the perspectives adopted, and have a shared will to contribute to the common good.

Image 1: The beginnings, or searching for a career path in the university based on cooperation

FC: During the 1980s, I developed my teaching through vocational training in a neighbourhood of Madrid, thereby maintaining my commitment to teaching and participating in both the life of the institute and in the social environment in which it was located. These were years of openness and modernization in Spain that were accompanied by great social and economic changes. Here, I can highlight a characteristic that has greatly influenced my professional development, namely, the importance of collaboration and teamwork as a common way of approaching tasks. On the one hand, cooperation with other colleagues has always allowed me to carry out my activities better and to encompass more initiatives and projects; on the other, it has also opened many doors to new horizons for me.

After spending a period of time in the United States, I enrolled in an MBA programme and began my doctorate at the UAM, where I later obtained a part-time teaching position. At the same time, an opportunity arose to teach at the Spanish branch of an American university, Saint Louis University (SLU). These temporary contracts allowed me to request a leave of absence in secondary education to dedicate myself full time to university-level teaching and to the completion of my doctorate.

Afterwards, I got a full-time contract at the UAM, and I also joined the University Institute of Business Administration (IADE-UAM), where I coincided with Jesús, with whom I have collaborated on different teams since that time. With him, I have shared, as reflected in this text, many of the convictions and commitments about university work that have led us to develop similar and highly interrelated academic careers.

JRP: At the beginning of my academic career, I already had five years of professional experience in various organizations, which has allowed me not only to constantly seek connections between theory and practice but also to keep in mind the importance of the social impact of our activities. Such external professional experience is less frequent among Spanish business/organization academics than it is among those from other countries. When I returned at university setting, I tried to connect with dynamic people and groups who were aware of the importance of having ties with organizations. Fortunately, I was able to gain access to a university institute (the IADE-UAM) where I learnt to combine teaching, research and knowledge transfer. Intense effort was applied to a plurality of activities with the enthusiasm and commitment levels that are typical of the first stages of an academic career. In addition, two keys points explain, to some extent, what happened to me later: appreciating teamwork and not demanding a direct and immediate outcome to my work. You also have to learn with whom you can team up (and that also involves some bad experiences). Also, the long-term positive balance between what is contributed and what is received from the institution, as well as trust and mutual benefits within the teams (with different members, but in which my colleague Fernando has usually been placed), are essential. I tried to synthesize years full of experiences (and the corresponding personal maturity) within which there were also downsides, e.g., working with people for whom collective work was a lever for their own particular interests (which allowed me to verify that free riders are not only present in companies) or deviations and delays in professional progression. Such delays had various origins and consequences, such as curiosity that led the team to take advantage of a consulting or teaching opportunity for a certain organization even though that was not very productive from a research point of view (an overwhelmingly decisive criterion for career advancement).

Image 2: Efforts towards tenure and the tempos of the chosen academic career: successively developing the functions of the university professor or simultaneously advancing in all aspects?

FC: In my early years at the UAM and the IADE, I focussed primarily on teaching at different levels, e.g., undergraduate and postgraduate degrees at our UAM department and continuous training programmes at the Institute, while maintaining a great relationship with the realities of both the social and business worlds. At this time, my dedication to the other two missions of the university – research and knowledge transfer – could be described as balanced; I approached both missions with lower levels of intensity than with which I approached teaching, but I still tried to maintain certain standards of homogeneous quantity and quality with regard to the rest of the system by publishing in national journals with, if possible, wide circulation. In this way, in a few years, I managed to reach the position of tenured professor, which guaranteed me stability and security in my academic work. By becoming a civil servant, I could then request the evaluation of my research, in accordance with the national system assessment of every six years of research output; surprisingly, just after being evaluated very positively by the academic panel in the public concourse to attain tenure, I received a negative evaluation of my research by another panel. I think that there is a growing trend to assess the publications of the recent past with brand new criteria. The implementation of more stringent criteria year after year to assess research outputs generates greater levels of competition, insecurity and anxiety in teachers without tenure and a certain amount of discouragement in stable, tenured teachers. In many cases, this results in the loss of motivation to make an effort in this area when the expected results are not fulfilled.

JRP: During a promotion process, I encountered the scorn of evaluators (colleagues from other universities) who considered IADE to be exclusively dedicated to consulting and technical assistance and that it did not perform quality research. For those evaluators, a publication has a value narrowed to the impact factor and the number of citations received. I also suffered from the combination of legislative changes and scant care from those at my university who were responsible for budding academics at the time.

In short, I have chosen a heterodox path better portrayed as a contrast to the orthodoxy defended by those who have hardly set foot companies. In my view, orthodox scholars only publish esoteric articles in journals with high levels of academic impact but low levels of social and economic relevance. They usually work within patronage networks, despise students considering them a hindrance to their careers, and use positions in university administration in their own benefit.

Image 3: The manager as a critical management scholar (our passage through different university management positions)

FC: Faced with the dilemma of splitting my efforts between research, teaching and management, I have always considered the development of my functions at the university from a personal perspective that considers to which activities I can add more value at a given time, depending on my skills and possibilities. In this way, I did not hesitate to dedicate myself to university management when the possibility arose to join, as vice-rector, a rectoral team led by a new rector. He defended a disruptive perspective with regard to the previous university administration. He also had won election by weighted universal suffrage, which was celebrated for the first time in our university after this possibility was opened up by a modification of the law approved in Parliament. Those who know about university management already know how absorbing and conflicting such an activity can be, since on the one hand, the responsibility of the administration of an institution is assumed (equivalent in budget and personnel to a large company), while on the other, the authority and the necessary management tools are not available to carry it out. In my case, i.e., integrated into a reformist team and eager to face the changes, the situation became very complicated when, a year into our new career, the head of administration of the university resigned and, for reasons of professional competence within the team, it was decided that I would assume that position. This implied absolute incompatibility with my teaching activities and was a significant parenthesis in my academic career. However, my full dedication to the management of the university allowed me to learn in depth about the characteristics and problems related to both the higher education sector and the direction and management of the institutions that comprise it.

JRP: One of the features of my career (which I share with Fernando) is my extensive participation in different university management positions. I believe that such participation is due to my willingness to intervene in the public sphere by seeking the common good, which is understood as the progress of the public university. Positive consequences of such political actions have resulted in the following: a certain reputation (of different value, depending on who you ask), unequal experiences about my behaviour in certain situations, a wealth knowledge about my university (which, among other things, makes it easier for me to write this text), some positive personal relationships and an excellent touchstone for my role as an organizational researcher. Of course, my thinking as an academic has been enriched and transformed thanks to those experiences, which have spanned a dozen years.

On the other hand, negative consequences included the delay in the publication of the articles necessary to continue advancing in my career, the realization that much of the effort that I placed into those offices was worthy of a better cause, and some interpersonal conflicts (which, although painful, were occasions for personal and professional learning).

In February 2017, I was appointed vice-rector for strategy and planning at UAM, which was a position created to renew and modernize the university. In a way, this appointment could be seen as the culmination of my career in academic positions (which has included, among others, secretary of department, department head and vice-dean) that is present in a kind of relatively frequent *cursus honorum* both in my university and in others. Such a journey through different management and university representation positions is usually the gateway to the executive elite.

I worked on a registration system for all faculty activities. For about a decade, that system was a never-attained objective. Although it is true that such control systems are embedded in the managerial vision of the university, my approach diverged from this purpose. I think that the internal collective assessment and management of the services provided by faculty can successfully counteract the criticisms based on interested generalizations (e.g., that university professors do little work, their results are not of sufficient quality, etc.) repeated forever by the enemies of the public university.

I eagerly undertook the project under the premise of exhaustive dialogue, consultation and negotiation (which, as in many other universities, involves hundreds of meetings that negotiate difficult compromises) with different groups within the university. I patiently searched for points of agreement between the advocates of managerial control systems and those profiting from the absence of any control on their workloads. The system should be implemented in a transparent and democratic way by the university governing bodies. A year later, I managed to get the governing council to approve the academic workload model by a margin of 40 votes in favour, none against and four abstentions. For the first time, a model of that kind was approved within my university.

Image 4: Parrhesía as the meeting point between ethics and politics

FC: Upon my return to teaching activities, the knowledge acquired, and the contacts made during my time in the university administration opened up the possibility to focus my efforts on another of the university's activities, i.e., knowledge transfer, maintaining basic teaching and research activities through extensive collaboration with some of my colleagues. Therefore, without having previously planned it, I concentrated on the so-called 'third mission' of the university. At that time, this mission did not garner much academic recognition; a few years later, however, it was decided to recognize the institutional importance of this mission, and the activities that I carried out during this time allowed me to obtain a positive assessment by an academic panel when, as always a posteriori, criteria were established for the evaluation of transfer activities carried out previously.

JRP: During my years in office as vice-rector, I defended the university's interests based on my values and criteria. This experience clearly showed me to what the concept of 'organizational hypocrisy' refers (Brunsson & Karafillidis, 2007). Indeed, the performance of the directive function in my university has allowed me to closely observe the distances that separate what is proclaimed as the objectives to be achieved, what is decided upon for action and what is finally executed.

Image 5: A future as an intellectual?

FC: In this period of greater dedication to knowledge-transfer projects, we began to collaborate with a very powerful research group from another university that was interested in the same issues of public policies and the management of science and higher education. This convergence led us to consider a closer alliance that ultimately culminated in the creation of an inter-university research institute between our two universities, which aimed to combine our research and transfer efforts in the field of science and university studies. In this new and final career stage, my efforts have evolved towards research activities that are driven by the extensive experience and strong research skills of the team with which we are collaborating.

When I look back, I realize that my academic activity has been fundamentally characterized by my ability to adapt to different situations within the development of four university functions, namely, teaching, management, knowledge transfer and research, which I have experienced almost sequentially.

JRP: Among the enigmas that appear as one progresses through an academic career (and in life) is that of our relationship with time, or, put differently, what the changing relationship between the present and the future represents for each of us.

Having reached a stable position (but not the highest available in the career track), the cumulative experiences mentioned above and developing life perspective can help us to change focus from the future to the present. Following Weick (2004), the future serves as a means by which to achieve a satisfactory present through projects that fill the present time with growth, learning and encouragement. This approach can be damaging for those at the start of their careers, since the increasing competitive pressure obliges them to attain in the future a successful publication record, and passing through the present without enjoying it.

However, Weick's view on the relationship between present and future makes sense for any intellectual trying to "advance human freedom and knowledge", as Said (1996: 17) says. This is especially true if we consider how interesting the current times are in which we live.

Image 6: The professional career as the result of the combination of voluntary decisions and surrounding circumstances

FC: On finishing university, I always thought about dedicating myself to university teaching. I have been directing my steps throughout these past decades using that goal as a beacon or guide, regardless of the detours that may have arisen along my journey. On the other hand, I have not followed the path of a university professor that we could call conventional, i.e., one that would guarantee professional success culminating in the highest category within the teaching staff, namely, the position of 'full professor'. Such a path consists of a brilliant academic record, scholarships for university professor training and a focus on the achievement of specific outputs to attain full professorship. In my case, I did not join a university directly after finishing my studies; rather, I engaged with different situations or opportunities that appeared within my academic environment, always looking to make a commitment to the present institution and to personal and intellectual satisfaction regarding the work I do instead of focussing on promotions and professional status.

JRP: As of 2020, I have served 25 years as a university professor. All things being equal, I will retire in 2033 at the age of 70. In that case, I will have spent two-thirds of my academic career in this position. Although professionally, these years have increased my level of experience with the benefit of hindsight, I am still excited by the idea that my acme (ἀκμή) has not yet arrived. I have been a tenured senior lecturer or associate professor at the Autonomous University of Madrid (UAM) since 2006, and my prospects of obtaining a position as full professor (the next and last academic step) under the current circumstances are quite slim.

During this time, teamwork (of different composition and scope); a commitment to education as an instrument of social transformation; political action undertaken within the public university to defend its survival; the link between teaching, research and knowledge transfer that seeks results that are socially useful; and a still-present curiosity have placed me within the framework that could be referred to as the engagement with the collective academic ideal.

Given that in Spain (at least for the moment) there are no evaluations given after gaining the status of a civil servant that have an effective material impact on an associate professor,[1] the following question remains: why maintain the effort to progress in an academic career? Perhaps it is heretical for those who proclaim a certain academic ideal to ask this question, but I do think that the complacency of some professors at a certain age is relatively widespread in many countries.

Image 7: Character and ethics (our personal visions of what a university professor should be)

FC: The development of my professional career has been marked by the ideal vision of the university that I forged in my student years. This image consists of a public university in which people of different social origins meet and live together; it is participatory, both in the field of management of the institution itself and in the various educational, political and cultural activities that are constantly there; and it is dedicated to the acquisition and generation of useful knowledge for personal development and for the society in which it is framed. Indeed, Spanish universities in the 1970s were under great political tension, in parallel with the changes that were taking place in the country and actively participating in them. This situation pushed me to develop a university teaching vocation.

JRP: My answer to what a university professor should be has two complementary dimensions. On the one hand, there is individual character and ethics (if they can be separated), while on the other hand, there is the will to realize the freedom of the tenured academic, i.e., to pursue intellectual results that can be beneficial both personally and socially. After a quarter of a century of making efforts related to research, teaching and university management that tick all the career boxes, I feel obliged (which converges with my own desire) to engage with questions that I consider to be relevant but that are outside the scope of the mainstream studies of organizations and their management.

As a common and provisional conclusion: vocation, ethics, public service, adaptation to circumstances and cooperation (two ducks in the university setting)

When a scholar creates her career mixing teaching, research and service, she can enjoy the benefits of functional cross-fertilization. Good teaching requires – among other skills – to master the subtleties of the research work. And knowing where the difficulties to understand a real problem rest can shed light on the research process. University administration, service and engagement offer a wider perspective to comprehend who we are as scholars, how our tasks should be done in a social framework, and the evolution of ourselves in the university's historical dimension. Using a metaphor coined by Germán Schlatter, we are like ducks, who neither fly well, nor walk well, nor swim well…but, doing everything, we have survived.

If everybody in universities become ducks (this is, a lack of specialization in the scholar's main functions) maybe a productivity reduction would be experienced. Productivity as a number of certain items within the audit culture of the neoliberal university. The gains produced by a university of ducks should overcome any market-oriented view of productivity. These are an academic community prone to the common good, as well as a real contribution to the education of the citizens needed in a democratic society.

On the other hand, within the institution they could coexist with other types of academic staff (more individualistic and specialized), so that they complement each other to promote the different missions of the university.

If you want to engage in a conventional academic career under the current criteria, you should focus on complying with the established requirements, which in Spain currently consists almost exclusively of "publish or perish" with regard to high-impact and indexed journals (besides the fulfilment of some teaching experience requirements). This is what many teachers do, without stopping to reflect on the logic or the usefulness of this method to achieve their objectives, i.e., not only their personal objectives but also those related to the common good that the higher education system should promote. This generates a very strong competition between professors, all of whom share very similar profiles, such that they compete for a reduced number of spaces for article publications and positions in universities.

The other alternative, which we have aimed to illustrate within this portrait, consists of developing a university vocation through the balanced execution of the different university missions, placing an emphasis on each of them based on the skills developed and the commitment made to the institution and taking advantage of the opportunities that are generated through network collaborations and teamwork.

Resilience, such as the ability to recover after each hardship, is the concept the most often used in recent times to deal with the great changes that are taking place in our economic and social environment. According to Coutu (2002: 48), "Resilient people possess three characteristics: a staunch acceptance of reality; a deep belief, often buttressed by strongly held values, that life is meaningful; and an uncanny ability to improvise". These same characteristics are the ones that we want to highlight as the current keys to survival in the academic field outside the conventional neoliberal meritocracy.

We have survived in a Spanish university following a generalist academic path based on the collective academic's strong ties. This is not the only way to proceed with the academic career, but it is a path aligned with our personal values and, we think, with the common good. Our careers show that it is possible to survive fulfilling individual goals and serving social interests.

Note

1 In the Spanish public university, senior lecturers (professors and associate professors) are civil servants.

References

Brown, W. (2015). *Undoing the Demos: Neoliberalism's Stealth Revolution*. New York: Zone Books.
Brunsson, N.M.G. & A. Karafillidis (2007). Nils M.G. Brunsson im Interview: Organizing Failures. *Revue für postheroisches Management, 1*, 37–43.
Busch, L. (2017). *Knowledge for Sale. The Neoliberal Takeover of Higher Education*. Cambridge, MA: The MIT Press.
Coutu, D.L. (2002). How Resilience Works. *Harvard Business Review, 80(5)*, 46–55.
Foucault, M. (1999). *Discourse and Truth: The Problematization of Parrhesía (Six Lectures Given by Michel Foucault at Berkeley, Oct.–Nov. 1983)*. Downloaded Feb. 20, 2020 from https://foucault.info/downloads/discourseandtruth.doc.
Said, E.W. (1996). *Representations of the Intellectual. The 1993 Reith Lectures*. New York: Vintage Books.
Sassower, R. (2019). The Neoliberal University and the Common Good. *Social Epistemology Review and Reply Collective, 8(10)*, 90–106. https://wp.me/p1Bfg0-4yf.
Weick, K.E. (2004). How Projects Lose Meaning. The Dynamics of Renewal, in Ralph E. Stablein & Peter J. Frost (Eds.), *Renewing Research Practice*. Stanford, CA: Stanford University Press, 183–204.

EXCELLENCE AND DISRUPTION

A mid-career dialogue

Eugenie Hunsicker and Clare Hutton

Universities in the UK have been transformed during the course of the last three decades, and for academics now in their 50s, the landscape sometimes seems barely recognisable. "Excellence" is one of the new buzz words in this changed world. But excellence in what, exactly? Despite the tremendous changes in the sector, the understanding of what is meant by a successful academic career harks back to a model established in the middle of the last century, when largely male academics were supported and buffered from life's disruptions by stay-at-home wives. At the same time, more than ever, well run departments need a balance of excellent teaching, excellent research and strong leadership and administration. It is very difficult for one academic to fulfil all of those roles at the same time. And it is certainly impossible if a career has to work around disruptions such as illness or caring for children or parents. Confronting these issues, and how within the current context academic careers can be done differently, seems appropriate within the "Against Careerism" gallery.

CLARE HUTTON: Let's begin our dialogue with a set of questions. Perhaps they are disruptive questions. What do we mean when we talk of 'doing academic careers differently'? What do our experiences add up to and how are they instructive? How do they inform our understanding of 'excellence', the quality and value which is so deeply written into the strategy at Loughborough, where we both work?

EUGENIE HUNSICKER: There is a great paper called *"Excellence R Us": University Research and the Fetishisation of Excellence,* which concludes that the term "excellence" doesn't have any real meaning at all in academia, and instead relates to narratives of scarcity and hyper-competition. It concludes that scholarship and higher education are not well served by the use of the term (Moore et al., 2017). This basically summarises my understanding of the word as it is used in academia. For me 'doing academic careers differently' relates to a rejection of the currently dominant narrative of the careerist 'ideal academic' (Thornton, 2013), and of careerism as the only way to achieve excellence.

CLARE: Yes, to quote the paper 'it turns out that excellence is not excellent'. Fundamentally we agree.

EUGENIE: And yet, from our previous conversations, I know you have a sense of scholarly excellence in what you personally are trying to achieve in your research and teaching, in the decisions you have made and in the things that motivate you. What is this, and how does it compare to the way the word is often used?

CLARE: My doctoral research was in the field of early twentieth century Irish literature, and when I finished in 1999 I was very clear and confident about my ambition: to make a significant contribution to scholarly knowledge by writing full length and original monographs on two major writers of that era, W. B. Yeats and James Joyce. I have, more or less, remained true to that ambition in that I have completed the work on Joyce and I am now working on a book about Yeats. I remain comfortable with the disciplinary understanding of excellence imbued in me as a student.

At the same time, I have had to respond to the fact that the structure of English as a discipline has changed quite rapidly, and is generally under duress. Over the past few decades, government agendas have led to defining STEM disciplines as the paradigms against which excellence in UK research has been judged. It is in that context that I have had to learn how to continue my scholarly work through the gaps and disruptions in my career. Every time I came back from maternity leave, it felt like the rules of the game had changed.

EUGENIE: My own case is different. I sometimes describe myself as a recovering mathematician. I spent seven gruelling and demoralising years on my PhD in pure mathematics in the US. At one point I thought about leaving for industry, but the choices that appeared available to me, military or finance sectors, were even more demoralising so in the end I stuck with it and finished in 1999. I chose to go directly to a teaching intensive position at a liberal arts college. Ironically, at that point research started to look up, and after 7 more years up to getting tenure, I looked for a new position at a research-intensive institution. In 2006, ended up here at Loughborough in the UK with my new husband. Four years later, we adopted our three sons and I took a year off. This sequence of disruptions helped me realise that I wanted to do something different, that might actually have some impact. Thus started the slow process of charting a new research path in applied data science. My views of what is important in mathematics have had an almost diametric shift over the course of my career.

CLARE: There are some really interesting points of divergence and convergence here. I also have three children. We have both had to negotiate our ambition to achieve our own view of excellence during the 'disruption' of raising children. Literary scholarship does not necessarily move quickly, and I have been able to stop and start, to chop and change, to find my way back to the kind of work I did for my doctorate and as a postdoc, continue to publish, and gain some recognition. The impression I have in your case is that you felt you were not able to make an impact in pure mathematics. Is any part of that related to the deep structure or sociology of the discipline?

EUGENIE: After some time working in pure mathematics, I started to really doubt how mathematicians make the decision about what work in the area is interesting and beautiful. I started to feel that no ideas I proposed would ever be deemed good in these ways, not because of what they were, but because of who I was.

CLARE: That's so sad.

EUGENIE: What is particularly frustrating is that because of the abstract nature of the subject, the reactions to my work were presented, not as personal or cultural decisions, but as abstract absolutes: "This is not interesting", as opposed to "This doesn't interest me". I became really disenchanted with pure mathematics overall.

In data science, I know that even if other mathematicians don't think what I am doing is "excellent", it is accomplishing something. For example, I am currently applying for a patent with a colleague in chemistry for a device we believe can transform the monitoring of microplastics in the environment and help to solve a global challenge. Maybe the mathematics isn't novel, profound or beautiful, but really, who cares?

CLARE: Contributing to solving the problem of microplastics in the environment sounds like a kind of engaged scholarly excellence to me....

EUGENIE: Sure, but it isn't what the mathematical community, or our university, values, and rewards. So for me, "doing academic careers differently" is about challenging what an academic career could or should look like and how success in academia should be judged and rewarded.

CLARE: So the problem you are pointing to is social. The status quo is traditional-male-nothing-needs-to-change. What you are suggesting is that within the mathematics community those values are limiting. Thus we need to rethink 'excellence' in that sphere?

EUGENIE: Oh, yeah, we definitely need to open up our views of excellence in mathematical careers, or maybe drop the concept of excellence altogether, as it suggests a hard and protective line between what is excellent and belongs and what is not excellent and doesn't. I didn't have any sense at the start of my career that I had been indoctrinated during my doctorate about what academics were supposed to be like. I didn't realise I was not travelling along a well-trodden and inevitable path, but rather trying to navigate my way towards a rarely attainable ideal. Changing my idea of the ideal academic and of the ideal of mathematical research went hand in hand with realising I had been brought to believe in them.

In recent years, there has been a lot of media attention to African American women mathematicians Gladys West, who did the calculations behind GPS, and Katherine Johnson, who calculated trajectories for NASA space missions. And incidentally, I love the irony that they both worked in mathematical fields related to finding your way in difficult situations. But when we look at what mathematical work and careers are viewed as prestigious, such nonacademic positions and applied calculations are not among them. It is almost like the less useful your work, the more prestigious it is. And this is causing the discipline huge problems!

CLARE: Going back to disruption—it is a fascinating idea, and is clearly very central to ways of thinking that we share. Viewed institutionally I have had what is described as an 'atypical career': three maternity leaves, some time off work for health reasons, and a period of working part time. Is this really so very atypical? Also, during those 'disruptions' I was still reading and thinking about literature, and when I came back to work, I had new experiences, new insights, new energies. If we are to really value the idea of 'doing academic careers differently' we need to be able to value alternative kinds of experience instead of seeing them as 'disruptions' to the institutional norm.

EUGENIE: Right, your life experiences are not atypical at all. What is atypical is sustaining an academic career despite them. Which does point to a problem with academic careers as they are currently envisioned and supported. No wonder our disciplines end up with such narrow world views, if it excludes people with almost all collections of life experience. I feel that a lot of my struggles at the moment in diversity are concerned with the way in which alternative career trajectories are valued and rewarded—such as through promotion criteria, success in funding, esteem in academic work. But a fundamental issue is of what alternative career trajectories are even permitted. So this brings us again from personal disruption to disruption of the careerist norms of our profession.

CLARE: *Notes to Self*, a recent bestselling memoir by Emilie Pine, includes a searing critique of the contemporary academy wryly entitled 'This is Not on the Exam'. It is about the invisible and unwritten codes that dominate academic life post exam. She writes of 'being afraid of being the disruptive woman. And of not being disruptive enough' [Pine, 2019].

EUGENIE: I relish being the disruptive woman. I think academics needs to value disruption because of its ability to help people break free of traditional limits. But I think these lessons may be more helpful for those who have succeeded in traditional ways than for those individuals who are facing disruption in their own careers. My career as a mathematician is in a comfortable place now. I have a permanent position at Loughborough. I enjoy the research I do in data science. I have a wonderful marriage and three almost grown children. But I am always hesitant to hold up my career path in mathematics as a viable alternative to aim for, because of course, if it hadn't worked in my case, I would not be here in academics to write about it now, but there may be many more people for whom this route did not work.

CLARE: Until I had three children, my career had followed a fairly traditional structure for a humanities academic, in that I completed my BA, an MPhil, and a PhD by the time I was 30, and then went on to do a postdoc at the University of London. I arrived at Loughborough to take up a full-time lectureship in 2004, and was expecting my second child at the time. It did not really occur to me that having children and working full time might be incompatible. Nor did it occur to me that working part time might take me out of the competitive mainstream. I am one of six children and my mother was a full-time teacher when I was growing up, so there was definitely a 'have it all' role model there. When my third child was born in 2007, I decided to cut to a 0.5 contract. This was essential for sanity really, because I commute a long way from home to work, and I wanted to be able to have days when I could collect the kids from school, and days when I just did not feel pressure to be getting on with things. But I did not realise that being part time would mean being overlooked in the academic world, nor did I know that it would be so hard to persuade the university to allow me to resume full time work when the kids were older. I feel that the life experience gained by becoming a parent has not really been valued in the professional sphere. But when I teach and when I write, I know that that life experience has been completely formative. I think this is why I wanted to talk about disruption, and the connection between disruption and excellence.

There is, after all, a happenstance about research and discovery. Disruption is the route through which we find things that are genuinely new and transformative. To use a phrase which was important for literary culture in the 1910s, certainly I am now 'making it new'. I have designed and now teach some modules in digital literary studies (which could not have existed or been imagined in the 1990s when I did my doctorate). And more recently, during the first lockdown of the Covid crisis, I began to write a memoir about my experience of being ill in 2011. So, I have branched out from traditional literary scholarship to digital literary studies, and from writing criticism to writing creatively. All of that new work has originated from the experience of disruption.

EUGENIE: The conventional narrative of the ideal academic implies that disruption slows or prevents the achievement of career excellence. There are any number of initiatives now aimed at helping women who come back from a period of child-care leave to "get back on track" with their research, as if we were all on some narrow pass in the mountains with only one way through. Going back to the work of Gladys West and Katherine Johnson, a navigation analogy keeps coming to my mind. You know, when a ship or satellite or space vehicle goes off its calculated trajectory, there is no point trying to get it back on the original path. You need to calculate an entirely new one. And if it is far enough off, you may need to rethink the mission's goals entirely and move towards new ones. I don't think we are on a mountain pass. I think we are on the wide-open sea, or the vast expanses of open space. So much that could be explored, with excellence available in all directions. I'd like to see people who have had a period of leave, or of part-time work, given the encouragement and support to re-evaluate where they are and where they want to end up. Then these disruptions will permit us to discover excellence in places we would never otherwise have found, rather than preventing us from getting to some fixed goal.

In conclusion, academics of all types need to agitate for change from within for a broader view of the academic career map—one that recognises and celebrates the discoveries that can be made in the uncharted wilds where disruption can lead. With such a mindset, academia can benefit from the diversity that comes of doing academic careers differently.

References

Moore, S., Neylon, C., Paul Eve, M., Paul O'Donnell, D. and Pattinson, D. (2017). "Excellence R Us": University Research and the Fetishisation of Excellence. *Palgrave Communications*, 3(1):1–13.
Pine, E. (2019). *Notes to Self*. London: Penguin Books.
Thornton, M. (2013). The Miracle of Merit. *Australian Feminist Studies*, 28(76):127–143.

COLLECTIVELY CREATING CONDITIONS THAT NURTURE

The bushland as metaphor for the academic ecosystem

Sumati Ahuja, Mihajla Gavin, Simone Grabowski, Najmeh Hassanli, Anja Hergesell, Walter Jarvis, Pavlina Jasovska, Ece Kaya, Alice Klettner, Helena Liu, Jennie Small, Christopher N. Walker, and Ruth Weatherall

Academic identity has been understood almost exclusively through the written or spoken word. When we came together as a collective of 13 academics in an Australian Business School to reflect on our identity, we were determined to value and explore our diversity in career stage, familial commitment, gender, race, sexuality, (dis)ablebodiness, and age. As we began our conversations, we found that a focus solely on text limited the possibilities of the rich and diverse ways we could understand ourselves as academics (Power & Bennett, 2015). Accordingly, we sought novel ways of expressing and understanding academic identity through a combination of arts-based methods, text, and dialogue. This chapter offers insight into our collective journey through arts-based methods and towards understanding how our identities, when enhanced by interaction with each other, can create conditions that nurture diversity in academia. Our conversations highlight, however, that we also face challenges in academia related to our diversity. Arts-based methods offer an inroad to understanding that simultaneous value and pain.

To develop that understanding, we use a mixture of drawing, poetry, creative writing, painting, and photography. These arts-based methods have enabled us to interpret our experiences as academics and create a rich base from which to explore the relationships between our own experience and the experiences of others. A key takeaway from this endeavour was that while we are all subject to the conditions of academia, we experience these conditions differently in relation to our identity. In this chapter we use the metaphor of the Bushland, an important symbol long embedded in Australian consciousness (Davision, 1978; Lawrence, 2003), to unpick the conditions we need to flourish individually, and how we can create those conditions collectively. The memories are based on each author's personal experiences. We respect all narratives even if we do not identify with all. While the memories are personal, the Bushland metaphor draws on a common theme across the individual memories.

Prologue

The Bushland: soil, water, air, and light

We stand together in the Australian Bushland. The Bushland has symbolic power for us as well as a physical power. The Bushland connects us to our country, Australia. To what we dream our country should be. Here, we may fill our lungs with untainted air. Here, we may listen to the uncluttered sounds of nature. Here, we can seek something uncultivated and untouched.

But our tantalising ideals of the Australian Bushland are threaded with inequality, violence, and pain. Some have been excluded from taking roots in this land, some have had their roots violently ripped from the Earth. From First Nations Peoples, this Bushland, this country, has been stolen. The conditions of the Bushland are also at constant threat: from bushfires, from land clearing, from climate change.

Yet, as we stand here in the Australian Bushland in all its contradiction, grief, and hope, we think of how we can create the conditions to allow all to flourish. The Bushland is our place to stand. It is what replenishes us. It is how we know ourselves. It is a place where we have come to make a difference in this world. So, we take the pain and the possibility together and imagine how we could be otherwise.

We fight against reckless use of our Earth. We are against ruthless ideals that plants should grow at all costs. We push back on conditions which allow only a few plants to grow at the expense of others. We spurn places which push plants to grow and grow, and grow without sufficient support. We question histories of pain and exclusion which have only allowed some plants to flourish and not others.

Instead, we labour to cultivate sustainable conditions together. Life that feeds new life. We think of our *soil*, our *water*, our *air*, and our *light*. We think of our current home in Australian academia and our search for other ways of being, knowing, and dreaming.

Our heels and toes connect with the Earth beneath our feet. This Bushland we call home has a myriad of soils. We must find foundations which allow us to take root. This is the *soil* from which we grow. This is the soil that replenishes us. We till the soil with the tools available to us, turning the Earth ready for seeds or leaving the soil alone to return to nature. In time, we will burst forth in our lush diversity.

We touch the surface of the *water* with just our fingertips. Ripples radiate from our touch. Back and forth we move our hands, mimicking the way water pushes and pulls all life, to and fro. A gentle force. A gentle balance. Yet, we are rightly wary of the might of water. Water gives, but water can also take away.

A breeze gently brushes our face. Some of us long for cool *air*, others for heat. The wind has blown some of us off course, into this Bushland where we never imagined we would be. Some of us stand strong against the wind, others bend out of necessity or desire. Without the playful air, we could not breathe, or laugh, or cry.

Light warms our bare skin. We run, and play, and shout in the Bushland. Our ingenuity allows us to create new worlds, new life. The light which touches our skin, touches others too. The connection warms our bones. Our heads turn towards the light.

Similar as our basic needs are, the nuance of desire sets us apart. We flourish in different terrains. These are not differences which we erase, or differences we run from. No. These are differences which create the beauty of the Bushland. These are differences to protect. To nourish.

Follow us into the Brushland. Walk gently with us through our connections. Observe the small adjustments we make to accommodate our infinite variety. And of course, reflect. Feel the Earth beneath your feet, the water on your hands, the breeze on your cheek, and the light on your skin. Stand in our Brushland, considering how you and yours can cultivate one of your own.

Soil

I had only just started to dig my roots in this unknown soil and acclimatise to the department's conditions when Covid-19 struck and interrupted this gradual process. It was like a bushfire producing extreme heat and smoke, which left me stressed, struggling to breathe and anxious about my survival.

So, I focussed entirely on the day-to-day. During the first months of the pandemic, I channelled all my energy into teaching – teaching new subjects and moving them online, teaching my son at home. As a result of these efforts, I have grown one frond, my teaching frond. But I still feel fragile.

Nevertheless, this frond gives me the strength and energy needed to grow further fronds. So, the following semester, I started focussing on research and writing. While those new fronds are still protected within a coil and will take time before they unfurl, the lower parts of the fronds are starting to strengthen and increase my chances of academic survival and identity building. Also, other plants have settled in the soil next to me, providing a groundcover to keep my soil moist – these companions support me and make me feel like I belong here in this Brushland. So, while the Covid-19 bushfire has been an existential danger, it has also

FIGURE 10.1 Young tree fern. Photograph by author.

created a setting in which I could grow skills and self-confidence, unearth my resilience and adaptability, and develop long-term symbiotic relationships with companion plants. I know that the fire that has harshened conditions and threatened to burn me has also created space, light, and organic matter, encouraging long-term growth.

*****

Anais Nin's naturalistic metaphor speaks sagely to what is often at stake in human growth, character formation and indirectly to the facilitative function of education. I experienced and witnessed this through seeing the diverse global responses to Covid-19 and the earlier bushfire crisis in Australia which challenged my own assumptions about education – the need to 'blossom' and grow from the soil, even when the more natural response is to 'remain tight' when things are dark.

Tragedy, loss and challenge at a global scale reawakened and renewed my understanding about growth and learning – how in the face of risk, the greater risk is to 'remain tight' and buried in the soil. I witnessed the devastating fires across Australia (and elsewhere) which was then followed by Covid.

My reflection on these crises stimulated new insights and an even more demanding call to 'blossom' in the face of adversity. I thought it was a personal issue. I was regularly 'tearing up', weeping, sobbing at not only the raw vulnerability with unimaginable impacts on families and communities that I saw around me. But, crucially, at also what that fragility brought out in so many – spontaneous bursts of generosity and solidarity, especially manifest in how 'essential' workers has redefined dignity in work. Not celebrities, but 'salt of the earth' people, *dedicated* to public wellbeing). In stark contrast to much that financialises and commodifies education few if any of these essential workers are motivated by what is so often and widely disparaged, by ideals of health, education, safety, and service.

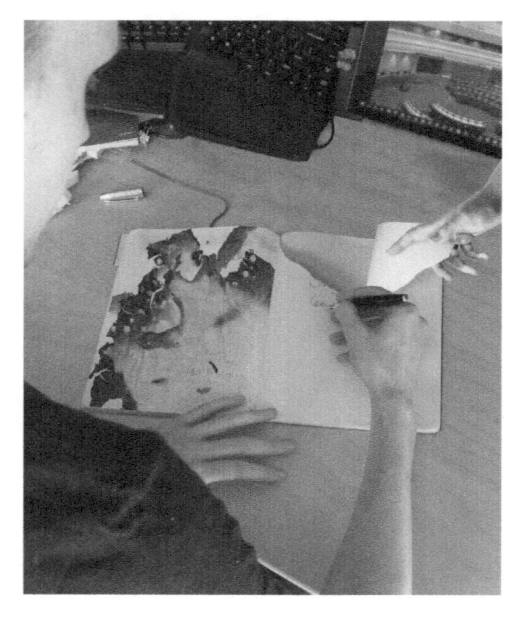

FIGURE 10.2 'Ardens Terrae'. Photograph by author.

These crises viscerally reinforced reflections on what I understand about the function of education, human growth and character formation. While there is a risk of being buried in the soil, it's important to see the primacy of intrinsic values – such as trust, dignity, and the integrity of ecological systems. That rediscovery exposed a harsh edge – an entrenched extrinsic focus on instrumentalist obsessions with measuring economic growth and productivity, blinding us to what was and still is at stake – ensuring essential conditions it takes to bloom, the intrinsic values necessary for life to flourish.

*****

I came by call for healing fruits, to aid their cultivation
but found Demeter just a mask – an Eris-borne deception

But the soil belongs to no-one
it was never theirs to promise
its fertile depths remain as true
and ripe for blooming solace

Yet how and where to lay my roots?
All soil here is not equal
much toxic land and shifting sands
obscure a place to start from.

And whereupon we find lush earth
it's also full of shit;
amidst rich dirt still grow the seeds
of change and social refit.

But still, these rise by blood and bone
Alphas through omega
a choice so old, so self-informed;
so violent; so distasteful.

Even if my roots take hold
how do I sustain them?
Each scoop I take of growing-aid
risks feeding hidden poisons.

So how am I to grow here?
and do I even want to?
to cut my teeth in violent feast
Is not what I signed up for.

It isn't, though, a hopeless bid
Degradation isn't total
between the weeds and trees' tall leaves
still fruits of every flavour.

It's not by chance these buds survive
but that they have is vital
by will to coexist they thrive;
repel encroaching wasteland.

*****

Water

At the end of last year, I had a mental breakdown – ironically this occurred during a Work-Life balance workshop run at work. It was the feeling of being dumped by a crashing wave while surfing without having enough breath to duck under the next. I could no longer ride the waves between deadlines (work) and children (home). Academia to me has no fixed, maximum workload. You are always in way too deep, but not quite past the breakers.

I cut back my work hours to part time this year so that I could spend more time with my kids. I've never really felt like I've spent time caring for them – apart from 3 to 4 months after each was born. They have been raised by grandparents, aunts, long day care centres.

FIGURE 10.3 Kids gardening. Photograph by author.

I began to love work again this year – the tidal flow had become a steady ripple. I wanted to do more of it, after hours. I signed up for more roles. Crazy maybe… But my day off is my day with my son. This year was a blessing; my 4 days each week were worked at home so that once the home-schooling (a not yet forgotten nightmare of Covid-19) had ended, there were lovely commutes to school with bikes, the dog, my husband.

This photo really captures the joy I have felt spending time with my children doing and sharing what I love doing – gardening. The veggie patch is right next door to my new home office, so I take every opportunity for a stretch to check the plants. And I spend time each morning watering before the long summer heat sets in for the day. Balance!

★★★★★

My academic journey can appear like calm waves – flowing, restoring, an open expanse ready for adventure. Beneath the surface are the depths of the water – the currents, the ebb and flow – that mask some challenges of the journey.

There can be 'tension'. Each aspect of the role is a push/pull through forces of the water. Is it possible to always swim between the flags?

My role as an academic sometimes feels like a push and pull – between teaching, research, and service – and a need for balance that others also strive for on this journey. I can craft my day how I wish, and feel extremely fortunate to, but currents can take me off course when urgent matters arise. I can craft aspects of my work – what I research, how I teach – but forces beneath the surface can sometimes threaten this calm.

Collectively creating conditions that nurture **81**

FIGURE 10.4 Ocean waves. Photograph by author.

The ocean is expansive, and you can't see the end. There is a lot of wonderful opportunity in academia. How can I create my own pool to swim in on this journey?

*****

Navigating the academic Bushland is hard but wonderfully free. My thirst for autonomy and freedom arises perhaps from my past career experience, struggles with health and the realities of being a working parent. In my first career I had no autonomy, I was miserable – the clock represents the time-based billing system that I detested. I was like water in a concrete jungle, sloshing along the surface with no control, feeling dirty as a defender of big business and its shady deals.

82 Sumati Ahuja et al.

FIGURE 10.5 Freedom-focussed. Image created by author.

In academia I feel I have found my way into a large and mostly clean lake – a natural place for water where it can sustain all sorts of life. I depict my varied interests and values as flowers that I can propagate and share through teaching and research.

In the early days of the pandemic, with schools closed, I was focussed on putting out fires – surviving the juggle of suddenly having two simultaneous full-time jobs. It was water that saved my sanity. Lucky enough to live near the coast, I plunged myself into the cold ocean every day – to breathe and float and stretch my spine.

I treasure the freedom and flexibility that working from home provides and have found a new equilibrium – I still swim at lunchtime, walk my kids to school, and catch up on work at a time of my choice.

I reject the idea of an academic or 'work' identity that is completely distinct from your 'home' identity – the pressure to hide personal responsibilities to appear more professional. I like that the pandemic has made it more acceptable to have those two streams of life flow as one. Of course, there will be patches of turbulence and rapids, but I try to stop splashing and wait – water will always find its way.

★★★★★

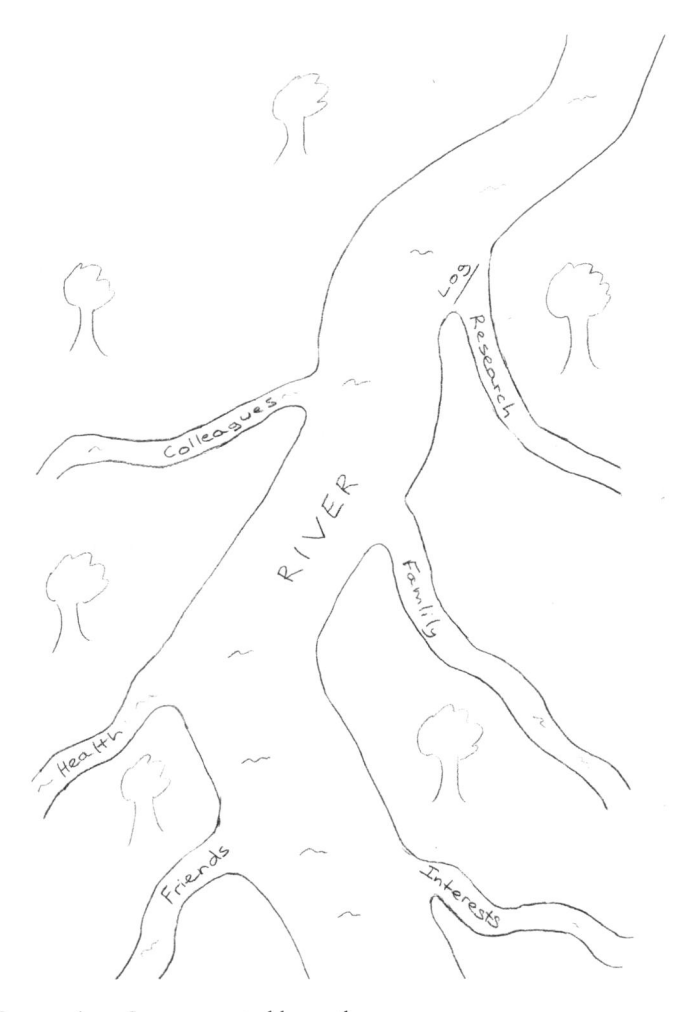

FIGURE 10.6 I am a river. Image created by author.

I am a river flowing through the Bushland. I am fed by many tributaries which sustain me and give my life meaning. These tributaries are my academic research, my colleagues, my family, my friends, my interests, my health. Life is sweet and I flow freely when they are in balance but often there is more ebb than flow if one tributary dries up or is blocked by logs from upstream. The flow of these tributaries needs to be in synchrony for me to achieve my goals. Now that I am 'semi' retired I am no longer flooded by the excessive demands of academe. As a river I am no longer out of control, breaking my banks. Nonetheless, this year my research 'tributary' is not flowing freely. It is partially blocked by a 'log' brought downstream by the family tributary. This 'log' is my new grandchild whom I adore and want to care for. I treasure every moment with her, but it has been hard to be productive and meet deadlines this year. This is reminiscent of earlier times when my children were young, and I tried to balance work and family.

84 Sumati Ahuja et al.

My river course has changed over the years as the academic tributaries (research, colleagues, institution) have impacted on my direction. I have been inspired by colleagues and enabled by my institution to create my own course – the subjects I wished to teach and research I wished to pursue. I feel a very fortunate river. In turn, I hope that I have contributed positively, at least in some small way, to the flow of the tributaries and the watering and nurturing of the Bushland.

*****

Air

The caricature drawn by my son implies a stillness and calm I don't feel. My academic identity is a constant toing and froing, still beguiled by the notion of a work life *balance*, a tightrope walk between order and chaos. My family, my friends, my colleagues are the wind beneath my wings. I need them not just to thrive, but they are the very air I need to survive. It's been a year of online teaching and virtual conferences. In the age of technology my social world is in 2-D. There is no air in Zoom meetings. I breathe the stale air reluctantly. I have no choice but to breathe it in. All living things need air. I cannot breathe.

FIGURE 10.7 No air. Image created by the author's son.

Collectively creating conditions that nurture **85**

   In this Covid year, I am teaching myself to breathe – not the sharp short breaths that leave me anxious but deep inhales that fill up my belly followed by slow releasing exhales that bring a sense of calm. I need to breathe, or I cannot live. I am learning to become an academic.

★★★★★

When I'm stagnant I lack breathing air, and so work is like oxygen to me. But I also carry with me a sense of guilt and anxiety of not working/achieving 'enough'. While having clear work expectations is the subtle breeze that helps me grow, I can easily break and fall if I feel pressured by the intense winds blowing at me from different directions.

FIGURE 10.8 Unfiltered & filtered air. Image created by author.

Earlier this year, we were hit by Cyclone Covid. My workload intensified to the extent that I felt on the brink of breaking...but I have managed to stay stable. Despite the initial destruction, Covid has had some positive influence through the (temporary?) relaxation of work expectations and performance metrics. Such changes have definitely helped me shake and bend less, but I also wonder whether this is the calm before the (next) storm. Who knows?

In such an uncertain climate, I have learnt to stay hopeful by starting my days with an air of determined optimism. I do so by connecting with colleagues who spread seeds of happiness and help me feel supported. I have allowed myself to become vulnerable, both in my reflections of who I am and want to be as an academic, as well as in my interactions with others. I have, as a result, become more accepting of myself and my achievements. I have learnt to filter out some of the pollutants that the gusty winds bring my way; I now feel more in control of what I expose myself to.

I know I should stay grounded and connected to my roots. I need to remain confident, but also stay flexible and free, in order to blossom.

*****

The breath is married to the health of our body and mind. It sustains us. It calms us. When the breath becomes synchronised with our movements, we can feel more space, we can reach further, we can stand taller. The synchronisation of breath and movement can be

FIGURE 10.9 Figure holding book. Photograph by author.

collective, as well as individual. We can chant together, protest together, laugh together. It is not only the quality of our breath, however, it is the quality of the air that we breathe. Our circumstances can render what sustains life, harmful and even lethal. To thrive and flourish in academia, we need air to breathe and the capacity to fill our lungs.

I breathe my academic myself into many spaces. I centre myself through breathwork during my breaks; body sticky with exertion of exercise, filling my lungs as deeply as I can. My extended exhale pushing non-violence into teaching and research. I start and end my working week at the ballet barre; connecting breath, to music, to the body. The carefully controlled lines help me hold my different roles as colleague, educator, and researcher. I inhale books; fiction and non-fiction, academic and non-academic. My air thick with a rich variety of ideas.

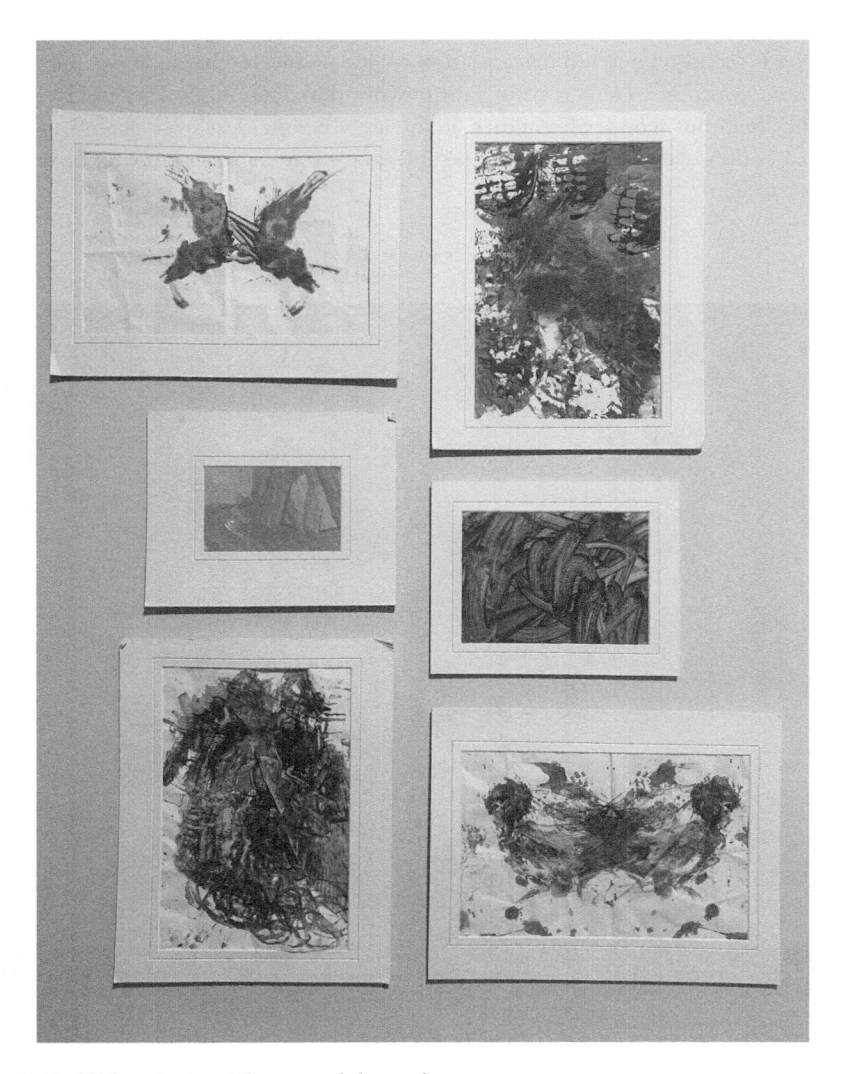

*****

FIGURE 10.10 Kids painting. Photograph by author.

Light

We've moved to a new house. Is this the new beginning, the light we are constantly searching for, in our life, parenthood, career, this pandemic?

I still remember our old apartment, which suddenly became too small for a family of four, two careers and lockdown. The times when I tried to concentrate on my research, and I would hear my husband's work calls – word by word. The times when I needed those precious two hours of work and I would hear my baby waking up from his nap – switching back to being a mama. Exhausted but feeling the light.

I arranged the furniture in my new 'office', my son's room, to have a white and clean background during my Zoom calls. The white slowly became grey, monotonous. Then the light came in. I found a massive pile of my son's paintings. They were just perfect to fill blank space, lighten my days. In my 'office', in my son's room.

During my evening classes, my older son would often enter 'my office', his room. He would ask: "Are these your friends, mama? I just need to take my dinosaurs!", and then he would leave. Recently, I entered my son's room. He saw me and he said with a serious tone: "Mama, I am working!". He was sitting at my work desk, playing, full of light.

I couldn't help but wonder: wouldn't be our new normal less overwhelming if we saw it through a child's eyes? And would we be able to find the light in our life, career, parenthood, this pandemic? Could we?

*****

FIGURE 10.11 Beginning of a storm. Photograph by author.

Covid-19 came like a storm. We were on a family holiday exploring Balinese culture. During a cycling trip among the very green nature of rice terraces and beautiful villages, we coincided with a burial ceremony that made our son start questioning life and death, thinking about what happens to us when we die, what people do when they lose their loved ones. It was also the time when I stepped into a new career path in academia: education-focussed lecturer. I remember the joy, excitement, and curiosity on the day I was offered my position. I felt I belonged until restrictions came into our lives.

My bedroom had become the workplace, giving me constant reminders of working more. The transition from face-to-face to online teaching and the lack of social capital were giving me frustration. My imagined academic identity was changing. I was missing coffee breaks and lunches with colleagues, having face-to-face chats with a mentor, conferences, networking, and travel.

Teaching was always like a theatre performance for me. Now I had to perform virtually. I embraced being an online knowledge transmitter, entertainer, storyteller, tech guru, and nurturer for my students. I also realised that I was present for my family and myself. Exercising, doing creative artwork, riding bicycles, reading, playing video games, surfing as a family, and long walks in the bush taught us to be mindful. That was the light healing the wounds, the light after the storm.

★★★★★

Before the pandemic, what the late bell hooks termed the imperialist white supremacist capitalist cis-heteropatriarchy was killing me. It suffocated me, left me limp and exhausted and starved of care. As a body out of place, I felt like the noxious weed that was trampled on and threatened to be torn out.

The pandemic unexpectedly became an opportunity for healing. Relocated to home, I found sources of light and life. In the mornings before work, I started my day feeling the gentle sun on my body as I took my daily walk around the local park. Soon, I recognised the regulars; neighbours who offered kind smiles and their dogs who bounded across the grass to receive pats.

I also found warmth in the home. Cold leftovers scoffed at my desk in between meetings were replaced with home-cooked meals, hot dishes generously heaped on my plate, salt, and pepper passed across the dining table as we traded stories and shared laughter.

Physically, emotionally, spiritually nourished, my mind and heart could bloom. My writings branching into new creative directions, teeming with strength, joy, and hope.

★★★★★

Epilogue

Our pictures, photographs, creative writing, poetry, and stories illustrate the rich variety of understanding and expression of our academic sense of self through arts-based methods. Most importantly, these portraits of our academic selves do not exist in isolation. They form a tapestry of experience that includes the elements of light, water, air, and soil. There was no singular 'ideal academic' that we were seeking, no one mould into which we were vying to fit (Knights & Clarke, 2014). We all experienced pressure to conform and challenges in negotiating a sense of self that often felt unattainable (Harding, Ford & Gough, 2010). We experienced frustration, failure, vulnerability and insecurity (Knights & Clarke, 2014; Harding et al., 2010). But together, we became something different: we were making the Bushland our own. Flourishing in the Bushland is a collective effort. Although individual reflections provide insight into our own challenges and successes, it is only collectively that we can understand the variety of conditions necessary to flourish and the manifold variations of academic identity. So now that you have walked through our Bushland, it is time to reflect on your own and to discuss these conditions with those who inhabit your ecosystem:

Bushland

What is the symbolic power of academia? What are its promises?
How is your own academia threaded with inequality, insecurity, and vulnerability? Who is subjected to that inequality and how can you (collectively) undo that inequality?

Soil

What tools do you have to change the conditions that surround you?
Where do you find it easiest to take root? How can you ensure that others can take root too?

Water

What pushes and pulls you in academia?
How can you make ripples radiate from your touch?

Air

Have you been blown off course?
How could you stand with others through the storms?

Light

What keeps you warm?
How can we introduce more play in academia? Or at least, more light-heartedness?

References

Davision, G. (1978). Sydney and the bush: An urban context for the Australian legend. *Australian Historical Studies*, *18*(71), 191–209.
Harding, N., Ford, J., & Gough, B. (2010). Accounting for ourselves: Are academics exploited workers? *Critical Perspectives on Accounting*, *21*, 159–168.
Knights, D., & Clarke, C.A. (2014). It's a bittersweet symphony, this life: Fragile academic selves and insecure identities at work. *Organization Studies*, *35*(3), 335–357.
Lawrence, S. (2003) At home in the bush: Material culture and Australian nationalism. *In Archaeologies of the British* (pp. 225–237). Routledge. https://doi.org/10.4324/9780203827529-22
Power, A., & Bennett, D. (2015). Moments of becoming: experiences of embodied connection to place in arts-based service learning in Australia. *Asia-Pacific Journal of Teacher Education*, *43*(2), 156–168.

III
Navigating belonging

Curated by Sarah Robinson

ACROSS HOSTILE WATERS TO BRAVE NEW LANDS? NOTES ON NAVIGATING ACADEMIC BELONGING[1]

Sarah Robinson

Open the heavy wooden door, come up some winding stairs and you will find yourself in the Navigating Belonging Gallery. This round observatory by day, has a midnight blue ceiling in which twinkle 57 navigational stars around the brightest of them all, the star Polaris Academicus. By night, the roof panels open allowing you to observe for yourself the night sky through the many telescopes on offer or with your naked eyes and to identify your own navigational stars and to plot your own routes. This is a space of navigation, choosing paths, grappling with navigational difficulties encountered and searching for new horizons and homecomings. Trestle tables groan with navigational tools, compasses, hour glasses, quadrants and rolls of nautical charts…. On the walls hang monumental works of ships on stormy seas, light houses, treacherous rocks, crowded lifeboats, desert islands and the horizons of brave new lands…

This gallery is about intrepidness and tenacity in navigating academia and of landing and finding a home within it. The brightest star, Polaris Academicus, beckons seductively offering bright futures and shining accolades. However, for some this cannot be their guiding star as they are not entering from the 'right' axis and so like many contributors in this gallery they must chart their own courses and make use of the other navigational stars to guide them. Choosing guiding stars, plotting meaningful routes can be stressful out there on the open sea where one is disorientated and exposed. It requires courage and skill, reflection and tenacity. Some travelers have succeeded unaided, others have experienced support from fellow travelers and allies whilst others are still traveling alone.

To capture the challenges of academic navigations and belonging I have chosen seven beautiful pieces for your attention in this gallery, four full portraits and three miniatures, which are written by scholars of different backgrounds, ethnicities, nationalities, and career and life stages. In their different ways they depict struggle, bravery and tenacity in the face of adversity. They tell of stories of racism, prejudice, censorship, ridicule and lack of understanding, resulting in self-doubt, lack of confidence and alienation. Yet, authors have docked in new worlds, foreign ports, unexpected destinations, some have found a home whilst others continue on their travels.

I invite you to engage with and take courage and joy from following these poignantly depicted journeys. At the same time these portraits invite you to think about how the existing structures they have had to navigate can continue to be challenged, broken down and removed from within the stormy waters of the Academy.

The first portrait you will encounter in front of the wooden door is entitled: *the collective academic*, by Jurdene Coleman, Mac Benavides, Aliah Mestrovich Seay and Tess Hobson. This is a critical account by academics of color: the 'Collective Academic' who, using a critical arts-based narrative approach unpack the experiences of Academics of Color and interweave the reflexive experiences of their white junior scholar allies, as they observe the ongoing oppression in higher education. As such they present a 'conversation across two worlds' and invite you to: 'look around and see where you might find yourself in the story as it unfolds'.

As you do indeed look around you will find the next portrait placed as a companion piece, the first single-authored piece in this collection: *Before you decolonize, let me into the game: Virtue, a key to unbridling the shackles of oppression* by Armand Bam. This is a powerful and moving portrait of Armand's own thoughts, feelings, and experiences as a black early career academic in South Africa, drawing on his wider history. He argues that while calls for decolonization within tertiary institutions grows in South Africa, the need to justify black excellence persist in "white spaces". He uses the concept of virtue, as it unfolds framing his chapter in the imagery of: 'a shackled slave who has come to identify the keys to my freedom lay in the consistent resistance as an activist overcoming victimhood to victory with virtue as my cloak'.

Continuing the theme of occupying and claiming academic space, the first miniature portrait you will see is *How to become an academic, and alienate people: the working-class academic* by Suzanne Albary, which addresses the much neglected issue of class within academia. Her portrait evocatively portrays how she is seen by her family: 'She's still at school', and her own 'attempts to navigate and assimilate into 'the Ivory Tower' – 'and I'm not good on stairs' – and a second assimilation as PhD in Art History and Theory into working within a Business School. She describes here 'clumsy attempts to negotiate learning what it means to be "an academic"', and her identity 'crisis'.

The difficulties in terms of dislocation and struggle on entering and continuing within academia if deviating in background, experience and orientation from a 'typical' academic profile and career route are exquisitely painted in *The back-door academic* by Sarah Stookey. Sarah's detailed and descriptive account of 'a life and work' uses the allegory of a house to discuss her own untraditional career and to illuminate the professional hierarchies that regulate academic lives and organizations. Her inspiring 'back-door' tale addresses the way being seen as 'lesser than' and her hope for different and more equal futures has allowed her to create an often-fulfilling relationship with her students, even when the front-door version of the profession feels alien.

Next door, Emma Newport's miniature portrait, *The Ingenuous Communitarian,* also carries the themes of an academic career chosen to be led differently. Here again, we gain insight into a value-driven career trajectory, forging her own pathway to a permanent post (thus highlighting the important issue of academic precarity) by 'working in ways that are community orientated and that focus on student empowerment'.

The adjacent miniature portrait, *the Journey of a Surprised Academic* by Laurie N. Di Padova-Stocks, picks up on the theme of academic hierarchies and tells the inspiring tale of a 'surprised' later entry academic who navigated many obstacles to achieve a lifelong goal, whilst at the same time coming the realization that 'the journey into academic life reveals a not-so-lofty script for aspiring professors'. For example, unknown pitfalls for the new PhDs include adhering to 'devotion to academic hierarchy'.

The gallery closes with a portrait of double navigation. *The self-made academic. From business to a business school* by Adrian Zicari, like the adjacent portrait, recounts a later journey into academia and also tells the story of both crossing continents and changing careers and reflects on the processes of navigation and the risks and opportunities encountered along the way. Rather than just following the research route, Adrian argues for the vocation of educating managers and the role of those with a background in business in that process arguing that 'Business schools need to nurture and support this kind of unconventional career path within faculty, which can be beneficial both for schools and students'. Adrian argues that it is reasonable that the professors who have to educate a wide pool of aspiring businesspersons for a life of non-linear careers, would have some variety in their own academic careers as well: 'Thus, business experience can be an asset, both in the classroom and in the research context'.

Taken together, the portraits in this gallery evoke a vivid space and atmosphere of intrepidness, courage and struggle. There is hope for the (unconventional) visitor as these portraits demonstrate that enduring orthodoxies and structures which ring-fence shining careers for a privileged few can be challenged and that multiple academic belongings are possible. At the same time, they collectively shed light on the shameful, treacherous face of our profession: on hostility, biases, prejudice and rejection of the outsider.

Note

1 I would like to thank the Navigating Belonging authors for their comments on the earlier draft of this introduction.

THE COLLECTIVE ACADEMIC

A conversation across worlds

Jurdene A. Coleman, Mac T. Benavides, Aliah Mestrovich Seay, and Tess Hobson

Introduction

Academic careers were designed by and for white men, and this is apparent when we take a step back to examine the structures and processes that constrain our voices within the Academy. In this chapter, we seek to come together and collectively inform new ways of doing academic careers that promote freedom, especially for those who have faced racialized violence. The culturally grounded ways of knowing, doing, and being that are central to of Communities of Color have been silenced and discredited through mainstream academia, imposing boundaries for when, where, and to what extent authenticity is allowed. All too often, higher education has "welcomed" People of Color through open enrollment, with the caveat that the invitation requires assimilation into Eurocentric norms. As a result, there is some experience of freedom from exclusion, yet the capacity to develop an authentic voice as an academic continues to be diminished.

Our team consists of two Junior Scholars of Color (JSOC), a Black woman and a Mexican American man, who were participant-researchers, and two white female junior scholar allies (wjsa). Recognizing the power of pluralistic voice to transform, we embodied the spirit of what we call the collective academic to surface and learn from stories that disrupt academic notions of normativity. Specifically, we used critical arts-based narrative inquiry to unpack how JSOC engaged with dominant norms in their fields, as they navigated predominantly white institutions. The collective academic emerged from a search for healing for the JSOC authors and a desire for wjsa to implicate themselves in the racial hierarchy. Together we recognized our inability to shift higher education on our own and the need to come together, collectively, to share our story. In this chapter, we present a dialog across two worlds, through which we make visible the violence of academia and call on academics everywhere to do differently. This is our story.

Reading this chapter

We use several mechanics of style in this chapter that defy traditional academic formatting. This is done intentionally. In critiquing the centrality of whiteness as a racial discourse, in this study we intentionally do not capitalize "white" or "whiteness" as a way of "reject[ing] the grammatical representation of power capitalization brings" to these terms (Pérez Huber, 2010, p. 93). However, we do capitalize terms used to describe racially minoritized peoples, including "Junior Scholars of Color," as a "grammatical move towards empowerment and racial justice" (Pérez Huber, 2010, p. 93).

The collective academic

Drawing from literature on collective identity, our metaphor of the collective academic recognizes how Communities of Color often use individual and collective ways of coping with racist systems (Harrell, 2000). The collective academic is not necessarily always a Person of Color. However, our conceptualization of the metaphor reflects an academic committed to actively centering the perspectives and stories of People of Color and other minoritized groups. The collective academic recognizes the pervasive nature of normalized whiteness and engages in the power of collective storytelling to disrupt normative and dominant narratives. Especially in a place where whiteness continues to be protected (Sensoy & DiAngelo, 2017), higher education Communities of Color need the collective academic to actively decenter Eurocentric ways of knowing, being, and doing. The collective academic understands the power of the long histories of Communities of Color using storytelling to pass on cultural perspectives that have traditionally been silenced (Carter-Black, 2007; Delgado et al., 2012).

Through the use of collective storytelling, we seek to inform policies of freedom in our institution by starting a dialog about how current structures and processes embody what Grosz (2010) refers to as a freedom from ontology. This idea of granting freedom from oppression, while well intentioned, focuses on the power of the socially dominant to bestow freedom upon those who are marginalized. We want to challenge our readers who operate within higher education systems to reflect on how their own institutions inhibit or encourage the transformation of the quality of activity of JSOC; creating spaces for us/them to experience freedom to be our/their whole selves. Inviting JSOC into the academy without disrupting the primacy of Eurocentric structure will never lead to meaningful transformation.

This empty gesture invitation is representative of the conditions that brought us to this work. On the one hand, there was the epistemological racism that the two JSOC authors faced throughout our doctoral program. From the lack of representation of scholarship reflecting our cultural backgrounds to the active invalidation we faced in classroom discussions, the need for doing academic careers differently was clear. We dream of a day when we, too, can see ourselves in the framing of these institutions who want our bodies but not our voices. On the other hand, there was the commitment the two wjsa have made to contributing to racial justice. As two white women engaged in critical whiteness studies, we acknowledged our responsibility to implicate ourselves and the epistemological comfort we feel within academia. We must break down the notions that white, Eurocentric frames are universal, objective, and normal. This is how we do academic careers differently.

This chapter represents the multiple layers of sense-making that took place through this project. To understand what transformation was needed regarding how we approach academic careers, we conducted a research study involving two intersecting processes. Our study in and of itself was disruptive because we refused to reduce the complexity of marginalized voices and experiences and instead engaged in personal and collective storytelling work to develop a polyvocal narrative. In this study, we collectively made meaning of the experience and engaged in a dialog about how to reimagine academia. Our re-presentation (Bhattacharya, 2017) of our findings embodied the collective spirit of Communities of Color taking the form of poems, letters, and creative nonfiction writings. The stories that emerged from this study presented insights into how we might transform academia to better serve a diverse and changing world.

In this chapter, we present an overview of the findings of a critical arts-based narrative research project that we used as a tool for doing academic careers differently. First, we outline the process and theoretical conceptualization undertaken by our two JSOC. Then we will turn to the complementary work of our two wjsa, exploring their experience with making space for the emerging stories. Finally, we present the dialog across two worlds that emerged from weaving together these two meaning-making processes.

Junior scholars of color: collective storytelling, collective transformation

In this section, the use of "we" will refer to JSOC.

Our process consisted of a complex, layered approach to storytelling. This began as collective meaning-making between the two of us as we navigated our experiences in graduate school at a predominantly white institution. We quickly became each other's support, sharing our frustrations, expressing our pain. As the work evolved, we recruited two JSOC who were also doctoral students at our institution. Leaning into the relational nature of our cultural orientations, we decided to limit the number of participants so we had adequate space and time to build trust and get to know each other. Together, our identities included a Black woman, a Latina woman, an Asian woman, and a Mexican American man. The four of us worked together over the course of a semester to share stories, imagine new realities, and create direction for future work. In this way, our research project served as a powerful platform for transforming academia.

We used art as a medium through which to continuously dive deeper into the lived experiences of our participants – the two peers we recruited and ourselves. Our data collection and analysis methods included (1) life story interviews using photo-elicitation to explore how whiteness manifested in participants' academic lives; (2) co-constructed poetic testimonios to re-present participants' stories; (3) an art-show where participants creatively shared their understanding of their testimonios; and (4) a focus group through which we collaboratively edited and made meaning of our collective narrative.

The Collective Academic recognizes the significance of relationships within academia and this project built upon those principles in its execution. Relationship-building and mutual understanding began during the initial interviews with participants, during which we engaged in a two-way examination of racialized experiences on a predominantly white campus. This sharing of stories between both parties during interviews provided a powerful and culturally relevant space for collective meaning-making. This led to a deeper understanding of the participants' experiences, which allowed us to construct rich, powerful testimonios depicting their stories in a poetic manner. The participants felt seen and heard by the testimonios, and these informed the way they approached the creation of their artistic representation for the art show.

Each stage of the research was relational in nature. None of the virtual meetings began on time or immediately moved to the business of research. We spent time checking in with each other. We devoted time to sharing joys, concerns, inspirations, and frustrations. We shared new perspectives we were learning and advice for navigating the journey of graduate education. Given the purpose of our study, we had to move beyond the traditional exploitative nature of academic work (Smith, 2012). Our art show was a prime example of this. It exceeded any expectations we could have had for the storytelling and community-building potential of this event. Each participant shared their art and their story, which in and of itself was a meaningful and healing experience. However, the discussion that happened after each presentation reflected the collective experience of coping with racist systems (Harrell, 2000). We found that each presentation struck a nerve for each of us. We shared our own stories that were inspired by the art, stories we likely would not have even thought to share had it not been for the art show. We moved into a realm of discussing issues of the heart and soul. We explored the embodiment of racialization, minoritization, and marginalization. The art show engagement achieved the goal of surfacing unheard stories.

After the art show, we used the initial testimonios and the discussion from the art show to construct the initial draft of a collective narrative. What resulted from this were four letters to white academics, two of which outlined challenges we faced due to the whiteness in academia and two of which represented corresponding stories of hope for change. Together with our participants, we discussed each letter and collectively edited it to align more with the collective story that had unfolded through the engagement. The result for each of us was a sense of empowerment reading a narrative with which we could each relate and which transcended the power of any of our individual stories.

Warren et al. (2016) explained that community engaged scholarship is fundamentally collective in nature, which "provides the vehicle for students to develop new, countercultural identities and commitments in the face of mainstream academic pressures" (p. 252). Through the focus group, our participants were able to collaboratively debrief the experience of exploring racialization in academia, feel relief that we were not alone in our shared experiences, and process the anger and pain that resulted from realizing that we all have endured these challenges.

Grosz (2010) examined the connection between freedom, autonomy, and integration. She stated that "freedom is not so much linked to choice as it is to autonomy; and autonomy is linked to the ability to make activities one's own, that is to integrate the activities one undertakes into one's history, one's becoming (p. 151)." We understand this dialog as the first in a series of steps toward supporting the autonomy of JSOC in higher education because we believe that this type of freedom opens up opportunities for creativity and ingenuity that otherwise do not exist. As Grosz (2010) noted, freedom is linked to innovation and invention. We acknowledge, as Grosz did, that freedom is a capacity inherent in JSOC, and we hope that by encouraging open dialog, these JSOC will allow themselves to take up space in higher education; that they will attain a new sense of freedom to be.

At the end of the focus group, we were moved to find opportunities to share the narrative, though we remained cautious navigating the politics of higher education and our status as graduate students. Keeping in line with Grosz's (2010) concept of freedom as the ability for self-determinism, we invited our participants to collectively decide what our collective narrative was capable of doing and what change it had the potential to bring about. In this way, we wanted to make a plan with them for "what's next." Ultimately, we determined that the risk to our perseverance in higher education was too high to share the letters with targeted audiences, such as faculty and coordinators in our academic programs. Instead, we identified several campus venues through which we could share the findings of our research and indirectly make calls for change through these academic channels. In this way, the focus group engagement achieved the second goal of determining how to disrupt the university's dominant discourse framed by whiteness.

White junior scholar allies: listening to create space

In this section, the use of "we" will refer to wjsa.

The dialogic engagement process that occurred between JSOC and wjsa was strategically co-constructed so that the interactive and collective process resulted in two narratives: one created by JSOC and one developed as our critical white intercultural listening response. We also used this project to build community with each other, challenge our perceptions and beliefs about whiteness, and provide a sounding board to unpack our own preconditioned racist ideologies. We used the construct of critical white intercultural listening, informed by critical whiteness studies (CWS) and intercultural listening (IL) (Mestrovich et al., 2022), for our engagement process. We utilized the key tenets of CWS adapted to higher education by Cabrera et al. (2016) including whiteness as colorblindness, whiteness as epistemologies of ignorance, whiteness as ontological expansiveness, whiteness as property, and whiteness as assumed racial comfort. These core components of CWS are intersectional and reinforce one another in a way that allows the problematic position of whiteness in the racial hierarchy to remain invisible (Cabrera et al., 2016). Our conceptualization of IL (Mestrovich et al., 2022) includes listening being (Lipari, 2010), active listening (Gearhart & Bodie, 2011), as well as constructivist and narrative listening (Hyater-Adams, 2011). These interconnected listening frameworks support the human experience beyond discourse and dialog with an intentional focus of supporting the cultural and emotional experiences of marginalized voices with the listener's acute awareness in systems of oppression. The result is the potential opportunity for new narratives to be explored which separate the speaker from the problematic situation with a focus on positive change and new stories of transformation to be told (Hyater-Adams, 2011).

Grounded in literature on CWS in higher education and IL, we took field and observation notes throughout the entire research process focused on responding to preliminary research questions which required them to explore how JSOC engaged with IL and what elements of IL were reflected in the natural forms of listening exhibited during the JSOC engagement process. Additionally, we explored how JSOC could have other natural ways of listening that differed from IL. Finally, we explored how CWS (Cabrera, 2016; Frankenberg, 1993) informed the ways in which we practiced and conceptualized IL and what action steps we would take as a result of this exploration to support the decentering and deconstructing of whiteness in academia.

We performed the intentional process of social un-conditioning in a variety of ways throughout the engagement process: taking field and observation notes while viewing the video recordings of JSOC and engaging in individual and collective critical reflexivity involving the racial dynamics at play. We were transparent and vulnerable with each other as we unpacked the role we have played and continue to play in the centering of whiteness in academia.

The process of critical white intercultural listening occurred in five different phases aligning within the engagement process of JSOC. First, during phase one, we observed the recordings of JSOC being interviewed about their experience at a predominantly white institution (PWI). It is important to note that we did not attend the meetings in real time because it was determined early in the research planning process that our presence could alter the community and group building dynamics as well as feelings of safety and belonging that could take place among JSOC. In phase two, we watched a Zoom recording of JSOC presenting their art related to their experience at a PWI. We went through a systematic process of taking field and observation notes while watching the videos and then debriefed after each viewing of each recording of the JSOC engagement process. Finally, in phases four and five, we interviewed (a) JSOC participant-researchers about their experience of listening and (b) JSOC participants about their experience of feeling listened to and the overall impact of listening on the co-construction of collective meaning. In phases four and five, we transcribed the individual interviews we conducted with JSOC. The outcome of this engagement process was a generation of themes about our own experiences involving the role CWS and IL play in decentering and deconstructing whiteness in academia.

The authentic engagement process of JSOC created a collective narrative that can inform the ways in which white academics understand our role in perpetuating systemic racism in higher education. We identified two major themes that emerged from this process: (1) white people must understand the importance of taking up less space and (2) there is an urgent need for us as white people to "take the work back" to deconstruct the racist systems that we created.

Through a process of field notes, observations, and participant checking, we were able to differentiate between culturally relevant listening and IL (Mestrovich et al., 2022) employed by and between JSOC. JSOC employed what they defined as culturally relevant listening which is a natural form of listening to build upon shared experiences of People of Color fostering a sense of interconnectedness, belonging, and community in their collective group. JSOC described culturally relevant listening as being comfortable, validating, and transcendental in nature. We also ascertained that JSOC utilized all four tenets of IL throughout the engagement process: listening being, active listening, constructivist, and narrative listening (Lipari, 2014; Hyater-Adams, 2010; Mestrovich et al., 2022)) to further individual narratives as well as the collective meaning-making process throughout the project. Additionally, after interviewing JSOC, it was evident that there were moments during the project that both culturally relevant listening and IL were employed naturally in unison intersecting with each other in a dialogic dynamic which fostered the development of the collective narrative.

It is important to note that we as white people cannot access this form of natural culturally relevant listening due to our lack of being the targets of harmful racialized experiences. It is these shared experiences of marginalization that allow JSOC to practice authentic culturally relevant listening with one another. Furthermore, in our IL practice, we made note that in the presence of white people (us), JSOC felt pressure to censor themselves and cater their expressions to our comfort. As such, it is important as wjsa, to recognize that our absence could support the creation of spaces in which culturally relevant listening leads to racial healing. We should not expect to be acknowledged for stepping back from these spaces; we should do it because it is our role to right the wrongs we have created and from which we benefit. Therefore, it is our charge as white people to be aware of the space we take, the burden we create for People of Color in doing so, and to learn to decenter ourselves and disrupt the oppressive systems we perpetuate.

Lastly, we practiced critical white intercultural listening as JSOC provided direct and indirect feedback to us regarding implications for white academics. There was a consistent focus on the importance of relationship building, implementing change at personal and systemic levels, developing more awareness around whiteness, deeply acknowledging the significant challenges we have created and that the playing field is not equal. Finally, we were asked to make a commitment to do the work necessary to challenge oppressive systems of racial inequality with urgency. As an action step, we have written responses to the collective narratives of JSOC.

Developing the collective narrative

As outlined above, the collective narrative was first developed by examining data collected throughout the project by the two JSOC researcher participants. This narrative took the form of letters directed to white academics and higher education administrators and centered on two stories of challenge and two corresponding stories of hope that emerged as themes from the data. The unified voice of JSOC in these letters offers a glimpse into these shared collective experiences. After a process of member checking and collaboratively editing the letters with participants, these were shared with the two wjsa researchers who then developed a response, in the same letter format, based on their own experiences and themes from their findings. These letters are shared below as a dialog between JSOC and wjsa. We used specific formatting styles to illustrate difference in voice and perspectives. The words of JSOC are left-aligned and written in an italicized version of the font used in this write up. The words of wjsa are right-aligned and written in a different font. The reader will notice the letters are structured on the page as a dialog, moving from challenge to recognition of the challenge to a dream of a better future. Finally, we were also intentional about the amount of space wjsa take up on the page in an effort to focus on the experiences of JSOC. We recognize that this dialog is only one step toward further understanding the experiences of JSOC and how white academics and administrators can recognize and respond to these, but we argue that it is an important one.

As the reader engages with the collective narrative below, we present several key implications that surfaced through this project related to doing academic careers differently. Academics should intentionally examine the broader social systems and structures in place that create asymmetrical power dynamics within the academy. Doing so is a crucial first step to understanding whose voices are needed to bring about lasting and meaningful change. It is also necessary to actively seek out the concealed stories of those who have historically been and continue to be silenced.

In our study, the use of the arts and relational storytelling were culturally responsive approaches to this work. However, we caution readers to avoid seeking universally appropriate approaches. Academics must make time and effort to understand what will be culturally responsive and sustaining within their own context, something that must be done in collaboration with minoritized communities. Additionally, academics must do the self-work needed to engage with these stories from a place of non-defensiveness. Because doing academic careers (as well as any other normative practice) differently may involve disrupting the cultural perspective of dominant culture academics, listening to these stories can feel like personal attacks. It is important to recall that listening in this way requires examining dominance as imposed social systems rather than focusing on its proximity to dominant cultural identities. It is because of this complex, interdependent nature that we describe this approach to academic careers as a dialog across worlds.

Dialog across worlds

Part I: The exhausting journey of belonging

Could you walk a mile in our shoes? Carrying the pain, honor, and expectations of generations everywhere we go. Expected to leave that at the door and soak up this westernized education that erases us from the pages of history. Listless. These grand universities with their whitewashed curricula are built on the backs of our ancestors but we still don't have a seat at the table. We are the culmination of generations of the weary.

Every day we walk around with a midwestern smile plastered on our faces, straining our mouths into a pleasant grin despite carrying the load. Burdened. Behind that smile we hide the real impact of the microaggressions we hear every day – Hey Beaner! Wow, you're kind of loud. Oh, so you're not Chinese? You don't need to get so angry. – It's exhausting filing each one deeper into ourselves, so we don't let on how much it hurts. We are tired of it.

The days are cloudy. It takes every ounce of energy to show up. Every ounce of energy to just be. Where is the sunlight? Where is the hope? Drained. It's overcast by unspoken expectations that we don't yet know but will be quizzed on. We pick ourselves up and get out there because that's what we do. We are warriors.

In our families, we are the first, the youngest, the only. We have so much to prove, so much riding on our success. It is bigger than ourselves or our families, our success is for our People. Our success is vital to prove you wrong. The weight... of all that... is heavy.

Who are we? We are exhausted, nice to meet you.

> *We see you, we hear you. But do we? We want to understand your experience, and at the same time acknowledge that you share pain and exhaustion we cannot fathom. The burden you carry sounds indescribably heavy and it is a load that we (white people) created.*
>
> *The prejudice, discrimination, and racism you have endured is abhorrent and deafening. We acknowledge that we have perpetuated a system that leads to your pain through our silence, complicity, and "well-intentioned, good white person persona." We say we care, and we do, but empty words fall flat. Even though we can't imagine walking a mile in your shoes, we want to walk beside you with urgency and behind you with commitment to disrupt this system of whiteness.*
>
> *Racism is a white problem. It wasn't ever yours to carry. We are the ones responsible for your exhaustion and we want to do better. We have to do better. We are ready to tune in differently to listen with all of our being as we acknowledge our limitations of understanding as white scholars. Could you tell us more? Could you help us understand?*

It often feels like we do not belong in these institutions of whiteness, at least as they exist today. They're not meant for us – they weren't built for us. They were made for you. They were framed in your cultural norms. But, imagine what it would look like if we disrupted these ivory towers. If we reconstructed them so that they represented multiple ways of understanding and navigating the world. We DO belong in higher education. Our experiences, our values, our cultural frameworks offer so much to the world. We can inform and transform practice and theory with our stories.

It's time for us to give the work back to white people. It's exhausting being asked to be your Google. To help you see our humanity. We've given you lots of ideas, solutions, feedback. Now it's time for white people to just do the work. It's time for you to accept that you created this problem. You created these systems that try to shut us out. You created the walls of this ivory tower which seek to cut off our connections to who we were and are. You brought us here to serve you.

But now, we're here to empower ourselves and our communities. We're making space for our stories and perspectives to be heard. We're taking up space that you have consistently refused to give us. We will build relationships with you so you can know us and so we can know you. We will walk with you as you come to terms with the changing world. We will remind you that your voice is not less valid just because our voices are heard.

Remember, People of Color disrupt whiteness by existing and making noise in white spaces. White people disrupt whiteness by listening to and celebrating our stories.

Part II: Our whole story belongs

We knew ourselves before. Connected. Authentic. Real. We entered the ivory tower and had to leave those parts of ourselves at the door. The tower is built on the backs of our people but there's not room for our people inside. A vast history of oppression, exclusion, and colonization stands between us and your great tower. We want a bridge wide enough to bring our values across, bring our perspectives across, bring our cultures across.

Instead, we walk a tightrope between who we were before and who you expect us to be now. It's a painstaking, tedious, treacherous walk across this bridge. Looking back over our shoulder, we see our values, our cultures getting smaller and smaller as the tower grows larger and larger. We wear a forced smile and maintain a self-preserving silence that allows us to survive in the midst of white violence.

We don't see ourselves in this place. We were sold this idea of developing new ways of thinking, yet we are invisible in every guest lecture. "Have you considered the gender gap for Asian American women? Trans Black women? Queer Latinx folks?" We're told "no, that wasn't considered" but what you're really saying is "we" weren't considered. We're still invisible to you.

You ask, "how are you" but you aren't really asking. You don't want to connect. You don't want to know us. But we are here. We show up to your classes and your office hours, yet you make no connections, no interactions, no effort to see us. We want to be seen. We are dying to be seen. But are you ready to see us? Seeing us means you have to acknowledge a history this institution ignores. Seeing us means you admit that you've been overlooking us all along.

We are ready to be seen, but we wonder if you're not ready for it; not ready for us.

We see you, we hear you. The fact that you have to ask us to see you is part of the problem. We are ready to see you, which means we are ready to see us — the us that has made you feel unseen. We are present with you now in deep, intentional, humble acknowledgement — listening as we learn to suspend our own white agenda.

You are beautiful people with beautiful stories that have been silenced in a system that disconnects you from who you are. We built bridges only wide enough for our oppressive eurocentric ideals. They force you to shrink and constrict your whole and beautiful being in order to get across and survive in this system. Crossing the bridge comes at a great cost to you sacrificing your culture, values, and perspectives to survive; you feel like you're fading away amidst being invisible, dying to be heard. We are ready to hear you.

As we listen, truly listen, we hear your stories of transgenerational trauma of emotional, mental, and physical violence that has been enacted and simultaneously silenced by white supremacy. In order to truly see you, we have to acknowledge the history, the pain, the violence that we have caused and perpetuated and challenge our fellow white people to do the same.

Let's not just make space at the table. Let's leave the table. Finally. For once. So that People of Color can share their stories in safety. Then we can get busy cleaning up the mess we've made.

Yet, here we are again taking up space: on the page, in the classroom, with each opportunity white comfort continues to be unchallenged and normalized. The game is rigged. When we do not listen, when we choose to not understand and remain ignorant, when we choose not to act, we are complicit.

Pretty words without action is the epitome of whiteness. We want your stories to inspire our action, inspire us to BE the work, daily, for the rest of our lives. We are ready to continue seeing and hearing you. We want to connect. We continue to acknowledge our limitations of understanding as white scholars on our journey of antiracism. Could you tell us more? Could you help us understand?

We're interested in stories and voices that are not always heard. In qualitative research, you have to bring all of yourself. That's frightening and overwhelming at times. We learn about research conducted by white people, framed in a white lens pretending to be neutral. You think that your white lens is objectivity. We recognize that we see what we are studying through ourselves. We know that because our stories are hardly ever centered, our lens can broaden how you understand this issue. Don't you see that you need us? But not just the parts you like. Not just the parts you are comfortable with. You need our whole selves. We need our whole selves.

But our whole selves don't fit here yet. It's a sacrifice we've been making — allowing parts of our story to fade away, parts of our hearts to be forgotten. That's just part of the process, right? It's normal to change and not recognize the person you once were, right? It feels like this isn't a sacrifice we should have to make. You need to make room for us to be who we were and who we are.

Why should we listen to our music with the volume turned down? We want to jump on the couch and sing at the top of our lungs. It brings us life. And yet, it's also sacred to us. It's not for you. Please, hear our stories. Listen to the lyrics that tell of where we come *from. But don't ask us to explain it all to you. We want to exist in a space where we can celebrate all of who we are without being under your microscope. Just feel the rhythm of our ancestors in your hips, the voices of our people in your heart. The spirits of those songs can carry you to a new understanding if you let them.*

But be content with not fully knowing what they mean to us. Some things belong to us – in our hearts, in our minds, in our souls.

References

Bhattacharya, K. (2017). *Fundamentals of qualitative research: A practical guide.* Routledge: New York.

Cabrera, N. L., Franklin, J. D., & Watson, J. S. (2016). Whiteness in higher education: The invisible missing link in diversity and racial analyses. *ASHE Higher Education Report, 42*(6), 7–125. doi:10.1002/aehe.20116

Carter-Black, J. (2007). Teaching cultural competence: An innovative strategy grounded in the universality of storytelling as depicted in African and African American storytelling traditions. *Journal of Social Work Education, 43*(1), 31–50. https://doi.org/10.5175/jswe.2007.200400471

Delgado Bernal, D., Burciaga, R., & Flores Carmona, J. (2012). Chicana/Latina testimonios: Mapping the methodological, pedagogical, and political. *Equity & Excellence in Education, 45*(3), 363–372. https://doi.org/10.1080/10665684.2012.698149

Frankenberg, R. (1993). *White women, race matters: The social construction of whiteness.* Minneapolis: University of Minnesota Press.

Gearhart, C. C. & Bodie, G. D. (2011) Active-emphatic listening as a general social skill: Evidence from bivariate and canonical correlations. *Communications Reports, 24*(2): 86–98.

Grosz, E. (2010). Feminism, materialism, and freedom. In D. Coole & S. Frost (Eds.) *New materialisms: Ontology, agency and politics* (pp 139–157). Durham, NC: Duke University Press. https://doi.org/10.1215/9780822392996

Harrell, S. P. (2000). A multidimensional conceptualization of racism-related stress: Implications for the well-being of people of color. *American Journal of Orthopsychiatry, 70*(1), 42–57. https://doi.org/10.1037/h0087722

Hyater-Adams, Y. (2010). Learning diversity and leadership skills through transformative narratives. *Tamara Journal for Critical Organization Inquiry, 8*(4). http://www.tamarajournal. Com/index.php/tamara/article/view/106

Hyater-Adams, Y. (2012). How to get going with personal narrative and scholarly writing. *Practicing Social Change,* 538–41.

Lipari, L. (2010). Listening, thinking, being. *Communication Theory, 20*(3), 348–362. https://doi.org/10.1111/j.1468-2885.2010.01366.x

Lipari, L. (2014). On interlistening and the idea of dialogue. *Theory and Psychology, 24*(4), 504–523.

Mestrovich Seay, A. K., Benavides, M. T., Coleman, J., & Eddington, S. (2022). Beyond perspective taking: Fostering equity through critical empathy and intercultural listening. In C. Ward (Ed.) *Achieving equity in higher education using empathy as a guiding principle* (pp 141–171). Pennsylvania: IGI Global.

Pérez Huber, L. (2010). Using Latina/o critical race theory (LatCrit) and racist nativism to explore intersectionality in the educational experiences of undocumented Chicana college students. *Educational Foundations, 24*(1–2), 77–96. https://www.questia.com/library/journal/1G1-227945959/using-latina-o-critical-race-theory-latcrit-and

Sensoy, O. & DiAngelo, R. (2017). *Is everyone really equal?: An introduction to key concepts in social justice education.* New York: Teachers College Press.

Smith, L. T. (2012). *Decolonizing methodologies: Research and indigenous peoples.* London: Zed Books Ltd.

Warren, M. R., Park, S. O., & Tieken, M. C. (2016). The formation of community-engaged scholars: A collaborative approach to doctoral training in education research. *Harvard Educational Review, 88*(2), 233–260.

BEFORE YOU DECOLONIZE, LET ME INTO THE GAME

Virtue, a key to unbridling the shackles of oppression

Armand Bam

Justifying black excellence

Frederick Douglass, address at the Convention of Colored Men in 1883 still holds relevance today. In his address Douglass suggests that while slavery had been abolished that as the colored man rose in prominence they encountered resistance and resentment, yet their fall in standing followed an unfettered path (Douglass, 1883). Today, Douglass' description of the struggles of the black wo(man) aptly points toward the drudgery of justifying black excellence in this world of academic bondage. Slavery has not left us; it has evolved while the invisible shackles of white approval rest on the wrists, ankles, and necks of many black early career academics. The master's house remains intact.[1] Freedom is an imperative for all humans but cannot be spoken of without addressing its context. Here, academia is often portrayed as an authentic and pure space and *the* house of freedoms into which one can enter unshackled. This testimony is an opportunity to address this myth and provide a personal account of the emotional burden associated with a grand battle for freedom. This portrait is not a manual for aspiring or early career academics, but instead a narrative of the experiences of tensions and contradictions; power and resistance linked to the terrors encountered in a university (business school) with its origins rooted in apartheid. The exposure to the persistent and insistent systemic whippings reveals the anxieties, vulnerability, and periods of disillusionment etched into my skin.

I am still the only person in my extended family to hold a Ph.D. Of the 13 grandchildren three of us have a university qualification. I often reflect on this as I was not the top "academic" in my family. What I believe is that I was the most determined, consistent, and insistent and I came to understand that education was a gateway to many things. My dogged determination was forged in the furnace of racial classification. We often use categories to make it easy for us to understand *things*, but people are not *things* and the complexity of being and experiencing life cannot be boxed. Here in South Africa, we have had to come to terms with an apartheid classification system that was aimed at promoting white supremacy while restricting the social and economic mobility of black citizens. We were made to live separate lives and our development as people was determined through restrictive policies dividing people into groups. In essence the Apartheid policy was directed at controlling who we could associate with, where we could live and work and significantly how and where we were educated. The effects of this policy are still felt today through a divided education system. While I am conscious, I have entered this system, the lingering danger is that it has not rid itself of the notion of supremacy. I have and continue to witness the mistrust and stereotyping and slaughtering with words that cut far more deeply than any physical brutality indicative of a system and institutions and one that lacks imagination. And so there remains a central question for me as a black early career academic. What does one do to shield yourself against such hate?

At the heart of this sketched narrative lay a few important questions: can freedom be delivered through simply 'playing the game' (Ratle, Robinson, Bristow, & Kerr, 2020) and must we guard against it by resisting the political and professional bureaucracy in the academy? As calls for the decolonization of South African business schools increase, black ECA's like myself are confronted with whether to resist or comply (Bristow, Robinson, & Ratle, 2017). The legacy of apartheid has ensured that networks in academia remain dominated by white researchers and without their patronage and mentorship, the shackles of bondage are tightened. This real rather than symbolic violence is inflicted as increased managerialism and performativity enters academia changing the rules and securing power and privilege. Black early career academics, as apprentices, are then often left on their own to figure out how to meet these requirements. As a black ECA I share my experiences entering academia as an activist and highlight the value of identifying purpose, individual and collective responsibility for doing the right thing at the right time which can act as a cloak shielding against many terrors. Moving from a postdoctoral fellow to a fulltime academic has required that I withstand different forces seeking the surrender of my autonomy (Alvesson & Spicer, 2016). In the end, I want to draw attention to the importance of virtue and integrity as the true keys to unlocking the chains of oppression, domination, and marginalization for all early career academics.

Decolonize what?

Close to the end of 2015 the rise of the #FeesMustFall movement intersected with the broader calls for decolonization of Tertiary institutions in South Africa. Universities across the country were challenged particularly through the student protests and calls to reduce fees and increase access to universities were made. The resounding call was that the university system needed change. It needed to rid itself from its colonial influences and ensure in some respects improved access to education for black South Africans. Students directed attention not only at those in power but at the symbols and statues that represented the system. Yet the institution and the injustices it perpetuates remains. Why is this? Will we ever see the point where "the last will be first"? Is it even possible to suggest such a notion? As a young black ECA the idea that entering an institution that has fortified privilege through education I am also not oblivious to the fact that I too write here in privilege, but a privilege that for me has come at a significant cost.

I often wonder whether universities can live up to the claim of being a community of teachers and scholars when some are considered in and others out. How does a university that perpetuates such inequalities help develop academics intellectual and moral lives (Mbembe, 2016)? How free can the pursuit of knowledge be as a young early career academic in an environment that is not yours. This environment does not always affirm my black body and so the question remains whether we can untangle the fabric of an unjust historical system which has evolved so much and resigning some to a certain fate. The struggle to continue in a system that is not meant to accelerate my progression in society serves only to keep the masters house intact. I am weary that I too should not fall prey to the trappings of this privilege. The need to ensure that other young black early career academics do not have to struggle in the same way is important. The risk remains that one falls in line and doesn't challenge these practices. The risk is there to internalize this oppression to the point of demoralization tightening the shackles of bondage even as we emerge with a consciousness of ourselves.

Dismantling apartheid is a long and arduous process and so too is the dismantling of other colonial practices in higher education. The work is not done. In recognizing this as early career academics we must be aware that privilege should not become a self-serving crutch. It must lead to the emancipation of others. With that cautionary note I keep reminding myself of what Edgar Villanueva (2018) cautions as the greatest threat to our society, the colonizer virus, one that urges us to divide, control and exploit. It represents the true embodiment of how we deal with the inequities in our society and perpetuates the trauma we have experienced over generations. Those who sustain this virus also have an important role in dismantling this project. But first they must come to recognize and face up to the complexity of their privilege. It cannot be ignored. Those who stand and benefit from an unjust system such as apartheid must address the hurt that others endure.

Freedom has a context

In South Africa a tendency persists in society to narrate our history from 1652 the year coinciding with the arrival of the first settling colonizers at the southernmost tip of Africa. If my freedom is to be understood, it must also be addressed within this context and the associated historical amnesia. There is a need to understand the foundation on which this *masters house* has been built. I believe this is important as a South African early career academic for at least two reasons. Firstly, I must recognize the indigene people, the Khoe, San and Kalanga people, whose knowledge systems, beliefs, and perspectives have been systematically erased from our ways in the pursuit of Western science. Secondly, I acknowledge that I work at a business school in a university with deep rooted ties to upholding the Apartheid government having weaponized science and writing indigene peoples and their stories out of our history. As a teaching and research institution the anthropological, linguistic, ethnographic, and other research conducted over the last 100 years has done much to uphold this system of oppression and dehumanize this country's citizens. In other words, this university has been complicit as an apparatus of social control (Freire, 2014) deepening the fault lines (Jansen & Walters, 2020) we see today. There is no denying or justifying this.

By its own admission, the University acknowledged *"its inextricable connection with generations past, present and future"* and *"its contribution towards the injustices of the past"*.[2] Although this olive branch has been extended, addressing the symbols, names of buildings and representation of academic staff has not been as forthcoming in this "white space". The representation of black academics remains ominously low with little prospect for radical change. Marginalization by numbers is evident. How then does a black activist early career academic experience belonging in a place where people do not look like me, speak like me and have endured experiences like me? What is it that can contribute to developing and nurturing an "active sense of belonging" where bureaucracy has evolved to neutralize the political and aid just a few professionals? The state of my freedom and any "process of becoming" clearly is not dependent only on myself but on those who hold the keys to opportunity, guidance, mentorship, networks and more. This process is not only mine to shape (Felstead et al., 2006). Any unshackling cannot be by my own doing and freedom must be understood collectively.

Resistance is cultivated

I grew up in the community of Grassy Park, on the Cape Flats of South Africa. A community beset with social ills and challenges. My parents were working class people with a protestant work ethic who believed in the mantra *education at all costs*. Both had only finished their secondary schooling, but they understood the importance of creating opportunities for their children. Although they were denied higher education, they were educated in more important ways, they were politically conscientized and my first role models as resisters. They were weighed down by an unjust system. I recount this aspect of my upbringing because I have come to understand that resisters are not just born, and you do not just arrive as an activist. Resistance and activism have been cultivated and my education started in my home with social justice and equality the core curriculum. In a certain sense you can say we were force fed this diet due to the circumstances of our country, not out of choice but necessity.

During the heart of apartheid, I witnessed family members being carried from their homes, incarcerated, and held in detention without trial for up to 90 days. I witnessed what it meant to resist and what the costs were. To physically surrender yourself to the obedience of a cause meant taking a beating, being dragged, starved, tortured, and relegated to isolation. I saw and listened to these stories. When compliance and the benefits of co-option were presented by an unjust system, I saw the immediate effects of resistance. Incarceration and liberation are tied together. Today those who resisted are no longer so and have claimed freedom for a nation. Their integrity and commitment to freedom bear witness to the freedom of their mind and souls the physical scars. But how does this help me or any other early career academic? The vivid images remain of the authority's arriving exerting their unjust power and the natural response was resistance and an associated and unwilling surrender as a means of self-preservation. I have come to accept that this experience of encountering a system that can exert its power unjustly is not much different to entering academia and the torture, starvation and relegation to isolation are not uncommon for those who are marginalized. One must fight and resist the unjust to truly appreciate liberation. These are scars you should be willing to bare for the freedom of those to come. As a person and an early career academic I know being black is exhausting and resistance has become a shield against the daily barrage of overt and subtle criticisms fueled by hate. Resistance can be our cloak that covers the scars of our existence.

White ears hear white voices

Entering a university and more specifically a business school I have been asked or reminded that "we should forget about the past". For those who have benefited from this unjust system it is an easy request. What is it that they stand to lose? Yet, when I ask how I would go about doing this without letting go of my identity, the response is often silence, visceral or met with agitation. This is most obvious when I ask in return to count the black bodies in the room and watch in silence as reflexivity departs. Why is it that I am called to let go of my experiences so effortlessly while others claim benefit in theirs? I have come to embrace the redemptive quality of resistance knowing action is required to challenge existing models of power and can lead to open dialogic engagement (Hibbert, 2012). What remains unanswered for me then is how to preserve myself in an institution where those in power hold the keys to my progress? Do I lack the "creativity, inventiveness, courage, political astuteness and reflexivity" (Bristow et al., 2017, p. 1202) to have made this place my home?

Why is it that black voices go unheard by white ears? What is it that allows the blood curdling calls of "I can't breathe" and other visible injustices to be willfully ignored? Surely, justice must come into the reckoning of all our lives as we are "caught in an inescapable network of mutuality".[3] Are our destinies not tied together in my bondage beyond a relationship of superior and subordinate; master and slave; professor and student? What can be said of those who profess but fail to display their humanity as they see my and others suffering? Do they just not see what is so obvious to me? Most culpable are those whom at all costs deny access to their networks and opportunities and narrowly set out to improve their careers with no consideration of those who must still rise. Privilege is their poison, and many are drunk on it believing their achievements are only attributable to their academic prowess and not the help of an unjust system. What sustains a system of privilege other than those in positions of privilege and those that allow it to remain? Are my colleagues aware that in their action or inaction I am suffocating? How much louder should my screams and calls be? How do I lift their knees of oppression off my neck? With established academics maintaining their grip on their domain, what motivation is there to allow a black early career academic into *their* space? And why should my freedom and success be so intimately linked to what others would allow? These are serious questions we must engage with as black early career academics in our attempts to understand whether to don the white masks in a white world and be seduced into playing the game or striving for freedom as gaining access to networks, support and willing mentors is required.

Tensions and contradiction

As an activist a just fight and allies are clear to identify. In a country of 60 million people South Africa has less than five million people who are white. Many efforts have been made to ensure equitable representation occurs in all aspects of society and the institutions functioning within it. It would therefore be reasonable to expect this profile would be reflected throughout higher education institutions. As an example, in my faculty it is estimated that at least 70% of the academic staff are white with few retirements due in the next five years. What prospects then truly exist for progress and promotion as a black early career academic? South Africa does have a unique history and tensions like these are not uncommon and our academic institutions are constrained by them.

Where then in one's life is tension never present? We are human beings after all, tension persists with tendons stitched to our bones and a musculature holding us upright. It is in constant states of perfect tension then that we can sit, stand, lay, walk, run, and jump. In other words, tension is ever-present, a part of the human condition. While this tension is desirable, it must always be guarding against injury or pain. Excessive states of tension lead to situations that become critical and breaking points become inevitable. Intellectually this is no different, tensions between thoughts, beliefs and actions linger. Injury and pain are not always avoidable and often come at the hands of others.

How is it possible to advocate for tolerance and divergent views without making a resting place for them? In academic institutions in South Africa structural inequalities only lead to increased tensions and contradictions witnessed through ongoing calls for decolonization and limiting the collective learning that can take place. Those in power seek to maintain dominance while others are targets in subjugation. Our resistance must move beyond raising objections and calls for change. In a country like South Africa, our economic, environmental, and social discord has largely been propped up by the policies of apartheid. When activism is not present injustices flow, and we all struggle to maintain or regain our humanity particularly if all we do is consider this a 'game'. It is this fight to humanize all our lived experiences that should be acted upon, and dehumanizing resisted.

Activist, victim, victor!

We can take what people say about us, internalize it and believe it or we can rally against it. Whichever way it is our choice not theirs. I have shared this sentiment with many of my students when discussing my own agency particularly in light of resistance and compliance and the perception of being a powerless victim or careerist based on the approaches taken as I carved out my identity in this school (Bristow et al., 2017). What is striking about the notion that one may not be a powerless victim or careerist is that we tend to overlook something fundamental about being a powerless victim or otherwise. Victims encounter and must overcome an assailant. My reality is that I have been a victim of nature and circumstance and held in subjugation by policies that sought to undermine my success in various aspects of my life. This is my reality whether it appears trivial or not. The choice though to seek emancipation from this victimization is what separates me and many like me from those who cannot. My emancipation is intimately tied to those who hold the power. Even though psychological liberation may occur the physical liberation is still required. Systems, buildings, institutions that have been stitched together by these divisive policies do not just rid themselves of this. So, the need for developing a new tapestry to clothe us all is clear. We do not let go of victimhood because we have said so, we let go of victimhood as we weave and reconstruct these institutions. To claim victory is premature. We are still treated like modern day slaves denied our daily rations and set to the mines to work for those who need no more. But let's accept that inequity is avoidable and that from our understanding a collective moral agency could emerge that reconstructs the structures and practices that place black early career academics at risk from not furthering their careers. If we are to be able to claim a just society and one that lifts those oppressed out of their oppression, we require action and collaboration from all those in these unbalanced relations and we cannot rely on the ways of the past. The oppressors would have to relinquish something. Power.

Next to privilege the annealing of power must take place. Offers to play the game or get to know the rules, belies the greater need for change. It has become evident that playing this game only moves to entrench the divisiveness of the past. The need to be an academic cannot outweigh the need for activism. I am an activist first and so the duty remains to address the inequalities of this institution before it is that I can play any game. How much of this activism is enough to maintain a trajectory of an academic? Do these questions betray the activist knowing the rise of managerialism brings about measures that do not make consideration for activism and social justice? Collegiality, publications, scholarliness, teaching, and learning are the markers for promotion. But what is it I seek promotion to or from? Is striving for a title still part of my ambition? Is it an indicator of success in a life that has been filled with the need to prove myself unjustly so that I meet the standards of others? Academia should not only be considered a place for intellectuals. It is a place for people. If we cannot see each other beyond our intellectual contributions, we are no better than those who developed oppressive and divisive policies. Our knowledge is to be shared and not generated in isolation.

Virtue in action

We all should endeavor to be living the good life and being happy. With it comes the need to cultivate human connectedness and do more than just act in the right way or behave to receive rewards. The ends cannot always be considered to justify the means. As we cultivate these virtues, we do so both in benefit of ourselves and the communities we live and work in supporting our personal wellness and the common good. Acquiring such qualities in essence becomes a reflection on our excellence in character and it is this excellence that leads to happiness. It is virtuousness that can advance the moral good, eliminate prejudice and conflict particularly when human interaction is valued and aimed at collective goals. The development of early career academics must be part of this collective goal. Trust and empathy are the foundations of virtuous organizations. This is often missing or betrayed by our history. We need to do more than just see the challenges that the 'other' experiences. We must be able to see ourselves in them. Virtues can be both human and organizational virtues. And so, beyond the people working within academia the institutions themselves must ensure that virtue can flourish.

Can virtues be taught or learned? I ask this question particularly as we tend to narrowly focus on values-based leadership at business schools. Values in my mind have always been subject to personal beliefs and dependent on context. In other words, values can be ranked or prioritized depending on where you are. Virtues on the other hand, are enduring and can be seen to be universal. Virtue directs attention at our character, who we truly are and what we represent. It is about our excellence in existence and can unbridle positions of power and privilege. When I cast my mind back to living through the heart of apartheid, excellence in being did not mean the same thing for all of us. Some could live out their excellence in privilege while others in poverty. What makes us good by all accounts isn't something we inherit or pass on. Here virtue can be understood to be personally cultivated from within. Intellectual excellence originates through teaching and requires time and experience. This is what we are told to strive for in academia and as the rules are laid out, our worth is measured this way.

But what of our moral excellence then? Moral excellence is cultivated through habit. It is here that I often reflect on how people and a system that promotes intellectual excellence falls short in the cultivation of a moral excellence. In return they uphold the foundation of the master's house. To be good, one must practice doing good daily. My university has a particular origin story one which lacks the ability to claim the preparation of fertile grounds for moral excellence to flourish (maybe only in pockets). It is evident that courage, bravery, valor (fortitude) is required to address such a faltering system. We speak and write so easily of having to be courageous in academic institutions, but words do cut deeply, and actions do leave indelible fractures in our bones. Our flesh, hearts and minds are not infrangible as young black academics! Our memories do not fade with ease while laced with pain! To be brave requires the rightful understanding and embracing of fear, even the fear of being isolated when the corridors whisper "he is *the* activist". As I reflect on those who are yet to come, I see that this is a rightful endurance of the suffering of terrors. My life is committed to this, whether in the academy or outside of it.

In approaching my role, I have come to accept that moderation, mastery and self-control (temperance) are needed while righteousness (justice) needs to be at the root and the application of any practical wisdom (prudence) to negotiate this terrain with integrity. It is possibly in moderation that I have found the greatest tension to address as an activist. Moderation for activists is not easy in the face of injustice, but how else do you convince a majority in power to bring about change? Moderation occurs best in action when we understand a duality in our roles, as activists we are at times called to be the mirror of pain held up to oppressive acts of terror speaking our minds when all others remain silent. As easily as we reflect our shackled bodies, we must be the carriers of light showing a path to freedom for all. In committing to the practice of chastising the failures and praising the successes one can also bring about change. The tempered radical understands this and the contribution of 'moderation' in strengthening the collective responsibility and allyship potential (Meyerson & Scully, 1995). While progress is not made with haste, we must also not be blind to the successes. Self-control must be applied when addressing institutionalized thinkers, the defenders of the past. I have at times had to consider restraint in situations where it is evident those in power willfully ignore the extent of their privilege. What would their motivation be to give up such a position? Why would they seek to open up the 'game'? I have taken the view that this 'game' is not mine to play. As I cloak myself in resistance, I must cultivate these virtues and build my character to endure. I must continue to address the nuanced misunderstandings of my colleagues at their first insistence that there are "not enough black applicants for academic positions ", or "black applicants are not qualified enough" or that "senior black academics are unaffordable" and that "we all have an equal opportunity now" to publish or voice our concerns, and that "we could do better in the future" when in fact the power is in our hands to do so now. Resistance is my consistent voice. Consistency is my shield in this struggle I remain committed to. Resistance is in my constant presence. I must be there where change is required, it is with my presence that those around are able to see themselves amongst an 'other' and recognize the need for change. Resistance is my contribution to change.

Notes

1 The imagery draws on the work of Audre Lorde "The Master's Tools Will Never Dismantle the Master's House", 1984.
2 University of Stellenbosch restitution statement.
3 Martin Luther King Jnr "Letter from Birmingham Jail," April 16, 1963.

References

Alvesson, M., & Spicer, A. (2016). (Un)Conditional surrender? Why do professionals willingly comply with managerialism. *Journal of Organizational Change Management*, *29*(1), 29–45. https://doi.org/10.1108/JOCM-11-2015-0221

Bristow, A., Robinson, S., & Ratle, O. (2017). Being an early-career CMS academic in the context of insecurity and 'excellence': The dialectics of resistance and compliance. *Organization Studies, 38*(9), 1185–1207. https://doi.org/10.1177/0170840616685361

Douglass, F. (1883). *Address of Hon. Fred Douglass, Delivered Before the National Convention of Coloured Men.* Louisville, KY: Courier-Journal Job Print. Co.

Felstead, A., Bishop, D., Fuller, A., Jewson, N., Unwin, L., Kakavelakis, K., & Lee, T. (2006). Performing identities at work: Evidence from contrasting sectors. *"Transitions Through the Lifecourse" Seminar Series, 44*(0). Retrieved from http://www.tlrp.org/dspace/retrieve/1606/Performing_Identities_Chapter_2nd_Draft.pdf

Freire, P. (2014). *Pedagogy of the Oppressed* (30th Anniv). New York: Bloomsbury.

Hibbert, P. (2012). *Approaching Reflexivity Through Reflection: Issues for Critical Management Education.* https://doi.org/10.1177/1052562912467757

Jansen, J., & Walters, C. (Eds.). (2020). *Fault Lines: A Primer on Race, Science and Society.* Stellenbosch: African Sun Media.

Mbembe, A. J. (2016). Decolonizing the university: New directions. *Arts and Humanities in Higher Education, 15*(1), 29–45. https://doi.org/10.1177/1474022215618513

Meyerson, D. E., & Scully, M. A. (1995). Tempered radicalism and the politics of ambivalence and change. *Organization Science, 6*(5), 585–600.

Ratle, O., Robinson, S., Bristow, A., & Kerr, R. (2020). Mechanisms of micro-terror? Early career CMS academics' experiences of 'targets and terror' in contemporary business schools. *Management Learning, 51*(4), 452–471. https://doi.org/10.1177/1350507620913050

Villanueva, E. (2018). *Decolonizing Wealth. Indigenous Wisdom to Heal Divides and Restore Balance.* Oakland, CA: Berrett-Koehler Publishers, Inc.

HOW TO BECOME AN ACADEMIC, AND ALIENATE PEOPLE

The working-class academic

Suzanne Albary

"She's still at school". This is how my brother described me to my nephew, when the little boy asked what I did as a job. I was in the last year of my PhD.

"You're a teacher, right?" My aunt, this time, three years into my first academic role at a UK University.

"You're still writing essays?" My mother, incredulous, last month when I attempted to describe putting the finishing touches to a chapter I was writing for a book.

Writing this portrait, this cameo if you will, I can think only of Gilmore et al.'s (2019, p. 6) words: "I feel like a traitor to my writing differently self". The traitor in me roils under the glare of the reflexivity demanded here. The writer of fiction is a traitor to the cold objectivity of academic writing, the academic writer a traitor to emotional writer of fiction. The middle-class academic a traitor to the working-class girl, my work-class consciousness traitorous to the academic I am trying to become. Bear with me as this messy story unfolds (Plows, 2018); the ghosts of the galleries in these pages will not let me tell it any differently. I am trusting you to read with care.

I stand in the gallery alone. Being a PhD student, you get used to the solitude, but you are not told that it never really goes away. I have learnt to be comfortable in my own company, but it makes the collaborative projects that define the 'successfully academic' more challenging. Be wary of becoming too used to your isolation, friends. Build networks, for the gallery is best enjoyed in groups. As I walk around the hallways lined with portraits, I notice that I am not the only one alone, not the only one struggling to be seen, to be heard, to understand how to navigate this strange place. Perhaps we should join forces, to topple the ivory tower, to be together in our "aloneness".

My family do not understand why I am here. It is where posh people go. I am the first in my family to go to university, so it seemed only right that I check off each rung of the achievement ladder. I had to make up for something, so I overcompensated with degrees. Standing in this gallery, surrounded by the great and the good of academe, I know that I am out of place. I am the working-class academic. Well, I was. Not so, anymore. I have been assimilated. I have learnt the lingo, I wear the clothes, I have changed my accent, and snuck my way into the tower. For a tower it is, and I am not good with stairs.

I still *feel* working-class. Class is in the core of who I am, an internal and integral part of my identity, and I live the contradiction of my middle-class life and my working-class consciousness (Hey, 2003) every day. I hoped that in my journey to *becoming* I would one day arrive. But it seems that there is no end in sight, that I will never quite be able to say 'I am' (McAlpine et al., 2014). There is only the potential to be *more* – more experienced, more widely published, more *highly* published. I have never been one to collect stars, but they are all anyone seems to talk about. Two is okay, three is better, four is for the gods.

I remember, though, a comment made by a colleague during an uncharacteristic rant about academic publishing: that *impact* had nothing to do with stars, and *impact* was a more important measure of success. I cling to that nugget of wisdom. If only I knew what *impact* means, and how to have it. So much of my academic identity is tied into being a successful researcher, and that, at least in the UK, is tied inextricably to the Research Excellence Framework (REF). The REF is a gallery unto itself. There are gatekeepers (Pullen, 2018, p. 124), bouncers, not to stop you looking around, but to stop you from fully understanding what it is you are looking at. The guidance is there, of course, but you still need to read the invisible ink between the lines. Despite all my training in Art History, I cannot seem to read the room.

It is not the only room I struggle with in this maze. Searching the warren of side galleries, I find the space in which I am *supposed* to inhabit. A grand entrance celebrates the 'Business School' wing. Inside, the portraits hang almost lifeless but for the hint of smugness, "disembodied and unemotional beings" line the walls (Gilmore et al., 2019, p. 4). What am I doing here? I have asked myself this many times, fuelled by the number of times *others* have asked this of me. What is a PhD in Art History doing in a Business School? It sounds like the start of a bad joke.

My PhD was a labour of love. It had to have been – unfunded, barely supervised, it took me almost six years to complete. But love it I did, and as with everything we *do*, it became part of who I was. It was to become, not that I would realise it, part of who I am. When I landed a coveted *permanent* role as an academic in a UK University, I barely questioned what discipline was taught in the department I entered. I'm not sure questioning it would have made any difference. My work-class roots tightened, and I focussed on the reassurance of having almost full-time, reliable employment.

Of course, it did not take long for those roots to turn the experience sour. I had been chosen, but the sense of guilt that I was not good enough and had somehow conned my way into this position has never quite left me (Hey, 2003, pp. 323–324). How had I managed it? Surely my academic training was limited at best, and my family still believed I was "in school". Now they think of me as a teacher at best. I can lay out the trajectory that got me here, but as an abstract, impersonal journey. I did that job, then that one. I studied these things. But in telling that story, I sound like I am making excuses, trying to justify why I am here. It exposes the realisation that I do not feel worthy, or that I belong. And as I imagine you reading this, that is not the 'me' I want you to see. It is not the portrait I wish to paint.

Instead, imagine me within the Business School wing, but not *of it*. My portrait does not hang here, nor do I want it to. I do not want to risk conformity to the norms that are found here (Pullen 2018, p. 124). There are unspoken rules to being in academia that, as a working-class academic, are difficult to fathom. Looking around, these rules are written in the subtext of the paintings. I know they are there but cannot decipher all of them. I feel their collective eyes on me as I stare down at my Doc Martens, heavy, clumpy things that send echoes to disturb the tranquillity of the gallery anytime I move.

My negotiation of my 'self' is inextricably embedded with how I look, in the body I inhabit. Our lived experiences cannot be separated from our bodies (Richardson, 1997, p. 143), and for so long it felt like mine was betraying me. Too tall, too large, too loud. Too feminine, not feminine enough. Women were art historians; men work in business schools. What was I doing here? I am, after all, a woman. For much of my early career, I conformed to the performativity of the business school in how I dressed, wore my hair, did my makeup. I had to look middle-class. I had to look like an academic (Nolan, 2018). But how could I, when men's bodies are the norm? (Pullen, 2018, p. 124). I will always be the deviant. And so, it is time I embrace it. No longer will I wear the pinstripe suit, the business heels. I will wear jeans. I will dye my hair blue. And *it will not matter*. My Doc Martens, my hair, my jeans may disturb the quiet balance of the gallery around me, but no longer will I be bound by the corrective strategies engineered by the status quo (Pullen, 2018, p. 125). Instead, I will seek out the places, the small (for now) rooms of disquiet rebellion, where I might explore and celebrate my classed dysphoria, where my sex and feminism might be spoken aloud rather than the hushed tones of compliance.

The business school gallery no longer feels so imposing, nor does it hold sway over me. My name is currently inscribed upon the plaque just inside the entrance, but my Art History training remains. Galleries are not static exhibits of paintings. Works are borrowed, moved, restored, cleaned. Their display changes over time. Artwork is not as fixed as it seems. With new technology, we can see beneath the surface, see what came before. Many works can be produced in the process of developing a final piece. My cameo might be small now, but one day it will be the practice piece for a larger, more intricate, embodied work of art that will be all of me, 'other' but content (Hey 2003, p. 327), no longer longing to belong to something violates where I have come from in attempt to justify where I am now.

I can hear the faint muffled chatter of other academics in galleries beyond my sight, an occasional laugh, as the little cliques discuss their favourite paintings, their merits and shortcomings, using bigger words and longer sentences than I know. I cannot keep up with the chatter on Merleau-Ponty or Taylor. Marx never looks at me as he whizzes past, eager to land on someone who understands and appreciates his works. But as I clutch a dogeared folder of assimilated articles and book chapters, I find I do not care as much as I once did. I stand on the shoulders of Pullen (2018), and Richardson (1997) and Hey (2003). I must do them proud. I walk my academic path differently, just as I will write differently. That is enough. I am enough.

References

Gilmore, S., Harding, N., Helin, J. & Pullen, A. (2019) "Writing Differently," *Management Learning* 50(1): 3–10.

Hey, V. (2003) "Joining the Club? Academic and Working-class Femininities," *Gender and Education* 15(3): 319–336.

McAlpine, L., Amundsen, C. & Turner, G. (2014) "Identity-Trajectory: Reframing Early Career Academic Experience," *British Educational Research Journal* 22(1): 952–969.

Nolan, S. (2018) "'What Does It Look Like?' The (In)Authentic Early Career Academic," presented at *Art of Management & Organizations: Performance*, 30 Aug–2 Sep, University of Brighton, Brighton.

Plows, A. (2018) "Coming Clean about Messy Ethnography," in Plows, A. (ed.) *Messy Ethnographies in Action*, Delaware: Vernon Press, pp. xiii–xxv.

Pullen, A. (2018) "Writing as Labiaplasty," *Organization* 25(1): 123–130.

Richardson, L. (1997) *Fields of Play: Constructing an Academic Life*. New Brunswick, NJ: Rutgers University Press.

THE BACK-DOOR ACADEMIC

Sarah Stookey

The academic house only looks like a unit from the outside to passersby. Inside, it is an arrangement of worlds: front, back, top, bottom. Hierarchies of use and population. Spaces for patterns of expression and interaction, segregation, and performance. Constructed according to a map of difference and identities that makes it difficult to cook in the living room or bathe in the library. Hallways and stairs for transitions and for marking boundaries.

Most people first enter through the front door, down a brick path, past trimmed hedges, up the steps to the porch. The front of the house is public-facing, ceremonial. The entry opens into the fanciest rooms. These are large and well-lit, with the better furniture, maybe crouching sofas (Parker, 2018), maybe antiques. The arrangement reflects the primary activity of conversation: clusters of seating, appropriate side tables. The owners of the house have made aesthetic choices: books (a few) on shelves, pictures on the walls, potted plants, but the effect is not intimate, tastefully unrevealing about the inhabitants. Maybe there's a desk in the corner, with a ledger and pens. But besides a stapler, no machinery, no tools, none of the raw materials of production. It is neat and ready to receive guests. The space doesn't encourage crowding or hanging out; entrance is monitored and purposeful. When people are there, they sit nicely and speak quietly.

I'd known other academic houses before this one: public elementary and then a Quaker school in Brooklyn, with seminars on the Byronic novel and skipping out between classes to roam downtown with Abigail. College at Harvard, book-confident, shy. A vague sense of wanting to study how people come together, how "I" becomes "we". I didn't know what the disciplines were and ended up lost in the government department. After two years, my best friend went to Florence to study art, and I joined a government program to work with a community organization in southwest Missouri for a year. There I met the smartest people, college debaters. They argued, backed by shoeboxes of handwritten research on notecards, and fueled by passion and beer. Also, we staged Ionesco on the front lawn. I was the one who found community.

This academic house is tightly organized in easily quantified terms, benchmarks of training and certification: classes, research, degree, defense, job, publish, tenure. Into categories of knowledge: schools, departments, disciplines, sub-disciplines. Into ranks delineating sanctioned achievement. Into spaces: buildings, offices, classrooms, allied businesses. Into schedules: academic semesters and breaks, tenure clocks. Into variegated products and activities: creative, load credit, service, PRJs,[1] and "other", documented in Digital Measures. Into A-B-C journals. Into indicators of legitimacy: impact factors, Assurance of Learning, ACCSB Continuous Improvement Reports.

Back in Cambridge I kept banging my head against the government department. I was a girl, so I was assigned one of the two female professors (out of 41), the younger, untenured one. She studied voting patterns and I didn't make much sense to her, but she invited me to dinner one night, and talked about how difficult it was to get tenure at Harvard[2] and when I offered to help with the dishes, she told me she saved them for later, that after hours at her desk it was a satisfyingly concrete task before bed. It's one of two things I remember about her, remember it often when I wash my dishes. The other is that she wore the black cloth shoes we used to buy in Chinatown. I didn't know professors could dress like me. Another touchstone: a grad student's seminar about Marx opened a door. "Consciousness is, therefore, from the very beginning a social product" (Marx, 1978(b):159). Audible intake of breath. Fireworks. But when the seminar ended, what then? American government to the right of me, political theory to the left of me?[3] Then somehow, on my own, I stumbled into the Divinity School and felt a path open. In courses on ethics, on the theology of liberation, in a fellow student telling me about what it had been like to be driven from their home in Palestine. In more women (students, the professors still all men) around me, even older ones, people who had had children. Classrooms where the topic seemed to be love. Our commitments – students' and the professor's (!) – in the classroom. I struggled to wrap this into an honors thesis in government about transformative belonging, but I didn't know how to make the translations.

In the academic house I inhabit now hallways lead from the front toward the back. The front halls are still ceremonial. As you get closer to the back, the space looks different, mainly less decoration. Different, messier activities happen back here, and it needs to be easier to clean: linoleum instead of carpet, paint that can be sponged down instead of wallpaper. Most people don't enter the back of the house through the front; they come in the side door by the driveway, near the garage. It's handy for unloading groceries and taking out the trash, close to the gate to the garden. The back of the house is not ceremonial. The kitchen is here. Surfaces are enamel and steel; the walls painted a neutral color. No decorative objects: they'd just get greasy. Drawers and cupboards of knives and pots, macaroni, and sugar. There are two sinks, one large and deep, made of slate, for washing flowers or other outside things. There's a curved bench by the window and a little counter where you can put a cup of tea while something is on the stove, watch the blue jays at the bird feeder. A pantry with stacks of the good dishes and a swinging door to the dining room. A door to the cellar where the washing machine is.

A Divinity School professor was going to Nicaragua, that summer. There was a chance to study Spanish and learn how the Sandinistas, come to power four years earlier, were remaking society. He knew (!) me enough to suggest I go. I was about to graduate; I didn't know what I should do next. Going to Nicaragua seemed like a bridge between the new landscape I was only just seeing and notcollege. I had $500 from my grandparents. I bought a ticket.

It's messier where the back-door academic spends most of her time. Front of the house metrics still rule but artifacts and activities unspool differently. The institutional and formal more evidently mixes with the commonplace and mundane. There are some bananas on the counter, beginning to go bad. There's a pile of assignments next to the stove. There's a 20-minute drive to the day care center and you must be there by 5:30. There is the problem of getting enough money into the bank by the 15th when the mortgage is due. "In creating an objective world by his practical activity, in working-up inorganic nature, man proves himself a conscious species being..." (Marx, 1978a: 76). At the back of the house thoughts are grounded in tangible necessity and practice has physical weight (often the same weight as a child).

Nicaragua was a startling, kaleidoscopic revelation. The first 24 hours felt like a huge mistake. But within weeks of living in Estelí, in the north, I felt I was supposed to be there. I couldn't speak, but life around me was fluent in words I'd been carrying inside. "Government" was people moving ideas from their hearts and pain, into words, onto paper, into cement and dirt, transforming farm and neighborhood and state. And love, encompassing, wholehearted, was climbing into trucks to go somewhere unknown because there was a need. Sharing, so much sharing: food and trust, rides and work, homes, and families). And with clumsy Spanish ("dust" = "dirt in the air") and no clue about anything (you can't eat a raw plantain), they let me help. With Donna, a wiser refugee from the north, I spent a year working on a potato and dairy cooperative, learning to milk and hoe. Generously welcomed as a dedicated but often inept junior member. Participating in meetings about organizational process and problems. The experience made me want to become an agronomist and I applied to the highly regarded Jesuit-run school nearby. I took high school classes in Nicaraguan history and geography at night to fill the holes in my education. During the day I collected and wrote up information about rural communities for the Ministry of Rural Development and Agrarian Reform. By the time I'd finished the prerequisites, colleagues had convinced me I'd be more useful doing that than as an agronomist.

The front and back of this academic house are connected by more than hallways. Woven together by functions and resources, alternately symbiotic and exploitative. Cleaning the drawing room involves hauling the vacuum from the closet in the back hallway. The money comes in envelopes addressed to the front of the house and the checkbook lives in a drawer of that desk in the corner. The circuits of the house are shaded by varieties of work: the groceries unloaded from the car bought with those checks, drawing room conversation sustained by roasts and sandwiches. What work brings money into the house, which doesn't? What does money say about value?

For eight years I worked in rural communities: first researching and writing about ownership and local economies, then conducting workshops on cooperative organization, supporting new communities established on former plantations, helping to figure out ways to use state-owned coffee processing plants and trucks to service the production of private farms, trainings for urban cadre, creating a community-based system for more democratic planning. Much of the work involved capacitación,[4] workshops to exchange information and introduce new administrative and organizational systems. I learned to teach from books and from Modesta and other more skilled colleagues; how to create time and space that honored experience, accounted for whether people could read, and made learning collaborative. We strived for concientización (Freire, 1985). Pre-internet and subject to economic blockade, we treasured the books we could get hold of: histories, reports, and theories from agrarian reforms around the world, brittle paperback copies of Marxist treatises, Latin American feminists, Cuban economists, the new books by Nicaraguan intellectuals were events; the Barricada[5] serialized them in special sections. And, also, to address the nuts-and-bolts questions of getting stuff done, we tried to learn how business did things. I took a course in statistics at the University. The Party sent my supervisor to study administration at Harvard-linked INCAE in Managua. We grabbed what we could, digging for what could serve our purposes, ecumenical as to origin, conducting "managerialism of the revolution" to "get (the important) things done" (Stookey, 2012). Without computers we made data tables and planning matrices with rulers, and I typed on my father's Smith-Corona.

The front and back of the house are different: one place for relaxed conversation, another for preparing the chicken. But they are not "different but equal"; fancy or plainness are understood to reflect relative value. The front is finer because it is better and it's better because it's fine, "ingots and rough lumps of gold" under the drawing room floorboards; "what lies beneath the gallant red brick {note: linoleum?} and the wild unkempt grasses of the garden?" (Woolf, 1949: 30). Finer, in turn, understood to require deference; the back of the house is subject.

There was a bloody and illegal war to break solidarity and my country lost my deference. In Nicaragua, despite the mines, a department of cinema sent projectors and generators to mountain communities on the backs of mules. There were massive vaccination programs and competitions to encourage cooks at public daycare centers to cook wild-growing leafy greens. Cooperative members did watch duty at night and pruned coffee plants during the day. People were learning to read and keep accounts and paint and they danced in army boots. People worked hard to do their job well, to be better people, to embody "la ética",[6] rejecting hollow hierarchy, elevating comradeship. Plain was finer. Some people sacrificed everything. But some people enjoyed air-conditioned jeeps too much. The war with the Empire was deadly and corrosive. I got married in Nicaragua. After 40,000 dead, the Sandinistas were voted out of power. The spirit shifted. My spirit shifted. I returned to the U.S. I started a PhD in economics (economists were god-like in the Revolution). There was a study group to read Capital but mainly there was too much math, and it wasn't clear to me where it was going. After two years we loaded up a truck with seed and hoses and a washing machine and returned to Nicaragua, to get a job, to farm, to start a family. There were a lot of new NGOs; I got hired to start a micro-credit program. I had a son. In some ways it was like before: early departures for distant communities, meetings around corrals. We invented lending procedures, studied Grameen, promoted Fair Trade coffee exports. But it was also different. Splintered, la ética less strong.

The academic house is zoned by space and function and by inhabitants. People may move through the hallways, but everyone has a designated home base, front or back. "Only the Fellows and Scholars are allowed here; the gravel is the place for me" (Woolf, 1949: 9). You may spend time in the front but *belong* in the back (rarer is *belonging* in the front but spending time in the back). Who is where? The assignment system is slippery; it results from and produces difference. If you're in library, you don't make sandwiches and if you're in the kitchen you don't write books. The person who mops the floor *could* give a lecture, no? The check writer *could* clean the refrigerator?

Several years of Nicaragua, part two. But too much was different. I was sad and ended up leaving for Washington D.C., hoping to get a job doing development work. But a Sandinista work history wasn't an easy sell. There was a sort of hallucinatory year in the secretarial pool at the International Finance Corporation, a globally diverse group of women married to and serving men doing front of the house work. We typed, got coffee, made travel arrangements. Rosemary saved me. She supervised the Salvation Army's U.S. AID contracts and hired me to create micro credit programs and monitor maternal and child health programs. For two years I worked with people in the Philippines, Indonesia, Chile, and Mexico who – like people I'd known in Nicaragua – believed a new society could be built out of love and who distributed soup and health care to trans sex workers on the night streets of Manila. But it was hard to travel to Indonesia and be a mother in D.C. When I had a second child I had to stop. I'd watched the proliferation of community-based lending programs in the U.S. and thought I could do that. But the U.S. wasn't Nicaragua, you couldn't just set interest rates, type up promissory notes and drive around with sacks of money. MBAs seemed to be getting the jobs I wanted.

We are corporeal bodies, needing soup and health care and loans, daily producing, and reproducing our lives (Marx, 1978b: 156). "The human frame being what it is, heart, body and brain, all mixed together, and not contained in separate compartments…a good dinner is of great importance to good talk" (Woolf, 1949: 28). What role, the specifics of our bodies? Gendered, racialized, classed, and wealth-ed. Layers of privilege sculpting where and how we occupy the house. Men in the finer front and women in the baser back? Yes, often women are balancing creativity with mundanity and repetition, "this activity of world-protection, world preservation, world-repair, the million tiny stitches, the friction of the scrubbing brush, the scouring cloth, the iron across the shirt, the rubbing of cloth against itself to exorcise the stain, the renewal of the scorched pot, the rusted knife-blade, the invisible weaving of a frayed and threadbare family life…" (Rich, 1977: xvi). With or without children, homes need food and maintenance and celebrations, domestic managerialism, getting done the shopping and laundry. With children the attending and the caring is more complicated. "Consider the facts, we said. First there are nine months before the baby is born… Then there are three or four months spent in feeding the baby. After the baby is fed there are certainly five years spent in playing with the baby. You cannot, it seems, let children run about the streets" (Woolf, 1949: 34). Feeding and playing and making new life is messy, unpredictable. It is back of the housework, mundane, audacious, and glorious. Of course, sometimes men are also in the back, and women occupy the drawing room, sometimes asking you to clean their office and pick up their sandwiches. People doing and transmuting gender. It's difficult to cultivate solidarity when segregation is assiduously performed.

Now not married, it was important to be near family in New England. Admitted to Dartmouth, I learned only two members of the cohort were parents and both had partners at home. UMASS Amherst was cheap, near sisters, and seemed a good place to have young children so I went there. I'd chosen the MBA for the accounting and finance skills and for the credential. I did not expect to be excited and mainly I wasn't. But in a required class I was introduced to organization studies and another opening: maybe past work and what I carried inside could be woven into this unfamiliar field, into a different kind of job. Plus, it was easier to mother as a student than as an employee. Easier to miss class when a child was home sick. I started the PhD. "Easier" still means dashing between the front and back of the house, landing in early class after "mornings of crisis and near hysteria, trying to get lunches packed, hair combed, coats and shoes found, everyone to school or Child Care on time, the baby ready for transportation" (Olsen, 1961: 10). It's not smooth. Recording academic and domestic responsibilities in a calendar divided into 15-minute increments, a professor asks (irritated when I've missed a deadline) if I have a system for organizing my time. And when I explain why I'm unavailable, that I need to write a paper, my son asks, "why do you always have to be so good at everything?"

The geography of the academic house is overlaid by divisions of paradigm and discourse. The front itself is not homogenous. Each school and department claims expertise and sovereignty over their patch of territory then links with similar units around the country and world, knitting together disciplinary authorities surrounded by high walls. Even the alternatives that push back against the mainstream are often codified, air sucked out in the process (Stookey, 2008). Beyond these differences, the front and back propagate their own languages: a drawing room vocabulary, a kitchen dialect. The structure of an academic paper. The pilings of a literature review. As with the spaces, concepts and names correspond to tribes and are to be invoked. The back-door academic long ago forgot what a distributed lag is, gets fuzzy about Foucault, sometimes confuses postmodernism and poststructuralism.

She tends to say different words: capitalism, Africa, middle school, you/yours/your family, me/mine/ours.

It took seven years for me to complete the PhD. Resources – money and time – doled out in clumsy chunks. Raising children costs money and reproducing society is not paid work. I had some wealth but not enough, so I taught many extra courses. "The extent of the power of money is my power" (Marx, 1978a: 103). Our corporeal, growing, coveting bodies need money and yet amidst all the financial equations and profit-privileging, business school courses didn't talk about it. I had to leave the building to find money as a topic. In the geography department the sparkling professor said, "people make their capitalisms" (Gibson-Graham, 1996). In economics the other, dry-humored ones walked through fundamental and subsumed classes (Resnick & Wolff, 1987). There was so little conversation between these and the school of business that I held a dinner party and invited everyone. I decided to write a dissertation on the social construction of money. I would knit it all together, a five-dimensional framework for seeing how money is made in society and organizations. Umm. Dissertations as tactical career choices vs visions carried since age 19. "Better not to do a conceptual dissertation". Years later I would ask students, "Why do you think you were told not to write in the first person?" and one responded: "Because they're not interested in what we think". As a student myself, I said, "I want to write about the social construction of money" and the professor said, "I really don't see what there is to say about money".

The house is organized to buttress authority, legitimacy conferred by tightly ranked professional training (how could you be an expert without it?). The degree must be terminal, the institution AACSB (Association to Advance Collegiate Schools of Business) accredited (who accredits AACSB?). Creative activity also ranked: "basic/discovery" at the top, then "applied/integration", "teaching and learning" at the bottom. Ranked, weighed, and counted. PRJs the gold standard, worth multiples more than anything else. With limited time you must do the calculus; is a book chapter worth it? Corporate consulting burnishes credentials, teaching for extra money does not. The back of the house academic never made a profit. What use the shelves of yellowed paperbacks? What authority derives from mountains and potato fields, from the secretarial pool or keeping the small ones clothed and fed? *Getting things done* is not typically esteemed (Stookey, 2013). Teaching also, often, a lower grade, back-of-the-house job. Especially undergraduates. Like the children at home, the young ones generally have their intro courses crowded around the kitchen table, attended to by adjuncts, junior faculty, or grad students. Spacious seminar tables in the front of the house are marked "reserved".

*I started to look for academic work, expecting I'd find the best fit in a liberal arts college where I could teach about business. I was deluded: liberal arts colleges don't hire people with doctorates from business schools. The academic houses stand far apart; the whole street is segregated by tribe. In the last year of my studies, I taught at an esteemed liberal arts college, a course in their "complex organizations" subfield ("business" or "management" being verboten). One day in the mail room I told a sociology professor that I'd seen his syllabus and that I too taught about Mondragon, the Basque cooperative. "Well, he hmphed", I'm sure **you** teach it differently". My degree was terminal and carried a prognosis. It gave entry to the front of the business academic house, and only that one. Where I could be hired was also determined by geography: which institutions could I commute to, not have to move from the community where my children were growing up, where their father lived?*

I was very lucky to get the job in the business school where I work (66 miles from home). Even though there were mornings, at the beginning, when I drove in a kind of shock: how had I become a business professor? The university is public, not the flagship state school, between that and the community college. A long history of educating the daughters and sons of the working majority. In a struggling post-industrial town with a proud history and new waves of ambitious immigrants. It's a school where the plainer work of teaching undergraduates is usually well-regarded. Even so, it is (without teaching assistants or multiple-choice tests), time-consuming, a lot of grading. Kitchen work. But also, if you claim it, freedom from the constraints of drawing room fanciness. When you can be messy it's easier to explore. You can even leave, go next door, find people in the education house, connect to local middle schools. With flurries of carpooling, Intro to Mgmt. students mobilized to help sixth graders understand what business is and create fantasy business plans. Or they organized Empty Bowls[7] fundraisers, coordinating bowl making and donations, music and serving. With a supportive administration and school district we created a downtown space for educators and the community to collaborate. Homing in on a glorious, unused bank building, classes developed proposals for student-run businesses and a café (unrealized). To highlight the city's industrial past, we staged a "Making Value with Our Hands" event to showcase manual skills. We even strayed as far as Nicaragua, groups of students and I, to sleep in the houses and visit the farms and learn about globalization on the ground. Pushing the boundaries also carried into the critical corner of the Academy of Management[8] with Get Out of the Hotels field trips to visit activist groups during hermetic annual meetings.

But it is the nature of life to be messy. Children have crises, and so do mothers. Attending to what needs attention means not doing other things. One morning you wake up and it's been too long since your last PRJ. You've become unqualified, the authorities say. There are consequences: more courses. Front of the house status must be earned. Except now it's harder because there is more teaching, more grading. But there is always flux. When life calms down and when the authorities mutate, space reopens.

How do I live in this academic house, more than 20 years after I first entered? I have two priorities. I want students to think about capitalism. We construct understanding by reflecting on their experience[9] of work and pay, capital and profit, democracy, and government and reading parts of books (including some of the yellowed paperbacks). They conduct "capitalism conversations" with friends and family and write papers about what was said and the experience. Encouraged by years of their work, I spent a sabbatical driving around the U.S. and doing flash classes in high schools and community colleges. I'm beginning to write about the capitalism work (even learning to use data software to help the insights be taken seriously in the front of the house). And I teach an international management course that emphasizes global political economy. Students read The Economist and they learn the countries of Africa. I talk about a world that wants them to be drones. I want them to know they're decisionmakers.

The academic house is constructed to keep people in their places, to elicit deference. The back-door academic tries not to defer. She tries to be clear about her bottom line (Robinson, Bristow & Ratle, 2015). Sometimes she looks wistfully toward the front of the house. Sometimes the back is lonely, not enough comrades. But her radicalism is not tempered (Meyerson & Scully, 1995). While she identifies with the students and their curiosity and hungers, she doesn't identify with the house and its segregations. Maybe one day there will be a different house, with easy-to-clean tiled floors throughout, paintings on the kitchen walls and banana peels in the drawing room. Maybe it will be a school for organizing (Parker, 2018). In the meantime, the back of the house is a good place to be, to be humble but not humbled. It's a place to make community out of our shared, messy lives. The back-door academic believes in the fineness of the mundane work, in the words of need and desire and us. Her guests, the many, the most, come by after their second job, sprawl on the curved kitchen bench, prodded to consider what Marx and Locke said about property and whether it relates to the condition of the person they are, what the job feels like and what should be different. They eat chocolate cookies. They say, "in my life it is like this". Sometimes they doze off. The kids play outside.

Notes

1 PRJ = peer-reviewed journal article. Use of the acronym highlights the cursory attention given to the substance of your writing. I've never been part of a discussion of a departmental colleague's PRJs.
2 She didn't.
3 The 1978 course catalog lists "The Individual and Community", taught by another then-grad student, Paschalis Kitromilides, now at the University of Athens.
4 Training workshops.
5 Daily newspaper of the Frente Sandinista de Liberación Nacional (FSLN), the Sandinista party.
6 *La ética*, formally "ethics", used to refer to a commitment to solidarity, self-sacrifice, and collective wellbeing.
7 Empty Bowl events are used to raise money for and awareness of hunger in the community. Instead of an elegant dinner, attendees get a locally made ceramic bowl and soup in exchange for a donation.
8 ¿*La Academia de Gestión?* 管理学院?
9 First, they read Plato and Kuhn and think about truth.

References

Freire, P. (1985). *The politics of education: culture, power, and liberation*. South Hadley, MA: Bergin & Garvey Pubs.
Gibson-Graham, J.K. (1996). *The end of capitalism (as we knew it): a feminist critique of political economy*. Cambridge: Blackwell.
Marx, K. (1978a). *Economic and philosophic manuscripts of 1844*. In R. C. Tucker (Ed.), *The Marx and Engels reader* (pp. 67–125). New York: W.W. Norton & Co.
Marx, K. (1978b). *The German ideology*. In R. C. Tucker (Ed.), *The Marx and Engels reader* (pp. 146–200). New York: W.W. Norton & Co.
Meyerson, D.E. & Scully, M. A. (1995). Tempered radicalism and the politics of ambivalence and change. *Organization Science*. 6(5), 585–600.
Olsen, T. (1961). *Tell me a riddle*. New York: Dell.
Parker, M. (2018). *Shut down the business school: what's wrong with management education*. London: Pluto Press.
Resnick, S. A. & Wolff, R.D. (1987). *Knowledge and class: a Marxian critique of political economy*. Chicago: University of Chicago Press.
Rich, A. (1977). Conditions for work: the common world of women. In Ruddick, S. & Daniels, P. (Eds.), *Working it out: 23 women writers, artists, scientists, and scholars talk about their lives and work* (pp. xiii–xxiv). New York: Pantheon Books.
Robinson, S., Bristow, A. & Ratle, O. (2015). Critical learning and tempered radicalism: an exploration of the roles and development of early career academics. *Academy of Management Proceedings*.
Stookey, S. (2008). Populism and elitism in critical management studies". *Organization*. 15(6):922–994.
Stookey, S. (2012). The people need to make the trains run on time for empowerment to happen: managerialism and revolution in Nicaragua. *Journal of International Development*. 24(5), 649–655.
Stookey, S. (2013). Getting the wrong/right things done – problems and possibilities in U.S. business schools. In J. Malin, J. Murphy, & M. Siltaoja (Eds.), *Getting things done*. (pp. 73–90). London: Emerald.
Woolf, V. (1949). *A room of own's own* (11th ed.). London: The Hogarth Press.

THE INGENUOUS COMMUNITARIAN

Emma Newport

Sometimes I reread things that I have published and it is like reading the work of someone whom I don't know. I have felt the need to write in a way that makes me sound like I think I belong and that I deserve to be here or there. Why use five words when you could use ten? Why use single syllable words when polysyllable possibilities abound? In producing this portrait, I was forced to reflect on the fact that my youthful belief in giving note-free lectures, of playing with ideas in the moment at conferences, has been displaced more recently by nervous perfectionism. I have sought refuge in prewritten words, carefully controlled and contrived to sound as clever and as difficult as I might imagine a scholar is supposed to. (And then, of course, we are surprised when students feel anxious in seminars and don't want to talk, so used are they to listening to the precisely perfected vocabularies of their lecturers.) For the purposes of this portrait, however, and the person who might be reading this online or in a library, I want to write closer to how I really think and speak, especially to students. I do not want to give the reader a portrait of the scholar as an old critic. That picture be seen elsewhere.

It would have thus been dishonest of me to promote the idea of being ingenuous and of being a communitarian if I didn't use this as an act of confession that, in the years since I received my doctorate, I have misstepped at times and become more cynical and have definitely, on occasion, sought to be less like myself than I am – and yet where else but in academia can we celebrate being just who we are? I think it is important to admit to the ways in which we compel ourselves to match the performed perfection and competitive overworking of others. The story that is often left untold in academia is that success is not predicated upon retreat from making mistakes, from avoiding vulnerability, or from following the rules, but instead *comes from* your idiosyncrasies, vulnerabilities, risk-taking, and error-making.

I have thus chosen to write this differently from how I write other chapters and articles. I am sitting here listening to my words spoken back at me and, in fact, I am saying those words in preparation for when I later listen to this on my voice recorder, ready to transcribe it. Normally, for me, writing is a gladiatorial combat, wrestling in some constricted battle with keyboard, notes and other people's ideas as I search to eliminate what has been said in order to find what is still left to say about a text. On good days, I triumph; on the bad ones, I feel more like the poor andabata, who fought blindfolded. For this portrait, though, I wanted to convey the sense that I am sitting here talking to you like I would talk to any of my students or newer colleagues, or to a school pupil somewhere who doesn't yet know that they will even go to university. Cynicism and self-protection, which have been building through the friction encountered along the path to a permanent post, needs sloughing off. Consider this to be me heading to the podiatrist.

A beginning

My pathway to a permanent post began in a place that embodies the life of a peripatetic early career academic: drinking tea with my Airbnb host, an English teacher with a doctorate who quit academia due to the job crisis and the desire for stability for his young family. I was staying with my host because I was too poor to move: ten-month contracts don't synchronise with affordable lets in expensive university towns. It was still better than my hourly waged lectureship somewhere else, when commuting costs often outstripped my pay and I had had to work two other jobs to make ends meet.

We discussed the decline of English as a subject in schools and the need for post-Gove reinvigoration.[1] Our solution: a radical collaboration between the Department of English and local schools. I went on to create Sussex Writes, a student-led creative writing outreach initiative that works in the local community. What began as a three-person pilot in one school has become a funded organisation with almost 30 undergraduates and postgraduates working in over 20 schools, including a large Academy trust and a pupil referral unit, where we have worked with adolescents who have been expelled from mainstream education. We also work with literacy charities and, as part of our COVID-19 response, we established a global creative collaboration called Lockdown Live with a pan-African youth-led NGO called The Youth Café. This has inspired our student team to develop since a full suite of student-led public engagement via podcasts, videos and social media, as well as resuming the in-person workshops post-pandemic. One of our undergraduate team members, Abbie O'Connell, says, "*Sussex Writes has enriched my degree in ways I never thought imaginable. The immense privilege of sharing my vocation with enthusiastic (and sometimes unenthusiastic!) young people reminded me daily of the value of words, language and storytelling*".

Though when proposing the pilot, I failed to predict the expansion of Sussex Writes in such important ways, ingenuousness is neither naivety nor ignorance. Sussex Writes aims to create stronger relationships between academics, students, and the wider community in which we live and work, and thus to share creative writing with a larger constituency. What we came to realise was that nobody else had ever done this at our institution; and what surprised us was the breadth of what we could with our work, and our impact.

Sussex Writer Sophie McClellan believes that working for Sussex Writes "*has given me the confidence and communication skills necessary to begin my education anew, in a completely different discipline. It has also made me a more independent person, who is confident in their decisions no matter how I may feel*". Sussex Writes is predicated on empowering students of all ages: a principle that underpins everything from how students design and run their workshops to how Sussex Writes has grown to incorporate digital as well as in-person platforms.

Consequently, community-centred creative approaches have proven unexpectedly useful tools for rearticulating who an academic is and how they might contribute to the institution.[2] Such a philosophy has helped me to forge relationships with senior colleagues who have celebrated and supported our programme's aims; in turn, I have been able to help new young doctoral researchers advance their careers.

With Sussex Writes came a route to my permanent lectureship.[3] As a first-generation scholar, I accidentally redefined how to navigate a temporary contract, mainly because I didn't know to do differently. And for those thinking that if I wasn't being clever, then I was likely being brave: it wasn't bravery. I didn't have a strategy for penetrating the inaccessible ivory tower mainly because I had no idea that I was supposed to break my way in and climb up it. I caught the odd voice floating down, warning me to *publish or die*. Another suggested I was doing *feminised labour*. But I tend not to pay attention to these voices.[4] The ingenuous communitarian, then, as a model for navigating academia, is not one of subjection, naivety, or guilelessness, but instead embodies openness, generosity, excellence, creativity, strength of purpose. I use the term 'ingenuous' in its older sense of honest, open and candid. Shakespeare uses it, at times, interchangeably with ingenious, and I like the way this blurring of usage inflects ingenuousness with inspiration and boldness of thought.[5] Most importantly, it means doing what you believe in rather than what you think will be strategically and personally advantageous, and of working together, in partnership with the whole community, towards achieving those shared aims.

Someone to whom I do listen is Sussex Writer and founder of Teach for Change Nigeria, Jennifer Emelife. Jennifer exemplifies all that makes a great academic: taking risks; caring about others; pulling others up with you and amplifying their voices; being open, candid, and honest. She is the very picture of an ingenuous communitarian.

And anyway, Jennifer says it better than me:

> The notion that academia is boring is popularised by the fact that it is full of like-minded individuals speaking and critiquing in a language only they understand. I think that the purpose of any kind of education should be to create a connection or a bridge that brings the world together. However, if academia continues to thrive on jargon understood only by scholars, how then does it hope to achieve the change it craves? Joining Sussex Writes during my Master's program at Sussex showed me the multiple ways that academic careers can be adapted to make sense to and impact positively on the common person. It is not enough to teach students about theories and academic trends. Sussex Writes helped me shape my ideas on how teachers can help students step out of the lecture rooms and get them involved in practical activities which reinforces what they have learned in the classroom. Sussex Writes showed me that academia can be diversified, flexible and truly impactful. It could mean running a project alongside your students and delivering important knowledge to people who might otherwise not have access to it. I still remember the joy of the teachers, students, clubs, organisations, and so on that we have worked with; their excitement at being part of something 'big' run by academic scholars. Out there, there was no jargon, no airs: just a group of people exchanging ideas, asking questions, writing, learning and unlearning. Imagine if there were no Sussex Writes and we all had our heads buried

in big textbooks and large screens, reading thousands of articles and writing tons of papers only we can understand? We would be living in a shielded world, almost blind to real life happenings. Often time, true change begins when we step out and engage with people differently.

Jennifer Emelife, Sussex Writes and Chevening Scholar, 2020
For more on Sussex Writes, see www.sussexwrites.org.
For more on Teach For Change Nigeria, see www.teachforchangeng.com.

Notes

1 As Minister for Education Michael Gove sought to make the curriculum more rigorous, which translated to less coursework, more exams, and more rote learning. Furthermore, he said that he 'want[ed] the political correctness out of national curriculum' (Gove, 20 January 2011).
2 "Communitarian" carries both philosophical and political implications. It has its critics and detractors, particularly when used to erase academic autonomy. Here, though, I am using communitarian in the sense that it is antithetical to aggressively individualistic neo-liberalism, and that it points to the value and power of working with, by and for the community, which might, in its most expansive definition, include the local neighbourhood and the global community, as well as current, former, and future scholars, wherever and whoever they may be.
3 Along the way, I won the Sussex Teaching Excellence Award (2017), the Sussex 'Better World' Award (2020), which is my favourite prize because I was nominated by our students; and I was nominated for the National Teaching Fellowship Award (2018) and the Sussex 'Teach to Disrupt Award' (2020).
4 I did listen, though, when a colleague of mine remarked: *It is always better to ask for forgiveness than permission.*
5 See *Love's Labour's Lost* IV. ii. 77 and *Timon of Athens* II.ii.226.

Works uncited

Armato, M. (2013) 'Wolves in Sheep's Clothing: Men's Enlightened Sexism & Hegemonic Masculinity in Academia'. *Women's Studies*, 42(5), 578–598, doi: 10.1080/00497878.2013.794055

Arthur, J. (1998) 'Communitarianism: What Are the Implications for Education?' *Educational Studies*, 24(3), 353–368.

Bagilhole, B. and Goode, J. (2001) 'The Contradiction of the Myth of Individual Merit, and the Reality of a Patriarchal Support System in Academic Careers: A Feminist Investigation'. *European Journal of Women's Studies*, 8(2), 161–180, doi: 10.1177/135050680100800203.

Bal, E., Grassiani, E., and Kirk, K. (2014) 'Neoliberal Individualism in Dutch Universities: Teaching and Learning Anthropology in an Insecure Environment'. *Learning and Teaching*, 7(3), 46–72, doi: 10.3167/latiss.2014.070303.

Cavalieri, S. (2019) 'On Amplification: Extralegal Acts of Feminist Resistance in the #metoo era'. *Wisconsin Law Review*, 2019(6), 1489–1550.

Cicero, M. (1977). *Epistulae ad Familiares* (S. B. D. Roy, Trans.). Cambridge: Cambridge University Press.

Derrida, J. (1998). Trans. Patrick Mensah. *Monolingualism of the Other: The Prosthesis of Origin.* California: Stanford University Press.

Finn, M. (ed.) (2015) *The Gove Legacy: Education in Britain after the Coalition.* London: Palgrave Pivot.

Gove, M. (2011) "Michael Gove: 'I Want the Political Correctness Out of National Curriculum' [video]". http://www.telegraph.co.uk/education/8272021/Michael-Gove-I-want-the-political-correctness-out-of-national-curriculum.html (accessed January 27, 2022)

Henkel, M. (2005) 'Academic Identity and Autonomy in a Changing Policy Environment' *Higher Education*, 49(1), 155–176.

Macfarlane, B. (2019) 'The Neoliberal Academic: Illustrating Shifting Academic Norms in an Age of Hyper-Performativity'. *Educational Philosophy and Theory*, doi: 10.1080/00131857.2019.1684262.

Messerschmidt, J. W. (2018) *Hegemonic Masculinity: Formulation, Reformulation, and Amplification*. London: Rowman & Littlefield.

Saussure, F. (1916) *Cours de Linguistique Générale*. C. Bally and Albert Sechehaye (eds.) with the collaboration of A. Riedlinger. Lausanne & Paris: Libraire Payot & Cie.

THE JOURNEY OF A SURPRISED ACADEMIC

Laurie N. DiPadova-Stocks

Ours is a lofty, values-driven profession, tied to national interests as well as to the betterment of humanity. Thomas Jefferson declared education to be vital to a free self-governing people, the life-blood of democracy. As United States Senator Michael Bennet observed, Jefferson tied education to democracy when he wrote: "Educate and inform the whole mass of the people . . . They are the only sure reliance for the preservation of our liberty".[1]

In founding the University of Virginia, Jefferson boldly stated: "this institution will be based on the illimitable freedom of the human mind;"[2] he viewed higher education as a public good, necessary for the betterment of society.

"Freedom of the human mind" provides the foundation of discovery, advancement, and innovation. Yet, the successful academic career is tightly scripted, arguably limiting the "freedom of the human mind" for academics: expectation that new PhDs will have an academic career at a major university in a top-ranked program (not in industry or at a community college—happily, the new First Lady of the United States, Dr. Jill Biden, teaches at community colleges); publish in top journals; and earn tenure in a prescribed number of years with dire consequences if tenure is not awarded. I well recall when the major academic association in my field conducted an all-day doctoral student consortium at its national conference. The consortium program provided strong reinforcement for this script; no other paths were acknowledged, much less affirmed as possibilities. As I jokingly commented to the speaker: if I were to adhere to his script, I would be fortunate to be awarded tenure before my 85th birthday.

Even the now accepted pedagogy of service-learning was off the table.

Perhaps the most challenging aspect of higher education is in its structure. We have created "silos": each academic discipline is a different lane, and we tend to stay in our lane. While some PhD programs may offer the interdisciplinary PhD option, these programs are rare and often limit academic career options, unless the degree is from a top-tier institution.

Alternative paths often require risk taking, abandoning the importance of rankings, and ignoring what mentors may think, prompting unexpected consequences. In my experience, former Stanford U. professor, Dr. Genevieve Bell, stands out as the proverbial poster child for such consequences. By her account, she was hired out of academia by Intel and thus became an embarrassment to her academic department.[3]

For a profession that embraces the values of enlightenment and inclusion, it was surprising to find that ours is one of the most hierarchical of professions. We rank faculty, journals, universities and academic programs, mostly it seems, for ratings and thus fundraising purposes. We protect tradition, along with the clergy and the judiciary; we even wear the same robes.

By outward appearances, I am a traditional successful academic: Full Professor 12 years after PhD completion; twice dean: a public affairs school and a graduate school; elective office over years in two national academic associations, each step of which was a surprise. This summary belies the challenges and risks of the journey, such as accepting a staff position. Even though it may be prestigious, I came to learn that staff positions carry vulnerabilities.

My experience is that of a first generation female college student who attended an all-women's college attached to a major state university that, surprisingly, prohibited admission to women. Ironically, that major state university was Mr. Jefferson's own University of Virginia (UVA). As an aside, my Mother was incensed, rightfully objecting to paying taxes to support an institution of higher learning that barred women from admission. As a further aside, UVA changed its admission policy in 1970.

Immediately after graduation, I pursued the master's degree, and taught at two colleges, the first of which was a community college.

How did I get here?

Family life as a child was nonconforming: I was born in the post-World War II era when divorce was unheard of in polite company. My parents divorced when I was four. I lived alternatively between them.

Due to frequent moves, I attended 13 different schools in 12 years. While this lack of stability was often a detriment to "fitting in", I later realized that attending different schools enabled me to "start over", meet new friends, and adapt to new environments. This awareness helped me adapt during difficult times.

As a child, I felt safety and freedom in school: the freedom to think, to wonder, and the world began to open up. I could not imagine life without reading and learning. Yet, college did not occur to me. No one in my family had attended college. We did not talk about it. College was never an aspiration.

My last two years of secondary education were in the same school, a circumstance made possible by a long commute; I was grateful for this consideration by school officials.

Many of my high school classmates applied for college. Fortuitously, one day my close friend told me I should go to college. She was the first person to utter those words to me. The very idea was foreign. My reply was that I did not know how to apply to college. What I meant was that I did not know how to go to college, or to be in college. She said: "Laurie, you have just been elected Most Intellectual in the senior class. You have to go to college!" She helped me apply—and much to my surprise, I was accepted.

The barrier to college then became financial. I did not have the necessary funds. While I was offered two on campus jobs (working in the library and in the dining hall), my funding still fell short.

In this period, the National Defense Education Act made college possible for many high school graduates. Launched in 1958 by President Dwight D. Eisenhower, this federal program offered funding to college students in mathematics, engineering and technology, as Soviet advancements in this arena were considered a threat to our national defense. My heart sank as I knew these were not areas in which I could excel.

Imagine my excitement upon learning that that the Act had recently been expanded to include the humanities and social sciences! This change occurred during the Kennedy Administration, championed by the United States Commissioner of Education, Dr. Sterling M. McMurrin. He argued that the nation's defense did not rest on scientific advancements alone, but also on an understanding of history, of the humanities and social sciences, and on the development of moral values. This was his testimony before various committees of the United States Congress.

So off to college I went, and then to graduate school for the Master's degree. I have a vivid memory of receiving the graduate school's acceptance letter. What joy! Truly, by far one of the most exciting days of my life. I never dared dream that I would go to graduate school.

The acceptance letter was signed by the Dean of the Graduate School. I sought the Master of Science degree in sociology, with an emphasis in the sociology of religion. I managed also to take courses in philosophy, all taught by the dean of the Graduate School, Dr. Sterling McMurrin.

Imagine my surprise—my shock!—to learn decades later that he was the one who made it possible for me to go to college!

After a few years teaching at a junior college, where I taught sociology and also religions of the world, my inner compass was pointing toward another advanced degree. My efforts were not successful. The biggest disappointment was not being considered by a divinity school. The school, associated with one of the most prestigious private universities in the Southeast, had a sociology component, and was associated with a protestant denomination. I spent the day with the one sociologist on the faculty, and knew this was the place for me.

At the conclusion of the visit, and with high expectations, I met with the dean of the divinity school. After a few pleasantries, he revealed that there were a limited number of openings for students, and their priority was accepting men who were already in the ministry and who needed an advanced degree. He offered further that since I would most likely marry and have a family, I would not be accepted. Deeply disappointed, I later wrote to the Dean's office, detailing the conversation, and asked if I had misunderstood what I was told. The reply came that I had indeed understood correctly. Obviously, this situation would not be tolerable today.

Fortunately, I was offered a full time teaching position at a four-year college. With only a master's degree, my maximum time teaching there would be seven years. Thinking about a PhD, I recognized that the commute to a doctoral granting institution would be a difficult commute.

It was at this college that I met my husband, an academic who was in another department. Due to life events and family matters, my doctoral studies began later than most, with PhD completion just weeks before my 50th birthday.

And then the script began!

Like most women at the time, I built my life around husband, and around his career, including typing my husband's dissertation. He received a job offer in another state. And the children came. Motherhood and life were consuming.

Fortunately, we had relocated near the major state university and once the children were old enough, I was able to pursue and earn the PhD, for which I am grateful.

My experience in college confirmed and fulfilled my every lofty thought and dream about education. The impact is generational. In a real sense, we do not educate students; we educate families.

My seeking the PhD was good for my children. Seeing their mother do homework added a new dimension to their studies. Education makes the world a better place, expands horizons and opportunities, has promise as "the great equalizer", and advances the betterment of human kind, just as Jefferson had written.

Taxpayers in the three states where I attended public college and universities subsidized my education. I am grateful for what these three states have made possible in my life. While there is no way to repay such a debt, my academic work is a humble effort to make the world a better place for some of my fellow citizens. It certainly made my world a better place.

Notes

1 https://medium.com/@SenatorBennet/why-education-is-essential-to-our-democracy-931cfb7a1e1.
2 Letter to Richard Price, January 8, 1789. Library of Congress. https://www.loc.gov/exhibits/jefferson/jeffrep.html.
3 Bell, Genevieve, "Through the Looking Glass: Reflecting on 15 years in Industry." Council of Graduate Schools, New Deans Institute, July 13, 2014. Portland, Oregon. Also, https://www.nytimes.com/2014/02/16/technology/intels-sharp-eyed-social-scientist.html.

THE SELF-MADE ACADEMIC

From business to a business school

Adrián Zicari

I completely identify with the title of this book, "Doing academic careers differently". I feel that this is a timely and necessary discussion, particularly in these times of increasing isomorphism in academic careers. On the surface, faculty in most business schools in North America and Europe is very international, and students would reasonably expect a wide range of expertise and experience from their professors. However, this is rarely the case. While the academic career is international, indeed global, career paths for young faculty tend to be increasingly the same, namely, joining a doctoral program straight after graduate school. Nowadays, concrete business experience is becoming rarer amongst faculty. This seems to be the standard, obvious path for success in academia.

In this context, a book about "Doing careers differently" is much welcome. Doing business is a "democratic" endeavor, in the sense that anybody is entitled to do business. Contrary to other professions (e.g. medicine, law), one does not need a degree to become a practitioner. In business schools, students learn the basics of the trade, and develop their skills in order to become better businesspersons. These aspiring businesspersons are by definition very different people, with diverse backgrounds and skills. In addition, business careers are nowadays less predictable and linear. For instance, a young graduate can launch a startup, then work in a big firm, and later enter an NGO. By the same token, it is reasonable that the professors who have to educate this wide pool of aspiring businesspersons for non-linear careers, would have some variety in their own academic careers as well.

For this Gallery: "Navigating Belonging", I would like to add my portrait of the 'self-made academic', which is possibly the most appropriate representation for my story. I could have also chosen other portraits, for instance, "the imported academic", as I was educated in a very different context, or perhaps the "accidental academic", as I would have never imagined to enter academia when I left high school. While those two latter portraits have some resemblance with me, I still feel that the 'self-made academic' portrait better illustrates my story. I had to find my own way, without having a clear, structured roadmap. It has been a matter of trial and error. Indeed, a lot of trial! As the Spanish poet Machado says "Walker, there is no path, it is by walking that you make a path" ("caminante, no hay camino, se hace camino al andar").

Dear reader, let me share my story with you. I was born in Argentina in 1967, into a family of immigrants from Southern Italy. At the time, Argentina was a land of opportunity. Social mobility was real: my father and my mother had been the first in each of their respective families to attend university. According to the tradition, being the first son in my family, I was supposed to follow my father steps and do something related to business. In my home city, at that time, the closest thing to a degree in business was a BSc in Accounting. After graduation in 1991, I worked in different companies for several years. I took a year off to do an MBA, which I completed in 1997.

At the beginning of the new century, Argentina was (and still is) a quite unstable country, with recurrent macroeconomic crisis. During the crisis of 2001, I lost my job, as many people did in Argentina at the time. In order to make ends meet, I began teaching business students. I liked this experience of teaching so much that I dared to make a career change in my thirties. I taught for seven years in Argentina, and in the meantime, I had the opportunity to do my doctorate in the local university (Universidad Nacional de Rosario).

When I entered the doctoral program, I already had a significant business experience. Consequently, I had come to the program with a few ideas about business, and I was not a stranger to the field. The program helped me to think rigorously, to elaborate my ideas and to write better. It was a good training for a career changer like me. I am grateful to my alma mater for all this.

With the benefit of hindsight, I realize how lucky I was in doing that program. My professors gave very good classes and provided excellent support for thesis writing. Furthermore, they were kind in not imposing nor "selling" any school of thought. I never had to follow any specific argument, adopt any specific theoretical framework or come to this or that expected result. As long as I followed good research standards, my work was fine. I owe a lot to my professors in Argentina, who had the courage to set their students free.

Academia in Latin America can be tough. There are very few full time positions in business schools and most available positions have short-term contracts, are perhaps part-time, and are usually for teaching only. While exceptions exist, there is scarce funding for research. I soon realized that if I wanted to have a career in academia, I should move abroad. And I began looking at opportunities in Europe.

Things changed for the better in 2009, when I came to a business school in France. Here I found a conducive atmosphere for work: supportive colleagues, resources for research and opportunities for growth. I gradually built up a research pipeline, began collaborative research projects and I found my place in academic conferences. It took me some time to understand the rules of the academic game in my new context. For instance, the priorities and expectations from my colleagues and my students. With the passage of time, I built up a network of trusted peers. I have research collaborations with many colleagues, both inside and outside my school. I found a focus for my research, with a consistent, coherent line of thought that I have been developing in the last years over several publications.

In terms of pedagogy, I got used to teaching both in English and in French (without mixing both languages!). I gradually learned how to address different audiences, as my school provides courses at undergraduate, graduate and executive levels. I tried to do things differently, oftentimes taking the less traveled path. For instance, I coordinated the launch of an online asynchronous course on Responsible Leadership, now followed by almost 900 students per year. It is a school-wide course, with colleagues from all the school's departments contributing to it, as well as many alumni. This course is quite different from a conventional one, and it calls for a completely different approach to teaching and learning. Another unusual pedagogical experience is a capstone course for an MBA program that a colleague and I designed. It is an intensive week, where students make complex business decisions, with the support of a realistic business simulator. The simulator runs online, 24/7, allowing students from anywhere in the world to take part in the experience. Now I see that being 'self-made' made me to be more open to different pedagogies, and less attached to traditional ways of teaching.

I am an 'imported scholar', not so much because I was born abroad (not an unusual situation in our profession), but rather because I was not "born" into academia. I began teaching in my mid-thirties and I completed my thesis after my fortieth birthday. I used to be a practitioner, and I do believe this experience to be an asset, both in the classroom and in the research site. Students appreciate whenever a professor can reflect on his/her experience, contextualizing the concepts and theories in the light of experience. Also, whenever I conduct research interviews, my interviewees realize that they are talking with somebody who knows their trade. This point is particularly important for my field of research, Sustainability, which is relatively new. It did not exist when I entered college, and I struggled to find a supervisor for my thesis. Besides, Sustainability is a field that changes all the time, and it changes fast. This change happens not only in academia (i.e. new publications) but also in practice (i.e. new standards, guidelines, initiatives). Indeed, I would say that it goes faster in practice than in academia! Thus, I am happy to be an imported scholar. Not being native to academia gives me an advantage. I easily understand the viewpoints of managers and that of my academic colleagues. I am a double citizen.

I am also an "accidental academic" because I imagined nothing of this when I was 18. Academia was completely out of my horizon. I imagined being a businessperson, and at some moment, I found another career path. This path is not a rupture from the past, but a continuation of my career in a different sense. I now have the responsibility of taking stock from my previous business experience while remaining in contact with business practice today. I like inviting practitioners to my courses, who are in many cases alumni from my school. I also profit from opportunities to meet practitioners and talk with them. Furthermore, given that my research is empirical and qualitative in nature, I need to continuously contact practitioners for research interviews. In other words, I did not leave the business world.

All things considered, I think that a different career, as mine is, has value both for business schools and for students. I do not fall into the easy criticism of ivory towers, theory detached from practice, irrelevant research and so on. Some of that criticism may be justified, but I do not tend to buy it. As business is a complex reality, we need different, complementary approaches by which to learn about business. We need of course good theorists, colleagues who can come up with sophisticated concepts and insights. For those colleagues, conventional careers (i.e. with little or no business experience) make perfect sense. However, this cannot be the only career path in academia. It is a case of blending different perspectives, much in line with the complexity of business and the need to change with the times. The rigor of science and the dynamism of business have to go hand in hand, and so much the better if a scholar has a bit of both worlds. Both conventional and unconventional careers in academia are necessary nowadays.

Dear reader, I do hope that my unconventional story about an unconventional career can echo with your (unconventional?) story. If you are reading this book, and particularly if you are visiting this "Navigating Belonging Gallery", chances are that you are considering a career change to academia. Perhaps you are a business practitioner who wants to pursue doctoral studies. Maybe you are a business consultant who would like to teach in the local business school. It could also be that you are not considering a complete change in your business career – but just wish to have a closer relation with academia, for instance, tutoring students or taking part in research projects. Many possibilities exist. I would like just to tell you that in terms of academic careers, nothing is written in stone. Do not be afraid to try. It can be complex, it can take time, but it is not impossible, as you may have seen in my story. If it is your calling, you should give it a try!

IV
Nurturing careers

Curated by Olivier Ratle

NURTURING CAREERS

On the importance of care and relationships

Olivier Ratle

As the visitor progresses in this exhibition, this gallery provides an opportunity to stop, and rest. A haven of peace, it is a place to resource and restore oneself, to feel nourished and nurtured. It may evoke the restorative power of nature: green and blue spaces conducive of calm, serenity, tranquillity, and peace of mind – all good things! Nature writer Richard Mabey's (2005) account of dealing with depression makes a compelling case for why we need access to nature. Those who spend time in nature – whether in the wood, mountains, or even at the allotment – know tacitly the benefits. Cultivating the land, for example, as a manual and contained activity, provides a sense of purpose and achievement that can be lacking in other endeavours (where tangible outcomes are sometimes visible only after many years). Being outdoor in nature feels good mentally, and its effect on the reduction of stress and anxiety are well documented (e.g. White et al., 2019). It also feels good physically – whether the benefit comes from the gentle workout of a promenade, or from the good night of sleep derived from harder physical labour.

This gallery brings our attention to this question: what does it mean to feel resourced, refreshed, nourished, and nurtured? And what practices are conducive of that? Perhaps, one may point out that nobody would have to think about how to feel resourced and refreshed if we were not routinely burning the candle at both ends to start with, and we all had the time and resources necessary to do our jobs satisfyingly and properly. Alas, this is the sad state of affairs: academia is rife with exhaustion, burnouts, stress, and anxiety (see the editors' synthesis of this literature and own take on this issue in Bristow et al., 2019). Trying to answer that guiding question, contributors to this gallery are firmly grounded into their reality – sometimes a harsh reality, and their wisdom has often come at a price.

We begin with a portrait from Maribel Blasco, which introduces us to permaculture – a set of ethical design principles for cultivation, which aims to integrate land, resources, people and the environment, maximising beneficial relationships, and working with nature rather than against it. *Permaculture* is a useful metaphor often applied beyond the field of agriculture, 'to support and inspire more sustainable lifestyles, to improve mental health, sanitize consumption, and design livable, humane social systems'. So how can it help rethinking academic careers? Maribel draws specifically on 3 of the 12 design principles of permaculture to reflect on her career trajectory, and on the choices she has made over time. For example, the permaculture principle of *obtaining a yield* invites us to think meaningfully about what result actually comes out of our efforts. Maribel details at length how she came to realise that she did not enjoy academic conferences, that she did not get enough out of them given the efforts required to attend them, and that it would simply be a better idea to spend her time differently. This is a text full of wisdom, but it is not a 'how-to' guide; it is a political statement. Just as land cultivation is political, so is the way we play out our careers. Maribel says:

> we do not have to buy into academia's current trajectory. We owe it to each other, and to our intellectual vocation, to push back against this, and make our own and others' thriving a priority. That means, first and foremost, recognizing that our wellbeing is intricately interwoven with that of others, human and non-human.

The second portrait we encounter is also about interwovenness and relationships. Three feminist academics – Jenny Helin, Nina Kivinen, and Alison Pullen – welcome us into their conversation and into 'the room they created'. During the Covid-19 pandemic, they found themselves isolated in their homes, longing for ways to building and maintaining relationships. Across different time zones, they started reading Virginia Woolf's A Room of One's Own, but never finished it. What came out though is a conversation that features themes directly emerging from the pandemic (e.g. the reconfiguration of 'home' and of the boundary with 'work'), but also enduring and universal ones: the turmoil of academic life, women in academic life, and the quest for a feminist ethics of care.

Mary Godwyn's portrait is a tale of endurance in the face of adversity, and as such, could have been equally at home in the 'Living precariously' gallery. All odds were stacked against an academic career, and its trajectory would have been very uncertain. Mary evokes her college years, 'traumatized by the relentless stress of poverty', where she experienced like so many students, 'constant food insecurity or outright hunger', and where she could neither afford textbooks, nor a warm coat. At 23, she became pregnant – something she had not planned and did not want to happen before being in a financial position to be able to support children. But this is where the story takes a different turn: 'And then there was the fact that I had the most amazing child. When my first baby was born, I felt as if life began anew. The world transformed from grayscale to Technicolor'. And here are the two sides of this moving portrait which on the one hand, details the hardship faced, but on the other, describe the joys, the fulfilment, and the nourishment that love for one's family can generate. A Professor in sociology, Mary has reached the highest echelon of her profession. By her own words, she has had, 'a rich and fulfilling career as an academic who has been able to balance research, teaching, and parenting'. This may sound too good to be true, but the guiding principle is simple: 'I went into academia with the conviction that I would not compromise my professional integrity or diminish my commitment to being an involved parent', Mary says. Empathy and understanding also go a long way, she concludes:

> I recognize desperation in the faces of hungry students and exhaustion in the eyes of junior faculty members juggling the demands of publishing and parenting. I do not consider myself to be especially nurturing and I am certainly not soft or overly

sentimental, but I know that we are all one helping hand away from falling down or burning out.

The fourth portrait in this gallery is Elizabeth Siler's, which like the previous one, is in large part autobiographical, where parenthood looms large, and where there are a lot of 'helping hands'. In my correspondence with Elizabeth, I questioned whether *The mom academic* was really the most apt image to represent this rich text. This is a beautiful multi-layered portrait where the author discusses a wide array of themes: the volume of writing required by academic labour that is invisible and ephemeral but that still leaves one exhausted, her experience of academic care and emotional labour, and the origin story of her career as an organisation scholar (which enables her to question how we generally understand careers). Given the number of themes discussed, it is not a surprise that Elizabeth acknowledges in the text that '[she] contemplated a thousand different phrases to make sense of [her] life'. She settled on the mom academic because moms, 'never feel adequate, never get to finish anything', and yet, manage to do well enough to keep kids 'intact and alive and mostly content' – something that will sound indeed like an adequate level of achievement to most parents. Her text portrays with humour and depth the fragmentation of academic lives, but also the importance of the care work involved. For the mom academic, 'everything comes before writing, the way that for moms everything comes before "taking care of yourself"'.

References

Bristow, A., Robinson, S., and Ratle, O. (2019) Academic arrhythmia: disruption, dissonance and conflict in the early career rhythms of CMS academics. *Academy of Management Learning and Education*, 18(2): 241–260.

Mabey, R. (2005) *Nature Cure*, London: Vintage.

White, M.P., Alcock, I., Grellier, J. et al. (2019) Spending at least 120 minutes a week in nature is associated with good health and wellbeing, *Scientific Reports*, 9: 7730. https://doi.org/10.1038/s41598-019-44097-3

THE PERMACULTURE ACADEMIC

Maribel Blasco

Introduction

I cannot sit still. A day spent flicking through PDFs, out of sorts, nothing much written to show for it. I long for a distraction but when it comes, in the form of my elderly neighbor walking up my path, I am irritated. Nobody 'worked at home' in her day, never mind corona. I am a sitting target. I smile and greet her, blocking the door with my body. I love her, and she is lonely. But I have already wasted a day. She leaves, and I am ashamed.

Much work on the dystopia that is academia today focusses on the ravages wrought by an implacable, performance-fixated system on the 'embodied individual' that lives it (Smith & Ulus 2020: 841), including stress, anxiety, uncertainty, vulnerability, fear and even suicide (González-Calvo & Arias-Carballal 2018; Smith & Ulus 2020; Sparkes 2007). Yet academia is not a closed system. The toll it takes, starkly outlined in this call for papers, reaches far beyond those embodied individuals. As Cunliffe (2018: 18) writes, "we do not live our lives in isolation but in relation to 'others' … people whose lives interweave with [our] own in ways difficult to fully articulate". We need to pay attention not only to individual academics' struggles within a relentless system, but also to the ripple effects of those struggles on the ecosystems in which academics are embedded: our significant others, others beyond them, animals and our planet.

This portrait uses *permaculture* as a metaphor to reimagine academic life as connected to, and impacting, zones of life far beyond its perceived remit; and suggests ways in which this metaphor might inspire alternative ways of being an academic. I came across the concept of permaculture by chance, and quite recently, during a conversation with a neighbour. Despite having gardened for two decades, I could not recall having heard of it. Fascinated, I got home and googled. Permaculture, I discovered, is a set of conscious ethical design principles, often used in sustainable cultivation, which aims to integrate land, resources, people and the environment by maximizing beneficial relationships, working with rather than against nature to enhance resilience, diversity, productivity and stability (Hopkins 2020; Permaculture Research Institute 2023). Permaculture advocates three overarching ethics: *earth care, people care* and *fair share*, and twelve design principles – the petals of the so-called 'permaculture flower' (see Figure 20.1). Ultimately, the goal is to foster responsible cultivation, production and consumption through a whole-systems approach. But permaculture is much more than that – increasingly, the concept is being applied beyond the field of agriculture to support and inspire more sustainable lifestyles, to improve mental health, sanitize consumption, and design liveable, humane social systems.

I use three of the design principles – (i) *edge effect,* (ii) *self-regulation* and (iii) *obtaining a yield* to chart my own ongoing journey, spurred partly but not entirely by the COVID-19 pandemic, towards an alternative existence with one foot in academia but another firmly planted outside. As should always be the case in permaculture thinking, the three overarching ethics are present in all these reflections. I chart my struggles with finding a niche in my academic 'edge' existence, and on how being in that uncomfortable space has made alternative types of 'yield' possible through 'self-regulation' – consciously cultivating certain types of activity and relationships and curtailing others. Living with discomfort comes at a cost, however, in this case, the waste of a great deal of energy through my failure, for a long time, to work with my own nature rather than against it. But, as I discuss in the section about 'self-regulation', correcting such dysfunctions is tackled in permaculture through small, adaptive steps, and I share here how I have attempted to do this.

> It is six o'clock. I feel permitted to leave the screen now. I step outside, unappeased.
>
> On my garden path, a perfect, enormous red apple has appeared. There is nobody there.

FIGURE 20.1 The permaculture ethics (adapted from Permacultureprinciples.com).

Edge

I am a shade plant burned by the sun. Here by some accident of nature, against my nature, immobilised, unable to help myself. The gardener has great responsibility, since my kind, for all our adaptive capacity, cannot uproot ourselves and leave a poorly chosen spot. But my gardener has overlooked me. Paralysed, I watch the flowers on either side of me thrive, grow tall, send down deep roots, and multiply. I am not envious – I do not want to be like them – just faintly surprised that plants exist that seem to flourish in such conditions. I struggle, but I cannot grow with them and support them. My colours and forms and desires are all wrong. I belong in another ecosystem. But which one? The edge pulls me back, here is comfort in discomfort, safety in stuntedness. Tomorrow I am teaching again, 180 students in a hulking auditorium, and as usual I cannot sleep. I open my wardrobe, searching for an outfit that can disarm my fear. Nothing feels right. I find a dark sweater and slacks; at least this will not draw attention. I give up and snap a sleeping pill in half. It's usually enough. In the morning, the terror has not subsided. I arrive at school. My walk stiffens, I am watched and watchful. But the discomfort is a comfort blanket, it has become part of me, I am no longer able to shrug it off and I am not sure that I want to, or that I would know what to replace it with if it were no longer there. Why can't I walk here as I do along the shore, light and poised, facing the wind, sinking into my hips and the earth.

Vignette 1

The *edge effect* is the tenth permaculture design principle. It refers to the transition zone or 'ecotone' where two ecosystems overlap – as where land meets water or forest meets heathland. Here, we find rich diversity, since species from both ecosystems occur. So do species unique to the edge itself, that are adapted to the conditions of the transition zone, such as amphibians who can survive both on land and in water (though we cannot know if they are equally comfortable in both, or what this ambivalent existence has cost them). Conditions in edge zones usually differ considerably from those deep within the surrounding ecosystems.

Edge zones are energy traps. They connect ecosystems by buffering and enabling flows of energy, materials, nutrients, across their boundaries. Shells wash ashore, leaves blow into drifts against hedges, earth and nutrients accumulate at the foot of slopes. Edges are also liminal spaces, thresholds between worlds, which seem to naturally pull one towards them – water's edges, forest clearings, the dappled places between shade and sun. Permaculturists value and nurture these edges. Edges permit tensions, contradictions, and idiosyncratic yields.

One of my clearest childhood memories is being entered for essay writing competitions by my father, who had a bad case of ambition by proxy. I detested every second. I could not sit still, and longed to be outdoors, in motion, anything but the dreary, dry, writing. But I had to learn to persist with things I didn't like, he said. And I did. I won a few second prizes, and got into the local newspaper, much to his delight. Discomfort, I learnt, brought approval. How easy it must be, for want of proper observation, to teach such things to one's children.

This sensation of discomfort has persisted, showing up in various – not always productive – ways throughout my academic career. My choices were steered not by what I enjoyed but by what I was good at, or what I thought I ought to study. It never occurred to me that I should pursue a non-academic career, although I lived and breathed for plants, birds and nature. I was, however, interested in social justice issues, and took my PhD in Development Studies. I still disliked the writing and rarely experienced any kind of flow, but the ideas were interesting, and the research felt meaningful. Coming from this background, I got my first (and current) job at a business school, and felt as out of place as it is possible to feel, despite being hired to a department with largely like-minded colleagues. Not long after, managerialism swept into Danish universities like a wildfire that torched intellectual life as we knew it, replacing it with metrics, angst and busywork.

In my efforts to adapt to all this, I went through a phase, fairly early in my career, where it seemed to me that if I wanted to succeed, I would have to be more pragmatic or even cynical about how I spent my time. So I practised 'saying no' to non-compulsory tasks that would have helped out students and colleagues – letters of recommendation, interviews for people's research, answering random email enquiries, and a million other invisible things that academics are asked to do for others every single day, *pro bono*. I hooked up with research projects that had little to do with my own interests but were steered by senior colleagues who seemed to have a handle on fundable topics. Even if the personal chemistry was off. I worked too much, and when I wasn't working a pall hung over my free time. I dutifully submitted my research to the right journals, having been (kindly, I must say) encouraged by my boss to be a little more ambitious. I went to conferences I would rather have avoided – big, boisterous events attended by confident-looking people in power clothes and a stronger sense of self than me. Internally, I berated myself for not being able to match their enthusiasm. I felt outed when asked to talk about my own work.

This adaptation strategy failed spectacularly. I did not become more comfortable or productive, just miserable. I was terrorized by conference small talk; sometimes it would take me an hour just to muster the courage to leave my hotel room. I felt fake, ill-fitting, clothes and hair all wrong, and why was I worrying about that anyway? I felt miserly for turning down simple requests from colleagues and students, and I was not a terribly good teacher. I bailed on a funded research project because I could not find my heart in it, and then panicked that I had sabotaged my own career. The few rays of joy I had gleaned from my academic job dissipated – the delicate intrigue of playing with an emerging idea just for the fun of it, the delightfully unpredictable exchanges with students and colleagues from whom I learnt something every single day, and whom I loved talking to.

Not surprisingly, like so many other academics, I ended up on stress leave (Acker & Armenti 2004), followed by a glacial recovery. I could not stop crying, I yawned incessantly (a stress symptom, I was told), my brain fogged up and I systematically forgot what I was doing. Everything was onerous. The HR department referred me to a psychologist, but getting myself to the appointment, across town in a bus, felt like an unsurmountable task. When I finally arrived, I could not speak. Therapy, rather unhelpfully, only works if the patient is actually able to engage in a conversation.

Most academics are resilient to a fault long before we enter the scholarly colosseum. Once there, we conscientiously set about honing that skill: we tolerate insomnia (Acker & Armenti 2004), overwork, anxiety, stress and breakdown (Gill 2017); we battle to prove our worth as our core competences are scrutinized and assessed over and over again, often resulting in punishing criticism or rejection (Carson et al. 2013; Kiriakos & Tienari 2018). We are obliged to compete, often with our closest colleagues, for tenure, professorships and other career prizes (Carson et al. 2013); we neglect our loved ones, human and non-human, and feel guilty about this (Acker & Armenti 2004). In short, we throw ourselves repeatedly to the lions, in some cases with fatal consequences (Times Higher Education 2018). We are life-long, driven perfectionists. We do not give up. But at what point does resilience become dysfunctional, and how can we know? And when discomfort becomes a way of life, part of our identity, who will hit the brakes for us when we cannot or will not do so ourselves? My breakdown forced me to find ways to accommodate the discomfort of being 'on the edge', and I believe even to make it work, more or less fruitfully, for myself and those around me. Permaculturists hold that edge zones can be as productive – or more so – than the conventional zones on either side, breeding their own singular species and yields. Here, where debris accumulates and categories fall short, there is a kind of freedom. I turn to this now.

Self-regulation

> My dog wriggles and fake-growls on the floor. She is having a silly moment, she is telling me I have been ignoring her for too long, stuck to my stupid screen. Why am I sitting staring at that dead thing? I toss her a toy and tug on it for a few minutes. Her tail thumps the floor in delight. I love her more than anything in this world. Too soon, I return to my desk, guilty for 'taking 5'. Her tail lowers. She would have played all day long. And so would I. On our next walk, I let her sniff every single spot she likes. Often, I have hurried her along, my to-do list beckoning, the landscape suffused with stress, oblivious to Kattegat's lapping waves and the sea buckthorn berries, the scent of seagrass on the darkening horizon. The walk just another task to be ticked off before I have to get back to my nightmare of an R & R. I stop to chat with another dog walker. "Lovely to talk to you finally", she says, "you're usually in such a hurry".

Vignette 2

The permaculture principle of *self-regulation* requires us to 'see what is in front of us and not what we wish for'. Distinguishing between the two can be a life's work. Self-regulation is about intelligently and patiently working to understand the essence of things, and to use that knowledge to work with nature, rather than against it. It means spotting when something is not thriving, incorporating feedback, and taking small, adaptive steps to correct it. Thus, Bill Mollison, the 'father' of the permaculture movement, recommended 'protracted and thoughtful observation rather than protracted and thoughtless labor'. On a personal level, self-regulation is about being true to one's values, in action as well as thought (Jacke & Toensmeier 2005). To take self-regulation seriously means moderating one's stance, one's behaviour, or both, thereby limiting or discouraging inappropriate growth or behaviour (Jacke & Toensmeier 2005). Allowing oneself to make mistakes is fine, but it is not OK to fail to take action to correct them.

I am invited to talk to a group of new PhD students about The Research Process. Having steered my own ship haplessly into an iceberg, I feel qualified to comment, if only so they may steer clear. 'Research careers', I tell them, emerge through choices that are more or less free, within certain systemic constraints. BUT you *will* run into the wall of your own temperament sooner or later. It's important to reflect on that – you are unlikely to enjoy, or be good at, all facets of the research process. Make your idiosyncrasies explicit to yourself, and make them work for you, not against you. That means thinking about the following:

Your intellectual proclivities:

- Do you naturally prefer explaining or exploring? Opening up or closing down?
- Do you incline most towards quantitative or qualitative methods?
- Are you most inclined towards critique or corroboration?
- Do you prefer generating your own ideas and theorising/conceptualising yourself *or* applying/testing existing models and frameworks?

Your work organization and preferences:

- Rhythms – do you write best in the morning or afternoon? In short bursts with regular distractions, or in long concentrated periods?
- Are you ok with sitting still – or must you expend physical energy in order to be able to write?
- Do you need unbroken time for research? (e.g. setting aside a whole day in your calendar?)
- Are networking and conferences enjoyable for you or not?
- Do you enjoy writing? If not, could you ally yourself with others who do?
- Do you prefer data collection (e.g. interviewing, surveying) or data analysis?
- Autonomy or collaboration: to what extent are you prepared to share your ideas and compromise on their execution? (this can vary from project to project)

The bigger picture – what does academic success mean to you:

- Collaboration with other researchers?
- Individual career advancement?
- Aesthetic/intellectual quality of a piece?
- Bringing an original idea into the world?
- Citations, A-journal publications, career advancement, prestige?

The above excerpt is taken from my presentation to the PhD students that day. Distilling these reflections on academic temperament seems simple now, but was preceded by a long string of faltering choices in my own 20-year academic career. Upon returning from stress leave, I knew that I would have to make changes if I were to survive in academia and maybe even (I hoped) to thrive. I figured I had little to lose – I was ambivalent about academia anyway so if this cost me my career I was resigned – it would be the final nail in the coffin that would propel me to do something different.

I started by *rethinking who I worked with, and why*. Having been involved in a calamitous collaboration – albeit one that ostensibly ticked all the right professional boxes – in the early stages of my career, I resolved to work only with people with whom I felt a genuine connection, regardless of status, convenience or funding. I would treat these relationships as 'ends in themselves' (Gersick et al. 2000: 1039). With that in mind, I continued to 'say no' – just for different reasons. Most of my collaborations since then have begun with random conversations that gained traction of their own accord, and where neither of us had any particular agenda other than to swap ideas for fun. Nowadays, if I like someone and our work styles are compatible, I will sometimes even deliberately try to seek out a way to work with them, for no other reason than that. Academic life is, in essence, one long conversation, and for that you need kindred partners.

The second change I undertook was to *avoid conferences*. There is a lot of pressure in our field to attend large, prestigious conferences. Of course, conferences are one way to kickstart the writing process, and there is inspiring learning to be had, in pleasant locations. But beyond that, conferences are, to me, among the most baffling and trying of all academic rituals – the long hours of travel, surreal hotel stays, hurried presentations, small talk and stylized performances (see also Henderson 2015), not to mention the blatant monetization of intellectual life. I have always been puzzled by those who see the travel and hotel stays as a major 'perk' of the job and who thrive on the atmosphere. Though I know there are also many others who, like myself, are sceptical about the usefulness of many conferences (e.g. Nicolson 2016) and probably do not enjoy them much either (cf. Settles & O'Connor 2014). Rarely have I come away feeling that my thinking about a particular issue has been significantly advanced, simply because there is seldom time to go into depth, though I have received much thoughtful feedback and often enjoyed the mental time out spent listening to other people's presentations, a rare opportunity just to 'take in' without having to produce something myself. I have also, on occasion, found myself sharing laughter and genuine relaxation among a group of strangers. But not often enough.

After one particularly strained event, where I struggled to leave my hotel room each morning, I decided that enough was enough. From then on, I routinely deleted calls for abstracts, and for several years I avoided everything except one event – the Research in Management Learning and Education (RMLE) Unconference, a tiny, informal gathering whose format – small group conversations with no targeted output – cultivated intimacy and rich intellectual exchange. I began to feel a deepening connection with the RMLE community, and particularly with a small group of people who started to meet regularly beyond the conference, taking turns to visit one another in Denmark and the UK. Within this group, we have deliberately not focussed on outputs, but on allowing space for simply conversing with one another, and for collective writing and authorship.

The third change I made was to *give myself the freedom to pursue idiosyncratic ideas*. While this is, of course, the goal of all research, the extent to which one 'allows' oneself to indulge in research on the riskier end of the scale is constrained by a metrics-oriented system that does not tolerate repeated failures. By 'risky' I mean time spent developing an idea that is non-mainstream and therefore possibly difficult to publish (Kiriakos & Tienari 2018) – which is of course not always a reflection of the soundness of the ideas or the research behind them. So, after having failed miserably at the pragmatic route of pursuing hot topics with hot colleagues, I decided to try to rediscover what was meaningful to me, starting by returning to my roots in educational studies. I developed research ideas from random remarks by students that made me curious, and teaching challenges that mattered to me; and I did some of that together with colleagues I cherished. A few years later, I also decided to stop pursuing funding, an activity on which I had spent a lot of time – usually unsuccessfully – and to focus instead on projects that did not require it. This freed up even more energy.

My fourth decision was to *turn down the opportunity to apply for promotion*.[1] In Denmark, the tenure track to become full professor involves a five-year period in which one must qualify by defining a research field and publishing in its top journals. I was invited a few years ago by my head of department to begin this process. Surprised, and pleased to be asked, I started drafting the application document. But I was soon filled with qualms. The position would mean an intensification of all the things I already found gruelling, with more pressure to boot. And for what? I wasn't motivated by the salary increase or the status. Also, through the small changes described above, I had managed to claw back a degree of freedom in my existing position. Well-meaning friends urged me to go for the promotion, and remonstrated with me for refusing to do so, thinking (aloud) that low self-esteem was probably holding me back. I couldn't make them understand that it simply didn't feel like the right path for me. In fact, I had been dreaming for a long time about doing the opposite – namely going part time and looking into other career possibilities.

Yield

> I have always picked wild things. When the corona crisis struck and we were all sent home from work, I began to forage in earnest – sea kale and beet, nettles and dandelions, ground elder, plantain, ramsons, rosebuds. It was free, liberating, and delicious. Bitter greens, gathered and prepared through time-less hours. The thought of buying shrink-wrapped produce forced in southern European hothouses began to repel me. How could we be duped like this? I went to shops less and less, relying on local farms when my foraging sources went out of season. With no commute, I had time to research and practice self-sufficiency, filling my tiny garden with raised beds packed with seaweed, hay, manure and prunings from my neighbour's lilac hedge. I crammed fruit trees and bushes – quince, cherry, apple, blueberries – into every available space. The more I planted, the more my garden seemed to grow. This is life, and it has been passing me by. Capitalism is learned dependence. Westerners like myself consider ourselves independent, but most cannot grow a vegetable, let alone build a shelter. Unlike independence, self-reliance obliges interaction with, and respect for, nature and people, thus enhancing resilience and minimizing dependence on fragile, exploitative systems.

Vignette 3

Obtaining a yield – that is, some kind of reward or value from work one puts in – is a key principle and goal in permaculture. Yield can take many forms – it may be material (e.g. food), psychological/emotional (e.g. increased wellbeing), intellectual (e.g. knowledge) or interpersonal (e.g. collaboration or partnerships). Fun, joy, beauty, energy, courage, community, confidence and understanding are all forms of yield. Yield is not just about maximizing production. Rather, it means thinking about what is sacrificed, and what is impacted, in the process of obtaining a yield (Practically Quantum, 2018). These questions force us to reflect on whether we are devoting too much energy to activities that aren't producing sufficient – or the right kind of – yield; whether more could be done to improve or redistribute the yield we produce; and whether other types of yield should be pursued. Is the time we spend producing 'joy or drudgery'? (Think of it as an adventure, 2015). Could that time be spent on a different, more rewarding yield? Are our activities resulting in yields that we haven't yet recognized?

Thriving is a duty – without it, meaningful yields are not possible, we cannot nurture others, attend to our environment, or generate a surplus that can be shared. From the adaptive steps I describe above, different yields resulted that I could not have foreseen, which each in their own way reflected the permaculture triad of people care, earth care and fair share.

First, my decision to work only with kindred others has become the driving force of my academic life. I have never since regretted a collaborative project. Rather, my collaborations have yielded joy, connection and learning, and have strengthened my integrity as a teacher and colleague. In the current academic climate, relationships are too often seen as strategic alliances engaged in to advance careers (Ibarra 1997; Gersick et al. 2000), and refraining from doing this may not even seem like an option. But there are many ways to be in academia, and we have more choice than we think if we recast the parameters of how we choose our significant academic others. With her habitual insight, Ann Cunliffe (2018: 16) writes: "this is a crucial aspect of our lives as scholars – finding colleagues who are interesting and fun to work with: people with whom you can talk, laugh, debate, and whine – even if across continents. Finding your community is important". Gersick et al. (2000) similarly write of the rejuvenating, life-changing and saving impact of some academic relationships that can provide emotional support, relaxation, fun and inspiration. And Chemi (2018: 22) writes, quite rightly, that "Pleasure is … a basic academic need. Pauses are needed in the craft of scholarship as much as productive moments, and are an integral part of academic work-processes". To me though, the two are inseparable – pleasure is a creative necessity that we should seek not just in the pauses but in the productive moments as well, and the people are a huge part of that.

Second, I was not, as I had feared, frozen out for declining promotion. Quite the contrary, my boss accepted my decision with the greatest respect and understanding, and I was subsequently given greater responsibility in the form of mentoring and research leadership tasks which connected me more with especially junior faculty, giving me a great deal of pleasure. Other colleagues told me that they were inspired to see that alternative career paths were possible. Neither did my conference moratorium bring forth fire and brimstone, or jeopardize my job. Instead, cutting down on conferencing enabled me to spend my time in less depleting ways and to give more of it to others, human and non-human, both within and outside academia. I wasted fewer resources due to unnecessary travel, and focussing on a single event enabled me to forge more meaningful intellectual and personal relationships with like-minded scholars.

Third, pursuing idiosyncratic ideas has become a cornerstone of my academic identity. Assuring intellectual freedom is a constant struggle (Williams 2016), in which tenure and political forces that increasingly dictate the funding agenda (Williams 2016) play important roles. But freedom to experiment is crucial to our sovereign creativity and enjoyment of our work as academics (Kiriakos & Tienari 2018). Chemi (2018: 22) writes that,

Using and producing academic works requires long-term thinking and feeling, such as inspiration and resonance. This is also a creative need. To find, invent and apply different and original ideas and solutions takes time: time to not understand, to tinker and wander, to think deeply, to think wrongly and re-think, adjust, deconstruct, destroy, re-build.

It is certainly slow – I am not an especially productive researcher – but it has been a better route, since what I eventually produce is uncompromised by the agendas of funding institutions or other researchers, and getting there is a labour of love and personal commitment, not obligation.

This self-regulation and the resulting yields made my academic life vastly more tolerable – sometimes even joyful. Yet my discomfort persisted. Recently, I experienced what can perhaps best be described as a dark night of the soul – within the space of four years, my fifteen-year marriage ended, and I had my heart broken by somebody new. This at an age when it hit me that there was no longer infinite time left to reinvent my life. I lost faith in myself and in any bearable future. Worse, during this period, I serially failed to honour my own values, further damaging myself and others. I was working on too many research projects, and then an R & R for a high-ranked journal came back with 'major changes'. I asked for an extension, although this would run deep into the autumn semester, when I had to coordinate and teach a course that had received tepid evaluations for several years and which I had been tasked (yet again) with overhauling. Hundred and eighty students on a quite hard-core business programme, who did not see much point in the soft subject that I taught which had 'no proper right and wrong answers'. Due to COVID, the whole thing had to be put online – a massive task. My heart was not in it, and I reproached myself for this too. The semester ahead churned into dread. I found myself alone at home, stuck in front of my screen, doing work I found stressful and taxing, but if I am honest also often crushingly tedious. Like many others during the first COVID lockdown, I missed face-to-face contact with my colleagues, which usually compensated. Only the bare essence of the work remained, stripped to the bone. Absent a relationship to distract me, I was forced to confront my discomfort and think about what it might mean to thrive rather than just survive. But taking even a tiny step to right my path seemed inconceivable, risible even.

I returned to therapy, this time able to speak, and emerged with instructions to stop tolerating discomfort and instead cultivate things I enjoyed. I set about doing this. I applied to go half time for the coming autumn semester, freeing me from some of the teaching. Instead, I enrolled in permaculture and garden design courses. I volunteered at an inner-city greening project. I gave unrushed attention to my family, dog, students and colleagues, neighbours and acquaintances. I gave free rein to my physical energy, running ad libitum. I walked slower. I spent time researching and practising eco-friendly living: shopping at local farms, foraging, sharing produce with my neighbours, and redesigning my own garden with self-sufficiency and biodiversity in mind. I changed to an ethical bank, determined to live more in alignment with my values. By the end of my semester of freedom, I had befriended new people with different outlooks, my existing relationships had deepened, and my CO_2 footprint had been slashed. I found myself able to give again. By allowing space for other things, I also suddenly found myself more at peace with my academic roles.

The way we approach our work, and who we are as scholars, is tightly bound to who we are as people, to our sense of self and our identity, and to our relations with others (Cunliffe

2018). From the outside, I doubt that my tormented dance with academia was particularly obvious to anyone. I have functioned fairly plausibly on the surface, both as a teacher and researcher, for nearly 20 years. It is only as I write this that I realize how aberrant my academic 'edge' existence has been, and how limited its yield, before I took steps (still ongoing) to right it. For a long time, I mistook my discomfort for stress, or impostor syndrome. I certainly felt myself to be a fraud when teaching business-related subjects with which I had no hands-on experience, and when working on research projects to which I did not feel particularly committed. Yet neither label could account for my intense and persistent discomfort, the physical sensation of simply *being in the wrong place, doing the wrong thing*.

My childhood restlessness, it turned out, was not a phase, but a matter of deep temperament. To thrive in today's academia despite this, I have had to let go of every preconceived idea about what I should be doing and feeling. I am aware that it may be easier in some contexts, such as my adopted country Denmark, to tread a different path. Still, we do not have to buy into academia's current trajectory. We owe it to each other, and to our intellectual vocation, to push back against this, and make our own and others' thriving a priority. That means, first and foremost, recognizing that our wellbeing is intricately interwoven with that of others, human and non-human.

I am still a reluctant academic at least half the time, struggling with sitting indoors (or anywhere else for that matter). The other half of the time, I am bowled over by the beauty of our profession, its generosity, diligence and resilience. I suspect that many other academics lead similar double lives: we are covert doubters, secret secessionists, vicarious escapists. Mostly, though, we do not tell.

Epilogue

> A grandmother passed me by. Her toddler hung back, staring intently as I pruned the hedge in the communal yard where I volunteered, dressed in my overalls and blissfully happy. "Look sweetie", she said to him, pointing at me, "that lady's a gardener!"

Acknowledgements

Ditte Kathrine Engelstoftegård for welcoming me into her team of volunteers. Laila Bruun for helping me see that there is a choice. S for pushing me over the brink so that I had no choice.

Note

1 To the position of 'Professor with Special Tasks' ('MSO' in the Danish system) – a five-year position during which one must qualify for a full professorship. 'Reader' is an approximate UK equivalent.

References

Acker, S., & Armenti, C. (2004). Sleepless in academia. *Gender and Education*, 16(1), 3–24.
Carson, L., Bartneck, C., & Voges, K. (2013). Over-competitiveness in academia: A literature review. *Disruptive Science and Technology*, 1(4), 183–190.
Chemi, T. (2018). Pleasure and academia? Really?. *Organizational Aesthetics*, 7(1), 21–23.

Cunliffe, A. L. (2018). Alterity: The passion, politics, and ethics of self and scholarship. *Management Learning*, *49*(1), 8–22.

Gersick, C. J., Dutton, J. E., & Bartunek, J. M. (2000). Learning from academia: The importance of relationships in professional life. *Academy of Management Journal*, *43*(6), 1026–1044.

Gill, R. (2017). Beyond individualism: The psychosocial life of the neoliberal university. In: Spooner, M. (Ed.), *A Critical Guide to Higher Education & the Politics of Evidence: Resisting Colonialism, Neoliberalism, & Audit Culture*. Regina, Canada: University of Regina Press.

González-Calvo, G., & Arias-Carballal, M. (2018). Effects from audit culture and neoliberalism on university teaching: An autoethnographic perspective. *Ethnography and Education*, *13*(4), 413–427.

Henderson, E. F. (2015). Academic conferences: Representative and resistant sites for higher education research. *Higher Education Research & Development*, *34*(5), 914–925.

Ibarra, H. (1997). Paving an alternative route: Gender differences in managerial networks for career development. *Social Psychological Quarterly*, *60*, 91–102.

Jacke, D., & Toensmeier, E. (2005). *Edible forest gardens (volume one): Ecological vision and theory for temperate climate permaculture*. White River Junction, VT: Chelsea Green Publishing.

Kiriakos, C. M., & Tienari, J. (2018). Academic writing as love. *Management Learning*, *49*(3), 263–277.

Nicolson, D. J. (2016). *Academic Conferences as Neoliberal Commodities*. New York: Springer.

Permaculture Research Institute (2023). *What is permaculture?*. Downloaded at https://www.permaculturenews.org/what-is-permaculture/ on 13th of March 2023.

Practically Quantum (2018). Principle 3: Obtain a yield. Downloaded at: https://medium.com/@dftchemist/principle-3-obtain-a-yield-6e6ca28673aa on 20 November 2020.

Settles, I. H., & O'Connor, R. C. (2014). Incivility at academic conferences: Gender differences and the mediating role of climate. *Sex Roles*, *71*(1–2), 71–82.

Smith, C., & Ulus, E. (2020). Who cares for academics? We need to talk about emotional well-being including what we avoid and intellectualise through macro-discourses. *Organization*, *27*(6), 840–857.

Sparkes, A. (2007). Embodiment, academics, and the audit culture: A story seeking consideration. *Qualitative Research*, *7*(4), 521–550.

Think of it as an adventure (2015). *Permaculture Principle 3: Obtain a Yield*. Downloaded at https://thinkofitasanadventure.com/2015/03/02/permaculture-principle-3-obtain-a-yield on 9 June 2022.

Times Higher Education (2018). Lecturer's suicide a 'wake-up call' on overworking in academia. *THE*, June 2018. Available at: https://www.timeshighereducation.com/news/lecturers-suicide-wake-call-overworking-academia. Downloaded on 19 November 2020.

Williams, J. (2016). *Academic freedom in an age of conformity: Confronting the fear of knowledge*. Basingstoke: Palgrave.

A ROOM FOR THREE

Living academic, feminist lives (or the unfinished reading of *A room of one's own*)

Jenny Helin, Nina Kivinen, and Alison Pullen

April 6th, 2020

In Turku, Finland, Nina wrote on Messenger: 'Hi Alison, Jenny and I talked yesterday and we decided to start reading Virginia Woolf's (1928) *A Room of One's Own* together next week and we were hoping that you would join us <<<3'.

Twenty minutes and 16,000 kilometres later, Alison responded typing in Sydney, Australia: 'Hi both, perfect I'll dig out my copy xx'.

That was it, our reading group across time zones had started. Jenny living on the island of Gotland, Sweden, Nina in Finland and Alison in Sydney.

Reading *A room of one's own* seemed like a perfect choice for this strange time. A text published more than 90 years ago about women and fiction, about women writing and our place in the world. Hauntingly relevant still today. So here we were, reading this text confined to our homes due to the pandemic, thinking that, possibly, somewhere, sometime, we were all doing the same.

Our reading occurred during the Covid-19 pandemic in the spring of 2020. From one day to another, 'home' had become something entirely different. 'Home' – in relation to work – used to be the place where we could sit and write, a space for thinking, reading and writing. In contrast to days at university, working from home used to offer at least the idea of peace. As full-time employed academics, in many ways we had what Virginia Woolf saw as necessary for women who wanted to write: a room and money. However, as universities closed and we departed our offices to work from home, much changed. Being isolated and stranded at home made it evident that 'home' as we knew it, and importantly, home in relation our work, was in need of re-negotiations. Sara Ahmed (2000: 89) wrote:

> We can think of the lived experience of being-at-home in terms of inhabiting a second skin, a skin which does not simply contain the homely subject, but which allows the subject to be touched and touch the world that is neither simply in the home or away from home.

Our chat conversation about life, and life in academia at home, became important during the months of self-isolation and lockdown. Through our short, swift messages we reached out, moved and touched each other. Messages written barely awake in the early hours of the morning, in the middle of the night, worrying whether the other two ever slept. Messages about work, about children, about partners and lack thereof. About loneliness and exhaustion. Yet the messages created an affectual relationship; a deep bond between women, a sense of solidarity and an ethics of care that we continue to share. A care for our families, our students, our colleagues, of each other.

Based on our own experiences of having to navigate the homecoming process where new meanings around the relationship between our work and home were created, this chapter contributes to the contestation of the 'ideal worker' – 'ideal academic' – as a gender-neutral person (sic man) towards relational, affective, collective encounters that constitutes feminist academic lives.

This text emerged during the first few weeks of the New Year of 2021, a year which we hoped would bring change. However, much of 2020 entered 2021. The brief messages from the previous year have emerged as longer reflections on ideas of home, academic life and working at home. During our time together we have contemplated on the need to develop key learnings about the importance of relationships for sustainable academic lives. Taking the form of a conversation between the three of us, we develop a collective account which surfaces the gendered realities of being women academics, the importance of developing feminist relationships and solidarity, and the ways in which feminist ethics of care surface, particularly in relation to working at home, and the meaning of home during times of global uncertainty and risks. Our chapter offers feminine, embodied writing which draws on recent publications (Helin, 2020; Kivinen, 2021; Pullen, 2018) that rupture dominant ways of knowing and writing. Drawing on writers that call for women's ways of knowing and writing as relational, embodied and affectual, we hope to cultivate an understanding and praxis for working differently: we propose the academic as a sisterhood fostering intimacy and togetherness, an embodied critique of masculinist university performance driven cultures.

Nina, January 12, 2021

In March 2020, we retreated into our homes, perhaps scared, definitely worried and anxious. But I wasn't worried about work really. I enjoyed working from home. My home was a safe space, quiet and peaceful. I wasn't worried about teaching either. My course on diversity and inclusion would have been a flipped classroom anyway so I only needed to re-plan two days of seminars. However, I was unprepared of the loneliness. As days and weeks went on, rather than experiencing my home as a safe space, it started feeling more and more like a prison. Furthermore, Zoom and Teams became tools of surveillance as the expectation of being available at any time became prevalent. There was no way of hiding from work, from colleagues, students, particularly as I could see that I was better equipped than many for coping with insecurity and fear. I am resilient.

The same week as the lockdown begun, however, I had signed a contract with a new university in a different country. Not far away at all, but with the borders closed and travel restricted, suddenly my new job was light years away, unreachable. The illusion of my home as a safe space became obvious and my vulnerability started to surface. I knew who I was as an academic, but now, suddenly, I had no idea where I was heading.

'Home' is a complicated construct. It is a reference to a space, a specific place where relationships matter. It speaks of an origin, a starting point, a place of belonging. It is a space where part, present and future are intertwined in a complicated entanglement of memories, precious belongings and people. We carry the idea of home in our hearts and we rebuild it over and over again during our lifetime. An important aspect is that we can police its boundaries, that we can control who we allow inside. I am reminded of bell hooks' essay about homeplace (hooks, 1990), in which she talks about the importance of private spaces in which to heal together in order to build resistance against white oppression.

Messages in our chat became a lifeline. A brief and short lifeline in the form of hastily written words, words that invited others in. Words that built solidarity, a temporary homeplace for resistance. A homeplace that for me was less lonely, that helped me to keep the boundaries of my home.

Nina, January 13, 2021

In September 2020, I relocated to Sweden and for a few weeks I was trying to adjust to a new job, new city, a new home. I was excited, busy and curious about all things new. But in late October came the new stricter Covid-19 recommendations for the region: only meet people in your household, do not use public transport. My world was again diminished to my kitchen and walks in the neighbourhood. No commuting to work, no more teaching on campus, no more meeting friends, no more visits to museums. But this time the world outside my new home didn't seem to take these recommendations as seriously as I did. People seemed to go about their business almost as before as if the pandemic was somewhere else. My family back in Finland were worrying about my safety, urging me to return. I spent five weeks alone in my kitchen, not seeing anyone. As things got even worse, I came home. Home to Finland.

It is difficult to make decisions about your life, work and career when you are in your 40s. You are settled, you have roots, family and networks. Yet, the exciting things always seem to be somewhere else, particularly as by now you are often so entangled with administration, committees, and workgroups. In Swedish, we have an expression stating that you have become part of the furniture, *en del av möblemanget*. Part of that which is fixed, stable, reliable in your workplace. For female academics that is quite often our role. Only I want to be dynamic, exciting, thrilled, while avoiding too much risk and strangeness. Probably impossible at this stage of academic life.

Jenny, January 14, 2021

When I read your words Nina, about how you moved to another country, I am impressed by how you actually did that during the pandemic. How did you manage to push that through? I feel more cemented than ever to where I live. Watching TV series about change, like Fab Five and The Queen's Gambit, I am also longing for making this kind of life transformation, at the same time, my main movement is between the couch in the living room and the kitchen table. Living on an island in the eastern outpost of Sweden, my life has in many ways become 'small'.

Thinking about the lack of movement more thoroughly, it strikes me that what I miss is maybe not so much the physical transportation of my body to another place. It is more of how my body is confined to this place where all the poetics have been taken away. My home has been transformed into a digital warehouse where my two daughters and I store laptops, iPads, TV screens, and mobile phones. From being the place where I could go home to disconnect and be absorbed in reading and writing, the technology involved in working these days has invaded our personal space.

Sara Ahmed (2000: 89) was absolutely right when she wrote that the 'home as skin suggest the boundary between self and home is permeable, but also that the boundary between home and away is permeable as well'. My sensory apparatus is responding to the technology brought home by gently saying; is there a way out of this digital landscape?

Digital disarmament. I am reading Gaston Bachelard (2014), who wrote in *The Poetics of Space*, about homes that makes us travel in imagination. The home that Bachelard points towards 'is not conceptual space (the space of geometry and physics), nor is it concrete space (the space of a building), but lived space of imagination and memory, the space we engage our consciousness with, the house, the home' (Kennedy, 2011: 38). I am realizing that in this switch to work entirely from home (or study at home for my daughters) I have had a functional orientation; we have to make the Wi-Fi and these sorts of things work. The interesting thing is, that with this functional outlook only, it does not work in the long run. It is not enough. I am lacking the kind of poetic feel at home where it is possible to find 'hide-and-seek places where the mind can go on holiday for a while and think about nothing – which means everything' (Kearney, in Bachelard, 2014, xviii).

Where can I find such spaces these days?

Alison, January 16, 2021

Time has passed and we are two weeks into the New Year; a year of hope and new beginnings. It seems that to retain this hope will need work. I have enjoyed reading your text. Actually, I have found them hard to read and now I find it difficult to articulate a response. Writing forces me to slow down to remember difficult days that have passed. I miss your voices. How are you? Is it snowing still Nina? Jenny will you have snow?

I am writing to you as colleagues but also dear friends who have sustained me in tough days. There have been too many difficult days these past two years and you have both been there. It is 10.30 pm Saturday night and the temperature has dropped to 26 degrees. I was walking today and kept thinking how I would like to feel the cold weather, maybe even some snow and I remembered you in the north. I feel so far away. Far away from where I usually am this time of year. January is the month when I head north as I take my son to visit his grandparents; time and space to be me and escape Australian summer. I read and reflect, plan, and gather myself for living so far away and being responsible for so much. You remind me of this distance. I have two homes – one the land I was born on, a land savaged by Covid-19 and lack of management, and the land on which I type and raise my son. This land, Gadigal land, does not belong to me. Remembering that I am a foreigner is important so that I tread carefully not to violate the land that cares for us. I usually make sense of my dislocation from Wales in the skies, suspended in-between, it allows me to have two homes but when I am in the north or south, I long for the other. Consequently, writing about home is challenging as I feel permanently dislocated from the home that I know. However, I am also very grateful that the Australian government has been proactive in managing the public health crisis. Masks are mandatory, 'track and trace' is required in any public space, social distancing is evident everywhere. Surveillance and control have been necessary to provide an active response to Covid-19, but it is also tracking everything people do. Freedom is limited. I feel trapped. What will happen this year? I long for the interaction of bodies – from being able to read the stranger's lips when they speak. To sit and be with colleagues and friends. It seems that elements of feminist ways of working are threatened, and this will last longer than the pandemic.

As a university worker I am witnessing widescale university restructuring involving large scale precarity. Who remains have new futures waiting for them. Can the future be feminist in the neoliberal university? Perhaps it depends on where your home is. Feminism is threatened. Who I am, and can be, is under threat.

Jenny, January 18, 2021

It's Monday night and I should be preparing for a meeting tomorrow morning, but I cannot get Alison's words out of my head. You make me think of homecoming and rhythm. How you usually go 'home' to visit family in January and will not be able to do that this year. The rhythm of starting the New Year with your loved ones has been broken. What does that do to you? I go back to Sarah Ahmed's (2000) book *Strange Encounters*. Like Alison she recognizes how definitions of home shift: home as the place where one usually lives, or where my family lives, or my native country. Then, she adds:

> Home is associated with a being that rests, that is full and present to itself, and that does not over-reach itself through the desire for something other. To be at home is the absence of desire…
>
> *(p. 87)*

Can you be at rest, Alison? I also wonder, Nina, what difference did it make for you when you came back to Finland? Did it feel homely, could you rest back home?

I think I am sensitive to home and life rhythms because I live a rhythm that I have not yet come to peace with. Since the divorce from my two daughters' dad, they live with me every second week. The same house, but my experience of home changes dramatically depending on the week. These ruptures in-between are difficult. I'll make myself busy. To rest, at home, has been almost impossible.

Alison, January 22, 2021

I have been thinking of you both and wanted to talk with you but we, each of our own ways, find ourselves out of rhythm – through ruptures in the everyday to more life changing events. To engage in dialogue is to face a homesickness. You are both living in contexts where Covid-19 is rife and yet the machine – university, journal, teaching machine lives on. I have certainly become part of this machine rhythm.

'Can you be at rest Alison?' Jenny this is such an important question. I see Nina's rupture experienced in Sweden and returning home to Finland where she has verbalized that rest is vital, but it is never satisfied as I feel that Nina is also a longing for change and to move forward in Sweden which has not eventuated? Jenny, this idea of resting troubles me, it makes me feel as if I will never move again. I said it. Did I want to say this? Keeping moving, to make oneself 'self busy' is exactly the obsessive everyday routines that make the longing feel more bearable. Longing for the north, home, visiting family, seeing friends. It is in the north I rest. In the south I work – university work, journal work, homework. What is it about me that prevents me from slowing down? Genetics, yes, my mother has form. A fear of being content or rested, to be with myself, yes. But also a culture in which resting seems impossible. Sydney life is busy – city rhythms, running cultures, excessive hobbies – it seems that to do nothing is impossible. You see I am stealing time, all the time. My mind is overloaded, my body is overloaded… it has been this away since my son was born (I felt compelled to do everything).

When I first came to Australia sending emails in January (summer) was taboo! January was a month for stopping, resting – I remember it being a month for pleasure and nothingness in terms of work. Then it would be followed by a slow February a month for preparing for the start of teaching. Now summer is busy, catching up, getting stuff done before teaching starts, the neoliberal university has colonized the calendar year, colonized private time. The public has consumed private life. I am here juggling. I am privileged to be able to juggle, but there is a strain – everything I do seems late, and the anxiety that ensues with every missed deadline. My body is affected – I currently have pain in my back, hip and knee, shoulder, and elbow. Too much typing, sitting, and I feel that I am really good working with multi-demands. It seems that university workers – now all precarious – are needing to look busy. Soon work will intensify; mass restructuring, voluntary severance, pre-retirement packages and compulsory redundancies. Has Covid-19 provided an opportunity for those universities who want to move towards a leaner, meaner, operating machine? How will feminist academics be affected? What will happen to feminist work? In my own university more women departed, especially at professorial levels. Will these redundancies enhance the university as masculine?

The first day the university opened in 2021, the first email of the year came from a senior administrator who advised on appropriate online courses to take to ensure that we could administer our own courses because administrative staff had been cut. Soon after, an email arrived from senior management announcing a new human resource system which requires learning. Following, a message from the university asking us to complete our performance appraisals and that the system had been automated. It is clear to me that there is widespread efforts to become more visible. I long to be invisible. I now process university administration, including progress reviews for students, ordering student feedback, booking rooms, ordering readings, uploading research activity. What is an academic? Given such de-professionalization and automation of academics (and we are the lucky ones with jobs), how can we begin to talk about the ways in which relationships matter to our work? I hide at home, but even my home has become automatized.

In the masculine university it will be harder to establish feminist spaces, including gaining respect for home and family boundaries. In all the months of homeworking during Covid, not one person asked whether employees with caring duties needed support. You need to be thick-skinned. The compassionate, empathetic, caring worker will be eaten. How can we develop thicker skins to ward off the toxic masculinity of academia? I am fortunate that you have cared for me in ways that goes beyond friendship or feminist care – it is an unspoken care that runs through every pore. To have someone who can be there for you – outside of one's home (always a contested space). Your texts demonstrate how the boundaries of home have certainly been consumed, work seeps into every crevice. Is resistance futile?

The Queen's Gambit was such an amazing television series and it revealed how respect for women follows exceptional performance. It also shows that women when they learn how to navigate male spaces can work on their own terms. Given that women have been co-opted by many governmental regimes, what would a feminist life, after Ahmed, look like in academe? Does it mean disconnecting? Does this mean leaving academic careers behind? Nina, given your work on affect, how can affective resistance become possible in these times? Jenny, you write about slow philosophy, can slowness become possible in neoliberal universities?

Nina, January 23, 2021

It is Saturday and the beautiful winter landscape is raining away. Again, it has been a week when I wasn't able to finish even the main tasks on my to-do list. A rejection on a paper that meant a lot to me has diminished my will to push past the challenges at hand. I am slow, or at least I work slowly. Even routine-like tasks take too much time and I think I am getting bored of being at home. However, I have been thinking about how important it is to me not to leave colleagues alone, not to leave anybody behind. Being here in Finland, in my home surrounded by photographs of loved ones, books I cherish, family and friends close by have given me strength to shift my focus from myself to others around me. I realize that I have been so wrapped up in my messy circumstances that I have neglected to care for others. Alison and Jenny, you have reached out to help me as have other colleagues and friends and this reassured me that solidarity is still here and it is important. The lack of embodied, affective encounters has us misunderstanding e-mail messages, misinterpreting spoken words, inadvertently causing harm with our own words. This week I decided to reach out a hand in solidarity and it feels good. I do feel ashamed that as a senior academic, I lost my way for too long. I wanted to be independent and selfish for a while, to only care about my own work and career, but it is not me. Affective solidarity is powerful, it connects, gives comfort, transforms us and it empowers us to move together, to resist the complex challenges we face in the neo-liberal university. But I am also thankful that I work in Sweden where universities are properly funded by the government rather than being imprisoned by a market logic. However, the Swede's somewhat relaxed attitude to the pandemic also means that there seems to be hardly any recognition of the challenges the pandemic causes for academics, female academics in particular (with the exception of talking about the difficulties of online teaching).

My future is most likely somewhere else than in my home in Finland, but I need to keep this place as a safe space to return to. New adventures await across the Baltic Sea and I will again embrace my role, but in the mean time I will cherish this time with my family and plan for all the things we will do when they visit me in Sweden. And I will start making plans to see Alison and Jenny. I can't wait to travel! It will soon be a year since my last visit to Australia and I have never been to Jenny's island. So here I am now smiling. Anticipating. Waiting. Hoping. I will see you soon and give you both a long, long hug.

Alison, January 25, 2021

I feel cold reading your words Nina, thank you and I am looking forward to us being together again. Not being able to be with others is affecting us all – even Rupert my little dog is more anxious. I'm sorry to hear about the rejection and not being able to keep up. Again, I think this is a sign of the times. The paper will however find its special home (some journals have special places in our hearts), but in a world of metrics (upon which many journals set their mission and strategy), it is hard to care about the home in the same way as we once did. In the early days of being an academic as long as we did research and some was published it met role expectations. Academics and their work are being siloed. But we push against this, right? Is this the same in Sweden and Finland? We find homes as feminist scholars for us and our work with others like us, against the grain of the current metrics-obsessed institutions that surround ourselves. With Covid-19, these institutions and cultures slide into our homes too. Care for our self needs to ensure that we push that which threatens ourselves out of the home, but it is very difficult. I find as well as caring in the home, for my son and students, friends, and colleagues, that home has become a site for care. I am doing more care of the home too, gardening, mounting pictures, as a continue to do home care for those who were not previously in the room. The isolation required for writing has gone, as care work has become central to academic work. This time has offered the possibilities to engage in ethics of care, feminist ethics of care, that were previously done mostly in relation to other bodies. But I am so tired of it, 11 months of it. Students writing organizing zooms meetings to be able to communicate, PhD candidates writing every week for meetings, colleagues messaging at midnight (those in the same time zone). We are craving contact. And while I need bodies to hug, to be, to relate, to feel, to care – I am tired. Care was always incorporeal, physical. But I am also mindful of the ways in which being at home manifests struggle and in some cases exploitation of others. How do we as feminist academics care, and know when not to care? Solidarity and care of others requires me to walk away. But, not from you – to have you here in my 'attic room' amidst the family dining table in school holidays means more than I can express.

Nina, February 1, 2021

Oh Alison, how your words bring you close. Through this *anno horribilis* I have felt that we really share this 'attic room'. This morning, alone in a cottage by the sea we have rented to get away from home, I watch the snowflakes slowly falling and the sea freezing over. I have peace and quiet here with no Wi-Fi, but when reading your words, I am also sitting at your dining table, present in your home as you are in mine. I am hiding from academic responsibilities for a few days, or more accurately, I am resisting the urge to be online 24/7 in order to catch up with some of my responsibilities. Marking and journal editing in particular. But also, some luxury isolated writing time as I am feeling the need to maintain the illusion that writing and thinking requires space and time. It is more about my body needing the quiet, peaceful space around me to get some rest. I will use the sauna every day and embrace the presence of your bodies with me in this small intimate space. I will feel the heat and the sweat on my body, and when I have had enough, I will step out into the snow with my bare feet, and I will feel alive.

February 1, 2021

> Across tables, we feel closer,
> As we write, our bare feet press in the clean fluffy snow.

Running into the sauna, a communal place for cleansing,
Flushing out the toxicities of the neoliberal machine.
Homes truly consumed by work and so many people,
To leave home to find home.
There was a time when January was for rest, now it is catching up,
Unrealistic deadlines and demands most possibly the result of the erosion of scholarship,
The first day of February and it feels like the end of the year.
Are we experiencing collective fatigue?
Perhaps we need to resist.
Be kind to yourself.
Do you remember Fleetwood Mac's Gypsy (Nicks, 1982) and the woman in the attic?
She wanted to go back.
Can we go back?
The freedom that we long for, to go back to what was.

References

Ahmed, S. (2000). *Strange Encounters. Embodied Others in Post-Coloniality*. London: Routledge.
Bachelard, G. (2014). *The Poetics of Space*. Boston, MA: Beacon Press.
Helin, J. (2020). Temporality lost: A feminist invitation to vertical writing that shakes the ground, *Organization,* DOI: 10.1177/1350508420956322.
hooks, bell (1990). Homeplace (a site of resistance). In: *Yearning: Race, Gender, and Cultural Politics.* Boston, MA, Chicago: South End Press. 41–49.
Kennedy, M. (2011). *Home. A Bachelardian Concrete Metaphysics.* Oxford: Peter Lang.
Kivinen, N. (2021). Writing grief, breathing hope. *Gender, Work and Organization*, 28(2), 497–505.
Nicks, S. (1982). Gypsy [song]. On: Fleetwood Mac, *Mirage* [CD] Los Angeles, CA: Warner Bros.
Pullen, A. (2018). Writing as labiaplasty. *Organization*, 25(1), 123–130.
Woolf, V. (1928). *A Room of One's Own*. London: Penguin Books.

THE NON-CONFORMIST ACADEMIC

Professor, parent, provider

Mary Godwyn

Having acquired both my PhD and first teaching position in 2000, this is my twenty-first year as an academic. By several measures, I am a success, but that description belies a rocky start and renewed insecurities. I am a composite of identities that are unusual in the academy: I am a single mother of four children, a full professor, and a sociologist who teaches at a business school. Taking a decade off between undergraduate and graduate school to care for my two children, I was an older, non-traditional student. Under-representation of women in the upper tiers of academic ranks is well-documented, and being a parent while a graduate student, as opposed to earlier or later, is the most damaging to women's careers in the long run (Mason et al. 2013). Being a single parent is harder still. Fewer female academics have children than do their male counterparts; for women, babies are a "career killer"; for men, babies are an advantage (Mason et al. 2013).

Earning a college degree was not a foregone conclusion and graduate school was even more of a reach. I had worked my way through college and was still traumatized by the relentless stress of poverty. For most of my undergraduate life, like so many students, I experienced constant food insecurity or outright hunger. El Zein et al. (2019) report that nearly 20% of college students in the US experiences food insecurity and over 25% more are at risk. I was often without the funds to buy textbooks and suffered through New England winters without a warm coat or boots.

As a philosophy major, I cherished the logic and discipline of that subject, but when considering grad schools, I was afraid of plunging back into privation and accumulating even more student debt that I would have no way to repay. The near guarantee of no available positions in my discipline sealed the deal. Graduate school in philosophy, it seemed, was for the rich – those with enough independent wealth to support their studies. As a well-meaning relative commented, with a touch of distain, philosophy was for people who could "afford to sit around just thinking all day." I would not, could not, afford to pursue a doctorate, at least not yet.

Like so many students who love rhetoric, argumentation, and theories about morality, ethics, and justice, I turned to law school. An education in law, I reasoned, would surely sate my intellectual curiosity while also providing practical skills and a way to avoid impoverishment. Having missed the law school applications, I had to wait a year to apply. I was determined to familiarize myself with the life of an attorney, and earn some money, so I took a position as a paralegal at a large law firm. Within a year, I had married. A few months later, at 23, I was pregnant.

It was a shock. I had planned never, ever to have children, and certainly, definitely, absolutely, not to have children before I could financially support them. My own childhood had been pockmarked with trauma and transience. I had lived in temporary shelters, foster homes, state institutions, and with several different relatives. In total, I had been enrolled in six separate school systems. According to the National Fact Sheet on the Educational Outcomes of Children, only 2–9% of those who have been "in care," a euphemism for being a ward of the state, ultimately attain a bachelor's degree (2014). Though national numbers are in dispute, former foster youth are significantly over represented in prison populations compared to those who grow up with their families (Steele 2019). I had earned a college degree and avoided incarceration; but I could imagine no greater failure than to put another child through the same instability I had experienced. Setting aside my personal ambitions to devote myself to parenting seemed like the only responsible course of action.

And then there was the fact that I had the most amazing child. When my first baby was born, I felt as if life began anew. The world transformed from grayscale to Technicolor. With a precocious toddler who began holding animated conversations that rivaled the Existentialists when he was only three, and who started playing chess at four, I was never bored. In fact, parenting was not only physically and emotionally demanding, but tested my intellectual focus as well – far from dumbing things down, I struggled to keep up. Having a front row seat to witness the development of another human being remains the most engrossing and challenging experience of my life. I was transfixed. Three years later, after a second child, I became a single parent. I had been out of the workforce for eight years. When my younger child started kindergarten, I decided to go back to school.

It was a radical decision. It meant delaying my ability to earn money for years and banking on the slimmest of possibilities: that I – a single mother who was roughly a decade older than her peers – might snag one of the few available spots in a doctoral program and then (here the chances became slimmer still) be rewarded with an academic position. The odds were awful, but I had waited so long; I just took a leap of faith.

In the decade since earning a BA, my interests had shifted. I was not as consumed by the analytical philosophy of my youth as I was with the practical life experiences that I accumulated. The casual sexism and misogyny imposed on mothers and the debilitating lack of social and economic standing that comes from being a full-time parent were corrosive. I bristled at the cavalier disregard of women's autonomy and competence leveled at me when I called for home repairs – the first question was often: "What's your husband's name?"

Parenting seemed to me a serious, urgent responsibility where mistakes and successes by definition had life-long ramifications. As powerful as I was in our tiny universe, in the larger world, I barely existed. In addition to being classified as "non-working dependents," on tax forms, full-time mothers are variously referred to as helpmates, parasites, busybodies, and brainless do-nothings. We were just housewives, the support staff, not the stars, of families. The life-sustaining, ceaseless, unpaid work of caretaking was constantly trivialized and discredited. I chafed under the daily indignities of living in a male-dominated, capitalistic system: the premise that the male pronoun is all-inclusive; the conventional lexicon that endlessly infantilizes women with the term "girl"; the incorrect assumption that I preferred the title Mrs. (which I despised), and had adopted my spouse's last name, or worse, that our children bore his name alone. I rejected the hierarchal nomenclature of husband and wife, and insisted on the term partner or spouse, but no one really listened. People often smiled condescendingly at my unusual demands and discontent. With a metaphorical pat on the head, I was nonchalantly dismissed. Economic dependency on my spouse had transformed our mutual respect and friendship into an oppressive cage for both of us. It was demoralizing and exhausting. After being a full-time parent under patriarchy, or as I came to know the feminist term, kyriarchy (Sch*ü*ssler Fiorenza 2009), I knew I had to study social and economic inequality. Going back to school was an act of resistance and hope.

Within the discipline of philosophy, I thought I might explore these practical issues in applied ethics and political philosophy. So, my first venture back to the academy was to visit the linguistics and philosophy department at the Massachusetts Institute of Technology (MIT), home at the time, to Noam Chomsky, Judith Jarvis Thomson, and Joshua Cohen. Professors Thomson and Cohen were kind enough to meet with me, and I decided to apply.

I was fortunate that some of my college friends offered advice and support. Cautionary stories made me change direction. One friend, who, like me, married in her early twenties, entered a PhD program in chemistry at MIT. Shortly afterward, she became pregnant. She reported that the head of the chemistry department reproachfully warned that faculty would not mentor her since she was obviously "wasting their time and throwing away her education." She advised me that many doctoral programs accept women, but then provide little to no support, effectively stranding them midway through their studies without funding and absent meaningful mentorship. MIT, she said, had a reputation for being one of the most male-dominated and hostile campuses toward women.

Indeed, during the mid-1990s, at the same time I was applying to graduate school, and at the insistence of a group of female faculty members, MIT conducted an in-house study on the Status of Women Faculty in Science and the inhospitability of the "masculine culture" at the university (Chisholm et al. 1999). The objective was to change the environment to one where women graduate students and faculty members could thrive. From 1994 to 1999, during the years of the study, the number of female faculty members in science rose from a paltry 22 to only 31. In 1999, the last year of the study, there were 73 female graduate students in chemistry compared to 176 male graduate students, and 2 female faculty members compared to 30 male chemistry professors. Clearly, MIT had remained a largely masculine culture and would not, I decided, be a conducive environment for a single mother rusty from a decade of primary parenting, and who, on top of everything else, lived an hour away from campus.

Focusing on my interest in social, political, and economic inequality, I discovered the sociology department at Brandeis University. In its heyday, Brandeis had been home to some of the most influential and theoretical sociologists of the twentieth century including Herbert Marcuse, Everett Hughes, Philip Slater, Irvine Zola, and Morrie Schwartz; graduates of the department included Barrie Thorne and Patricia Hill Collins. I thought I might find a home there. Before applying, I met with current faculty and described my situation. There I found moral and financial support. I was awarded a stipend that allowed us a bit of financial breathing space and a teaching fellowship that provided invaluable experience in the classroom. I felt welcomed and respected. In fact, the year I applied, I was not the only single mother who was accepted.

I relied heavily on my friends for childcare. The suburban public school my children attended had "early release" days on Wednesdays: children were dismissed at noon, and there was no afterschool programming. The standardization of this schedule assumed either a stay-at-home primary parent, almost always a mother, or a family with enough wealth to pay for a nanny or babysitter. Our family had neither. A devoted social network of other mothers was essential to the premise that perhaps one of us could pursue full-time education. My children were cared for, without financial remuneration, by friends every Wednesday throughout the five years I studied at Brandeis. Even when my children were sick, and theirs went to school, my friends continued to provide childcare for us. Caring for a sick child who is not even yours, as any parent knows, is the ultimate selfless act.

Student life was not all childcare and home maintenance: making up for the fact that I had spent my twenties changing diapers, I had a social life during graduate school. I made friends with other students, threw parties, went on dates, traveled to conferences, attended concerts, and visited museums. But, I was constantly exhausted. I worked after my children went to bed, which was usually from 10:00 pm to 2:00 am. To get up in the morning, I placed an alarm across the room; that forced me to leave my bed to turn it off. I slept in my car between classes. The ache of exhaustion became my constant companion. Invariably sometime in October, I would get a cold, and it would last the entire year until the spring. Several times, it advanced to pneumonia. I was always sick with something: strep throat, sinus infections, bronchitis, etc. Once, while we were food shopping, I dispatched my six-year old to the next aisle to get a loaf of bread. I told him to come right back so he would not get lost, and he said, "don't worry, I can find you by your cough."

The last year of my doctoral program was punctuated by four tragic events. First, after fighting illness for several years, my father died suddenly from a pulmonary aneurysm. Next, my dissertation advisor abruptly left for another institution, and I had to scramble to replace him. He invited me to come, too, but with school-age children in tow, a move was not feasible. Then, less than a year after we married, my second spouse had a brief foray into infidelity. Five days before I defended my dissertation, I came home and found all his things gone: he had neither the courage nor courtesy to tell me our marriage was over. With no time to explore the sorrow or betrayal, I called a real estate broker and put our house on the market. Finally, the years of sleep-deprivation, stress, and constant work took their toll. I became very ill with a bout of influenza that quickly morphed into a bacterial pneumonia. Too breathless to walk, and barely able to speak, I was hospitalized and feared that, like my father, I would die struggling to breathe. The situation was so grave, my doctor counseled me to set up guardianship for my children. I owe my life to a powerful fluoroquinolone antibiotic that had recently become available. It took me 3 months to regain my health, during which time I had a relapse and was again hospitalized. The pneumonia permanently scarred my lungs.

The tasks before me were daunting: regain my physical health and retain my mental health, shepherd myself, and my children, through the emotional trauma of a second divorce, sell my home and find more affordable housing, finish and defend my dissertation, and, secure an academic position near-by so at least my children did not have to change schools. These challenges seemed so formidable, not only did I think I could not manage them, I wondered if anyone could.

What I did not realize then, is that graduate school is a divorce generator and women are disproportionately affected. Women who start tenure-track positions are 144% more likely than are their male counterparts to be divorced (Mason et al. 2013: 61). Moreover, married women in tenure-track jobs are 35% more likely to get divorced than tenure-track men, and have double the chances of divorce than do women who are non-tenure track faculty. Mason et al. write, "Whatever makes the marital behavior of female faculty unique appears to begin in graduate school, given that the gender gap in marriage and divorce is largest right when Ph.D. recipients are beginning their careers" (2013: 63).

The authors underscore how demanding and all-encompassing academic work is as female academics have a substantially higher divorce rate than women with doctorates in other professions. This suggests that the intensity of the work is to blame; however, based on my own experience, I would also suggest that academic work might embolden women to critically assess and ultimately reject the restrictions of heterosexual marriage, especially as they represent a traditional division of domestic labor and the presumption of male superiority. Perales and Baxter find that lesbians in the UK and Australia report higher relationship satisfaction than do heterosexual women, and their research was gathered prior to the legalization of same sex marriage in those countries (2018). Using the gender-as-relational concept (West and Zimmerman 2009) the authors suggest, "the relatively poor relationship quality reported by heterosexual women may be driven by being partnered with a man rather than a woman" (Perales and Baxter 2018: 66). Moreover, they speculate that the relative satisfaction of same sex couples might reflect, "levels of egalitarianism in domestic work and better conflict management strategies" (Perales and Baxter 2018: 64).

The expansion of Jürgen Habermas' concept of communicative action was central to my dissertation, and the sociologists in my department felt unsure of how to evaluate such a theoretical work. They asked that my outside reader be a philosopher, and that is how one of the professors from my undergraduate days came to sit on my dissertation committee. He was an engaged and interested reader. He alone offered me mentorship and career advice reduced to just one persistent suggestion, which he unfailingly repeated every time we spoke: send out your CV to every place you would consider working.

I was incredibly resistant to this advice. It seemed like such a waste of time, effort, and paper. It was a forgone conclusion that my CV and carefully crafted cover letter would arrive on some department chair's desk only to travel the short distance to the nearest trash receptacle. I was so exhausted and over worked by the spring before I graduated, I could not imagine devoting an entire day to such a whimsical and pointless endeavor. Eventually, his patient, relentless, insistence wore me down; purely out of deference to him and with certainty that it was an utter waste of time, I complied.

I sent out 12 CVs with cover letters. Two days later, I was invited on my first interview. In all, I received four responses, which yielded two interviews, and I secured both positions. Within a year, I was delighted that one of my visiting positions became tenure-track. My career trajectory provides an important lesson about how to find academic work. Department chairs are often given a budget that stretches over two to three years, and they usually have knowledge about funding for tenure-track lines before these positions become officially available. Choosing upon whom to bestow that rare and precious commodity in academic life, the tenure-track line, is fraught with uncertainly and second guessing among department heads, deans, and faculty colleagues. Search committees are often lead by junior faculty who are, in essence, searching for a department colleague (friend, collaborator, co-conspirator) with whom they will spend the next 20–40 years – a much longer commitment than most marriages entail. Interviews are intensive daylong affairs beginning with winnowing hundreds of applications down to 3–4 candidates. After a stress-filled overnight stay, candidates are scheduled into meetings and presentations with faculty, administration, and students from breakfast to after-dinner drinks.

Despite this scrutiny, it is not uncommon for mistakes to be made thereby wasting the precious resources of money, time, and mentorship needed to turn a junior faculty member into a tenured professor. Moreover, a bad hire is an embarrassment to the chair and search committee members that can diminish their reputation and undermine their relationship with the administration for years to come. This high stakes process can be managed effectively by hiring a vising professor for the position well before advertising the tenure-track line. Visiting professors are paid less than assistant professors are and can be hired on a part-time basis reducing the monetary investment even further. Departments might cycle through three or four visiting professors before a potential match is found, then they animate the line and advertise the position.

It is far from a *fait accompli* that the inside candidate will get the job, but it is often a wise strategy to hire someone who is already familiar with and successful in that unique and particular environment rather than take a chance on someone new and untested. This how I secured a tenure-track job. I had not imagined that I would teach sociology and gender studies at a business school, but it was refreshing and invigorating to introduce theories and ideas that provided critical perspectives to the capitalist assumptions of students and colleagues.

When newly minted PhD's ask me for advice on how to get a position, I tell them what my mentor told me: send out your CV to every place you would consider working. It seems like a fool's errand, but it might work because it can be easier to get a part-time gig that turns into a full-time position than it is to be one of the three applications chosen from among hundreds during a job search.

Early in my career, I was largely unable to travel because of childcare responsibilities; it made sense to stay put and focus on teaching. I had a couple of journal articles that were expanded from graduate papers, but my research productivity was low. When my younger child left for college, I threw myself into research and began to publish. My first book entailed traveling all over the country, staying in cheap hotels and interviewing minority women entrepreneurs. I went to Texas, Oregon (Michigan), Florida, Maryland, Vermont, and Montana, among other places. My rental car was vandalized in a remote Montana town; I had to sleep overnight in an airport chair on my way to Oregon, I was desperately lost in Florida, and nearly arrested in Colorado. It was a glorious. I interviewed Native women, differently abled women, Muslim women, and women in hiding from abusive partners. I walked beside them and wrote their stories of mutual support, community solidarity, and economic independence. A major university press picked up the book. No longer just behind a desk, but in the field, I was a complete sociologist.

From 2011 to 2015, I produced a large number of publications: including three books. I also received substantial research funding, a best paper award, and two women's leadership awards. In 2011, I earned tenure. I had attained my dream of being a faculty member. People call me many things, but the two that make me happiest are "Mom," and "Professor." I celebrated for an entire year with everyone I knew: colleagues, friends, family, and friends of family. It had been such a long adventure; it took me a while to adjust to the fact that I had made it.

But then, something felt off. It felt like something was missing. Things felt *too* easy. My sister told me I was not allowed to feel that way. I was accomplished: I should accept that and enjoy it. Friends told me that women sabotage themselves. I read about the dangers of imposter syndrome. Yet, as I watched my children enter their own graduate school experiences, I was plagued by the feeling that something was unfinished. I had left something undone.

I was drawn to social service websites that publish stories of children who are waiting for home placements. The foster family who took in my brother and me were not remarkable in any way other than their kindness and generosity. They already had six biological children of their own, including a son my brother's age and a daughter two years older than I; their youngest child was only two. We were a mess: young traumatized teenagers, the very least attractive demographic. Yet, they tossed us in with the mix and hardly seemed to notice a little bit more laundry and two extra places at the table. They made it look easy, but I know it could not have been. They gave us a stable and loving home. It is hard to find words to describe the difference between living with a family and being in institutional care. I can just say the difference is everything. They saved my life.

Buoyed by the promise of job security and in a stable marriage, I now had a little bit of extra money and a little bit of extra time. I reasoned that could provide for another child. I spoke to my partner, a virologist who works on vaccines. Devoted to his work above all else and traveling a good deal, he did not want more children, but he also did not want to stand in the way of something I felt was so important. He would join me, but from the beginning, there was that tacit understanding that often seems to accompany heterosexual marriages: children are the woman's responsibility. Only two months after filling out the application, we were offered the opportunity to adopt two young sisters. I was in my early 50s, old enough to be their grandmother.

I was not a parenting novice. I had grown children and had done most of the childcare for my stepchildren during the time they were with us. Over the years, I had cared for my friends' children and my children's friends. We had a foster daughter about a decade earlier who was ultimately reunited with her family. I thought I had achieved pretty close to expert status as a parent. Maybe not summa cum laude, but probably magna. I had seen things. I had been through puberty and adolescence with all of them. There had been bullies, dyslexia, drinking, depression, failed romances, failed courses, car crashes, college applications, and sports injuries. After all that, I thought I could manage two toddlers.

In retrospect, my naiveté is embarrassing and a little humiliating. My adopted daughters had experienced severe deprivation and witnessed violence. As neglected and traumatized children, they had profound delays in speech acquisition and in emotional modulation. But, they were so young, I thought, in a stable family home they would flourish in no time. They were immediately and intensely attached to me, as I was to them. It sounds trite, but as soon as I saw them, as soon as I held them, I knew I was their mother, and they seemed to know, too. There was no doubt in my mind that they were the source of the unfinished business that had dogged me. When they came to live with us, our family felt complete.

The transition was difficult. My daughters had never lived in a home with a family before. They had never eaten at a table or used a toilet. They were not used to shoes and clothes irritated them. They would run around turning on and off light switches and marveling that water came out of the sink. Starved for much of their lives, they had to be taught not to eat paper and other non-food items, and how not to hoard food in their pockets. Adults were not automatically viewed as benevolent. I remember how all the parents, myself included, at the suburban elementary school my older children attended would lecture about "stranger danger." Some adults cannot be trusted, we would warn, and, do not go home with anyone except me – not even a neighbor! They would look at us with bewilderment and disinterest. Like the turtles of the Galapagos, they thought the world would always be safe. My daughters knew that adults could be hurtful. They did not need any reminders: they were already afraid.

The girls were loving and joyful one moment and defiant and angry the next. They had experienced homelessness, neglect, hunger, and trauma that was so severe they had learned to navigate the world on their own and, at an inappropriately young age, assume responsibility for their day-to-day survival. The intervention of even the most well-meaning adults was met with deep ambivalence. Violent tantrums that included hurting themselves and their adult caretakers were part of every day.

Before my daughters had arrived, I had already lined up two childcare providers to care for them at home while I worked. The first one, who had two decades of experience in daycare centers, quit within hours. The second one, a retired Navy intelligence officer with four grown children of her own, lasted only several months. Ultimately, her employment ended when, one afternoon while caring for the girls, she was overcome by physical and emotional stress. She got in her car and drove away. Thank goodness, I was working from home at the time. We went through six nannies in six months.

Somehow, we muddled through spring semester. Despite adopting two children, I continued the same intense research productivity. In 2017, I applied for and was promoted to full professor, only the second woman in my department to attain this distinction. I celebrated this victory by committing to buy all the course books for the students in my all classes going forward, thereby eliminating one of the obstacles that had plagued me as an undergraduate. By this time, my spouse had taken a position in another state. I was back to juggling single parenting and professional work, but I still thought I had it made.

Though I had always been an outspoken advocate at my institution, as the only full professor with young children, it was my responsibility to help junior colleagues. As a member of the Faculty Senate, I already had a platform. One change that was long overdue was to offer parents and other caregivers the option of using research funds to cover caregiving obligations. In 2018, female political candidates had successfully advocated for the ability to use federal campaign funds to cover childcare and political candidates in my state were demanding the same (Leung 2018).

The first rule of organizing is never go it alone. I sent an email to all the faculty members I knew who had family obligations. After mentioning the changes in campaign finance laws, I argued that the same logic holds for the travel and research policies at our college. This would not mean asking the college to pay additional money to faculty members. It would only mean that funds *already allocated* to faculty members for the purpose of research and travel be allowed to pay for family related expenses that would enable faculty members to accomplish research goals. Our current policy had the accounts payable department interrogating faculty members about whether the meal or the grocery store receipt they had submitted had been used to just feed themselves or had they also fed their family members? In the latter case, the expense would not be reimbursed. I had a rental car bill rejected because it included the additional cost of a child's car seat.

Given the imperative to keep up research credentials and the cost of childcare and other family expenses, I argued, research travel proves a disproportionate burden on those who are primary caregivers, and in practice that means that more female faculty members are disadvantaged. Most parents of young children are early in their career and therefore especially vulnerable to both cost and publication pressures.

I circulated a petition asking faculty members if they would support a change in policy. Roughly one third of the faculty signed the petition and many vociferously supported the change during the subsequent discussion at the Senate meeting. Faculty members provided data on benchmark institutions that permitted research funds to be used for family expenses. Administrators resisted, and like so many reasonable requests, the idea was tabled. Over the next year, several faculty members and I continued to remind the administration of the proposed policy. In my experience, even when suggestions make sense and are budget neutral, institutional change requires patience and persistence.

With the advent of COVID-19, my fragile juggling act came crashing down. The bout of pneumonia from my graduate school years had left me with scarred lungs and meant I had an increased risk of complications from the coronavirus. School closures meant that I became the sole provider of childcare and educational instruction for my two daughters. My youngest had not even finished kindergarten. Before the pandemic, I was spending about 40 hours a week caring for my daughters. A dependable babysitter and after-school programs made it possible for me to continue working full-time. Once schools closed and my babysitter left to care for her granddaughter, I was clocking about 100 hours of childcare a week, while also teaching two classes a semester and trying to maintain my publication pipeline. As my institution struggled to re-open, my health vulnerability and my parental obligations made me a less attractive faculty member. The job security that informed many of my adult life decisions was in peril. The pandemic drove millions of women out of the paid labor force, and I vowed not to be one of them.

In the spring of 2020, the administration issued our new contracts with a disclaimer that the college could "adjust, revise, reduce or eliminate in whole or in part the terms and conditions of this appointment" based on the impact that COVID-19 might have on the budget. Panic spread through the faculty members and staff. We agonized over whether to sign the contract. We consulted with colleagues at comparable institutions, employment attorneys, and the American Association of University Professors. In the end, an outcry lead by senior faculty members, myself among them, caused the college to modify the language, and we agreed to sign the contracts. As of this writing, no faculty members have been cut, but given the health risks and the technological skills needed for remote work, some opted for early retirement. I was allowed to work remotely, but only after providing an American with Disabilities Form from my physician. More than half of our faculty taught on campus during the most intense periods of the pandemic. Research and travel funds were initially suspended completely, but as I write this in spring 2021, a portion has been restored. As the vaccine becomes available, we are planning to resume normal classes in the fall.

During this pandemic year, I have maintained my teaching responsibilities while also caring for and educating my daughters, both of whom continue to have profound behavioral issues and academic challenges. I am re-experiencing the same level of sleep deprivation I did in graduate school. It almost killed me then, but I have stayed well so far. Out of necessity, I set aside research that required travel. Given the dip in publications, I lost my research funding, and as a result, my teaching load will go up. The increase in teaching might well end my career as a researcher. That would be a devastating loss, but it is tempered when I remind myself that there are junior faculty members who need the time and research funds to start their careers, just as I did.

I have had a rich and fulfilling career as an academic who has been able to balance research, teaching, and parenting. My childhood experiences set the odds of graduating from college at less than 10%. Yet, I reached the highest academic rank despite being a non-conformist in the classroom, in my research, and in my personal life. I went into academia with the conviction that I would not compromise my professional integrity or diminish my commitment to being an involved parent. Because I have had some rough patches myself, I recognize desperation in the faces of hungry students and exhaustion in the eyes of junior faculty members juggling the demands of publishing and parenting. I do not consider myself to be especially nurturing and I am certainly not soft or overly sentimental, but I know that we are all one helping hand away from falling down or burning out. I have benefitted immeasurably from the generous acts of others, and I want to give that generosity back to my children, my students, and my colleagues. After 20 years, four children, three marriages, one pandemic, myriad conference presentations, numerous publications, and over 3000 students, I am still counting.

References

Chisholm, S., et al. (1999). A Study of the Status of Women Faculty in Science at MIT: How a Committee on Women Faculty came to be established by the Dean of the School of Science what the Committee and the Dean learned and accomplished, and recommendations for the future. Massachusetts Institute of Technology.

Fostering Success in Education: National Factsheet on the Educational Outcomes of Children in Foster Care. (2014). https://cdn.fc2success.org/wp-content/uploads/2012/05/National-Fact-Sheet-on-the-Educational-Outcomes-of-Children-in-Foster-Care-Jan-2014.pdf. Accessed 12 Feb 2021.

Leung, S. (2018). "Mass Political Candidates Can Expense a Tuxedo, But Not Child Care. That Need to Change," *Boston Globe*. July 12, 2018. https://www.bostonglobe.com/business/other/2018/07/12/state-law-allows-political-candidates-expense-tuxedo-but-not-child-care-that-needs-change/4xqAzbURNRKPd1HuJWAG6L/story.html. Accessed 3 January 2021.

Mason, M., Wolfinger, N. and Goulden. M. (2013). *Do Babies Matter: Gender and Family in the Ivory Tower*. New Brunswick, NJ: Rutgers University Press.

Perales, F. and Baxter, J. (2018). "Sexual Identity and Relationship Quality in Australia and the United Kingdom," *Family Relations*. (February 2018). 55–69.

Schüssler Fiorenza, E. (2009). "Introduction: Exploring the Intersections of Race, Gender, Status and Ethnicity in Early Christian Studies". In Nasrallah, S.L., Schüssler Fiorenza, E. (eds.). *Prejudice and Christian Beginnings: Investigating Race, Gender, and Ethnicity in Early Christian Studies*. Minneapolis: Fortress Press, 1–23.

Steele, J. R. (2019). "'In the Little World': Breaking Virginia's Foster-Care-to-Prison Pipeline Using Restorative Justice." *University of Richmond Law Review*, 54(1), 313–vi.

West, C. and Zimmerman, D. H. (2009). "Accounting for Doing Gender." *Gender & Society*, 23, 112–122.

El Zein, A., Shelnutt, K.P., Colby, S., Vilaro, M.J., Zhou, W., Greene, G., Olfert, M.D., Riggsbee, K., Morrell, J.S., Mathews, A.E. (2019). "Prevalence and Correlates of Food Insecurity among U.S. College Students: A Multi-Institutional Study." *BMC Public Health*, 19(1), 660.

THE MOM ACADEMIC (FRAGMENTATION)

Elizabeth Siler

When I was working on the proposal for this chapter, I contemplated a thousand different phrases to make sense of my life: the knitting academic; my career as a mosaic, a pastiche, an archive, a collage. The unlicensed social worker. The drowning academic, in blood and amniotic fluid, in paper and ink and toner, in my own emotions crying back in response to my students' pain. The "Biblical gardener" academic, sowing seeds that will grow or wither or be carried by the wind or eaten by birds and planted elsewhere. The good teacher. The hidden rebel, inserting critical theories into the invisible spaces between Student Learning Outcomes. The academic mystic, who knows that teaching and writing is my calling, so that in the face of frustration and doubt and inadequacy, I take a deep breath and remember, yes, I am doing exactly what I am supposed to be doing, and I become calm.

Texting a philosopher friend, the night before the proposal was due, tossing metaphors back and forth between time zones, while semi-watching *How to Train Your Dragon 3: The Hidden World* and eating cake and pizza in front of the TV because it is my only child's 8th birthday in the middle of a pandemic and he hasn't seen anyone his age in nearly four months, so of course this is what we do to attempt to compensate, and feeling guilty that I am working on his birthday and feeling guilty that I am enjoying the intellectual game far more than the movie and… and then my friend says, "Mom academic is a metaphor too, for that matter. This conversation is an example. You are with your child, and he is unconcerned, yet the guilt hit and the 'casual' means of conversation kind of work," and he is right. This is my academic life, my mom life.

Mom academic as in I never feel adequate, never get to quite finish anything, yet I am a good writer and good teacher and good colleague and good employee. Because how can a person ever feel adequate to the responsibility that is another person's life? You can't; you can only keep your kid intact and alive and mostly content. How can an academic ever feel adequate, when learning is infinite and writing can always be better?

Seatack

It is the mid-1970s. It is Friday afternoon happy hour, week after week. I am 5, 6, 7, 8, years old. I sit at the kitchen table, listening to my mom talk with her best friend and co-worker.

They (we) are white. They teach third grade at what had been a Black public school until 1971; it was the last to be integrated in our Southern American city. They do not mention who is Black and who is white, but I know, because the people they talk about have been to our house, and I have been to school with my mother.

They gossip and complain: about the other teachers, the administrators, the students. I learn that there are amazing principals and horrible ones. I learn that one principal is unpopular because she demands that everyone do good work and follow the rules. (My mother has no sympathy for that view.) I learn that teachers are people, imperfect, and with lives outside of their classrooms. In my own school, because of this learning, I neither fear nor revere my teachers. I learn through listening and through experience that there is good teaching and bad teaching, and, occasionally, bad teachers.

Week after week, I listen, hard, pulling in their words like they are my beloved storybooks, like they are food. I drink up the emotions and the complexities. I love knowing things that other people do not.

Week after week, I stay silent and try not to eat all the snacks. I want my mom and her friend to be able to pretend to forget I am there, so they will speak freely, so they will let me stay. I prefer listening in the kitchen to playing with the kids in the other room. I like the feeling that I understand these very grown-up conversations. I like the feeling that the adults let me listen, that they trust me to not repeat their words.

They talk about being forced to stop teaching, windows open in the unairconditioned classrooms, when the Navy planes fly overhead. They half-laugh at one teacher's imaginary plan to put a giant "GO ARMY" sign on the building's roof. My mom tells a story of a very young boy, trying to learn basic math, who said, with no self-pity, "it was my brother's turn to eat today."

Looking back, I see my fascination with people and organizations from the very beginning.

I learned, without knowing it, that organizations get better or worse because of the people who make them up. I learned, without knowing it, that people in organizations suffer because of external circumstances beyond their control. I learned, without knowing it, that externalities matter for learning: students who are hungry can't learn.

Portrait

At first, when I thought of writing this chapter, a portrait of myself and my career, I thought of a "snapshot"—a description of a moment (a day? An hour? A semester? A year?) in my academic life, a glimpse of "now," of the way my working looks now, in this place and time. Snapshots, photographs, portraits—they are all pictures of people in the "now" when they were made.

I've spent the months since March of 2020 working in a room that was never meant to be an office, never meant for work, even though a wall is lined with books. It is a room where a portrait, an oil painting, hangs on the wall. A girl wearing a red dress stands by a chair, one hand on her spaniel's head as it reaches toward the biscuit she holds in her other hand. She looks over my shoulder while I type or video conference. When I read, or knit, or collapse in a chair across the room, I sit facing her.

The portrait is not a "snapshot." It is so much more than a moment in her young life. It took time to paint, layering on and letting dry, building up over days. It is a means of time travel, a document of hair and clothing styles, of textile and furniture design, of the status of pets. It connects generations of my husband's family—I can see his niece in the girl's face, in her eyes and lips, in her coloring. It is of course unique, but its details are general enough to tell you its time and place of origin, and the name of the artist, if you have the skill and context to interpret them.

The portrait has people in it that you can't see, but who are there nonetheless: the painter, of course, who made the work. The child's mother, who gestated and birthed and raised her. The child's father, whose business was prosperous enough that he could afford to commission this painting. The people whose work enabled the father's business to be so prosperous. The artisans who wove the carpet, who dyed the fibers, who built and upholstered the chair. The seamstress who made the red dress and the white leggings.

I write about this other, older, physical portrait because it helps me make sense of the irresistible urge to go backward in time, as I write this portrait of myself.

If I am writing about "doing careers differently," with, I suppose, the purpose of being an example of how to do this job in a different way, how on earth is it helpful to write about my childhood, when anyone reading this is already far beyond their own childhood? It is not as if you, reader, can go back and find different parents.

At times, I have been envious when I've heard people tell their stories of how they came to be here, now, at the time of the telling. Their lives seem to be clear-cut and linear: first this, then that, from one thing to the next. Their journeys, even when the stories include detours, seem inevitable. Many of these stories begin when their tellers were extraordinarily young, when tiny humans have so little agency that those necessary, formative childhood events were caused by their parents. "I started figure skating at age 4," an Olympic skater might say, and tell a funny story that has been repeated by their parents.

Hearing those stories felt frustrating, because I could not go back and begin again; because I didn't have a "passion" from birth until eternity.

We don't hear the stories of the other 4-year-olds, also skating at age four, with their own cute anecdotes. These are the youngest children, dragged along because there was no child care, and thrown onto the ice as soon as they could walk, performing next to older siblings and parents and grandparents. These are the children who lost interest in skating by age 12, moved their attention and time to working off the ice, to painting sets and building props, and who look back with no regret that they, too, are not Olympic skaters. These are the children who grew up to be adults with successful lives and careers despite their "late" introduction to their areas of expertise. We don't hear those stories, but they are everywhere.

In one way of reading and writing, my career was inevitable. If I choose to write about only the moments that seem the most directly relevant, if you choose to ignore the moments I left out. These moments are the layers, they are the people and experiences that you can't see in the "now" of my career, but who are present in it nonetheless. Without them, or with other people, my career today would be different.

That feeling of linearity, of an obvious sequence of steps, and the confidence that comes from such a solid and seamless narrative, that is what I envied in other stories. But what happens to that inevitability if I confess that it wasn't until writing this chapter that I saw any connection between those Friday afternoons and my work in the field of management and organization studies?

Finding my way to this career was not inevitable, of course. The stories here, and the ones that are not here, could have been the foundation for an infinite number of other possible futures.

The lie

My journey toward an academic life teaching management courses began with a lie. "Oh, I'm planning to go get my MBA someday," I would say when asked, with absolutely no intention of doing any such thing. I would, I was sure, return to the world of non-profit arts organizations, perhaps somewhere more glamorous, or at least doing work that I could understand and enjoy, for its own sake.

When I told this lie, I was working as an executive secretary, a job that did not require my degree in English with a concentration in comparative literature (medieval Italian), but that did require a typing test. I worked for a Vice President at the headquarters of an international financial services corporation, and while I was there, I read and watched and listened and learned.

I read my boss's copies of the *Wall Street Journal*, of *Harvard Business Review*, of trade journals, after they were delivered to my desk and before I placed them on his. I learned about our industry; I learned that business is like a big puzzle to solve, with lots of ways to get the right answer. I learned about power: the power of my boss's position, which brought instant compliance even when it probably should not have; the power of the relationships I developed on my own; the power of just being friendly and polite to people who I now can see were probably often ignored. I learned about breaking promises and avoiding conflict. I learned that people can be so isolated and sure of their beliefs that their only reaction to something different was to denigrate it.

I watched the organization's culture change as a response to an economic downturn that destroyed the industry's financial complacency. I watched it change from the kind of country club that welcomes the whole family to the kind that is mainly for the benefit of the high-ranking men, in exchange for longer hours and more acceptance of harshness disguised as quality. I learned that people can be blamed, fired, and ridiculed for circumstances completely out of their control. I learned about (broken) psychological contracts, and so very many ways to ignore the humanity of the people whose work enables the business to function at all.

And then, because I was bored and had perhaps listened to my own lie too long, I enrolled in a part-time MBA program, at night. It advertised itself as an MBA for women who want to work in arts or other non-profit organizations, and I was hooked. I read the thorough marketing materials over and over, reading the course titles with words like "strategy" and "communication" and "change," with such a strong desire to learn about these things and change the world! (Looking back, being excited about the courses may have been a hint that school was a good place for me.) I read the profiles illustrated with black-and-white photos of successful alumnae and imagined myself in their stories: a senior officer at an international bank (doing what? I had no idea), an entrepreneur who renovated beautiful and historic houses. (Does redecorating the kitchen of my 1987 house count as renovating a historic and beautiful house? No, actually, it does not.)

During the three years of part-time coursework in the evenings, I was fired from my job, and found a position as research and teaching assistant to two professors who taught only undergraduate management courses. The assistantship paid less than a full-time job, so I borrowed money for tuition and living expenses because, I thought at the time, it won't matter! I am never going back to school again, so this debt really won't matter in the long run, especially once I find my high-paying dream job. At least this time, my inaccurate prediction wasn't a lie! I added six years of school and $100,000 of debt before I finished my doctorate.

What I write (Virginia Woolf was right)

At the time of writing this chapter, I am a tenured full professor, and I have published exactly one article in a peer-reviewed academic publication. As unusual as that may seem, these two facts exist at the same time. Please don't assume that I dislike writing and doing research; I love that part of being a professor. This absence of published work is not caused by a lack of ability, or a lack of ideas, or a lack of motivation (whatever that means). It is definitely not caused by a lack of suggestions by other people about how to write more.

One semester, I followed all the "how to make yourself write" advice. "Prioritize your writing." "Develop the habit." "Have an accountability buddy." "Set yourself up for success." "Protect that time." "You don't need hours of uninterrupted time to write, if you do it every day!" "Write first thing in the morning!" I recruited a friend. She came to my office before going to her own, so that we could sit and write, in parallel, three mornings a week for just 30 minutes. I even closed the office door and covered the window, so no one would interrupt us.

It should have worked.

It didn't.

I would like to say that we didn't blame ourselves for "failing," but we did. Of course we did—everything I'd read said that if I could just take *this* advice, I'd be a consistently productive writer. It turns out that the ability to set aside time for writing is not the problem. It was not, and is not, a lack of self-discipline, or "time management," or "prioritizing." Instead of writing, we talked. We talked about ideas that inspired us, and an interdisciplinary course we were planning to develop and teach together. But most of the time we talked about the weight of our work, the ridiculously heavy emotional and intellectual labor that is our teaching and advising. We talked as a way to legitimize and validate our own experiences of just how exhausting it is to do work that requires so much emotional and personal effort. At the time, we wouldn't have used these words to describe what we were doing. It felt inevitable and like something to apologize for at the same time. We apologized to each other during these conversations for doing things that weren't writing, and yet when we talked it was the most important thing we could have done at that moment.

This is what I write.

I write policies: my late work policy; my end-of-semester missing work policies, for courses with and without a major final project; the computer programs that students can use to submit work or else I cannot read it; the places to go on campus if you need help with writing or a disability or library research or counseling. I write my course values (writing, being present, learning from each other, transparency). I write student learning outcomes.

I write assignment instructions, revisions of assignment instructions, adaptations of assignment instructions, examples of assignments, annotations to the examples of assignments. I write these because my students have a very difficult time following instructions. I write them because of tacit knowledge (Polanyi) and habitus (Bourdieu).

I write discussion board prompts, "Welcome!" responses to every single student in the "introduce yourself" discussion boards, no matter how bare-bones the student's post was. I write calendars for my courses.

I write self-test questions with cheerful, informative feedback on incorrect answers, and upbeat, congratulatory words (with exclamation points) for correct answers.

I write major assignment rubrics, low-stakes assignment rubrics, discussion board rubrics. I write these not because they help students (they might) or fend off questions (meh); I write them because they make my grading faster and more consistent. I write low-stakes, in-class, small-group activity instructions; low-stakes, in-class, small-group activity content; low-stakes, in-class, small-group activity examples. I write the answers I expect students to get from doing these activities, and I write why they should care about doing these activities to actively engage, because so many of them would prefer a nice, easy, transactional relationship with school. It's not until years later, when they have been working at non-internship jobs, with people who are different from them, that they say, "wow, Professor Siler's class was one of the most important ones I took!"

I write out-of-office autoreply messages for summer, explaining that faculty are on a nine-month contract and listing resources for students who might be in touch over the summer, in a way that is polite and accurate while also indirect, because saying, "I don't get paid for answering student email in the summer" sounds as if I don't care about my students enough to answer their questions year-round. I write out-of-office autoreply messages for between-semester breaks, explaining why I may not answer student emails immediately, because I am no longer allowed to be "off the clock" on days or weeks when the university is open and classes are not in session. Sometimes, I write out-of-office autoreply messages for long weekends, explaining to students that it is a weekend, and I will write back on Tuesday.

I write documents for research proposals for my university's human subjects review board: consent forms, debriefing forms, interview questions, survey questions. I write course proposals, and program proposals; I write comments on and questions about course proposals and program proposals and policy proposals. I write research proposals and tiny grant proposals and book chapter proposals.

I write recommendation letters on behalf of the university-wide faculty committee on tenure.

I write conference papers, conference presentation proposals, conference PDW proposals, conference PowerPoints, conference handouts, conference paper reviews, conference symposia proposal reviews, conference caucus proposals, conference stream proposals. I write reviews of conference papers, reviews of conference workshop proposals, reviews of submissions to academic journals.

I write emails giving students permission to follow the course policy and turn in their work late. I write emails to students saying, "Thank you for staying home when you are sick! Of course you can turn in your work after you feel better!" (I have been writing this for my entire teaching career; being ill is not something to apologize for.) I write emails to students explaining the unwritten exceptions to our university policies, and opportunities to appeal missed deadlines related to those policies. (Bourdieu, again; this time making visible to my students the unwritten institutional rules based middle-class values, which are not the same values and rules my students learned in their families and communities.)

I write emails to our registrar asking for grade changes, authorizing exceptions, asking for a manual override be applied to the single aspect of one course that our antiquated computer system does not allow to happen automatically.

I write polite email responses to student emails that begin, "Hi Elizabeth!" from students who have either not watched or chosen to ignore my "welcome video" that, among other things, explains all the choices for addressing me. Those choices do not include "Elizabeth."

I write emails to students, referring them to Counseling Services. I write emails to students, referring them to Counseling Services and to the Title IX office (the one that handles the logistical and legal aspects of sexual discrimination, harassment, and abuse) because their boyfriends are stalking them. I write emails to students whose parents are dying. I write emails to students after their parents have died from natural causes. I write emails to students after their parents have died by violence. I write emails to students after their parents or friends have died by suicide.

This is writing.

It is invisible. It is not valued. It is, for the most part, not counted. But it is writing. It is the same work, whether for email or a journal paper. It is putting together *these* words in *this* order for a particular purpose. So, my writing comes last, when it comes at all, not because of any failure on my part. It comes last because all of all the writing-that-is-not-writing, is exhausting.

Fragmentation

I work at Worcester State University, a former state teachers college, in the center of Massachusetts, 50 miles from Boston. I work in the Business Administration and Economics Department in the School of Humanities and Social Sciences. We do not have a separate school of business. We offer a Master of Science in Management. We do not offer an MBA. We do not have doctoral programs at any of the state universities. We do not have large lecture classes, and we do not have graduate (or any) teaching assistants/assistance. Tenure-track faculty in all departments are free to take whatever theoretical approach to whatever research topics they choose, and "unpublished" research counts toward tenure.

Worcester State is what is called a "teaching school," which I write in quotation marks because it seems redundant. Aren't all schools for teaching, by definition? And yet, when discussing teaching loads with colleagues at conferences, I've been met with expressions of astonishment and pity, at the revelation that I teach four undergraduate classes each semester, as if somehow this work is nothing more than a burden, a barrier that prevents me from doing the "real" academic work of writing.

These are some of the ideas that I teach: that, not only is it 100% legal in the US to talk about pay, but that secrecy about pay only helps the people who are paying the salaries, not the ones who are earning those salaries. That people make the rules, so people can change them. That, when they are in charge, they can make their organizations better. That bodies don't get in the way of work; bodies are what enable us to do work at all.

Most semesters, I teach four undergraduate courses, which is 12 hours in the classroom, over 15 weeks. Those four courses are almost always three different preparations. Sometimes, I teach a fifth course in the evening division (for extra pay); usually, this duplicates one of my day courses. Each course has between 20 and 32 students, so most semesters I teach 80–100 or more students. I learn their names.

I hold three office hours spread over at least two different days, per our union contract. If I stack my courses on three days (three classes twice a week, and one class on the third day), then I am too exhausted to do anything else on those days. If I stack my courses over four days, I am less exhausted from teaching, but I am present in the office more days per week, with all that entails.

In addition to teaching, these are other normal demands on my time: recurring monthly meetings: union, department, at least one and sometimes several committees (governance, advisory boards, accreditation), what-are-my-colleagues working on presentations. One-off training seminars: how to teach better, how to follow Title IX regulations correctly, how to help prevent student suicide. One-off but long events: at least three teaching demonstrations for each position we are trying to fill, if I'm not on the committee; many, many more hours and meetings and phone interviews, if I am on the search committee.

Each semester, there are two scheduled weeks (which stretch into four) of academic advising for preregistration, during which I have at least 40 and up to 60 meetings of 15+ minutes each. In these meetings, I am expected to help students choose courses for the following semester, which includes supplementing the antiquated computer system's information with information that is invisible to the students. I am also expected, during these 15 minutes, to become a mentor to students, even if I have never seen them before and never will again, in contrast to the ones I see all the time during classes.

This list excludes any writing or reading to prepare for any of these events; it excludes course preparation time, lunch, and just being human and talking to my co-workers.

This is how my time is fragmented. It's actually not so awful in terms of spoken-for time; a "regular" (non-academic) job would also have many hours a week committed to working with and meeting with other people. It isn't the committed time on its own. It's the mental and emotional effort that most of these commitments require.

The difficult part, the exhausting part, is that good writing, and good teaching, like good parenting, requires giving of yourself. It requires showing up, and paying attention. It requires finding words that are age-appropriate and emotionally appropriate to express whatever it is that needs saying. It requires being present, and finding and enforcing boundaries. Over and over during the pandemic, when reading about student mental health or how to teach effectively through crises and asynchronously and over Zoom, the same basic message came back: it's about the relationships. And that is true regardless of the state of international epidemiology.

Mom academic

"Mom academic" as a characterization of my career works, in that I literally do both at the same time. The cognitive load of parenting a small child is often low enough that I can work in my thoughts and be present for my child at the same time, and it is enough. In that there really is no substitute for me and my presence—to have someone take over my mom duties and my class duties if I could not do them would be possible, but my classes and my child would become something else, something different, in my absence.

"Mom academic" because so much academic work is care work, like that of a mom. I say "mom" rather than "parent" or "mother" intentionally, because care work is gendered, and because academic care work is casual, by which I mean implicitly required or expected, but not formally acknowledged. Because academic care work depends on my own performative caring, regardless of my actual emotions—the inverse of the love that I feel for my son, which over and over, again and again surprises me in its magnitude and intensity.

"Mom academic" as a metaphor works, in that everything else comes before writing, even though writing is the thing that keeps my sanity and my sense of self. I squeeze it in just before deadlines and stay up late because that's when it's quiet. Everything comes before writing, the way that for moms everything comes before "taking care of yourself." I work during movies because my kid needs my presence and I want to be there. My physical presence is more than enough. I take a deep breath and remember that I am good at my work and I am right where I am supposed to be, and when I do that, I become calm. Ignoring the movie, texting a friend and writing a proposal, I take a deep breath and remember that the most important thing is taking care of him, and that when I do that, I become calm.

V
The hall of mirrors
Curated by Sarah Robinson

MIRRORING ACADEMIA

Reflections from a hall of mirrors[1]

Sarah Robinson

Take a peek through the flap in the red and yellow striped canvas and you will be entranced by the fairground attraction that is the Hall of Mirrors. The air is heavy with the smell of burnt sugar and punctuated by the chatter of excitement, laughter and shrieks of horror. Don't be afraid to enter, bring your toffee apples and candy floss, and be prepared to get lost in a maze of long and short, fat and thin distorting mirrors… by each twist and turn you bump into a different you… will you recognise your reflection?

But mirrors do more than distort, they reflect, giving you the chance to adjust your clothing and correct your make up, removing anything which might be unseemly and thus honing the image you wish to present to the world. They encourage compliance to standardised appearance norms but also provoke change… as a wakeup call as to how much you have conformed, become jaded, to how tired you are and how Gollum-like hunched you have become after the long stints of Covid homeworking. But remember, it's just a mirror image, far from the embodied experience of yourself – unless of course, you play creatively with mirrors to arrive at the 'real' you as others see you!

Mirrors also diffract, spreading the light around obstacles and corners, and refract (causing rainbows); they can be written on (in lipstick) as parting shots or billets-doux, plastered with motivational sayings or engraved by with a diamond for eternity. Mirrors can cause fire, they can magnify, they can crack and shatter (seven years bad luck!) causing multiple images, and 'through a glass darkly', they can produce an imperfect or distorted vision, becoming a conduit into the dark side. Mirrors don't lie – remember 'mirror, mirror on the wall…' – or do they? Like reviewers, they might tell you things you don't want to hear/see and distort the 'truth'? Are mirrors doing nothing but lying? Approach with caution and choose carefully which you look into – now you see me, now you don't!

Unlike the other galleries, the 'portraits' here are reflections from mirrors, which with their different frames, shapes and sizes are in themselves works of art. I have selected six reflections on and of academic life for you to gaze into and form your own reflections.

The 'reflections' I have chosen in this gallery show the tensions and dilemmas of academic life, they reflect on the paths taken and those not (yet) pursued. They show how mirroring an ideal academic type is expected, how the profession is being reflected back as homogenous – and yet personal struggles can bravely shatter such normalising images. The resulting shards show alternative career structures and possibilities for those whose image does not reflect such norms. These portraits also mirror different ways of reflection: there are poetic and artistic reflections, autoethnography and diarising. There are reflections on the diffraction of the disruptive effects of the Covid era and the fears of that period, and of the normative effects of the neoliberal university. Visions of others are reflected as role models that can diffuse the light of hope and inspiration, like glittering confetti, for others, while perhaps the choice of subjects also reflects the values and orientations of the portraitists themselves?

The role of mirrors in thinking about the tensions of academic life is beautifully illustrated in the miniature portrait you will find in the entrance: *Reflections, distortions – the mirrored academic* by Victoria Pagan. This shows how an academic career can be reflected in an embodied way by academic mirrors showing: 'both smooth images and some of the tensions and distortions that may not always be foregrounded'. Placing emphasis on the continuing challenges of paradoxes and contradictions within academic careers, particularly around the themes of publishing, promotion and teaching, Victoria intriguingly suggests ways of doing academic careers differently through 'cultivating the shadows'.

Following the contradictions and tensions of academic identities please, dear visitor, tread gently as you will find under your feet a shattered mirror reflecting multiple academic identities and challenges which is the thought-provoking collective reflection by the self-proclaimed 'Academic Misfits', namely: Magnus Hoppe, Anton Hasselgren, Fatemeh Seifan, Steffi Siegert and Serdar Temiz. They pose the fundamental question: what makes an academic? Is it vocation and work style preferences or socioeconomic privilege and racial profile? And, they ask how (and if), are the received images of academics changing? Through shards of broken mirrors, they encourage viewers to look at a group of misfits that are 'the odd one out' in most academic contexts that defy common classifications. Raising issues of prejudice within the academy relating to race, ethnicity, sex or social economic class, they break the academic mirror but hope and continuity is diffracted across the shards creating a 'misfitting family' to which they 'hold on for dear life'.

Look up from the shards and you will find a delicately painted miniature: *Becoming a (never) good enough critical scholar? On precarious academic subjectification processes* by Mie Plotnikok, which continues the themes of normalisation and subjectivation in academia, focussing on the specific example of Critical Management Studies. Using an autobiographical approach, Mie discusses becoming 'a (never) good enough critical scholar', reflecting on precarious identity, body and writing work performativity in relation to her academic subject positionings and career path. In so doing she engages with ongoing debates about academic subjectivity, power, and writing differently, as resources with which to think of and challenge subjectification processes of academics dominated by certain ideals of critical scholarship.

Moving from being 'never good enough' to 'being never-complete', you will find the colourful and beautifully illustrated full portrait: *The Art of Being a Reflexive Academic: Painting a never-complete self-portrait* by Russ Vince. Russ illustrates how, through a process of writing and painting in his reflexive journal, the subject of the portrait notices and creates the lived experience of his role. The portrait captures layers of experience over time that inform and disturb his contributions to knowledge and to pedagogy. This is 'a never-complete self-portrait' constructed from images and words of an ongoing academic career. Russ generously shares his art of reflection in which experience is painted as a way of understanding and transforming. He presents his reflexive journal as a medium for thought, imagination, emotion and connection and in so doing explores the process of being an academic as 'creative understanding in the making'.

Continuing creative arts-based reflection, Friederike Landau-Donnelly's evocative miniature: *The Poetic Academic* gives poignant insight into the manifold struggles that academics encounter while writing. Written against the backdrop of the first Covid-19 lockdown in early 2020, her poetic approach surfaces lingering questions of how, when and why to write academically and repeatedly 'strays' into poetic explorations of how concerns for necessity, rigor, motivation, urgency and solidarity were reshuffled vis-à-vis the pandemic. You will see reflected in this portrait the acute struggle, and different bodily and mental states of 'wanting to write, wanting to write differently, wanting to lie down, wanting to travel, move, move on from lockdown mode'. Friederike interweaves a critical reflection on the partially narrow silos of knowledge production via journal articles, and the desire to stay relevant in the face of global meltdowns producing 'a medley of irritation and inspiration, hoping to advocate for a mindset of being [un]grounded as a means of staying afloat amidst the challenges academia articulates from within'.

The final portrait in this gallery is in fact a double one: *I am you, as you are me: Academic lives as a mirror of ourselves* by Oscar Javier Montiel Méndez, Duncan Pelly and Araceli Almaraz. Here the long careers of two academics from very different backgrounds sit side by side, lovingly painted by their friends and former students. Drawing on in-depth interviews with José Manuel Valenzuela and David M. Boje, from Mexico and the USA respectively, the double portrait reflects how both academics have progressed differently from the standard career routes within their national contexts, reflecting their relationship to academic and social norms. Both have found ways of mixing social activism, beliefs about society, and research values through taking risks and overcoming challenges. They are painted as creatives and warriors from which the authors have taken much inspiration in the development of their own careers and so in gratitude offer this dual portrait as inspiration to others that any individual no matter their background, or age, can learn from their experiences, and follow their examples.

With that, the Hall of Mirrors is complete and is ready for you to explore at your leisure and for your pleasure. Take your time to engage individually or collectively with the images reflected back at you, to laugh and cry at distortions, to heed the warning signs and to delight in the diffusions. Catch some confetti, follow the rainbows and enjoy indulging yourself in toffee apples and candy floss!

Note

1 I would like to thank Hall of Mirrors' authors for ideas, suggestions and corrections on the earlier draft of this introduction.

REFLECTIONS, DISTORTIONS – THE MIRRORED ACADEMIC

Victoria Pagan

At this point ten years into my research-active business school academic career I am acutely aware of the trappings that I carry, not seen as material pieces on my body but as embedded/embodied within me. I can be perceived as 'successful' but on what mis/representation may this based? To what extent am I doing my academic career differently or perpetuating dominant norms? Perhaps practising difference and practising norms are not mutually exclusive, but what is of more (arguably most) importance is which practices are of most interest and existential impact – the focus of this piece. While the challenges of academic organisation and the elements associated with careers therein are well-documented, doing my academic career differently means highly personalising the implications. It means confronting the practices not willingly seen, those of which I am ashamed, that demonstrate hypocrisy, contradiction, performances, inauthenticity. It is this confrontation that the hall of mirrors brings into being and the purpose of this is to demonstrate that many of the accepted norms are contributing to a toxic work environment and ought to be eradicated (e.g. Jabbar et al., 2018; Dar et al., 2021; Savigny, 2019). It recognises my place in perpetuating these norms and calls to action to do better by doing differently.

In my mind, the hall of mirrors is a room in academia that forces self-reflection and a transparency of haunting, veiled, backgrounded, unspoken practices. The mirrors are transparency devices (Flyverbom et al., 2015) that work to show illustrations of uncomfortable elements of an academic career. As I slowly move, I look at how my different practices and crafts of being an academic are reflected. From the moment I walk in, I am confronted by images. The walls, floor, and ceiling are all mirrors, showing the academic parts of myself from all angles and projections. The room itself features dividing panels to create a maze-like pattern through which I move tentatively, at times with clarity and at times with some confusion. The indistinct edges of the mirrors create a fluidity of movement that reveal images differently, quickly, and dynamically as if simultaneously. The room has light and shade that also both foreground and obscure different parts and whole images reflected in the mirrors depending on the position of the viewer. The hall offers an opportunity to explore glimpses of events that are dislocated from the time and space in which they happened, like memories, in order to understand something more about their significance (Davis, 2007).

In this hall, some mirrors are flat, some are curved, some have a crazed surface, some show fractures. There are glimpses of people holding some of the mirrors, these are composite impressions of those with whom I have worked throughout my career to date. To varying extents, they are all those whose influence has played a part in the construction of my academic career. Each mirror from the multitude shows me at my most flat, distorted, crazed, fractured. While the flat glasses show the deliberately ordered presentation of an academic career, the variety of other images, like ghosts, disturb this and temporarily blur the separation of norms and alternatives (Davis, 2007). There is a coalescence of the misshapen and the transparent in the mirrors, they offer a degree of indistinctness, with both clarity and ambiguity at the same time (Birchall, 2011). In the hall of mirrors, I play with my hypocrisy through deliberate stillness, strategic questioning, the mirrors show me thinking and doing academic practice in both mainstream and marginal ways.

The flat, even-faced mirrors show the standard elements of an academic career, those that conform to received wisdom and expectations in the ways that I perform them. These mirrors are designed, positioned, and held by some senior colleagues whose careers have simultaneously built and been built from the mainstream expectations of business school academia. As a first example, in one such mirror, a published article is shown – a 'good' one as judged by the holy book of UK business school research, colloquially known as the ABS list, that ranks journal quality from 4★ to 1★. On the smooth face of it, this is 'good' for my academic career, I fall into line, I fulfil the expectation of being a 'good' academic. The work is judged 'good' by colleagues echoing those holding the mirror, it will make me 'REF-able', a further measure on the academic career ladder. A second example of another smooth mirror surface shows my job promotion through the exercises of engagement, management and leadership roles. This includes the delivery of strategic work in relation to equality, diversity and inclusion, women in leadership, research culture, and quality in teaching and learning. This links to the third example even-faced mirror, which shows my engagement with students in teaching and scholarship, helping them connect their studies with their future employment, promoting a business school education, celebrating successes on LinkedIn – performing the most common understanding of a business school academic. Those holding these mirrors celebrate these practices as they show me playing by the existing, accepted, comfortable rules of the academic game.

Simultaneously, as I and the light and shade move through the hall, other mirrors show the processes of academic careers that are often shaded, screened, not captured in the flat surfaces despite them being the same practice examples as above. These mirrors are also designed, positioned and held by colleagues – but by those who are doing their academic careers differently. Nevertheless, each offers an authentic image, some of which are uncomfortable to see. They are a source of inspiration and change towards admitting my shadows and using this to cultivate different, better academia. With regard to the first example above, a curved mirror shows the experience leading up to the publication of my 'good', ABS-rated article. In its distortion, the uncomfortable contradictions are presented, this one showing the initial feeling of flattery verging on hubris at being asked for my input to its production. A crazed mirror reflects my unseemly pleasure in the strategic gain of being part of a REF-able submission prioritised over any sense of belief in the research. A fractured mirror shows my lack of belief in the argument and theoretical position of the article despite its career advantages.

The light moves to shade these but in doing so casts itself on another set of warped surfaces, revealing elements of the second example above, my career progression not shown in the flat mirror. An asymmetric mirror shows the unevenness of my deservingness in a system full of inequities. A notched mirror showing the ways in which I manipulated the presentation of my practices to fit the criteria. A broken mirror showing the dissonance of feeling grateful for the promotion while feeling under such pressure from the work it entails. A final corner turns, the light shifts again, and the next of mirrors show other elements of the third example above, my engagement with students in their teaching and scholarship. A patchy mirror showing my frustration at the commodification of education, while bending over backwards for student approval. A buckled mirror showing my cynicism of graduate schemes and the assessment centres that they seem so pressured to apply to, a cracked mirror showing my anger at their unrealistic demands and expectations of their university experience. All of these distorted mirrors are held by those who show that I am playing superficially by the current rules to a degree of self-interest, but that by centring the disturbance the rules could be changed and academic careers could be constituted by different, more equitable, values. Gordon (2008: 205) describes this as "profane illumination", that "it is telling us something important we had not known; because it is leading us somewhere, or elsewhere". These colleagues show this in practice – they have done/are doing their academic careers differently and they are 'successful'.

In my academic practice, I may veil and unveil to allow for different elements of my work to be revealed or hidden. This may be deliberate or unintentional but the mirrors do not distinguish. Where premeditated, in selecting what I foreground or background, there could be "an implicit association between invisibility and malevolence" (Cruz, 2017: 619), that is, there is hypocrisy in my desire towards challenging norms yet my complicity in actions within them. I practise the pretence of following the publicly approved academic career rules, and this practice is crafted from gnarled, knotted means. The partial elements of revealed/concealed that would not match if put together, they may clash, they may sit uncomfortably with one another. The hall of mirrors shows both the accepted pictures and the warped although authentic glimpses of the events that serve to materialise these challenges.

For those reading this, how might this help you think about your own academic career and how it is reflected in and by others? This piece of writing is *mea culpa*, but I am not sure it is the act of contrition it perhaps should be. In my writing I am not apologising for the duplicities revealed, but I am regretful and aware that this is risky to put in the public domain – I am commenting critically on aspects of academic careers that I continue to live, have complicity within, many of my colleagues work hard on these aspects and believe in them. It is not my intention to undermine them and their achievements, but rather think about what academia has become/is becoming through some of these norms and expectations. I cannot take too strong a position of judgement; as glimpsed in the examples above, my career is a product of doing most of my academic practice the same rather than differently. However, this has been troubling and the hall of mirrors shows all of the good, the bad, and the ugly.

I encourage sitting with the discomfort of recognising the popular ideals of an academic career while doing your career differently by foregrounding your individual strengths, motivations, and vocations within your work. I do superficially comply with the baseline 'key requirements' by partially participating in the mainstream expectations of an academic career despite despising rankings, self-celebration, and the classics of business operation. But I aim for this to become a reducing proportion of the work I do as I prioritise the elements that I see as valuable and that those colleagues have shown me are part of a 'successful' academic career: writing for the journals and books that I love; doing social science; and working with students for their knowledge and critical thinking skills. These are the practices that may be currently shown as corrupted images, but are the most legitimate to me and my academic career. Maybe if there are enough academic careers being done differently and progressing to senior roles, the acceptance of variety and multiple value will become the new norms reflected undistorted in the mirrors.

References

Birchall C (2011) Introduction to 'Secrecy and Transparency' The Politics of Opacity and Openness. *Theory, Culture & Society* 28: 7–25. https://doi.org/10.1177%2F0263276411427744

Cruz JM (2017) Invisibility and Visibility in Alternative Organizing: A Communicative and Cultural Model. *Management Communication Quarterly* 31: 614–639. https://doi.org/10.1177%2F0893318917725202

Dar, S, Liu, H, Martinez Dy, A, & Brewis, DN (2021). The Business School Is Racist: Act Up!. *Organization* 28(4): 695–706. https://doi.org/10.1177%2F1350508420928521

Davis C (2007) *Haunted subjects: Deconstruction, psychoanalysis and the return of the dead*, Basingstoke: Palgrave Macmillan.

Flyverbom M, Christensen LT and Hansen HK (2015) The Transparency–Power Nexus: Observational and Regularizing Control. *Management Communication Quarterly* 29: 385–410. https://doi.org/10.1177%2F0893318915593116

Gordon AF (2008) *Ghostly matters: Haunting and the sociological imagination*, Minnesota: University of Minnesota Press.

Jabbar A, Analoui B, Kong K, et al. (2018) Consumerisation in UK higher education business schools: higher fees, greater stress and debatable outcomes. *Higher Education* 76: 85–100. https://doi.org/10.1007/s10734-017-0196-z

Savigny H (2019) Cultural sexism and the UK Higher Education sector. *Journal of Gender Studies* 28: 661–673. https://doi.org/10.1080/09589236.2019.1597689

ACADEMIC MISFITS

Magnus Hoppe, Steffi Siegert, Serdar Temiz, Fatemeh Seifan, and Anton Hasselgren

Introduction

There are many intentional and unintentional ways of making you feel that you do not belong to a certain place in academia, that you are an outsider, a misfit. Some of these ways can be traced to well-meaning expressions like "I don't see a black person when I look at you" or "Oh, your Swedish is really good!". They might be more indirect such as "I also have a Muslim friend" and "Yeah, I have friends who have gay friends", or the remarks that come off the top of one's head like: "You don't look that old" or "I am not racist but…" Then, of course there are the comparatively blunt ways, usually from those senior or well-established, that let you know that you do not belong. This is done on a daily basis through expressions of institutional normality using specific references to theory, methods, associations, and jargon that you have not yet had the chance to explore, adapt to, or maybe just do not find much interest in. We may have our dreams about what academia could and should be, but the reality does not conform.

Willard van Orman Quine wrote these lines in 1974, without possibly imagining that half a century later, his words would still perfectly describe the working life of many academics:

> If a man could get a teaching job, his struggles continued. He would prepare nine to fifteen hours of lectures a week, besides grading papers and serving on committees. He would do his professional writing in the evenings and on Sundays and during such weeks of vacation as were not taken up with summer teaching. He would type it himself and buy the eventual reprints out of a meager salary. If more money were diverted into academic channels, one thought, how Academia might bloom! Talent would be attracted and relieved of burdens, and a renaissance would be assured. Fat chance, in our profit-oriented society, but a man could dream.

People spend a long time at grad school before starting their academic careers. They spend those extremely stressful early years to ramp up their portfolio, to prove that they are worth the long-term investment of the system and the organisation. But what will actually happen after those years? Putting the conflicts between work cycle and life cycle aside, do they finally fit in after getting a permanent job? We shall venture to say not necessarily. This is just the beginning of a long journey, and there will be plenty of other reasons that make you feel like a misfit despite all the effort you put in.

But what is a misfit? Can you ever be a misfit in academia, the – allegedly – most diverse of all industries? Academia has always been elitist and exclusionary in one way or another. In the middle ages, academia was open only to men, with very few exceptions, such as Elena Cornaro Piscopia, who obtained her doctorate degree in 1678 (Guernsey, 1999) (funnily enough, the academic middle ages lasted until about 1883 in Sweden when the first woman, Ellen Fries, earned her doctorate degree at Uppsala University). Piscopia was exceptional in many respects (e.g., she spoke seven languages fluently) and pursued a doctorate degree in theology, but it should come as no surprise that the Roman Catholic Church got in the way of a woman's success. They forbade her to receive a doctorate in Theology so Piscopia got herself one in Philosophy. The first women to enter academia, without any prospect of a future in academia, were from the upper classes, though still misfits. Academia wasn't just exclusionary when it comes to sex but also class.

In an effort to avoid the exclusionary practices of society in the past, Sweden, as many other European countries, does not collect information on race or ethnicity. The hope is that this will limit the potential for discrimination based on race or ethnicity. However, if we don't collect data on historically oppressed groups, how can we know that we are treating everyone equally, and by extension, how do we characterise a typical career in academia?

In this chapter, the reader enters a hall of mirrors with us. Mirrors, broken in shards, that each try to illuminate and reflect challenges that academics face to accommodate aspects of their real identity which may not match the typical image of a successful academic. The reader will meet some of the darkness that we have met throughout our careers in academia, but we also want to stress the point that nothing could be seen in a mirror without light. And there is light. There is hope for misfits. We invite the reader to come and look into our mirrors, or more correctly the shards thereof, and stay with us till the end where we show how we have found hope.

As a group, we call ourselves Academic Misfits. The group was formed before we knew about this book. A few years back we found each other through the shared feeling of not being fully accepted by academia, of being the odd ones out, and that there were stories to tell about other types of academic life. We are not poster children, our stories aren't told to those who aspire to academic positions. Part of our storytelling can be found in the coming paragraphs as a bricolage of shards from our different academic lives, here assembled to form a few mirrors for you to look into and reflect upon.

The mirror of close encounters

Academia is characterised by insecurity in jobs and requirements and a blatant disregard for the academic as a person with a life and dreams outside the office.

Shard 1

Through the back door. Coming back to university after several years on the outside, my task as a project manager was to design a three-year bachelor programme. With no PhD,

I think that defined me as an academic misfit from the start. At that time, I didn't reflect much upon it, I was just glad to do the work, and believe me, I worked. I not only created all courses for the programme, but I was also head teacher for all courses the full first year. If you'd ever wondered what a useful idiot looks like, take a good look at this person. I didn't reflect much on it at the time. In retrospect, it seems odd that I ever was allowed to do this; someone ought to have had some responsibility for the scientific grounding of the programme. It was just up to me, and as I (at that time) was not one of the PhDs, my impression was that they didn't bother. Odd though, as it might risk the reputation of their school, but maybe they felt no threat to their personal reputation. Still, even without a PhD I understood that the programme needed scientific grounding and that I needed a doctoral degree if I was to have a future in this environment.

Next door. I started to discuss the possibility of starting my own doctoral research. At first this was received benevolently but I soon learnt that my research questions didn't fit into the formal research programme, which is why I ought to reframe them towards what was considered suitable for the department. At this point, I started to realise that the academic freedom was illusionary for those in less favourable positions. I didn't accept their premise, I instead started to look elsewhere for a doctoral position. Fortunately, I had a connection at another university that made it possible to start my research education there instead. I financed it myself, working part time. Nowadays, this opportunity is closed. You need external funding. Without financing, you do not fit in, and to get financing it is of course better to already have connections inside academia that can advocate for your potential fit. Your research interest alone will not give you a place on the inside. Instead, you need to find your way in somehow, become associated, a part of the network. It helps a great deal to be an academic by proxy, at least be a "hang-around" and thus be nudged and favoured when a position is advertised. Being an assistant on the inside is one relatively fail-safe way to get admitted to a PhD programme eventually, but there are probably other options as well. As long as you are there and are present, you will know when announcements are drafted and maybe even get invited to be part of a funding application, and if you are lucky – ka-ching – there will be some money to finance you. Money comes first, wit second. Therefore, there is an unknown number of academic misfits out there, that were financially cast-off even before they got a chance to prove their worth inside the system.

Shard 2

We are told that we should raise money. How can I be independent when all the research is tied to external funding coming from organisations with their very own agendas? How can I be an independent researcher when I have to conduct research on the topics dictated by the funding agencies? Imagine, we have created positions such as post-docs just to hire qualified PhDs without any job security. At the same time, my students that graduated five years ago are making more than I make after years of education and industry experience. Tough choice. We have so-called individual set salaries while being bound by a collective pay scale, which is way below the salary of the industry. I like research, I like to teach, I like to learn and share my knowledge, but I should not pay that big a price for having this passion. I did not have any job security until I was 40 years old! When you don't have job security, you can't get a mortgage, you can't make long-term plans. Why is it presented as a necessity, outright desirable and easy to change countries every other year, just to make a career? Which academic organisation is helping to find accommodation, to maintain relationships with romantic partners and friends, and develop a social network?

The mirror of dissociation

Do not expect there to be something inside academia you could attach to easily without giving up some part of yourself, if that even is an option.

Shard 3

I am a scatter-gun researcher. I am a cat-like researcher. Quickly excited, quickly scared. Did I bite off more than I can chew? The perpetual imposter syndrome, known by many academics; I am no exception. Only that I don't fit, my language doesn't fit, my mannerisms don't fit, I don't belong. Others before me have described their feeling of misfitting in white collar professions. I am not the first and I won't be the last. It's nevertheless worth describing. I am holding up a mirror, I don't look like you but there are similarities. You are not alone; you are part of the involuntary family of misfits that try their best to struggle along without fitting in. Fitting in is not a merit in and of itself. It's important to remind oneself of that every so often.

The first time a senior academic pointed out that I don't speak like an academic, I was ashamed, I felt found out…caught? Now I understand that it is a form of language policing, of destabilising an already fragile façade of belonging. I have learnt from those experiences. I use coarse language, I use simple words, and I use clear sentence structures. I don't write fancy; I don't speak fancy. I don't pretend to be what I am clearly not. I am an immigrant, to my chosen country, to my new social class, and the language I work in. I tell my students and I don't hide it from my colleagues. Misfitting should be hidden less, not more.

My mannerisms are ill-fitting in my chosen new home and the professional environment I am allegedly a part of. I speak loudly, I laugh raucously, I use my whole body to communicate. Everyone around me seems to *know* how to do an "academic career". I lack strategy, I lack focus, I want to change the world, one class of students, one critical chapter at a time. This is not how you become a professor in academia. This isn't even adjacent to an associate professor. Still, it is a career, isn't it?

Shard 4

I am at a conference. Will they ask me where I am from even before they ask me about my research? I have been in several situations where others start to talk about my family background, my ethnicity, my religion, and I responded kindly, but the conversation ends with me asking them about their research, and them asking me about my past. They remember only my ethnicity, my religion.

Do you know how strange it is that I have to answer their questions about a country I don't live in, and a leader that I did not vote for? How can I know details about ISIS when I have been living in Europe since before they even existed? Do these people realise that I do not think or practise religion the way they picture me? Once, there was an anonymous survey and international researchers were complaining that there were discriminatory and racist comments and jokes in the workplace. Do you know what the lesson learnt from this survey was, according to the official analysis? "They don't understand our humour and culture". What kind of ethnocentric stupidity is that, written by well-established scholars? Is this all they could get out of the survey, one might ask?

I am in the social sciences but also good with computers. When there is a technical problem, I can solve it. It has happened many times that I have been the one to fix technical issues for colleagues at work or at conferences. Instead of appreciation, I have sometimes been faced with researchers commenting that "Oh, I see that you are more of a practitioner". How do they know? Have they seen how I write and conduct research? Why do they judge me even though I helped and solved *their* problem?

Shard 5

I got my PhD and have since made some kind of academic career including full time, open-ended contracts and formal positions. I have in many respects found a way of living my professional life inside academia. But throughout this personal journey, I have never felt, and still do not feel, that I have had much backing from any institution or group. Friends yes, and trust from people I work with, yes. But my research profile and interests still do not really fit into the expected standards. I keep on researching and writing what I find interesting and not what is in fashion or what funding institutions ask for. In some way, I have stayed an independent researcher, which is exactly what is expected from all researchers. But this so-called independence is an illusion for many academics, as you also need connections for making a career. You need to become an accepted part of at least one established field, and thus getting asked to take roles as an opponent, chair seminars, being part of evaluation boards, etcetera. And not the least, get financing for your research. If no one knows you, sees you, and particularly if you move around without attaching yourself to anything, people will have a hard time trusting you, and without that trust, you will probably stay a misfit throughout your academic life no matter how good your research is. Thankfully, many people just don't care. They stay disconnected, stay misfits and thereby create a body of real independent researchers. Too bad, governing and financing bodies do not see that there is much worth in this and support it. I guess, anyone with power and money likes to define what kind of research they deem society needs and ultimately support their own agenda, not your agenda or your interpretation of what society needs. Hence, there are several actors that exercise control over what is to be considered as good research and good knowledge, making truly independent research even more scarce. I quite like being a misfit under these circumstances.

Shard 6

I fit in. I am welcomed, accepted. I am not questioned or disputed – I am excused. I blend and I mingle. So, what's that feeling? What's that thought in the back of my head? (I don't belong).

Am I a misfit now?

I belong with the misfits – but I don't fit in. I don't know adversity, loss, or struggle. I don't have the right to call myself a misfit. Because I fit in. So where do I belong?

Am I a misfit now?

I am portraying myself as a victim. I wallow in entitlement. With self-importance and vanity, I infiltrate and insert myself in others' struggles. Because no one wants to be a misfit. Right? So where do I belong?

Am I a misfit now?

I don't belong professionally. I don't belong socially. I think about different things, and I care about different things. I don't relate. But I fit in. I blend and I mingle.

Am I a misfit now?

I connect with the misfits, the outsiders and the different – but I don't fit in. Because I am not different.

Am I a misfit now?

I am the double imposter. The fake misfit. A warped reflection.

Mirror of dreams

Becoming an academic is filled with expectations and dreams of something better, on all sides. Becoming disappointed at some stage seems to be part of the process for everyone involved.

Shard 7

I am an accidental academic. I am not alone. We are an involuntary family of misfits and accidents. I had no plans on becoming an academic. I grew up in a rural, working-class environment. Becoming an academic is not a typical childhood dream where I grew up. I dreamt of becoming a firefighter, being in movies, becoming royalty. My parents dreamt that I'd become a high-school teacher, a doctor, a lawyer. Those are professions we knew; we had a concept of. I am a curled working-class child, two generations of women in my family dreamt of education, higher education. A path that was closed to them due to social class, sex, political affiliation. My family made sure that their children didn't get stuck on the sticky floor that the working class association constitutes in my country of origin. My higher education is my family's achievement. They were excited for me to come back after my master's degree and get a well-paid desk job close to home. My family was not sure about my academic career. My family is still unsure. The definition of success is to work at a desk away from the elements, shower before work (Jordahl, 2003) and employment security.

Shard 8

I apply for jobs, lots of jobs. According to the requirements, I know that I am a strong candidate, but will they categorise me separately, will they discriminate against me? I know that SÄPO, the Swedish Intelligence Agency, once recommended universities not to accept Iranian students to master's programmes if the programme was connected to nuclear and missile technologies. Well, what is *not* related to nuclear energy? Biology, chemistry, mathematics, and innovation can all be related to nuclear energy. Basically, what they are saying is to "not accept any Iranian students to master's programmes". So, one might ask, are there some hidden rules that people do not talk about but accept and act accordingly? Are these evasions based on hard facts, or are they based on feelings of who should be in and who should be out?

I have applied to several positions, to then see the positions cancelled. What does this mean? I once applied for a job and was told that I was not on the shortlist. I then received a call telling me that this was due to a tech glitch and was invited for an interview. During the interview, I understood that I was supposed to have received a summary from the evaluators. I was told that it was a "small mistake" by HR. I had to have an unprepared interview because I had no idea which issues were raised in the expert reviews. Was it a coincidence? Was it on purpose? Was it a formality so they could hire the person they had already decided upon before the formal process had to be adhered to?

Through the looking-glass

As in the novel written by Lewis Carroll (1871) about the curious and brave Alice in Wonderland, in academia logic sometimes seems to be reversed but you first discover it once you climb through the mirror.

Shard 9

Universities usually tell you that they are about collaboration and industry knowledge and networks, but nobody promotes you when you are good at that. They tell us: "If you can raise money, then it will be easier to employ you". Well, in some funding applications the university picks the nominee. So, if funding agencies decide what is funded, which research is valuable, how can we talk about independent research? I spent hundreds of hours on funding applications and collaborations for co-applications, but nothing has come of it. Shall I stop my research plan and career because it is not "en vogue" right now?

As academics, we enjoy a great deal of freedom of expression; it is part of our job to shape the public discourse. We are supposed to contribute to debates in society; it is considered our "third objective" next to teaching and research. However, I noticed that when some researchers raised their voices against their government's actions in regard to Covid-19 by sharing petitions, they were "advised" by their managers to not sign if they are not an authority in the domain. If they still wanted to sign, they were not allowed to use their university affiliation or their academic title. Well, I may not be an authority in virology or infectious disease, but I am capable of comparing statistical data between countries, I am capable of finding discrepancies within the shared data. Do these managers suggest that everybody else can say whatever they want, everybody else can raise their concerns, but academics who have academic qualifications, who have advanced knowledge on methodology, on data collection, on analysis must shut up? Interestingly, academic unions did nothing. At one university internal meeting one representative said: "We have decided to support any who face charges by the university". Well, I know many people decided to be silent following their managers' "advice". They were silenced.

From the perspective of the Western world, it seems as if academic freedom is only under threat in non-Western countries. That is a matter of perspective. There is a cancel culture that erases certain voices that do not conform to existing or newly created standards. Discussions are curtailed, suffocated. Even alleged attempts to work towards the greater good, need to be analysed, criticised, and discussed. We should always strive towards transparent, open and fair debates.

Shard 10

Lots of studies have established the existence of systemic sexism and racism in Academia (see Melaku and Beeman (2020) and Laland (2020) for instance) and the problem is not a surprise anymore. Books have been written, thousands of pages of papers have been published, and still there seems to be a big gap between the practice and the preach. There is a disconnect between the reports and the actions, and even though academia acknowledges the problem, it has the tendency to put the ownership of the issue on individuals. As a woman you receive unfair responsibilities and evaluations due to gender perception and discrimination, as a person from the middle east you miss conferences while waiting for your visa application being processed, and as an individual who doesn't fit into the existing setting, you don't get any support from your institution because your research questions and teaching methods don't fit into the formal frame. And at the end, *you* are asked to try to fit in the organisation that does not help you to feel a sense of belonging. *You* are asked to understand how subtle systemic discrimination operates both formally and informally in the organisation and find a way to cheat the system, a system that does not take diversity seriously. You convince yourself to follow the unwritten rules, to fight and find a way in. You are awarded a grant or a position. What will you hear then? "Well, it is much easier for women!". But what is the reality? What do the statistics say? Do you bother to respond to such a common comment? Yes? Let me tell you, every time you try to respond to such comments, it feels like you have to start from the bottom again.

The mirror of doubt and hope

In academia, you have an enormous freedom of becoming who you want to be, while finding yourself entwined in a web of relations, ideas and norms that will distort whatever idea you had of academia. The huge variety of academic careers might not come as a surprise.

Shard 11

You do not have to fit in. You have a choice but choosing to stay and become an academic misfit will make it harder for you to advance inside academia. Still, it is possible, and you will retain your personal integrity and in your heart be sure that you are an independent researcher in your own right. You are not alone, even though it might feel like it at times.

Shard 12

I am a misfit, but I am not giving up just yet. I am holding on to my family of misfits. We celebrate our collective misfitting and try pushing the boundaries of what is considered acceptable for a successful academic career.

Shard 13

All the tensions and problems I have experienced led me to doubt if I wanted to stay in academia. Do I want to fight to resolve these problems? Yes, of course. Do I need to stay in academia to continue this fight? Not necessarily. I was at the end of a two-year research position. I had to decide whether I wanted to apply for another short-term research position/grant or if I would rather take a totally different path. I chose the latter, but I am still concerned about all these problems, and I think everybody who sees the issues should be.

Beyond the shards

It's easy to write about all the things that don't work but every time one mentions some form of discrimination, one has to start from the bottom to explain as if this was a completely new phenomenon. It is not. There is hope to be found in shared experiences.

While the stories shared here are based on our experiences in Western academia, we do not presume they are exclusive for this setting, nor that conditions are worse or better here. These are our experiences. But it does not mean that it is all bad. It is not without hope. Working in academia and living in our context is often fantastic, inspiring and fulfilling. We want to experience more of the good things, less of the bad. Despite the struggle, the delay, and the pain, you are not alone, and you can be resilient and stay in academia. You can also leave, and we wouldn't blame you. It makes you no less resilient.

In this chapter, you have met our misfit family. We give each other encouragement, try to provide opportunities, laugh, and cry together. This is our way to muddle through and is our suggestion to you. You don't need to change the (academic) world all by yourself. And you don't need to feel alone either. There are others like you (us), we just have to find each other in the discriminatory, exclusionary, neo-liberal, quantifiable, results (papers, and papers only) oriented mess academia has become. Resilience, that is the one thing that connects all of us. Resilience can look differently. We like being academics, we have met each other, and we get to write book chapters like this. Academic life has its perks.

But what is the misfits' role in academia? We venture to say that it is crucial. Is it not the misfits, unconforming and diverse, that embody the ideal independence sought after in researchers? Ellen Fries, the first woman to receive a doctorate degree in Sweden, was a misfit. A woman in a man's world. She was the first, but not the last. Through her, change was not only possible; it became inevitable. We will struggle, but we may also force change.

There is hope. Find your family of misfits or come and join ours. Together we will change the world shard by shard, one classroom, one book chapter, one academic encounter at a time.

References

Carroll, L. (1871) *Through the Looking-Glass*. London: Macmillan.
Guernsey, J.H. (1999) *The Lady Cornaro, Pride and Prodigy of Venice*. New York: College Avenue Press.
Jordahl, A. (2003) *Klass: är du fin nog?* Stockholm: Atlas.
Laland, K.N. (2020) Racism in Academia, and Why the 'Little Things' Matter. *Nature*. 584(7822): 653–654. https://www.nature.com/articles/d41586-020-02471-6
Melaku T.M. and Beeman, A. (2020) Academia Isn't a Safe Haven for Conversations About Race and Racism. *Harvard Business Review*. https://hbr.org/2020/06/academia-isnt-a-safe-haven-for-conversations-about-race-and-racism
Quine, W. (1974) Paradoxes of Plenty. *Daedalus*. 103(4): 38–40. www.jstor.org/stable/20024240.

BECOMING A (NEVER) GOOD ENOUGH CRITICAL SCHOLAR? ON PRECARIOUS ACADEMIC SUBJECTIFICATION PROCESSES

Mie Plotnikof

Critical questions mark the becoming

?	[uncertain, must concentrate
A question	[heart beating, will I/they understand
A mark	[sweating, but cold
On the body	[moving, but still
In my mind	[empty, but full

We must know, what we don't know, before we can know it.
Which literature, which debate, which critique, which contribution.
Solid and critical theorizing. Classic yet innovative methods.
Data. Analytical consistency and saturation.
Findings. To argue one point.

Am I scientific enough?
A body that is conventional,
      sure, designed, clever,
        sharp, arrogant, knowledgeable.
          Always available, tough, persistent, continuing.
Am I critical enough?
A body that is challenging,
      questioning, changing, playful
        certain, experienced, creative, insightful.
          Not pregnant, parental, tired, insecure, humble.
Is this the becoming of a critical researcher within the right body of knowledge?
                Am I masculine, feminine, queer,
                        post, post post, or
                                edgy, funny enough?

Am I in a field, a community, a reference list, a citation metric, a high-ranked journal?
Am I average, blue eyed, longhaired, smiling, networking, interesting?
Am I? I am. Yes. Maybe. Or. Not. But still I am. Maybe just average.

Research	[the right, the best, the top
Privilege	[for some, for them
Critical	[precarity
?	[me

How to become a critical scholar? Notes on identity work

"She is so nice, blue-eyed, long-haired, clever, quiet, sharp, engaged". During my ethnographic fieldwork as a PhD student, taking place across hierarchical levels in local governments, I was often positioned by field actors in contradictory ways. Whatever label or characteristic they used, I was always struck by the performative effects it had on my interactions with them; ignoring me, inviting me, telling me secrets, asking me, smiling at me, mansplaining to me. I was often affected in precarious ways – feeling uncomfortable, confused, insecure – yet it helped me produce rich, multimodal data by including those situated positionings (Davies, 2000; Dille & Plotnikof, 2020; Plotnikof & Zandee, 2016). Likewise, ambiguous positionings emerged in academic contexts at research seminars, conferences, meetings; "you are so caring, strategic, engaged, dynamic, critical" – yet typically with a normative undertone or explicit correction of "but you should be more like…" added, no matter how much more I tried to do and be. Frustrated, estranged from myself, and insecure of ever "making it" I wondered again and again, how to ever become a good enough critical scholar?

The crafting of "good" critical research is rife with norms and conventions about constructing contributions (Locke & Golden-Biddle, 1997), mysteries (Alvesson & Kärreman, 2011), and critique (Bell & King, 2010; Cabantous et al. 2016; Parker 2016) with power-infused rules of excellence (Ashcraft, 2017). That reproduces a continuous flow of precarious academic subjectification processes and fuels imposter syndrome, as well as streamlines academic identities and performances in recognizable ways (Bristow, Robinson, & Ratle, 2017; van den Brink & Benschop, 2012). While this manifest certain quality criteria, these powers also risk limiting academic becoming, voices and identities, thereby counter-producing efforts of challenging, rethinking or queering them, which are all the more important to critical research (Parker, 2016). Such endeavors are often disciplined by review processes (Brewis, 2018) and likely remain the privilege of the already established scholar, and rarely celebrated in struggling, early-career academic subjects.

So how to become a critical scholar in this mix – and how to navigate all the toxicity it is saturated by? For me it entails posing that question again and again in ongoing precarious identity work that balances self-care with extreme self-critique; materializing in continuous reworkings of my work, my questions and emerging versions of 'me' positions to become critical through, when engaging in various debates.

How to embody a critical scholar? Notes on body work

"Don't behave girly or sexy, but always be available – to feedback, to critique, to collaborations. And be ready to cut your hair at a later point in your career" sounded the advice from more experienced female scholars early in my career. My body tried to fit, although I struggle with being compliant, so I still have my long hair. Later, I had to mention in an e-mail to a male scholar, who was going to host me at a foreign university – that my body image was changing due to pregnancy. In that period I was told by a senior scholar "to read some articles during maternity leave, as breast feeding makes you braindead". My changing body became a critical matter of academic professionalization, a matter that I had to recognize in myself to assure that others would recognize me. My gendered body and its changes (pregnancy, motherhood, weight, haircuts, etc.) have been noticed again and again over the years, not just in negative ways, but always surprisingly – confusing me, making me question how changing female figures can embody legitimacy in elitist, critical scholarly environments?

Academia is a gendered organizational world, like many others, within which the body is surely a bio-political site (Butler, 2004; Fotaki, 2013) that is disciplined in a multitude of ways, not least in critical communities (Bell & King, 2010; Pullen et al., 2017). Even critique as the most prominent sword in certain communities of organization and management studies must be carried, voiced, and embodied in certain ways to meet the norm (Ashcraft, 2017; Brewis, 2018). Yet norm-critical body work leaks and saturates the neo-liberal academia with its dominant rule of excellence (Phillips et al., 2014). The female body with its curves, blood, and other changing reconfigurations – turns into a queer body in these typically masculine environments.[1] Its ongoing elasticity and disorder, which some scholars live through daily, are only starting to be recognized as legitimate critical scholarship (Huopalainen & Satama, 2019; Pullen, 2018; Vachhani, 2018). Yet, those continuously moving bodily expressions, signs, sensitivities may foster new life to and new forms of critique, when unleashed, when allowed space, when legitimized as enough.

So, how to embody such criticality now and in the future? I am pregnant again. As soon as I knew, I felt the anxiety, the pressure, the stresses of not fitting into academia once again, of not being available 24/7, of not feeling sharp constantly, of having to go on leave despite R&Rs, data collection, and supervision responsibilities (Plotnikof et al., 2020). But I find strength and hope in a sparkle of feminist killjoy (Ahmed, 2017), and the critical power it spurs in me to keep on claiming legitimacy, although my body is doing motherly stuff in the meantime, however unwieldy it may be.

How to account as a critical scholar? Notes on writing work

"Your writing is too creative, too unclear, too boring – you cannot start as a maverick writer, but must prove yourself first", said the editor from a four star journal at a writing and publishing seminar. Demanding something more, else, better. My writing changed, struggled, disciplined itself, but also lost its breath. Small breakouts occurred, but writing differently easily meant no writing to me. However, recently new paths are being forged, new potentials are acknowledged (Gilmore et al., 2019; Pullen, 2018). Yet "Refer to the known works, the seminal pieces, so the reader can identify you quickly, what is he to do with this?" asked an editor. I hesitated. I hesitated to consider whether again I should discipline my account, I hesitated as an ethic of (self-)care (Kofoed & Staunæs, 2015; Plotnikof & Utoft, 2021) for my own critical becoming and my way of challenging forms of critical knowing and writing through other modes than what is usually recognized as good scholarship. Was the critical idea not also to question, trouble, reformulate our experiences and insights into politics and scientific discourses of positivist logic and rationality?

Academic writing of critical research accounting is not supposed to follow the mainstream rules and the classic gap-spotting, but rather to mystify and create research in critically performative ways (Alvesson & Kärreman, 2011; Locke & Golden-Biddle, 1997; Ashcraft, 2017). Indeed, these features do help many emerging scholars to move beyond the all-to-easily constructed strawman, as we learn to write up papers with one point and play the politics of referencing (Brewis, 2018). However, writing differently is currently materializing as a collective form of resistance to the toxic performance pressures and disciplinary powers of the patriarchic, neo-liberal university (Amrouche et al., 2018; Gilmore et al., 2019; Plotnikof et al., 2020). By walking the risky walk, rather than talking the talk, of writing differently, this work is shaping a multitude of new pathways in solidarity with marginalized, oppressed, or colonialized academic voices and forms of critique. As an ethic of care (Plotnikof & Utoft, 2021) to scholars emerging in this field as well as to the potential critical work, we may all be grateful to have read one day.

So what is critique really in organization and management studies, and how to write as and maybe even become a good enough critical scholar? Who the hell knows – I suspect I will never know, and actually I don't want to. But I do hope that you and I will keep on questioning it and rewriting its many potential puzzles and answers in multiple ways.

Oh, the bitter-sweet joys of becoming a (never) good enough critical scholar.

Note

1 This is written from a white, middle-class, CIS-female scholar's experiences, who fully acknowledges that these issues are far more complex as they intersect with other identity markers, such as ethnicity, capability, religion, sexuality, age, etc.

References

Ahmed, S. (2017). *Living a Feminist Life*. Durham: Duke University Press.
Alvesson, M., & Kärreman, D. (2011). *Qualitative Research and Theory Development: Mystery as Method*. London: Sage Publications Ltd.
Amrouche, C., Breckenridge, J., Brewis, D. N., Burchiellaro, O., Breiding Hansen, M., Hee Pedersen, C., Plotnikof, M., & Pullen, A. (2018). Powerful writing. *ephemera*, 18(4), 881–900.
Ashcraft, K.L. (2017). 'Submission' to the rule of excellence: Ordinary affect and precarious resistance in the labor of organization and management studies. *Organization*, 24(1), 36–58.
Bell, E., & King, D. (2010). The elephant in the room: Critical management studies conferences as a site of body pedagogics. *Management Learning*, 41(4), 429–442. https://doi.org/10.1177/1350507609348851
Brewis, J. (2018). On interference, collegiality and co-authorship: Peer review of journal articles in management and organization studies. *Organization*, 25(1), 21–41. https://doi.org/10.1177/1350508417703472
Bristow, A., Robinson, S., & Ratle, O. (2017). Being an early-career CMS academic in the context of insecurity and "excellence": The dialectics of resistance and compliance. *Organization Studies*, 38(9), 1185–1207. https://doi.org/10.1177/0170840616685361
Butler, J. (2004). *Undoing Gender*. New York: Routledge.
Cabantous, L., Gond, J.P., Harding, N., & Learmonth, M. (2016). Critical essay: Reconsidering critical performativity. *Human Relations*, 69(2), 197–213. https://doi.org/10.1177/0018726715584690
Davies, B. (2000). *A Body of Writing*. Lanham: AltaMira Press.

Dille, M.H. & Plotnikof, M. (2020). Retooling methods for approaching discourse – materiality relations: a new materialist framework of multimodal sensitivity. *Qualitative Research in Organizations and Management*, 15/4, 485–501.

Fotaki, M. (2013). No woman is like a man (in academia): The masculine symbolic order and the unwanted female body. *Organization Studies*, 34(9), 1251–1275. https://doi.org/10.1177/0170840613483658

Gilmore, S., Harding, N., Helin, J. & Pullen, A. (2019). Writing differently. *Management Learning*, 50(1), 3–10.

Huopalainen, A.S., & Satama, S.T. (2019). Mothers and researchers in the making: Negotiating 'new' motherhood within 'new' academia. *Human Relations*, 71(1), 98–121.

Kofoed, J., & Staunæs, D. (2015). Hesitancy as ethics. *Reconceptualizing Educational Research Methodology*, 6(2), 24–39.

Locke, K., & Golden-Biddle, K. (1997). Constructing opportunities for contribution: Structuring intertextual coherence and "problematizing" in organizational studies. *The Academy of Management Journal*, 40(5), 1023–1062.

Parker, M. (2016). Queering queer. *Gender, Work and Organization*, 23(1), 71–73. https://doi.org/10.1111/gwao.12106

Parker, S., & Parker, M. (2017). Antagonism, accommodation and agonism in critical management studies: Alternative organizations as allies. *Human Relations*, 70(11), 1366–1387. https://doi.org/10.1177/0018726717696135

Phillips, M., Pullen, A., & Rhodes, C. (2014). Writing organization as gendered practice: Interrupting the libidinal economy. *Organization Studies*, 35(3), 313–333. https://doi.org/10.1177/0170840613483656

Plotnikof, M., Bramming, P., Branicki, L., Christiansen, L. H., Henley, K., Kivinen, N., Lima, J. P., Kostera, M., Mandalaki, E., O'Shea, S., Özkazanç-Pan, B., Pullen, A., Stewart, J., Ybema, S., & Amsterdam, N. (2020). Catching a glimpse: Corona-life and its micro-politics in academia. *Gender, Work and Organization*, 27(5), 804–826. https://doi.org/10.1111/gwao.12481

Plotnikof, M., & Utoft, E.H. (2021). The "new normal" of academia in pandemic times: Resisting toxicity through care. *Gender, Work & Organization*, online first: 1–13.

Plotnikof, M., & Zandee, D. (2016): Meaning negotiations of collaborative governance – A discourse-based ethnography. In: Pedersen, A.R. & Humle, D.M. (eds.): *Doing Organizational Ethnography*, London: Routledge, pp. 137–158.

Pullen, A. (2018). Writing as labiaplasty. *Organization*, 25(1), 123–130. https://doi.org/10.1177/1350508417735537

Pullen, A., Harding, N., & Phillips, M. (2017). *Feminist and Queer Theorists Debate the Future of Critical Management Studies*. Bingley: Emerald Publishing Limited. https://doi.org/10.1108/S2046-607220160000003001

Thomas, R., & Davies, A. (2005). What have the feminists done for us? Feminist theory and organizational resistance. *Organization*, 12(5), 711–740. https://doi.org/10.1177/1350508405055945

Vachhani, S. J. (2018). Rethinking the politics of writing differently through *écriture féminine*. *Management Learning*, 135050761880071. https://doi.org/10.1177/1350507618800718

van den Brink, M., & Benschop, Y. (2012). Gender practices in the construction of academic excellence: Sheep with five legs. *Organization*, 19(4), 507–524. https://doi.org/10.1177/1350508411414293

THE ART OF BEING A REFLEXIVE ACADEMIC

Painting a never-complete self-portrait

Russ Vince

Introduction

A hall of mirrors provides many simultaneous reflections of oneself in the same moment. The art is in finding ways to perceive these reflections and their interrelations. In this full-length portrait in 'The Hall of Mirrors' Gallery, I respond to the invitation from the editors to come out from behind my profile '*to paint an individual or group self-portrait which reflects individual and/or shared struggles, contradictions and hidden stories…*' Since 2013, I have been keeping a *reflexive journal* that both captures and helps to create my lived experience as an academic. Through this journal I am literally painting a self-portrait of my being an academic. The process of painting captures many layers of experience over time that inform and disturb my ongoing contributions to knowledge and to pedagogy. It is a never-complete self-portrait that applies layer upon layer of experience to build a mosaic of images of an academic life. I hope to inspire others to add a reflexive journal to their everyday practice. I think of my journal as creative understanding in the making.

A reflexive journal is a very personal object. I start by painting each page of a new hardcover notebook with an abstract watercolour wash. I write my ideas for papers, my experiences, my notes from teaching, meetings and conferences (and much more) into my notebook. I collect my thoughts and feelings. I paint and draw over the words with watercolour pens... to reflect on them, to notice them, to visually embellish, to frame and to transform them. (I may do this several times.) The value of my reflexive journal is that it paints my experience as a way of understanding and transforming it. It is the art of reflection. Through my journal, I have learnt to make connections between parts of my day-to-day, academic life that were previously not well joined up (even though I thought that they were). Before the journal, I found that interesting conversations, collaborations, conference presentations were lost; ideas vanished quickly; emotions were ignored or forgotten. I realised that, as academics, we can neglect to perceive connections over time; we do not keep our notes in one place, go back to them, or remember them. A reflexive journal helps me to think, to imagine, to feel, to connect.

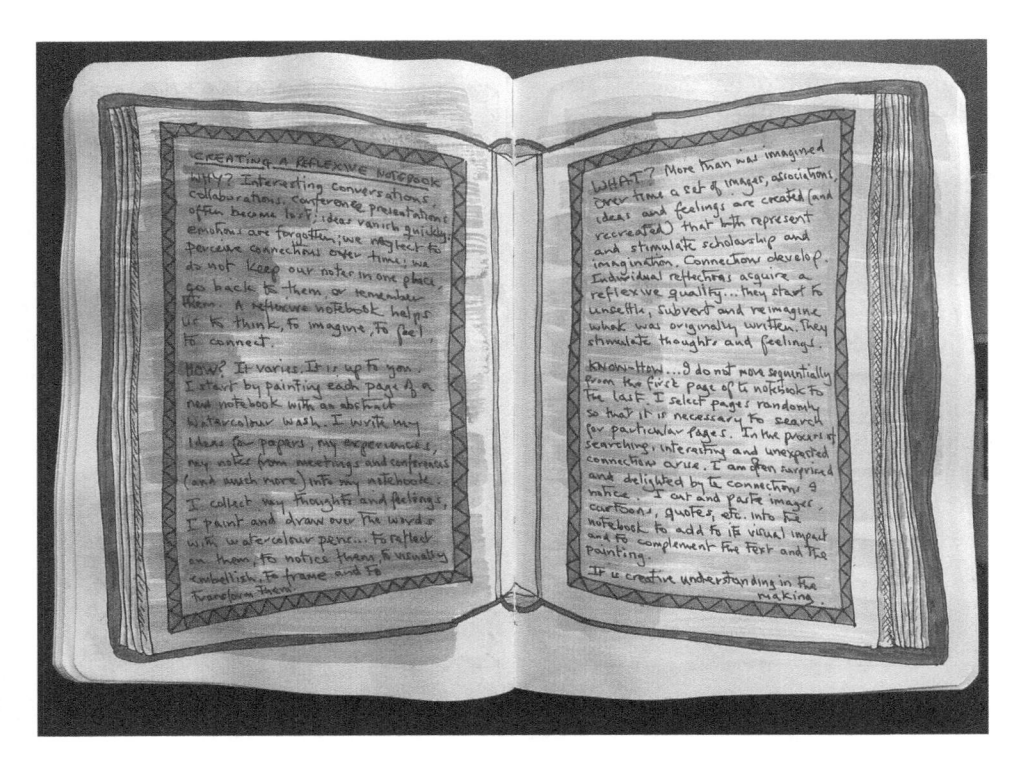

FIGURE 28.1 Creating a *Reflexive Journal*, photo taken by the author from his journal.

The journal has delivered more than was imagined. Over time, a set of images, associations, ideas and feelings are created (and recreated) that both represent and stimulate scholarship and imagination. Connections develop. Individual reflections acquire a reflexive quality – they start to enhance, unsettle, subvert and reimagine what was originally written. They stimulate thoughts. They stimulate emotion. I do not move sequentially from the first page of the notebook to the last. I select pages randomly so that it is necessary to search for particular pages. In the process of searching, interesting and unexpected connections arise. I am often surprised and delighted by the connections I notice. I cut and paste images, cartoons, quotes, etc., into the notebook to add to its visual impact and to complement the text, the drawing and the painting. Through the various iterations of my painting and writing I am building a relationship with the lived experience of my academic self that helps me to perceive what is important to me. In summary, here's an example of what creating a reflexive journal looks like and involves for me (Figure 28.1).

Thinking and writing differently

One of the things that I discovered from my reflexive journal is that there is a lot going on; and how much of it is connected. Of course, this idea was not new to me. What was new to me was putting it all down in the same place and reflecting on it. The main activities of my everyday academic life that are captured in the journal include: my ideas for papers, my initial work on papers (both alone and with others), my notes and feelings from conferences, records of my thoughts and feelings in my MBA module and PhD teaching, Editorial Board meetings, conversations with co-authors and colleagues, quotes I don't want to forget, my emotions and associations, supervision with my PhD students, Divisional Away-Days, School meetings, presentations by external speakers, internal seminars, course/module development, Research Centre masterclasses, thoughts and questions as an External Examiner for doctoral students, and notes from my readings.

One example of ongoing connections in my journal is represented in Figure 28.2. This page shows the initial ideas for a theory of historical reflexivity (Durepos and Vince, 2020). I had recently completed a paper with my friend and long-time co-author, Michael Reynolds (Reynolds and Vince, 2020), where we had used the phrase historical reflexivity, but not clearly defined or developed it. It was a way of describing our process of engaging with our publications over many years in the journal *Management Learning*. Our Associate Editor, Gabie Durepos, was fascinated by this idea and its potential, so Gabie and I had a conversation about it. This page provided the starting point for our conversation (at the Academy of Management meeting in Chicago, 2018).

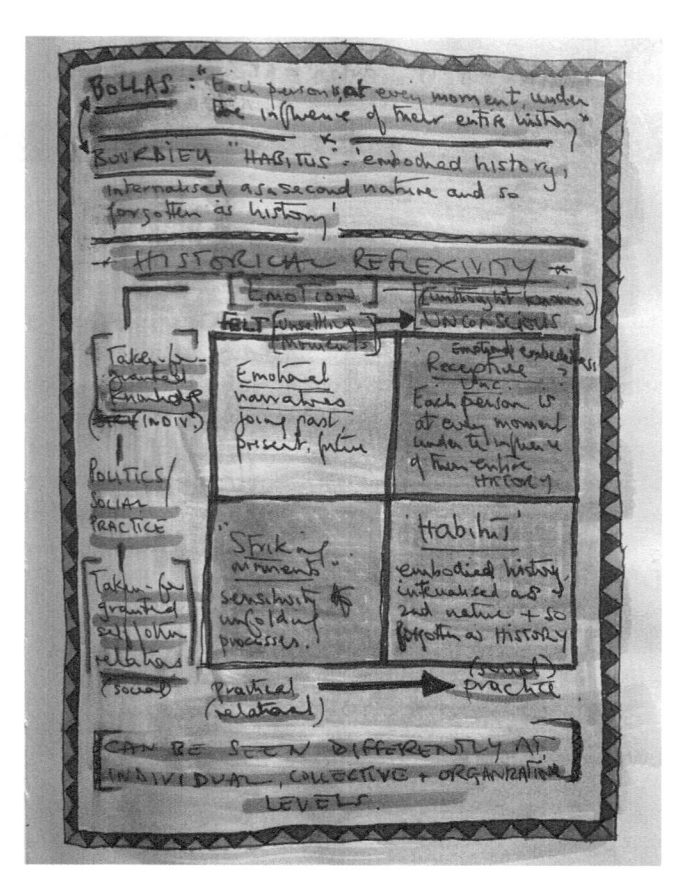

FIGURE 28.2 Starting a conversation about historical reflexivity, photo taken by the author from his journal.

The initial theoretical model emerged from the intersection of two quotations. First, an idea from the psychoanalytic writer, Christopher Bollas that: 'each person is at the same moment under the influence of their entire history'. Second, a description by Pierre Bourdieu of his concept of habitus as: 'embodied history, internalised as second nature and so forgotten as history'. These thoughts formed part of a provisional 2 × 2 matrix. Over time we discarded the matrix but recognised in the image and through our conversations the importance of a non-chronological view of history as a key assumption in historical reflexivity (Durepos and Vince, 2020). Painting the initial theoretical frame and interpreting the image together felt very creative and thought-provoking.

Of course, my experience with my reflexive journal is not all positive. I remain acutely aware of a mistake I made at an EGOS conference (Athens, 2015) when I had been invited to speak about emotion and paradox. I photographed and showed the audience two pages from my notebook that I had painted during the conference. I used the imagery to free-associate on the paradoxes of my emotional experience of being at an academic conference. This was not a wise choice… as I could see from peoples' faces when I had finished speaking. Sometimes it is best that the emotions captured in a reflexive journal remain private. Also, it is not necessarily a good idea to free-associate with such personal imagery in public. I do find academic conferences *both* excruciating *and* delightful at the same time. I did want to share this perspective with others (especially in the paradox sub-theme) because I suspect that I am not alone in feeling this way. However, it was the excruciating more than the delightful that returned for my future reflections. I cringe whenever I look at that page. I am sure that there is something valuable about going to an academic conference and making a complete ass of oneself. At the moment, I just can't remember what it is. However, this experience is not alone in the journal. It sits alongside painted and repainted notes from other EGOS conferences and two, one-day conferences at Cass Business School on paradox. It testifies to the contradictions of emotional and intellectual experience within such academic networks. It is a reminder of the mixed emotions that underpin my lived experience as an academic.

My journal offers opportunities to directly capture my emotional experience (Figure 28.3). I felt full of fear and sorrow at times during the March 2020 lockdown in the UK. This image reflected the intensity of the mixed emotions I felt, and it inspired a short contribution to the *Journal of Management Inquiry* on emotion, paradox and coronavirus (Keller et al., 2021). I created elaborate frames to embellish the tweet from Deva Dalporto and the quote from Phillip Larkin. I gave myself a lot of time to reflect on the emotional intensities of lockdown and on the deaths caused by the virus.

When I came to write my short piece for the *Journal of Management Inquiry*, it was this page that inspired me. For example, the line from Larkin's poem, 'most things will never happen, this one will' is a continuous reminder of how the pandemic has made death more present in our lives. I wrote:

> In the early stages of lockdown, when the first deaths from the virus were being reported, the BBC news showed photographic montages, head shots of those who had died. It was too painful to watch. Later, as I sat in front of my computer for a virtual conference, the 'gallery view' in Zoom evoked my visual memory of the faces of those early deaths, shown in full screen on my television. In these discomforting times, I am *both* talking with the living *and* haunted by the dead.
>
> *(Keller et al., 2021)*

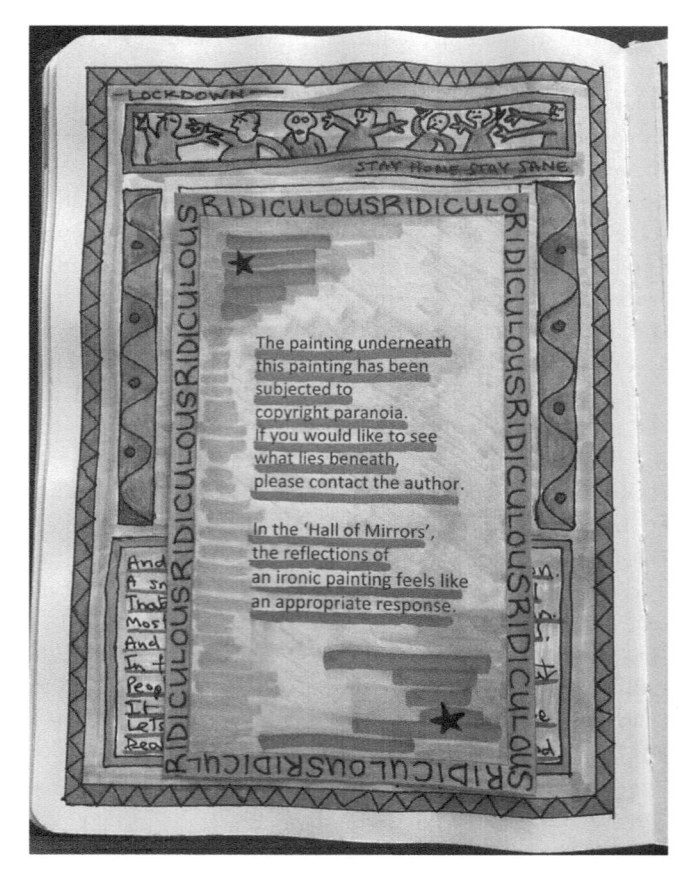

FIGURE 28.3 Some feelings during coronavirus lockdown, photo taken by the author from his journal.

Such reflections emerge from taking the time to paint, to see these representations of how I feel, and to listen to them.

My process

Look. There is nothing new here. Artists have always had notebooks, academics have always written ideas down, connections can be made without painting on words to reflect on them. Look again. The new is here somewhere. It is in visualisations of my lived experience and ideas that I can return to, reflect on, renegotiate with. It is in uncanny juxtapositions. It is in colour and composition. There is something in this process that energises my academic role and outputs. Art becomes a focal point for reflexivity, revealing striking moments and unsettling connections embedded in the everyday. Everyone who keeps a reflexive journal will develop a different, very personal way of doing it. My approach is very different now compared to when I started in 2013 (Figure 28.4). I spend much more time painting to reflect than I did originally. As I felt the value of painting, I moved to a more paint-filled and framed style of capturing my experience. Also, I make more effort to pre-paint the pages on which I am going to write (see Figure 28.4) and to select them. Selection might occur because of colour, by proximity to other things in the journal, by whim or by accident. Who knows what my journal will look like in another five years? I hope that it will become different again.

I use watercolour paint to apply an abstract wash to every page of each new journal (I have filled two journals over the seven years). I use *Windsor & Newton* watercolour pens for my painting, both to create pages on which I want to write (see Figure 28.5) and to highlight and reflect on what I have already written. I like these pens because they are vivid, easy to carry around and work with. Sometimes, if I am particularly angry or dissatisfied with what is on a page, then I paste a new page on top and start again. For example, one of my PhD students went through a particularly difficult viva examination that made me feel angry with the external examiner for how he interrogated rather than conversed with the student. I pasted new pages over the notes from the viva so that I know that they are there, but I never have to see them again.

I paste artefacts into the journal that reflect me back to myself: the rainbow tag from a Paul Smith shirt; the label from high-alpine green tea from China sent to me by a former PhD

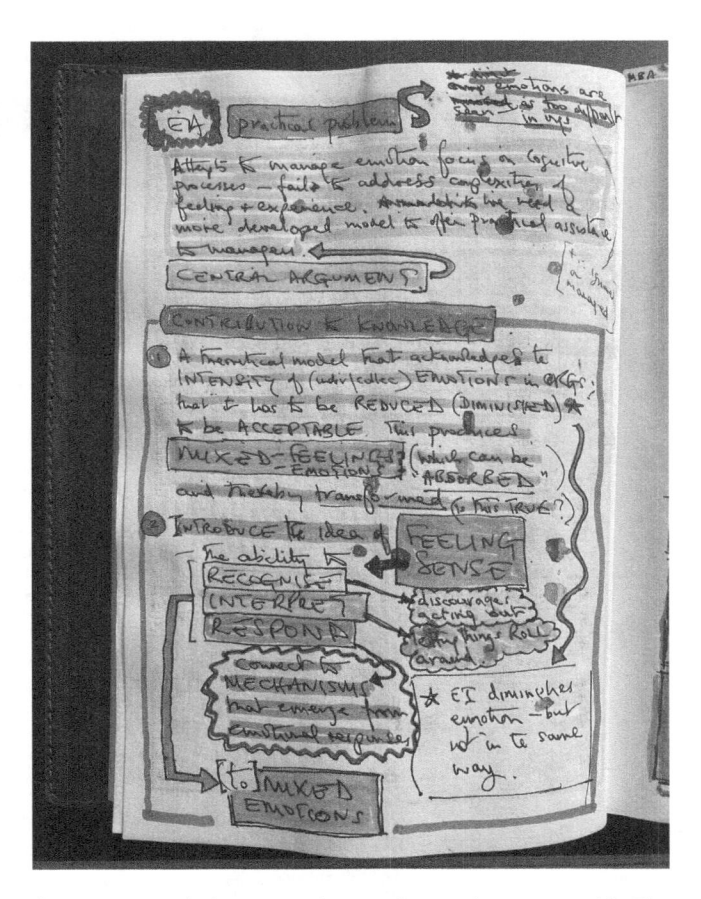

FIGURE 28.4 Differences in style between then and now (compare with Figure 28.3), photo taken by the author from his journal.

FIGURE 28.5 'Where did all these feelings come from…?', photo taken by the author from his journal.

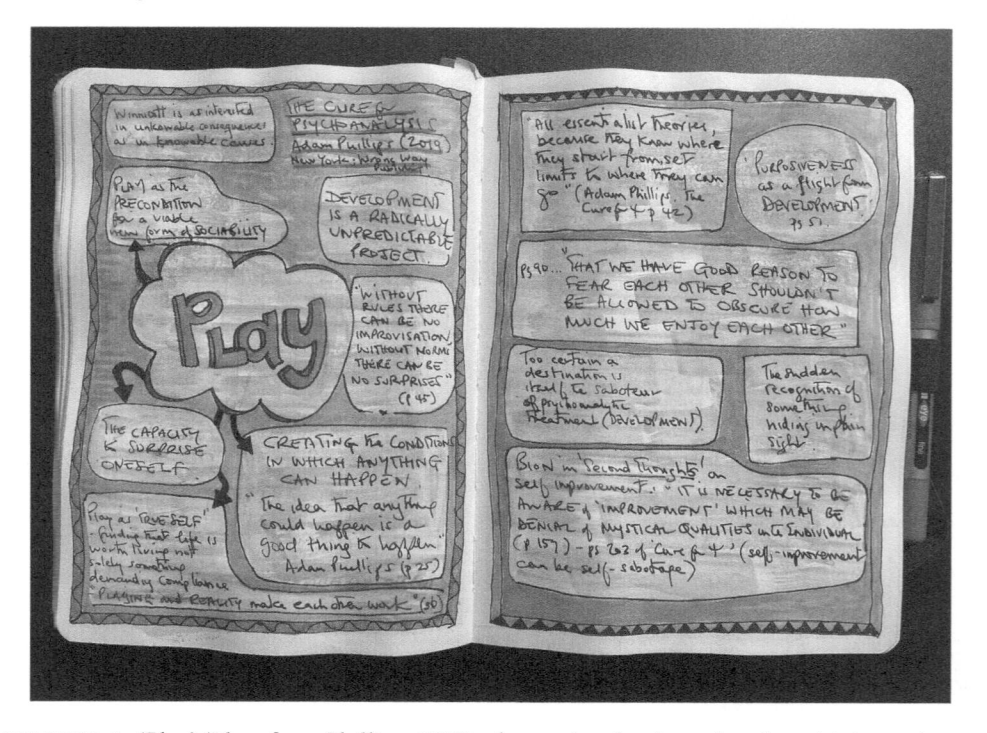

FIGURE 28.6 'Play' (Ideas from Phillips, 2019), photo taken by the author from his journal.

student; cartoons by Tom Gauld, Stephen Collins and Chris Riddell; or other appropriate images (see Figure 28.5). I write and then paint quotations from novels, from academic works, from Neil Gaiman's 'Art Matters' (2018). As you see, the left-hand page remains blank, a space that is waiting for some future feelings.

I have found different ways of thinking about the development of academic papers. In Figure 28.6, I play with ideas about play, purposiveness and learning from Adam Phillip's book *The Cure for Psychoanalysis*. This sits alongside my typed notes from the book, as well as other readings, that will help me to develop some current writing on the role of imagination in organisations. The difference between this imagery and my typed notes is that the image speaks to my unconscious and my emotions, and the typed notes speak to my intellect and capacity for reasoning. I am at my best when they work together. The arrows in the image were added to recognise an emerging theoretical point about three related components of play: as a precondition for sociability, as the capacity to surprise oneself, and as a way of 'creating the conditions in which anything can happen'. This feels like a good starting point for an exploration of play in organisations. We shall see.

There is no conclusion

I return to the Hall of Mirrors. What can I see? Many reflections of myself with little clarity about which way I am facing, and considerable creative potential in the multitude of views.

Let's face it. The art of being an academic can't be captured, for example, in the Research Evaluation Framework (REF); in wrangles about workloads; in our obsession with A-rated outputs; or in pressures to comply with rhetoric about working in a 'world-class' organisation. We're stuck with it, we know the rules of game, but we also know that there is more to an academic life than this. An academic life should be replete with ideas and imagination; with productive international friendships; with collegiality; and with unselfish support of those who are early in their careers. This is much more about the relationships that lead to quality outputs than the outputs themselves. The art of my reflexive journal is that it helps me to think, to identify new ideas, to write, to connect with the people I want to work with, to reflect on the lived experience of being an academic. It keeps me open to the complexities of being an academic. It reassures and unsettles me at the same time.

Postscript

I appreciate the support I have had in the creation of this portrait. I want to mention some insightful viewings. First, a big thank you to Anne Pässilä, who introduced me to the idea of art as an ongoing process of reflection and learning. Gabie Durepos provided me with a review of my first draft of the portrait and told me that 'there *is* something new here', prompting me to look again. The 'Hall of Mirrors' Curator, Sarah Robinson, reflected on this portrait with care and thoughtfulness. Sarah saw that the journal is 'a space for remembering, working through and sometimes covering emotions – we have very little space for doing this in a profession in which a rollercoaster of emotions is almost inevitable'. Finally, my 97-year-old father, Ron Vince asked to read it. I quite often talk with him about what I am writing. It is a good way to ensure that it makes sense beyond academia. He said that he enjoyed reading it. He thinks that I write well! My father was a journalist, my mother was an artist, so I guess that an arts-based journal reflects something of the marriage that created me. He asked me the question: 'what does the painting bring?' It is a good question that prompted an enjoyable conversation. I could also hear my mother (sadly, no longer with us) counter-question with 'what do the words bring' (when images speak so eloquently for themselves)? I am grateful for them both.

References

Durepos, G. and Vince, R. (2020). Towards a theory of historical reflexivity. In S. Clegg, M. Maclean, R. Suddaby and C. Harvey (eds.) *Historical Organization Studies: Theory, Methods and Applications* (pp. 39–56) London: Routledge.

Gaiman, N. (2018). *Art Matters: Because Your Imagination Can Change the World*. (Illustrations by Chris Riddell). London: Headline Publishing Group.

Keller, J., Carmine, S., Jarzabkowski, P., Lewis, M. W., Pradies, C., Sharma, G., Smith, W. K. and Vince, R. (2021). Our collective tensions: Paradox research community's response to COVID-19. *Journal of Management Inquiry* 30/2: 168–176.

Phillips, A. (2019). *The Cure for Psychoanalysis*. New York: Wrong Way Publishing.

Reynolds, M. and Vince, R. (2020). The history boys: Critical reflections on our contributions to management learning and their ongoing implications. *Management Learning* 51/1: 130–142.

THE POETIC ACADEMIC

Friederike Landau-Donnelly

Intro: pandemic [dis]locations

COVID moved me in many ways
I moved in COVID many days
it made me go on planes unexpectedly
it kept me from going places
it made me go into the woods
trees stacked hopelessly neat
the useless irony, yet silent continuation of some orders of destruction
others made completely redundant
how do we write when the world around you is falling apart?
what is a desk when the world is locked down
what is a tree when the world is knocked down
COVID drew me away from my desk when I thought about public spaces
places I was going to know
grass I was going to lay in
sensing distance
growing in and out of distance
growing distances
the subtle evilness of filigree silence
passion and passivity share a whole stretch of the way, coming out of the same source

I crashed into the reality of COVID-19 when I abruptly interrupted my postdoctoral fellowship in Vancouver from one day to another in March 2020. Until this point, the distance of almost 8,000 kilometers to family, friends and my partner had not played as big of a role as it did once the pandemic started to become tangible in everyday life: scarcity of toilet paper and yeast, flights and classes being cancelled, worried calls at night. With this unpredictable crisis approaching, over the course of an 18-hour-journey, dosing off in a half-empty plane, I found myself back at my parents' house in a small German town, laying awake in my brother's old bedsheets sprinkled with cotton hearts. As a result of necessarily jet-lagged nights, cascading thoughts ran through my head. I was thinking not only thinking about COVID's yet-to-be-determined everyday politics, but also its implications for academia: when would we be able to go into the field again? What should researchers responsibly do with their time in this pandemic? How can academics speak now, who can speak, who can't and about what would we speak? Briefly, I wondered how systemically relevant academic research and writing is in a pandemic. I started to feel an uneasy blend of physical discomfort upon the realization that I would not be able to leave my proper skin without much further ado, and a sudden push of motivation, a sense of new beginnings. In other words, my stamina was pretty out of control. I felt like I started ten new project ideas and finished none (which, luckily enough, turned out as not quite true, but who would've known that at the beginning of lockdown). At the time, I was working on a book about notions of space with two colleagues, but instead of eagerly finishing chapters and completing literature reviews, I felt a sudden urge to sense space and its absurd (in)finity by laying on the ground in my old childhood room, or stroking grass in the nearby forest. Space felt so full and so empty at the same time. I felt literally ungrounded, which ironically had been selected as the title of our book long before we were all hit by a pandemic. Now all things being uncertain, the feeling that only words were not enough anymore crept up in me.

Irritations, inspirations, inspiring irritations or *how do we write in a pandemic?*

In the first weeks of lockdown, I found it difficult to focus. The existential question of meaning of what I was doing (i.e., sitting in my brother's old teenage room, trying to tame months of experiences, sensory excursions and conversations with artists, activists and bureaucrats into the well-established format of 9,000 words of peer-reviewed journal articles), the crucial 'Sinnfrage' of *why* I was doing this right now remained in limbo in my head. I started reading seemingly off-topic literatures on depression and vulnerability, looking up terms like critical care and sat on my parents' balcony with no laptop on my lap. I felt like wading through moving grounds, less safe in front of my computer

> *flat aesthetics of crisis*
> *say no to solidarity with capitalism*
> *going back like a knife through butter*
> *shadowy sides*
> *time chimes between the silent blizzard of collective Angst and the realization that we were helpless, after all.*

I was trying to bring myself back to the mantra I had developed for myself throughout my PhD:

> *The world is a huge pile of unresolved questions. I am equipped with a little shovel in my hand, and as long as I dig a little every day, the pile is never quite the same at the end of the day. One day, the pile will look very different – and the day in day out shoveling with a very small shovel will have meant something. Every day, I'm shoveling.*

So, there I was, in a provincial, self-made home office, top-notch décor but no colleagues, no exchange with real people (except for my gardening parents). COVID made me realize that I was surviving in and enjoying academia largely because of the encounters with inspiring people I had from around the world. In times where this kind of connection was not possible, it felt like micro-observations were a way to reconnect, with myself, and potentially others. I think I realized I was missing a crucial source of inspiration, which usually came to me via great new people I'd meet through research, which I now tried to leverage from within.

Interestingly enough, I found myself being sucked into the Twitterverse, connecting with new people, initiatives, discourses. At first, it felt like a geeky chatroom, and I wondered whether I should have a bad conscience about spending so much time on my phone, but the jungle of hashtags created many new associative ways of thinking for me. Engaging with new routes to research topics, often accidentally, on my own schedule, directed me to think differently. As I was already unfocused and impatient to sit in front of a screen for a longer period of time, the rapid verves of online news, critique and visual images helped me to 'charge up' with inspiration. Especially in lockdown, social media proved (again) to be agile and close to the ground in reporting on the global #blacklivesmatter movements in the summer of 2020 after the violent police killing of George Floyd, or #WetsuwetenStrong, in solidarity with indigenous nations in Canada protesting against pipeline constructions on their territories with road blockages, or the devastating fire in the overcrowded refugee camp of Moria on the Greek island of Lesbos in early fall. Being connected – or temporarily grounded in a global community of solidarity – via social media gave me space to not only stay informed about ongoing activisms, but also express solidarity and support. While COVID-19 has certainly reinforced already-existing injustices of racial and environmental inequality, it has also pulled our brains to think about new ways for digital solidarity and organizing, shedding new light on how to fight the fights we chose to fight precisely *in spite* of the pandemic. Amidst it all, I came to position myself in new ways in the various layers of privilege I experience as a queer, cis, white able-bodied, married woman with academic education.

kill your privilege
instead of stabbing yourself in the back

The pandemic made me reflect upon, and write about vulnerabilities, exposure and exhaustion. While I had never understood myself as an ivory tower scholar– living the postdoc life had taught me various more or less precarious, always-temporary contracts, affiliations, and identities – yet I was always very lucky/privileged/self-disciplined. But in light of the globally enmeshed crisis of crises, the ways to connect or become (dis)connected or (un)grounded burgeoned and almost paralyzed me at first. The academic harness had unexpectedly become alien and heavy, cutting into my writing flesh; I just could not go on writing with the scaremongering of double-blind peer review on my shoulders. Interestingly enough, after leaning into the absence from my computer, taking hours of walks in the forests, accepting that I would simply not be 'productive' in the prescribed ways of pushing out articles. Instead, I rushed into writing *differently,* from a position of (un)groundedness maybe, which made my ways of speaking more poetically – I was more aware of the uncertainties surrounding us

> dɔn't let nothingness eat you up for breakfast
> what is broken, what is just numb?
> You can't belong to this disillusion don't return, Damian
> finally, I couldn't do it anymore

The initial feeling of being trapped was ultimately transformed into a state of writing things off my chest, proceeding in (un)groundedness, regardless of where my thoughts would travel. I wrote poems every day. When I was finished with my first reflections about the implications of COVID-19 on the arts and cultural sector, I was given the opportunity to publish two consecutive essays in the Berlin-based homelessness magazine *Arts of the Working Class*. After weeks of feeling isolated from big city talk and face-to-face discussions, I encountered this platform, which is both being sold on the streets and hooked into social media, as an intermediary space to connect differently with people and concepts via poetry, in a much more personal, direct and unabridged way. In our precarious times, I noticed that malleable forms of knowledge production and dispersal such as blogs, zines and social media compilations are crucial spaces of survival for immediate expressions of critique and suffering, which many of the more institutionalized channels of academic publishing are not really made for. Poetry for me was a way to shape the living creatures of public opinion. Besides allowing for flexible, self-organized and overall more 'breathable' formats and times to publish, it also helped me to connect not only with other academics across the globe, but also with directly concerned people, whose everyday working and living routines of individual and collective experiences of vulnerability I was trying to speak with, about and to. In line with the theme of this volume, by writing more unruly, vulnerably, and poetically, I found my own way of *doing my academic career differently*.

Outro: Thinking a_part_s

While I still find it difficult to accept that many planned conferences and field research trips were cancelled or postponed until further notice, the pandemic also taught me that there are not many good excuses to remain disconnected. Especially with regards to my planned collaborative research project with the *Conflictorium – Museum of Conflict* in Ahmedabad, India, personal encounters were difficult to be replaced. Nevertheless, the museum's founder Avni Sethi and I co-organized the beautiful format of an online discussion about notions of conflict and care in museums in times of crisis[1] together with the Vienna-based MA program *educating-curating-managing*. From this experience, I found that such digital ways of being together also brought about new opportunities, free from some financial or time restraints to meet, while it surely also reminded us that we would also continue to *remain apart* in this global crisis. One the one hand, I have found it utterly discouraging, politically problematic and disheartening that efforts at advancing decolonial research methods, practice, and theory development might be further strained and thwarted by a virus that does not stop at territorial borders. At worst, COVID might reinforce existing asymmetries of power and visibility between scholars from the Global South and the Global North. On the other hand, though, I have found inspiring times, places and communities of scholars and activists who continue the fight to make the academy less hierarchic and less obsessed with seemingly irrefutable parameters of performance, output, or value. My experiences to adopt poetry not only as temporary coping mechanism or method, but come to think of the poetic academic as mode of doing academic writing differently, and thus challenging academic conventions of how we are writing, and also who we are writing for, from within academia. For me, becoming a poetic academic self in the midst of feeling (un)grounded, has mobilized new times and places to do academia differently. Regardless of the concrete places in which we struggle to live a livable life during or after lockdown, I have not found myself irrevocably 'thrown back' onto producing (academic) knowledge like before (if a pre-COVID mindset is even possible). Instead, I am reminded of how I wrestled through lockdown and a quite existential feeling of ungroundedness thanks to becoming more open to poetry, connecting differently. While the implications of the virus linger and will continue to shape all aspects of our lives, we might have yet to invest ourselves to acknowledge the different ways in which we are all already vulnerable (in existentially different ways) and work toward new ways of being apart together. So I keep shoveling, a little bit every day.

walk, don't write
dried up think
lay there t_here here air
words will come
stay st_ill
when do we think?
whose slowness is virus-proof?
selection is no coincidence
concrete falling apart
concretely falling apart
teeth in all the wrong places
moving in_to absence
the fetish is present
is crisis management academia's new professional development baby?
will there even be babies after the blaze
staring, healing, laying on the moving ground
stealing, bearing, feeling the moving ground
bouncing, crying, me moving grounds
grounding bearing healing the grounds

Note

1 https://www.ecm.ac.at/ecm-diskurs/archive/

I AM YOU, AS YOU ARE ME

Academic lives as a mirror of ourselves

Oscar Javier Montiel Méndez, Duncan M. Pelly, and Araceli Almaraz

Introduction

We are academics. But more than that, throughout our careers we have been motivated to be warriors and entrepreneurs and do things differently. Within our trenches, our works always have that sense of bringing novel ways of seeing things, reflecting upon what has been done, and what can be said or done to improve our contexts.

That is the reason we have chosen to paint a contrasting double portrait (consisting of several mini portraits each), through two in-depth interviews with our colleagues José Manuel Valenzuela (JMV) and David M. Boje (DB), each with 30+ years as academics. Manuel and David are long time admired colleagues who have been always willing to share with us their impressive knowledge, work, and experiences of the research road, with its never-ending miles ahead, a road that they have traveled before.

Our double portrait aims to add to and develop critical academic career studies by challenging orthodoxies and power relations in academic career trajectories, illustrating possible alternatives and the risks involved. Both career portraits are different and abstain from conforming to stereotypical academic norms and roles. Both tell their stories in drastically different contexts (the USA and Mexico), socio-economic backgrounds, and conditions, and in doing so, can inspire and encourage others to forge their career paths through re-thinking and taking ownership of their careers. However, both have paid costs for taking the risk of doing things differently outside of and inside of academia.

In the interviews, we asked them how they were able to be creative and juggle the dominant discourses (for example, of the neoliberal academy), and we asked about the different parts of modern academic life. We paint their narratives and our reflections and explore how they confronted academic power structures and norms. Moreover, they used the micro-practices of writing and reflection to build upon their research.

Throughout the chapter, we sketch out the tensions and contradictions of the heroes of our portraits. What paths have not been taken or what stories lie hidden or untold? What lies behind the homogenized institutionalized masks (profiles) they show to the world? We learned by painting these portraits that we are not alone in this fight, and that there is hope in doing things better to have a positive impact on our students, institutions, and society. When things are getting tougher, you can think of Manuel and David's stories.

The actors: our portraits are based on JMV and DB narratives

JMV,[1] MEXICO

I (Araceli) met José Manuel in COLEF in 1994 when I was a master's student. Still today I am surprised by his discursive capacity, his perseverance, and eloquence. A piece of advice he gave me that I will never forget is "to build networks with social actors, step out into the street and join the processes of social change from within." The positions achieved do not matter, what matters are the contributions to knowledge, Manuel once told me. "Fight to give light to your studies, you have a good rhythm, in your field of specialty, business history, your work is already a benchmark, and please do not stop writing poetry." I am grateful that at key moments in my academic life, intellectuals such as Manuel have been by my side and have encouraged me to move forward.

One of José Manuel's teachings to me is that his tenacity and social commitment were forged in a hostile environment to the social classes he studied later. In the 1970s–1980s, academic career life in Mexico still depended on family ancestry and the positions linked to Mexican centralism. Doing a career in the north of the country and living in a different environment than most Mexican intellectuals was not easy, even still now, with obstacles that are sharpened by being a woman. In a sense, my career has developed in a similar sense to Jose Manuel's. Social activism-academic activism. A binomial in the academic career of JMV overlaps sociological analysis, with social solidarity.

Portrait 1: Juan Manuel, the tenacious

The first portrait depicts a man faced with tremendous adversity, but who overcomes obstacles to find ways in which to thrive.

We had the opportunity to interview JMV, which was an amazing experience. He explains his humble origins:

> I had an extremely happy childhood in the small town of Tecate, on the Northwestern Mexico-USA border. This context of precariousness is widely appreciated, because, in the end, it had to do with ways of life in which we build a sense of happiness, deep security, of certainties.

Manuel's first job was at the Tecate Brewery, where he understood what it was like to belong to the working class. Despite the economic limitations of Manuel's family, he applied to be a student at Mexico's National University (UNAM), in metallurgical chemical engineering: "But when I got there, I realized that it wasn't my thing. One day, someone heard me make a speech (he won several oratorical competitions in high school) and invited me to the Faculty of Philosophy and there I entered what was a cadre school, a political training school, and there I started something that completely transformed my life, I dropped out of college and dedicated myself to doing political work to support the working-class movement....I was in a context completely crossed by the student movements in Mexico (1968 and 1971, where he confronted the Mexican Army), and this was very important for my professional life. It was a collision that accelerated my work, 'the intensity of social time.'"

He did not give up and kept working and participated in meetings discussing activism strategies.

> There, unlike the usual academic work you do with students, where many people can say anything and there are no direct consequences, you must think about what you are doing, because it has a very direct impact, and if you make a mistake, maybe it'll cause consequences for the workers.

We think that this social activism has been embedded in all our research, where building novel approaches to advance knowledge and with it improve society's quality of life has always been our vision. But JMV's experiences deeply inspire us and demand us to innovate and improve our role outside academia.

Portrait 2: Juan Manuel, the academic entrepreneur

His persistence in achieving an academic career is also very striking:

> In Tijuana, I found a job as a librarian (1981), in an institution that was in its early days, which now is one of the best research institutions in Mexico named El Colegio de la Frontera Norte (COLEF). For three years, I continued writing academic papers and participating as an assistant in institutional projects. Then in 1984, Jorge Bustamante, the Principal at COLEF, suggested that I apply to the Regional Development Master program. But I said to him I did not have even a bachelor's degree. So that was my challenge. Over the next years, I had to finish the master's program and conclude the bachelor credits (simultaneously) to continue to be a part of COLEF.
>
> I called the University of Sonora asking about open bachelor programs, but they told me they didn't have any; then I asked for the Sociology Dean. Against all odds, the Dean supported me, even against her superiors. Later, I asked her why. I did not know she has been also a social activist. She was Margarita Urías, a former political prisoner. She told me: –there I learned that when you can swing it for someone, you should and I decided that I would swing it for you.
>
> Then in 1988, I finished my master's degree program and was hired as a researcher at COLEF, and in August, I went to El Colegio de Mexico (in Mexico City) to start a Ph.D. in sociology.

Manuel has some characteristics that mirror some of the struggles I (Oscar) have faced in my academic trajectory. I also have a nonlinear way of advancing through academia. I used to work in the family business (electrical contractor), and never thought I would be in academia formally. I once saw a newspaper ad where my present university was promoting their PhD program in alliance with Mexico's National University (UNAM), and I applied to it because just like Manuel, I wanted to have a new challenge in life.

Those experiences shaped JMV's life and ultimately, his approach to teaching:

> "I have always tried not to ask my students to do what interests me. You have to try to place yourself in the logic of what they want and support them in their processes

FIGURE 30.1 Personal archive JMV, 1981, 2nd St. Tijuana, Mexico. A movement to support border workers.

of analytical construction. I can say that I and the people I have worked with and graduated with maintain a very good relationship. Their careers must follow their course, nurtured by other perspectives". Just as JMV, we can see ourselves related to how satisfied we are when our students transcend, achieve professional/academic goals, and grow.

We all identified with his ethics and vision toward his profession:

> I am in an environment where I feel deeply grateful that I can do the things that I like. I have worked on the themes I like (gangs, cholos, immigrants, the homeless, maras,

> rockers, graffiti artists). I went to work in an institution where they never imposed a topic or a way of doing research, where my methods and way of working were always respected, I have deep gratitude to COLEF. And the way we do it, I do it, is in privileged conditions.

The tenacious trajectory of Manuel (and COLEF itself) made visible the new social processes in the north of Mexico which had been little analyzed until before the 1980s. The vision of Manuel's academic work became to transform, with others, the social border epistemology,[2] and that also can be reflected in our research upon issues related to the world's most dynamic, unequal border.

Portrait 3: Juan Manuel, the daredevil

> In 40 years at COLEF, nobody forced me. I experienced conflicts and authoritarianism at other times, for example, with companies or the federal government. Yes, there were attempts to silence me or at least seek my separation from the institution by external actors, but in COLEF I found support, I think that we should be grateful to Jorge Bustamante, beyond his political affiliations, he was a visionary man that made possible a space in which freedom of ideas, thought, and work was allowed.

COLEF was creating its intellectual thinking by embracing cross-disciplinary border studies (USA-MEX) research just as JMV started to do.

> So, my political activity and positioning, the persistence of my positions have not changed and prevailed fundamentally from an ethical, political, and academic commitment. What did happen is that I began to separate from actual activism and spent more time working on it. My research themes reflect social activism and so is a different way of doing it.

He narrates a specific event where the heat and pressure were turned on:

> Being the coordinator of the northern office of Popular Cultures,[3] we organized an event in 1993 where former president Ernesto Zedillo was at the inauguration. Popular Cultures merged with the Tijuana Cultural Center (CECUT), an important turn in the activity. We introduced very strong activities about and from popular culture, including conferences, exhibitions, wrestling matches, crops exhibition, Mexican popular toys, and workshops on popular art.
> Also, we had a strong relationship with indigenous groups, Yuman, Kiliwas, Paipai, Kumiai, Cucapá. This was a moment of pressure, because the CECUT was like a temple of "high culture" in Tijuana, following schemes that came from the era of enlightenment. In this division between the named "high culture" and "popular culture" or even the "no culture" for many, there was an important dispute against the Mexican centralist view.[4] In this context, there were very strong expressions of protest against my job, in particular when I organized with local Yuman groups, the first indigenous meeting on the Mexico-United States border. Then, a group tried to boycott the

event. They carried out activities without authorization from the communities themselves (and without the organizer's consent), they supposedly spoke on behalf of them and local groups interposing regional interests of people who had been occupying the lands of these communities.

The political pressure was extremely strong at the federal level, obviously for the reason that we are talking about an unprecedented event, an encounter that had not occurred before or after the border delimitation (USA-MEX war, in 1848). The situation was that around 54 indigenous groups gathered to discuss their situation. A few days before the event, there was a call to tell me that the political pressure was strong and to ask me to suspend it. My answer was 'no!', that I would not do it, and that I would resign the day after the end of the congress. The director of Popular Cultures took a supportive position and said, "in any case if there is an impact it is with me, not with you", and I said, "well, let's go both go". The congress went on.

The dispute over the environment, popular cultures, small businesses, women entrepreneurs, the desolate border spaces, and the inequalities in the academic field, are the points that unite our careers (Araceli). A former director of my university's business incubator, I (Oscar) too was confronted internally with agency problems, trying to start the 1st entrepreneurship movement in 40 years. I was criticized all the time, no matter how successful my work was. Up to today, seven years after I left my office, my institution keeps my vision alive. I always looked to the institutions' best interests, not on personal or groups benefits.

DB,[5] USA

We would like to tell you about a man who is a legend in academia. He is known as the last living postmodernist. He is in the top 4% of all academics worldwide in terms of citations.

I (Duncan) am proud to call David, my friend, and colleague. I first met him at the European Group for Organization Studies Conference (EGOS), in 2017. Everything David wrote inspired me. As a result, I was determined to meet the man behind the legend. David and I crossed paths at the conference. "Oh, my goodness you're David Boje!" I stammered. David, unsurprised that he was indeed the name by which he was known, said "Hello." Thus, began our friendship, professional discourses, and collaborations.

David's story is unique to academia. His childhood years were difficult (to say the least), characterized by a challenging relationship with his parents and frequent moves. Young David struggled with school and with the law. Surprisingly, he discovered his talents in an unusual place – The War in Vietnam. After high school, David enlisted in the Army to garner a fresh start. Although it was far from an idyllic experience, it helped him discover a hidden talent: reading voraciously, absorbing and digesting massive amounts of information, and reviving a love for learning.

After his return to the USA, David was offered an early discharge if he entered college. As a Ph.D. student, David began teaching management courses and immediately became aware that those students were inattentive. He told them "I don't think you guys are learning anything," to which one student responded, "That's because you're not teaching anything." Instead of becoming frustrated, David asked the students what they would

FIGURE 30.2 David took this picture in Copenhagen in a park dedicated to the Stone Age. He loved this experience and picture because it was an opportunity to go back in time.

like to learn. This was the first step in his uniquely successful approach to project-based and Socratic Method instruction. He said, "I was popular because out of 14 sections, I was the only one doing non-lecture. I guess I was popular because I was different." As a result, he became the coordinator of the 14 sections of the management curriculum. Upon completion of his Ph.D., David accepted a position at the University of California, Los Angeles (UCLA).

At UCLA, David challenged the status quo. He taught phenomenology, ethnography, and storytelling. He was extremely popular with students, but his success and willingness to experiment made him less so with his colleagues. Consequently, the combination of his classroom success and collegial resentment resulted in his tenure being denied, despite his publication prowess.

Portrait 1: David the tenacious

The first portrait depicts a man faced with tremendous adversity, but who overcomes obstacles to find ways in which to thrive.

"Life is about ups and downs; if you're going to make a career you have to take risks." David explained the difficult choices faced during his first tenure track position at UCLA:

> The Dean told me that I was in the phenomenology group and that I was the worst teacher and scholar, and the worst human being – and there was no way I was going to get tenure. That was only in my second year, my two ASQ (Administrative Sciences Quarterly, the premier journal in business) articles didn't count because they were co-authored, and none of the work I published with doctoral students counted either.

Before UCLA decided to deny his tenure, a faculty member from a competing department reached out to him and made the following offer, "David if you want to switch to my department, I can make sure you get tenure." David replied,

> I appreciate the offer, but I was hired by the phenomenology group and I don't think I should turn my back on them. . . The funny thing is that faculty member never spoke to me again – even when we sat next to each other on a plane ride.

This was the beginning of his downslide – he was denied tenure, went bankrupt, and his private businesses failed. Once his former colleagues at UCLA discovered he was moving to Loyola Marymount University, they offered memorable words of encouragement, "When you go to Loyola Marymount you are going to fail miserably because that is a teaching university. They expect people to know how to teach and you have been an academic teaching phenomenology and systems theory. You are going to fail big time," to which David responded, "Okay, but if I'm going to fail, I'm going to do it my way."

David was a different kind of teacher, implementing new ways of teaching (much like myself (Oscar)– once a colleague told me, "Don't teach with Harvard case studies, the students don't care, and they don't value that"). Also, in 2014, I (Oscar), begin to promote within my department at UACJ, the need to do research on entrepreneurship, as part of a new trend in the academic arena but also to improve the regional social and economic setting (Juarez, Mexico was considered the most violent city in the world). No one except one colleague (Claudia Rodriguez) followed my request (everyone thought it was going to be one of those projects that will never start, something common in Mexico's culture). Four books were published. Later, in 2018, this project went into the global arena when I met Araceli, and Emerald Publishing (UK), who decided to publish a book about the history of entrepreneurship in Mexico. Everyone thought we will also fail big time. Now, we continue to be involved in two more projects, with the same publishing house.

One of the many things that inspire us most about David is his unbeatable tenacity. The academic career path is fraught with frustrations. David could have taken the easy way out, but that would have meant sacrificing his principles. Moreover, it would have ended his unique identity, and he would have ultimately become just another cog in the academic machine. Many would have simply given up in the face of such pressures. Instead, David saw this adversity as a source of strength. He had confidence in himself and his ability to forge a new path.

David's example gives courage and inspiration to all. A failure at one institution is not a failure of the Self. As David et al. indicate (Larsen, Boje, and Bruun, 2020), the most important thing is to seek "truth" in a Heideggerian sense. This is not true in a universal sense, but rather being true to oneself. We have found that every career change has been epitomized by trepidation; and, I (Duncan) realize that there is more success in strength and grit than in fear. In 2013, I (Oscar) implemented (from zero) and oversaw, for both teachers and students, the first institutional entrepreneurial movement in the university's 40 years of existence, successfully confronting institutional obstacles.

Portrait 2: David the academic entrepreneur

In the second portrait, we see a man whose gaze and mind extend far beyond the frame, a man not bound by rules, but a man who thrives in their rupture. "I was the teacher of the year for my first year at Loyola Marymount. Then I was the teacher of the year every year."

For David, being the best teacher at Loyola Marymount was not enough. He wanted to make the world a better place. His first project was creating a vocational training program in South Central Los Angeles (one of its most dangerous areas) – the ultimate goal of which was to help people living in the housing projects acquire jobs in those same projects.

> I had this idea to get jobs for the residents in the bureaucracy of public housing. I was negotiating with a lawyer for the city who is saying it could not be done – it will cost too much money. What I wanted to do is create a job development training program that was free. It would not cost the city a dime. I will have some professors from the local universities to help; we will have the residents of the housing projects provide additional workshops on showing up on time, writing a resume, interviewing, anger management, and basic skills. We wanted the residents to get jobs as maintenance workers, janitors, clerical staff, and administrative support. The first seven graduates from our job training program were so important because the hopes and aspirations of 5,000 people rested upon them.

Fast forward, this program grew and spread hope across the Watts Housing Development in South Central Los Angeles. David wrote a grant for the Peace Corps (PC) to create programs for economic development.

> One of the most significant outcomes was that PC volunteers did not receive teaching certificates (as was the norm at the time), but rather MBAs from Loyola Marymount for their service-based learning projects. I then mobilized my core course sections of more than 50 students to perform their service-learning projects – they learned management by doing, and they loved it. This was how I recruited for service-learning projects – it was impossible to not be excited.

David's story is the embodiment of the "plus zone challenge" (Pelly and Fayolle 2020). It is not enough to engage in inert education (Whitehead, 1967) geared toward academic neoliberalism (Pelly and Boje 2019a) or academic silos (Pelly and Boje 2020). As academics, we must make the world a better place. David was not only a thought leader who helped others – he served as an example that encouraged others to do the same. I (Duncan) have yet to achieve a similar societal impact. However, his example did encourage me to create my YouTube channel, "Dr. D University," which has had an international following and has enabled me to help students in developing countries.

Portrait 3: David the daredevil

In the third portrait, I (Duncan) see a blank canvas and an artist's palette beckoning to me. This is David's invitation to paint my canvas.

"When students would participate in class, I would hand out participation slips. You could redeem them for a piece of chocolate or a condom."

> . . . So, I got in trouble at Loyola Marymount big time, because the one thing you don't do in a Jesuit university is pass out condoms in your classroom. The Jesuit order called me: 'I got a report that you're passing out condoms in the classroom. I don't

mind you going to do tutoring in South Central LA and all this other stuff. And you brought murderers into your MBA leadership class. But I'm willing to overlook all that. There might be some value in a person who has been to prison and is a murderer talking about leadership. You people had a beer bus as an event. You had kegs in the classroom. We're Jesuits, we don't mind the drinking, but you cannot have condoms in your classroom. Promise me you won't do that again.' Of course, students handed out condoms all the time at student events.

This humorous anecdote reminds us that it is important to take risks. Sometimes these risks lead to successes and sometimes they do not. This anecdote shows it is acceptable to take chances – pushing the envelope and finding these roadblocks is what ultimately makes us human (Pelly, 2016). More importantly, it highlights that David found a way to avoid the stereotype of the high-power distance professor, forged a path to relating to students in new ways, and crippled inter-organizational barriers. If we can understand the way others think, then we can craft solutions that represent integration or better ways to help educate all parties involved (Pelly, 2017).

I (Duncan) am unable to imitate David's exact approaches to motivating student participation, but it did motivate me to ask more challenging and engaging questions and to try to understand the underlying dreams of those I teach. I am then capable of tailoring my lectures to reflect their aspirations and not those of my own.

Final thoughts

We are amazed at how both JMV and DB have made such a difference in our lives (to which David responded:

> I didn't make a difference in their lives – they did that themselves. But they did make a difference in my life. They taught me important lessons – both political parties have disrupted the poor. Yet despite this tremendous adversity, these people were resilient. It is okay to speak against the powerful).

Perhaps the most powerful testament came from David's advisor, the late Louis R. Pondy:

> Dave, you're truly an amazing fellow, Dave. You have a rare ability to have creative ideas and put them into practice. I'd like to do my little part in giving you as much room to operate as possible. You can be a multiplier for large scale organizational change."

I (Duncan) can think of no greater compliment to my mentor and friend.

Both portraits showed how they fought against the system, which was a centralized and sometimes bizarre, vision of the borders (territorially, academic, teaching), and its dynamics. To us the academic lives of DB and JMV are resumed in the phrase: "The system is against us." They both encountered in life many barriers, but everyone seems to have been just a good excuse to overcome them and grow. The analysis and understanding of culture and social commitments are movement and resistance at the same time. That's how we've felt, our mirrors are clear and our portraits are that of a permanent and constantly evolving fight,

Notes

1 He is a professor at El Colegio de la Frontera Norte (Tijuana Campus), a Mexican international renowned federal government research center, with 6 campuses throughout Mexico-USA border, and 2 more in Monterrey and Mexico City. He received in 2021 the distinction as Emeritus in the Mexican National System of Researchers, a federal program under the National Council on Science and Technology (CONACYT).
2 Although the term border leads us to the idea of limit, social borders invites us to think in open spaces and constant mobility of ideas, beliefs, and social senses. It leads us to a definition of multi-speed transits. The idea of social frontier is therefore the image of moving and inexhaustible meanings. It is true that a border politically divides countries, regions, and localities, in social terms the borders are alive and represent movement. Although at certain moments dormant, social borders are never fixed and never concluded, at certain moments they are slower, at others they re-emerge more accelerated and dynamic than ever.
3 This Department was created by Mexico's federal government in 1978 for the promotion, study, conservation, dissemination, and development of the popular cultures of Mexico. Today it is strengthened with the creation of the Ministry of Culture, with policies to promote cultural diversity and safeguard the Intangible Cultural Heritage.
4 The Mesoamerican Civilizations, where the Aztecs and Mayas are the most renowned and famous, were located in today's Mexico's central and south regions. No relevant culture developed in the north. That is why in Mexico it was common to say that there was no culture in the north.
5 He is an emeritus professor of management at New Mexico State University, USA, and a professor at Aalborg University, Denmark. He has worldwide recognition as the pioneer on the Storytelling Theory, and created the field of "antinarrative" research. David was Editor of the *Journal of Organizational Change Management* for 14 years, and founder and editor of *Tamara: Journal for Critical Organization Inquiry*. He was past chair of the Academy of Management Research Methods division. He was also awarded an honorary doctorate from Aalborg University.

References

Larsen, J., Boje, D. M., & Bruun, L. (2020). *True Storytelling: Seven Principles for an Ethical and Sustainable Change-management Strategy*. Routledge.

Pelly, R. D. M. (2016). A bureaucrat's journey from technocrat to entrepreneur through the creation of adhocracies. *Entrepreneurship & Regional Development*, 28(7–8), 487–513.

Pelly, R. D. M. (2017). The story of captain baby face and the coffee maker: An entrepreneurial narrative perspective on corruption. *Journal of Management Inquiry*, 26(4), 390–405.

Pelly, R. D. M., & Boje, D. (2019a). Neoliberalism in the North American University: Toward integrating divisions in agent orientation via a Follettian differentiated relational ontology. *Communication & Language at Work*, 6(2), 28–41.

Pelly, R. D. M., & Boje, D. (2020). A case for follettian interventions in public universities. *Journal of Applied Research in Higher Education*, 12(4), 562–571.

Pelly, R. D. M., & Fayolle, A. (2020). Ethnography's answer to the plus zone challenge of entrepreneurship. In W. B. Gartner & B. T. Teague (eds.), *Research Handbook on Entrepreneurial Behavior, Practice and Process*. Edward Elgar Publishing, 82–101.

Whitehead, A. N. (1967). *Aims of education*. Simon and Schuster.

VI
The transgressive gallery
Curated by Alexandra Bristow

IN THE GARDEN OF DREAMS

Transgressive careers

Alexandra Bristow

Welcome to the Transgressive Gallery. By now, you may have become accustomed to the dizzying architecture of our exhibition. If you have followed the suggested route through the interconnecting rooms, nothing should phase you after the non-Euclidian maze of the Meandering Gallery, the stormy waters of Navigating Belonging, and the mind-tricking reflections in the Hall of Mirrors, to name but a few of the preceding adventures. If, instead, you have chosen a different route, you might have already communed with the ghosts of the Haunted Gallery, or with academics Living Precariously. If you have, you are well prepared to explore the portraits in the Transgressive Gallery.

It is also possible that this is the first gallery you have chosen to visit. If you were drawn here by the radicalism suggested by its title, this gallery will not disappoint. In terms of doing academic careers differently, transgression arguably constitutes the most radical departure from prescribed career norms, short of leaving academic employment completely (as academic ghosts would remind us). The academics you will encounter in this gallery share this impetus to transgress boundaries, particularly between academic and non-academic careers, but also between disciplines and between academic careers and personal lives. Their stories are brimming with creativity and wonderment, and portray two activists, a philosopher, a journalist, and two performing artists, all combining these with their academic work.

If you look around you, you will see that the space in which you stand embodies this spirit of openness. We are in a room that spills beyond the confines of the building. Its fourth wall is broken, opening into an adjacent garden, inviting you to step outside and explore. Come with me and I will give you a tour.

As we cross the threshold, you feel the warm sunlight on your face and blink your eyes, realising how dark it had been inside the building called 'academia'. Dark, confined, stale. But out here you can move, stretch out your limbs and your mind, glimpse a red kite soaring high overhead. The air is sweet with the scent of roses, lavender, and rosemary blooming in the borders, and there is a meditative susurration of a fountain somewhere just out of sight. A gentle breeze stirring the treetops adds to the music and brings aromas of pine and sea air from beyond the crest of a distant hill. Multiple paths run through the garden and into the woods and fields beyond. If you follow them to their destinations, who knows where they will take you? Your head fills with possibilities.

So, where shall we start? How about here, through this hidden doorway, where in a brick-walled niche under the arching branches of a climbing rose hangs a miniature by Sophie Del Fa. Written in a mixture of French and English, poetry and prose, it is both bleak and beautiful. Touch it and you will be transported to less clement climes on the shores of a cold river, the setting for a journey from transgression to contestation and back. It tells of Sophie's experiences of her first year as an assistant professor trying to find her path as a grassroots activist academic, and of anxiety and personal sacrifices involved in this search. It speaks of the emotional and physical toll of contestation and transgression, but also of how pain is itself transformative: 'La douleur, dans l'fond, c'est un tremplin vers autre chose. Toute douleur transforme.' ('Pain, basically, is a springboard to something else. All pain transforms.')

Pain as both the cost and the impetus or means of transgression is a theme that echoes through all portraits in this gallery. The idyll of the garden setting in which we find ourselves, the dreams of openness and freedom are grown on the roots of suffering. When these dreams come into full bloom, they do so by drawing nutrients from the composted memories of harder times, of failure, of non-belonging, of loneliness, which still cast dark shadows under the trees and shrubs around us. Are they worth it? Each one of us must decide for ourselves.

From one portrait of an activist academic to the next, let us move along a path less travelled. There is a bright thread caught up in the foliage to your left; if you pick it up it will start pulling. Following it leads us to a shaded stream, where an ancient tree stands, its trunk immerse, its branches dominating the view. It is not healthy: 'The roots are far too rotten'. That is the diagnosis of academia you will find as you regard Camila Fredes Ortiz' portrait, pinned to the bridge starting from the opposite bank of the stream. The bridge does not reach the tree-side, stopping part-way over the water, symbolic of the partial connection between activism and academia. Relating her struggles to respond to the violence of the Chilean state and the revolt of 2019 while located in distant Barcelona, Camila shares the hope and possibilities for social justice in academia and beyond, which come through feminist descolonial, connected, collective activism. She puts forward a 'felt-thought declaration of consequence towards academia', a manifesto for staying, despite 'its rotten nature, its walls and limitations', in order to break, to transform its hegemonic careers and institutions, reclaiming its territory as a place of questioning, creativity, and social change. Can we, collectively, achieve this massive undertaking? Can we, together, complete that bridge that will take us to other places? Perhaps, for now, we just need to make a leap of faith.

...We land on the other bank. Leaving the stream through some shrubbery, we come to a fragrant rose garden in full bloom. Beyond a gate, a wide path seems to run unimpeded, but the warning is stark on a sign fixed to the entrance:

> From an outsider's point of view, academic life is an extraordinary career option. For them, it is an easy pathway through a rose garden. But as we, academics, know, it is indeed surrounded by roses – roses with thick, sharp thorns.

Those are the words of Jaime Bayona, the initially canonical, turned failed, and now absurd academic. To get to his portrait, we must be brave. It takes a while before, scratched by the thorns of 'stress, deadlines and personal struggles', we emerge from the roses at the bottom of a steep upward slope, where the portrait is etched into the surface of a huge round boulder. 'Happy Sisyphus', reads the inscription. Drawing on the philosophy of Albert Camus, Jaime tells of how he has come to accept the absurdity of academic life, 'as a point of equilibrium between the stress of the canonical option [of academic dogma] and the emptiness of the suicidal option' of leaving academia. Despite the overarching meaningless of academic life, he contends, an absurd academic can be happy in finding meaning 'in the small activities of academia, especially impacting the lives of our students, via teaching and research'. In this way our constant 'pushing a boulder up a steep hill' becomes balanced with going 'back down the hill again and again, giving guidance and meaning to our students (with the new knowledge we collected during the last round of pushing the boulder up the hill)'.

And so, like Sisyphus (happy or otherwise), we press on. Onwards and upwards, to the top of the slope, where a bench stands overlooking the vista of pine forests hugging the shores of a restless sea. Following the climb, there is an opportunity to sit here a moment, to catch your breath. Conveniently, there is a newsstand by the bench, to help while away the time. Have a look at *Academic Times*. The lead article on the front page of the newspaper portrays Todd Bridgman. Trained and experienced journalist before he became an academic, Todd shares his journey from a sense of academic failure (to publish in 'top' journals as his writing was considered too journalistic) to crafting a successful career in 'academic journalism', which, he says, 'means producing research that challenges the status quo, that holds those in authority to account and that seeks a broad audience beyond the "ivory tower"'. He argues that 'the rise of "impact", the open access movement in academic publishing and disruption of mainstream print and broadcast news media' 'provide fertile ground for the growth of "academic journalism"', including of the 'slow journalism' variety. Todd's portrait offers encouragement to find an academic career path that plays to individual strengths and interests rather than waste time trying to be something you are not.

Transgressing academic boundaries to find and be yourself is also a strong theme in the remaining two portraits in this gallery. To see them, we make our way down the hill, via paths meandering through maze-like rockeries interspersed with small waterfalls. Careful now, for someone (a passing Norwegian wolf?) has dropped a banana skin right in the middle of the walkway (at least we know the grandma is safe for now). As you lift your gaze you see it out there on the margins of the path, the portrait of a smiling face peering through the blinds. The blinds partially conceal it, 'avoiding co-optation', 'preserving mystery, keeping the inexplicit free of its own chains'. This is Stephen Linstead, opening with the banana skin of a near-death experience that is dramatic, humorous, and life-changing. From there, he paints the story of a life built between the worlds of management academia (and academic management) and performing arts, 'dipping into one then the other, trying to figure out who [he] was'. Over the years of 'never-at-homeness' he tells of expressing creativity and criticality 'on the margins, after dark', sometimes feeling 'as though [he's] been eluding the searchlights of a system that would do [him] harm if it only knew what [he] was up to', before more recently succeeding in combining his two lives by becoming a filmmaker. His portrait sparks hope for 'an alternative future in which intellectual alterity… helps to enable a better, less functionally obsessed but more humanly functional, world in which we stop judging each other so harshly whilst taking more precise care of the worlds under our stewardship'.

To create alternative realities and futures that are more humane and caring may require coming back to ourselves, reconnecting with our own feelings, however difficult they may be to face. And so, making our way to the bottom of the hill, and following a brook through an arbour, then a field, then a meadow, we return to the broken wall, to the last portrait. Lured away by the beauty of the garden, we didn't stop by it on the way out, graffitied there Banksy-style on the remaining stub of the wall. It portrays Ralf Wetzel, a clown in full regalia, face lit up by an enormous smile, tears spraying theatrically from his eyes. By his feet clad in oversized shoes, within the portrait and spilling out into the garden, are scattered huge grey rocks that had been part of the broken wall. Look closer and you will see that they are 'nothing but compressed and petrified feelings': fear, frustration, anger, love, desire, lust. Ralf tells of his long journey of self-denial, self-alienation, and emotional disconnection, starting from his self-repressing primary schooling in East Germany during which he has barricaded away his emotional self, through the alienating years of mainstream academic career, until he found healing and liberation in performing arts, which changed his personal and professional life. Now a theatre and clown performer who uses these skills in academic work, Ralf speaks of the performing arts' 'immense immanent powers for personal and societal transformation', and for 'breaking free of alienating and devaluating contexts, finding personal ground and a stance to operate truthfully from'.

…And so, visitor, we have come full circle, arriving where we started. And do we know the place for the first time? As Stephen Linstead, also reflecting on Eliot's words, observes, the past is another country. Following our tour, the garden around us is altered. The sun is westering now, the shadows are longer, the air cooler. The garden is less idyllic, and yet somehow more alive and vibrant for it. The transgressive dreams it grows are full of darker undertones and sharp thorns and yet are deeper and more hopeful. As the day begins to fade, the rocks by Ralf's feet light up in many colours. There is the strangely reassuring building of academia right here that we can re-enter to shelter from the night. But a tawny owl calls from the woods. And the fountain somewhere just out of sight whispers of the many paths there are to tread from transgression to contestation, and back.

SEEK & **DESTROY** – FROM TRANSGRESSION TO CONTESTATION. *AND BACK*

Sophie Del Fa

In this chapter, I take inspiration from Lorde, who says in *Sister Outsider* (1984, p. 37):

> For women, then, poetry is not a luxury. It is a vital necessity of our existence. It forms the quality of the light within which we predicate our hopes and dreams toward survival and change, first made into language, then into idea, then into more tangible action. Poetry is the way we help give name to the nameless so it can be thought. The farthest horizons of our hopes and fears are cobbled by our poems, carved from the rock experiences of our daily lives.

This chapter, therefore, is a reflexive poetical and hybrid proposition, a personal foray in the first year of an assistant professor who wishes to find her path in academia. Inspired by Foucault, I try to make peace with what was a traumatic year which still resonates in me today. I propose a poetic journey from transgression to contestation… and back to show how the urge to *exist* as an academic can interfere with (and destroy) personal life.

Le 18 avril 2019, j'ai eu 30 ans.

Hélène Dorion (1988) se demande si la trentième année apprendrait à refuser le va-et-vient de l'émotion?

Le 18 avril 2019, je me levais tôt, dans une petite ville au bord d'une rivière encore froide, pour une entrevue. Une entrevue de professeure d'université.

Le 18 avril 2019, j'aurais dû mettre ma vie entre parenthèses. Comme toutes les femmes devraient le faire à 30 ans.

In "A Preface to transgression" (1965), Foucault defines contestations and transgressions as two sides of the same coin:

> Contestation does not imply a generalized negation, but an affirmation that affirms nothing, a radical break of transitivity. Rather than being a process of thought for denying existences or values, contestation is the act which carries them to their limits and, from there, to the Limit where an ontological decision achieves its end; to contest

is to proceed until one reaches the empty core where being achieves its limit and where the limit defines being.

(1965, p. 36)

Transgression opens onto a scintillating and constantly affirmed world, a world without shadow or twilight, without that serpentine "no" that bites into fruits and lodges their contradictions at their core. It is the solar inversion of satanic denial.

(1965, p. 37)

April 22, 2019. 1 week before the thesis defense

Last week of my PhD. I am shaking. What do I need to read for the day of my defense? What do I need to know more? I have never been so scared. Gabrielle Roy's book lies next to me. I am at the edge of the rest of my life. Final count down. I feel so lonely. I don't have the strength to go on. I need to start my defense by speaking about the meaning of life. Living means becoming.

Who will I become?

April 23, 2019

I got the job!

April 26, 2019

Thesis Defense. I should surely be writing on a silver paper that I have just defended my thesis. But the only thing I remember of this day it's me holding my friend's newborn baby.

July 2, 2019

"Dear Miss Del Fa. Welcome to our department. I am one of your future colleagues […] We will have a lot of work to do during the school year. We work non-stop. Sincerely"

August 15, 2019

New professors, welcome day.

I am sure that in ten years I would read this and smile… I would tell myself that it was nothing. But here I am overwhelmed by anxiety. Anxiety of responsibility. Last night, I dreamt of my psychoanalyst. I also dreamt of Montreal which is so far away. And I dreamt of a small child, a restless little girl whom I was able to calm down while everybody had failed. Nostalgia. I don't want to grow up. Am I this little girl? Will I succeed in calming myself alone?

I am already so tired. I won't last long. One year max. I want peace. All of this is absurd. I need to sleep.

August 19, 2019.

First departmental assembly.

Where did my well-deserved holidays go?

As I walk through the green corridors to reach the meeting room, my new colleagues greet me and smile at me. They are surely thinking how young I am.

I enter the room. Everybody stares at me. "The new one". I hate when people stare at me. I feel like a circus freak.

The assembly is a combat arena.

I need allies.

This seems like the beginning of the end. I am now an assistant professor. What do I do? Now? Contest? Transgress? I chose both.

★★

Transgression	*Contestation*
"The solar inversion of satanic denial" (see Foucault above)	"An affirmation that affirms nothing, a radical break of transitivity" (see Foucault above)
	July 6 & 7, 2019, Saint-Fulgence
	Anarchist camp. Pure life. Concepts' deconstruction. The poetics of revolution.
	GNL Québec project: 1) A pipeline of 782 km from Ontario to Saguenay. 2) construction of a natural gas liquefaction complex at Port Saguenay. 3) increase of oil tankers on the Fjord du Saguenay
	50 million tons of GHG
	Threatens 30 vulnerable species of plants and animals because of the route and gas activities
	La *Coalition Fjord*, a grassroot group organizes the fight against this project.
September 3, 2019	
I barely know what day we are. One day follows the other while I am doing "my work". Loneliness. Gloomy office without windows. My head hurts.	
	September 9, 2019
	Where are you who fight in the dark?
September 11, 2019	
He does not care about me. I feel sad. This city is ugly. I am tired. I wanted to write. I do not write. I wanted to love, I don't know if I love. I don't like my body. It calls for help.	

                                                                    November 8, 2019
                                                                    1 year of the *Coalition Fjord*

November 11, 2019

Mais je veux aussi continuer d'explorer, de
transgresser*, de vivre mon univers retourné. De*
vivre le monde et la vie.

Je te demande ma liberté. Mais je ne la prendrai pas
si elle détruit notre commune.

                Betrayal.   **November 20, 2019**
                                                                    First draft of the letter.

November 22, 2019

    Exhaustion.
    I am drunk.
    All alone.
  I scream. No one hears me.
    I blame him
  He won't be there

                     CHAOS   CHAOS

January 29, 2020   **January 29, 2020**

His grandfather dies.   The letter against *GNL Québec* is sent. That is
I am away with someone else.   the academic I want to be.

                Black out   Black out

J'hurle dans l'ombre sans me faire entendre.
Le cri traverse les murs sans heurter personne.
On m'a dit, aujourd'hui, que j'étais toxique.

                                                                                              Tox-i-que

Le mot sonne aigre. Il fait mal aux oreilles. Il brule le corps. Comme des ongles trop longs qui grincent sur un tableau de craie.

                                                                                              Tox-i-que

Le lire m'a fait vibrer le cœur. Qui se tortillait. Qui se rapetissait. Mon cœur est devenu tout petit.
Petit.
L'hiver, les larmes gèlent si tu pleures dehors. Mais mes paupières givrées brisent la glace.
Qui craque.
Si tu fermes les yeux tu peux les entendre, les craquements, ceux qui usent les bords des plaques de glace suspendues au-dessus de l'eau. Si tu ouvres les yeux, tu les vois glisser sur la rivière, ce tapis noir.

Tu t'imagines t'y étendre. Mais la réalité est plus froide que le rêve.
Cette eau, noire, est-elle toxique, elle? Y gouterai-je pour le savoir?
Si je plonge dans l'eau, je meurs. C'est simple. On mettra du temps à me retrouver. À moins que je me mette à flotter, dans ce cas, je passerai pas inaperçue. J'aurais le ventre gonflé et la peau bleue. Violette. Une belle palette.
La poésie brille dans l'eau sombre. Je me suis sûrement trompée.
L'hiver, la terre est morte. On a dû dire plusieurs que la neige ressemble à un linceul.

Linceul.

Ce mot est laid. Comme toxique.

Mais je dois reprendre ma promenade hivernale et suivre ce cri aux échos muets.

La neige bruisse sous les pieds froids pendant que le chien y plonge son museau. La pleine lune éclaire le chemin. Pas besoin de lampes frontales.

Je veux tout contrôler. ***Je veux me faire remarquer. Être importante.*** Mais souvent tout t'échappe et là, tu souffres. Inévitable souffrance.

January 29, 2020

The university's administration does not endorse the letter.

Doing several interviews.

January 31, 2020

The letter appears in *Le Devoir*

February 12, 2020

Ce week-end, j'ai pensé au suicide. Plusieurs fois et à différents endroits.

Sur cette route, vers le nord puis vers le sud ou encore vers l'est et de retour vers l'ouest.

Je lis dans les autres ce que je ne suis pas.
Je lis dans les autres ce que j'aimerais être.

Je suis vide.
Une lame perce ma poitrine.

« Poésie érotique révolutionnaire. En pensée. Lutte diagonale. »
« Puisses-tu savoir que je t'aime, en avant, le poing levé. »

Him

His poetry reminded me of Audre Lorde's quotation:

> We can train ourselves to respect our feelings and to transpose them into a language so they can be shared. And where that language does not yet exist, it is our poetry which helps to fashion it. Poetry is not only dream and vision; it is the skeleton architecture of our lives. It lays the foundations for a future of change, a bridge across our fears of what has never been before.' (1984, pp. 37–38)

March 2020

I am engaged with la *Coalition Fjord* on a
collaboration with a local brewery.
La Micro du Lac.
Organizing the launching of the first beer!
A lot of fun
I like that.
Working on the website too.

May 5, 2020

La douleur, dans l'fond, c'est un tremplin
vers autre chose. Toute douleur transforme.
Changement d'état. La douleur est une
débâcle en relief à surmonter. Dans mon corps
c'est la débâcle. Les eaux s'agitent et emportent
tout. La débâcle peut tuer, mais elle est aussi
éphémère et saisonnière. **Comme les trente
ans d'une femme.**

Today.
Contestation through transgression.
I remember when I was told not to trust anyone in the university.
I remember how scared I was. I remember not to follow this advice.
I trust my colleagues.
I listen to their pain. And to my own pain
Pain is transformative. My thirtieth year is over. I am not the new one anymore.
Breakup can kill, but it's also fleeting and seasonal. **Like a woman's 30 years.**

References

Dorion, H. (1988). *Les Corridors du temps*. Écrits des forges.
Foucault, M. (1965). Préface à la transgression. In Gallimard (eds). *Michel Foucault, Oeuvres II* (pp. 1195–1213). La Pléiade.
Lorde, A. (1984). *Sister Outsider*. Berkeley: Crossing Press.

MEETING THE THREADS THAT PULL

A feminist declaration of consequence towards academia

Camila Fredes

Introduction

Many voices are invited here today. An attempt that feels right in my body and feeling, my felt-thought being. Of a movement that brings a shift. That here finds feet and begins to untangle. Accompanied. Because this belongs outside, in the community, the same one that inevitably lives in me. And to carry consequence to the places I occupy. This writing is that. From situated reflections, to move *the speaker* beyond. Trying for it to be respectful, from attending the threads that pull me back to a collective living. I am not alone and putting myself in this sense of groupness has made me understand. I don't wish to speak in the name of anybody, but as much as mine, somehow, it all feels shared. I hope that more than one of you reading feels found here.

La semilla. These days I have felt like an invisible thread/root pulled me strongly

I see a crack. It has always been there, but now it feels ripped in me.

While being in Barcelona, España, I felt deeply drawn to the place I had left a year before, Chile. There, on the 18th of October 2019 a social revolt broke out. A very exhausted collective and individual resistance, that through extreme repression, broke an apparent stability. A new rise in the price of the public transport -of 0.034 of euro- in Santiago, the capital, was the tonic that fueled discontent. They were young students, the ones that initially evaded the payment in the metro and buses. And after what was justified as insufficient police presence, the military took the streets, shortly after an emergency state was decreed, and later a curfew. An *uprising* took place and today still remains awake.

This found me an ocean away, and it still shook me to the bone. A rift, in between a *here* and a *there* that felt indistinguishable from each other. In this, social media took a central place, connecting me in real time with what was happening in the streets in different cities around the country. And that made my experience one immersed in virtuality, the same one that fed a quick organization of the diverse afflicted community spread around the world.

All of this happened at the beginning of my second year of a Masters in gender studies. And in an imperative way to be part, somehow, somewhere, this – my experience of the distant crisis – turned into the seed of my thesis. One produced from the guts and feelings before words – especially *these* words, since English is not *my language* – in a deep methodological exploration through autoethnography. A writing of memory intended from a descolonial[1] feminist living. Not focusing on gender as the sole axis of oppression but giving account of the simultaneity and codependence of the multiple systems of oppression (Astrid Cuero Montenegro (2019) and Yuderkys Espinosa-Miñoso (2014) have inspiring reflections on this). The amplitude and specificity of the approach allows a vision of the tangled panorama that reality actually is. Giving an understanding that figures the multiplicity and complexity of the Chilean revolt, its political sphere, and the many continuous and violent ways it keeps building an unequal, segregated and precarious living. These reflections have inevitably questioned how to approach an issue like this one in a way that is actually organic to the activist position where it is born. Thus, a critique of academia takes place, as a multiple hegemonic institution not open to the claims of the social fabric in which it is immersed.

Here, a shared feminist-activist standpoint on my conflicted relationship with academia. Not mine as in authorship, but as it lives in me through my collective being. And a declaration of consequence. One that reaffirms the notion of using our platforms, our own voices, to replicate and amplify struggles that have a place where we stand. An invitation to this on-going learning process of articulating consequently an activist, feminist and descolonial living, toward acting for social justice in academia.

Mescolanza: Untangling the road to this writing

Scission. A weird feeling of my mind being apart from my body, finding myself walking through the streets of the center of Santiago, while my body remains located in Barcelona. A multiple and complex mixture and connection, unwanted in a way, but so much inevitable in others. This has been the starting point of a felt-thought search and inquiry. Anchored, first of all, in the feeling of being part of the discomfort that originates the revolt. And sustained in social media, that as a bridge, has invited me to eliminate more than one border, possibilitating proximity though being far away.

Very quickly, Facebook walls, Instagram stories, Twitter, WhatsApp messages, now Telegram and Signal, were filled with images, videos, audios and testimonies. Of a violence that woke up the still very damaged social fabric of this eternal democratic transition we seem to live in.[2] Because we still grow under dangerous ideals and practices, as the constitution that weighs on us was built during the military dictatorship. Same political class and same old patriarchal, white and male centered politics, one completely not accountable of its privilege.

> A brief stop. I need to situate myself. In diverse directions, this context invites me to rethink and question, in and out of ourselves. Power hierarchies repeat and extend in many ways and we can easily forget the coordinates of where we stand. Understanding them in their complexities, being aware of the tangled tissue. Touch the fabric of who we are, and how we actually connect.
>
> My case, a distant-relation, not physically but still very present. *With the privileged option to leave voluntarily, and a good excuse which is studying,*[3] I came with a degree in

psychology that has served me little or not in the kingdom of España -nor in the kingdom of Nederland, that is where I am right now-. Fortress Europe. Where the student visa that allowed me to be here territory is deceitful, as a faithful product of the immigration laws. Just being able to apply for a visa is indicative enough for relative security. Which would allow me to work legally, have a contract, access social security. Just theory, because the bureaucratic obstacles did not make it happen, pushing to another relative precariousness. That is never said and good luck finding out by yourself (in my case, being part of a large migrant activist collective, I got help and orientation from friends to navigate this awful world that is migrant bureaucracy. Thanks to all of them). Now, the way I landed and settled in these new territories is related to my own background and genealogy. Particularly, the privileges I brought with me, like my white body, the access to higher education, the savings I brought with me that indicates my previous access to work, among others. As well as those that kind of faded away by the change in my coordinates (and I don't only mean the physical ones).

This small sharing is part of a multiple and extensive exercise (part of my thesis) of personal descolonization. That starts in the present but quickly connects to the past to actually understand how we benefit and have interiorised the oppression systems (Tuhwai Smith, 2016). How we replicate this in my/our living, standing and acting towards anything, in this case in relation to the revolt. How me/we talk about it, how we write and share about it. In a plural inner descolonization. To think of it from different dimensions and not only *locally and particular* to the social out-brake. Knitting towards the "erasures, obstacles, fractures and dissonances that cross this thinking since colonization"[4] (Ciriza, 2015: 85 in Martínez, 2020: 2). María Catalina Tabares Ochoa (2019) points here to the connection with communitairy and border feminisms, reminding us of the urgent task to actually "build bridges that allow us to envision common paths aimed at social change" (p. 85). Celebrating the heterogeneity of our contributions, the political potential of getting together with whom we would not be establishing connections under the rules of hegemony, in what Maria Galindo (2005) would call 'unusual alliances'.

The social claim quickly exceeded the territory, and a smaller-scale replica was heard in Barcelona, to the song of 'el derecho de vivir en paz'.[5] Protests, concentrations and interventions in the consulate, plaza Catalunya, the rambla, and in diverse migrant houses around the city, expanding all that was/is repeatedly experienced throughout the territory occupied by the state of Chile.

In between participating in an incipient migrant activism, I followed and accounted the first month of this uprising in an autoethnography, focusing on different moments that have given shape and depth to the major struggles and claims at the base of this social movement. A route from my own experience of the distant crisis, to what was being shared in my social media and diverse news channels, and to an active situated activism in the out-side territory. For this, it has been important to uncover the *multi-territorial* experience that migration *can* be, fed by an underlying privilege that allows a connection to a territory left by choice and not by obligation. That now stretches and resents, a bond that is deeply afflicted. Touched in a way that was impossible for me not to recognize myself in something beyond my own body, and my own voice, even my own thoughts and reflections. A truth that came from out-side. That even though I felt/feel in my own experience, it was/is profoundly shared, and not at all *individual*. Acting on this, taking the work back to that place became mandatory. Since all of it, the triggering event, the feeling, the connection, belonged in the collective place where it was *being*. That is how the Laboratorio de la Revuelta was born. An alternative, informal, plural and artistic conversation with 8 Chilean women living in Barcelona, around our diverse living of the distant revolt. This multiple exploration would lead to an extensive critique of the Chilean political system: for the imposition of undignifying living conditions; the refusal by spheres of power to establish dialogs with the people in relation to social demands; the criminalization of legitimate protest, and the exercise of violence that has gotten its way over and over again.

> A mention of violence. Because it is one of the keys where politics becomes inevitable. As something that boils inside the body due to the unworthy conditions, it is necessary to put the loudspeaker – not taking the microphone – everywhere where we reach. That organized lying, misrepresentation, denialism and the tendency to forget and manipulate, in the hand of murder, torture, kidnap, and many ways of physical damage cannot take place in our lives. But they have, through the criminal organization of those who have imposed themselves and we have mistakenly chosen as authority. 34 people killed between October of 2019 and March 2020, and at least 400 presenting eye trauma from buckshot impact as well as permanent blindness during the same period. According to the Institute of Human Rights of Chile (2019), there were 1200 victims of torture and cruel acts of diverse kinds including sexual, while the Ministry of Health calculates 11.000 as the number of injured protesters of varying degrees. Added to this is the political imprisonment of protesters in cases that have not yet been resolved. And all of this without mentioning the historical victims of the state of Chile and its politics.
>
> Violence is also the forced displacement and land grabbing of communities. The economic and neoliberalist abuse; the almost non-existence of state guarantees; and the existence of disastrous institutions such as Sename and the AFP.[6] A legal system with a questioned reputation for reproducing a patriarchal, racist, classist system that has never been held accountable for the disaster and social crisis it/they have failed to contain. And that it/they have deliberately promoted.

How to take part in this? How to raise our voices being so far away? It is clear that getting involved while not being in the territory is a possibility, through diverse ways of online-distant activism as much as local extensions of the social claims. To occupy these streets too and amplify the scope of struggles, but mostly, to account for the horrible consequences that standing up was/is having. The absolute break with any way of compliance with this rotten structure, the negligence of the self-called *authority*. Standing that needed to be shared, in a public and repeated funa.[7] That while trying to find its way in an *academic* format, found itself claustrophobic inside the boundaries that have been imposed in social science. So a further questioning was mandatory, of the most problematic and hegemonic institution I was/am being part of: academia. Writing before, writing now. Lending my place in a set of rules I don't share but despise, but in which I still participate by being here. Not alone and not without bothering, while bringing the not much welcome feminist notions and ethics into the practice of this exercise.

About feminisms. Saying this out loud feels almost empty, since it's clear that *feminism* has not been up to the task of advocating and practicing what it preaches. So many diverse and contrary ideas and experiences make it so difficult to describe. This subsection is a multiple construction from many examples surrounding us. @soyciguapa, Yuderkys Espinosa, Ochy Curiel, SIlvia Rivera Cusicanqui, María Lugones, Lorena Cabnal, Sirin Adlbi Sibai, @cafeoscuro.cosasclaras, Karina Ochoa, Aura Cumes, Oyèrónké Oyèwùmi, @powershiftsproject, and so many more that may have already a presence throughout this text. And important to say, most of these reflections have been gestated –not as an answer, but as an autonomous and original experience- from indigenous communities from the global-South, and from afro-descendents in different locations that bring a necessary anti-racist positioning.

De(s)colonial feminisms. Anticolonial and non-hegemonic attempts to comprehend the oppression intersectionaly, while carefully, emphatically and actively engaging to visibilize and act against injustice. Injustice that feeds on male-white-privilege-western-northern visions that focus their violence towards the populations outside of these coordinates. A plural and shared living, that understands the claims of its bases, critically viewing history and the recent local events that only justify social discomfort towards inefficient and damaging systems (López Rodríguez, 2018). Awareness of our communities, because we are part of collectiveness. An understanding that coloniality is a still current state, 'a tangled bundle of various forms of hierarchies and devices of domination on a world scale' (Garzón Martínez, 2014: 225).

This that I name as descolonial feminisms, following Yetzi Villaroel (2018), are diverse in terms of place of enunciation, 'in which they move away, get closer, or intersect approaches and practices, but always in dialogue' (p. 109). That even includes nearness to postcolonial feminisms, as Kiran Asher (2019) would tell us, extending the need of not closing the borders to avoid repeating the same mistake of creating another universalism.

Not surprisingly, these notions do not quite fit in the *ideals* of research, intervention and teaching-learning dynamics in social sciences. All of them fundamental parts of the matrix of colonial domination, born and shaped to the perverse gear that holds the western-north-modern fiction. But we keep on trying, because we are many against that tide. And we take a stand, we do not remain indifferent. An-other commitment is needed, against a multiple monster, in a junction that demands an extensive epistemic disobedience. Here is, then, where this chapter stands. After taking the long road to account the context of the reflections taking place, the core of the matter comes to surface. How to act on consequence, in and out of the streets, and have an activist living while in academia? Inviting to a descolonizing mindset and practice in academic life. I wonder if it is even possible to act on allyship and social justice in this context, with humility and actively committing to a descolonial feminism.

Manifiesto funa a la academia. And a standing against institutional gaslighting

'Putting the body[8] is to give voice to the gut' (Joyce Jandette,[9] 2014). In an unleashed word, that accounts for the self-thought being.

No recipe is there to make room and noise for the claims against injustice and un-dignity. Responding to this transversally from standing against denialism and institutional gaslighting that has inevitably taken place in all that is *formal education*. All this academic structure has been a historical constant in the reproduction of hegemony, in a Western-colonial and white patriarchal standard. It has exercised a coloniality of knowledge and power, in an obvious way, but that has had inevitable consequences as a coloniality of being. An ethnocentric universalization – as Mohanty (2008) would say – that has crushed and diminished cultures and ways of living, and has only allowed us to understand the world we live in in very limited coordinates. A dichotomic categorical logic, 'central to modern capitalist and colonial thought on race, gender, sexuality' (Lugones, 2016:106, in Tabares, 2019: 90). That has imposed an absolute truth with a linear and developmental temporality, that sets a pace, way and order to the procedures of social knowledge and intervention. Notions that prevent a genuine approach to whatever matter by isolating it and removing all the bonds we have with it.

This has meant awful, life-threatening life conditions for those in misrepresented and systematically reproduced positions of subjugated power. Racialized, colonized and occupied communities and territories, all those outside the hegemony codes. Dynamics that reproduce and are sustained through the micro-practices and discourses of all the research, intervention and education done in the name of *social science*. Disciplines like psychology, sociology, anthropology, geography, history, education and many others were gestated as institutional instruments of extraction of knowledge and ways of being to a language only understood among its northern walls.

From diverse places of society we rise and claim due to the non-accounted position of the academic platforms in the re-production of these practices. The presentation of the Red de Feminismos Descoloniales /Network of Descolonial Feminisms/ back in 2014 would describe with embodied detail the appeal for a critical descolonial academic task, one that cannot be understood among its barriers. But whose colonizing scaffoldings 'are scattered everywhere: in the references, the readings and methods for Bachelor's, Master's and Doctoral degrees "with a gender perspective", "feminist research" or "women's studies", guiding the research questions, setting the methodologies and demarcating the criteria for knowledge validation' (in Millan 2004: 324).

The fight is against the limitations of 'the possibilities to see: to see the emotion, to see the desire, to see sense, to see the body, to see the singularity, in synthesis seeing the experience, or worse, seeing in it, "something wrong"' (as Tabares Ochoa, 2019: 92 would say). An aware position – not without failures, since we are not exempt from reproducing these same logics- is to start in exactly that which is rejected. As an act of protest. An exploration at the rhythm of everyday life, in what would seem slow passed for the accelerated non-realistic timing of academic life. Not fracturing the social fabric, in an imbricated reading and organic account of a multiple and tangled reality. That needs a critique that extends to spheres usually unrelated: economy and accumulation, sex-gender system, nation constitution, production of knowledge, body experience, state violence, and many more.

Other codes are needed. And we are surrounded by leads and examples of ethical and anti-racist, anticolonial and feminist practices and felt-thoughts, in a movement that brings a shift. That comes from everyday life and finds a consequent extension in this **scenario of protest, claim and intervention that is academia** and its devices. These words, that thesis, this chapter and book, is actively using the spaces that we have. To annoy and 'push past comfort and politeness and challenge the structures and norms that we've all grown up taking for granted, and be a part of creating the society you want to live in' (Williams 2020: 29). A territory we can perform in and make noise. As much as any other, this is a place to install questioning, and join forces into opening the room from its border walls. Break windows and doors. Let the very established building fall. And use the territory to create. To transform. And from here, break academic habits.

For this, it is necessary to exercise the **centering to de-center. Attending those threads that pull** and being accordingly. Taking everyday life into academic performance, being aware of the place we stand, the room we occupy, the benefits and privilege we hold and from there knit toward the collective. Stop and listen, stand and locate yourself. How *are we* in what we talk about? How does it affect us? There is potential in breaking and making evident the non-existent neutrality we have with any matter. We are involved, distance is therefore absolutely impossible. The affection for social life, then, needs to have a place in social sciences and in the world of intervention, research and learning-teaching many of us live in. Favoring the visibility of problems that exceed us and that find a loudspeaker in these pages. We are involved and we don't remain oblivious. We take a stand that holds the microphone when there is something that directly affects us, but that leaves room and listens when it is not ours. The commitment to replicate and add volume to the claims and narratives of common life is the moving force that seeds change. Not as a choice, but as a consequent act of taking the already old invitation of holding an accountable living.

What is it that sets the pace? What is it in the center, as the horizon of direction? Life

In all the extension and understanding of the concept. The lives of those who are put in the middle of this gear. Who from marginalization have been historically underestimated, due to the asymmetry that exists with those who hold expert knowledge. Ourselves. Whose life is also secondarized through these dynamics, in a continuum that dictates the relevance of the matter.

A politic of care, building *other* standards that hold dignity. That embraces the reproduction of common living and all those tasks that guarantee the sustenance of life. It implies a change in the conception of what is essential work, and who is actually doing it. In a reading from gender, race, class and beyond, and its imbricated impact in the scission of the roles of production/reproduction. And in view of a historical reparation of socially stigmatized tasks. A structural change that is thriving from diverse sectors of civil society, in particular relation to organizational processes of women and dissidents from rural and Indigenous backgrounds. Beyond mainstream feminism, finding its way to urban and popular contexts. Having feet also here, in hegemonic careers and formal institutions like the ones we sadly seem to represent. Those are the ones we need to break, and we are here to stay.

Last considerations: 'To overflow all the spaces' (Joyce Jandette, 2014)

Consequence, I take, as the word that sets the pace of this writing. To be an ally, relative to a distance that invited me to explore and crack *alternative* ways of noise and critique. That by taking me back to the notion of community, one agglutinated due to a triggering event, has allowed me to account a so much personal and individual experience as it is collective.

An activism with feminist and descolonial convictions. This would set the ground for ways that would break my relationship with the institutions of formal education, through an extensive and still continuous attempt of inner descolonization. And though the learnings and reflections of this process are multiple and diverse, so much that they don't fit in these sheets and barely fit in my body, two ideas I highlight for this closing.

First, to claim feminist and descolonial critique as tremendous possibilities to insert doubt. As positionings that bring notions from the antiracisms and from territorial and communitarian activisms, moving us toward social justice and the necessity of a dignified living. That embraces the collective construction of a desired present, in a continuum that requires academia to be sensitive to what it has historically tried to make invisible.

Second, that all of this writing and understandings are not in service of this system. The one that has shown over and over again not to be useful or prosperous to dismantle the serious social crises that are replicated in it. Where the same ones hold the microphone and occupy space *in the name* of others, obtaining the earnings and recognition for work that completely exceed them while not giving up any earnings or benefits.

At the very end, a shift of power is needed. In every aspect of life, while I still wonder how to make a bridge to academia and its devices. Because I don't believe it can actually be descolonized. As much as I don't expect feminism to have room for itself in this fort, without following at least some of the rules it aims to break. The roots are far too rotten. Dismantling the whole system seems a more suitable possibility, by the hand of searching for alternative ways of intellectual activity. An active though sometimes uncomfortable commitment. But one that certainly is not lonely as long as we can find ourselves and take shelter in our communities.

Notes

1 The use of the terms decolonial, descolonial and anticolonial are not innocuous. Each of them has particular genealogies of origin and use. From my background of Latin-American feminist influence, in Castellano/Spanish I would use descolonial as a result of a large debate of different academic/activist encounters. The issue is actually in its use in English, where I have come to realize that both decolonial and descolonial are reduced to the first one. This is not a problem of translation, though. It is an issue of academia, and how it has narrowed these terms in order to 'include' them.

The text 'About the decolonial/descolonial distinction' of Paula Meschini and Luis Porta (2017), and also Juan Vicente López (2018) in his text 'Convergences, divergences and positions between the decolonial, the descolonial and the postcolonial from feminist views of the South' have reflections on where these 3 concepts meet and their distances. Following them, throughout this chapter I will use descoloniality to understand an on-going, diverse and plural process and project of intersectional and imbricated reflection and rupture of modern colonial ontology. An ethic and political commitment towards grassroots organization and situated transformation.

2 Referred to the period after 1988, the year of the vote to have democratic elections and finally end the dictatorship. After this, the *transition to democracy* would begin, in a still unfinished process.

3 Poem for Migrant Stories /Microhistoriasmigrantes/, a cycle of collective reflection on our migrant living.

4 All the quotes contained in this text are originally in diverse forms of Castellano/Spanish/ and have been translated by myself.

5 Song 'The right to live in peace', Victor Jara (1971).

6 Sename is the National Service of Minors (in its literal translation) that protects the rights of children and adolescents, deals with the judicialized youth and national adoption. It has been the subject of numerous scandals related to the death of children in their locations. Also because of

taking custody of kids and giving them an adoption without letting the families earn their right to keep them.

AFP is the Pension Fund Manager, private institutions that invest your pension money in a macabre game where people lose their life savings while these institutions earn money out of ours.

7 Funa: public complaint. Usually used to denounce gender violence in the context of sex-affective and family bonds. Here adapted to an-other context of violence. For more on this, check Carol Schmeisser (2019) and Ivana Jancik (2020).
8 Putting the body means presence. Embodied action, of going, being, doing. From the politics of activism, acting according to what mobilizes us (the gut).
9 From the performance of Joyce Jandette, transcript by Xochitl Leyva Solano, 2018, translated into English by me.

References

Asher, K. 2019. *Reivindicar la cercanía entre los feminismos poscoloniales y decoloniales con base en Spivak y Rivera Cusicanqui*. Tabula Rasa, vol. 30, 13–25. Doi: https://doi.org/10.25058/20112742.n30.01

Espinosa-Miñoso, Y. 2014. *Una crítica descolonial a la epistemología feminista crítica*. El Cotidiano, núm. 184, marzo-abril, 2014, pp. 7–12.

Galindo, M. 2005. *Así como tú me quieres Yo no quiero saber de ti*. Publicum.

Garzón Martínez, M., 2014. *Proyectos corporales. Errores subversivos*. En Espinosa, Y, Gómez, D. y Ochoa, K. (eds.) Tejiendo de otro modo: Feminismo, epistemología y apuestas descoloniales en Abya Yala. Editorial Universidad del Cauca, 223–236.

Jancik, I. 2020. *Feminismo y punitivismo. Análisis del surgimiento de funas a varones en Argentina*. Revista Némesis, vol. 16, 49–59.

Jandette, J. [JoyceJandette], 2014. qué carajos es poner el cuerpo? [video]. Youtube. https://www.youtube.com/watch?v=JabMdko3xRc&ab_channel=JoyceJandette

Jara, V., 1971. El derecho de vivir en paz [song]. In El derecho de vivir en paz. DICAP.

López Rodríguez, J. 2018. Convergencias, divergencias y posicionamiento entre lo decolonial, lo descolonial y lo poscolonial desde miradas feministas del Sur. Analéctica, ISSN 2591-5894.

Lugones, M. 2016. *Hacia un feminismo descolonial*. La manzana de la discordia, vol. 25, n. 4, 85–112.

Martínez Espíndola, M. 2020. *Perspectivas feministas en/de/desde Latino América. Notas para pensar genealogías*. Estudios de Filosofía Práctica e Historia de las Ideas, vol. 22, pp. 1–21.

Meschini, P. y Porta, L. 2017. Acerca de la distinción decolonial/descolonial. En M. E. Hermida y P. Meschini (Comps.), Trabajo social y descolonialidad. Epistemologías insurgentes para la intervención en lo social [Social work and descoloniality. Insurgent Epistemologies for Intervention in the Social], pp. 20–24), EUDEM.

Millan, M (coord.). 2014. *Más allá del feminismo: Caminos para andar*. Red de Feminismos Descoloniales.

Mohanty, C. 2008. *Under western eyes: Feminist scholarship and colonial Discourses*. In Suárez Navaz, Liliana, y Hernández, Rosalva Aída (eds.) Descolonizando el Feminismo: Teorías y Prácticas desde los Márgenes. Madrid: Ediciones Cátedra, pp. 117–164.

Montenegro, A. 2019. ¿Es posible una intervención feminista descolonial? Una reflexión desde la experiencia y la práctica política antirracista. Millcayac, vol. 5, n. 10, 21–40.

National Institute of Human Rights, 2019. *Informe anual 2019: Situación de los Derechos Humanos en Chile en el Contexto de la Crisis Social*. INDH.

Red de Feministas Descoloniales, 2014. *Descolonizando nuestros feminismos: abriendo la mirada. Presentación de la Red de Feminismos descoloniales*. En Espinosa, Y, Gómez, D. y Ochoa, K. (eds.) Tejiendo de otro modo: Feminismo, epistemología y apuestas descoloniales en Abya Yala. Editorial Universidad del Cauca, 455–463.

Schmeisser, C. 2019. *La funa. Aspectos históricos, jurídicos, sociales. Memoria para optar al grado de Licenciada en Ciencias Jurídicas y sociales*. Universidad de Chile.

Tabares Ochia, M. 2019. *Feminist critical theories: Transgressors, creatives: A contribuition to the challenges of social theory in Latin America*. Revista Novos Rumos Sociológicos, vol. 7, n. 11, pp. 82–109.

Tabares Ochoa, M., 2019. *Teorías críticas feministas: transgresoras, creativas: Una contribución a los desafíos de la teoría social en América Latina*. Revista Novos Rumos Sociológicos, vol. 7, n. 11, 85–112.

Tuhwai Smith, L. 2016. *A descolonizar las metodologías: investigación y pueblos indígenas*. Translated by Kathryn Lehman. LOM Ediciones.

Villaroel Y. 2018. *Feminismos descoloniales latinoamericanos: geopolíticas, resistencias y relaciones internacionales*. Relaciones internacionales, n. 39, 103–119.

Williams, S. 2020. *Anti Racist ally. An introduction to action and activism*. Harper Collins.

THE ABSURD ACADEMIC

Jaime Andrés Bayona

Introduction

A university professor is a highly prestigious occupation in our society that is commonly regarded as well paid, with low levels of stress, a good work environment, with a stable demand in the labor market. However, it is not an easy task to obtain this type of job (i.e., tenured and secured), as an academic career is full of challenges that potential candidates should overcome to obtain such positions. As with any other job, an academic career shapes the self of those individuals who follow it, a process that sometimes implies profound changes in the values and life goals of those who want to become full-time professors at a university. In this chapter, I interpret this transformation through the absurdist philosophy of Albert Camus.

The absurdist philosophy deals with the problem of the lack of objective meaning of human life. In this chapter, I use this philosophical framework to understand different interpretations of the academic career in Management Sciences, and how these interpretations lead to different outcomes for academics (i.e., personal and professional). I use the autoethnographic method to analyze how I faced the meaning of academic life through three different *solutions* proposed by the absurdist philosophy: the canonical, the suicidal, and the absurd.

The chapter is divided into five sections. The first presents a brief explanation of the absurdist philosophy of Albert Camus, as well as its relationship with the existentialist philosophy and its roots in previous works of Søren Kierkegaard, Friedrich Nietzsche, and Jean-Paul Sartre. In the next three sections I present some of my own experiences dealing with the absurd using each one of the solutions proposed by Camus but exchanging the concept of *meaning of life* for *meaning of academic life*. Finally, I present some concluding remarks of these analyses.

The absurd philosophy

In philosophy, the absurd refers to the conflict between (a) the tendency or need of humans to find inherent value or meaning to their lives, and (b) the apparent inexistence of such value or meaning. The absurd emerges when humans acknowledge this conflict, and the philosophy of the absurd explores how individuals respond to it. Absurdism is commonly connected to existentialism[1] and has its roots in the earlier works of Søren Kierkegaard, Friedrich Nietzsche, and Jean-Paul Sartre. Humans, when aware of the conflict between the search for inherent value and the meaningless of their lives, look for ways to reduce this conflict. Kierkegaard and Camus proposed three possible solutions to the absurd: (1) religious or spiritual solution; (2) suicide or escaping existence solution; or (3) the acceptance of the absurd.

1 The religious or spiritual solution

In this option, the person believes in the existence of a realm which is beyond the physical world, generally governed by a god, who can put an end to the absurd, since the ultimate causes of existence and meaning of life could be explained by this supreme being. The Danish philosopher Søren Kierkegaard, a fervent Catholic, preferred this option and, in his writings, always defended it. He stated that, to opt for this solution, a "leap of faith" is necessary, as no empirical evidence of a realm beyond the physical world is possible. He also stated that, if the origin of all things in the world were based only on passions and in natural processes, then the entire existence would be empty, and the only expected result of this should be despair (Kierkegaard, 1843/2016). For Kierkegaard, faith is the cornerstone to overcome the absurd, "as faith begins precisely where reason ends" (p. 134), and "faith is man's highest passion" (p. 238). When there is no faith, despair emerges, which he called "the sickness unto death"; faith is the only cure for despair and the sickness. You need to believe in the divine, not to understand it; understanding is for all human-based creations, but not for God (Kierkegaard, 1849/2008).

The religious solution is also present in the work of Nietzsche, specifically in his book *On the Genealogy of Morals* (1887/2006), where he stated that ascetic ideals are key to the spiritual life. While these ideals are generally considered as a bridge to the afterlife, Nietzsche believed that they were even adopted among academics, not to improve or reach spirituality, of course, but to reach true knowledge.

2 Suicide, or escaping existence solution

In this option, the person is aware of the absurd, and ends her or his life because he or she cannot tolerate that life has no ultimate meaning or purpose. An example of this is presented in the play *The Possessed*, by Camus (1959/2013), in which Kirillov, one of the main characters, states that people should kill themselves to be free; you must commit suicide, as since there is no life after death it is the same to live or to die. This is a nihilistic point of view that Camus did not like, as in the play he called Kirillov's nihilistic perspective a disease. Killing oneself is admitting that life overcomes us and that we do not understand it.

3 Acceptance of the absurd

In this solution, the human acknowledges the absurd, and accepts it. In the acceptance of the absurd, the person embraces life as it is (Camus, 1956/2018). The acceptance of the absurd is presented in *The Plague* (Camus, 1947/2018), in which the plague is a metaphor for the absurd. In the novel, the plague advances in a town without contemplation. One of the protagonists, the doctor, continues to fight the disease, albeit knowing that he cannot do anything to stop it. But despite the uselessness of his efforts, he continues to work constantly (e.g., taking care of the sick, giving the medicines, and disposing of the dead bodies). That is, he does not succumb to despair and suicide, nor does he beg God to intervene. In another segment, some of the protagonists try to understand the plague (i.e., a metaphor about the meaning of life), but later, they learn that there is nothing to understand (i.e., life has no meaning), and the only thing to do is learn from it. You should not die from the plague (i.e., suicide), but neither should you put your hopes in false answers (i.e., religion). As you learn from the plague, you also learn how not to die from it. The plague is the absurd, and living in the absurd does not mean succumbing to the plague but accepting it, using support from each other and freewill in opposition to the options of indifference (suicide) and authority (religion).

For Camus (1942/2020), the acceptance of the absurd is better understood by the myth of Sisyphus, in which Sisyphus is condemned by gods to push a rock up a mountain for all eternity. Upon reaching the top, the rock would roll down again, leaving Sisyphus to start over. In this story, the task of pushing the rock is seen as life itself, it is an absurd task since it is useless, but you should accept it as it is, without any real end or great purpose. Camus states that once you accept this, you could be happy since, although the task is absurd (e.g., as our paid jobs), putting an end to that useless search for meaning is the real relief that allows us to enjoy life, like Sisyphus, whose acknowledgement of the truth gives him a sense that his destiny belongs to him, and that he owns his days (what Camus calls a "happy Sisyphus").

In the next three sections, I present some personal life events that shaped my academic career as management faculty in a business school in Colombia. I present these events, each framed as one of the three solutions to the absurd. The events presented in the following sections occurred mostly in sequential order, but some of them overlapped.

The canonical academic – the religious option to the absurd

During my undergraduate years at a public university in Colombia, an idea was planted in me by almost all my professors: Psychology is a Science, and Science is the right path, it is not the only path, but it is the path of truth and rightfulness. Why had I studied psychology? Because it was interesting. So, once you combined these two situations: an individual with curiosity, and a context that fosters this curiosity, a potential academic begins to blossom.

A few years after my graduation, I received a scholarship to pursue master's studies in Europe. There I visited many institutions with highly competitive academics who published dozens of articles per year, which was pretty astonishing for me. During that time, I had a couple of friends in another university who had an incredibly high workload and I started calling them *marines*, which was a metaphor that I adopted for myself; an individual who has a mission: to learn and serve as a tool for the army – the army of science. My life objective became to improve my research skills to ascend into the science-military ranking and someday become a general.

During my studies in Paris, I read Nietzsche's *On the Genealogy of Morals*, in which another powerful metaphor was planted: the acceptance of *ascetic ideals* is needed to fully embrace knowledge. Nietzsche originally talked about the need to embrace ascetic ideals for philosophers, but, from my own interpretation, I adapted it to my academic career context.

For example, given that I lived in a university dormitory, I started to think about the residence as a monastery, and my room as a cell in which I could embrace the ascetic ideals of science. With this new metaphor, I was ready to fully commit to science and academia, or perhaps more appropriately: I was ready to fully commit to God (i.e., science) and religion (i.e., academia). I was happy at that moment because those metaphors and their meaning gave sense to my whole life.

I tried to stay in Europe to follow my doctoral studies, but I could not balance this with the needs of my wife and son and stay away any longer (they stayed in Colombia during my master's studies). So, I returned to Colombia, and I filled a vacancy as assistant professor in a private university. At the same time, I started my PhD with a sandwich scheme. The university that allowed me to pursue my doctoral studies in this format during my paid work as professor was *Pontificia Universidad Javeriana*, which, very fittingly, is a university managed by the Society of Jesus. I remember the next four or five years as the purest canonical academic period of my life, as (a) I was a true believer in the power of our science (faith), (b) I was admitted as a regular priest in a congregation (religion), and (c) I embraced the ascetic ideals as a path to continue my spiritual journey (canon).

As my context changed, the marine metaphor started to decay. It had been useful during my master studies in which it is expected that students do everything that professors ask. But with my new role as professor, I needed a new metaphor that could reflect my gained autonomy, and the ascetic ideals were the answer. I started to see myself as a priest that follows those strict ideals. During the next few years, I tried and tried hard to balance finishing my dissertation, fulfilling my academic duties at the university, and my family responsibilities as a father and a husband. But I was not afraid: I had faith, my ascetic ideals, and my congregation. It was tough, but my main objective was related to the "greater good" of science… any sacrifice in its name would be greatly rewarded after I received my PhD and tenure at the university.[2]

The highest point of this canonical stage was the involvement in my first North American conference in which I had an oral presentation, a couple of paper development workshops and various social commitments with different colleagues. The conference spanned five days, but after three, I was totally exhausted. I already had experience with conferences in Europe, but "this one was the one", for which I would prove myself as a real researcher that could be inserted in the academic world with my own voice. Despite the exhaustion, I considered it a success, as I completed all the commitments and could face the final stage of my PhD with renewed energy, convinced that I could be a good researcher-general-priest. In fact, just two years later, I obtained my PhD, got promoted to associate professor and everything was fine. I was very happy, I thought: "I made it!"

In retrospect, I see that period of my life as dominated by dogma, both at the personal and professional levels. In my personal life there was a dogma: the idea of *family*: I must work for my family (i.e., wife and son), the family was the cornerstone of my personal life, the family was good, and every sacrifice was worth the price, as the most important thing was to keep the family united (i.e., ascetic ideal). On the other hand, for my academic career, I saw the traditional theories and methods of management science (i.e., positivistic and quantitative) as the only way good research could be done (i.e., the canon). The implication was that there was only one true academic path, related to a highly competitive knowledge-creation market in which the higher the H-Index and impact factor of your publications, the higher impact of your research on the advance of science, and, as a direct consequence, the construction of a better society. This career path is coherent with the actual neoliberal economy in which the winner takes it all and is highly appreciated by organizations and universities.

The failed academic – the suicidal option to the absurd

However, the amount of effort and resources I had to invest in my canonical career drove me to a mental and familial breakdown. Things started to change – and not for the better. At the professional level, my workload was higher, as I needed to fulfill my academic commitments with the university (classes and administrative work). But also, I needed to focus on my dissertation, which led me to work for 12–16 hours per day, including weekends. I felt constantly exhausted. Around the same time, my wife was experiencing something similar, as she was also in the final stage of her PhD, and in addition, around that time, my nine-year-old son attempted suicide for the first time (there were three in total), the latter event being the day that everything went downhill.

During those days, I was frustrated about the purity of science, as I began to see that a major part of research was conducted by graduate students who just wanted to finish their PhD (including myself). The initial internal motivation for the sake of truth changed to a more extrinsic motivation related to just finishing the dissertation. In addition, I felt frustrated by my students, as they were not engaged with my classes, probably because I also did not feel engaged with teaching, and I saw my research as just a job – a very boring job. From that point I started to experience symptoms of depression: apathy, irritability, and I started to see life as pointless. I stopped seeing science as my main motivation in life. I saw no purpose in science, or at least in Management Sciences, as I felt that I had failed to improve workers' quality of life. I thought that our societies were not advancing, and the knowledge I was producing was intended to perpetuate the structures of power within organizations and not directed to produce a real change in society (at that time, I discovered Critical Management Studies). So, my life and academic career, in my eyes, were meaningless.

During that time, I saw two films that helped me to channel my feelings: *The Turin Horse* (2011) by Béla Tarr, and *Hard to Be a God* (2013) by Aleksei German. *The Turin Horse* deals with the slow disintegration of the world, the senseless rituals of everyday and the uselessness of religion. From that film, I started to see how my own life and family were being progressively destroyed by mental illness and excessive workload. On the other hand, German's film deals with a group of scientists who travel to a middle-ages earth-like planet where every bit of science or art have been eradicated, leading to a cultural stagnation and general ignorance among the population. From this film, I projected my work as a professor, as one in which students were not interested, a job that was senseless, as no matter how hard I tried to improve the learning of my students, it was a useless task, and the majority of my students were not interested in it. Likewise, I felt that my papers and presentations in both academic and professional events did not lead to any real impact in the world.

These pessimistic metaphors about my public and private life led to an increased sense of depersonalization in both realms. At the personal level, I felt like a failed father (I couldn't prevent my son's suicidal attempts), and a failed husband (I completely lost interest in my wife and her personal struggles). In addition, I also felt like a failed academic, as I felt that I was not competent enough and my research projects were theoretically weak and based on questionable statistical artifacts. Although I finished my PhD and obtained the promotion to associate professor, nothing made sense. I felt empty and depersonalized, as my roles were dead (neither my son nor my wife expected anything from me, and my classes were just boring presentations). I felt that I was either an imposter, not interesting, or just incapable of any of these roles. I just wanted to put an end to all those responsibilities: quit my family and quit my work duties. Life overcame me. I did not understand it.

This perspective is a direct consequence of the letdown from the canonical academic. As the core feeling in this perspective is deception: deception from the first stage of canon and ascetic ideals. In order to feel deception, the academic needs to have been highly engaged in the initial dogma of academia. For academic careers, this path is the one with the highest emotional toll on the individual, as it is the consequence of the high amount of workload of the canon approach, which can lead to exhaustion and mental health problems.

The confronted academic – the acceptance of the absurd

My son gave us an ultimatum: he was going to end his life on January 1st. The months before that deadline were a nightmare. I could not sleep; I barely could complete my work commitments, I argued with my wife almost every day. Life was a complete blackhole from which I could not escape. My mental health started to deteriorate rapidly. I had to do something. I started psychological, psychiatric, and pharmacological treatments. However, in addition, I needed to "change my mindset", so I started reading Seneca and Camus, who helped me question myself about my previous conception of the world and how I was relating with it. During that time, I learned that all this suffering was self-inflicted, as I placed all my hopes in others and my happiness was based on how successful and accomplished I would become.

January the 1st came and went, and nothing happened. My son continued to go to school as usual and did not mention anything about suicide again, although it was still an idea in his mind. After a couple of months, the medication and psychotherapy started to work on my depression, I felt calmer. And then, the pandemic came… as for everyone else, it was a period of change and adaptation. I was not accustomed to working from home, but at the same time I enjoyed staying at home. So, the adaptation process was not so bad. However, I got divorced during quarantine and from that point I started to re-assess my whole life, my family and work relationships, as well as the roles and expectations that others and myself had placed on myself.

I adopted the metaphor of a happy Sisyphus: existence does not actually make any sense at all, but you must keep moving, you have to accept things as they come. The adoption of the Sisyphus metaphor at this point does not mean that I have just left the previous metaphors, as they are kept real in my interpretation of the world. That means that sometimes, I feel like a priest, and sometimes I see life as *The Turin Horse* and *Hard to be a God*. What changes is the anxiety that came from the acceptance of those metaphors in isolation. In the "macro-metaphor" of Sisyphus, I accepted that Science is not pure, that academia is a job like any other, that I cannot change the world to be a better place because that is just not possible: a mere human is incapable of affecting societal change. Besides, my son, who now seems to enjoy life, can choose to end his life at any moment, and he has the right to do so, as he is an independent being who is old enough to reflect about his own existence (now he is an 18-year-old). My own happiness should not be based on the accomplishment of titles or concepts like "husband", "professor" or "father". The world is in decay, as in *The Turin Horse*, and the job of being a professor can be just as frustrating as it is for Don Rumata, the main protagonist in *Hard to be a God*, to observe an Earth-like planet, whose denizens have abandoned science and all common sense and blissfully trudge about in mud, muck, and feces. But it does not mean that I have to be sad, or depressed.

Does it mean that I do not care about the world, my family, or my cats? No, I do not want to see the world burn, but I have to gain consciousness of my role in the world, and what I can do to improve the lives of others around me and to improve my own life. But for this, the prerequisite is happiness. Just like Sisyphus, I contently push the boulder uphill. This is a perspective dominated by acceptance: the acceptance of the senselessness of academic life. I had to admit that I can't change society by myself. However, I began to see that I can change the life of some individuals in society, such as my students, and they can also change the life of others based on the seeds I planted in them. (For example, a master student who worked for a consulting firm told me that because of my classes on corporate social responsibility and organizational justice, she pushed the board of directors of the firm to increase the wage of their cleaning lady. It was a very small step, but for this woman, it was a great improvement in her life conditions.)

With the absurd option to deal with the meaning of academic life, the professor should first accept that academic life has no intrinsic meaning, that the power structures present in universities are the same as those present in private corporations, where performance is the highest asset. In universities, performance is also key, but in terms of university rankings and impact factors. Accepting the absurd is putting an end to the search for meaning, that the rock that we carry (our teaching, research, and administrative tasks) can be seen as useless, which may in fact be an accurate assessment. But that should not mean that we cannot share our experience and knowledge with others.

Concluding remarks

Doing academic careers differently means that although academics tend to perform similar activities (i.e., research, teaching and administrative work), the paths that lead us there are very different depending on our context, our own talents, and limitations, and especially, on the interpretation and acting of our beliefs, emotions, and thoughts. This chapter has presented one such interpretation using the philosophy of absurd of Albert Camus, which offers three solutions to the problem of the absurd. My interpretation should not be taken to mean that there aren't other possibilities. But acceptance of the absurd is one common consequence for academics. I have colleagues that look very happy within the canonical approach (generally they are single and have no kids). This analysis came from my own experiences in a business department and would not necessary fit exactly other scientific areas where power structures may be less predominant.

In the philosophical works of Camus and Kierkegaard, the solutions to the absurd are seen as excluding each other, as you cannot choose at the same time the religious and suicide options. However, little is said about the change from one solution to another and how this process could work. In this chapter, for an academic career it was shown that two of the options can occur at the same time or they can overlap depending not just in the work context, but also on the events that occur in their personal life, which in inherently tied to her / his academic career. The use of metaphors that help us confront the absurd could change, adapt, and activate or deactivate depending on our needs.

From this analysis, a dialectic triad can be presented (Figure 34.1), depicting the canonical view of academic career as a thesis, the suicidal option as an antithesis, and the absurd point of view as a synthesis. This re-interpretation of the absurd option as synthesis supposes that the absurd academic path is somehow a more integrative or preferable to the other two options. This is not necessarily true from the point of view of interpreting the quality of science as better or worse. But it could be better in terms of the consequences for the academic, as the first two interpretations result in higher levels of stress, whereas the absurd point of view gives a state of greater well-being.

The increase in mental health problems in academics during the last couple of years is on the rise, and the associated problems of depression and anxiety have been considered common (Cactus Foundation, 2020). So, in addition to formal qualifications and impact factors, nowadays successful academics are individuals who can overcome the challenge of properly caring for their mental health. These are requirements to be fully accepted in the science-religion dimension. But what worries me the most is that the suicidal option has also been normalized, i.e., "Well, you can't make an omelet without breaking some eggs". Nowadays it is normal to be stressed, normal to be depressed, normal to quit the academy due to internal and external pressures. So, we have a situation in which the religious and suicidal options for academic career live together in a strange symbiotic relation where a large number of PhD students and young faculty opt for the religious solution. Yet, as time goes by, some of them switch over to the suicide solution. By far the less popular option, of course, is to just accept the absurd, many because most academics don't acknowledge the absurdity of academia, its power games, and limited theories and methods. However, if one wants to obtain and maintain a career in science, the absurd solution is a perspective that is not entirely reinforced by educational institutions or our neoliberal economic model, both of which are fully committed to higher impact factors and position rankings.

Finally, the influence of COVID-19 in our academic lives has also changed how we see science and teaching. During this time, most academics have been generally seen by governments as non-essential workers who do not need to attend physically to their jobs. This gives us an opportunity to reflect more about our own existence, as humans in general, but also as academics. How can we help our colleagues and students? How are we coping with the absurdity of online classes? How are we fostering the religious, suicidal, or absurd solutions for ourselves, our colleagues, and our students? How do we perpetuate each one of these options and all their consequences?

From an outsider's point of view, academic life is an extraordinary career option. For them, it is an easy pathway through a rose garden. But as we, academics, know, it is indeed surrounded by roses – roses with thick, sharp thorns. The final reflection of this chapter is not that the absurdist solution is by any means "the best option" as I already state. Some of my colleagues seem pretty happy working 50–60 hours per week, writing papers and

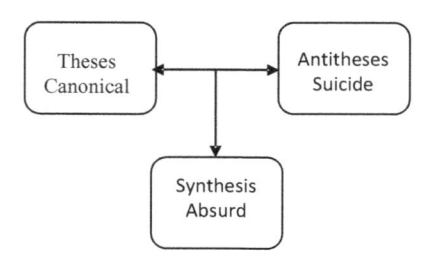

FIGURE 34.1 The dialectic triad of the absurd.

conference proposals under tight deadlines and are fully convinced that they are helping to improve our society at large. And on the other hand, those who have chosen the suicidal option and now are out of academia are also happy about their decision, as they feel relief about the pressures that they felt during their academic years.

Accepting the absurd of academic life has its advantages, as it can be seen as a point of equilibrium between the stress of the canonical option and the emptiness of the suicidal option. Although academic life has no meaning per se, one can find a meaning in the small activities of academia, especially impacting the lives of our students, via teaching and research. The meaning is not in the nature itself of academia as a supreme science-religion, but neither it is as devoid of meaning as in the suicidal option. We can find some meaning in our activities asking some of the questions that I previously stated and helping our students to think critically about their surrounding world. As in the Sisyphean myth, we constantly are pushing a boulder up a steep hill (i.e., writing a research proposal, looking for funding, conducting the research, writing the paper, submitting the paper for peer review, publishing the paper, and start the process over again and again – recall the thorny rosebush path, full of stress, deadlines and personal struggles), but we also go back down the hill again and again, giving guidance and meaning to our students (with the new knowledge we collected during the last round of pushing the boulder up the hill). And in doing so, at the same time, we give meaning to ourselves and to our work. We can be a happy Sisyphus, granting full acknowledgement of the lack of meaning in academic life, but also happy about our role and responsibilities in society as academics.

Notes

1 Existentialism, from the standpoint of Sartre (1946/2018) is a philosophical doctrine that declares that the existence of the human precedes its essence, i.e., that humans first begin to exist, and then define themselves by confronting the world. Humans are no other than what they made of themselves, and thus they can choose and change their morals as they see fit. The implication of this is that humans are fully responsible of their actions and their existence. There are no supernatural or godlike figures who can be responsible for their actions. For existentialists, life has no meaning per se, and as such, humans can choose the meaning of their lives. Existentialism does not attempt to prove whether God exists or not (that does not matter), since humans are solely responsible for defining their own existence.
2 In Colombia, the tenure-track system is not well entrenched, but like in the USA, for example, the level of associate professor is given only to PhD awarded professors.

References

Cactus Foundation (2020). *Joy and Stress Triggers: A global survey on mental health among researchers.* https://www.cactusglobal.com/mental-health-survey/index.php
Camus, A. (1942/2020). *El Mito de Sísifo* [The mith of Sisyphus]. Alianza Editorial.
Camus, A. (1947/2018). *La Peste* [The Plague]. Penguin Random House Grupo Editorial.
Camus, A. (1956/2018). *La Caída* [The Fall]. Alianza Editorial.
Camus, A. (1959/2013). *Los Posesos* [The Possessed]. Alianza Edictorial.
Kierkegaard, S. (1843/2016). *Temor y Temblor* [Fear and Trembling]. Alianza Editorial.
Kierkegaard, S. (1849/2008). *La Enfermedad Mortal* [The Sickness unto Death]. Editorial Trotta.
Nietzsche, F. (1887/2006). *La genealogía de la moral. Un escrito polémico* [On the Genealogy of Morals]. Alianza Editorial.
Sartre, J-P. (1946/2018). *El Existencialismo en un Humanismo* [Existentialism is a Humanism]. Edhesa.

CRAFTING A CAREER IN 'ACADEMIC JOURNALISM'

Todd Bridgman

Introduction

> Your writing is too journalistic.

Rejection decisions on academic papers are never easy to read, but the one I received in 2010 was especially tough. It was tough because it followed several rejections. I was acutely aware of the phrase 'publish or perish' and was having serious doubts about my ability to publish. It was also tough because before I was an academic, I was a journalist. I had always considered my journalism experience to be an asset. Seemingly, it had now become a liability.

In this portrait I reflect on my academic career thus far, which has had some terrific highs and very deep lows – from the high of graduating with a PhD from one of the world's most prestigious universities with dreams of a stellar career publishing in 'top journals' to the low of believing that I was incapable of publishing research.

Things have got a lot better in recent years and I attribute that change in fortune, in large part, to developing an approach to my academic career that played to my interests and strengths. For the sake of clarity, I call it 'academic journalism', which for me means producing research that challenges the status quo, that holds those in authority to account and that seeks a broad audience beyond the 'ivory tower'.

I will argue that three transformations in academia and the news media provide favourable conditions for the identity of the 'academic journalist' to flourish. First, within academia, and especially in business schools, are recurring demands for academic research to have 'impact' and 'relevance' to stakeholders outside the university. Second, the traditional subscription model of academic journal publishing is threatened by demands from stakeholders for research to be 'open access'. And third, the growth of social media and disruption of mainstream media provides opportunities for academics to generate new audiences for their work.

There are, therefore, fresh opportunities to do an academic career differently – to be the 'academic journalist'. I will explore this though my work experience, first as a polytechnic-trained journalist on a small community newspaper in New Zealand and for the past 15 years as a critical management academic in a business school. As can be seen by the amazing diversity of contributions to this book, there are many possibilities for doing academic careers differently. I'm certainly not claiming my career trajectory to be better than any others. Nor am I offering a recommendation for others to pursue it. I hope that by sharing my experience I can encourage those who want a rewarding career in academia, but who worry that the heroic model of the prolific star researcher is not for them. And beyond the potential career benefits for individuals, I believe there is a broader public value to be gained through a convergence of the roles of academics and journalists.

My journey to journalism, then to academia

At the end of my schooling, I didn't do what my family and friends expected me to do – go to university. Instead, I headed to my local polytechnic to enrol in a six-month journalism course. It felt like the right choice for me. One of my most memorable days at school was taking part in a newsroom simulation. My teacher was the editor, announcing the breaking news stories. We were the production crew – we had to write the stories, work out which to assign to the front page and put that front page together using scissors and glue. I loved the excitement of working to a deadline.

I was also attracted to journalism because of its role as the Fourth Estate, which derives from the European concept of the three estates of the realm – the clergy, the nobility, and the common people. The free press came to be regarded as the fourth estate, providing a check and balance on the other three and serving an important role as a watchdog of government and protector of democracy (Debatin, 2016). The final years of my schooling were turbulent times in New Zealand politics with the implementation of a neo-liberal policy agenda by a Labour government elected on a traditional Labour policy programme. Journalists played a key role in holding those politicians to account. Journalism looked to me like an exciting career, as well as being of value to society. I wanted to get out into the 'real world' and get working, so the six-month polytechnic course suited me perfectly. We learnt typing, shorthand and how to write a story.

In 1991 New Zealand's economy was in recession, so it wasn't the best time to be hitting the job market. I wrote letters to every media organization in the country seeking work. Many were kind enough to send me a rejection letter, thanking me for my interest and wishing me the best. Eventually a job came up at the *Taupo Times*, a small community newspaper in a tourist town. I applied and was delighted to receive an offer. It wasn't the adrenalin-pumping role that I had dreamed of. Most of it was standard community newspaper material, but I felt lucky to have a job, even if it did pay barely above minimum wage. After 18 months I began to get bored. I interviewed a political science academic who was visiting Taupo to give a seminar. He had an interesting story to tell, which made me reflect that I was just the medium – I didn't have an interesting story of my own. Having told my father two years earlier I would never go to university, he was pleasantly surprised when I told him I was quitting the *Taupo Times* to study business and political science at University of Auckland.

The journalist training came in handy. I took lecture notes in shorthand and my typing became an asset with the introduction of personal computers. Academic writing looked different to the newspaper stories I had written – it had more jargon – but it was far better, I thought, to discuss complex ideas in simple language than to dress simple ideas up in convoluted language. The undergraduate degree led to a Master's in management studies at Auckland and eventually to a place in the PhD programme at University of Cambridge, under the supervision of Hugh Willmott and Chris Grey.

I had emailed Hugh after reading a journal article he wrote on the commodification of higher education that gelled with my own thoughts. New Zealand universities are distinctive for having a statutory obligation to act as the 'critic and conscience' of society (New Zealand Education and Training Act, 2020). 'Critic and conscience' is most commonly interpreted by New Zealand academics as an obligation to make public commentary. I saw the role as being under threat in an increasingly commodified higher education sector, especially in the business school.

I wasn't aware of 'critical management studies' but thankfully that didn't seem to bother Hugh. He introduced me to the discourse theory of Laclau and Mouffe as a theoretical framework for analysing the changes taking place in higher education. It was dense, abstract and learning the concepts felt like studying a foreign language. I will never forget presenting my first conference paper at a postgraduate discourse theory conference at University of Essex. Everyone seemed to be an expert on Laclau and Mouffe apart from me. At the end of my presentation I couldn't understand the questions I was being asked, let alone give coherent answers.

I returned to New Zealand with PhD in hand and a lecturer job at Victoria University of Wellington. During my time in the UK I had met so many smart, ambitious doctoral students. I enjoyed my opportunities to teach in the UK but had learnt that to progress in academia you needed to publish in 'top journals' and that is what I aspired to do. As you will know already, it didn't work out that way. I lost contact with my intellectual support network in the UK. I was also struggling to get a clear head to think. My wife had given birth to twin boys, which gave us four children under five and a chaotic home-life, trying to balance the demands of parenting with two careers. Paper after paper was being rejected and I took the criticism hard. I considered looking for a new career, but I wasn't sure what else I could do – apart from return to journalism which wasn't an attractive option.

Crafting a new academic identity

While the research part of my academic career was imploding, I was thankful that I continued to enjoy teaching. Little did I know that teaching would provide the spark for the creation of a new research identity and a different academic career. It started with a conversation with my colleague Stephen Cummings. I teach an MBA course 'Leading Change' and had always taught Lewin's 'change as three steps' as the foundational model of the field. I prescribed a set of readings rather than a textbook and was interested in reading what Lewin had written about the model. I asked Steve, who teaches strategy, and he replied he had wondered the same thing but hadn't been able to locate it.

Reflecting on this project now, it had several features that resembled a piece of journalism. There was a strong *investigative* component. We hired a research assistant to read Lewin's extensive body of work, and it turns out that he said very little about 'change as three steps'. Kenneth G Brown of the University of Iowa joined us on the project and trawled through Lewin's archives there. We then set about trying to piece together how 'change as three steps' went from a fragment in an article Lewin wrote shortly before his death in 1947 to the foundational model of change management.

I had been fascinated by textbooks as an undergraduate. I took issue with my business textbooks because of the unquestioned assumptions they made about the inevitability and desirability of free-market capitalism and the need for managers to single-mindedly pursue profit-maximization for shareholders. I scribbled my critique in the margins, hoping that those who bought the books on the second-hand market would appreciate an alternative perspective.

Textbooks played a central role in the creation of 'change as three steps'. It provided legitimacy for a top-down, manager-knows-best prescription to changing organizations that bore little resemblance to Lewin's fragment of an idea. I never liked this managerialist approach to change. The research was, therefore, a *challenge to authority* – to best-selling textbooks in management. We were also challenging Lewin scholars, who we felt had overstated the significance of 'change as three steps' in Lewin's oeuvre.

It wasn't easy getting that Lewin paper published in *Human Relations*. One reviewer said that if our paper was published it would be "likely to reduce rather than enhance the reputation of the journal". Thankfully, we had the two other reviewers on board and eventually the Associate Editor. We sought a broad audience for the paper, beyond the small group of scholars with specialist knowledge on Lewin, and beyond the field of management studies, because we knew 'change as three steps' was influential in many disciplines. We argued that if we went back to Lewin's own work, we might create a different foundation for change management. And we raised the possibility that if students learnt about change management differently, there was a chance that if they one-day became managers, they might practise change management differently – in a more inclusive manner. We attempted to write the paper in a style that would not exclude or bore readers. It was a journalistic style.

We also were active in promoting the paper. The publication of the Lewin article coincided with my introduction to Twitter. In 2015, on Steve's encouragement, I created an account but didn't understand how it could help me and did nothing more with it. I got interested again in 2017 when on sabbatical in the UK. My first tweet was about an editorial I had just written in *Management Learning*. It got 'liked' and 'retweeted'. It was being shared by people I didn't know. The power of Twitter suddenly dawned on me. Here was a medium to share my work, to share others' work and to further cultivate a network – not just of academics, but practitioners, consultants, journalists and other interesting people. I realized that I had my own media. I no longer needed to ask the university's communications staff to write press releases about my research.

I soon discovered that publisher paywalls were a major obstacle to getting my research read. We produced a free-to-view animated video to summarize the Lewin paper, but it was no substitute for the full paper. Thankfully, that paper won *Human Relations'* Paper of the Year Award for 2016, which came with a lovely plaque, but more valuably, a removal of the paywall. The paper has now been downloaded more than 300,000 times. That's a lot of downloads for an academic article. It has already been cited more than 400 times on Google Scholar.

The paper was a great success, even though it has not done wonders for my H-index. One of the parts of academic life that I've found difficult to deal with is the emphasis on quantity of publications. The most pernicious of these is the H index – a measure of a researcher's contribution to field of study. A Google Scholar H index of ten means the researcher has ten papers that have at least ten citations. The H index supposedly measures how productive and influential a researcher is, but the emphasis seems very much on 'productive'. This mattered because my Dean at the time was a strong believer in the H index as a yardstick for assessing applications for promotion. Citations can take years to materialize, so there's an incentive to focus on churning out the research articles. The H index was problematic for me because I've never been strongly motivated to publish lots of papers. I didn't really see the point of it, because from what I can tell, much of the research produced by business school academics isn't read. Academics in most countries are under pressure to publish and the massive growth of business schools in recent decades has meant masses of academics publishing. Sometimes I feel I don't have time to read because of the pressure to publish.

On the back of the success of the Lewin paper, Steve and I have done similar investigations into other well-known foundational theories in management. We highlight misrepresentations and put forward explanations for why these have happened. We do this to create a space for alternative ways of learning about management and of practising management to take hold. The one to have gained most traction is a paper in *Academy of Management Learning & Education* on Maslow's hierarchy of needs (Bridgman et al., 2019), probably the most well-known theory in management and a staple of introductory textbooks. 'Maslow's pyramid' is probably the most well-known symbol. Steve and I were fortunate to connect with John Ballard, who knew much more about Maslow than we did, lived close to Maslow's archive in Akron, Ohio, and was eager to join our team. To cut a long story short, we concluded that Maslow never used a pyramid to represent the theory – it was the creation of a business consultant in the 1960s.

The decade which started with the low of being criticized for producing work that was "too journalistic" finished on a high with the Maslow paper being described as "the academic equivalent of a scoop" by the committee which judged it the Best Paper for AMLE in 2019. The award committee commented: "It's a fine paper and it is particularly so because the authors have done the required leg-work to move from speculation to informed claims". Maybe my first career as a journalist hadn't been such a detriment to my academic career after all.

Favourable trends for the 'academic journalist'

This retrospective account of my career is somewhat misleading. It overplays agency – that my success was the result of my skills and effort as opposed to good luck, or broader forces at play. In this section I want to correct that imbalance. In my view there are significant transformations underway in academia and the news media that provide fertile ground for the growth of 'academic journalism'. They are the rise of 'impact', the open access movement in academic publishing and disruption of mainstream print and broadcast news media. These have provided a strong tailwind for my career and I will consider each, in turn.

1 The 'impact agenda'

Discussions about research having influence beyond the community of scholars have intensified in the past decade. In the UK, the Research Excellence Framework (REF) in 2014 was the first time that the impact of research beyond academia influenced the allocation of core funding to universities (Pearce & Evans, 2018). There are, of course, disagreements about what impact means and what types of impact should be privileged. And, as with any measure, there is a risk that it encourages 'game-playing' by academics and institutions seeking to gain advantage or becomes a 'box-ticking' exercise that academics comply with. I am optimistic, however, that the rise of the impact agenda will weaken the hegemonic grip of publication in 'top journals' as a measure of academics' success. It irks me that in this dominant model, one's status as an academic is measured by *where* one has published. I have often heard comments at conferences along the lines of 'She's such a great academic. She's had two AMJs and an AMR'. If you need to ask what those acronyms stand for (*Academy of Management Journal* and *Academy of Management Review*) then you're probably not considered to be much of a management academic!

Now, it might be common-sense to assume that research published in 'top journals' has the biggest readership and impact. But there are good reasons to question that. Certainly, rates of citation in these journals are high, since the journal impact factor is a direct measure of citation. But I'm not convinced that research published in 'top journals' is the most read. A recent development has been academic publishers making publicly available data on how many downloads or reads a paper has received. It might surprise you how small these numbers are for some highly ranked journals. Perhaps their higher rates of citation might be explained by "coercive citation" (Wilhite & Fong, 2012) – the implicit or explicit pressure on authors, when submitting to journals, to cite other papers published by these journals. I acknowledge that this might be a rationalization to make myself feel better for not having published much in so-called top journals!

The impact agenda has created a space for me to do my academic career differently. I am relatively unusual for focusing my research in management education, which has generally not been regarded as high status field. I am fortunate that *Academy of Management Learning & Education*, where I have published several papers, is ranked A★ on the Australian Business Deans Council list that is the 'gold standard' for academics in New Zealand. I have also spoken with American academics who would like to publish on teaching and learning in AMLE, but don't because in their tenure process these papers would be considered part of their teaching portfolio, rather than research.

This is unfortunate because as Paul Adler (2016) noted in his presidential address to the Academy of Management, if we consider the extent to which our research has made a difference to the lives of our readers, and compare that with our influence in the classroom, most of us would conclude that our greatest impact (whether positive or negative) is on our students. There is a strong case to be made then for management education research as having high impact. While some academic fields might be criticized for producing knowledge that is not sufficiently relevant or related to practice, the same cannot be said for management education research. It appears well-placed for the increased emphasis on impact.

2 Open access publishing and the development of digital media

I know from my own open access publishing experience that it massively increases the *potential* audience for academic research. Paywalls are an enormous barrier for those academics not privileged to be at institutions that can afford journal subscriptions. They are also a deterrent for anyone outside academia interested in university research. Thankfully, the open access movement has gained significant momentum. Open Access initiatives such as Coalition S, a group of European research funding organizations committed to making all scholarly publications funded by grants available free of charge, are gathering pace.

I do not possess a crystal ball to know how commercial publishers will respond to threats to their subscription and pay-per-view models. Article processing charges, where a fee is paid by authors, their institution or research funder are likely to part of the mix. No doubt, leading journals will be keen to retain their status and prestige and remain the most sought-after outlets for publication.

What I can say with confidence is that the trend towards open access will continue. If we think about this shift together with the impact agenda, it is reasonable to anticipate that over time it will become less about *where* you publish your research and more about ensuring that your research is accessible, so that it can generate impact. You have more opportunities to do that if your article is not behind a journal paywall. In this environment, the AMJs and AMRs of this world might not hold the allure that they have in the past.

In this environment, it becomes important for academics to generate audiences for their research, rather than to see publication in a journal as the last stage in the research process. This involves producing supplementary material to disseminate key conclusions and implications. Journalism skills – communicating succinctly and in language that can be understood by lay people – add value here. There has been a steady growth in demand for online material in the form of videos, blogs and podcasts. A prominent example of this is *The Conversation*, which publishes free comment and opinion pieces written by academics and researchers, based on their areas of research. Launched in Australia in 2011, it reported a monthly online audience of 11 million users in 2019. These outputs are replacing the traditional press release written by communication professionals employed by universities (many of whom have trained as journalists). Academics with these skills are well-positioned in this new environment.

3 News media disruption

The third favourable trend for 'academic journalism' is the ongoing disruption of mainstream news media. Traditional print media companies have seen their subscription models threatened by online news outlets providing free content. For broadcasters, the growth of satellite channels and more recently digital providers such as YouTube has splintered their audience and lowered advertising rates. Many advertisers have deserted traditional media for Facebook and other social media, who are perceived to offer better value. These cuts in revenue have necessitated cuts in costs, leaving newsrooms decimated. Those journalists who remain are under pressure to produce more in less time with the advent of a 24/7 news cycle. Adding to the sense of crisis is the 'fake news' phenomenon, where stories are created to deliberately deceive for political motives.

These trends generate concern about the future of resource-intensive investigative, public interest journalism. Thankfully, it is not all doom and gloom. A recent development has been the growth of 'slow journalism' (Le Masurier, 2016), a noteworthy example of which was the 8,000-word *New Yorker* feature that detailed sexual harassment and assault allegations against Harvey Weinstein and gave impetus to the #metoo movement. This article was the culmination of a ten-month investigation by journalist Ronan Farrow (2017) – a dedication of resource well-beyond most media outlets nowadays.

The crisis of public-interest journalism presents an opportunity for academics to help fill the void (Remler et al., 2014). I see a possible point of convergence between 'slow journalism' and new forms of academic research made encouraged by the impact agenda and the development of digital media. By way of illustration, In April 2020 I read an article in *The Guardian* by journalist Julia Carrie Wong about how the unproven drug hydroxychloroquine became Donald Trump's coronavirus 'miracle cure'. Wong examined the flaws of the French study that was used to promote the drug. She traced how the study was promoted by *Fox News* and other American right-wing media networks, and then by the White House. Hydroxychloroquine was a piece of viral misinformation concluded Wong; a conclusion validated by subsequent studies that failed to replicate the findings of the original French study. Wong's research shared similarities with the research I have done with colleagues into the misrepresentation of well-known theories in management, such as 'Maslow's pyramid' and Lewin's change-as-three-steps model'. While our academic journal articles are a different form of writing to Wong's, we could have presented our research in a form that would closely resemble a long-form newspaper feature – potentially supplemented by blogs, podcasts and video content. Combining the traditional academic article with these forms of dissemination is consistent with demands for increased impact and relevance that universities, and business schools in particular, face. Those academics with journalistic skills can thrive in this environment.

Conclusion

In this chapter I have reflected on the twists and turns that my academic career has taken thus far. After coming to the realization that I wasn't very good at writing papers for 'top journals' and couldn't really see the point of it anyway, I have crafted a different sort of academic career, that of the 'academic journalist'. Along the way I have learnt some things that might be of value to others. First, I would have achieved more fulfilment had I pursued earlier a path that utilized my interests and strengths rather than to waste years trying to be something that I wasn't. Second, I've learnt that the meaning of terms in academia such as 'impact' are up for grabs. I wish I had been more proactive earlier in my career in defining what it meant for me and convincing those around me (including Deans and promotion committees) that my research was worthwhile, even if it wasn't published in 'top journals'. And third, I've learnt that journal publications need not be the end of the research process. Sharing my research in various forms has greatly contributed to its impact and it also been a fun and rewarding experience. My journalism background helped me, but these are skills that can be acquired through training. I expect that far-sighted universities, that understand the ways in which academia is changing, will support interested faculty to develop those skills.

I am fortunate that there are some favourable trends that make it more viable to pursue this variant of an academic career. I am not suggesting this could or even should displace more traditional forms of academic work. But is has worked for me, and for that I am very grateful.

References

Adler, P.S. (2016). 2015 Presidential address: Our teaching mission. *Academy of Management Review*, 41(2): 185–195.

Bridgman, T., Cummings, S., & Ballard, J. (2019). Who built Maslow's pyramid? A history of the creation of management studies' most famous symbol and its implications for management education. *Academy of Management Learning and Education*, 18(1): 81–98.

Cummings, S., Bridgman, T., & Brown, K. (2016). Unfreezing change as three steps: Rethinking Kurt Lewin's legacy for change management. *Human Relations*, 69(1): 33–60.

Debatin, S. (2016). Fourth estate. In *The International Encyclopedia of Political Communication*. NJ: Wiley-Blackwell. https://doi.org/10.1002/9781118541555.wbiepc198

Farrow, R. (2017, October 10). From aggressive overtures to sexual assault: Harvey Weinstein's accusers tell their stories. *The New Yorker*. https://www.newyorker.com/news/news-desk/from-aggressive-overtures-to-sexual-assault-harvey-weinsteins-accusers-tell-their-stories

Le Masurier, M. (2016). Slow journalism: An introduction to a new research paradigm. *Journalism Practice*, 10(4): 439–447.

New Zealand Education and Training Law (2020). https://www.legislation.govt.nz/act/public/2020/0038/latest/LMS170676.html

Pearce, S., & Evans, D. (2018). The rise of impact in academia; Repackaging a long-standing idea. *British Politics*, 13: 348–360.

Remler, D.K., Waisanen, D.J., & Gabor, A. (2014). Academic journalism: A modest proposal. *Journalism Studies*, 15(4): 357–373.

Wilhite, A.W., & Fong, E.A. (2012). Coercive citation in academic publishing. *Science Magazine*, 335: 542–543.

Wong, J.C. (2020, April 20). Hydroxychloroquine: How an unproven drug became Trump's coronavirus 'miracle cure'. *The Guardian*. https://www.theguardian.com/world/2020/apr/06/hydroxychloroquine-trump-coronavirus-drug

BLINDS AND BANANAS

Metaphor in the margins

Stephen Linstead

It was hairy, and sticky, and it passed with preternatural slowness in front of my face. I was upside down, about 4 metres above ground, travelling around 100 miles an hour, spinning, and in that serene space that I've only been in twice in my life. The one where you think you will die, you know there's nothing you can do, and you simply let go of life. Where myth has it that your past life passes in front of you, it's a mistake to think that your head fills with pivotal moments and precious memories. It fills with trivia, because that's what life is,

FIGURE 36.1   The author (image by Bryan Ledgard).

mostly. The sticky fruit sweet was closely followed by a stripey child's sock from under the passenger seat. It belonged to Ben, my youngest.

I was wondering how to lever them into my famous last words when having vaulted three lanes of traffic, my brand-new Ford Sierra hit the hard shoulder and rolled 50 meters, coming to rest four square on its wheels, neatly parked facing horizontally towards the carriageway. Amazed that I was alive, unharmed and unmarked, I unclipped my life-saving belt and wandered into a nearby copse to collect myself. When I returned around 20 people were looking for my body. I joined them, relishing the invisibility, thinking this was what it would be like witnessing your own death. That, I thought, was some banana skin.

I had been on my way to a conference. It was my last duty in an exciting but ill-fated job as a very well-paid trainer and research director for a generously funded start-up company combining behavioural and computer simulations. The glitzy storytelling that had lured me from the headship of a large academic department had been a sham – the simulation software never worked beyond quarter seven and the expensive beachfront hotel where we ran the exercises for the country's blue-chips (each room had a spiral staircase) was chosen because it was owned by the MD's discreet friend, who accommodated his chum's adulterous affair with his secretary in return for the trade and corporate exposure. This MD had put his sales pals on the road in BMWs, and evaporated £1 million of venture capital in six months. Dream job became melancholic intermezzo. I had formally been declared redundant a week prior, and the previous night I had stayed awake until 5 am filling in job applications, writing up initial research drafts from the company's work for publication, and preparing an examiner's report on a plagiarised thesis. I was an accident waiting to happen, and it did.

Four years previous, the world had looked a bit different. I had a piece that was ground-breaking in the study of organisational humour published in a major sociology journal – it sundered novel turf in boasting three jokes, seven quips and two "fucks". Ultimately this scatological gem was republished and anthologised three times and is still being cited 35 years later. But on first submission to a leading organisation studies journal, it was rejected, with one reviewer asking – "is this one big joke?". It was my first submission to such a prominent organ, and I was crushed. I wept. Nay, sobbed. And, perhaps too predictably, cursed. Violently and repeatedly. Three years of field work doing shifts in a factory, struggling to "write-up" my PhD under the pressures of my first academic job, my family's sole breadwinner, a new born, and a hostile work environment that drove me to desperation in seeking an exit. And that was the response to my efforts. Not simply unscholarly, but disrespectful, arrogant and hostile. I could so easily have given up there and then, and the margin was wafer-thin. I didn't, of course, but that memory haunts me – even writing about it now I feel it in my stomach. I also remember I was sitting and looking forlorn when a well-published colleague, who was regarded as a bit of a misfit in our small college, came over and asked me what was wrong. I told him, and said I had been feeling bad for two or three days. He said for him it took two or three weeks – and "if you push the boundaries you need to expect it, just don't give up". He was a quantitative psychologist who used hypnosis in his work and had written an impressive textbook. He didn't fit either. I felt reassured. The following term the weirdo got a job at UC San Diego. My latest rejection, just last week, displayed the same arrogance, dismissive tone, lack of scholarship, paucity of professional ethics and plain human insensitivity as did the first one. I was just as hurt and angry – but these days I have the tools to know how to handle it. If you work the margins, it's how you know you're still there.

I always felt a bit of a misfit, and even, on bad days, a fraud. I had, and still have, confidence issues, and I'm basically introverted. I like interacting with people, but it exhausts me. In later life I was diagnosed as having a form of Asperger's but quite a quirky variant at that (of course, it had to be, didn't it?). I'm obsessive but not compulsive in that I don't need the rigid regularity other sufferers do. I really struggle to fit into others' formats and systems which just seem alien to me, and I can get anxious if my own needs aren't met in that regard, finding it hard to maintain my thought processes. Filling in forms literally puts me on the road to a panic attack and formal meetings give my body physical pain. But I can isolate myself even in the midst of confusion and accomplish prodigious feats of concentration and focus that have been called scary by shuddering traumatised witnesses. I tackled my painful introversion – it was hurting me back then – by becoming a performer, acting and singing, fronting bands and doing stand-up semi-professionally. I could be in role the person I struggled to be in private. Yes, it's a classic depressive cycle response, but these masks and that focus were functional, a shield from the world I loved but which hurt me, and a way to escape the continuing fallout from a violent, drunken father and the breakdown of my parents' marriage. Behind the doors of a softly furnished professional home, and a prosperous middle-class lifestyle, my mother, brother and I were physically and psychologically tortured, but the outside world was not to know – we were expected to put on a brave face, and he'd "come round". He didn't.

Scholarship was part of my attempt to regain some control over my identity, as was manual labour. Both threw me upon my own resources, which made me feel oddly validated, and a little bit safer. During my undergraduate years I lost my way somewhat, and family and personal circumstances precipitated a minor breakdown. After I graduated, I worked as a fork-lift driver and dairy operative, humping churns and working tipping machines, playing in bands and sessions at night, where I loved being out front and in control, riding the risk of audience reception. I got a Master's degree to repair the damage, but that particular stream was exhausted for me, and I drifted into the old pattern of manual work and semi-pro music. Again, I was trying to build a life in between worlds, dipping into one then the other, trying to figure out who I was.

What I learnt from 14 years of full and part-time jobs was invaluable. First, was the dignity of labour and the need to respect the workers who are on the job at 4 am getting the milk out of the cooler for the roundspeople to start loading at 5 am to be on customers' doorsteps at 6. People used talk of being "up with the milkman", forgetting that there were invisible ghosts who put him on the road. Although there are few people left on the road delivering milk there's always a backstage full of unsung grafters in any job. I was one. I loved being out back, and anonymous – a schizoid counterpoint to my performing side. Second, you may not be *obviously* in a team, but you are. Figure out what that team is, build trust with your workmates, and have fun – you can have fun even in the worst of circumstances and conditions if you support each other. Third, you can always motivate yourself by doing your best work, however menial. When set the job of cleaning a toilet, symbolically hardly prestigious, I decided to be the best toilet cleaner in the world. I finished the job and went back to my station and got called into the Regional Director's office. I was internally shaking as I entered, as I had troubles with authority as a result of my upbringing, and still do. The toilet I had cleaned was his personal restroom, his regular cleaner was off sick and he had an important visitation coming in. He said it was the cleanest the toilet had ever been, and in an arm on the shoulder moment, literally, he told me that if I approached the rest of my career with the same attitude, I'd go a long way. Although I perhaps wouldn't need the brush. I maybe didn't go all that far, but I never forgot that moment – not so much for the content, but for how it made me feel. My father constantly made me feel guilty, and not good enough – I was once punished for coming fifth overall in class although I'd been off sick for part of the year, as only first was acceptable to him. I had a report full of As but was grounded. The Director had no idea of my psychology, but he wanted to give me credit for my efforts in a small way anyway because he knew it mattered. You never know how much good you may do with a tiny gesture. If it's genuine, it's never trivial. So I guess there's also a fourth point – extraordinary outcomes can start with ordinary actions, and a fifth – good management really does make a difference.

Because much of my work has been in the food industry, where hygiene is critical, I got used to starting work in a pristine environment, making an unholy mess of it, then restoring it as though we'd never been there. Identity, for us, was invested in our imperceptibility. Our best game went unnoticed. As authors, we were dead. That affected me too, long before I read Barthes, Derrida, Foucault, Deleuze and the rhizome, self-as-site and life-as-wayfaring literature. But when I found them, I found my (un)self.

Since my first job, I had become fascinated by two things: one was how organisations that appeared well run on paper were far from well run in reality, and relied on what I would come to call "culture" in order to function. And this wasn't just me thinking this – the people I worked with were discussing it with me in tea-breaks. The organisations I worked for were run from the margins. As I was getting drawn more deeply into one organisation by successive shopfloor promotions, I decided to get a management qualification and after doing some personal research I opted for a masters in Organization Development which changed my life. I discovered structuralism, Lévi-Strauss and Roland Barthes, semiotics, and became convinced of the link between the literary texts I had previously studied and the social and psychological studies in which I was now engaged. But the model of the "text" in play did not feel quite right. Then I discovered poststructuralism and a new concept of textuality, which fed straight into my emerging take on organisational culture, which was suddenly becoming the hot organisational topic. I really discovered Derrida in 1981 when I sat down with *Margins of Philosophy* having purchased it in the students' union book market at the University of Hull. I sat in a toilet cubicle with a magnificent piece of life-size graffiti of angry Betelgeusian Tharg the Mighty, fictional editor of *2000 AD* (the comic) towering over his sheepish assistant, the waste disposal droid Ro-jaws. It could have been the work of the immortal Pat Mills himself, except that his trembling speech bubble encased the unconvincing apology "I'm sorry Tharg, I didn't mean to call you a cunt". Sandwiched between subcultural legends in text and art felt like a homecoming until vascular circulation ceased in my lower extremities and I was forced to hobble out blinking into the oblique glare of our own red dwarf.

Needing to feed an expanding family, I accepted a promotion running an MBA programme, happy to get back to working with post experience managers. But before I arrived in post, I was nudged into a different trans-European role, involving partners from France, Germany and Spain. I didn't know that the penultimate incumbent but one had been the founder of this pioneering programme, and had been removed by the current Dean because he was basically running a fiefdom. He was still in touch with his friends in the School and in Europe, and was determined to embarrass the Dean by making the programme unmanageable. As a consequence of these political machinations the penultimate incumbent lasted only nine months before a nervous collapse. Before I'd been in post three months this hit me full-square. I was dragged through an unnecessarily tortuous negotiation where there appeared to have been a leak from my senior team to the European partners as every move I made was anticipated and my propositions were ambushed. Our students were effectively being held hostage to policy-bending to please our partners' heavyweight stakeholders. Careful questioning and listening led me to one suspect. At the last minute, the day before the next meeting, I fed the prime suspect individually with an irresistible titbit of information that was false, but I knew would startle the European partners should it reach them, and it did. In the joint meeting, they immediately raised with alarm this fictitious issue, effectively exposing the mole, and were able to respond that they must have been misinformed. I then presented an entirely different set of disarming proposals that were accepted as the basis for progress. Not only had I effectively stopped the leak, but I shifted the basis of my relationship with the partners to a new level of respect. But other problems remained, including a law lecturer who was the founder's best friend. He maintained his own professional practice using this as a vehicle to send demands regarding his workload (which he wanted to minimise) to my home via recorded delivery. The feral lawyer had been feeding malicious gossip to students regarding proposed changes to the course and encouraging them to get their parents to write to the VC, while surreptitiously taping, editing and releasing private conversations. With the help of the Head of Law, who had, fortuitously, written the standard textbook on relevant issues in focus, his claims were dismissed. He had had a good deal – by overplaying his hand he ended up with one that was far worse, and he was off the programme.

I moved on to a major Head of Department role in a sprawling institution. It was about to emerge from local authority control and become central government funded. In this process properties in use by the institution had to be divided as assets with the Council, which effectively meant we had to demonstrate that all our retained sites were being used for degree teaching. In my department I had a site that was a couple of miles away, a former school on prime residential land, that was used for short post-experience courses for languages for the general public and business. What I had to do was create a restructuring of our degree programme so that business with language students would be bussed over there and some staff relocated, while other staff were made redundant and the short courses closed down. One of the targets was the very popular head of site, Cyril, who I liked rather a lot. The VC personally charged me with persuading Cyril to request consideration for voluntary redundancy, whereupon the VC would create some customised advantageous terms. The VC was a former MP with powerful connections, and a habit of delivering instantly executable marching orders to his senior staff over dinner at a particularly classy restaurant in the city. Strong men trembled when they received a dinner invitation from this clubbable Stalinist's PA, wondering if they were on the menu.

I felt the weight of my role bearing upon me, and accordingly sat down with Cyril and told him what I thought of the situation. I didn't want to lose him, but I knew what was coming down the track – yet I didn't want to threaten him either. Again the prevailing atmosphere was of rampant rumour, leaks (to the press this time as one of the language students was a journalist), and as part of the general uproar the VC and I had to face a packed and hostile public meeting set to rail against the partially leaked plans. The VC was brilliant. His rhetoric was flawless. He owned the hostility of the group, turned it against the government, won their support and even had them establish a support group of activists to lobby both the City Hall and Westminster. We got our way, and eventually they got theirs, with replacement provision coming from a different city college. The site was ceded to the institution on independence day, and three years later it was sold to residential developers for millions. But I had had my conversation with Cyril, he had had his chat with the VC, and a few weeks later his retirement was announced. Around that time I was passing the VC's office on the way to a planning meeting. Unusually he came out and called me, then even more unusually put his arm round my shoulder – which felt very different to the dairy manager's embrace – and said "Thanks for delivering Cyril. I won't forget". I went cold. Again, I remember how that felt to this day.

Up to that point I had, surprisingly, been enjoying the thrill of Management, doing some real problem-solving and change management. But I missed the thrill of teaching, and my research had shrivelled to a dribble. So the VC's arm was pivotal: I had crossed the threshold, I was in the club, I was in line for bigger things. I was 36, so 2–3 years and a Deanship was likely, PVC in a further 5, and maybe all the way by 50. But the price was probably being locked into that sector, leaving behind the teaching and executive work I missed so much, and almost certainly the chance of producing any distinctive scholarship, into which I still had so much of my identity invested. And I now had three children and a mortgage. An impressive ad appeared in a quality Sunday paper for a job that sounded ideal – simulation-based management education, practical but research-led, to be based in the North, with a car and a 25% boost in salary. The selection process was rigorous, with seven stages including personality and presentation tests. To my delight, I got the job, reporting to a former Brigadier who to my surprise was one of the best managers I ever worked for. Unfortunately, his boss, the MD, was the worst.

So I'd been wriggling between the blinds of research, teaching, academic management, and real-world management education – figuring out who to be, and not settling. I later found out that this never-at-homeness was one consequence of childhood trauma, although I never considered myself traumatised – I just thought my father was an arsehole. Then again, the worlds I found myself in didn't exactly featherbed me into a sense of security. In my first academic job, I discovered that it didn't actually help to be academic. At that time PhDs were not required for entry to the profession, and even studying for one could provoke resentment in colleagues who hadn't had the opportunity. Being good at your job could be a disadvantage if others defined the job differently. It was never as simple as research versus teaching. Some of the "teachers" were gifted, dedicated and generous, others secretive, envious and avaricious. But the real problem ones were those who used the job as an anchor for private consultancy work. They would obstruct any changes that made it more difficult for them to operate commercially – so any pedagogical innovation was a hostage to private interests and many colleagues were bought off by being given a slice of whatever consultancy work or perks were going. One of these included siphoning off fees from a student residential weekend to run a free "staff bar" in an empty hotel room for both programme deliverers and "drop-ins". In another institution one of the AV staff was day-trading from his repair workshop. One of his scams involved evading limits on the purchase of shares in privatised public utilities by buying them in the name of academic staff, to whom he paid an immediate premium. This was illegal. Within 12 months he made £240,000 profit (at 2021 prices). The issue was discovered when a new head of section logged into his computer for some necessary technical information while he was off sick. He was fired, but the money was gone. He handed back his lab coat, but kept the cashmere polo-necks.

After the commercial adventure, the old university sector provided a safety net, but in a new section devoted to management development, running MBA programmes for blue-chip corporate clients. This was demanding and at times very intensive, but because it was arrhythmic it enabled me to develop my scholarship. Early in my career I had realised that my bread and butter teaching would be in personnel management as well as OB, and it would help me to deal with both students and colleagues if I acquired a professional qualification. I won the national prize in the exams, and specialised in training and development from that point. My new job allowed me to tie down mainstream professional publications while allowing scope for the marginal poststructuralist work I had been developing. I had stumbled across a new and exhilarating network at a conference in 1984 called SCOS, and this provided intellectual sustenance for the next 20 years, and still does, to some extent. It set a pattern in that my research collaborations have since been decentred, located in my networks rather than my home institutions. Energy and support was out there if I phoned "home". In 1992, my marriage fell apart and I was left in a disastrous financial situation, but contacts at UCLA enabled me to secure a visiting position in a new university in Hong Kong that provided the immediate returns I needed. I developed core programmes and residentials that again secured me space to write, to pay for childcare, and to travel to conferences. As a result of a late-night conversation on the Paris Metro, I found myself a single parent with a chair in Australia.

Both Hong Kong and Australia were good for me – I got to do management development with major clients, taught talented students, and had space for scholarship. I had a spell as Head of Department, which introduced me to Australian academic politics, and experienced Chinese academic politics intercalated with global politics. Experiences I wouldn't have missed, and leaving Australia was very difficult, but family circumstances back in the UK required my presence. I took a research led Associate Dean position in an emerging new university business school, which nevertheless left scope for scholarship to continue but not the management development work. I moved on to a research director role in a major and well-established business school, then took a chair in a new management school in a leading university. The politics were frustrating: I saw harassment up close and a Dean dismissed for scholarly fraud. But once the core business was out of the way and the needs of each University to hit its targets were satisfied, there was room for creativity and criticality to be expressed – in the spaces, on the margins, after dark. Only relatively recently have I managed to combine the two lives I've been forced to lead, in becoming a filmmaker, but across the years I've managed to create and record musical performances, publish poetry, direct theatre and film, and curate multimedia exhibitions, including founding a conference almost 20 years ago that focusses on bringing all the arts to bear on MOS issues. I still feel as though I'm a little in the wings career-wise, but I like it that way, and I'm not rushing to pull the curtain down.

I have had a few banana skins, but my best theatre moment wasn't slapstick. It was in Hong Kong. My University was next door to the legendary Shaw Studios, and we had a deal that allowed us to share their limo company for airport trips. Immediately before a Christmas visit back to the UK, my 11 year old son had his end of term show, in which he was playing a general. We literally had to collect him at the stage door – he walked off stage and into the limo like a Shaw Star without time to remove his uniform or his bristling moustache. As we arrived at the old buzzing Kai Tak airport, fellow travellers were much entertained, but as we reached the immigration desk I realised that his appearance might not sufficiently match his passport. The Chinese immigration officer looked at the document, then looked at my son, with a perfect stone face. In a forensically precise Oxford accent, he enquired "He's rather mature for his age isn't he?"

So avoiding banana skins has continued, although if I had slipped on an actual skin, quite possible in some areas of Hong Kong, it would not have been the same type as the first recorded fruit based tumbler – Billy Watson – slid on. The banana, of course, with its bright yellow skin, sends out a clear warning of its presence, so if a person on stage or on film slips on one, it is their own failure to pay attention to the world around them that is at fault. As Bergson notes, they become an automaton, the world reminds them it is not under their control, and the absurd flailing of limbs to regain balance, usually unsuccessfully, is what we find funny as pretension is punctured. The mask is not removed, but slips briefly – once we have seen what's underneath we don't forget it, even if we renew the mask.

The banana hides its true nature in several ways. First, despite its appearance the plant is a herb not a tree. Second, the actual banana fruit is a berry. And the banana skin in real life is only quite briefly yellow, being green until ripe, with quite a short shelf life. Once discarded, it very quickly becomes dark brown, the worst colour to spot in situ, and research has confirmed that it is indeed one of the most slippery fruits. It's a very singular fruit too in that it is cloned, and exists in monocultures. The bananas that Chaplin, Lloyd and Keaton slithered on, and Americans consumed in their millions between the wars, were the Gros Michel varietal, larger, straighter, fatter and tastier than our current favourite. It was this humble plant that provided the narrative for the United Fruit Co and the CIA to topple the government of Guatemala in the 1950s and deliver the epithet "Banana Republic" to the English language. But it was already too late for Big Mike. Clones share and transmit common vulnerabilities, and the popular plantain was wiped out between the 1920s and 1960s by Panama Disease, to which the Cavendish variety was resistant, and it eventually usurped the throne. But the mutation Panama Disease Race 4 is currently attacking the Cavendish, and has claimed plantations in Malaysia, Indonesia and Australia. It could be just a matter of time, and although the GM specialists are hard at work, modification is more likely to take decades rather than years. Is academia, too, being slowly devoured by its own skin?

So has this love affair all been a waste of effort? Or am I back where I started, knowing it for the first time? No, Eliot was wrong – because that "I" doesn't exist that way... and neither does the place... the past *is* another country. But is there any hope – is there something in what keeps me going that connects to an alternative future in which intellectual alterity receives more than at best, repressive tolerance, and helps to enable a better, less functionally obsessed but more humanly functional, world in which we stop judging each other so harshly while taking more precise care of the worlds under our stewardship?

Sometimes I feel as though I've been eluding the searchlights of a system that would do me harm if it only knew what I was up to. I wonder why doing what I do has to hurt, and why almost uniquely in the developed world, is scholarship viewed with such open public disrespect in the UK? Do we only dream because we know those dreams *must* elude us? Why does real creation always come from the despised margins? Maybe it's because so many scholars role model in practice the very behaviours they criticise in print.

But peering between the blinds is about more than avoiding co-optation. It's about preserving mystery, keeping the inexplicit free of its own chains. Dreams keep coming – they aren't goals and objectives, they are the pure flow of desire, to be followed not analysed. And creation comes from the margins because it is subliminal. It comes from dreams not diagrams. The future is always offstage, out of frame. We need to stay open. We need to stay on our feet and avoid banana skins. And steer clear of Thrillsuckers.

A CLOWN'S TALE[1]

Ralf Wetzel

At that moment, the vibration of the floor around me became stronger and stronger, louder and louder. I had to put my hands upon my ears, I went down on the floor, looking for a place to shelter. The vibration was roaring by now, I heard the furniture moving in the dark. The plaster on the walls cracked and gushed down, dust filled the air. Suddenly, the walls also started to crack, bricks slammed to the floor, until finally the walls collapsed around me.

Then – silence.

When the two of us were children, we were sitting on top of this huge heap of sand in the middle of the yard of his family's house somewhere in East Germany. As soon as we touched it, the sand turned into castles and dungeons, rain forests with rough rivers and fragile rope bridges, spaceships and pirate ships, the moon and the sun, prairies and oceans. After a few weeks of playing there, he pulled me away saying "George, look!" pointing at the creek behind his garden and the meadow behind the creek, the wood behind the meadow and the wheat field behind the woods. In the blink of an eye, we were there. We put our hands deep into the ice-cold water of a little well in the middle of the woods, we listened to the deer calling loudly in the August wheat field, we built an armada of spaceships from forest loam, we liberated the creek of human waste. When I was imagining a band of evil cowboys ready to attack my village of Apaches, he was already jumping to the opposite side of the creek, giving commands to his imaginative fellow cowboys preparing to go to bloody war with us. Whenever we sat at the well and he started to collect wood to build a little ship, I already had big leaves from the trees in my hand for the sails.

One summer evening we stayed in the cave beneath the trunk of an old oak. We were lying on our backs, our arms behind each other's necks in our sleeping bags. We listened to the rustling leaves in the dark. A tawny owl told the whole forest we were there. With our heads out of the cave we looked into the clear black sky, counting stars. We looked at each other, smiling, and I saw the same stars glistering in his eyes. Without any words, we fell asleep.

Hardly a day went by that we returned home not covered in mud, with wet or torn pants but singing, laughing and with sparkles in our eyes and with millions of stories to be shared.

Then the day of Ralf's school enrolment came. He carried this huge sugar bag in his arms, filled with sweets, dressed in new checked pants and his beige shirt. But what I remember most was his pale face and the frown on his forehead. He was nauseous in the morning before we left the house to go to school. His stomach was aching and just minutes before he had to go, he threw up and pooed at the same time. In the weeks and months to come, the kids in his class were often congregating around him. "You're slow as a turtle with your short legs!" the girls laughed.

"Your glasses are thick as magnifiers, you blind worm!" the boys yelled while pushing him around.

One morning, he even lent forward because of stomach cramps while walking to school. Halfway to school he stopped, looking at me with tears in his eyes.

"You're not feeling well, right?" I asked.

"I don't want to go there" he replied.

"Then don't!" I said. "It's not a good place for you to go, I can see that."

He paused for a moment, then suddenly straightened his back and lifted his chin.

"You are right." he said with a tearful voice.

"You're not happy there." I added and slowly caressed his back.

"School is over for me!" he shouted and stomped his feet on the ground.

"Why don't you tell your mom?"

"Yes. Let's go," he said.

He turned around, grabbed my hand as he ran back home. Only at the door he let go of me, ran into the house and threw himself into his mother's arms, wrapping himself around her, constantly sobbing. "I will never go to school anymore, never! Never! Never!"

His arms and shoulders relaxed when she caressed his hair and back. Then, without saying a word, she took his hand and his school bag, pulled him out of the house and dragged him all the way to school. He cried, screamed, yelled, dug his heels into the ground, but without success. She just pulled him along. When they arrived in front of the school entrance, he had completely given up. His face was pale again, without any expression. She sent him in on his own without saying anything.

"Be a strong boy. You need to go in" was her only comment before she stepped back, not giving him another chance to escape.

His stomach was rebelling when he entered the classroom, head bowed while going to the teacher to apologize. He never said a single word in class unless he had to. I waited for him in his room that evening. He came in, wordlessly, and threw himself onto the bed, hiding his face in the pillow.

"What happened?"

"It was a stupid idea to go back home." he sobbed after a while.

"Why?" Minutes passed as he continued sobbing into the pillow.

"My father talked to me just now."

Him and his father rarely spoke. When it happened, it was clear that something was wrong and that his mother had handed the matter over to stronger hands. His father was an entrepreneur and ran a small family business that his grandfather had started a long time ago. It was hard to sustain a business in East Germany since it was against the communist ideology to own a company. Entrepreneurs were seen as bourgeois and as such taken as being against the state. Everyone in the family knew that there were spies around, carefully observing the family and the company, just waiting to find any reason to shut down the business and punish the family.

"He said I can't do anything like today again. I have to pull myself together."

"But why?" I asked. "What is the problem?"

"I am putting the family at risk. He said that they only wait for us making mistakes to destroy us." My chest started to tighten.

"And? What are you supposed to do when you don't feel well at school?" I felt my jaws starting to clench and my throat closing up.

"He said I never should allow anyone to read my mind, to know what I think and feel. 'No one should ever be able to read you. Just pull yourself together, put down your head and carry on'. That's what he said." The pitch of his voice went higher and higher as he said that. He buried his head again in the pillow.

"But this is terrible!" My voice grew louder. "You just can't do that, it's going to be painful!"

He lifted his head and said: "What else should I do?" – his eyes staring fiercely at me. "*You* made me return in the first place, *you* brought me into this mess."

I held my breath as my eyes grew bigger. Really? Did he just snap at me?

"Because I saw that you were not well" I justified. "And it was clear to me that you needed to do something, whatever that might be!"

"And what's the result?" He paused but did not wait for an answer. "Now I am on watch at school *and* at home! *Thank* you!"

"But you can't just do that, you just can't! It's going to kill you!" The pitch of my voice went higher.

"You are not helping!" He stood up and walked towards me: "Don't you see that? You are making it worse!"

"But I am your friend, I can't just let you go into this!" I almost begged.

"No, George, you're not my friend." He came closer. "Not anymore. You are just bringing trouble to me" he slowly said, in a dark voice.

"What …?" I gasped.

I slowly started retreating. I have never seen him that way. His hands had turned into fists, his chin was lowered to his chest while his eyes were drilling holes into mine.

"Leave me alone!" he yelled.

"Out!" his pointing finger prolonged the stretched arm showing me the door.

"But …"

"*Out!*"

Closing the door from outside, I couldn't believe what just happened.

We hardly saw one other after that but I tried to watch him from afar. I noticed how his health was deteriorating. He was constantly coughing, with a dripping nose and sometimes even with fever. After some time, he simply disappeared. I had no idea what was going on. In the next days I pondered going to his mom and asking, but I was afraid. Something was terribly wrong. Weeks later, after I had eventually again seen him in his yard, I went to his house but was sent away by his mother. I returned to my room. I bricked up the door and windows of my room, painted everything black and switched off the lights. I just sat in my dark, slowly losing my sense of time.

Some ten years later, after the Berlin Wall fell, his father wanted him to study business administration, and since he had no idea about what to do himself, he followed. His studies became the most boring time of his life. None of the courses he followed with any passion or own inner ambition, he just did what he had been told. He remained pale, thin, and mostly without any smile on his face. Instead of making decisions for himself, Ralf sat on the old, deserted swing in his garden, wondering about what all people do when they go to work.

At the end of his studies, as he was about to write his thesis, a new psychology professor, John, arrived at the university. Breathlessly he sat in on one of John's classes. He was intrigued by the task to find the hidden meanings in an interview with an employee working in a sausage factory about his work. The employee talked about how he cared about his tools, how he meticulously cleaned them each day and put them in precise order for the next day. Ralf raised his arm and said:

> The tools are a manifestation of the pride the employee has built through his work. The tools are an extension of himself, the tools and how he treats them are expressions of his identity. His work *is* his identity.

After class, John stopped Ralf as he left the room and asked him whether he would be willing to work as his research assistant. Ralf's jaw dropped. "Of course I am!" he answered with eyes wide open, smiling.

During his time as John's assistant, he felt like he was awakening after a long and paralysing sleep. He discovered that life happens in episodes, not bound to one family narrative, where everyone has his place, predetermined from beginning to end. When one story ends, a thousand new ones might start – it's about how you choose to live. Once, bursting out with laughter, he said to John with all the colours of life in his eyes and cheeks: "I finally know what I am! I am not what my father wants me to become! I am a researcher, a scientist, an academic!"

After some time John asked him to remain as his assistant and invited him to come up with an idea for a PhD, "otherwise the time you spend here doesn't make much sense for you."

During this time Ralf and his colleagues spent many hours discussing research methods, debating about philosophy, epistemology and intervention. He pryingly went out to do interviews in companies and was frantically writing research papers at home. Ralf was constantly laughing and joking with his colleagues, scribbling on the whiteboard in his office until it was covered with multi-coloured circles, arrows, unreadable words. The idea of becoming an academic and eventually professor invigorated him. Soon he was going to get married too. He probably never felt that happy.

Then, without any warning, John left, and soon many of his handpicked researchers left too. His successor was about John's age, but when Ralf was once asking him in the hallway to explain one of his thoughts, he just frowned and yelled dramatically "Read my texts!" Ralf stood there as if hit by lightning. The research assistants and research collaborators were treated like a commodity and like useful idiots.

The new professor asked him to take over some of his teaching duties. In his first lecture the students refused to pay attention, irritating him. He lost his train of thought, his hands and his voice started to tremble. The longer he talked, the more he coughed nervously. The students responded by mockingly copying his coughing and his trembling voice. The minutes till the end of the class seemed endless. The next morning, his boss called him in.

"Well done, Ralf, you lost the class. It's going to be very difficult for me now but let's cut the crap, I have to take over," he said. Ralf sat there in his office, silently, trying to hold back the tears.

Ralf switched back to becoming the pale, silent collaborator he was before. He realized that this is academic normality. Competition about publications, exploitation of researchers, teaching assignments without didactic training, underfunding, political games all over the place. He realized that John was an exception, and that *this* was normality.

After finishing his PhD and after years of inner exile he had to leave this university. He went to Switzerland to become the head of a small research and consulting department at a university there. Yes, Switzerland. 850 kilometres away from his home. His wife did not agree to come with him and so he commuted each second weekend back to Germany to see his family. He threw himself into his new role. He had meetings with his team, drawing models on the whiteboard late into the night, with wine, pizza and potato chips. He spent time with his researchers to find out where their passion was, what they would love to focus on. He was fighting with his bosses to free up funding for their workshops and conferences and defending their research strategy. It was like during the times he worked with John, but this now was his own, he could create his own dream.

His pillow turned yellow beneath the pillowcase from the sweat he lost during the night. It was as if he had no family, as if he had no other life when he was in Switzerland with his team. To return to Germany, he used to take the night train. Since he couldn't sleep while commuting, he wrote papers and reviewed the work of his team. When he was back home with his family, he touched his wife less and less, and she didn't reach out to him either. They were managing the kids, deciding over holiday destinations, what new household equipment to buy, how to deal with teachers. But they never kissed. At night, they were just lying next to one other. In Switzerland he had more and more meetings, came home later and later, more and more failing to take the calls from his children.

One evening in Switzerland, while watching Yasmina Reza's "Le dieu du carnage" in the metropolitan theatre and seeing the merciless fights between the characters, tears rolled down his cheeks. In the days to follow, he had to stop in his daily business, since tears were welling up unpredictably. He was transfixed by the destructive fight of the couples in the play. He started a collaboration with the theatre about the play, obsessively. He was happy as the theatre agreed to set up a joint Sunday morning matinee open to students and the public, in which the actors showed parts of the play and he, together with his team, would give short monologues in between about the parallels between families and organizations. He started spending days and nights with the actors, the directors and his team. To work with actors, directors, producers, stage designers took all his energy and invigorated him.

Somewhere deep inside him a door appeared, and suddenly, a key was in his hand. He didn't hesitate for a second. And there he was, in an unknown room that felt so familiar to him. The day came while there were 35 people in the audience, curiously waiting for what was about to happen. The play started, the actors played, the story unfolded in its most painful moments. His colleagues talked about what was going on in the play, they revealed the patterns beneath, explained theories. He smiled all the way through. His cheeks were red, his eyes wide open, heavily breathing in and out. Then, it was his turn. He walked onto the stage, his heart beating fast, his lips dry. His place was on the couples' toilet. He found himself surrounded by a golden toilet paper holder, tall green decorating flowers, and shiny bourgeoise mirrors. He held his monologue, about the difference between a marriage and an employment contract.

"I found a quote recently," he started, "saying 'my marriage has fouled me beyond all recognizability'. This is what we're discussing here."

The room broke out in laughter, while he did not even smile. The longer he talked, the calmer and more relaxed he became. This was his place.

In the months that followed, he engaged more and more with the theatre and he started to use theatre exercises and methods in his teaching. This unconventional way of working brought him in full conflict with his university. The fights with his bosses escalated. It was not about budgets anymore. It was about who was right and who has the final word. When he was home in Germany, he hardly talked anymore. He just sat there, or slept on the couch, in the middle of the day. A constant headache became his daily companion.

It took two more years until he broke up with his wife and moved out of his home in Germany. He also quit his position in Switzerland. But he didn't return to Germany; he threw himself again into work at a new place, in another country.

One day, when he visited his daughter in Germany, she was waiting for him smiling, with glitter on her cheeks, a pink wig and a red nose in the middle of her face. A clown had come to her school and played with them. His daughter always had been a silent child, introvert and shy. In the past they often played together with few words, just with glances and with the twinkles in their eyes. But the nose and the costume seemed to liberate her. She jumped onto his lap, tilted her head and asked him why the sun is yellow, why the moon looks so cold and why he was so silent for so long. His jaw just dropped.

Later, when he killed a mosquito, she broke in tears and in the very next second yelled at him for daring to kill a fragile animal. Jumping for joy one moment, yelling in anger the next? He did not know her that way, that open. She never had the sort of sparkles in her eyes that he saw then. When he was with her, he could let go of his thoughts and worries, he laughed, smiled and cried. He had forgotten he could still do that. Something deep inside of him began to warmly hum and vibrate. When he came to be with her, he asked her to slip into the costume and don the nose. He soon brought oversized shoes, a wig and a red nose for himself too. They fooled around in her room and even went out on the streets dressed in their costumes. More and more she asked him how he felt about things. His only response was to stutter and sweat. He just enjoyed being next to her with his eyes wide open in admiration, smiling constantly.

He started to follow theatre clown courses where he lived. There, when in costume and with his red nose on, the teacher asked him to let show any feelings he had. He was stunned. He looked inwards and didn't find anything there. He saw all the other participants in the class laughing and crying, being sad, flirty, jealous and angry. He searched around within himself, but time and again all he felt was nothing. He took more clown courses to search deeper and deeper inside himself to find what the others so easily expressed. All he found was a humming sound and it took him a long time searching within himself, until he felt that he stood in front of a black wall. As he touched it, he felt this vibration coming from behind it. He started to check his phone for teaching or client appointments less and less, cancelled travel plans and booked in sick at the office. Instead, he threw himself into clown work and encounters with his daughter.

One day, he signed the two of them up for a clown street festival in the town where his daughter lived. In the afternoon before their gig, they were sitting in the kitchen having tea, giggling and rehearsing the tricks they wanted to perform, until his phone went off. He pulled it out – and froze. The picture of his boss appeared on the screen. Tiny drops of sweat turned up on his forehead while she was watching his every move.

"Yes" He mumbled soundlessly into the mic. "Peter … errr …"

His daughter came to him and sat on his lap, tilting her head, looking into his eyes.

"Ralf!"

Peter's voice came across short and sharp.

"Eventually! Goddammit I haven't heard from you for ages and I just wanted to check in with you whether everything is all right for the meeting with the pharma client tonight."

The drops of sweat on his forehead formed battalions and armies. The ticks of the clock on the wall, one slow tick after another became louder. He took a deep breath.

"No. I can't make it."

She put her head on his chest.

"Tick, tick, tick" said the clock.

The voice on the other end of the line exploded.

"I'll be back next Monday, Peter," Ralf added calmly after a while.

"Let's talk then."

Her arms were wrapped around him after he hung up.

"Let's go" she whispered quietly, smiling at him and jumping off his lap, grabbing the prepared bags with their props and off she was out of the door.

In my own darkness, I felt a deep humming vibration around me.

And so he became a clown and decided to work on his own clown show. He was frustrated about not having his own theatre or clown troupe where he was living and turned to Lee, a clown teacher and director he had been working with before. With her, he found himself one day exposed to different noses and masks she wanted him to try out in a workshop she ran. As he glanced at the different masks, he stopped suddenly and couldn't take his eyes off one specific mask. He had to put it on. In that very moment, his body cringed forward, his fingers became stiff and as he tried to talk, his voice became estranged. After he put on a wig and a costume, something changed in the atmosphere in the room. The lights dimmed as he slowly moved with the mask. He became unrecognizable to anyone around. As soon as he had the mask on his face, he was instantly pulled inside himself, deeper and deeper, darker and darker.

At that same moment, the vibration beneath and around me became stronger and stronger, louder and louder. I had to place my hands over my ears, I went down to the floor, looking for a place to shelter. The vibration was roaring by now, I heard the furniture moving in the dark. The plastering on the walls cracked and gushed down, dust filled the air. Suddenly, the walls also started to crack, bricks slammed to the floor, until finally the walls collapsed around me.

Then – silence.

I could barely see anything as the dust slowly settled.

I looked around. Then I saw someone standing some meters away.

"Ralf? Is that you?" I said.

The person turned to me. No doubt, it was him, covered in dust.

"George? What on earth are you …" he coughed.

We both found ourselves amidst debris inside a large room, scarcely illuminated by a dark red light, unclear where it was coming from. There was a chill around us.

I stood up, ran towards him and embraced him firmly.

"I missed you" I said.

"I missed you too" he whispered and cleared his throat. Still in embrace, we looked around. As our eyes got used to the light, we noticed huge grey rocks lying around, piled upon one another. As soon as we saw them, they started to hum. Suddenly we started vibrating just like them, the vibration had caught us. There was an energy radiating from these rocks that pulled us towards them. As we came closer, I realized that they were nothing but compressed and petrified feelings.

I saw a huge rock consisting solely of compressed fear. And another one was filled with condensed frustration and another huge one with anger. Right next to us was a block of ice consisting of nothing but love and next to that a granite of desire and a marble of lust.

Whenever we looked at a rock, it was as if it was responding, its vibration becoming stronger, and louder, and I wanted to avert my eyes off, but couldn't. We were drawn to them, interlocked with them, as if we carried the energy they needed to be released and liberated. My eyes widened and my breath quickened. The longer we looked at them, the more the rocks changed colours. They turned from dark purple to dark red, into light red, into dark and into yellow, light yellow and it felt like small particles were breaking away from the rocks, hitting us until the colours turned into flashing lights. Then, with a deep groaning sound, the rocks exploded. We held each other tight as amidst the explosion a whirlwind pulled us in, pulling us up and around. Tighter and tighter we held each other until I could not feel any difference between him and myself anymore. I felt nauseous, my mind was spinning until I lost consciousness.

When I awoke, I found myself alone on a theatre stage, in front of Lee, with the mask on my face.

"Ralf, that was good!" she told me. "Now take off the mask, sit down and write everything down so that you can replay everything as you just did. Its great!"

In the hours and days to come, I did things that I never imagined I could possibly do: I messed up a wedding, I fucked a man, I had orgasms, I killed a friend, I ended up in prison. I became the earth, the air, water, a tree and an elephant. I was desperately in love, full of fear, hopelessly lost, entrapped in anger, I was shy in one second and filled with relentless lust in the next, I got humiliated, became furiously destructive and violent, I hid in panic and turned agonic. All the things that were hidden in the dark alleys of my soul seemed to have been awakened and broken through on stage. All of that happened within two days on that black, lonely stage, and almost all of my show was there. It literally broke through me.

Lee and I continued to work on the show, I don't know anymore for how many days. She yelled at me when she was dissatisfied, she pushed me hard beyond my limits, but she always knew how far she could push me to find the unknown treasure that was waiting inside me to be revealed.

We decided to bring the show to the Edinburgh Fringe Festival. Twenty four shows on 24 evenings in a row. Each time with the mask on my face, I turned furious on stage and time and again went through all the emotions that had been woken up within me. Some people became quite upset at the character, some laughed, some cried.

I realized that I could deeply touch people. It was addictive. In the nights after the show, I cried, I laughed, I smashed glasses and threw chairs around in my flat. And I just wanted to have more.

Last week, more than 15 years after my first disastrous teaching experiences, I taught a group of executive MBA students, experienced managers, in their early 40s. I was supposed to teach about how to create and maintain a truthful connection to your client. Like always, I removed the tables from the classroom to have space for moving around and to activate the physical energy in the room. We played a round of exercises and games to train how to deeply listen to your partner, how to be aware of your feelings when interacting and about how to tell your truth about what is happening. As always when teaching, I smiled when explaining and side-coaching the exercises, I laughed, jumped, made faces, danced around the students. Since I reconnected with George, I enjoyed teaching as a physical experience, as a co-performance created on the spot together with students, providing a physical way of learning.

After the usual moment of hesitation and doubt at the start, people became cheerful, laughter filled the room, the movements of the participants became relaxed, they suddenly became trees, rockets, animals, dogs, the sun. From these images, participants built bigger pictures. The tree was suddenly standing in a haunted forest, the rocket brought scientists to Mars, the animals took over a zoo and turned the humans into the creatures being visited. Bliss was in the air, eyes widened and jaws dropped when students accepted and built upon rather than blocked each other.

Then it happened. During a movement exercise, people stopped in the middle of it, more and more leaving the room to have a break. I noticed that my jaw had tightened and my whole body froze, blood was leaving my face. I stopped the class and announced a break. While standing in the empty room, I could not think. But I felt a deep and warm vibration growing in my guts. Continuing as planned was no option, that would have made it worse. Suddenly I realized that thinking would not bring me forward. I pulled out my red nose from my bag, put it on and closed my eyes. I took a deep breath and it didn't take long that, from deep down, something came up.

"Yes, George." I said, "Great idea, let's go to where the fear is. Let's do that." I slowly exhaled.

After the break, the participants were sitting in a half circle in front of me. Some sat with tilted heads, some with raised eyebrows, some smiling at me, some with no movement in their faces at all.

"What do you think happened just before the break?" I asked.

"It was too much for me" said one.

"I dropped out because I didn't see the meaning anymore. What has this funny and childish stuff to do with my work?" added another one.

"So, what did happen between you as class and me?" I continued.

Silence. "Tick, tack, tick, tack" the clock on the wall said.

"The connection between you and us broke." Someone said.

"Exactly" I confirmed. "Remember? That's the subject of this class."

I could hear a needle drop to the floor. "Tick, tack, tick, tack." No one moved.

"How often in your daily practice does it happen that you talk to a client and at one point, the client backs off, doesn't follow you anymore, withdraws and disengages?"

People were leaning forward on their chairs, eyes wide open. Nodding filled the room.

"They feel they have enough of the funny stuff we propose to them too." Another one said and the class broke out in laughter.

A man with grey hair gasped "Those were the most horrible moments in my career."

All eyes were on him.

"Tick, tack, tick, tack." I heard a tawny owl crying from somewhere.

"This is the end of the class as I had planned" I said. "Now it's about me and you only and what we both could do to get back in a proper connection. What do you think I could do to repair the connection? And what could you do? We have 60 minutes left."

Suddenly, I no longer saw participants anymore in front of me. They had turned into a bunch of cowboys sitting around the fire, discussing how to attack my apache village.

"Ok. Let's play!" one of them said.

Note

1 I am very grateful for the side-coaching in writing this text by the wonderful Pierpaolo Buzza, writer, actor, director and artistic director of Improbrussels.com. Thank you so much!

VII
The late entrance
Curated by Olivier Ratle

THE LATE ENTRANCE

Muddy water and dry grass?

Olivier Ratle

We are so glad you found the Late Entrance door. Wherever you were, you have had to find an exit, go around the building, not being distracted on your way by all the bright colourful flowers in garden, and make your way through a hardly accessible door – not such an enviable location considering how much the management likes to publicise the existence of the gallery this door opens onto.

The first exhibit in this gallery is a miniature portrait by Catherine Heggerud. Or perhaps we should say 'a portrait of the author *as a portrait*, describing life in the gallery from the perspectives of its framed inhabitants'. In a delightful satire, Catherine paints a vivid and poignant but also nuanced picture of what is it like to join academia at a later career stage, and of the years that immediately followed. From the (absence of) welcoming into her new role, to the struggle for tenure (with all implicit and hidden rules governing this process), Catherine expresses genuine surprise at different aspects of her role. She is surprised to find so few people around her sharing a similar career trajectory. She is surprised by the suspicions displayed by colleagues towards industry experience. She is surprised by the complexity of university structures – a gentle euphemism perhaps to label some of the most dysfunctional aspects of academia, such as goal displacement, incommensurable objectives, and conflicting reporting structures. She is surprised by how hard it is to overcome the internal barriers we create inside the University. She is surprised by the arbitrariness of the tenure process, which under a veneer of impartiality and procedural objectivity, is riddled with far more arbitrariness than it is acknowledged. And ultimately, she is surprised by the subtle hierarchies that determines who is allowed to produce knowledge and occupy the 'creative spaces', and who is forced to reproduce it, inhabiting the space of the work-intensive classroom where the work can be sometimes less rewarding.

Catherine's portrait depicts an experience that will resonate with many others who came late into this occupation. There are many reasons why people choose to come to academia as a second or late career choice, however, what late entrants often have in common is this sense of surprise or even bafflement at the inner workings of a world they did not really know – or that they thought they knew. Digging into the meaning of this 'bafflement', we may find different things: genuine surprise, but also anger, agony, and disappointment. Whatever talent and expertise late entrants bring from their previous career, by definition, it is almost bound to become a bête noire and a source of frustration. One can simply imagine the tales of the senior manager wondering why she is at the receiving end of some debilitating micromanagement. Or the former finance director, who isn't being trusted with his own budget, however derisory small it is. And the accountant asking herself: 'but where is all the money going?' The bafflement reveals the *doxa* – the set of rules internalised by those who have been playing the game for a long time. Taken for granted, they are rarely spoken of, at the risk of heresy, and Catherine's satire exposes this *doxa* with insights and humour.

In the middle of the gallery stands a full portrait, by Margaret Ying Wei Lee, Olivia Davies and Kathleen Riach. Margaret is a late entrant (or 'second-careerers', to use their own term) while Olivia is an 'early exit' (leaving academia for another career after her PhD), and together they provide insights into the ambivalences and contradictions of second-careerers' experiences, as doctoral students. Those contradictions are well illustrated with two pastiches, where one author recounts for example that 'I am explicitly celebrated yet also "put in my place", often at the same time', and that 'No credence was given to my previous professional work experience during the PhD application process, even though this same experience has made me a favoured research associate within the Faculty'. The stories presented through these pastiches enable the authors to identify what they call three modes of 'embodied disturbances' ('relating', 'appropriating' and 'betrayal and biting back'), which are not only responses to those contradictions, but also help laying bare constitutive organising principles.

As an academic located within a business school, I am reminded by this text that on the one hand, there is an abundant literature lamenting the absence of meaningful connections between academics and practising managers. On the other hand, very little attention has been paid to what happens when managers/practitioners join faculty ranks. A quick survey of the literature reveals the existence of a few studies spread across different fields and disciplines, but overall, those who embody the interface between academia and practice are almost a missing subject in those discussions. This text, in addition to all the insights it provides, also lays useful conceptual foundations for future studies of a group overlooked. Understanding their experience is important, because as the authors suggest, the way resources are allocated, and achievements are recognised often reproduce certain norms or 'ideal subject positions that shape conditions of possibility and legitimacy'. A pluralist University cannot be one that consciously or not, overlook and suppress the potential contribution of one of its constituent group.

Finally, for the third portrait in this gallery, Mark Stringer gives us another miniature, allowing us into the intimacy of a (pseudo)psychoanalytical session, where he occupies both roles of analysand and analyst, and which reveals issues around identity, lack and desire, and acceptance. Mark asks a question that many late entrants will have contemplated: why would someone who has spent nearly 40 years in a business career find themselves striving to become an academic? While academia can be an escape route or can be seen by outsiders as a very cushy occupation, for those who experienced various and genuine career successes, the answer is less obvious. As Mark puts it, 'why, given the messy, emotional, and more precarious state of contemporary HE careers (…) would I even want to make such a move, into a role that will be, in all probability, the last stage of my career (…)?' Readers will find a tentative answer in his text, but perhaps the title of the portrait itself is revealing.

Mark evokes the lyrics from the song *Up the Hill Backwards* by David Bowie, which one music critic suggested appears to address, 'the simultaneous emotions thrown up by private developments and intrusive press scrutiny in the aftermath of [Bowie's] messy and public divorce' (Pegg, 2002: 194). Another enlightening interpretation may be that, '[the song] explores two different aspects of existential angst: indifference to the way of the system, and a commitment to fighting against it' (Genius, 2018). Whatever Mark has in mind, we are bound to agree with his conclusive remark: 'the journey into academia in the next ten years will be anything but dull'.

As we exit the gallery, we can reflect on the fact that the Vietnamese proverb that inspired the title – 'the buffalo that arrives late will have to drink muddy water and eat dry grass' – may not be entirely true. The three portraits displayed here present a more complicated, nuanced and even optimistic story, inviting us to continue to be attuned to what late entrants bring into academia, to their challenges, and to how every workplace is enriched by being made of people from different backgrounds and with different career trajectories.

References

Genius (2018) Up the Hill Backwards, web site available at https://genius.com/David-bowie-up-the-hill-backwards-lyrics. Retrieved on the 13th of June 2022.

Pegg, N. (2002) *The Complete David Bowie*. London: Reynolds & Hearn.

LATE PORTRAIT ARRIVAL

Catherine Heggerud

I was harried as I arrived at the portrait gallery. The butterflies of anticipation had shifted into a deep pit feeling in my stomach. "I'm late," I thought to myself. Years of conditioning reminded me that being late was not acceptable. Yet, when I entered the gallery, no one was there to receive me. The building was unusually dim. I struggled to find the lights. Yet, I felt strangely at peace. Not at home, but calm. My path to the gallery had been a career well-travelled. I was accustomed to unusual circumstances. My onboarding experiences at various other organizations had ranged from well-organized welcoming parties to yellow sticky notes on the desk with handwritten scrawl, "decided to take vacation, back in a week." I had missed all the usual fanfare that is afforded to new portraits as the gallery was set to open in two weeks. Other portraits typically arrived two months in advance of the gallery opening which gave them time to understand the building layout, chat with the other portraits and really understand their place in the building floor plan. The building was beyond dark, it was lifeless. It was lonely but peaceful.

I believed I was resilient though as I had found myself in similar situations during previous journeys. I gingerly picked my way through the building, finding portraits with similar experiences for shared camaraderie. This was not an easy task though. New portraits were much younger with tiny offspring at home and not much in common with this older portrait. The seasoned portraits had established rituals and routines. They were suspicious of new portraits, particularly one covered in soot from industry experience and without appropriate academic credentials to reside in an ivory tower.

The early days in the gallery were challenging. There were competing priorities and incongruent expectations. Having worked in complex, large matrixed organizations, I thought I had seen all possible permutations and combinations, but I was wrong. At one time, I had simultaneously reported to an executive vice president, a vice president and a director so thought I could manage complex reporting relationships. In industry, there is generally one overarching goal – to stay financially viable – that helps to guide all decision making, but in the portrait gallery, there is not one implicit goal. For some, it is teaching, for others it is research, and financial viability seems somewhat irrelevant. Everything I had understood about the way the world works was effectively wrong. This was difficult to overcome. If you ask an outsider to the gallery, they might tell you a business school should function like a business. If the school feels compelled to research and teach it, then surely the school should practise it. Yet, this is clearly not the case. The underlying belief structure seems to be that we know best but do not follow it because we are unique, special, and quite frankly, not a business.

When I arrived at the gallery, like other portraits, I was given a two-year window to see if I would become a permanent exhibit rather than a temporary one, to make sense of the gallery, and to find my way within it. The countdown clock was continually going off in my head. Outsiders to the gallery would comment that it must be nice to work in an environment where you cannot be fired. Yet, I generally felt that I was watching a bomb in the corner of the gallery, ticking away, just waiting to go off in the temporary exhibit room. I had to guide the patrons and defuse the bomb simultaneously. Guiding the patrons through their learning was an insufficient condition for bomb diffusion. The other conditions were not well defined though, and knowing whether to cut the blue or pink wire felt like Russian roulette. After 25 years in industry, I had always known, whether I agreed or not, what the conditions were. In the first two years, I must have sent out dozens of resumes to have a plan B. Not feeling in control of the outcome was painful. Constantly looking for another gallery to hang in, just in case, was exhausting.

The two years passed and another contract arrived. I could remain in the gallery for another four years to work on fulfilling the obligations required for tenure. This was a huge relief as the bomb seemed smaller now. I felt like I had wire cutters to deal appropriately with the sense of impending doom. I began to better understand how portraits thought, how they worked, and how decisions were made. These next two years were filled with finding the appropriate portraits to collaborate and commiserate with. There was a sense of belonging but also a sense of indignation. The portraits that were late entrants like me, carved out unique niches and were crystal clear in their vision for being in the gallery. These conversations were critical to finding a gallery tribe. I also learnt within these next two years that the custodial staff of the gallery are critical to my well-being. I forged relationships with non portraits as this helped me to maintain perspective and keep my indignation in check.

Now, four years in, I have learnt much and questioned more. The velvet ropes designed to steer patrons to various parts of the building keep portraits in their respective rooms. The rooms are important to the well-established portraits as they are documented and referenced relative to the room they are kept in. Portraits never move between galleries. If portraits attempted to move between rooms, portraits believed that anarchy would ensue. Some portraits, based on pedigree, were allowed more freedom than others. Some portraits, with the appropriate publication record, never set foot in a room with patrons. Yet other portraits continued to be paraded in front of patrons, despite the colour being gone from their faces and their frames in need of repair. Much of portraits' daily existence revolved not around doing things right, but around doing the right things to make it through the tenure process. The tenure process removes the bomb from the gallery permanently. Tenure affords portraits freedom to speak-up, freedom to experiment, and freedom to be oneself. At lunch prior to her retirement, one senior portrait said to me, "you are untenured and female, keep your mouth shut until those conditions change." The tenure process is best described to a gallery patron as a sophisticated hazing ritual predicated on patriarchal norms.

The tenure process exists on two planes. The first plane is well documented, enshrined in a tome known as the collective agreement along with a faculty specific set of tenure guidelines, referred to in our school as a *blue book*. Blue is a fitting colour for the patriarchal nature of its contents. Grounded in "father knows best" thinking and classic normative business school theories, the blue book is the set of quests the portrait must complete, document, and have approved by others to demonstrate worthiness before being granted the holy grail of tenure.

The second plane bubbles below the surface. The informal processes that "govern" who sits on the tenure committee. The watercooler chatter on whether a portrait is collegial to others. The unwritten benchmarks on publishing, despite the very clear collective agreement rules that publishing is not a requirement for teaching faculty. As the teaching portraits gathered for lunch, the discussion weighed heavily on who would put a name forward to sit on committees where the decisions were made. Cohesive power reigns.

To put oneself forward for tenure requires vulnerability to judgement. The closest ritual is the electoral process. Your peers critique contributions, write letters in support of application or not. They write letters blocking your worthiness. If you attempt to go early for tenure, you are viewed as an upstart, challenging the status-quo. If you want to go later, you are viewed as lazy, not worthy of the prize at the end of the tenure process. The land mines are everywhere!

Despite the challenges and the loneliness, this portrait recognizes all of this and questions it all. Not only in the context of what it means for a portrait to get tenure but also in the broader context of what it means to be a good corporate citizen, a good role model, a good mentor. We, the business school, say we want our organizations to be more engaging to employees, we want our leadership students to be more ethical, we want to hear the voices of diversity, we want to be inclusive but in the classic flawed parenting style, we say, "do as we say, not as we do."

As I reflect on the process of jumping through the patriarchal hoops to achieve the outcome, I have decisions to make. Without a pedigree, I will never be a peer. Portraits without a pedigree but with tenure are still insubordinate, disposable, stuck in the trenches, on the factory floor. The creative spaces are reserved for those with a pedigree. Indignation still bubbles up at the unjustness of it all. Regardless of how many hoops I jump through, I will always be disposable, easily dismissed in favour of portraits with publications and doctoral degrees. As we closed out the current calendar year and started planning for the next one, I created my wish list of courses to teach combined with my other obligations to the school. My wish list was dismissed as the hiring had begun for real faculty – those with publication records and research agendas – and their desires would trump mine. As the wave of hurt rolled over me, I kept my eye on the horizon. This too shall pass.

Yet I know I need to create. I need to innovate. I want the workplaces of my children's future to be more democratic, more inclusive, and less hostile than the ones I encountered during 25 years in industry. The only way to do so is to rearrange the gallery. Mix the masters with the up and comers. Take down the velvet ropes. I know in my heart I must produce the normative package of father knows best. I have tried my best to be collegial, I have been seen but not heard. Once I pass through the gates of tenure, I remain optimistic that there is hope for the future. I am optimistic that business schools can change to be more reflective of where we would like our corporations to go. In a decade, when it is time for retirement, I dream I can leave via the main entrance.

DISTURBING BODIES? PROSPECTIVE AND RETROSPECTIVE SECOND-CAREERING WITHIN THE DOCTORAL CANDIDATURE

Margaret Ying Wei Lee, Olivia Davies, and Kathleen Riach

Introduction

In this chapter we seek to tease out some of the tensions, contradictions and possibilities involved when the normativity of academic trajectories is disrupted, and the consequences for the bodies, practices and institutions involved. Specifically, we focus on the movement in and out of academia by doctoral researchers rendering visible ambivalent spaces of disturbance in which institutions seek to simultaneously benefit and undermine second-careering. On the one hand, these seek to demonstrate plurality, relevance and professional credibility through their faculty and their practices. On the other hand, they demand a compliance and reproduction of rankings and assessment systems that prioritise traditional siloed scholarly pursuits such as publishing in 'elite' peer reviewed journals that forefront new theoretical vistas as opposed to direct practical application.

Second-careering refers to the material practices and negotiated identities of those whose careers traverse two different professions or sectors over their working lives. These may be retrospective, whereby an academic position is undertaken after a period of time outside the Academy; or prospective, whereby individuals embark on advanced study or faculty positions with the expectation or growing awareness that they will not remain exclusively within academia afterwards. Common (but by no means exclusive) second-careers in the Business School include those who move from chartered occupations (such as accountants) into lectureships where they simultaneously work on a doctoral qualification, PhD graduates who return to become academic staff after a period of consultancy or working, or financially solvent business owners and executives that return to full-time 'professor of practice' positions. These groups, among others, are seen as providing valuable ways of integrating and encouraging academic thought with workplace practice, a critique long being charged at more traditional modes of dissemination (e.g. Rynes et al., 2007; Hughes et al., 2011). And while 'connections to the coalface' have historically been an ongoing discussion since the emergence of Business Schools taking over from departments or centres of management, finance, accounting and economics, we now find second-careerers being positioned as central to the particular economies of 'credibility' and 'relevance' that have accompanied recent rhetoric surrounding academic capitalism and the neoliberal university more broadly.

It is important to note that other disciplines have navigated academic/praxis relationship in a variety of ways. Here we see that second-careering includes Engineering faculty who are expected to have an association with a professional chartered body requiring a number of years of professional practice or Arts faculty with 'works of practice' as central to their academic standing (Lam, 2020). In medicine, parallel careering is often the norm where faculty will also have an affiliation and position within a hospital or other healthcare setting and maintain a connection with clinical practice (Smesny et al., 2007), while other scholars may move back and forth in a pattern that Green (2016) calls 'turnstile careers'. What locates Business Schools in a particularly curious position is that high numbers of students (and associated institutional revenue) mean they are often under pressure to maintain aggressive growth and satisfy a consumer-orientated demand for 'relevant[1]' programme content, while ensuring positions in rankings that can be determined in relation to often narrowly defined research metrics.

Second-careering reveals the contradictions in variegated messages surrounding what constitutes 'academic excellence' within universities and broader systems of academic valuation in the Business School. This has particular consequences for the experiences and subsequent interactions with institutions for individuals coming from and thinking of careers beyond academia. First, it shapes how the opportunities and initiatives associated with securing success are organised, distributed or prioritised. This may be overtly through the way resources (e.g. time, buy-out) for particular activities, or more subtly through what achievements are headlined, communicated, publicly congratulated or otherwise recognised. As a result, such practices often reproduce ideal subject positions that shape conditions of possibility and legitimacy given that "forms and practices of organizing academic work not only affect the quality of the products but also constitute the subjectivity of the producers" (Muller-Camen and Salzgeber 2005: 271–272). Significantly, those within doctoral programmes who are either retrospective or prospective second-careerers are likely to be the most vulnerable to any institutional misrecognition surrounding second-careering, as well as have the potential to disturb and render visible these forms of misrecognition.

To explore this further, we write from our own positions as a current doctoral student who came to the PhD after significant professional experience (Margaret); a former PhD graduate now undertaking a career in filmmaking (Olivia), and a supervisor from a rather normative career trajectory going straight from study into an academic job (Kathleen). We used two analytical vignettes as a point of entry to our reflections, framing these as pastiche: imitations of encounters that both seek to 'give flesh' to the idea of prospective and retrospective second-careering. While written in the first person as Margaret and Olivia, they are composed through reflecting on both our own and our contemporaries' experiences then 'corrupted' through rewritings that echoed broader discussions and debates that circulate Business School careers and academic second-careers, as well as serving to protect the identities of those who shared their experiences and thoughts with us. After the pastiche we reflect on three modes of disturbance they reveal, allowing us to further contemplate how second-careering in the business school is experienced and what consequences or possibilities they might hold for thinking about the possibilities and parameters for how academic careers might be done differently.

Pastiche 1: Prospective second-careering: Preparing for non-academic chapters

I took the direct train into doctoral study. Progressing from my undergraduate, into Honours, then immediately into a PhD programme may have seemed to those around me, and certainly in my own mind, that I was on my way to applying for postdoc or tenure track positions. However, with the prospect of graduating looming, I had the growing awareness that I was coming up to a now-or-never moment. Through the PhD programme, I already had a taste of what could be if I continued into a tenure-track academic position. However, I had not yet put any significant energy into pursuing another long-held interest to be involved in factual film, and there hadn't been much space to think beyond how to try and secure anything but an academic position. Within myself I could already recognise a sense of restlessness and impending regret should my professional involvement in film not go beyond its use as a multimodal methodological tool or as a supplement to traditional academic publications.

As excited as I was, accepting a professional traineeship in social documentary filmmaking brought with it some sadness and doubt, exacerbated by well-meaning but misguided questions such as, "So why did you do a PhD if you're not going to be an academic?" and, "What are you going to do now you've spent your whole life at school and have no real-world experience?" What made explaining this transition, to both myself and others, significantly easier was my view that moving into film is a continuation of, rather than a break in, my scholarly career. I have maintained ties to the Academy via reviewing and co-authoring a small number of academic publications, and I continue seeking to buy into the currency of academic capital in other ways. For instance, I have my sights set on working collaboratively with academics to produce and translate research into film for various purposes and audiences.

Yet even in the absence of these activities, I would still understand my professional identity as one connected to academia. And I know from friends and colleagues that my own path is often given as a 'success story' at the university, even though at the time it felt a lonely decision. The process of completing my PhD animated my academic spirit, the continuation of which is not dependent on a formal Business School affiliation. It may appear as though I have deviated from pursuing an academic career, however, I understand myself as tracking along a parallel path which allows me to engage in research and theoretical thinking with a similar rigour, but that just happens to take place less in an office and more in the field and editing suite.

Pastiche 2: Retrospective second-careering: Being and knowing your place as a doctoral student

I embarked on an academic career after several years of working in the private sector in Australia and Asia. While individuals like myself can be considered 'second-career' professionals, academia is in fact my fourth career. My first was as a journalist, writing longform news stories on the healthcare beat at a national broadsheet; this was followed by some years in professional services where I consulted for medical and biotechnology companies; my third career was as a health economist in 'Big Pharma' where I worked with teams in Europe, the US and Asia to lobby national governments for funding for new medicines while completing my Master of Public Health.

My experience is certainly not unique, yet there remains a poverty of language to describe the mosaic of work experiences individuals have prior to their academic lives – for example, I have been variously and vaguely described as 'coming from industry' and a 'mature-aged' student' (despite being in my early thirties). We seem to occupy a liminal space between 'professional' and 'student'. More specifically, we serve as 'convenient capital' in which our work experiences are alternatively leveraged in select institutional settings, and then dismissed in others.

This selective valuation also manifests in ways I am explicitly celebrated yet also 'put in my place', often at the same time. No credence was given to my previous professional work experience during the PhD application process, even though this same experience has made me a favoured research associate within the Faculty, specifically my 'client-facing' consulting experience and knowledge of public health settings. For instance, being able to communicate health research in a topical manner for 'lay' audiences led to me conducting a series of live radio interviews within my first six months of commencing study. My work experience, being technically varied yet also industry specialised, is considered by my supervisory team and other parts of the University to be a unique skillset. This has secured me positions on various projects which benefit me financially and through the connections made with senior faculty members. On the other, my experience is flattened and confined in an hourly pay structure determined by a binary measure of doctoral qualification – 'have' or 'have not'. In other public spaces such as seminars, I witnessed other students with similar work experience disparaged for their more 'prosaic' observations that related academic theory to the practicalities of industry. By comparison I have been explicitly praised for being more 'academically-minded' compared with other second-career doctoral students.

Ultimately, while my work experience is regarded for its production value, it was immediately discarded by the institution under a framework of work, health and safety. While employed as a sessional staff member, a recent workplace injury served to affirm the shifting nature of my position within an academic system. My attempts to access support for my injury as a professional were rebuffed and I was framed as a 'high maintenance' and 'unaware' student. University administrators took great pains to highlight 'complicated workplace procedures' which I 'may not understand' – despite having worked for a Fortune 500 company and with the highest levels of Federal bureaucracy, such as the Office of the Minister for Health. In the academic system, however, I was 'processed' as a student, meaning I became the *subject* of work safety discussions, rather than an equal party with whom to negotiate workable solutions, and denied the rights of a 'real professional' within the institutional system.

Exploring Second-Careers through Doctoral Disturbances

The above accounts highlight the ambivalent positions that second-careering individuals are beholden to during the doctoral candidature, both pro- and retrospectively. To us, they emphasise how the doctorate is not simply a programme of study which one comes through either before or after another site of work but is felt and experienced in and through our bodies (Stanley, 2015; Burford, 2015). Barnacle and Dall'Alba (2014) suggest that doctoral candidature, like academic practice more broadly, is as much an embodied process as a skill-based one. Given part of doctoral candidature is relinquishing one's own perceptions to be 'open' to new knowledge, systems and ways of knowing, it represents a space where individuals may be seen as more susceptible or porous to embodied effects. This is particularly the case for those coming from a markedly different context or be more profound for those planning to venture into different terrain in the future. In other words, the emphasis on transformation is likely to carry particular resonance for second-careerers.

From our analytical pastiches, we see three embodied 'disturbances' playing out that help us conceptualise prospective and retrospective second-careering in doctoral lives: relating, appropriating and biting back. As Tavuchis (1991: 12) suggests, disturbances help us see "disparities, asymmetries, contrasts, oppositions, ambiguities and compensatory reactions that lay bare, if only fleeting, organizing principles". Yet these are not simply processes or practice, they are people: embodied beings that are corporeally situated within particular contexts while required to navigate culturally mediated expectations of the body.

Relating

Immediately, we found that in curating each pastiche, positioning retrospective and prospective trajectories signalled various parameters of relating the troubled distinctions between academic and non-academic 'changes'. Here the disturbance lies in how to negotiate our personal ways of connecting our careers with instituted expectations of how we *should* relate as doctoral candidates.

In both cases, no definitive lines are drawn between being 'in' or 'out' of different occupational or sectoral spaces. Both prospective and retrospective pastiches refer to an intention to 'dabble between', which is often possible due to the constant need for collegial and flexible labour in academia (in the form of reviewing or short-term teaching contracts, for instance). This ability for second-careerers to continue to traverse two occupational spaces provides an opportunity to experience different temporalities. For example, non-academic spaces can provide immediate feedback and provide a visible connection to practical impact, while life within the Academy affords moments to reflect and contribute to broader ideas or trajectories.

It is in this relating that second-careerers can find real pleasure. In lieu of institutional scaffolding to help articulate these connections, individual experiences in finding connections (deliberately or unexpectedly) are a creative and sometimes delightful process. For retrospective second-careerers, an interest in doing something 'different' was often marked out in discussion with supervisors and colleagues. This afforded particular skills that helped when undertaking reading and fieldwork, rather than feeling solely socialised into a lack of reflexive awareness within one institutional setting. For prospective second-careerers, this relating can bring a constant sensitivity around the writing of the thesis that is likely to extend beyond the eye of the supervisor or examiner.

At the same time, our accounts suggest that within the doctoral programme, 'right' and 'wrong' ways of relating are demarcated along institutional lines. One aspect is the care required in publicly declaring a 'critical eye', including when situating their past or possible experiences. This requires self-moderating contributions in public settings and 'reading' the room for receptivity about 'outside' experiences. Would these be greeted well or met with assumptions of naivety (about not 'really knowing academia') or slight irritation (being positioned as arrogant about our own knowledge of other sectors or workplace contexts)? This was often coupled with a feeling that doctoral students did not yet have the authority to voice an 'academically informed' opinion.

This reveals the expected embodied subject position of a doctoral candidate and the tensions in connecting to the past. The corporeal experience of undertaking the doctorate often reflects broader challenges that academics face, highlighted by Barcan (2013: 6) who asks if faculty "as flesh-and-blood people can actually sustain the role of holding onto the past while embodying the future". This past, of course, is the past of academic knowledge and one that often displaces one's own personal experiential learnings. As such, the undisturbing doctoral subject is situated as a neutral and muted body, a deferent sponge ready to soak up the knowledge and environment they study in, or to pad out seminar rooms for guest speakers and absorb their ideas: rightly and wrongly, public relating in the Academy often advocates for passive relating, especially in the early years. By comparison, the experience of coming into a programme and immediately engaging in active relating broke the silence expected of a doctoral body.

Appropriating

The second mode of disturbance relates to the recalibration of an individual into circuits of value, allowing such trajectories to be institutionally utilised, and how this comes to be experienced by second-careerers. The prospective trajectory, while openly questioned by colleagues and peers, is latterly celebrated, while the retrospective careers become evidence of the doctoral programme attracting high calibre students. Important to these narratives, however, is that the institution (rather than their previous careers per se) frames this valuation in its own terms.

This appropriation happens in ways that may be seen as exploitative. On the one hand, such accounts can be read through a lens of how institutions identify surplus labour, highlighting the malleability of the current system to extract from experiences that they have not paid for, contributed towards, or even supported. In some ways this may be structurally embedded. For example, in some institutions, industry work experience is awarded zero points in a points-based system that evaluates doctoral candidates for scholarships and funding decisions. At the same time, however, business schools are keen to emphasise and seize upon the 'real world' experience and industry connections of their doctoral cohort in increasingly important discussions of research impact and to build networks for income generation opportunities. Second-careerers also help promote employability agendas that can be used to attract by current and future applicants to a doctoral programme or the face of branding about impactful research agendas.

Yet there is also a strong affective dimension that underpins the ways such bodies are also negated. Here we suggest an economy of feeling appears to be deliberately employed to create a precarious subject position of 'second-careerer' who is more an interloper rather than legitimate community member. This may also draw on broader technologies that academics experience, such as performance metrics or the other forms of unpaid labour that Gregg (2009) refers to as 'production cultures'. They amalgamate to situate second-careerers as 'lucky' to be (semi-) welcomed into the Academy.

Central to this appropriation is *simultaneously* claiming and dismissing past experience. The dynamic produced here is one that denies place and fixity; an ability to claim one's space as either valuable or not valuable. Our reflection is that being positioned between valuable and invaluable (as referred to in the pastiche above as liminality) produces the most significant disturbance: in some ways, a constant dismissal might be easier to tolerate since it does not cause the disorientation of not knowing how to act as a doctoral candidate. A cynical reading would be that such simultaneity produces a feeling of being 'out of place' that then lubricates the way for appropriation to take place unhindered by inconvenient assertions by individuals.

Betrayal and Biting Back

The final element considers the way that second-careering as an embodied process has the potential to disturb normative practices and expectations. This is through drawing on resources that help to question the lines of hierarchy, power and authority in doctoral-institutional relations. In other words, by virtue of not being fully inculcated into existing systems in the ways discussed above, they can provoke and disrupt the norms that are usually sedimented into organising practices.

This manifests in slightly different ways for retrospective and prospective second-careering. For those projecting possibilities of moving away from academia, they find themselves in conversation about what elements of doctoral education have a value beyond the narrow silo of the Academy. From our reflections and woven into the pastiche, this appears to be more an affront for others, rather than the individual themselves, reminiscent of what Akerstrom (1991: 4) sees as 'betrayal as not honoring the we'. Here the projected move from academia is experienced as rejecting the collective socialisation towards an academic post, exposing the assumed trajectory as not the only path, nor even the best one. In choosing to think otherwise and 'desert' this path, the value of that trajectory itself is brought into question by those around us.

By comparison, retrospective second-careering presents the opportunity to call on resources that question current practices in a wholly different way. The past lives of these individuals disturb conventional hierarchies and notions of doctoral candidates as a tabula rasa upon which to imprint institutional knowledge. For example, in the second pastiche, the author was able to mobilise skills developed from years of diplomatic but highly competent political e-mail exchange to simultaneously challenge and leverage the 'student' position to gain material support for her injury. Specifically, recognising that the student positionality also entails pastoral care responsibilities for University administrators, the author used this and her knowledge of workplace health and safety to compel administrators over a period of months to provide a meaningful solution to her workplace injury.

In both cases, the responses suggest a desire – perhaps even an anxiety – to regulate doctoral bodies and render them compliant and nondisruptive. In the second pastiche, the injurious effects of this are not simply discursive, but etched on the body whereby the differentiation of bodies results in physical harm. While the harm of academic work is explored elsewhere (e.g. Gill, 2009), there is also the potency of 'calling out' negligent university behaviour based on experiences from other sectors. As our pastiche shows, just as the body may 'bite back' on being treated marginally by the institution, so too does the institution bite back through individualising and attributing disturbance to the body in question through situating *them* as the problem. While possible to resist, the efforts to do this are exhausting. For example, in the second pastiche, we hear of mobilising both knowledge and previous experience from previous workplace to consistently resist being 'put in her place' as a different/lesser organisational body compared to paid full-time faculty.

Conclusion

In this short chapter we have sought to reflect on some of the challenges that second-career doctoral students face. We view these reflections as only a partial insight into second-careers and doctoral candidature made through our own situated positionality in terms of our geographical position, as well as our relative privileged position of being English-speaking in English speaking institutions. We also note talking of 'second-careers' may itself be problematic, perhaps reproducing the lines drawn between academic and non-academic careers that are either out of touch with the ways current business scholars should think about their working lives, or not fully appreciating that crossovers have always been an important part of Business School trajectories.

That said, second-careerers, wherever they are situated in the Business School, present a particular kind of disturbing phenomenon. Here we consider 'disturbance' not as an individual problem, but more in its etymological sense as disrupting or interrupting normative patterns of authority, power and hierarchy. Through this lens we suggest there are three takeaways that might help potential disturbances become less disturbing for all involved.

First, it is clear to us the embodied presence of prospective and retrospective second-careering exposes some of the normative mechanisms at play within doctoral education and socialisation within the Academy. We note that much of this may be inadvertent, the culmination of a number of voices or careless comments. However, we also recognise the need to be more reflective of the ways that keep individuals 'in their place' by rendering them always in danger of falling 'out of place' of immediate lines of power and authority. Just as this occurs in terms of gender, ethnicity or class, so should we be mindful of assuming a chrononormative and singular career trajectory whereby detractors are made to feel 'not quite right' in ways that are negating, anxiety provoking, or physically painful. We consider this particularly urgent against the backdrop of portfolio-based modern careers in which a job or singular vocation for life might be considered an anachronism – particularly for women who are more likely to experience a constellation of (unrecognised) career experiences. To move away from the problematisation of 'disturbing' second-careerers is needs explicit consideration from the Academy is needed in order to be far clearer about how these individuals might play an important strategic role in the present and future of scholarship.

Second, there needs to be clearer institutional lines surrounding who, when and under what conditions second-careerers are recognised. Repeatedly we heard about second-career PhD students constantly negotiating their positionality in a normative system that treats them as a buffet from which to 'pick and choose' their various selves for institutional benefit. Candidates are, in these instances, expected to resurrect or project these 'dead', possible or alternate selves (the 'competent professional'; 'industry codeswitcher'; 'academic ingenue') with varying benefits. Supervisors may also feel caught between institutional protocol and advocacy for their student or feel inadequately skilled to supervise in a way that utilises their past experiences or supports their future ambitions. Other supervisors may be less scrupulous and view second-careerers as a way of increasing their own reputation through networks or 'trophy' candidates alongside devaluing and dismissing the student's own trajectories and associated positions as fanciful or irrelevant to their current candidature.

Finally, and perhaps more optimistically, in meaningfully recognising prospective or retrospective second-careers, there is an opportunity – to use business school parlance – to broaden the 'value proposition' of the Academy. This is particularly salient when considering mounting institutional imperatives surrounding research 'impact' and broader contemporary challenges in combatting misinformation and declining trust in institutions and expert opinion. Second-careerers sit at the intersection of the Academy and their chosen Other Career/s and represent a unique 'diplomatic channel' for hybrid careerists in Business Schools. We posit that formally and systematically recognising and honouring second-career experiences requires a seismic shift in institutional strategy and material commitment to cultivate a legitimate (hybrid or second) career community and pathway; in the words of then US Senator Biden: "don't tell me what you value, show me your budget and I'll tell you what you value". Note that on a broader level, this may also carry consequences for how we view sources of knowledge and authority differently (including the quotations we use for inspiration in academic work, for example).

In conclusion, it is not surprising that doctoral students have such experiences: disturbances often come from the margins, or those that are not fully inculcated into particular spaces but still have 'skin in the game' in terms of a lot to lose. Doctoral researchers not only invest years of their life for study, but often rely on the institution to provide financial support, are subject to systems of regulation that are highly subjective and often open to bias, such as candidature reviewers, and in many countries are situated in a grey area between fully recognised employees and fully recognised students, thus gaining the protective characteristics of neither group. Yet doctoral research can also be a fulfilling, validating, transformational and joyous experience: wouldn't it be great if part of this positive experience was helping to shape the Academy of the future and finding an institution receptive to this? As Ahmed (2010: 32) suggests, "while you can cause disturbance, you can also turn disturbance into cause". We would like to think that in being present in the Business School, second-careerers not only provide a valuable conduit for relating beyond the Academy, but also a foil through which internal and systemic flaws can be productively questioned.

Note

1 We agree with other commentators (e.g. Hughes et al., 2011) that 'relevance' should not be conflated with years of experience in the private, public or third sector beyond academic, but acknowledge it is often recognised as such.

References

Ahmed, S. (2010) Creating disturbance: Feminism, happiness and affective differences. In Liljeström, M. & Paasonen, S. (Eds.) *Working with Affect in Feminist Readings: Disturbing Differences*. London: Routledge, pp. 31–44.

Akerstrom, M. (1991). *Betrayal and Betrayers: The Sociology of Treachery*. London: Transaction Publishers.

Barcan, R. (2013). *Academic Life and Labour in the New University: Hope and Other Choices*. Farnham: Ashgate.

Barnacle, R., & Dall'Alba, G. (2014). Beyond skills: Embodying writerly practices through the doctorate. *Studies in Higher Education, 39*(7), 1139–1149.

Burford, J. (2015). "Dear obese PhD applicants": Twitter, tumblr and the contested affective politics of fat doctoral embodiment. *M/C Journal, 18*(3), https://doi.org/10.5204/mcj.969.

Gill, R. (2009). Breaking the silence: The hidden injuries of neo-liberal academia. In Flood, R. & Gill, R. (Eds.) *Secrecy and Silence in the Research Process: Feminist Reflections*. London: Routledge, pp. 228–244.

Greer, L. W. (2016). Turnstile careers between academia and practice. *Pedagogy in Health Promotion*, 2(4), 221–238.

Gregg, M. (2009). Learning to (love) labour: Production cultures and the affective turn. *Communication and Critical/Cultural Studies*, 6(2), 209–214.

Hughes, T., Bence, D., Grisoni, L., O'Regan, N., & Wornham, D. (2011). Scholarship that matters: Academic–practitioner engagement in business and management. *Academy of Management Learning & Education*, 10(1), 40–57.

Lam, A. (2020). Hybrids, identity and knowledge boundaries: Creative artists between academic and practitioner communities. *Human Relations*, 73(6), 837–863.

Muller-Camen, M., & Salzgeber, S. (2005). Changes in academic work and the chair regime: The case of German business administration academics. *Organization Studies*, 26(2), 271–290.

Rynes, S. L., Giluk, T. L., & Brown, K. G. (2007). The very separate worlds of academic and practitioner periodicals in human resource management: Implications for evidence-based management. *Academy of Management Journal*, 50(5), 987–1008.

Stanley, P. (2015). Writing the PhD journey (s) an autoethnography of zine-writing, angst, embodiment, and backpacker travels. *Journal of Contemporary Ethnography*, 44(2), 143–168.

Smesny, A. L., Williams, J. S., Brazeau, G. A., Weber, R. J., Matthews, H. W., & Das, S. K. (2007). Barriers to scholarship in dentistry, medicine, nursing, and pharmacy practice faculty. *American Journal of Pharmaceutical Education*, 71(5), doi: 10.5688/aj710591

Tavuchis, N. (1991). *Mea culpa: A sociology of apology and reconciliation*. Stanford University Press.

BETTER LATE THAN NEVER

The 'up the hill backwards' academic

Mark Stringer

Reality

Grasping or securing? Why, at the age of 54, after a business career spanning 30 plus years, do I find myself striving to become an academic? In the song 'Up the Hill Backwards', David Bowie proclaims that,

> The vacuum created by the arrival of freedom
> And the possibilities it seems to offer
> It's got nothing to do with you, if one can grasp it.

His enigmatic lyrics raise many questions, for a start: is the sense of freedom within an academic role a thing of the past? If so, why do I deliberately put myself in an uncertain, liminal position, betwixt and between one identity and another (Söderlund & Borg, 2018) whether it be in departmental meetings, at conferences, as a teacher, or in standing alongside my colleagues on cold, mid-winter days? In truth this brief chapter provides me with an opportunity to explore what I might rather describe as a growing sense of coming to, despite the fact that by 'doing an academic career' late and in a non-traditional manner, I am not only moving 'up the hill backwards' (Bowie, 1980) I also have weights on my ankles. So why, given the messy, emotional, and more precarious state of contemporary HE careers (Enright & Facer, 2017) would I even want to make such a move, into a role that will be, in all probability, the last stage of my career (with lower pay and fewer prospects of achieving a senior status)? And this, within the academy that can be defined as being 'cruelly competitive, (with) winner takes-all structures, fortified by neoliberal ideals' (Smith & Ulus, 2020, p. 840).

Where is my 'thing'?

So, I could say I am partly on the outside of academia, happily pushing in – but what is the reality of my experience, especially in these complex days of limitation and separation?

And how can my psychoanalytic research into employee engagement, utilising the thinking and theorising of Jacques Lacan, provide a way for me to reflect on the lot of the late career academic? The plan for this chapter was to create a mise en scène reminiscent of a typical analytical session – with me performing the roles of both analysand and analyst in an autoethnographic format, to understand my own challenges and motivations. In methodological terms, and in using a psychoanalytic lens for reflexive tools, questions were formulated in terms of liminality in thinking on how I make sense of being in a liminal career position and the questions of desire, in attempting to move into academia and how will I respond to the demands found within the discourse of the university (Lacan, 2007) and whether I am 'good enough' (Winnicott, 1973, p. 278).

On returning

I decided on using material consisting of fragments from an interview undertaken with myself during the first Covid-19 lockdown period in the UK. However, on beginning the session that day, things took an unexpected turn. In hauntological fashion, when I started recording, time and space appeared to slip out of joint. Seemingly, this rupture, the levelling of norms created and perpetuated by lockdown, allowed for a 'visitation' by the Lacanian 'Other' – the keeper of rules. And the shape and aim of the interview process began to provoke unconscious thoughts about what really motivated my late career shift, if only in incomplete glimpses. In viewing myself both as subject and researcher (Brown, 2008) I found I could indeed grasp tightly, in accordance with David Bowie's guidance.

Transcript from recording: May 31, 2020

ANALYST: So, who are you trying to be?

MARK: Perhaps I am trying to fulfil the desire of the Other; address a lack between the ideal ego and the ego ideal. Academia has a very seductive nature – the books, the structure, the ability to be in control of one's own work and time and to some degree the subject. Or taking a more hauntological stance – perhaps I am simply grabbing the chance to follow a path not previously taken – making up for 'lost' time or to attend to a 'lost' future. There is a painful element too, of recognising that existing ephemera and facts in my head are slowly being replaced by the needs of an academic life. There is a lot of 'stuff' in there which needs to be archived to allow a new set of material to take residence. That changes who you are.

THE OTHER: Did I hear residence? I was just in the neighbourhood.

MARK: Surely, as the big Other, you are the neighbourhood.

THE OTHER: Mind if I join you both?

MARK: Is there a choice?

THE OTHER: Not really.

MARK: My career trajectory has taken what one could call a peregrinatory path. As in 'to embrace the uncertainty and spirit of discovery as articulated in the practices of dérive and peregrination' (Gries, 2015). There have certainly been some wild deviations, coupled with a lunge at some unexpected opportunities and, yes, a lot of hard work. Even in saying that, my mind is deconstructing peregrination into 'pere'/'grin' – the benevolent smile of the Father? The Other? Ah, those two devilish Jacques! What have they done to me!

THE OTHER: Let us hope the readers nod sagely and applaud you for these oblique references. Or are you aiming to maintain a dual position as nascent academic and as an acolyte of the UK comedian Stewart Lee through the use of Brechtian alienation in this session?

ANALYST: Quite the spectacle.

THE OTHER: I do the jokes around here…

ANALYST: Interesting then that you use the term dérive. We can perhaps recognise this alongside derive.

MARK: As in, 'What am I hoping to derive from this move into Academia'?

ANALYST: Yes.

MARK: Marc Bolan once said 'the music is in my head all the time – it never fucking stops man, it never fucking stops'. That is where I am. I need an outlet for all this knowledge and thinking. I need to make up for lost time. I need to prove myself. There is a lot riding on this. It is a risk.

THE OTHER: This calls back to Bolan and Bowie, are you sure you are not just a consummate music geek crossing inter-disciplinary boundaries?

MARK: Now you say that…

ANALYST: Focus please… Lost time you say?

MARK: I left school at 16. This is 1984. My secondary school careers service had me down as a tree surgeon. Any thoughts of further education were knocked out of me, and I got away as swiftly as I could, but with a chip on my shoulder about not going to university.

ANALYST: Issues surrounding mourning and melancholia?

MARK: On reflection, yes. But at the time, I had no idea, I just went to work.

ANALYST: No idea of what?

MARK: Of what I wanted to do. So, I just got on with work instead, various roles in banking, music, eventually The British Library and then as Director of Operations at Sotheby's Institute of Art. I became professionally qualified in my field of HRM and moved quickly up managerial ladders (as opposed to arboreal ones) but there was always a lack and a desire to find a new language, to be able to challenge my world view culturally and intellectually.

ANALYST: So, what was the catalyst for change?

MARK: I became a mature student at 44, studying for an MSc in Organizational Psychology at Birkbeck.

ANALYST: And then?

MARK: The doors of perception were flung wide open at approx. 18:00 pm on a Tuesday in September 2011. I sat nervously in my lecture theatre seat with my fellow students and in rode the 'Four Horse Riders of the Epistemology' – Liefooghe, Mackenzie-Davey, Kahn, and Priestley – our lecturers. I finally knew what I *wanted* to do – become an academic.

ANALYST: You found a new language.

MARK: And a sense of focus. I completed my studies, took on tutoring roles in the department and was encouraged to undertake my PhD. This process has invigorated me but has also created this liminal status, as I complete my degree and become a member of the academic team. Until then, it is still a halfway house. On positive days, I feel like I am a prospective member of an exclusive club. On less confident days, I am a Dickensian street urchin peering through frosted windows at a sumptuous Christmas dinner in a well-to-do household…

ANALYST: Identity issues prevail?

MARK: Probably. I may only feel that I have truly entered academia on completing my degree – we shall see. But also, by undertaking a role within HE, I have now become exposed to what it means to be an academic in contemporary practice – the issues, the pressures, and of course the delights. I do not think I could happily return to a role in business although my great advantage is my practical acumen which I owe to my background in business. Alongside this though, is the encroachment on a life of scholarship of external factors and challenges such as the positioning and structuring of HE both within the UK and globally. Access and the commodification of learning are major problems for the industry, as is the role of the business school in perpetuating intellectual inconsistencies, the gruelling cycle of writing and publishing…the REF for example…

THE OTHER: My dear friend Lacan would say that, as the 'big' Other, I am the 'REF!' He always was a fan of wordplay. But aren't you are getting close to your wordcount limit for this piece? I do not want to penalise you but….

* *Suddenly, there was another entrant into the conversation. Although, on reflection, they had always been there…*

SUPEREGO: Did someone say 'penalise'? I arrived just in time! You do realise that no-one is going to read this, don't you?

MARK: Oh…

An issue with the recording equipment took place at this point. Time stopped. Mechanisms whirred. The big Other bade their adieu. The Superego was last seen smiling and mouthing 'What did I Do?' and I was left with a methodological concern. Will I be seen as a reliable author?

Where are we now?

Undertaking this process and its outcomes has provided a realisation that, while the traversing of this liminal space and time may symbolically end on the receipt of my PhD, the journey into academia in the next ten years will be anything but dull. And that aiming for 'good enough' (Winnicott, 1973, p. 278) while making that journey, will indeed be good enough.

References

Bowie, D. (1980). *Up the hill backwards* [song]. On: *Scary Monsters (and Super Creeps)* [CD]. New York: RCA Records.

Brown, T. (2008). Desire and drive in researcher subjectivity: The broken mirror of Lacan. *Qualitative Inquiry*, 14(3), 402–423.

Enright, B., & Facer, K. (2017). Developing reflexive identities through collaborative, interdisciplinary and precarious work: The experience of early career researchers. Globalisation, *Societies and Education*, 15(5), 621–634.

Gries, L. (2015). *Still life with rhetoric: A new materialist approach for visual rhetoric*. Boulder: University Press of Colorado.

Lacan, J. (2007). *Seminar XVII: The other side of psychoanalysis*. Trans. Russell Grigg. New York: WW Norton.

Smith, C., & Ulus, E. (2020). Who cares for academics? We need to talk about emotional well-being including what we avoid and intellectualise through macro-discourses. *Organization*, 27(6), 840–857.

Söderlund, J., & Borg, E. (2018). Liminality in management and organization studies: Process, position and place. *International Journal of Management Reviews*, 20(4), 880–902.

Winnicott, D. (1973). *The child, the family and the outside world aspects of juvenile delinquency*. Harmondsworth: Penguin.

VIII
The living precariously gallery
Curated by Olivier Ratle

LIVING PRECARIOUSLY AND OVERCOMING THE ODDS

Olivier Ratle

Contributors to this gallery reflect on how different kinds of precarity have made their careers different. The image that guided its assembling is one of someone being slowed down by something encumbering them. It reminded me that I have often visited exhibitions carrying a suitcase, trying to squeeze-in one last visit before heading to an airport. I have found myself wheeling or dragging one when the fee for the cloakroom was too expensive for my student wallet, or when the lockers were too small. I have also been plainly refused entry, when security measures meant that no one with any sort of baggage could be let in. When I have been lucky to make it through the door and be let inside, I have met the gaze of suspicion of the security guards, and accepted the heightened awareness that here, I am not simply someone who loves museums and exhibitions; I am a tourist, and one to be possibly apprehensive of. The six contributors who made the portraits featured in this gallery may share similar feelings in their professional life – whether they feel that they should not be here (or are made to feel like that), or whether they are encumbered by something slowing them, preventing their progression (in all the different meanings of the word) and reducing their possibility of enjoyment.

We start with a miniature portrait by Emily Yarrow, who discusses candidly her early career experience as a precariously employed academic. Her focus is the *academic precariat* – the numerous colleagues employed on short-term contracts, hourly contracts, or exploitative contracts, for who the value of their labour is not always recognised, but without who university activities would be grounded to a halt. Emily calls this reality 'gig-academia', which she sees as a short-termist way of organising academic labour which endangers the future of the profession and put an enormous strain on its aspiring members. Through her accounts, she makes visible the tensions between survival and anxiety, and career development and scholarly engagement. There is no easy fix for this system of exploitation sedimented over the years, but Emily's text is a reminder that for those of us who can, 'we have a moral responsibility to support our precariously employed colleagues of whom there are many'. And that to be kind to oneself and to others is a good start, whatever we manage (or not) to achieve in the fight against exploitation.

DOI: 10.4324/9781003267553-51

In a similar vein, Gabriella Kiss uses the image of the game of the sack race to describe her experience of academia. It may be fun for a child to try to run with their legs in a sack, but for the grown-up, she says, 'It's not a funny game, it is a real race, but I have a handicap'. Gabriella opens a window into a context and system that will be foreign to many readers, but her articulation of the relationship between the specific patriarchal culture of post-socialist Hungary with the experience of being a female academic and a mother will sadly sound too familiar. Her analysis may stem from a specific context, but the themes discussed are universal: women bearing the responsibility of parenthood disproportionally; being unable to progress as quickly as male colleagues; or women with children suffering various forms of discrimination for being a woman, and for having children. Gabriella recounts how her professional survival has required accepting a number of trade-offs, or balancing acts: balancing the demands of family and career, balancing the need to pursue individual agendas and academic 'service', and balancing doing meaningful but more demanding work with simply getting the work done. It is the awareness of those trade-offs that helped her keeping a sense of focus and direction.

Motherhood is also the central theme in Chrisavgi Sklaveniti's text, which offers us a Bakhtinian dialogical analysis foregrounding the hidden and marginalised voice of mothers. The position of working mothers in society, she says, 'is always inferior, and (…) always causes us anxiety'. This anxiety, she adds, 'is what unites us in the face of patriarchy, together with feelings of underestimation and underachievement'. The stories she presents aim to raise awareness about what motherhood feels for working mothers in academia; it is not a depiction of how working mothers appear in the academic world, but of how the world appears to working mothers. Those stories would be utterly depressing and discouraging if Chrisavgi did not follow with an attempt to imagine what it would mean to overcome patriarchy in terms of cultural norms, work practices, and public policies. For example, she suggests that we need to appreciate that motherhood is not a uniform experience, and that the different stages of child development all pose specific challenges for the possibilities of managing work and motherhood. She suggests that acknowledging the father's role in relation to parenthood would be a decisive step towards modifying societal expectations about gender equality. Chrisavgi also addresses the blatant anomaly made visible by the Covid-19 pandemic: the disjuncture between current work arrangements and the possibilities offered by technology to positively restructure and reorganise work.

Garance Marechal takes us into a different territory with a portrait that is by her own description, reminiscent of Francis Bacon's visceral paintings. It is a rich and poignant account of the struggles of her academic career and trajectory, dealing with depression, various health problems, and years later a formal diagnosis of multiple sclerosis. It is a tale of struggle, of hardship, but also of resilience, courage, and temerity. It is a tale that may bring tears, but also admiration and humility in the face of adversity. In my correspondence with Garance, she told me how writing this text stirred painful and difficult emotions. It makes me feeling even more grateful and privileged that we are able to read it. There is no happy ending here, but a sense of perspective:

> There isn't any resolution. My long struggle with acceptance is still ongoing, and layers of impairment never fully dissolve. They elude the will and my determination. Both hopelessly and expectantly, I am still trying to find ways of healing in the midst of my daily encounters with a rebellious, evasive mind and body.

As in Samuel Beckett's 'Waiting for Godot' from which she takes inspiration, Garance's tale can be read as a cautionary one. The play's character Vladimir and Estragon are just like us. In the academic world of deferred and uncertain gratification, how often are we putting our life on hold for something that will never come?

In the second miniature portrait of this galley, Ann Armstrong reaches a similar conclusion, but from a different starting point. A one-sentence summary of her text could be: academia is a harsh place, and it does not get better. She discusses her journey, portraying herself as, 'someone who was naïve throughout her journey from being a doctoral student to taking early retirement', and who never really overcame the shock of encountering the toxic aspects of academia. Her account features vivid and angering descriptions, healing poetry, but also some useful advice. One may never be entirely able to avoid the most dysfunctional and toxic aspects of life in the University, but one can at least be mentally prepared for it.

The final portrait and third miniature is Molly Hand's invitation to problematise the fact that the majority of academic scholarship is produced and published by a privileged minority – in the US context she writes from, those on the tenure track – and to reflect on what is lost in this process. Molly recounts her own career story, occupying different positions in government and outside of academia, and still trying to maintain a research agenda and a rich publication profile. The title 'Why even bother?' takes its cue from the general attitude Molly has faced as an independent scholar – someone who does not have to write and to publish scholarly work as part of their job, but who nevertheless wants to. She has pursued what she calls 'a practice of defiance', which consists in, 'persisting in doing the work that was important to me, continuing the research and writing and editing and publishing I'd been trained to do and had no desire to leave behind when I started working full-time outside the academy'. Molly makes it clear that it has not always been easy. Here, as we exit the gallery, the tone is different though: defiant, joyful and seditious. Her conclusion is an invitation to democratise the production of knowledge and tear down walls. In an era where we assess the value of knowledge based on its 'impact', an apt image is the one of knowledge being like a keg of powder, and there is only one thing to do with it: fire it up!

THE HAPPY AND SMILING, BUT INWARDLY CRUMBLING GIG ACADEMIC

Reflections on early career precarity and anxiety

Emily Yarrow

Introduction

08:05 am, Monday morning. I stood at the top of the hill, my blouse soaked once again in sweat, shaking, my heart beating loudly in my aching chest, retching and wracked with anxiety for my 9 am lecture I was due to give. I pressed on, knowing that an hour later everything would be fine again and my lecture would be flowing, the lecture hall providing a stage for my masquerade. This was me. Wrestling internally to function, and externally to 'present a front' – the tensions of precarity and micro terrors (Ratle et al., 2020), an exhausting way of living, exacerbated further still by precarious employment and uncertainty.

This mini portrait will explore my experiences of hustling in the gig academy (Yarrow, 2020) and my experiences of early career precarity and academic anxiety, three years post-PhD. I explore the tensions between survival in the precarious academic world, career development, anxiety and scholarly engagement in the neoliberal academy. The marketised, capitalist, gig academy is being held-up by an army of gig academics (Kezar et al., 2019), scholars who are not employed permanently, full time, or in roles with time allocations for research, but rather who are manifestly exploited, in turn, often stripped of their self-confidence, and proletarianised (Wilson, 1991). However, gig academics are present and active at the forefront of teaching and interactions with students, which in the neo-liberal, marketised academy (Willmott, 2003) could even be, albeit objectionably and distastefully, described as being in 'customer facing' roles on a production line (Barry et al, 2001). The realities of life and individual circumstances of academics are often not recognised and are at odds with the common perceptions of idyllic life in the ivory tower. In many respects, this is a short-termist way of organising academic labour, which endangers the future of the profession.

I felt lucky, I had found a teaching fellowship role at a top university after a previous short-term contract elsewhere, initially for four months while writing up my PhD. I was eager to get more experience, acutely aware of the precarity and difficulty of finding jobs, let alone permanent jobs in the sector. I also felt privileged and naïvely thought that this would quickly lead to more permanent employment, though what followed was a series of short-term contracts, the constant threat of redundancy and extreme anxiety that manifested itself both physically and mentally.

The regular sweaty blouse was anxiety playing itself out, a metaphor for deeply problematic performativity. Each day I would follow a very similar pattern-walk to work shaking and sweating, arrive at work already exhausted from worry, teach, try to write but not really managing much, teach some more, and then head home. After a while, I would wear a t-shirt to walk to work, the damp cotton hidden in the depths of my bag, swapped for a crisp, starched blouse, truly a symbol of the tensions between how I felt and the front I needed to present, of the outwardly driven, entrepreneurial, happy, yet inwardly crumbling, gig academic. I told myself that as long as I showed up at work looking polished, it would be somehow be ok. After the first four months, my contract was extended, then extended again, and extended again; seven or eight times in a three year period, with the prospect of permanent employment luring me to keep trying, to keep going and to find that permanent job, the first lectureship. However, the not knowing, the re-applying for my role, not being able to get for example mobile phone contracts as they were longer than my contracts of employment, was exhausting, dispiriting and ultimately, extremely anxiety inducing. This anxiety played itself out in various ways, in both my academic and personal life; I was unable to focus on writing, let alone really write anything that I could publish, I was unable to maintain relationships, exhausted by maintaining a front and not knowing what the future would hold beyond the next few months. After the first year, burnt-out, I was signed off sick for six weeks. I didn't work, I couldn't work, but all I knew was that I needed to get away from precarity for the sake of my health; it would take me another two years, but things did get better eventually.

My dissertation students, of whom there were many, wrote about precarious working, the gig economy, and retention in organisations; I remained silent as to the fact that these were and indeed are issues that are endemic in their own university which they cherished so much. I struggled with presenting myself outwardly as being a driven, happy academic, while inwardly being constrained by anxiety, emotionally shackled by the promise of permanent work and my own self-blame and adopted identity as a failure. I felt like I was deceiving not only the students, but also myself. I looked for many, many jobs, jobs in locations where I would know nobody and have to start over again completely; I applied for many jobs, but nothing came until 2019. I had many colleagues and friends who tried their best to help and support me, sometimes even lobbying management to give me a job, something that I am very grateful for, but in real terms, there was little they could do.

It has taken its toll on me, as I know it has and does on many other early career researchers (Hollywood et al., 2020). I was exhausted by the effects of prolonged precarious employment and the deep marks this leaves on your scholarly identity, wellbeing and confidence. There is an 'epidemic of poor mental health' (Morrish, 2019), characterised by widespread academic anxiety and insecurity (Bristow et al., 2017; Knights and Clarke, 2014; Smith and Ulus, 2019) which will have long term effects on universities, academics, and in turn, also students.

I was, and indeed remain, hyper aware that publications [of the '*right*' calibre] have become traded commodities (Willmott, 2011), making and breaking the start of academic careers, but also driving narrow and prescribed ways of working and living scholarly life, which are not only unsustainable, but also deleterious to mental health. This is particularly notable in Business Schools, where the use and abuse of the, now infamous and widely used, ABS (Association of Business Schools) list is driving excesses of managerialism and the 'publish or perish' [in 3★ and 4★ journals] rhetoric, which has also become not only deeply engrained in business school culture, but also fetishised (Willmott, 2011), not only in the UK, but also in a range of contexts around the world. This is particularly damaging to those at the start of their academic careers. In my experience, this is one of the key drivers for performance anxiety and when paired with precarious modes of employment, is deeply damaging to the mental health of academics and, in the longer term, scholarship.

For three years, across eight short-term contracts I carried on, trying to build my network, being nominated for teaching awards, trying to write papers, becoming increasingly anxious and aware of my need to find a permanent lectureship, let alone progress within an academic career. The following excerpt from a paper I cited in my PhD played heavily on my mind:

> Good teaching evaluations do not compensate for a shortage in research output, because research productivity over the course of an academic career is paramount for appointments, the cumulative effect of prioritising teaching over research could generate a significant difference between the genders in terms of promotion. Women's dedication to teaching could thus become a handicap in attaining the status of excellence required for a professorship.
>
> *(Van den Brink and Benschop, 2012, p. 514)*

I still didn't have any publications, other than a co-authored government report and book chapter, which anecdotally, people said '*wouldn't count*' [towards existing metrics of research evaluation in the UK]. It was true, I applied twice again for the lectureship that would absorb my teaching, each time rejected because of my lack of publications. I needed to figure out '*the game*' and how to find a tenable position within it. '*The game*' is not an even playing field, and precarious employment further stacks the odds against junior academics, and indeed anyone who does not fit the idealised figure of the unencumbered, white, able-bodied, male scholar, who is able to dedicate themselves fully to academic work. I still struggle with reconciling 'being strategic' as a mode of survival in a deeply problematic and tumultuous sector and question my own positionality in the system and how I can take a non-performative stance while surviving. Something that has helped me a lot is to connect with people, online, in person, wherever possible and let them know what you're working on, and that you're looking for work; its free and may lead you to an unexpected position or opportunity. It is however still imperative to be aware that for many people they are still in precarious positions, battling at the same time with caring responsibilities, mental ill-health and various other issues, and now, also in the context of a global pandemic. Precarity in academia is literally making academics and next generation of academics sick; Humboldt would be turning in his grave.

Finally, in September 2019, I was made redundant. I had already applied and finally been offered a lectureship at a different university, over 500 miles away from my home, and after coming to terms that I would have to look at different types of universities, taking a 'side step'-moving to a teaching-focussed university for security; a bittersweet symphony? (Knights and Clarke, 2014). I was met with questions of 'oh, why would you go there?', 'that will kill your career', 'that's an *interesting* choice' and 'I didn't realise they were making people redundant here'. I moved from an elite research-intensive University to a teaching-focussed university, a move which many considered 'unthinkable' or 'career suicide', which is demonstrative of the deeply engrained prejudices in the [deeply divided] sector. I was de-spirited and angry, at times, shamefully, even embarrassed, but I knew that having a permanent contract would help my mental health, my ability to write, and my overall wellbeing. A key point however is that there are opportunities available in various types of institutions, which in itself can be helpful to know or be reminded of, and explore. It's important to remember not to be defined by the institution and its reputation, but rather focus on the work that you do and the impact that it may have.

Precarity and the gig academy had forced my hand to make weighty decisions, decisions that may not have been possible if I had family ties or caring responsibilities or not been geographically mobile for any reason. Indeed, mobility is an assumed norm, which is exclusionary, ableist and problematic, but endemic of the sector. It is here where the covid-19 pandemic may however provide some scope for change with increases in online working for example, though it is clear that it is not only the covid-19 pandemic which is shaping the sector, but managerialism in the neoliberal university is one of the most dangerous threats to academic life, and the health and wellbeing of academics.

Thankfully the sweaty blouses are a thing of the past for me, but it is not a time I will ever forget. I hope that I can share with you some insights about the importance of being kind to oneself, and acknowledging that sometimes we have unreasonable expectations of ourselves. My main advice to you is seek support from colleagues and friends, and remember that there are a range of institutions that you may not have thought about which can offer a potentially different, but satisfying and healthier path. Sometimes we need to readjust our own definitions of success and remember that our work does not define us, a re-focus or re-calibration of our perceptions and values can help us seek opportunity in unexpected places; remember, it is not just elite universities that have excellent students, colleagues and opportunities.

For those of us who are in permanent positions, we have a moral responsibility to support our precariously employed colleagues of whom there are many, and to continue to call out and critique the neoliberal gig academy in which we find ourselves. Be kind to yourself and to others, the academy will be a better place for it.

References

Barry, J., Chandler, J., and Clark, H. (2001). Between the ivory tower and the academic assembly line. *Journal of Management Studies*, 38(1), 87–101.

Bristow, A., Robinson, S., and Ratle, O. (2017). Being an early-career CMS academic in the context of insecurity and 'excellence': The dialectics of resistance and compliance. *Organization Studies*, 38(9), 1185–1207.

Hollywood, A., McCarthy, D., Spencely, C., and Winstone, N. (2020). 'Overwhelmed at first': the experience of career development in early career academics. *Journal of Further and Higher Education*, 44(7), 998–1012.

Kezar, A., DePaola, T., and Scott, D. T. (2019). *The gig academy: Mapping labor in the neoliberal university*. Baltimore, MD: Johns Hopkins University Press.

Knights, D., and Clarke, C.A. (2014). It's a bittersweet symphony, this life: fragile academic selves and identities at work. *Organization Studies*, 35(3), 335–357.

Morrish, L. (2019). *Pressure vessels: The epidemic of poor mental health among higher education staff*. London: Higher Education Policy Institute.

Ratle, O., Robinson, S., Bristow, A., and Kerr, R. (2020). Mechanisms of micro-terror? Early career CMS academics' experiences of 'targets and terror' in contemporary business schools. *Management Learning*, 51(4), 363–530.

Smith, C., and Ulus, E. (2019). Who cares for academics? We need to talk about emotional well-being including what we avoid and intellectualize through macro-discourses. *Organization*, 27(6), 840–857.

Van den Brink, M., and Benschop, Y. (2012). Gender practices in the construction of academic excellence: Sheep with five legs. *Organization*, 19(4), 507–524.

Willmott, H. (2003). Commercialising higher education in the UK: The state, industry and peer review. *Studies in Higher Education*, 28(2), 129–141.

Willmott, H. (2011). Journal list fetishism and the perversion of scholarship: Reactivity and the ABS list. *Organization*, 18(4), 429–442.

Wilson, T. (1991). The proletarianisation of academic labour. *Industrial Relations Journal*, 22, 250–262.

Yarrow, E. (2020). Knowledge hustlers: Gendered micro-politics and networking in UK universities. *British Educational Research Journal*. https://doi.org/10.1002/berj.3671

THE "SACK-RACE" ACADEMIC

A post-socialist portrait of a single mother facing social expectations and the trade-offs of an academic career path

Gabriella Kiss

Dedicated to my Mom

Introduction

When I first read the call for this book the gears began to spin in my brain, and I started to reflect on my career path[1]. I was wondering what can be instructive to others that I have experienced in my work life. In the first point, I felt that my career can't be separated from my private life, and the most critical steps I have taken have been in connection with the significant events of my life as a woman or as a mother. If I look back to the decision points of my work, I often make comparisons with my private life and what situation I was in that time personally. Consequently, I concluded that if I am willing to write a book chapter about my career path, I must put on the table many aspects of my private life that we usually don't talk about in a workplace. To be honest, at first sight, it frightened me a little bit, but after that, I saw it as a great possibility to try something new in writing, and try to find my voice "differently", a mode of expression different from my academic face. Moreover, I found it extremely exciting to cut into the topic and show how privacy challenges affect my work as a university teacher.

The second thing that came into my mind was that I must explore – for the readers' sake – what the researchers and university teachers' life is like in Hungary, a post-socialist country. When I thought of my career in a wider context, I realised that it is necessary to talk about these obstacles. I began to think through how the post-socialist environment had an impact on my career.

The dilemma that I wanted to share – and which I've experienced many times in my career is best interpreted in terms of trade-offs. By this, I mean trade-offs between family and career, between university public service and researcher/education, and in the context of studying transdisciplinary issues, between having social impact versus working in the mainstream topics.

To be able to write honestly about my career, I must point out that I am not an outstanding researcher or educator. I think I am good at what I do, and I do everything that I do to a high standard. But I'm not a member of the elite of my profession and I never wanted to belong among them. That's why my story isn't intended for those who want to be the best, as I can't tell them anything. I speak instead to those who want to be "good enough" at what they are doing. In this chapter, I present the trade-offs of a university career in a post-socialist environment from a critical perspective. In addition to gender differences, I will also address the situation of single parents and the pitfalls of a universalist approach to performance measurement.

The sack-race academic

Several times in my academic career, I have felt like I'm either not on a good track or else running with my legs tied in a running race. If I try to visualise myself on this route, I can imagine myself in a "sack race". This funny race is usually based on a situation where every racer must pull a sack to his waist and must run from start to finish that way. In that scenario, all riders start with the same handicap as everyone must run in a bag. However, academia is not quite the same as this. In the "race" to build an academic career, all of us must run on the same track, one envisioned by a recent policy, but a few of us run with different handicaps, while others are unencumbered. From my perspective, we are in a running race with each of us on our track, and I am the one who is running in the sack, while others are running without one. It's not a funny game, it is a real race, but I have a handicap.

I have a very kind colleague whom I consider to be a benchmark. We are the same age, we went to the same schools, we worked before in the same place. Whereas he is already a qualified professor, I was appointed associate professor this year. He has three children, I have two. The big difference is that he's a man and fits the academic career pattern almost perfectly. I see our situation as we are on the same track, but he is not wearing that sack.

I realised this sack-race feeling a few times in my work life. My first experience was when I wanted to go back to work after my first child. The others who didn't give birth were already light years ahead of me in building a career, while we had "rowed in a boat" before. Not because they were more talented or hardworking than me, but because they were in that boat all the time while I got out for 1.5 years and stop reading, thinking, writing in my profession for that time. While undergoing the PhD process, 18 months seemed to be a long time. but I didn't get the same feeling nursing a baby. I had the opportunity to stay at home for three years, so from that point of view I returned to work early, but I didn't feel that way. Additionally, I was not able to go back to the same position, as my project was finished and there was no unoccupied position at the department at that time. That point I decided to pause my PhD process and I began working for a research centre as a project manager, performing management tasks.

The second shock didn't come from work. After my second child, I divorced with two young children (1 and 4-year-old). It was a very difficult time for me psychologically. Starting a new life as a single mother was a huge challenge. Additionally, in my PhD process, I had to perform, and I had to work to a deadline. I won a predoctoral scholarship for writing the thesis. I remember I was sitting in the library and trying to read papers about very important topics for my thesis. I was not able to concentrate, I felt like I didn't have enough intellectual capacity to handle my personal life: marriage/divorce, two young children and PhD writing. In the literature, I found that phenomenon described by workplace productivity theory (Becker 1985). I wasn't productive at work due to my private life challenges and family obligations. The hardest moment was to admit to my supervisor that I was a single mother with two young children, and I was not able to do the job to the planned schedule. I felt like a disadvantaged (handicapped) racer again. Maybe in another profession, it would still be an obstacle anyway.

Finally, I obtained my PhD. I saw it through because it was important for me, and I fought for that. I admitted to myself and my family that I need help, and I was able to ask for help, and luckily my family could help me. My mother-in-law helped me with babysitting regularly. I decided to separate my working days from family days. On working days, I went out from home, and I concentrated on my thesis for all day and night, and on family days I was with my children. In this way, when working I was able to feel that I could do my job without limits or obstacles, and on other days I could be a caring mother. To finalise my dissertation, I travelled to the countryside for four days to work day-and-night, while my mother took care of my children. She was my help as many times in my life before and after this critical period.

Social expectations

Of course, all these career issues are difficult to understand without a deeper knowledge of higher education and the social welfare system in Central and Eastern Europe and especially Hungary where I live and work. The interpretation of women's careers in post-socialist countries and the roles and expectations of mothers and women in society make the situations described above understandable. I searched for the literature on these social aspects, and I summarise here what I found.

In a traditional society where gender roles are significantly separated, it is an important social expectation that the man should be the main breadwinner (Spéder 2011, Szalma & Takács 2018). Parental care in Hungary appears to be strongly related to women, and it is widely believed that a woman cannot live a full life without a child, while men seem to have less stringent expectations of this type (Szalma 2014, Szalma & Takács 2018).

In these societies, women are primarily responsible for caring for children, so because it is more about women than men, stereotypes about motherhood are closer to the general social perception of women. It is closely linked to gender inequality, as most women are also mothers, and they provide the lion's share of childcare. Women pay the "price" of child-rearing, while men and organisations largely offset the costs of social reproduction (Nagy et al. 2018). There are a wide range of services for working women, but little or no formal commitment to gender equality. This way the vertical and horizontal segregation stabilises the disadvantage of women (Nagy & Primecz 2010). Pay inequality also entails the vulnerability of women when compared to men: single mothers are at higher risk of becoming poor than single fathers (Nagy et al. 2018).

A difference in status can also be observed between women without children and with children (Correll & Ridgeway 2004). It can be called a motherhood penalty (Koplányi 2018). The motherhood penalty is when mothers with children are less likely to be hired or promoted, receive less pay, and their employment is more easily terminated than childless women with the same characteristics (Correll et al. 2007). In Hungary, Glass and Fodor (2011, 2014) examined the emergence of the motherhood penalty within companies and find that there are several discriminatory mechanisms in place for selection, promotion, and pay that HR staff did not conceal at all (Koplányi 2018). At the same time, it is important to point out that there are also sectoral differences, as the research of Glass and Fodor (2014) showed.

All this is confirmed by the inadequacy of state social policy and legal measures. In Hungary there is public maternalism (Koplányi 2018): the state explicitly supports childcare with long maternity leave but does not adequately protect women in the labour market by maintaining childcare facilities, especially nurseries and kindergartens, and family support systems. Mother-friendly policies have been excluding women from the labour market for a very long time, inhibiting their reintegration and reinforcing gender inequalities (Glass & Fodor 2011, Nagy et al. 2016). As a result of unequal share of household duties, the traditional gendered expectations and the long parental leave scheme mothers labour market participation is low (Nagy et al. 2017).

Another aspect that has an impact on a women career path and social expectations is the political discourse about family and gender. The anti-gender discourse has been present in Hungary since 2010, as in several post-socialist countries (Kováts & Pető 2017). This is an important factor in this issue, which is a step backwards in the shift towards gender equality. In Hungary, building an illiberal state also puts women at an increasing disadvantage in the labour market and career building. At the heart of the family support system is the "traditional family", which means whole middle-class (high-income) families where men and women build the family. This system reinforces traditional roles and ignores other family models (which are also becoming more common in Hungary). As Grzebalska and Pető (2018, p. 167) stated that "While some policies undoubtedly benefit women, they also conceptualize them primarily as mothers, and not as citizens whose equal rights need to be assured".

This model does not support single parents (especially women) and often even presents them with administrative difficulties. Family mainstreaming policy in Hungary has meant that single parents have never received selective benefits and their benefits have always been integrated into the wider family benefits system in contrast with the public opinion. As Herke (2020, p. 18) stated that "single mothers have a coherent positive (deserving) public image in the Hungarian public opinion: they are imagined as poor mothers, who work a lot to make a living for the family, and who lack financial and emotional support". It is in contrast with the fact that in public opinion the traditional family is the preferred family type.

This family policy background also has a major impact on a single mother research career, as long absences from the academic community can make career-building very difficult for women, and single mothers are not supported by the family policy either. If we examine the scientific sphere as a segment of the labour market (and my workplace) we can see a more nuanced picture.

The academic career path of women in Hungary

In the context of the Hungarian scientific sphere, the number of Hungarian female academics belonging to the Hungarian Academy of Sciences still does not reach 10% of domestic academics (Lamm & Nagy 2019). However, this is not so surprising, as we can say that in Hungary there are just as few women at the top of the scientific hierarchy, as in parliament.

The debate that erupted in 2016 in connection with the election of the correspondent members of the Hungarian Academy of Sciences (HAS) is telling (Somogyi 2017 and others). In 2016, there were no women among the new members. This drew attention to the fact that in 2016, only 6.6% of academics (members of the HAS) were women. Since then, there has been an ongoing debate in academic circles and a committee has been set up to investigate the issue (Presidential Committee Facilitating Women's Academic Advancement at the HAS). Several proposals and measures have been made to improve the situation. The results of Lamm and Nagy's (2019) study related to the work of the Committee show that only 16 per cent of the owners of the scientific title of the Doctor of HAS are women. But going further back in the academic career pathway, the proportion of women with a PhD is 37%. In contrast, the number of female and male PhD students is balanced. As Lamm and Nagy (2019) note, this declining trend is alarming and sad, as women are virtually disappearing from academia above certain stages of their careers.

This phenomenon of the leaky pipeline (Paksi 2014) has many reasons: childcare affects the career after PhD, or women did not take responsibility and did not go for positions. As Pető (2018, p. 553) added, "The model of a scientific career is based on the idea that someone is constantly present, reads the literature, and publishes, because only in this way can they be competitive. This model places research as a value before a person's value, which indicates what problems a female researcher faces when she wants to live a balanced life".

Another way in which women disappear on the academic career path involves them doing invisible work at higher education or academia (Pető 2018): "They can be the assistants, secretaries and wives" (p. 557). Or they support a leading man's work by writing proposals and papers with him. Or they do different jobs related to caring: they listen to the concerns of PhD students, they give them advice, they do the administration of the accreditation material and keep the minutes in scientific meetings (Pető 2018).

Compounding this situation in Central and Eastern Europe, university salaries are also unfairly low. A family cannot make a living from earning a university salary. Thus, those working in higher education typically either have more jobs or undertake more externally funded projects if they want to support their families from this salary. The other model typically found in the universities that women are content to accept lower pay in exchange for flexible working hours and will not be the breadwinners in the family. Again, the situation of a single mother does not conform to the assumed model. One single parent cannot be a breadwinner with that low salary alone or take more jobs if she is caring for two young children alone.

In post-socialist countries, another difficulty which is country/region-specific is the low level of knowledge of English in society. Hungary has the worst ratio (20%) of competent English speakers in the EU (Eurobarometer 2012, Nikolov 2011). Other post-socialist countries are in almost the same situation; while in the Czech Republic, Slovakia, Bulgaria and Poland almost 25–27% of the population is said to be able to speak English. This is a disadvantage in the English-speaking scientific world for the post-socialist countries. The situation in Hungary has steadily improved since 1990, but the last survey (Eurobarometer 2012) shows that we still lag behind the EU average. Improving one's language skills to become a scientist at a "good enough" level involves the investment of both time and effort. Many of my colleagues aged around 40 or more are struggling with a language disadvantage, something which may be regarded as a legacy of socialism and Russian language teaching, or else the inefficiency of English teaching in Hungarian schools.

Consequently, when I am talking about my benchmark colleague and the obstacles and challenges of my career path as a single mother, I am not a unique "sack-racer" in my profession. The social expectations and the policy narratives pave the way for these comparisons. I can admit that I have only faced these narratives a few times directly but taking on roles within a job can reflect these patterns. For example, amid the top management of our school, the domination of men is totally evident. To be able to move forward as a sack-race runner, one's attitude towards the immediate work environment is very important. You cannot change the system itself, but you can find a place where you feel comfortable. The reason why I decided to stay at my workplace is the supportive and accepting atmosphere I sense from my colleagues and direct superiors, which persists even though a very strong professional community has also developed. Today, I feel that this is more important than what exactly is taught by the department I belong to.

Decisions in a career path: trade-offs

Before I arrived here, in my career path, I had to make serious decisions. After my second child, I decided not to go back to the research centre to do project management tasks, but I instead focussed on thesis writing and looked for another job. I worked in a college for a few years before taking the job to be a research manager at Corvinus University for three years and last year, I ended up at the department where I am working now. I changed my job many times, and these decisions have allowed me to place a different emphasis on activities such as education, research and service as well as raise many questions that could be useful for building my career in academia in the long run.

The important aspect for me that lies behind these decisions is best interpreted by the concept of trade-off. Trade-off means according to Cambridge online dictionary "a situation in which you balance two opposing situations or qualities". In the dictionary the example given corresponds to my examples: "She said that she'd had to make a trade-off between her job and her family". It is said to be common sense, but the first trade-off for me is family versus career.

To exemplify such a trade-off with a real-life situation in my career, I can recall the feeling I had when I started working in a new department and first attended a meeting where we agreed on seminar dates. I had to admit to everyone that I couldn't take classes in the evening. Or in another situation, I had to say "no" to a job on an international project, where I would have had to travel abroad frequently for days. I just couldn't solve these issues: as a single mother, I couldn't afford to take on such commitments. I felt uncomfortable: it was a similar situation to the thesis writing dilemma I had to face earlier. But I had to ask myself: how much is my time with family worth, how much am I willing to give up on parenting/caring for the sake of building a career? How much is the time spent on work worth paying someone else for doing the housework for me? Is having children is more of a barrier for a woman who wants to develop her human capital?

Another critical trade-off I have experienced relates to taking part in university public activities, or as we call it: "service". I worked as a research manager for three years, spending many hours organising scientific events, judging applications, developing, and operating a research support system for the school. The main advantages of this position were the extremely rich network I was able to acquire, the integration of different knowledge and the opportunity to develop different skills. I learnt a lot from my colleagues and my professional life became richer thanks to important experiences. I felt what I was doing was useful and was helping the development of the university. I enjoyed building relationships in international networks and within the organisation as well. I got positive feedback from my colleagues about my job many times. But still a nagging question remained: how much were these relationships worth if I hadn't published for three years and my contact with students had been minimal? I was a unique case when it came to performance measurement. Criteria for promotion include metrics for educational and research performance. And in the meantime, I looked across at my benchmark colleague, who was "just" teaching and publishing, and I felt like I was running with my legs tied again. I found myself asking again: how much added value does each job brings to my career in the long run? Should the focus be on education, research, or management activities? How can I evaluate this properly? And is it worth it to me?

My third trade-off is in connection with my mission in my work. I am committed to sustainability issues, and I am working to foster the transformation to a more environmentally and socially sustainable future. I do think that higher education and especially business education has a crucial role in educating the decision-makers of the future. I think different knowledge holders can add to this education, and students can learn deeply by their own experiences. Consequently, I invite representatives of civil society organisations (CSOs) to my courses and have built my courses around an experiential and transformative learning approach. These efforts seem to have paid off in the sense that students and civil partners are satisfied, and we can have a bigger social impact. On the other hand, I have generated more work for myself that isn't evaluated or rewarded by the system of performance measurement. In researching sustainability as a complex issue, it is inevitable to cooperate with partners that possess different knowledge. I have two master's degrees: I am an economist, and an agricultural engineer on environmental management as well, a background which enables me to understand environmental issues from different aspects. However, when engaging with publication processes it is sometime difficult for sustainability researchers to clearly define our role: are we social scientists, or do we have a message for natural scientists as well? In performance measurement in a business school, these publications do not always align well with the strategic direction of the school. It is not always clear how much these publications count in terms of the academic measurements we are in practice subjected to. The effort that we put into teaching or research in the field of sustainability that aims to have an impact on society does not contribute directly to the performance measurement system that will ultimately evaluate our achievements. On my own career track, it doesn't count towards my promotion how big my impact is on my students or civil partners, or ecological problems. What matters more is how many international scientific articles I have published, which only a few will read. It is a big trade-off for a university teacher anyway: is it worth making the effort to advance the cause of ecological/social change if I am unable to advance in my career in the meantime? Is it worth developing a better course for students, involving correspondingly greater efforts, for the same achievement? Are we back in that sack-race again?

Conclusions or takeaways

During my career, I have switched and tried out different options on several occasions. These decisions were mostly not consciously made but were rather born out of external coercion or else the appearance of opportunities. However, my reflections on them went on to inform future decisions that were taken more deliberately and more consciously later in my career. Awareness of the trade-offs involved helped me to set the focus and the direction I want to go. I concluded that I need to find in every situation the challenge that provides an opportunity for self-development.

Based on my previous career decisions, I think I was able to learn from every role I took. My career path may not have turned out as expected, but it did increase my human capital and my experiences made me more valuable in human terms, too. What I learnt from these roles is to be aware of myself, my situation, my strengths, and my weaknesses. These insights may yet be carried forward to future positions where I can once again figure out what needs to be strengthened, abandoned, or consciously evolved.

If I have taught too much, I have realised that research is an important part of my job and experiencing creativity and intellectual recharge plays a big part in this. When I moved away from education, I felt that "university" as such was moving away from me when I didn't have a living connection with students. I really like working with students and getting to know their thinking, their world. This sense of connection also keeps a teacher feeling young and inspired to renew their courses every year, I think. From the many management tasks that I have done, I have come to realise that without education and research, the field is not passionate and creative enough for me, but these skills that I learnt from that position are very important in organising teaching activities, but most of all in creating and leading research projects.

I have discovered what is important to me on this track and I now try to find it in different positions: passion and creativity. However, this career provides a very good opportunity for achieving this: to constantly develop yourself, to find inspiration in different fields of your work, to teach passionately and to research creatively. And after a while, you can run without your sack, if you reach a certain point. Now I am an associate professor, and I am proud of it. If I look back at my running race up to the point I have reached today, I also see myself running with my legs tied in a sack-race, but at some point I freed myself from this. Maybe my children are older, maybe my salary is higher, I don't know what exactly made the vital difference. But today I keep running forward despite all of my "handicaps" and now more and more enjoy the new possibilities in my career path.

Note

1 I would like to thank Henriett Primecz for her encouragement and ideas for writing this chapter.

References

Becker, G. S. (1985). Human capital, effort and the sexual division of labor. *Journal of Labor Economics*, 3(1), 33–58. https://doi.org/10.1086/298075
Cambridge online dictionary: Trade-off. https://dictionary.cambridge.org/dictionary/english/trade-off. Downloaded 01.18.2021.
Correll, S. J., Benard, S. & Paik, I. (2007). Getting a job: Is there a motherhood penalty? *American Journal of Sociology*, 112(5), 1297–1339. https://doi.org/10.1086/511799
Correll, S. J. & Ridgeway, C L. (2004). Motherhood as a status characteristic. *Journal of Social Issues*, 60(4), 683–700. https://doi.org/10.1111/j.0022-4537.2004.00380.x.
Eurobarometer, 2012. Special Eurobarometer 386. Europeans and their Languages.

Glass, C. & Fodor, É. (2011). Public maternalism goes to market: Recruitment, hiring, and promotion in postsocialist Hungary. *Gender & Society*, 25(1), 5–26. https://doi.org/10.1177/0891243210390518

Glass, C. & Fodor, É. (2014). *From exclusion to accommodation: Employer practices and motherhood penalties.* Unpublished manuscript.

Grzebalska, W. & Pető, A. (2018). The gendered modus operandi of the illiberal transformation in Hungary and Poland. *Women's Studies International Forum*, 68, 164–172. https://doi.org/10.1016/j.wsif.2017.12.001

Herke, B. (2020). Investigating the welfare deservingness of single mothers: Public image and deservingness perceptions in Hungary. *East European Politics and Societies and Cultures*, online first, 1–25 https://doi.org/10.1177/0888325420937773

Koplányi, E. (2018). Nesze nekem anyaság! – Az anyasági hátrány Magyarországon. In Nagy, B., Géring, Zs., & Király G. (eds) *Dilemmák és stratégiák a család és munka összehangolásában*. L'Harmattan Kiadó, Budapest, 304–328.

Kováts, E. & Pető, A. (2017). Anti-gender discourse in Hungary: A discourse without a movement? In Kuhar, R. & Paternotte, D. (eds.). *Mobilizing against equality*. Rowman & Littlefield, pp. 117–131.

Lamm, V. & Nagy, B. (2019). 2019 ismét a „nők éve" az Akadémián – Törekvések a nők tudományos pályafutásának támogatására. Once Again, a 'Year of Women' at the Hungarian Aacademy of Sciences - Efforts to Promote Women's Academic Career. *Magyar Tudomány*, 180(11), 1649–1665. http://doi.org/10.1556/2065.180.2019.11.6

Nagy, B., Géring, Z. & Király, G. (eds) (2018). *Dilemmák és stratégiák a család és munka összehangolásában*. L'Harmattan Kiadó, Budapest, pp. 304–328.

Nagy, B., Király, G. & Géring, Zs. (2016). Work-life balance and the gender regime after the economic transition. *Intersections, EEJSP*, 2(3), 5–20. https://doi.org/10.17356/ieejsp.v2i3.283

Nagy, B. & Primecz, H. (2010). Nők és férfiak a szervezetben. Kísérlet a mítoszok feloszlatására. *Vezetéstudomány - Budapest Management Review*, 61(1), 2–17. https://doi.org/10.14267/VEZTUD.2010.01.01

Nagy B., Primecz H. & Munkácsi P. (2017). The downturn of gender diversity on boards in Hungary. In Seierstad, C., Gabaldon, P., & Mensi-Klarbach, H. (eds.). *Gender Diversity in the Boardroom*. Palgrave Macmillan, Cham. https://doi.org/10.1007/978-3-319-57273-4_9

Nikolov, M. (2011). Az idegen nyelvek tanulása és a nyelvtudás. *Magyar Tudomány*, 172(9), 1048–1057.

Paksi, V. (2014). Miért kevés a női hallgató a természet- és műszaki tudományi képzésekben? Nemzetközi kitekintés a „leaky pipeline" metaforájára. *Replika*, 85–86(2013/4–2014/1), 109–130.

Pető, A. (2018). A nők a tudományban. Women in Science. *Magyar Tudomány*, 179(4), 550–565. https://doi.org/10.1556/2065.179.2018.4.9

Somogyi, P. (2017). Representation of Women in the Hungarian Academy of Sciences. *Magyar Tudomány*, 11, 1490–1493. http://www.matud.iif.hu/MaTud-2017-11.pdf

Spéder, Z. (2011). Ellentmondó elvárások között. In Nagy I. – Pongrácz T. (szerk.): *Szerepváltozások. Jelentés a nők és férfiak helyzetéről 2011*. TÁRKI – Nemzeti Erőforrás Minisztérium, Budapest, pp. 207–228.

Szalma, I. (2014). A gyermekvállalás társadalmi normái és a mesterséges megtermékenyítéssel kapcsolatos attitűdök vizsgálata Magyarországon és Európában. *Replika*, 85–86: 35–57.

Szalma, I. & Takács, J. (2018). Is there voluntary childlessness at all in Hungary? In Sappleton, N. (ed.). *Voluntary and involuntary: Th e joys of otherhood?* Manchester: Emerald Publishing Limited, 309–337.

RE-IMAGINING THE DIALECTIC OF WORK AND MOTHERHOOD IN ACADEMIA

Chrysavgi Sklaveniti

Introduction

If I had to answer what it means to be a working mother in academia, I would not have one particular description to give. There are diverse life stories and looking for common characteristics among working mothers would not lead anywhere. Instead, I would say that it is worth turning attention to the shared experience of working mothers' position within society; a position which is always inferior, and which always causes us anxiety. I do not know what we would feel as working mothers if we did not face the harsh realities of patriarchy, its social norms, perceptions, and anticipations. What I do know is that as working mothers we share with each other a feeling of anxiety – sometimes even fear. We all share the same question, whether having children and a career can co-exist in our lives. Anxiety is what unites us in the face of patriarchy, together with feelings of underestimation and underachievement. We wonder what qualifies as success for a working mother and at what expense, and we are certain that our failures are an outcome of our identity as working mothers.

In an era, when we talk about the progress made on women's rights, there is practically such a long way until equality. According to the Global Gender Gap Report 2022 (WHO), which evaluates among other economic participation and opportunity, not only is the gender parity not recovering, but it will also take another 132 years to close the global gender gap. As noted in the Report, societal expectations, employer policies, the legal environment and the availability of care continue to be critical in the evolution of women's career trajectories. Considering these findings, this text calls for re-imagining the dialectic of work and motherhood and aims at raising awareness for working mothers *living precariously* in academia and at encouraging effective actions that promote change.

We all come with our unique life stories and our unique life choices; being a mother is yet another choice a woman may take (or not). While there is nothing special or shocking about the choice of motherhood, the becoming of motherhood is overlooked in the requirements of an academic career; more importantly, in the critical early career stage where an academic is called to forge one's identity and career pathway. The possibilities available assume masculinist norms of someone without caring commitments, while implicitly indicating that work and motherhood are at odds, and that coping with the two requires compromise on both fronts. The chapter paints the self-portrait of working mothers *living precariously* in academia by drawing on the dialogic thinking of Bakhtin (1981, 1984, 1986, 1993). In doing so, the hidden, marginalised and unofficial voice of feminism is presented and discussed vis-à-vis the dominant voice of patriarchy.

The living stories of working mothers in academia aim at raising awareness about what motherhood in conjunction to work feels for working mothers *living precariously* in academia and make a direct plea against living precariously (Gatrell, 2019; Miller, 2019). It furthermore aims to show that work-family conflicts need not be inescapable. Acknowledging that parenting is a progressive journey and that each family's experiences are unique, alternative academic trajectories support mothers in creating appropriate plans and patterns which afford them their own space in academia.

Bakhtin's dialogical thinking

Bakhtin (1981, 1986) sees the social world developing in a process of unfinalised dialogue, where different worldviews meet and contest with each other. For him, dialogue is more than a means to communicate with one another; it is a way of living and socialising. In dialogue, there is never only one voice, but multiple ones reflecting diverse worldviews. This is because when expressing ourselves, we draw on diverse ideologies, life experiences, value systems, cultural norms, and histories. Society's status quo is constituted by dominant voices, which are questioned, resisted, and even battled from minority voices. From here, social life goes on in an ongoing dialogue of competing voices evaluating the world around us.

Voices are not linked to individuals; they are rather linked to the relationships between individuals (Bakhtin, 1993). This means that a voice does not belong to one specific individual, but it represents worldviews evoked as an individual expresses oneself. Signifying certain worldviews, voices have an evaluative weight giving insight into what matters in the engagement and interaction with others. Dialogue is not about consensus among voices; it is about encountering one another in the making of a social world, where dominant voices reign over minority, suppressed or silenced voices (Holquist, 2002). Considering that voices stand for diverse worldviews, it is understandable that the encounter of voices implicates conflicts, struggles and even battles.

Drawing on Bakhtin's dialogic thinking, I develop living stories of working mothers *living precariously* in academia as seen through the eyes of working mothers and their outlooks on life. What becomes important in these living stories is not how working mothers appear in the academic world, but first and foremost, how the world appears to working mothers, and how working mothers appear to themselves (paraphrasing Bakhtin, 1984: 47). By placing emphasis on how various experiences generate complex conjunctions of work and motherhood, I suggest that academic institutions are constituted by the dominant voice of patriarchy which comes into interconnection and collision with the feminist voice.

Voicing academics living precariously

To voice working mothers *living precariously* in academia, I drew on my personal experiences as a working mother to reflectively and critically navigate an empirical enquiry into how the world of work appears to working mothers and how working mothers appear to themselves. From the summer of 2017 until the summer of 2019, I engaged in intimate and lengthy discussion with working mothers *living precariously* in the broader world of academia, starting from existing acquaintances and extending into new acquaintances made during academic conferences. The most important events for collecting empirical material were three management conferences taking place in Europe, between 2017 and 2018. In total, I talked with 37 working mothers *living precariously* in academia around two thematic areas: experiences and confrontations with the academic system after becoming mothers, as well as feelings and ideas about a more hopeful future. I kept a reflective diary of our talks, and I took notes in the following two ways. First, I noted the words and quotes that struck me both as researcher and as a working mother, following Shotter's (1993) method of following arresting moments in dialogue. Second, I returned to these original notes, reflected on them, and wrote down how they made me feel about my research enquiry. I analysed my notes abductively, by first identifying how the world of work appears to working mothers *living precariously* in academia. From there, I uncovered the voices navigating this world as well as their relationships. The voice of patriarchy was the dominant one, reigning over the minority voice of feminism, which was marginalised, silenced, and struggling to be heard. The voice of feminism corresponded to the worldviews of working mothers *living precariously* in academia and thus, I then proceeded with analysing the efforts to be heard. The overall analysis produced living stories of working mothers *living precariously* in academia.

To present these living stories, I built a broader narrative bringing together the life stories of the women I talked to. I enriched the narrative with direct quotes so that the voice of these women is (finally) heard. I chose not to include participant codes to emphasise the fact that a voice is not connected to a particular individual, but to worldviews expressed by the individual. As such, the quotes presented here represent the voice of feminism as it struggles with the dominant voice of patriarchy to express the worldview of working mothers *living precariously* in academia. The aim of the living stories is to problematise cultural norms and work practices, to raise awareness of the marginalised voice of feminism, and to seek alternatives for a more hopeful and inclusive future for working mothers. Each woman comes with a different story; the aim here is not to present a homogenous whole, but to hear the thoughts, worries, and hopes of working mothers as they live their individual stories.

> Sometimes I feel that others make judgements about me or draw conclusions about me from a very quick observation: from a photo I post, from what I am wearing, from what I am working on and so on. Sometimes there is so much to do, that I look kind of desperate and then others are quick to say that I am tired. I am tired, but not in the way they mean it. Not just physically. Mostly emotionally. Tired to see others defining what motherhood is or must be for me. Every mother has her story. I have my own story. And it is mine, my story. Only I can tell my story. Because only I know my story, and only I know who I am. Because only I know how I feel about motherhood and what motherhood means to me. But nobody seems to be listening to me. As if I have no voice, or as if it doesn't matter. As long as there is a perception out there, what I have to say about my own story is indifferent. And then, yes, I am tired of this; of not having a voice.

The journey to motherhood is one option among many a woman may – or may not – take in her life. Remarkably though, this option extends well beyond the personal decisions of women. It becomes a matter that concerns the whole of society, spanning from a woman's duty to reproduce the nation, to a woman's duty to perform the role nature planned for her, or even to a woman's service to maintaining society's status quo.

> Suddenly, everyone has an opinion on my uterus. The question about when I will have a baby is far more meaningful to them than the fact that I am a scientist, that I have an opinion about how the world works.

The fact that the personal matter of motherhood becomes a societal matter of concern affects the way women experience the world of work, even before becoming mothers. Their experiences show that there is a level of fear of the prospect of motherhood; a fear about the implications motherhood may have on their career prospects in academia.

> I had just finished my PhD and I attended this Conference again at that year. The comments I heard were something between funny and scary; I don't know how to describe it. It was something like an "advice" to attend as many Conferences as I can now because after I have children who knows when and if I will be back again. I hadn't even thought about having children. I also found it rather intrusive; it was such a personal matter and we had just met. No man received such comments by the way. Because of course, fathers do not make sacrifices. This is the mother's responsibility. It was the first time I sensed that being a woman made me different from my colleagues. It was a feeling I could not understand until I became a mother, and then yes, I felt completely different.
>
> I was pregnant, and I was so happy about it. But I felt scared to speak about it at my Department. I didn't know how or what to say. I was afraid that I would lose my chances for promotion. I was on track for a lectureship position, and I felt that having a child would be seen as a burden. I was right. When I shared the news with our Head of Department, there was a cold atmosphere in the room. He said that he didn't expect this and that changes needed to be planned. I became anxious. Why did I get pregnant then? I should have secured my promotion first.

For many women, motherhood is a threshold in the career; a turning point for the way they had planned or envisioned their career path and/or progression in academia. Specifically, for early-career academics, work decisions are based on Universities' official policies and informal rules around parenthood.

> I reduced my workload; I couldn't cope otherwise. It was expected from me to do so. I put my ambitions to the side. I thought that I was good, I thought that there is a future ahead of me. Now I just want to get by. Do what my contract expects me to do. I can't see a professorship in my future. Not that I don't want it. I do. But the culture here is "work hard". It is very competitive and there is no talk about flexibility, there is no understanding that I also have the role of mother. On the contrary, to get ahead, I need to work twice as much to prove that I am worthy. I don't need this; it is way too toxic. So, I take a step back.

The period of maternity leave changes the rhythm of everyday life. There is no uniform policy around its length: some Universities offer weeks of maternity leave and others offer several months. For many women, the choice of academic Institution is based on such formal policies. After these, there is an attempt to reconcile work and family lives.

> I had four months of maternity leave. Four months. Some women don't even get that. Others get two years. I really don't know what to say. What was I supposed to do with a 4-month baby? What options did I have? Practically speaking, there were not even childcare facilities I could turn to. I decided to restructure my contract. I asked not to have teaching for one year, and instead focus on research. It was a difficult negotiation. Our Head told me that I needed to find the resources and the substitutes myself. Then I came up with another idea. I still designed all the course material and turned to a colleague to deliver it. It worked; our Head accepted it. In this way, I was more flexible with my time. I was able to schedule my office visits around childcare availability, and I did the same for my research. Our Head was reluctant at first. He said that he didn't believe it could work. He put a lot of pressure on me, which was surprising. He knew me, he knew my work. I thought there was trust between us. But I had to prove my trustworthiness. I became more cynical afterwards. As a copying mechanism, to protect myself. I was still the same person, still with the same abilities. And even better ones. I was more focused and well-timed on my work. But now, there was doubt if I could be both a mother and an academic.

The primary reason behind the struggles in the conjunction of work and motherhood is that childcare is considered exclusively a mother's responsibility, which mean that whatever choice a woman makes, she will always feel guilty. If she decides to become a stay-at-home mother, her every day is considered simple, relaxed, and easy. If she decides to become a working mother, she is considered to abandon her children. The whole construction of patriarchy is based on the guilt and critic every woman is faced with, which is augmented further by comparisons among the choices available to women. The possibilities are there, but they do not belong to women themselves; they are up for approval.

> Whichever choice I considered, I always felt guilty. Whether I become a stay-at-home mother or a working mother. I could not avoid the guilt that comes with any choice I would make. Guilty all the time. What I eventually wish for us is that we don't need to justify our decisions and more importantly we don't need to justify our decisions in comparison to other women's choices. My decision will not feel more "right" because I evaluate yours as "wrong".
>
> Men do not feel guilty for working too much and not seeing their family enough. They consider it "normal" because they are good at their job and their priority is to engage with what they are good at. Practically, they cannot spend more time with their family and children, but they do not stay up feeling guilty and insufficient.
>
> Why don't men feel equally guilty? Why doesn't my husband have the same torturing thoughts as me? He would also like to spend more time with our children, and he is also concerned with working much and missing out on our children growing up. The difference between us is that he doesn't think it is his responsibility to engage with childcare. He has accepted missing out; he believes it is the way things are, he

doesn't see it as a personal responsibility. This is how I feel; I see childcare as my responsibility and from here comes guilt....

It is not the feeling of missing out that is a social construction. It is rather the feeling that a woman is more responsible for her family and so she feels guilty for what is simply "normal" for the father. Women from a very young age have internalised the patriarchical stereotype that taking care of the family is their responsibility. Men have internalised the same stereotype, albeit from the opposite direction. Thereupon, while these stereotypes are well-known and well-recognised, it is difficult for a woman to overcome them. On the one hand, she needs to go against her own selfhood and all the perceptions she has been raised with, and on the other hand, she needs to go against her husband's perceptions, who has been raised with the same stereotypes which, however, work on his favour.

> I just wonder… aren't all people – women and men – born by a woman? A child is born by a woman who needs to take time off her work. Why did I feel guilty during my maternity leave? Why did I feel as if I had let my colleagues down? Why do I feel that now I may experience discrimination, even though I try so much? Yes, I am a woman, I was pregnant with my child I needed to be absent from my work for a certain amount of time. No, this doesn't mean that I am no longer good at my job or that I don't care about my Institute and the goals we are trying to achieve.
>
> During the first few months with my baby, I reflected on the ways society operates for children. I suddenly felt that all the hype disappears after giving birth. There was so much information around the pregnancy. And complete silence for what comes after. What happens afterwards? How do children grow up? Do they grow up on their own? I felt that there were no talks about it. I didn't know how to navigate society anymore. I felt so many contradictions, I picked up so many paradoxes. I felt insecure. It felt obvious to me that discussions needed to take place. But there was nobody and nowhere I could talk to.

Voicing louder against patriarchy

Taking a broad look at the living stories of working mothers *living precariously* in academia, it becomes understandable that what binds the diverse life stories together is women's experiences struggling with the dominance of patriarchy. The attention dedicated to the lived experiences of working mothers *living precariously* in academia and the representations they reveal invite sincere reflection on the ways academic worlds of work are constructed and orient the possibilities available to caring academics. The understanding and practice of motherhood has changed dramatically the past decades as women have become part of the workforce. However, the cultural norms, work practices, and public policies essential for women to navigate work and motherhood have not kept pace. As in all professional fields, women in academia have not stop fighting for a more contemporary and inclusive paradigm, where choices about work and motherhood are made without fear, shame or anxiety. The struggles facing working mothers in academia reveal a silenced battle against what is framed by the dominant patriarchal voice as women's "selfishness".

Currently, the prevailing possibilities for managing work and motherhood fall under the two extremes of either resorting to childcare or staying at home (Gray, 2006; Wattis and

James, 2013). These two options, however, are limiting and unsatisfactory considering the developmental stages of child growth, as well as the mobility and connectivity technology offers in the digital economy. These possibilities do not relate to the wishes a woman may have, but to the internalised misogynist categorisation of a woman being "selfish". If a woman's life plan does not fall into the categories of "resorting to childcare" or "staying at home", she is considered "selfish". Why would a woman want to fulfil her life plan in another way, when specific plans are already in place for her? Why does she want to have a voice saying something different than what patriarchy has already built?

> Why do you insist on something else? You go on and on about something else than what is already here? You are not the first one nor the only one. These are the options that all mothers have, you are no exception; live with it. These are more or less the words I have heard to every alternative suggestion I gave. I was just asking for a flexible workload, which was pretty straightforward and doable. But there was no movement from the Dean. I wanted to say stop. Stop telling me about my life plan, my self-fulfilment. Stop telling me how I am supposed to live. I know better because the choices are about me; my choices, not anyone else's.

In the choice between resorting to childcare or staying at home, motherhood is seen as a linear and uniform journey. However, although women's experiences bear resemblance to one another, no two mothers' or no two working mothers' stories are identical. To voice the feminist voice louder against patriarchy, it is time to move the discussion on working motherhood further and to consider how parental demands change over time as children grow up (Ladge and Greenberg, 2019). A "one-size fits all" approach overlooks developmental stages of child growth, each of which demands different family responses (MacDonald and Callery, 2008; Taylor, 2004). Even the different words used to describe a child growing up – infant, toddler, pre-schooler, school-aged, tween, teen – are telling of evolving parental engagement. Therefore, a first step towards including the feminist voice relates to achieving a culture change with integrating the notion of developmental stages in the possibilities for managing work and motherhood. Exposing and critiquing ideological biases, reporting and upraising research from child psychologists as well as planning intervention activities and building networks are all envisioned actions for such cultural change.

For moving forward, it is worth clarifying that while a father's role in modern families is increasingly participatory (Coles et al., 2017), parenting responsibilities continue to fall primarily on mothers (Miller, 2011; Nešporová, 2019; Schober and Scott, 2012). Providing meaningful solutions to current dilemmas, struggles and controversies requires a wholistic understanding of the diversity of roles and expectations in modern families (Müller et al., 2018). The problem is not that there are no exceptions or examples of fathers participating in the demands of parenthood. Of course, there are, but this is not the point. The point is that this has not become the social norm to the extent that the upbringing of children and the care of the household are not *primarily* the woman's responsibility. To put it into perspective, fathers who actively engage with childcare and with the household either are either seen as doing the mother a favour or are either considered a rare type, worthy of some kind of award for what is standard practice for women. Acknowledging the father's role in conjunction to parenthood takes a decisive step towards modifying societal expectations about gender equality, motherhood, employment, and family (Gatrell, 2019; Miller, 2019).

The second anomaly needing to be addressed in the prevailing possibilities for managing work and motherhood is their inadequate fit to our technological era where the technological affordances of mobility and connectivity revolutionise the conception of work (Wajcman, 2018). Above all, technology alters working processes giving rise to flexible arrangements such as part-time, job sharing, working from home, compressed working weeks and flexible hours (Golden and Fromen, 2011; Puranam et al., 2014). While these were increasingly being implemented (Kelly et al., 2011), they were not the work norm until recently the COVID-19 pandemic brought them into force. The pandemic made available (without scepticism) the possibilities of connecting work and motherhood in daily life, by making use of the connectivity technology offers in the digital era. Flexible work arrangements were activated in the face of restrictions due to the pandemic, revolutionising the conception of work. It is remarkable, though, that it took a pandemic to centre flexible work arrangements, which although key drivers to gender equality (Chung and van der Horst, 2018; Nowak et al., 2013), were previously a result of debate and negotiation.

To voice the feminist voice louder against patriarchy it is time to address and answer vital questions about how different technological affordances can drive political and social change. Thereupon, another step towards including the feminist voice relates to achieving policy changes with elevating flexible work arrangements from exceptional circumstances or fortunate situations to unquestionable norms available to working mothers. Examining the practicalities, associated costs and organisational requirements of flexible work arrangements, exploring the lived experiences of mothers (both working and staying at home), fathers, occupational psychologists and organisational stakeholders as well as planning intervention activities, public outreach and the formation of social networks are all envisioned actions towards this direction.

Bringing this chapter into conclusion, the inspiration I bring forward for settling the anxieties of working mothers *living precariously* in academia develops in two directions. First, I encourage exploring possibilities that feel better for oneself. From re-structuring a work contract and adjusting teaching or research workloads, to taking on specific contract assignments, there are more possibilities which should become available than a uniform work model. The exploration of alternative trajectories is certainly not easy; if anything it is emotionally straining, and it may create tensions in the workplace. This is a natural outcome when moving towards changing the dominant voice of the patriarchy, however it strengthens a sense of self in a pragmatic way, towards looking for solutions in current practical dilemmas. Second, I recommend patience and resilience. Both the raising of children as well as the development of career trajectories are long-term process, which require just that – time. Taking the time to think about career prospects vis-à-vis motherhood protects the self from feelings of failure or under-achievement. All the same, allowing realistic timeframes for career objectives reduces the pressure of accomplishment. Starting from a realistic basis can ease the tensions which arise from while trying to realise one's academics dreams and facing the current workplace environment. Taken together, it is important for me to emphasise that I do consider it a personal responsibility to better deal with the conjunction of work and motherhood. That is, there is nothing wrong or nothing to fix in the feelings of unsettledness, I do understand and empathise with the living stories of working mothers *living precariously* in academia. There is a whole world around us needing to change, this (too) is not our responsibility. On the contrary, my inspiration stimuli merely aim at highlighting that it is ok to feel unsettled, that the feelings of unsettledness are valid and important, that the struggle is real and painful, and that navigating it in ways that are not so difficult are among the few possibilities we have.

References

Bakhtin M. (1981) *The dialogical imagination*, Austin: University of Texas Press.
Bakhtin M. (1984) *Problems of Dostoevsky's poetics*, Minneapolis: University of Michigan Press.
Bakhtin M. (1986) *Speech genres and other late essays*, Austin: University of Texas Press.
Bakhtin M. (1993) *Toward a philosophy of the act*, Austin: University of Texas Press.
Coles L, Hewitt B and Martin B. (2017) Contemporary fatherhood: Social, demographic and attitudinal factors associated with involved fathering and long work hours. *Journal of Sociology* 54(4): 591–608.
Chung H. and van der Horst M. (2018) Women's employment patterns after childbirth and the perceived access to and use of flexitime and teleworking. *Human Relations* 71(1): 47–72.
Gatrell C. (2019) Boundary creatures? Employed, breastfeeding mothers and 'abjection as practice'. *Organization Studies* 40(3): 421–442.
Golden TD and Fromen A. (2011) Does it matter where your manager works? Comparing managerial work mode (traditional, telework, virtual) across subordinate work experiences and outcomes. *Human Relations* 64(11): 1451–1475.
Gray A. (2006) The time economy of parenting. *Sociological Research Online* 11(3): 1–15.
Holquist M. (2002) *Dialogism: Bakhtin and his world*, London: Routledge.
Kelly EL, Moen P and Tranby E. (2011) Changing workplaces to reduce work-family conflict: Schedule control in a white-collar organization. *American Sociological Review* 76(2): 265–290.
Ladge J and Greenberg D. (2019) *Maternal optimism: Forging positive paths through work and motherhood*, Oxford: Oxford University Press.
MacDonald H and Callery P. (2008) Parenting children requiring complex care: a journey through time. *Child: Care, Health and Development* 34(2): 207–213.
Miller AL. (2019) Stereotype threat as a psychological feature of work–life conflict. *Group Processes & Intergroup Relations* 22(2): 302–320.
Miller T. (2011) Falling back into gender? Men's narratives and practices around first-time fatherhood. *Sociology* 45(6): 1094–1109.
Müller K-U, Neumann M and Wrohlich K. (2018) The family working-time model: Towards more gender equality in work and care. *Journal of European Social Policy* 28(5): 471–486.
Nešporová O. (2019) Hazy transition to fatherhood: The experiences of Czech fathers. *Journal of Family Issues* 40(2): 143–166.
Nowak MJ, Naude M and Thomas G. (2013) Returning to work after maternity leave: Childcare and workplace flexibility. *Journal of Industrial Relations* 55(1): 118–135.
Puranam P, Alexy O and Reitzig M. (2014) What's "new" about new forms of organizing? *Academy of Management Review* 39(2): 162–180.
Schober P and Scott J. (2012) Maternal employment and gender role attitudes: dissonance among British men and women in the transition to parenthood. *Work, Employment and Society* 26(3): 514–530.
Shotter J. (1993) *Conversational realities: Constructing life through language*, London: SAGE Publications Ltd.
Taylor C. (2004) Underpinning knowledge for child care practice: reconsidering child development theory. *Child & Family Social Work* 9(3): 225–235.
Wajcman J. (2018) Digital technology, work extension and the acceleration society. *German Journal of Human Resource Management* 32(3–4): 168–176.
Wattis L and James L. (2013) Exploring order and disorder: Women's experiences balancing work and care. *European Journal of Women's Studies* 20(3): 264–278.
WHO. (2022) *Global Gender Gap Report*, Geneva: World Health Organization.

WAITING FOR GODOT

The impaired academic

Garance Maréchal

'Mais écrivez!', said Raymond-Alain, with a stern face. There was something he didn't understand. 'What are you waiting for?'

Raymond-Alain had been my supervisor and mentor since I had taken my first steps one year earlier inside the new wing of the former NATO HQ that now housed DMSP (Dauphine Marketing Strategy Prospective). He was co-Director of one of France's most respected research centres in Marketing and Management, based at the prestigious Paris IX-Dauphine university. He always carried himself very humbly in a way that seemed at odds with the fact that the former Ford Fellow and Fulbright Scholar that he once was, had built such a stellar career that had left him one of the French thought leaders of the field of Strategic Management, respected, and well-liked on both sides of the Atlantic. I was lucky, and I knew it. So what had happened? Why was Raymond-Alain still imploring?

A haunting echo, perhaps re-emerging from my teenage years, and my love of theatre, bounced back into my head:

> I am beginning to come round to that opinion. All my life I've tried to put it from me, saying…, be reasonable, you haven't yet tried everything. And I resumed the struggle.
> *(Beckett, 1959: 27)*

This chapter, in pursuit of an answer, explores several layered forms of impairment that have punctuated, and sometimes shaped, my academic life. Some were, unbeknownst to me at the time, self-inflicted. Others were reactive to exogenous and critical events or experiences that sometimes abruptly, imposed themselves upon me. Writing this journey was difficult, and demanded to be different (Gilmore et al., 2019), so I depart from existing discourses that conceptualise experiences of critical illnesses and their effects on subjectivity and self-identity as biographical disruptions (Bury, 1982; Charmaz, 1995). I often had some self-awareness of the different types of ailments when I was experiencing them, however vague and emergent, and they contributed to various states of 'corporeal dysappearances' (Williams, 2000: 41, 43). But structuring my story around coping strategies whose typical forms were being associated with different mindsets that had evolved periodically led to artificially trying to carve stable and enduring states from more fluctuating moments to achieve linear forms of ordering. Aiming for a neatly ordered narrative that would be guided by progressive enlightenment felt like an illusory and constraining, but also pointless, task. The meaning that I gave to those moments wasn't stable and I soon discovered that many of those coping strategies involved some camouflaged form of erasure, some of which reminiscent of what Hibbert et al. (2022: 5) call 'containment': psychological processes that aim to suppress 'traumatic experiences associated with painful emotions'. The nagging, and often haunting, struggles I recurrently experienced kept morphing… shifting from one form to another and reappearing under different guises, in ways that overlapped, and never fully disappeared from one period to another. They clamoured for a hybrid, more fragmented narrative form (Beauchamp, 2021) that would engage the 'bits and pieces' that congregate around my experience of pain and suffering, time and the body. And so to Beckett (Weiss, 2000).

Samuel Beckett's play 'Waiting for Godot' is an existential vigil, a waiting for life to show its own meaning in which two protagonists attend upon the arrival of an imaginary third – Godot – who never comes, putting their life on hold for a chimera that never materialises. As the play unfolds, Vladimir and Estragon each become increasingly stripped of their humanity as they are limited in their movement. Stuck in a barrel, they lose more and more of their ability to move and gradually find themselves immersed into sand up to the neck. This play, which stuck with me from being a teenager, offers an apt metaphor for my journey. The image of the sand piling up into a barrel and restricting movement up one's neck is striking in its resemblance to how it felt to be trapped in my body during my recent relapse with Multiple Sclerosis (MS), a terrifying experience where the numbness, and muscle tightness and heaviness, kept progressing up, from my feet and ankles up to my knees, then my thighs, my waist, my chest, my hands, my arms, soon reaching my neck, and my face as the days progressed. Thankfully, I have been able to heal and disentangle myself from this tight barrel over the past three years in a way that shows some symmetry with the first three years of my PhD, during which my vigil for Godot began. But this is where the symmetry stops.

There isn't any resolution. My long struggle with acceptance is still ongoing, and layers of impairment never fully dissolve. They elude the will and my determination. Both hopelessly and expectantly, I am still trying to find ways of healing in the midst of my daily encounters with a rebellious, evasive mind and body.

Refreshing the page… The clarity that never came

October 1996. Elated, I was starting my PhD. I now belonged to one of the largest French doctoral communities in Marketing and Management. Paris-Dauphine's leading academic research was incubated within the confines of its v-shaped, concrete architecture, on the edge of the Bois de Boulogne. This was where I would spend so many days, nights and weekends but the space was already familiar to me. When I joined its flagship Master of Research the year before, our research centre had moved into the first floor of a brand new, shiny, transparent new wing. Hello the 'Bois de Boulogne'! The side show of some of its notoriously colourful activities now structured our day.

I had been awarded a prestigious Graduate Teaching fellowship: the Allocation-monitorat[1] and Professor Raymond-Alain Thietart had also agreed to become my PhD supervisor. Raymond would be my mentor during the full length of my PhD journey, including its most difficult years. He made sure that I could I start my empirical fieldwork at a one of the top six global management consulting firms less than a year later. Their Paris office was based in the Place du Trocadero, a mere 15-minute walk away from my university. I had been given 24-hour access to the premises and full access to all the company's corporate library resources.

For the first three years of my PhD, I awaited the 'Aha!' moment that would seamlessly bring the different parts of my research design together and create a beautiful text. I kept searching for this pure moment of conceptual clarity. It never came. My endless search for it fed the doubts I already had about my own academic abilities. 'Am I on the right track?' A question so familiar to anyone supervising students undertaking independent academic work. Was I translating a discomfort and fear of uncertainty in the face of a lack of structure into a dissolving sense of control? I became one of these students, with their gnawing, recurring feelings of doubt. These feelings have never left me.

Paradoxically, I resisted the very structure and guidance that was generously provided to me by my supervisor. I didn't want to feel that I *needed* any help – acknowledging this need would have threatened my fragile sense of self and unstable self-esteem. I just needed to feel that I could shine on my own, in my own terms. And while I genuinely enjoyed the creative freedom that funded academic research enabled, I also found it daunting. Such freedom provided a blank canvas onto which I could conveniently throw some well-rehearsed, grandiose projections: a romantic view of the creative and writing process, and a belief that the PhD process was an opportunity to 'reset' myself and reconstruct my identity to remedy some perceived flaws and past academic failures.

So, how did it go? Within two months of fieldwork, I had conducted a substantial series of individual interviews with various consultants at the Paris office and I had been on several field trips, meeting with clients. I was spending an average of three days a week on-site in the hope of capturing the problem-solving and knowledge-building processes that shaped the everyday of management consulting practice. I was well-liked in my empirical 'field', was taking part to the office social life and rituals, and I had built a friendly relationship with research staff, and consultants at different levels and across several divisions of expertise.

Still, I felt unsatisfied, unprepared and uncomfortable with the ambiguity and emergence that often characterise qualitative empirical fieldwork. I was afraid that the methodological approach I was using wouldn't enable me to capture the elusive phenomena that I wanted to grasp. And this made me frequently question the appropriateness of the methodological design that had been suggested to me (my supervisor and I agreed that I would use a standard interview-based qualitative methodological approach). I also didn't seem to be able to commit to one clear theoretical perspective, let alone an epistemological one. Eighteen months into my PhD, after completing more than six months of ethnographic fieldwork, I still felt intimidated by the size of the task of writing a thesis. The uncomfortable feeling of struggle that I experienced every time I tried to progress any conceptual writing was unlike anything I had experienced during my previous years of academic training, when I was always proficient at structuring arguments and writing essays. But this time I genuinely felt out of my depth. I didn't seem to be able to find any satisfactory conceptual angle, any stable theoretical perspective or a stepping-stone that would 'stick' and anchor my work in a way that wouldn't feel wobbly or limiting. My research question and research objectives were clearly printed on a small rigid card stuck inside a diary that I always carried with me. But the more academic work I read, the more possibilities emerged, and I felt very intimidated by the constant instability and ambiguity I encountered. Where to start? And where to stop?

Was something seriously wrong with me? I would think: 'If I was worth the recognition and legitimation I have received, I would have succeeded. But still I struggle…' The course on which I had set myself was crippled with self-fulfilling prophecies. 'I am not cut out for academia… It is not for me… I am not good enough'. Imposter syndrome.

My doctoral journey had been subsumed into an egocentric trip, a channel through which I persuaded myself that longstanding identity issues would be healed and resolved. I wanted it to become a site where my brio could explode, and finally be revealed in a way that would magically erase all those academic years during which I failed to genuinely excel. It was my moment, and I couldn't miss this chance. My progress seemed to be self-assessed through the prism of those grandiose projections and perfectionist standards. Sadly, my struggles with writing didn't fit this narrative. I also had ideas that may have been far too ambitious. I intuitively engaged with a variety of sources in philosophy which I found attractive but didn't fully grasp, and the literature on cultural or critical approaches to learning and knowledge was still limited in access and fragmentary in France, where different research traditions still prevailed. One had to fully justify one's choice to depart from objectivist quality criteria and I felt that I was going against the grain. Choosing a reflexive methodology floating within a relativist ontology was my way to deal with this sense of mismatch.

Raymond-Alain struggled to understand the origins of my struggles, and why I doubted myself so much. During our frequent conversations, I always came across as theoretically aware and alert, as well as convincing! Every week, he would profess the same mantra: 'Mais écrivez!' Please, write! Sadly, I was still clinging to the idea of finding a hypothetical moment of clarity, when, my brain would be able to gain a panoramic, spatial view that would enable me to integrate all the necessary, complex information I needed and collapse it into one perspective. I was trying to regress a matrix by finding the right equation. I was persuaded that, once I reached this point, I would start writing and build a road map. This moment never came but my brain kept fuelling this chimera for another six months… if only…

In the meantime, and unbeknownst to me, half of my data had disappeared! As I was agonising to find a theoretical direction away from the Paris consultancy I was analysing, they had moved office. In the process, they threw away some of the boxes that contained internal documents that I had painstakingly accumulated. These were meaningful and rich data, some of which were longitudinal. I genuinely thought I had the time to refine my theoretical perspective before coming back to collect new data but in the consulting world, six months of absence probably suggested that I had left. This made me realise how differently consultants and academic approached time. Rather logically, one of the secretaries threw away a few boxes of data to facilitate the move, thinking that I would not come back.

How could I get over this? I didn't at first. After working compulsively and at a frenetic pace for a few months, I cumulatively experienced personal problems that would lead to a mental breakdown. My relationship with my fiancé had ended two years before – the effects of academic uncertainties and self-esteem upheavals during the PhD had taken their toll. I was still young, enjoying Parisian life when I could, modelling on the side and once single, had a few flings before embarking on a problematic relationship as a distraction from stress and an overwhelming sense of failure. It all ended badly. I lost a baby in the early stage of pregnancy. This was in January 1999 and depression soon began to engulf me. It was initially misdiagnosed, and it would periodically return, on and off, over the next decade. I stopped working on my PhD and took a one-year break.

Morbidity, suppression and negation. Reflexivity as a limit experience

I had an anxious type of depression. I would mask it by obsessively maintaining what looked like normal academic activity from the outside. I had become anxiously attached to the routines and daily discipline that helped structure my personal life, some of which revolved around a regular practice of martial arts, morning stretches that would help me breath and improve the flexibility of my joints and muscles, and swimming. I transferred this systematic obsessiveness to my research too. I was feeling so empty inside that my newly found bodily discipline was a marvellously safe way to erase any problematic feelings I may experience and maintain a skeleton of cognitive movement. Such movement was religiously recorded and inscribed every day, over a period of several years, into a reflexive notebook. By doing so, I took any ongoing life out of my thinking by systematically screening it, sanitising it, controlling it.

> It took a life span with no cell mate
> The long way back
> Sandy, why can't we look the other way?
>
> *(Bank et al., 2004)*

Every time I would feel a glimpse of hope or excitement about an idea or make a creative association, this would be pulverised, atomised under this reflexive protocol until I was able to push any positive emotions aside and obsessively change my train of thought. A controlled form of punishment, this would erase any glimpse of vitality or desire by the same token. I had found a way to reset myself, detach myself and reflexively observe my thinking, my ideas, my choices… in a self-critical way.

This obsessiveness erased any dangerous liveliness from my thoughts and transformed it into a deadened, lifeless but coherent, written recording of it as a trace. But a trace of what?

> I can feel them slip
> I can feel the hands pulling them away
> Crawling into the interstices of my viscera
> Searching for a penetrating grip
> They are harvesting my organs…[2]

Reboot. When I killed the life that was growing inside me, it ripped away a part of myself. I blasted to pieces any need for connection. Abject errands from my personal life, and the deadened and buried feelings that it carried, were tied to me so tightly that they suffocated my creativity. Guilt. And a sense of failure. This is all I could feel. I tried to survive by sublimating the psychological and emotional pain I was experiencing into an artefact. I was deadening it by drowning it under obsessive recording rules and a methodological protocol that enabled me not to express or feel this pain. By doing so, I was also persuading myself that I was transforming the cognitive aspect of my research process into an artistic performance. I enjoyed seeing myself as a conceptual artist who would push the cognitive boundaries of their sanity and psychological limits by experiencing and handling two different levels of thinking simultaneously: my train of thought as it was unfolding and my own reflection on this very process in real time. Sticking to this protocol would enable me to experience a schizoid 'état limite'. By the same token, this gave me licence to ignore and erase any bodily limitation or the materiality of my body. Looking at it now, it was probably very unhealthy, but at the time, this provided me a sense of empowerment as it produced an illusion of performance, a simulacrum.

In 2002, a few months before I was expected to present my work during a pre-defence, I was still searching for a qualitative way to analyse both my ethnographic and autoethnographic data. Attending the second day of a qualitative methods workshop at my university, a visual curtain fell over my left eye and I abruptly lost sight and colour vision in the span of an afternoon. It took two weeks for the ophthalmologist to establish a diagnosis of optical neuritis (inflammation of the optical nerve). I was sent to the Rothschild Foundation for additional tests. Multiple sclerosis was considered but excluded at the time, and I was put on an intensive course of steroids. I was 32. Neurologists categorised the incident as being 'isolated' but sadly, 16 years later I was diagnosed with the disease following a second episode.

> You're nothing but a wreck,
> Dead dog in the water…
> When memory ends
> And the ocean of forget,
> Breaks our hearts and our heads.
>
> *(Gainsbourg, 1994)*

A week after my grandmother's death in early November 2002 I pre-defended my thesis. I was out of funding after my ATER (Attaché Temporaire d' Enseignement et de Recherche) contract had expired. I applied for lectureship positions at several UK universities and in Spring 2003 I was offered two jobs. I chose the University of Liverpool. The Management School had been launched the year before and it seemed like an exciting opportunity to work there. I left the Banks of the Seine for Merseyside in September that year.

Displacement and estrangement: creating geographical distance

The music seemed to be coming from Frank's office. The Management School had two main entrances: one located in the newly built Atrium and the original Chatham street entrance, with its large, wooden, claret coloured, arched ecclesiastical double door. The grand, light glass-domed Atrium space was the architectural pinnacle of the extension that symbolised the newly formed identity of the Management School. It adjoined the Chatham building, a converted nineteenth-century church. Those Church doors are now permanently shut, as is the Atrium entrance, following the building of an additional extension in 2015. I often use the pod door, an old arched and curved side entrance, as a reminder of all those years of using it to enter and exit the building after hours. My office was next door to Frank, teaching veteran and great support from the start. He was a big Dylan fan, but today Bob was singing for me.

I was burned out from exhaustion, buried in the hail
Poisoned in the bushes an' blown out on the trail
Hunted like a crocodile, ravaged in the corn
Come in, she said I'll give ya
Shelter from the storm.

(Dylan, 1975)

Frank was a down-to-earth, colourful, warm-hearted Northerner. The culture of the Management School was distinctive in its own Mersey way: sociable, kindly and inclusive. Staff across the School were incredibly welcoming, inviting me to after-work activities, introducing me to Scouse life, its peculiarities, and customs. Still, very few had a good understanding of the specific kind of difficulties that I would encounter as a displaced, non-native speaker, parachuted into a whole new cultural system. Both I and many of my senior colleagues underestimated the cultural shift that I had to absorb to fully adapt to the UK academic landscape. I had abruptly relocated from Paris where I had lived for eight years, leaving a large, leading doctoral school with a vibrant, research-led culture. Within two months of arriving, I was teaching a final year undergraduate compulsory Strategy module taken by around 200 students. Being part of a new, freshly formed School was exciting but many of my colleagues had families and a very separate, settled, life after work. And everyone was overstreched. I had significant teaching experience in a French academic context but I was not yet fluent in English. I didn't feel comfortable asking for additional support as it may have come across as expecting special treatment in a context where time resources were already scarce. Another echo…

Born dead of night….
Gropes to window and stares out.
Stands there staring out.
Stock still staring out.
Nothing stirring in that black vast.

(Beckett, A piece of monologue', 1979, 1)

Trying to balance two cultures and two languages, I felt that I had been thrown at the deep end of the pool without adequate training. It seemed that the stakes were too high for final year students. Complaints began to flow and couldn't be ignored. There was no room for my taking time to learn and make some mistakes. My self-confidence took a hit. In response, I tried to absorb as much Englishness as I could, spending most of my life on the campus and limiting opportunities for French conversations to try to perfect my accent. Some of the lecture theatres were exquisitely antiquated, with heating equipment difficult to adjust, and muffled sound systems. I remember marvelling at the small, quirky shops in the Guild of students, where I could buy so many different tuna sandwich combinations. Deliciously exotic. And great music gigs were featured on campus! This was my first job experience at an Anglo-Saxon university, so different from French ones.

Frank and I soon shared a large introductory module. His improvised approach to teaching was so different from mine, but as a storyteller he was loved by students. He introduced me to the 'Critical Management' literature and helped me understand managerialism as well as the evolution of the English Higher Education landscape as it became incredibly privatised. When I wasn't failing at teaching, I would compulsively work on my PhD, with the help of daily kebab takeaways from nearby 'Kimos'. I defended it in February 2006. Now a Doctor, I felt more confident. Sadly, I was not being seen differently, or as more legitimate academically in my institution. I had just ticked one necessary box. Unhappily, I didn't get confirmed in post that year. The word was that I was not good at teaching, and I had not met the necessary targets research-wise. I vividly remember the room where my confirmation meeting took place, its formal tone and predominantly male panel. It felt very intimidating. I was still teaching the same final year undergraduate strategy module and had remained traumatised by my earlier experience. This led to insomnia before every lecture, and sometimes tutorials. I was teaching without sleep. Of course, I adequately taught other modules and successfully supervised dissertations as time went on, but I often doubted my competence. Some colleagues totally trusted the quality of my teaching but that negative reputation stemming from my earlier failures lingered on, the feeling being that I was at times too theoretically demanding for students. The debilitating anxiety that I was experiencing only fully subsided in 2014, after I successfully started teaching Critical Perspectives in Management as Frank moved to another University.

Dis-membering 'The Dark Side'

"F★★★ them" Steve said. "If they don't know a great idea, we'll do it ourselves". We'd just had a proposal for a stream at the major European conference in our field rejected. I was devastated. He was already organising the resistance.

Since starting at Liverpool, I had been committed to achieving the required academic research performance in a context where I had to build my British academic network from scratch and it took me several years to do so outside of my institution. Most of the papers I submitted to international conferences were accepted and I was granted funding to present them. I was able to network at key conferences but securing collaborations with colleagues at the Management School was not fruitful. When I left France, I also lost my privileged position in the French academic network where both my research centre and my supervisor were central players. In Liverpool, I was often not included in projects, events or papers in my area of expertise. Colleagues would not come to me and I always had to go out of my way to try to get involved. For long, I felt I had very little legitimacy and this made me feel isolated and lonely..

> You're coming with me
> Through the aging, the fearing, the strife.
>
> *(Banks et al., 2004)*

In September 2006, Liverpool organised the first Organizational Ethnography Symposium, where Frank had chosen Steve as the opening keynote. Having missed his presentation I was pleased to discover that we were placed together for dinner. I knew his work on reflexivity and he was so encouraging about mine that I told him a crazy idea I'd had and was working on with Dave, an American colleague who had been on my doctoral panel and who turned out to be a friend of his. He liked it. He was one of those people to come with me on my journey. Later Dave actually suggested we should ask Steve to join us in drafting a conference stream proposal. We did. We liked it. Then it was rejected.

But Steve wasn't done yet. He believed in my idea and he knew just the place to put it on. And a year later we gathered with 40 presenters and keynotes among the oak panels and stained glass of Wortley Hall, an aristocratic country house on the edge of the Dark Peak now owned by trade unions and used for worker education. He we would peek 'behind the scenes between the lines' to discuss *my* idea – The Dark Side of Organization! The conference bristled and fizzled with creativity. We knew it couldn't stop there, and shortly after we had a special issue approved by a high-quality academic journal. An American heavyweight, Ricky, came on board to broaden our international appeal. First submissions set a record for the time. Two years of hard work assembling reviewers, selecting, rejecting, debating and editing, and the issue was put to bed. The citations began to roll in. Within a further two years our introduction was included in an international collection of major contributions to organisational psychology. From despair to elation – we'd believed in the project against the odds, we hadn't given up, and we had made things happen. And I was on the 'Critical Management' community radar.

Nevertheless, on a cold station platform in Wigan in October 2006 I didn't know what would happen. I was on my way to complete a part-time Masters in Sociological Research at the University of Lancaster. I thought that getting a degree in the English language from Lancaster would give me a first-hand experience of being a student in the UK and help increase my academic legitimacy. It didn't really do so at my institution – my colleagues, including the new Dean, thought that I should have devoted my time to publishing instead, especially after failing to get confirmed in post.

But it worked for me. The time it took me to complete my Masters was productive: with the right backing and support, I got involved in writing one textbook chapter, three encyclopaedia entries, and two papers. These were based on two of my assignments, all published between 2008 and 2010. In 2008, I became external examiner in Strategy at Salford Business School. I was even asked to extend my term, and it was so good to have a role where I felt that my expertise was valued.

Even so, I was still having panic attacks every time I needed to write. This combined anxiety stemming from my problematic performance in writing and teaching was crippling at times and remained with me for years. Increased stress levels would periodically bring depressive feelings back. I took herbs and exercised religiously, but I realised that this health regime might not be enough and began a course of antidepressants (Prozac) to help stabilise my academic performance. In 2009, I both completed my Masters with distinction and my PGCert in Higher Education, and I was confirmed in post. I also stopped antidepressants cold turkey.

In 2014, I redesigned and led Frank's module on Critical Perspectives in Management, after he left. I have been leading it ever since, with great success. From that point, my teaching ratings became excellent, resulting in a teaching award in 2016. In 2016, I also became Deputy Director of Studies of a large undergraduate programme, got involved in programme design, and in 2017, became Representative at Large on Ethics and Inclusion for the Critical Management Studies division of a leading international management conference (Academy of Management). For teaching and administration, I was now considered a safe pair of hands.

Disability and numbness: being diagnosed with multiple sclerosis

It's January 2018 and those safe hands are numb and heavy, as are my legs, feet and arms. My muscles cramp, they burn, they get stiff... it is as if I was wearing boots filled with sand. I can't fully feel my fingers anymore. My joints struggle to bend, as if concrete had set over them, and compromised their function. This has been progressing almost daily over three weeks. I'm getting terrified to go to sleep and wake up to find that I've lost a little more sensitivity or mobility. This happened several times, sometimes in the middle of the night. Once in hospital I woke up to a tight sensation in my chest. Was I having a heart attack? I began having trouble swallowing. It took eight days of hospital tests and observation to diagnose me. In the meantime, every bodily area where I would first feel pins and needles would slowly get numb one or two days afterwards. Parasthesia. As this reached my hands, I started writing my will on a piece of paper, in fear that I might soon lose the ability to communicate. When my face started getting numb... my eyelids got heavier and more difficult to lift. The prospect that I might soon be locked inside a numb and rigid body, after losing the ability to move any of my limbs, became scaringly real. I felt powerless and terrified through a myriad of tests and MRIs. Two months later, my back still hurts, I can't sit for very long and I am still experiencing a tight band across my chest. This is called the 'MS hug'. I cannot stand for very long periods, and I struggle to walk. In the evenings, I often experience my body as a mixture of pins and needles and electric shocks... or it burns all over. It is as if it short circuits. Those strange sensations (paraesthesia) seemed unpredictable at first but the intensity of some of them has since decreased. But for how long? Multiple Sclerosis (MS) is a treacherous disease. One never gets 'used' to it but the strange symptoms now are less surprising. While I was first disappointed in my body for rebelling, I have learnt to accommodate my new physical limitations. I still struggle to accept the unpredictable fatigue that suddenly floors me. I still experience significant muscle stiffness and pain daily. Sometimes eye strain. My body feels crippled most of the time, like one much older. I must work through pain and fatigue. In the process of writing this text, I cried at the loss of my reminisced younger, fiercer self. I cried when recalling the vanity of some of my past sources of dissatisfaction. I still struggle with the constant feeling of inadequacy that I experience. I still lament the disconnect between my will and what my body can do.

But in a sad, bittersweet way, my MS diagnosis may have led me to live my academic life more authentically. In sharp contrast to what I did with my previous mental health struggles, I cannot hide this disease. My institution has been supportive since my relapse, and I benefit from reasonable adjustments to be able to continue to work full time. With this condition, one has to accept physical limitations. These force me to stop working constantly and give me a legitimate reason to do so. Does it feel less arbitrary? No. I often feel stuck in a slow lane, with more limited opportunities for progression. This is discouraging. I have to compete with often younger, fully able colleagues and meet the same performance targets. It felt that way after I moved to England, when as a foreigner working in a second language I had to perform as well as native English colleagues. And I have pushed that boundary. But it is now my *body* that feels foreign. A body that sometimes doesn't respond well. A body that brutally stops functioning and whose limits cannot be pushed. I haven't fully given up the hope that I can push this disease back a little, but is it mere wishful thinking?

I have many regrets. Did I mistreat my body with too many years of professional stress? For what result? I have gained substantial academic expertise but feel so impaired every day…

There's sand in the barrel. But I am still standing. And I stopped waiting for anyone.

Notes

1 Paris-Dauphine University specialises in organisation and decision sciences, and is the only institution in France to hold both the status of Grande Ecole and University.
2 Psychotic, sensory hallucinations experienced in 2001.

References

Banks, P.J., Carlos, A., and Dengler, C.A. (2004) *Evil [song]. On: Interpol, Antics [CD]*. New York: Matador.
Beauchamp, M. (2021) Doing academia differently: Loosening the boundaries of our disciplining writing practices. *Millenium: Journal of International Studies*, 49(2): 392–416.
Beckett, S. (1959) *Waiting for Godot: A Tragicomedy in Two Acts*. London: Aber and Faber.
Beckett, S. (1979) A piece of monologue. *The Kenyon Review*, New Series, 1(3): 1–4.
Bury, M. (1982) Chronic illness as biographical disruption. *Sociology of Health & Illness*, 4(2): 167–182.
Charmaz, K. (1995) The body, identity, and self: Adapting to impairment. *The Sociological Quarterly*, 36(4): 657–680.
Dylan, B. (1975) *Shelter from the Storm [song] On: Blood on the Tracks [LP]*. New York: Columbia Records.
Gainsbourg, S. (1994) *La Noyée [song] – On : Carla Bruni (2002) – Quelqu'un m'a dit* [CD] Paris: Naive.
Gilmore, S., Harding, N., Helin, J., and Pullen, A. (2019) Writing differently. *Management Learning*, 50(1): 3–10.
Hibbert, P., Beech, N., Gallagher, L., and Siedlock, F. (2022) After the pain: Reflexive practice, emotion work and learning. *Organization Studies*, 43(5): 797–817.
Trusson, D., Trusson, C., and Casey, C. (2021) Reflexive self-identity and work: Working women, biographical disruption and agency. *Work, Employment and Society*, 35(1): 116–136.
Weiss, K. (2000) Bits and pieces: The fragmented body in Samuel Beckett's not I and that time. *Journal of Beckett's Studies*, 10(1/2): 187–195.
Williams, S.J. (2000) Chronic illness as biographical disruption or biographical disruption as chronic illness? Reflections on a core concept. *Sociology of Health and Illness*, 22(1): 40–67.

SOME COUNSEL TO DOCTORAL STUDENTS FROM A NAÏVE AND SHELL-SHOCKED ACADEMIC

Ann Armstrong

In this portrait, I discuss my experience in academia as someone who was naïve throughout her journey from being a doctoral student to taking early retirement to returning as a sessional. On showing my proposal for this portrait to some colleagues, their reactions only served to underscore the toxic reality of academia for so many of us, whether we are mere sessionals or full professors.

My journey has been one of being an institutional failure even though I have enjoyed some success both as an instructor, as a colleague, and as a researcher. My failure comes more from my naïve approach to navigating my career and hoping that what I had experienced would change. Or at least that I could be somewhat authentic in a space that was, to my considerable surprise, conformist, and punishing.

I learnt that free thinking was anything but free as any semblance of non-conformity was punished. Of course, the punishments were often subtle slights that alone seemed benign or even invisible but together made for an uncertain start for my career as an academic. For example, when there was some concern in the doctoral programme, I was on the wrong end of the halo-horn effect although I had never mentioned the concern. The course instructor berated me and seemed not to believe me when I said that I was not the person who had raised the matter. Fortunately, I was able to persuade the person who had voiced the concern to tell him. She did and/but enjoyed her halo effect even so. I found that the doctoral experience was so painful that I shut down for several years and had to be re-instated to complete it.

There is much that I wish that I had known about the doctoral experience. I had naively thought it was about content mastery followed by research imagination. I was wrong! It became clear that I was supposed to play a game of politics against savvy or seasoned individuals. I learnt quickly that neither students nor faculty could be trusted allies. Of course, there may be elements that are special to my school, but I hear not dissimilar stories from others.

Looking back, there are two reality checks that I so wish that I had acted on or had known. One senior doctoral student said that I should do a behavioural lab study, using some sort of quantitative methodology. If only I had listened… Instead, I ended up doing two studies – one qualitative and one quantitative – as one committee member did not trust my supervisor. In a moment of rare candour, the member told me that he had indeed made me do what was essentially two dissertations in one. That candour cannot undo the unnecessary work, the lost time, and the lost self-confidence.

The other reality check that I learnt too late was to spend six months selecting my dissertation committee. The six months were to be spent in a stealthy analysis of the political dynamics of the department's faculty. Then it was time to mix and match so that the committee could be manipulated. While both these reality checks may seem – are – mercenary, I share the advice with current doctoral students. I also remind them that a done dissertation is a good one, however much its content is removed from their ideas and ideals. I also remind them that the acknowledgements page is the one place their voice – their ideals – can shine as it is inviolate. I struggled with what to say about my committee, so in the end I said nothing but thanked the departmental administrative assistant who supported every doctoral student, encouraging us through our difficult journeys. Of course, even though I was naïve, I recognized then that my act of omission would be costly – and it was!

What was the most costly was the impact of the doctoral experience on my mental health. I suffered from moments of acute depression and long episodes of inertia. At the time, mental health was still largely a taboo topic. Rather than wondering why I was MIA, I would receive emails that started with "Hi Stranger". My hope is that now faculty recognize that depressed students are neither weak nor delinquent – we are sick. My other hope is that faculty will look at their own damaging behaviours and address how they contribute to maintaining a system that can damage the minds and hearts of students.

> To any doctoral students who have read this far – please do not jeopardize your health – you will not be rewarded or supported. And recovery time is slow and stumbling.

Fast forward a few decades. Only last week, I received indirectly an email from a faculty member who wrote "…I was wondering if we will follow up on the transition (from Ann to myself) in the X program for next term. Needless to say [,] I'm super excited and ready to go if you wish!" This email was sent to the programme director alone who included me in his reply. I have taught in the programme from its launch 20 years ago and am the last "original". I have said that I am getting closer to moving on but have not made a formal declaration. Even more unsettling, the programme administer is apparently telling students and faculty that the author of the email is teaching the course next term.

I am not only that last original in the programme, but I am also the only woman – my proposed replacement is male so that a programme that enrols many women would be taught entirely by men. So now I fight a battle that I have no wish to fight. My naïveté will not help – but my memories of my students' many kindnesses will keep me determined.

Sometimes I write poems to release the sadness and the anger – the unspoken rage. The poems are, in a way, my sense-making tool. They provide voice and therapy! To become bitter is too great a cost, on top of the others. In what follows, I have tried to synthesize what I did not understand in how to succeed in academia. Of course, I have met some kind colleagues, with stellar careers in research, teaching, and service but they are a handful.

A Colleague
Too late, I see his wolfish stance.

> I shudder at my naïveté.
> Why did I not see?
> He seemed genuine.
> He moves from person to person, oozing wokeness.
> He lies – with charm and inspiration porn.
> Food is his weapon of choice.
> Flattery is his bullet.
> He smiles, he weaves, and bobs.
> He parades his piety, his badge of protection.
> He mimics the powerful, his suits and glasses cheap copies.
> His seduction completed with food, hand-written notes, and compliments.
> He exploits the insecure.
> He moves on unchallenged and lauded, his piety his shield.
> He seemed genuine.

What I find hard is not so much dealing with such colleagues as I can avoid them, but that others do not see the reality. Of course, some do but if a senior management team has been seduced, there is nothing to do but try to manage my emotions.

> To any doctoral students who have read this far – please understand that hard work is insufficient – understand that what you see may very well not be what you get. And coat yourself in Teflon.

As I navigate academia, I see many men who are esteemed who have significantly fewer publications than I have and wonder why. I think I know. One of my professors when I was a doctoral student, who was an expert on power, put it well – "to get ahead, suck up and fuck down". His words, while hardly scholarly, have stayed with me as they contain a profound, if simplified, truth. I guess I should have followed his implicit advice – he used it to his considerable advantage and was a renowned scholar of considerable power and prestige.

However, my experience as a professor was not without its pleasant and serendipitous moments. For example, I was approached to work on some research when one of Canada's finest scholars on the social economy read a newspaper article by a journalist who had written a story about taking a class with me! At his death, I wrote a short tribute that captured how his singular act of kindness gave me hope, several research opportunities, and various publications. "Whatever success I have had in the [field] I owe entirely to [him]".

While I am much more aware now of the acute political realities of the academy, I still cling to some naïve hope that for every self-aggrandizing, backstabbing, and ingratiating faculty and staff I have encountered, there are others who will allow us to be ourselves, support our dreams, and let us develop non-conforming ideas and practices.

So, what now…my future is behind me. I can't recoup the lost time and the many shocks to the mind and the body. I can keep trying though. I continue to teach and to write. The pay is not great and there is no recognition of my publications as I am no longer required to participate in the progress through the ranks process. To my delight, my students have been open to new ideas and I have a few paper acceptances with minor revisions. So now I work to salvage what I can. When I am working with my trainer, I try to end each circuit with a strong finish. Just as I hope that the recency effect works there, I am using it so that when I actually retire, my recent memories will be ones that I want to keep. They cannot erase my reality, but they can combat any potential lapses into bitterness. Again, bitterness is too great a price to pay as then I lose my self-efficacy and my dignity.

Looking back, I am surprised that I have survived – even if just. I was once introduced by faculty member in a rather unusual way. He said, "I'd like you to meet Ann, a survivor". I didn't think too much of it at the time – many years go – but I now appreciate his observation and his prescience. Of course, he won't remember that moment, but it turned out to be rather defining. I am not alone in keeping on keeping on. Tough questions remain though. Why should we keep on keeping on? Why should we have to negate ourselves to get promoted, to get accolades, to gain legitimacy?

When I told various individuals that I was excited about the chance to write about my lived experiences, some cautioned me that I was committing a career limiting error and urged me not to write these words. At this stage, I have little to lose but, more importantly, I am grateful to have had the opportunity of voice. I speak up not just for myself but, in particular, for those following their doctoral journeys now. My hope is that my lived experiences as a naïve, shell-shocked and – oftentimes broken – academic can serve as a warning and as a guide.

> To any doctoral students who are still (!) reading – always, always put your health first and remember that your capacity for resilience will be taxed but will serve you well.

These are not startling insights but to survive academia, they are necessary! While my academic experiences – and my reactions to them – may seem extreme, I know that I am not alone. Finally, I see articles addressing mental health issues in the doctoral journey. I see organizations promoting non-academic careers for doctoral students. There is hope but the old joke that change proceeds at glacial speed in academia is actually not funny. I end this depiction with a clarion call to all of you with power in academia – change what you can. Remember the powerful words of the late John Lewis: "make good trouble, make necessary trouble".

And…

> To any doctoral students who have gotten this far (!) – please remember that you are not your dissertation – you are so much more. And hang on to your sense of humour – for dear life.

"WHY EVEN BOTHER?" THE DEFIANT PRACTICE OF THE INDEPENDENT SCHOLAR

Molly Hand

For those of us who are not on the tenure track, but who maintain a research agenda and continue writing and publishing, a frequently asked question, in variations more and less tactful, is "But why are you doing that?" A more pointed version is "Why even bother?" Colleagues and friends might say things like "Well, for you, it's just a hobby." Or, "Consider yourself lucky that you don't live under the threat of 'publish or perish.'" Such comments, however well-intentioned (or not) are informed by the structural inequities of the academy, whereby a chosen few are producers of knowledge, and an ideal of the "typical" tenured or tenure-track academic – white, male, straight, cisgender, abled, mobile, free of responsibilities (often with a partner who assumes the burden of care and household maintenance), possessing an extended network, senior male mentors, funding – still powerfully shapes institutional policies and gatekeeping practices.

Many of us who do not conform to this normative standard succeed anyway. Stay curious anyway. Work outside academia, but do research anyway. Write anyway. Publish anyway. Yet, even despite the abysmal state of the academic job market, the decline in tenure-track jobs, the adjunctification of higher education, the rise of a precariat comprising adjuncts as well as one- or two-year "visiting" and other contingent and non-tenured scholars, and more and more PhDs making careers outside of academia, there persists a certain attitude toward those of us who are active as scholars though our jobs don't require it (and indeed, may create barriers) that is, by turns, discouraging, condescending, and elitist. And it's not just an "attitude" that concerns me: as troubling are the practices that reproduce the oppressive boundaries and hierarchies that undergird academe.

So, why even bother? In this brief chapter, I want to reflect on my own efforts to research and publish while working off the tenure track, and to think, then, about the implications of such work for the *majority* of us who are "doing academic careers differently." According to the Association of American University Presses, more than two-thirds of university faculty are non-tenure-track (AAUP 2020), and women/female-identifying scholars and Black, Indigenous, and Persons of Color (BIPOC) scholars constitute the majority of that majority (NCES 2020). I address with empathy independent researchers, those in "alt-ac" positions (fully acknowledging the problems with that categorization), and those in non-tenure-track faculty (NTTF) positions that neither require nor support (nor reward) research. Whose voices are amplified through existing academic structures for production of knowledge, and whose voices are muffled or silenced? And how can those of us who persist in our research outside of the tenure track meaningfully draw attention to the latter and effortlessly address the inequities inherent in academia? (Moreover, how can we encourage activism and advocacy regarding precarious scholars among tenured and tenure-stream colleagues?) In what way can our continued research and publishing be thought of as a practice of defiance?

I have long considered myself a "defiant academic," someone who persisted in my work despite considerable odds at different stages in my career. Briefly: after completing my PhD in English in 2009 (just after the American academic job market had plummeted), I moved into a full-time editorial position in state government, stayed in that position for five years, and was promoted in 2015 to a position working closely under the director of my office and managing contracts, among other things. (It's true: I was actually certified by the state of Florida and managed multi-million-dollar contracts. I pull out my certificate in a kind of show-and-tell when I discuss versatility and career possibilities with English students.) As I worked full-time outside the academy, I continued to teach, research, and write. I called myself a "peri-academic," travailing on the periphery of the inner sanctum of academia. My practice of defiance in these years took the shape of persisting in doing the work that was important to me, continuing the research and writing and editing and publishing I'd been trained to do and had no desire to leave behind when I started working full-time outside the academy. I busted my ass. I worked 12 hours a day plus weekends. I took on editing and writing gigs, taught as an adjunct at two different institutions, worked full time, AND did my own writing and research. My husband was supportive but also gently suggested that this was unsustainable. My friends encouraged and commiserated. My mentors kept in touch, made introductions, celebrated my accomplishments. I occasionally felt that I would buckle under the strain, but I was younger then, and kept going with a fortitude (and level of energy) that escapes me now. Beneath a calm public face, I determined to persist. Whatever else I did as my day job, I was going to do All. The. Things.

Then, in 2016, I interviewed for the position I currently hold: a full-time NTTF position. Mine is a 12-month position with a teaching load of four courses per semester in fall and spring, and two in the summer. I direct the Editing Internship Program in my English department (which counts as two of my assigned courses each semester). I teach upper-level undergraduate English literature courses along with the occasional graduate seminar. My Assignment of Responsibilities is 100% teaching, but I also do service and, more to the point, I do research though it is neither rewarded nor institutionally supported. I'm chipping away at a monograph, which might take another year or five more years to finish – who knows? In the meantime, I publish articles, present my research at conferences, and teach classes that connect in fruitful ways to my research. I wish I were more productive (even as I acknowledge the drive to produce as part and parcel to the academic culture of overwork). My CV is not as impressive as my to-do list and the folders of research in my drives. But still, I do my work, even if the pace is a bit slower than I'd like.[1]

In some ways, I think it is precisely *because* I worked as an independent researcher while I was employed outside the academy that the career change didn't mark a major transition with respect to my research: there were obstacles before and after. I just carried on, defiantly doing the work. I do it by the skin of my teeth. The work of the scholar is never easy. I've read all the strategies and pro-tips – write first thing in the morning, write for at least 30 minutes a day, write before checking your email or doing anything else, etc. – and certainly there's much to be said for having a disciplined practice. But those of us whose paid work demands 40-plus hours per week already might not have the luxury of a regular practice. Instead it's a scramble, a weekend hunkered down, one long stretch per month, perhaps, in which we crank out the draft, make the edits, send out the proposal.

Since I've spent roughly the same amount of time working outside academia and working in it as NTTF, I've accrued some experience in defiantly continuing my scholarly work in climates ranging from neutral to hostile. If, in those early years working full time in state government, my sense of defiance was mostly selfish, I now think about the possibility of defiance as *praxis*: how can more of us, in and out of the academy, become defiant academics, opposing the structures of power that would preclude us from doing our work, from publishing, from having our voices heard? At stake here are particular voices. Again, women/female-identified and BIPOC scholars make up about two-thirds of those in NTTF positions (NCES 2020). These groups are also more likely to be overburdened by both stated work requirements as well as carework and other forms of tacit labor in the academy. What can be done to better enable this *majority* to contribute to academic discourse, to participate in and shape the production of knowledge, and thus to be equitably represented in disciplinary conversations?

Outside the academy, similar barriers to research and publishing exist with respect to lack of institutional support and lack of reward. A persistent "myth of the independent researcher" as someone who happily stepped away from the academy (as a matter of personal choice, rather than the abysmal job market or other external factors) to work in a different environment but who dabbles in research – as though it is a pastime no different from yoga practice or taking up watercolors – combines with an elitism that insists on the identifying of both institutional affiliation and rank in practically every academic publication under the sun. Apart from the lack of respect, the greatest obstacle for the independent scholar is probably paywalled databases and lack of access to information. The industry of academic research is "pay to play," and punishes those who don't have access to the protected resources of top-tier research institutions.

The current state of things is, in other words, grim. The growing body of academic "quit lit" attests to just how harrowing have been some academics' efforts to obtain jobs and to the concomitant feelings of failure and hopelessness that ensue, particularly with respect to research. Erin Bartram's viral blog post, which elicited many responses and clearly resonated with tens of thousands of readers, is just one example of the genre. In her piece, she considers the value of her work: "Valuable to whom? To whom would the value of my labor accrue? And not to be too petty, but if it were so valuable, then why wouldn't anyone pay me a stable living wage to do it?" (Bartram 2018). An entirely reasonable question, and let it be said that even as I suggest maintaining a research agenda as an act of defiance, I am not saying that anyone is owed our research. Bartram's lamentation takes issue with the notion that even though the academy has rejected her, she should still give her research as an offering at its altar.

But I'm thinking here about the larger implications. I want, in other words, to defy the suggestion that those who obtain graduate degrees and go on to NTTF jobs or careers outside the academy – that is, again, the *majority* of PhDs – have nothing to contribute because their work has not been properly valued by the academy. In a profession producing many more PhDs than it needs to sustain itself (and arguably doing so precisely in order to sustain itself at lowest cost), are we meant to believe that all of these scholars are going to complete their doctorates and throw their hands in the air and exclaim cheerily, "Hey, I wrote a whole dissertation on early modern colonialism and the exotic animal trade, but oh, well! Leaving it all behind to start my new life as the editor of instructional manuals for administering statewide assessments!"? Are the myriad Visiting Assistant Professors, the adjuncts, the teaching faculty, and the independent researchers supposed to abandon their goals of writing and publishing altogether? Absolutely not. And this is not to say, on the other hand, that those who wish to leave their prior work behind, for any reason at all, should not. It is not to endorse the academic culture of overwork. It is not to support silent expectations or "stealth requirements" of research within departments (Haviland et al. 2017, pp. 515–516). Neither is it to encourage overproduction such that institutional administrations have more fuel for cutting tenure lines and hiring NTTF with enormous teaching loads *and* expectations of research.

My primary concern here is *what and who we are missing* when the majority of academic scholarship is produced and published by the tenure-stream minority. Because women and BIPOC scholars are the majority of the NTTF workforce, this concern regarding research and publishing for NTTF is not only to take issue with rank and pedigree. It has implications in terms of increasing justice and diversity and destabilizing racist and sexist structures of power. I adjure readers, finally, to think about what a practice of defiance would look like for them:

- How can you introduce practices that oppose structures of oppression within the academy with respect to your research and publishing? Who are you citing? Who are you teaching? Are you aware of their rank, their institutional affiliation, whether they are tenured or not?
- Where are you sharing your research? Do you publish in journals that consciously work to include scholars of all ranks? Do you notice how and when identifications of rank and affiliation are called for as a matter of course, and do you resist such conventions? Are you vocal in your professional organizations in calling for fair representation and funding of NTT scholars? Could you become an editor, or associate editor, or book review editor, or performance editor for a journal (or even create a new journal) and help dismantle barriers to access and promote equitable representation?
- Do you discuss diversity, faculty demographics, and matters of rank with graduate students? Do you discuss with them what maintaining a research agenda outside the academy or off the tenure track might look like? Do you let them know that their career will very likely take them off the tenure track? Do you do this in a way that does not uphold the tenure line as the *summum bonum* and every other option as a form of failure?
- Have you joined your faculty union? Are you partnering with or helping to create graduate and contingent faculty unions? Do you remind yourself that we are all workers in a particular industry, one that, like most industry, is interested primarily in its bottom line?

There are many more questions. What would you add to your own working list? What drives your practice of defiance?

Note

1 On "slow academia" as a deliberate response to corporatized universities, see Maggie Berg and Barbara K. Seeber, *The Slow Professor: Challenging the Culture of Speed in the Academy* (Toronto, ON: University of Toronto Press, 2017). Sharon O'Dair proposes "slow Shakespeare" as one way that early modern scholars can take concrete action in response to anthropogenic climate change in "Slow Shakespeare: An Eco-Critique of 'Method' in Early Modern Studies," in Ivo Kamps, Karen Raber, and Thomas Hallock (eds), *Early Modern Ecostudies: From the Florentine codex to Shakespeare* (London: Palgrave MacMillan, 2008), pp. 11–30, and reiterates her call for scholars to "engage more slowly and cautiously and generously – less competitively, consuming less – with their environment, including animals and their fellow humans" in "Mourning Becomes California, or New Reflections on Slow Shakespeare." *Oecologies Blog*, April 2020, https://oecologies.com/2020/04/27/mourning-becomes-california-or-new-reflections-on-slow-shakespeare/. Some precarious scholars have responded to the slow movement, pointing out that "slowness" is itself a luxury afforded to tenured faculty; see, for example, Andrew Robinson, "Slow Professors? Yeah, right." *Precarious Physicist Blog*, April 4, 2016, https://medium.com/precarious-physicist/slow-professors-yeah-right-539a1b84dd24.

References

American Association of University Professors (AAUP) (2020) Annual Report on the Economic Status of the Profession, 2019–20. Available at https://www.aaup.org/report/annual-report-economic-status-profession-2019-20 (accessed January 15, 2021).

Bartram E (2018) The Sublimated Grief of the Left Behind. In: Erin Bartram: *Doomed to Distraction*. Available at http://erinbartram.com/uncategorized/the-sublimated-grief-of-the-left-behind/ (accessed January 20, 2021).

Haviland D et al. (2017) "Separate but not equal": Collegiality experiences of full-time non-tenure-track faculty members. *The Journal of Higher Education* 88(4): 505–528. Available at http://dx.doi.org/10.1080/00221546.2016.1272321 (accessed January 15, 2021).

National Center for Education Statistics (2020) The Condition of Education 2020 (NCES 2020–144), Characteristics of Postsecondary Faculty. Available at https://nces.ed.gov/programs/coe/indicator_csc.asp (accessed January 20, 2021).

IX
The haunted gallery

Curated by Alexandra Bristow

HAUNTING CAREERS

The realm of academic ghosts

Alexandra Bristow

Down, down, down the narrow spiral staircase. The rough-hewn stone walls bare and cold, the way sparsely illuminated by torches set in iron brackets, their light only enough to reach a few steps ahead. Descending the steps is like going back in time, sinking into a place of memory. The confined air is increasingly thick and electric, as if before a thunderstorm. It is oppressive with saturated sadness, disillusionment, anger, but also charged with invisible energy that seems coiled up for a sudden release. There are whispers just on the edge of hearing, sighs, an occasional wail. And below, darkness. Are you sure you want to head this way, visitor?

Below the Tower of Precarity lies an out-of-bounds area. To be here, you must have snuck past the red rope barring your way, ignoring the sign that said 'no entry'. Yet beware: to come here is not just to traverse boundaries, as in the Transgressive Gallery, it is to cross the ultimate divide. This is the part of academia that does not exist. The academics you will meet here do not exist. And yet they do, inhabiting the shadow economy of academic life.

Down, down, down the darkening steps. You struggle to see where you are going so you run your hands along the walls, to guide you. Your fingers brush over smooth, curved objects embedded in the stone. As you near the next torch (they seem so far apart now) you peer closely to see what they are. You wish you didn't as you realise you have been guided by bones and skulls, fused into the foundations of the building of academia. Death surrounds you. Yet there is also life, of a surprising kind. The coiled energy around you condenses into an undeniable sense of an absent presence. It presses down on you, presses on your temples, demanding to be noticed, to be recognised. Unable to bear it, you flee down the steps.

In darkness, by touch, you find what feels like a heavy door at the bottom of the stairs, with an iron ring set in it. You fumble it open, stumble into the room on the other side. The change is subtle but immediate. It is as if, when you pushed through that door you also pushed through another, unseen barrier. The absent presence fills this space even more than it did the staircase, but it is no longer oppressive. Diffuse silver light filters in from somewhere, and along the walls, many portraits are discernible through its mist-like quality. Although the backgrounds on which they are painted are stark, the faces that look at you from them are not unhappy. Surprisingly, many are even joyful. And here am I, walking towards you with a smile.

Welcome to the Haunted Gallery. This is the realm of academic ghosts, who leave academia and yet continue to haunt it by doing academic work outside of formal academic employment. I can see that you are relieved to see a living soul in this ethereal and uncanny place, but I, too, was once a ghost. Finding myself in the wrong place at the wrong time, there came a point in my early career when the choice between my value(able)s or my (academic) life became unavoidable. Following my own call to resist preoccupation with professional survival[1], I chose my values. A surprising thing happened then: even though my sense of failure was immense and I thought I was leaving academia forever, after a period of recovery and healing I began to feel liberated rather than destroyed. I realised that when I gave up my academic job the academic that was me still remained – and, furthermore, could finally flourish. I began to do the kinds of academic writing and work for which I had had no time, and which had not been appreciated while I was employed. Eventually, I found my way to resurrection, at a place that could not be more different to the institution that had hounded me to my professional demise.

Like their folklore and popular culture counterparts, academic ghosts have many stories to tell. Pain, disappointment, sense of failure, and departure are common themes, but professional non-survival followed by ghostly existence can happen at any stage of academic careers and for various reasons. Some become ghosts by falling or being pushed off the neoliberal Tower of Precarity. Liminal spaces and transitional stages are fraught with danger in this regard. PhD students become *de facto* ghosts when they are expected to meet job market requirements unrealistic to achieve by the end of the PhD and are left in limbo post-completion to, for example, work on high-ranking publications in the hope of landing the coveted and increasingly scarce academic positions. For others, transitional paths between temporary contracts or to parenthood can pass through the haunted realm. Yet others become ghosts following reflection on the meaninglessness of contemporary academic employment and/or its conflict with their values and ethics, choosing to step off the conveyor belt of institutional academic life to tread a more independent path.

For Subir Rana, in the first portrait in this gallery, it has been a mixture of circumstance and motivation. His portrait paints his experiences as 'a reclusive rebel and an 'outsider or *brut* academic" who, in Subir's case following the completion of a PhD, has not been able to secure employment and 'for lack of a better word and to escape embarrassment' presents himself as a 'freelance' or 'independent researcher'. Subir's portrait is a fierce critique of Indian academia, which he says 'is trapped in a Brahmanical structure' creating 'a silent apartheid like situation… where tribals and Dalits including minority communities' are excluded from the modern education system, othered, and discriminated against. On the other hand, Subir argues, India's 'glorious ancient tradition of dissent, debate and scepticism', including 'the central figure of… "Argumentative Indian"… has been forced to die down' due to the corporatisation of Indian academia. Although as critical of what he sees as his own conceit and privilege, Subir points to the important role of outsider brut academics as rebels who are beyond the academic conventions and therefore can question them in forceful and compelling ways. For Subir, this also frees him to co-mingle arts and aesthetics (his passion) and sociology (his discipline). He concludes that 'it is better to be acknowledged as an unemployed maverick outsider than to be a mediocre or run-of-the-mill academic basking in the dazzle of an elite status symbolised through affiliation with an established institution'.

Alexia Cameron is similarly critical of the suffocating developments in contemporary academia, but in the Australian setting. In her miniature portrait she sketches her growing distancing from institutionalised academia during and after the final stages of her PhD as she watched the decimation and casualisation of her department. The subsequent period of unemployment interspersed with adjunct work further deepened this distancing. She felt like she 'was being institutionally killed-off, on a never-ending firing line, or at least experiencing a slow ego death', and 'crushed by a system that either made career academics, or forever adjunct casuals living out of their cars, with works that were rather depersonalised and ultimately built to fit the script'. Despite this, Alexia's commitment to and belief in the value of sociology only grew stronger. She felt freed to take risks and found alternative spaces and radical voices that helped her engage in independent, passionate critical work beyond the dictates of capital and journal regimes dominating the field. She also joined a private online education start-up, which ironically, she argues, is developing a less commodified and more meaningful approach to teaching than what is available in a contemporary university. Drawing on the work of autonomist thinkers, Alexia has reinvented herself as a 'non-collaborative academic', embracing the legacy of academia and its democratic foundations, while reappropriating it and affirming her own creativity, 'both as an independent self-directed researcher, and in course design and delivery in online higher education'.

Tone Dandanell's miniature is exhibited next to Alexia's, and in many ways echoes it, particularly in terms of holding onto and reaffirming the love of one's academic subject through engaging in teaching outside academia. Tone's portrait transports us to Denmark, initially to haunting and painful questions and memories. As she observes, 'at times, life itself can feel like a haunted gallery', when ingrained academic norms reassert their hold, telling us 'that there is really only one way of doing an academic career, and that if we don't end up being affiliated with a well-renowned university, we failed'. The haunted images that fill her canvass make for difficult viewing. She narrates her experiences as a woman postgraduate researcher in the male-dominated field of academic philosophy, which include her own censuring of her femininity, and demeaning and abusive treatment at the hands of senior male professors. Yet it is these experiences, she writes, that have led her to question the mainstream academic norms, re-evaluate her own academic role, and find fulfilment and joy teaching philosophy at a Grundtvigian folk high school beyond the university walls. Tone hopes to 'inspire others to think more creatively about what an academic career might consist of' and 'to fight philosophy's persistent gender-bias'.

Some ghostly paths pass through truly shadowy places. This is the case with the next portrait – an unusually large and detailed canvass by Martha Emilie Ehrich who takes us to Germany and the Netherlands, bravely providing a rare and fascinating insight into the normally hidden world of an academic ghostwriter. Using an autoethnographic, triple-inverted interview technique to enable distancing from and reflection on their experiences, Martha explores the legality, ethicality, tensions, contradictions, feelings, and vulnerabilities associated with this truly ghosted work. When after nearly a hundred failed job application at the end of their PhD Martha became a ghostwriter, they were simply grateful to be able to finally pay the bills. Yet as a critical scholar, Martha has also derived a great deal of satisfaction from ghostwriting, taking pleasure in 'producing endless streams of nonsense data interpretation' in record time, but more importantly in relation to interesting pieces bringing Martha 'closer to the essence of academia', to 'write and carry out intelligible scholarship for the sake of the research itself – not the career building, not the indices and impact factors, not the publication list', while acknowledging the pain of having their name and voice removed from their work. Interestingly, from an ethical perspective, Martha condemns only ghostwriting for academic professionals but not for students, seeing this practice as embedded in 'interlocking matrices of neoliberal academia', in which 'the apparatus producing the demand for academic ghostwriting services is what has removed the ethicality from academia in the first place'.

All the above portraits have in common particularly untimely departures – becoming ghosts very early on in the academic career. Things are a little different with the remaining two, UK-based, portraits. Ruth Slater's miniature invites you on an adventure beyond the surface of an old, cracked mirror that you can see hanging in the corner opposite the entrance. By her own acknowledgement, Ruth's portrait could also belong in several other galleries of this exhibition, and that is perhaps why, if you step through her mirror, you will find yourself in her world between the worlds, her own reflected haunted gallery. Speaking to you in a disembodied voice, through mirror-writing and a note flung out from the mirror's murky depths, Ruth tells of her journey accidentally late-entering academia as a second career, then departing it through a voluntary redundancy to become an 'unwaged and repurposed' academic. The feelings and reflections Ruth shares in many ways epitomise the academic ghost experience. On the one hand, she expresses her sadness for things lost, being 'haunted by the spectre of what she has missed and of what she could have been', and despondency of not belonging. Yet she also critiques the 'glass tower' of academia with its missing collegiality, 'half-empty lecture halls, the spoon-feeding, the poor writing, the epidemic of mental health issues, no time, [and] no academic freedom'. Conversely, she tells of her enjoyment of her current way of working, where she fills her days with slow scholarship, reading, researching, and writing things that matter, and more professional development than has ever been required of her in academia or industry.

This mixture of sadness and enjoyment of newfound freedom is also very present in the last portrait, by Mark Hughes – or should this say Emily Play, a fictional academic who interviews Mark in this humorous but also poignant piece? Like Ruth's portrait, it explores experiences post voluntary redundancy, but this time during the later stages of an academic career, when it is almost but not yet time to retire. Conveying 'the angst of an aging academic facing the identity threat of losing his academic identity', Emily's canvas lets us into the alternative 'academic wonderland' Mark has created to counter that threat. This 'intellectual playground' includes a website called woodlanddecay.com (the name a subversion of mainstream views of organisational change) that parodies and transcends a business school staff page, YouTube broadcasts with Mark 'merrily reviewing academic books sat beneath a tree, in the middle of a wood', and his 'publishing wing' of self-curated, self-published notebooks. Emily, often sceptical of the 'Marky-World', is at other times sympathetic, noting the deeper, more serious elements in Mark's pursuits. These include his 'Graveyard of Disappointed Hope' where 'his unpublished papers go to rest in peace', and which he appends to all his self-published books. It is through this mixture of the serious and the playful that Mark's 'alternative post-institutional academic life emerges characterized by disobedience, creativity, autonomy and freedom, but most importantly now embracing fun'.

And so, visitor, our circuit of the Haunted Gallery is complete. What is on your mind, I wonder? The tension, the energy of the absent presence that has chased you into this room has anything but dissipated, but do you now recognise it for what it is? The pressing unbearability of the status quo of academic life, and the equally pressing need for an alternative academia. For an academia which scholars do not need to leave to become happy academics. For an academia that already exists somewhere just beyond the veil, on the edges of memory, hope, and imagination. For an academia of which the ghosts whisper, tantalisingly, and playfully, but also mournfully, just out of reach.

Note

1 In Bristow, A. (2013) On life, death and radical critique: A non-survival guide to the Brave New Higher Education for the intellectually pregnant. *Scandinavian Journal of Management*, 28(3), pp. 234–241.

HIGHER EDUCATION IN INDIA

The *academic outsider* and the lived experiences of a reclusive rebel

Subir Rana

Introduction

A profession and vocation in higher education (HE) in India has become a risky decision in neo-liberal times particularly due to the systemic malaise and administrative rot that aggravated in times of globalization and its attendant neo-liberal policies. The power and politics of knowledge in the lives of nations was evident since the colonial times but its mimetic effects along with its hubris can be seen and felt even today in the Global South in general and the Indian education system in particular.

I have been on this journey of peripatetic band of knowledge seekers for long despite having encountered and survived personal tragedies and professional trauma in the past. In this light, I feel it my bounden duty to highlight some of my lived experiences as a reclusive academic dwarf strutting on the turf for a good quarter of a century or so and dwell upon some of the issues that plague and haunt Indian academia. Many of these challenges pose embarrassment to old tuskers like me whose faith in a world of rationale, argumentation and logic has been shaken and who is bored of academic romanticism and now want to turn a new leaf.

I sincerely feel that there is more to life and learning than getting stuck in a rut. I am of the firm opinion that academics can be pursued in many ways and alternative forms. Hence, I have decided to explore other avenues which are likely to be an admixture of academics and my fondness for art and literature. I have always liked writing, sketching and painting and believe that what can be done in a formal institutional setting as an 'insider' can be done with much greater freedom and elan in an informal position as an 'outsider'.

I want to embark on an uncharted journey which entails experimentation and adventure but also a bit of risk. This endeavour involves clubbing academics and art or in other words vocation and passion which might take me on virgin trails and can prod me for some soul-searching and self-reflexivity. I think that taking academia as an art form replete with its diorama and panorama will be the best way for 'doing academia differently' and which can be justified and made meaningful.

This chapter is an auto-ethnographic account of the lived experiences of the academic journey that I have covered thus far and my engagement with this field particularly concerning issues of professional integrity, values and ethics apart from questions of employability, merit and accountability. It is an open diary of the challenges and angst of a reclusive rebel and an 'outsider or *brut* academic' like me who undertook an arduous mission but now finds himself lost and rudderless in a super competitive world. However, I am equally to be blamed and duly responsible for my past failings and shortcomings and for not having a practical approach towards academia which I have mentioned in passing at the end. This, I believe should also be a message for other budding researchers who want to or have just joined this peregrination of knowledge and truth seekers.

The life of an 'outsider' brut academic: defying academic gatekeepers and mediators

It is only in the last two decades of the twentieth century that the intelligentsia as a 'new class' began to emerge in India which expands on the previous Marxian framework of two classes having bases in agriculture and industry respectively. Unfortunately, this breed of academics (not intellectuals) have of late come under pressure and criticized for crawling when asked to bend. The genesis of this class of academics according to Nisbet (2017) began after WWII and started mushrooming with the onset of globalization and its attendant neo-liberal policies leading to what he called 'academic capitalists' (ibid.) after replacing 'academic dogma' or the pursuit of knowledge for its own sake.

The marketization and commodification of knowledge along with the processes of increased centralization and bureaucratization has resulted in tectonic shifts in the motto, meaning and field of HE. These developments in HE has led to 'academic capitalism' and 'new managerialism' and the birthing of the 'corporate university' (Tuchman 2009) or 'entrepreneurial university' (Slaughter and Leslie 1997). This corporatization and cartelization[1] of education or in other words 'Macdonalization of University' (Holmes and Lindsay 2018) meant sale and trade of traditional educational values for loyalty to the neo-liberal market. This marketization of knowledge resulted in a vast army of reserved labour force that comprised of Anglophone precariats[2] churned through academia's post Fordist assembly line technique. Moreover, obsession with 'measurable success' that laid stress on auditing and accountability resulted in policies of surveillance and control cloaked in the guise of scientific administration. However, this managementization of academic landscape dotted with entrepreneurial sweatshops are characterized by a loss of academic freedom to write, speak and even think critically so much so that even the idea of challenging disciplinary orthodoxies and hegemonies are fraught with censorship, loss of job, incarceration and threats to one's life.

Corporatization of education is responsible for blunting and corroding the 'guilds' of critical and analytical thinkers and leaves the world of learning, episteme and ontology much passive and pauperized. As a result, the renaissance spirit and 'scientific revolution' (Kuhn 1962) which provides logic and reason for knowledge to progress and grow stifles. Academicians and researchers become 'Yes-men' and spokespersons of administration and governments and coparceners in corruption, nepotism, bogus appointments, and farce committees. In few cases, these motley crowd transform into mobs and vigilante groups on university campuses as we have seen in the case of Jawaharlal Nehru University (JNU).

We have seen this lumpenism in many other Indian university campuses in the recent past where educational spaces have been transgressed, violated and criminalized to target and terrorize dissenting students many of whom belong to minority and marginalized sections of the society. Violence and gun battles on campuses are also used as a ploy to divert people's attention from urgent and imploding issues. In North India, incidents of hostels being used as shelter for dons and future law makers particularly during student elections are aplenty and many a times, student goons get trained as henchmen under a local councillor or a politician only to roll out later as a seasoned ruffian turned political master.

I thought that academics and academia were like a scalpel or a palette knife with which to shape individuals so that they could become responsible citizens who could grapple with the complexities of the world they lived in and bring transformation in their own societies. But times have changed as did the ancient University of Taxila founded in tenth century BC on the banks of the Indus River whose glorious history reminds us of the sheer commitment of scholars and teachers and the nature of scholarship it produced. Today, a sizeable section of the happy-go-lucky jobbers are in academia for earning their livelihood which is not faulty at all for, after all, one must earn her or his bread and butter. But the problem begins when education becomes a parasitic mode of survival or a means to flaunt one's status in the society which of late has attained an elitist and obnoxious character.

I always wrestled with the question of how to locate myself in the grand scheme of things when it came to academia and the closest that I could get by was as an 'outsider or *brut* academic' much like the 'outsider or *brut* artist' albeit with a difference. An outsider artist is a self-taught or native artist who hasn't received any formal training as an artist and with little or no contact with the mainstream art world or art institutions, can still earn by selling the artwork with the right aptitude, passion and acumen. However, in my case, this explanation had to be subverted. An outsider academic, on the other hand, is not only outside the hallowed 'ring' of the academes but hasn't been lucky enough to have been habilitated, institutionalized and employed and who for lack of a better word and to escape embarrassment proclaim themselves to be a 'freelance' or an 'independent researcher'. However, in doing so, they become an outcaste and a non-person by friends, peers and colleagues who are well-heeled in academia but who now draw boundary whereby the brut academics cannot become co-travellers in the exploratory journey of the unknown or the lesser known.

A unique commonality between outsider art and brut academic is their rebellious character as they are outside the domain of established academic art conventions and mores and therefore can be forceful and compelling. I have always believed that one must go against the grain and established truisms of the age and epoch in order to contribute something new, genuine and meaningful to the world of epistemes and learning. This is equally true for science as well as for arts and humanities for only disciplinary ruptures, rebellions and revolutions have the capacity to produce new knowledge. In India, a job in academia is taken to be like any other employment but with a crowning display of complacency in the fact that they have fulfilled the ultimate middle-class goal of 'settling down' in life besides meeting other sundry promises.

As I glean over the sulky and bumpy rides of my past, I immediately gather that the 'outsider academic' in me has attained a nomadic disposition and is a restless soul but one who has grown wiser from the lessons learnt in the journey. However, while turning the pages of the bygone era, I also stumble upon names like Thorstein Veblen who contributed to the epistemic pool even though he remained an 'independent' soul.

Veblen, the social theorist and political economist best remembered for *The Theory of Leisure Class* (1994) was a committed researcher who remained an academic rover throughout his lifetime. He was admired by an increasing number of discriminating disciples but never won the hearts that were handed out to his less able but more circumspect colleagues. Veblen was a multi-disciplinarian who remained a perennial student throughout his youth and contributed to the development of universities and worked towards political economy. However, he remained a footloose and recluse academic for most of his academic career due to his marital discord and rumours of sexual profligacies (Gutkin 2020).

On a personal note, I gained my intellectual and literary consciousness within the fascinating broad rubric of social science or Sociology, a discipline which was an 'art form' according to Robert Nisbet (1976) and which at the end of the nineteenth century danced on the 'fence between science and humanities, between explanation and interpretation' (Burawoy 2016). A brief auto-ethnographic account of my academic rites de passage and peregrination from my kindergarten days to my doctorate narrates my experiences as a student who left the margins that is my hometown Patna to migrate to the metropole for higher studies.

As a child and teenager, I was never particularly bright in my studies during my school days having all those paragon qualities that would get me noticed and applauded by my teachers and my family. It would be apt to say that I managed to 'scrape' through and was almost 'air-lifted' and 'parachuted' from one class to another. I wasn't too good at extramural activities either like elocutions and debates, general knowledge competitions, music or sporting activity. After my Graduation, when I had volunteered to go to Delhi for higher studies, my parents readily agreed although I wasn't sure myself if I could sustain long. Initially, university education in the national capital was a cultural shock for me but also gave excitement, thrill and curiosity – of embarking and exploring a bohemian climate, a different space along with encounters with the stark realities of life. The first pit stop was the Delhi School of Economics or DSE as it is popularly known which is part of the University of Delhi and from where I completed my Master's. In all manner, DSE is an elite institution and continues to remain so. It was a thrilling experience as I was actually 'living' my discipline being a participant observer and watching things from the margins although I couldn't gather much except the dazzle and spectre that it was bedecked with.

My actual learning (if I can call it so) happened at the JNU from where I received my MPhil and PhD degrees alongside the ideational rebels and creative revolutionaries who believed in the possibility of another world.

Academicians as ideational rebels and creative revolutionaries: have we become 'non-argumentative Indians'?

I firmly believe that the world of sapiens who inhabit this free, creative, evolving and protean space are inherently ideational rebels in search of knowledge and unique pedagogical tools and techniques so that they can effect some change in the popular understanding of things, processes and phenomena. They are creative disruptors or thinkers who have the social imagination to de-colonize academia by the very nature and commitment to their vocation. However, this might not be true in today's times as any rupture or contestation of ideas, policies and the 'given' ancient knowledge is akin to being read, seen and taken to be anti-state and hence an act of treason. This treatment and popular perception of creative disruptors cum thinkers and public intellectuals as renegades and rogues and who as 'habitual offenders' transgress their 'limits and challenge authorities isn't new and their dissent has always been vented through different forums in different ages since the times of the Greeks and Romans.

India has had a glorious ancient tradition of dissent, debate and scepticism which was manifested through renunciation, setting up of separate religious sects or monasteries, migration of peasants against heavy taxes which disrupted the kingdom's economy and breaking of caste rules by joining monasteries which were open to all castes (Thapar 1979). India's multiple or pluralistic traditions and democratic sensibility entails that there are many ways of looking at and living in the world. Thapar shows the continuity of rational thinking and logical explanation across different countries and periods, which was invariably opposed by religious fanatics and bigots.

Knowledge by its very nature is nomadic and confrontational in its orientation and as such is bound to create dialogue between the past and present. In the words of Sher (2016) the two foundational principles of knowledge are 'epistemic friction' and 'epistemic freedom'. History informs us those who questioned the hegemony of established knowledge system and powerful and entrenched philosophical wisdom of the times had to bear the tyranny and oppression of the state apparatus. The reality is that it is the shifting sands of knowledge and epistemes which accounts for academic progress and scientific development and the concomitant 'incremental changes' in our lives that shape our present and will usher us into the future. Knowledge, ontology and epistemology are part of the 'circulatory regime' that are exchanged and challenged leading to ideational ruptures and churnings and which, in turn, produce new nodes, systems and forms of knowledge. The philosophical edifice of knowledge necessitates dialogical encounters, dissent, trial and error, discourse and argumentation or what Popper (1962) refers to as 'conjectures and refutations'. In this respect, academicians and intellectuals are to be seen as rebels who militate against ossified ideas and knowledge systems.

It is these 'ruptures' or 'discontinuities' according to Kuhn marked by a set of alternating 'normal' and 'revolutionary' phases in which communities of specialists in particular fields are plunged into periods of turmoil and uncertainty in discourse that mark 'paradigm shifts' in knowledge creation. Much of what we enjoy and relish today in life is the result of constant argumentation of the scientists with the knowledge in their respective fields which ultimately led to the paradigm shift in knowledge. Unfortunately, the central figure of Sen's 'Argumentative Indian' (2006) and the torch-bearer of the millenia-long Indian tradition of scepticism and introspection has been forced to die down in many quarters.

Debate and argumentation is an integral part of Indian tradition due to the compulsion of conversion to the views of the opponent or the challenger. According to Sen (2006) there is ample evidence from the earliest Hindu texts that the Indian traditions begin with enquiry, doubt and challenge: plurality. These traditions continued and grew with other major religions that had their genesis in India whose founders dissented against rituals and caste rigidities of orthodox Hinduism to discover new paths of spirituality, social organization and liberation. Sen further points out that there was also a strong and multi-layered tradition of disagreement and debate in thought, conduct, knowledge and morality in pre-modern India. Unfortunately, this rich tradition of debate and discourse has been governmentalized by the power that be, where even the slightest inkling of posing questions and challenging the 'given' creates political flutters and administrative unease.

Today, Indian academia is being controlled and managed by the power elite and the fact that most of the private universities in India are run by corporate houses is a proof of the sanitization and embellishment of academia with the tag of 'world class university'. The cordon sanitaire drawn around higher education mean that learning is restricted to getting 'good' grades and hence no concept of ideational intercourse, critical interrogation and any attempt to discourse is seen as blasphemous and rendered dysfunctional leading to the death of public sphere.

Power, hierarchy and banking concept: hubris and *Imago Dei*

HE in Asia in general and India in particular is saddled with many glaring pedagogical flaws one of which is the normalization of the obnoxious divide between the tutor and the taught. There is a strong element of hierarchy and power dynamics embedded in the Indian educational system which seems to be highly invested in pontification and the 'banking concept' (Freire 2005) of knowledge which defines what is knowledge. At the places from where I received my higher education, the tutor was and is taken to be the *Imago Dei* (Image of the God) which for long has led to their colonial designations – Sir or Maa'm who by their sheer puffy knighthoods are (supposed to be) the fountainhead of knowledge, a rainmaker who performs all the magic and knows everything under the sun. This 'know all' attitude of the colonial knights is intra-generational in nature and entitles tutors to behave and interact with their students in the manner of their choosing thus incubating and reproducing hubris in academia. Indian society being driven by the caste system and influenced by class has witnessed numerous instances whereby the social position of the student and even faculty has compelled her / him to face undue pressure and harassment, indignation and public humiliation as well as ostracization by peers among the student and teaching community (The Times of India 31 Aug, 2021).

Another important feature of colonial domination and linguistic arrogance is the entrenched feeling of superiority and inferiority or the master and serf relationship in the world of HE leading to shrinkage of discourse and argumentation in Indian academia where while it offers a sense of masochistic thrill for the master, it also leads to dampening of higher education. However, this practice has feudal connotations too and becomes a reminder of the master-slave dynamic and subservience of the pupil to the teacher.

The student plays the serf who faithfully and unquestioningly carries the legacy of his mentor or master and in doing so finally becomes a tool of reproduction of the same hierarchy of which he was a part. This enforces and encultarates what Freire (2005) termed as 'culture of silence'. There is an entrenched power relationship and hierarchy in Indian academia and this gets amplified in Orwell's (1951) *The Animal Farm* when the author says, 'all animals are equal, but some animals are more equal than others'. The Indian 'Academic Farm' is populated by approximately 800 Universities and 40,000 Degree colleges that rears and breeds the same species. Most of these universities are in appalling condition with poor staffing and severe lack of funding and suffer from lack of adequate infrastructure. They are also known to display anathema towards academic freedom and critical viewpoints on issues of historical and contemporary relevance.

In my personal experience of having studied at three premier universities of India, I strongly feel that there is an urgent need to re-think and re-furbish academic spaces including its ancient pedagogy, curriculum and intellectual culture so that they are equipped and made dynamic to adapt to ever changing and uncertain times. In India, there is a tradition of the teacher carrying the image of a superhuman or a Martian who is ordained with extra-terrestrial faculty and is supposedly on a 'civilising mission', instilling fear and low self-esteem in the minds of the taught. The epitome of wisdom and the torch bearer of civilization and modernity – the tutor or master becomes a pompous, moribund and closed gateway who doesn't accept or encourage criticism, questioning or alternative viewpoints just like some of today's authoritarian governments. This inevitably means the dominance of a top-down approach which symbolizes an authoritarian and closed mindset that doesn't give space for dissensus, new ideas, alternative voices and opinions.

HE system in India is trapped in a Brahmanical structure which draws sustenance through the practice of caste system so much so that there is a silent apartheid like situation in Indian academia where tribals and Dalits including minority communities are unable to avail and take advantage of the modern education system and hence are othered and discriminated. Indian academia is an extension of the caste system and is marked by blatant inequities, hierarchy apart from various forms of oppression, othering and discrimination (Singh, 2020). The (mis)treatment of researchers as 'inferior' mortals by the tutors, the self-proclaimed Hermes over a period of time develop into a personality trait and where they see themselves as lesser mortals. This feeling of negative self-perception has a boomerang effect where it reflects or shows up in different ways to stay with the student for a greater portion of his student and teaching life.

A sizeable section of the students who come to the public universities hail from the most backward regions of India disenfranchised and minority communities who have stayed away from the glamour of urban lifestyle and have received their academic training in their regional language which inevitably leads to inferiority complex among such students. Those who are from the backward regions are weighed down due to the linguistic cleavage and academic hubris inherent in the academic fraternity dominated by the high caste folks.

Not too long ago, studies highlighted several cases of harassment and torture in elite educational institutions of the country many of which are also invisibilized and go unreported where faculty members have been accused of abusing their own students and colleagues particularly those from the most discriminated and deprived sections of the society (*The Free Press Journal*, 27 April 2021). Cases like these inevitably instil a deep psychological scar on the minds of those hailing from subaltern communities and have resulted in dropping out and even suicide, a case in point being Rohith Vermula's suicide (The Wire Staff, 17th Jan 2019).

Doing academia differently: as an art form

The horrors of the pandemic and the looming threat of complete erasure of an entire nation of Ukraine by Russia along with a global recession, staggering increase in rates of unemployment and poverty has arguably endangered humanity more than ever before. In these times, when there is a grave existential crisis of humanity it is difficult to predict the future of education in general and universities in particular. Based on my lived experience as a reclusive nomad in academia who has been nomadizing in the landscape of academia without any job at hand, I feel that it is better to be acknowledged as a maverick outsider than to be a mediocre, run-of-the-mill academic basking in the dazzle of affiliation with an established institution.

It gives me solace in the fact that I never cowed down even during painful and challenging moments, but I also realize and accept my own shortcomings in my approach towards things. I was an unchanging and procrustean being who refused to adapt, sync and hum with the times. It seemed as if I was under a spell of over-confidence and self-conceited smugness. I was thinking that my academic credentials would 'do the talking' but little did I realize that academia has a life of its own which is different when it extends beyond library spaces, lecture halls and university walls. It dawned on me quite late that I needed to be social and mobile for I wasn't going the right way about my vocation. In brief, I was extremely poor on social skills and wasn't doing smart work. I had confined myself to a silo, didn't have the 'right' political leanings and did not 'move' in the right circles; something that was sneered and booed few decades ago but has become a virtue now which could have facilitated my visibility. All these follies and brazen inconsistencies turned me into an outcaste of sorts. I was deliberately shying away and looking the other way as if I was doing something exceptional and different. My lazy and laidback approach stemmed from the fact that I had enough in my 'kitty' whereby I did not require to 'please' anyone and that the job would chase me rather than the other way around. However, realization of my own tomfoolery dawned upon me quite late but by then I had already 'missed the bus'. But maybe not quite so as this could be a strong signal for me to try and experiment with doing academia differently.

Doing academia differently can be a new talisman for all those who haven't been fortunate enough to get academic positions and are ready to embrace an alternative vocation which touches upon their disciplinary training in some ways. If not anything, my nomadism and freelancing has imparted useful lessons in strategizing my personal and professional life. Above all, it taught me to think differently and creatively and write critically and fearlessly.

Acknowledgement

I am indebted to my alma mater – JNU which taught me the freedom to think critically and write fearlessly and from where I got my highest degree. I am thankful for the guidance and camaraderie provided by the faculty members particularly my supervisors and friends who filled me with strength and tenacity to face and fight an increasingly complex, violent and unfree world. I owe this specially to my father, a publisher, a self-taught artist and a fine gentleman and above all, my dearest friend who set off on a different journey last year but has left behind a rich legacy of memories and social imaginaries within which we were nurtured and grew as adults.

Notes

1 HE has the qualities of a guild or a cartel and in India, the mushrooming of private universities in different parts of the country in the last two decades has shown that HE in India is run like cartels.
2 There is an increased reliance on English not just as a medium of learning and communication, but it is also the Western accent with which one speaks that matters. However, the cut-throat competition in academia particularly in jobs is such that even this linguistic quality is found to be lacking.

References

Burawoy, M. (2016) 'Sociology as a Vocation', *Contemporary Sociology*, 45(4), pp. 379–393.
Freire, P. (2005) *Pedagogy of the Oppressed*. New York: Continuum.

Gutkin, L. (2020) Thorstein Veblen and the Myth of the Academic Outsider. Available at: https://www.chronicle.com/article/thorstein-veblen-and-the-myth-of-the-academic-outsider (Accessed: 14 June 2022)

Holmes, C. and Lindsay, D. (2018) '"Do You Want Fries with That?": The McDonaldization of University Education-Some Critical Reflections on Nursing Higher Education'. *SAGE Open*, 8(3), pp. 1–10.

Kuhn, T.S. (1962) *The Structure of Scientific Revolutions*. 1st edn. Chicago, IL: University of Chicago Press.

Nisbet, R.A. (1976) *Sociology as an Art Form*. New York: Oxford University Press.

Nisbet, R.A. (2017) *The Degradation of the Academic Dogma*. London and New York: Routledge.

Orwell, G. (1951) *Animal Farm*. England: Penguin Books.

Popper, K.R. (1962) *Conjectures and Refutations: The Growth of Scientific Knowledge*. New York: Basic Books.

Sen, A. (2006) *The Argumentative India: Writings on Indian History, Culture and Identity*. New Delhi: Penguin Books.

Sher, G. (2016) *Epistemic Friction: An Essay on Knowledge, Truth and Logic*. Oxford: Oxford University Press.

Singh, Y. (2020) A system of Hierarchy. *The Indian Express*. Available at https://indianexpress.com/article/opinion/columns/nep-education-system-caste-hierarchy-inequality-6789387/ (Accessed: 14 June 2022)

Slaughter, S. and Leslie, L.L. (1997) *Academic Capitalism: Politics, Policies, and the Entrepreneurial University*. Baltimore, MD: Johns Hopkins University Press.

Thapar, R. (1979) *Dissent in the Early Indian Tradition*. M.N. Roy Memorial Lecture, Vol. 7. Indian Renaissance Institute.

The Free Press Journal. (2021) 'Bloody b*****ds': IIT Kharagpur professor hurls abuses at SC/ST and physically challenged students; video goes viral. Available at: https://www.freepressjournal.in/viral/bloody-bds-iit-kharagpur-professor-hurls-abuses-at-scst-and-physically-challenged-students-video-goes-viral (Accessed: 14 June 2022)

The Times of India. (2021) Former IIM-T Professor Writes to TN govt against elevation of colleague facing caste bias allegations. Available at: https://timesofindia.indiatimes.com/city/chennai/former-iit-m-professor-writes-to-tn-govt-against-elevation-of-colleague-facing-caste-bias-allegations/articleshow/85787625.cms (Accessed: 14 June 2022)

The Wire Staff. (2019) My Birth is My Fatal Accident: Rohith Vermula's Searing Letter is an Indictment of Social Prejudices. Available at: https://thewire.in/caste/rohith-vemula-letter-a-powerful-indictment-of-social-prejudices (Accessed: 14 June 2022)

Tuchman, G. (2009) *Wannabe U: Inside the Corporate University*. Chicago and London: The University of Chicago Press.

Veblen, T. (1994) *The Theory of the Leisure Class: An Economic Study of Institutions*. New York: Penguin Books.

MORALS OF THE DEMORALISED

The non-collaborative academic

Alexia Cameron

Starting from a position of weakness, embracing unconventional qualities and ego-death has led me closer to experiencing elements of freedom. As a young independent researcher, I came into academia from a non-traditional pathway, and I continue to practise in a non-traditional way. I left high-school in New Zealand at a young age, was accepted in a Certificate of University Preparation programme at 17—allowing me a pathway into university—and eventually moved to Melbourne, Australia, on a scholarship to undertake a Doctor of Philosophy in Sociology. I always intuitively feel grateful for this alternative pathway into higher education at 17, learning that it was almost always the students who went through the Certificate of University Preparation programme that would go on to achieve highly in the field and undertake postgraduate study. The funding for the university's pathway programme ceased to exist around a year or two later, during the Global Financial Crisis.

As someone who struggled to make sense of group-life from a young age and from an unconventional childhood, as an introvert, I fell into undergraduate sociology out of a simultaneous fascination and, almost, fear of the social, and I was excited by the idea that an entire field could exist dedicated to the study of social dynamics and society. This excitement I felt towards embracing the great breadth of the sociological perspective—and what it could offer the world—carried into my Doctoral studies and teaching. It was sacred to be honoured with fostering open dialogue in an inclusive and free classroom, this a touchstone of democracy. Operating out of passion, I wanted to impact students as I had been, and this blurred what it meant to work. I felt a deeper and less surface, or superficial, impulse. There's a tendency to wear one's heart on their sleeve as a tutor or graduate student in the humanities and social sciences, among other parts of the university, practising with an obsessive and dedicated focus and in the pursuit of intellectual emancipation. It's an innocent and obsessive love of a subject. Contractual adjunct work reveals itself as a something of a never-ending labour of love insofar as where the pay ends and the intellectual practice and property stops. I watched a shrinking and deflating world-class sociology department where esteemed intellectuals took voluntary redundancies and the workforce became increasingly casualised. I withdrew from the university setting to almost entirely envelop myself in the process of writing my thesis in the final year. Routledge published the research as a book, presented in the style of public sociology, before the thesis was officially awarded with PhD acceptance. I emailed academics across the world who I felt strongly about, who transformed and inspired me through their work, expressing my gratitude to them and I received generously warm-hearted and encouraging communication back from them.

Out of Graduate school, although for some time already physically distanced as I wrote my book (renting a cheap old horse stable on one of Melbourne's South Coast beaches), my experience with academic journal publishing was confronting because often the metrics endorsed research that felt redundant, like I had read much of a similar thing before. I wondered why the personality and radicalism in the voices of so many greats from earlier decades seemed forgotten in the journal articles published today. After all, sociology is a vector for thinking about almost everything—a form of consciousness, a martial art, and a lens through which to view the world anew. I searched for where those I admired had published their unharnessed voices and found alternative spaces and radical collectives that were distinct from some of the more mainstream and somewhat arbitrary journal regimes that have dominated the field for some time. I was enabled to publish passionate critical research—still grounded in rigor—but with potentially unconventional qualities. Spaces where research wouldn't be written off solely based on the unusual structure, prose, expression, use of mixed methods, or neighbourhoods of literature etc. Here, I was accessing feedback that actually seemed empathetic towards what I was trying to achieve on its own grounds and encouraging of singular vision; rather than what I had observed in peer review as something of a gatekeeping exercise in projecting another's knowledge, or intellectual—even ideological—bent, or the quest to make research impossibly difficult as a kind of benchmark for qualifying as a (sufficiently experienced) academic.

Detaching from institutional traditionalisms freed me to take risks and escape the tendency for work and research being programmed to fit preidentified agendas, or productivity targets, that seemed antithetical to the academic pursuit. I made meaningful networks with specific research clusters around the world by veering away from solely choosing journals based on ranking. This is when I started receiving invites from special groups to peer review research, as well as invites for publishing opportunities with specific networks of practitioners who seem collectively focused on a danker more transversal programme of contemporary sociology. From the sideline and passionate, present but not obvious or at the centre, this haunt helped me find others whose stance, work and approach inspired me.

After a period of unemployment and caught in the wheel of mass casualisation of higher education, the meaning and weight of sociology and my research and writing programme was only reinforced. I did, though, feel like I was being crushed by a system that either made career academics, or forever adjunct casuals living out of their cars, with works that were rather depersonalised and ultimately built to fit the script. More confusing, perhaps, were the stark differences in how feedback was communicated among mainstream and alternative publishing, even between academic book publishing and journal publishing. At times it was as if I was being institutionally killed-off, on a never-ending firing line, or at least experiencing a slow ego death. Being able to honestly stand by my work and the archive of experiences informing it, was all that mattered and could save me.

In my work, I began to theoretically explore these affected labours—that so many of us, often wilfully, undertake as sites of resistance—as places where the value of our shared susceptibility to feeling, that is to 'being affected', hold potential creative avenues (as well as their all too obvious exploitative dimensions). I theorised how they could be reconfigured as spaces that reveal the labours of love that go into them—through engaging in what Autonomist thinkers have described as non-collaboration. Many labours, in addition to their obvious exploitative dimensions, at the same time, hold immense potential for affirming and exercising creative departure, passions and desires, even transcendence, as sites of meaning. Hence, when non-collaborating, work itself isn't entirely rejected, but rather reappropriated and reaffirmed by workers themselves such that the product or job is reconfigured and taken in a new direction.

This long stretch of adjunct work and a period of straight unemployment was initially deflating. A devastating realisation after years of dedication to the field and psychically quite torturous given the personal connection I had with sociology and teaching—in addition to the grieving I had been doing for lost friends, family and lovers over this period. I found great comfort in pursing strong independent work that I could whole-heartedly stand-by as original and born out of care and passion, in shifting the paradigm of my work and outside of the optics of capital. Approaching academia from the outside and publishing research without capital incentive freed me to think deeper about my work, pedagogy, and reinforced that it exists separately from capital, not dependent upon a fixed term or adjunct university position.

Out of the blue, I discovered teaching online for a start-up who collaborate with on-campus universities and I now Project Manage the delivery and design of, in conversation with a range of academics, a portfolio of units offered online. While initially sceptical, having been enculturated through more traditional and institutional university environments over the decade, I saw online learning spaces as holding such potential to enable expression and the confidence required for engaged learning, which the university setting seemed to be challenged by with less attention paid to students given the mounting pressures faced by academics and students—overwhelming fiscal, administrative and temporal burdens. It seemed ironic that virtual could be less, rather than more, dehumanising. The emphasis on high touch teaching and learning meant that honest and rigorous discussion was able to take place in a raw and more natural way through the comfort of physical detachment. There is safety in communication outside of emotionally sterile environments with so many norms and forced sociality. Online, discussions become spaces where reflection and freedom of thought are exercised, and from multiple perspectives all lined-up in the discussion together; transparently, one after the other. There's time to think before replying, rumination and reflection are encouraged and valued. In this way, I feel grounded in the pursuit of unharnessed and self-directed research that's still part of the scientific process of peer-review et cetera, yet, not preceded by capital motive, a fixed-term position, a journal ranking, co-authorship or productivity targets, or more generally as just a box to tick. Teaching, too, is anchored by the humanism and emotional/critical openness of an online higher education environment where student-centricity is fundamental, without the pressures of university quotas, short-term contracts, gatekeeping measures and publishing metrics based on ranking—what is very commonly referred to as the publish or perish model—yet, still very much operating in academia from the periphery.

The commodification of universities globally isn't new, but it felt like at least online education (in the company I work for anyway) wasn't in a state of denial about it, passive towards the mass disruptions and paradigm shifts, or paralysed by it. There were pathways online that seemed to identify the gaps in traditional higher education, while respecting its fundamental premises and points of meaningful value—and with a significant investment in student success, which I found deprioritised in disrupted university settings given the funding cuts over the last decade at least. Academic institutions are spaces for radical free-thinking and critical enquiry, but they are clearly vulnerable spaces in undergoing commodification. There's a backdrop of postmodern irony to this experience: that it's the private company who is developing, in a sense, a less commodified approach and programme of teaching and education than the traditional university setting. Paradoxically, in the private company, the endless thirst of capital incentive doesn't completely drain—or exclusively determine—the *immaterial* product of higher education.

My work now feels dislodged from the grip of institutionalised capitalism and is a labour of love that I do passionately. My measure of success is if I can stand by it wholeheartedly and feel proud to share it with the friends and scholarly networks I admire most. Through online work, I see the potential for alternative spaces where research and teaching *can* take place. The commodification of higher education drove my divergence from the mainstream to becoming an independent sociologist, non-collaborating with academia. Non-collaboration is founded in the idea that forms of work and production, in a meta sense, hold innately creative, desirable, and liberating elements, only they must be affirmed, appropriated and reorganised by individuals themselves. Using the metaphor of a non-collaborative academic, I can embrace the scientific legacy of academia and pay homage to the past and present greats in the field, and the democratic foundations upon which it rests, while redirecting its flow and affirming the creative capacity of my own affected and emotional labour, both as an independent self-directed researcher, and in course design and delivery in online higher education.

I'm both present and absent in my strong desire to stay in academia, but on freer less monolithic terms. Without simply rejecting the university as a crucial site of critical enquiry and intellectual freedom, I engage with research and teaching beyond institutional walls. I embrace subversion of the status quo, always with underlying respect for the historically pertinent legacy of scholarship. I can research economies of desire, eco-systems of feeling, and immaterial labour from the periphery of academia, independent from competing professional agendas or capital incentives—research and teaching that isn't motivated by the wrong things. Seeing theory and research play out in everyday life, in full circle, I've non-collaborated with academia through my own 'being affected'. Imagine what traditional academia could look like if it were driven by, in addition to scientific rigor, a law of value that measured (the vastly differing) degrees of care, too? Until then, impassioned teachers and researchers could consider their approaches the creative self-affirmation of non-collaboration on the ground.

DOING PHILOSOPHY DIFFERENTLY

Learning to fight gender-bias by giving up on stereotypical academic norms

Tone Grosen Dandanell

Introduction

At times, life itself can feel like a haunted gallery. When images of the past present themselves, they can take the form of a question or a reproach. "Why did you really leave academia?" "Why weren't you just stronger, fitter, more productive?" I think many people, who are now doing an academic career differently, are familiar with this type of questions. Even though I am happy to be doing my academic career differently today, I am sure still sometimes haunted by them. To me, my personal haunting bears witness to at least two more general problems. First, it reveals the strong hold of the stereotypical academic norms. The norms that tell us that there is really only one way of doing an academic career, and that if we don't end up being affiliated with a well-renowned university, we failed. Second, it tells a story of the more general problems of being a woman in the male-dominated field of academic philosophy. In this chapter, I want to tell my story of what it was like for me to be a woman in academic philosophy, why I chose to leave that world, and how I found more joy in teaching philosophy outside the walls of a university. By doing so, I hope to fight the stereotypical academic norms and inspire others to think more creatively about what an academic career might consist of. I especially hope to inspire young people in philosophy to fight philosophy's persistent gender-bias.

Being a woman in philosophy

I originally chose my subject of study because I was in love with philosophy, especially the philosophy of Søren Kierkegaard. I am not from an academic family myself, but somehow Kierkegaard made me feel at home in the academic world as a student. He was a thinker I deeply resonated with, and I truly believed that I had something to offer to the international research in Kierkegaard's writings. Fortunately, I got to work as a student-helper at the Søren Kierkegaard Research Centre in Copenhagen, and I even went on to do a PhD on Kierkegaard's concept of wonder.

As an undergraduate, I never worried about being a woman in philosophy, and I didn't even think much about the fact that our curriculum almost only consisted of middle-aged, white men. Apparently, that was just how the key philosophical ideas had decided to incarnate themselves throughout the history of Western philosophy. But as a graduate student, when I was trying to establish myself as a philosopher in my own right, my gender did become a cause of worry. I was slowly becoming aware of philosophy's gender-bias, of how the philosophical canon was full of long-neglected female voices, but that knowledge didn't translate into a true change in my idea of the philosophical subject. I was so accustomed to think of this subject as someone non-feminine, that I was hesitant to seriously think of myself as one. I tried to tone down my feminine appearance in order to be taken more seriously as a philosopher. But I also felt the pressure to conform to certain gendered norms for a woman, such as appearing pretty, non-bossy, sexy – but not overly so, et cetera. As such, I actually tried to negate and accentuate my femininity at the same time, which was of course impossible to do. But trying to walk that impossible line occupied my mental activity and made it difficult for me to get lost in Kierkegaard's concept of wonder. It is hard to lose yourself and truly immerse in a subject, when you are at the same time outside of yourself, watching and judging your own gendered performance.

When you are a woman in a male-dominated field such as philosophy, you are an exemption to a rule. When you are an exemption – and you feel like you are being viewed by others as an exemption, you bear the risk of becoming *other* to yourself. That happened to me in graduate school. I felt split in two, an alienated experience best described by Simone de Beauvoir in *The Second Sex* (2011: 349):

> She becomes an object; and she grasps herself as object; she is surprised to discover this new aspect of her being: it seems to her that she has been doubled; instead of coinciding completely with her self, she is existing *outside* herself.

However, it was not only internalised sexism that made me hesitant to a life in academia. I want to tell of two episodes, where older philosophy professors exploited their institutional power towards me. By sharing this, I definitely find myself back in the haunted gallery, where the episodes now live on in present time as haunted images. There are so many more illustrated episodes in that room. I hope that the two I have picked paint the picture.

The harming images

Image 1: A very bright classroom, I have just given a paper on a philosophical connection between Kierkegaard and the feminist philosopher Luce Irigaray at my own department. It is time for questions from the audience, but in reality, there is no such time. A male professor takes up all of the minutes to give a passionate lecture of his own. He lectures me on how feminist philosophy is not a serious matter for a philosopher to engage in what true philosophy is, and how I have to stay humble to the philosophical tradition. He doesn't even have one single question hidden in his words for me, only demeaning remarks. I am so shocked by the whole situation and so tired from the meticulous preparation of the paper, that I only feel like crying. I manage to supress my tears until the end of his lecture.

Image 2: I am attending an international summer-school in philosophy. However, I can't concentrate at all on the subject of the ontological turn, as one of the teachers, a now world-famous Yale-professor, is constantly making advances at me in front of all the other (primarily male) students. One night after class, he bluntly asks me to sleep with him, which I politely decline. I must admit, that I am flattered by the fact that someone so well-respected – someone I look up to professionally – would even look my way. Years later, he will ask me to have coffee with him, so "we can discuss my possibilities at Yale". Even though he is clearly exploiting his institutional power, I am intrigued. Did he believe in me as a scholar? Did he believe I am good enough for Yale? I agree to have coffee with him and to later visit him in his home country Sweden. He tells me he is in love with me and I naively believe him. I fall for him. We have sex. The moment he gets what he wants, he ends it all on the spot. "I can pay for your ticket home", he says. "No, I'm good", I reply.

But I wasn't good. My self-confidence was broken. It didn't help that the professor had read my master-dissertation the day before he broke it off. I felt like less of a woman and less of a philosopher. I think that was the time where I began to lose interest in pursuing a university career in philosophy and began to think more creatively of what my academic career could be like.

The return of the love for philosophy

The moment I started questioning the stereotypical academic norms, I felt free to think about what I actually liked to do for a (philosophical) living. Truth be told, I didn't always feel like I was existing outside of myself in graduate school. When I was teaching philosophy, I was able to escape my own excessive self-conscious and to feel that passion of thought that brought me to philosophy in the first place. I therefore knew I had to keep on teaching philosophy, but also that it had to be somewhere less hierarchical and less anti-feminist than what I had come to perceive academic philosophy to be. I believe to have found this place today.

Today I teach philosophy and gender theory at a popular folk high school for non-formal adult education in Denmark. The school builds on the educational ideas of the Danish writer, philosopher, and pastor N.F.S. Grundtvig (1783–1872) and its aim is to provide life enlightenment, public enlightenment and democratic education. There are no exams and no grades at the school, so I can be sure that the students are only attending my classes because they really want to. They are all passionate about their subject and I find it immensely more rewarding than to teach a graded course at a university. Here the students live at the school, which means I get to know them not only as students, but also as individual people. I am not only doing my job when I lecture on Kierkegaard, but also when I lend an ear to those in love or in a crisis. As there is no fixed curriculum at folk high schools, I get to decide it completely by myself. I am of course working to increase the diversity of the curriculum and to fight philosophy's gender-bias.

I definitely found more joy in teaching outside the walls of the university. Today, I don't feel doubled, I feel in control and I am proud of what I do. My main goal today is to inspire young female students to believe that there is a space for them in the field of philosophy and that they are indeed thinkers.

My advice for those who can identify with my story or are facing similar career choices, is to try to think more creatively about what an academic career might consist of. We should all ask yourselves: where am I needed? That might be within the university after all. But in a world burdened by fake news and competing truth claims, we need theory in the streets more than ever.

Reference

Beauvoir, S. de (2011) *The Second Sex*. Random House USA Inc: New York.

BEING AN ACADEMIC GHOSTWRITER

Be(com)ing me(thodology)

Martha Emilie Ehrich

Introduction

The following autoethnographic interview seeks to explore the hidden experiences of an academic ghostwriter. Through a method of triple-inversion, I interview myself, though speaking about myself in third person, hereby anchoring more deeply into my unconscious feelings and thoughts about my profession and academic values. With this methodology, I do not seek to solve problems of any kind and refuse to follow the orthodoxy of science, which creates manifold demands on the production of knowledge and how to write about it (Honan & Bright 2016; Pierre 2011, p. 613). I strive to depart from the neoliberal insemination of science to accumulate ever more data about the world instead of corresponding with it (Ingold 2016, p. 10–11). The underlying research severely questions the scientific legacy according to which "[…]hard masculine reason (qua science) is established as the road to truth and knowledge, yet where soft feminine emotion (qua art and storytelling) is considered frivolous and inferior" (Phillips, Pullen & Rhodes 2014, p. 318). Through the triple-inversion method I replace common spectator knowledge with raising questions and complicating matters, actively drawing on people's emancipation in research (Shiva & Mies 2014, p. 39). In other words, my work is a continuous becoming as interview, as text, as me... as negotiating how much my thoughts and truths still pass as scientific enough within and beyond the academic project.

Understanding my research as becoming-research means to take up (ethical) responsibility towards our pasts, presents and futures (Honan & Bright 2016, p. 738). Therefore, my experiences, traumas, and healings are inevitably elements of this research performance, entangled with many more elements, which are all linked to my emancipation as a (ghosted) academic (Środa, Rogowska-Stangret & Cielemęcka 2014, p. 120). Following new materialist methodologies, I do not analyse or code "the interview" as commonly done in social sciences nor treat "the data" as explanatory of my experience. Instead, I treat the research performance as a whole, forming an assemblage, an amalgamation of stories (Mazzei 2013, p. 739). I as interviewer, interviewee, and ghostwriter am always already one, hereby destabilizing common assumptions about "[...] the relations between researcher and researched, methods and methodology and writer and researcher" (Honan & Bright 2016, pp. 736–737). This autoethnographic text might confuse you at times. Yet, feel invited to be(com)ing me(thodology).

The interview

I: First of all, thank you – well me – for joining me today to conduct this exciting interview. This autoethnographic interview is not recorded, but immediately transcribed as the conversation proceeds in my minds.[1]

I understand Martha has been working as an academic ghostwriter for quite a while now? Can you elaborate on this job a bit?

ME: Yes, well thank you for having me. I am happy to share some hopefully insightful information on Martha and their career. Martha indeed started working as a so-called academic ghostwriter in February 2020. After nearly one hundred failed job applications leading up to Spring 2020, Martha googled – as people do nowadays when in dire need of answers to fundamental life questions, I guess – the terms "self-employed" "academic" "social science". One of the first results in the list was a newspaper article on a ghostwriting agency. So far Martha had only heard of this concept in relation to memoires written in the name of famous people and pop songs for musicians. The article suggested that the academics, who work on a freelance basis for the agency, are not liable when it comes to possible allegations of fraud arising from the submission of academic work at universities that was actually written by someone else – a ghostwriter.

In fact, Martha quickly realized that there are no questions of illegality attached to the work as an academic ghostwriter, but – as if that is less daunting – solely questions of ethicality. Submitting academic work which has been written by someone else as your own work is a violation of universities' academic integrity policies. In most countries, such practices do not fall under criminal law. Thus, the prevailing question Martha asked themselves before taking up this profession, but also while working as a ghostwriter, has been whether or not they condemn this practice from an ethical point of view. In short: Martha doesn't; maybe there is time in the following passages to elaborate why Martha thinks that way?

I: Yes, definitely! Let me suggest we first tackle some more factual information about the job and the procedure of becoming an academic ghostwriter before we dive into the ethical questions surrounding this job. Could you elaborate on Martha's previous academic career as well as the application procedure for becoming an academic ghostwriter?

ME: Yes, sure. No need to rush through this, I guess. Well, Martha obtained a bachelor's degree in Sociology with a minor in Political Science at a German university. Martha then pursued a two-year master's degree programme in Criminology, which was supplemented with an additional two-year master's degree programme in the same disciplinary field, but with a different focus. Martha thus finished all degrees within five and a half years, leaving Martha well-educated, but without a very clear career prospect by the age of 23. For the second master's Martha had moved to the Netherlands, deciding to apply for several PhD programmes there. As Martha wanted to pursue an academic career outside of Criminology, they foremost applied for PhD programmes in the fields of Political Science, Sociology and Organization Studies. Within half a year of graduating Martha had been chosen for a PhD programme in the field of Corporate Strategy due to an expertise in both qualitative and quantitative methods. With a growing interest in Philosophy of Science and a background in System Theory, Martha was excited to carry out the proposed Network Research in the field of Corporate Strategy. During their PhD, Martha was exposed to Critical Management Studies as well as Economics and Business Administration. This rather diverse scholarly upbringing of Martha's and steady interest in exploring ever new fields of scientific enquiry, turned out to be quite essential for the later job as an academic ghostwriter.

I: This is a rather interesting point you're raising here. While applying for the job, was there ever an indication of what the profile of a successful ghostwriter should look like?

ME: Well yes, Martha applied with an agency that advertised to be looking for academics with expertise in the fields of Political Science, Law, Business Informatics, Medical Science, Business Administration and Linguistics. To apply with this agency, one has to fill in a digital form, including a CV, copies of all degrees (Martha didn't have a PhD certificate yet since Martha was still waiting to defend) and an exemplary, scholarly text. Within a few days, Martha was invited for a phone interview. Martha was rather nervous, as Martha was not quite sure what the work of a ghostwriter would actually look like. Martha only knew that procrastination and a general atmosphere of dissatisfaction had prevailed during their academic writing experiences and was pretty sure that both these factors would be detrimental to the work of an academic ghostwriter.

Yet, the phone interview with the agency's HR manager was quite convincing and Martha's enthusiasm to work from home as a freelancer with lots of freedom in terms of daily routines grew even more. As a complete novice to this industry, it also helped feeling that people at the agency were rather laid back and easy going. The HR manager said that Martha is the perfect candidate for such a job as they are always excited to collaborate with people who have quite a diverse academic orientation. The HR manager, for instance, holds two bachelor's and three master's degrees and is currently doing a PhD.

I: Wow, so it seems like this industry is a pool of lifelong students?

ME: I guess you could call it that. It makes sense though from two different angles. On the one hand side, being enrolled as a student (while working as a freelancer) is rather practical in terms of tax regulations, health insurance costs and for having easy access to literature, one of the main resources needed as an academic ghostwriter. On the other hand, there is also a qualitative argument to be made about it: When you're really into learning about new scientific concepts and diving into various disciplines you get to develop a kind of meta-level perspective on science. You get to see connections between disciplines, which usually remain hidden for students, possibly even accredited academics. Martha's multi-disciplinary upbringing really contributed to the work as a ghostwriter since Martha was able to take on quite a variety of projects as well as navigate even previously unknown fields of research, such as Philosophy. So by the time the phone interview ended, Martha had been subscribed to three different email-lists through which Martha would be able to apply for incoming projects, namely one on Social Science (including Sociology, Political Science, Linguistics, Social Work and Ethnology), one on Economics (including Management, Business Administration and Statistics) and one on Humanities (including Philosophy, History and Religious Studies). After signing a confidentiality agreement with the agency, Martha received access to a personal online account, through which all communication with clients and the agency would run. According to the agency, these accounts are highly secure to prevent sensitive information about the identity, payment methods and whereabouts of clients from leaking.

I: Can you still recall how Martha felt when all this started? Did it feel weird for Martha to engage in an activity under such relatively high standards of concealment?

ME: I am not sure. As I recall it, Martha just felt relieved to have finally found a job, which would pay the bills. Martha was also excited about how well-organized the agency appeared to be, feeling that it almost seemed too good to be true: Martha would be paid quite a lot of money for something they had been doing anyway for years – writing research papers and theses. What Martha felt more concerned about was how, for example, empirical work would actually be conducted in such a constellation. It was about two to three months into the work that Martha realized that most clients provide their own data and that it was quite common for clients to make use of other agencies, which actually fabricate empirical data. Only once Martha saw a project pass by, in which qualitative interviews with experts were to be fabricated. To Martha this seemed a disproportionate amount of work for the money offered, since pretending to be multiple other people with an expertise in a specific field is pretty difficult, don't you think?

I: Yes, definitely! But something else strikes me as relevant here: the ethicality of this profession. Maybe you could elaborate on Martha's considerations regarding the ethical intricacies of this work?

ME: Well, as far as I am concerned Martha understands the ethics of this work as embedded in, as Martha would say, interlocking matrices of neoliberal academia. For one, the so-called professionalization of work necessitates ever more people to obtain university degrees for non-academic professions. This, on the other hand, crystalizes in the fact that foremost people, who do not pursue careers within academia, make use of academic ghostwriting services. This might seem an obvious fact, but it fundamentally matters to the ethicality of academic ghostwriting in the sense that academic integrity as a whole remains intact. In other words, Martha does condemn writing pieces for academic professionals from an ethical point of view, but not for students, who are indeed interested in obtaining the relevant training for their future professions, but are simply not interested in the scientific-analytical aspects of doing research.

It boils down to the question, if and why professionals throughout various sectors are required to demonstrate that they can perform scientifically valid research, even though their day-to-day work routines do not demand such skillsets. This point is closely interlinked with what Martha understands as *neoliberal* academia: An academic apparatus, which – instead of being guided by the value of raising scholarly awareness towards the critical investigation of scientific status quos – is undermined by capitalist principles of growth and heightened competition. This neoliberal derailment of academia foregrounds the production of ever more data, ever more knowledge and ever more human resources for labour by competing for monetary funds and at the cost of neglecting the underlying power structures reproduced through this neo-colonial, capitalist and patriarchal science machine.

In short, Martha feels that academic integrity and the ethicality of being a scholar remain untouched by the profession of an academic ghostwriter because the apparatus producing the demand for academic ghostwriting services is what has removed the ethicality from academia in the first place.

I: Um, thank you for this unravelling analysis of the current status of academic work. I am not sure that we have enough time to go into further detail on this very critical issue, so please forgive this abrupt shift towards another topic: Could you elaborate a bit more on the daily work of Martha as an academic ghostwriter, so that our audience can gain a better grasp of the actual work routines this job entails?

ME: Sure. Usually, at least in the beginning, Martha preferred to take on small projects. Short 3 to 15-page papers, presentations or theoretical theses. Empirical work seemed too time-intensive to be worth engaging with. Small projects just spoke to Martha, especially because they had just finished their PhD thesis and the last thing they wanted was to feel the burden of a big scientific project again. Nonetheless, Martha's first project, which was assigned to Martha by the agency with the comment that the client is really easy going, was a theoretical Bachelor thesis in the field of Social Work. Martha had no previous experience in this field, yet the topic was interesting. It concerned the relationship between having a family migration background and experiences of societal inclusion. The final thesis had 40 pages and the project paid 1147 Euros.

How it works, is that the agency divides the project into several steppingstones. First, the ghostwriter needs to familiarize themselves with the topic of the project and the information provided by the client, such as university guidelines. Then the agency moderates a phone call between the ghostwriter and the client, in which both are to use their first names or a fake name. These conversations are meant for the ghostwriter to clarify any missing information, but more so to reassure the client that their choice to make use of such a service is not unethical, but understandable and totally justified. This is also the moment to ensure the client that you, as the ghostwriter, are an expert in the respective field and will deliver the product as requested.

I: This is really interesting. How was it for Martha to interact with these anonymous clients on the phone?

ME: Well, Martha experienced these conversations as quite diverse. While some clients were really rational about it and just made sure that all important information was conveyed properly, other clients were more communicative and even emotional. Martha did notice that a lot of clients felt the need to justify why they are making use of such a service. The majority of these people worked fulltime and thus simply did not have the capacity to carry out their own research projects. Some people would actually be so happy with Martha's style of working and the end results Martha delivered, that they would become regulars. In one case, a particular client booked Martha for five projects, and throughout the months of collaboration they would use these phone calls more as a nice opportunity to chat about how things were going personally.

Oh, and I should mention, of course, that these personal phone conversations are also important for the agency because they actually justify the comparably high price paid for the service. Some agencies only offer their clients to deliver the written piece by a specific date, often using automated copy-paste strategies for text composition as well as plagiarism. More professional agencies guarantee to have the pieces written by an actual human being or even a person with substantial expertise in the field. Hence the phone calls...

I: I would not have expected that personal relationships could form in such anonymized circumstances...

ME: Martha neither. Both to Martha and the client it must have felt quite like bonding to undergo this ghostwriting process together for the first time, as both were novices to using and providing the service. In fact, their bond became so strong that the client requested Martha to write a very personal reflection piece on her experiences of racism and mobbing during student course work as well as in her private and professional life. Martha, having (un-)consciously benefitted from white privilege their whole life, has never experienced racism geared at themselves, but surely has been complicit in perpetuating white supremacist structures to some extent by simply not speaking up and not actively encouraging anti-racist behaviour in themselves and in others at points in Martha's life. To be asked to write a personal reflection piece on the racist experiences of the client, a person of colour, seemed therefore quite presumptuous, if not offensive. Yet, the client assured Martha that due to being very emotional about her own experiences, the better fit to reflect these instances with the right balance of personal involvement and professional distance would be Martha. As a second-generation immigrant of Turkish descent in Germany, a woman and a Muslima, the client had faced multi-facetted forms of oppression, disrespect and discrimination due to racism, sexism and islamophobia.

I: Don't you think that particularly the fact that the client feels her standpoint and experiences are too emotional to be counted as a legitimate personal reflection piece, is already a prime example of the underlying racist atmosphere prevailing in society at large and thus also universities? And don't you think that Martha was complicit in reproducing this racist culture by getting paid to write a reflection on personal experiences of racism which aren't Martha's?

ME: Well yes, of course it is fucked up that the client does not feel confident to write about her own experiences of racism. Yet, the client did voice her traumas and experiences to Martha, who was able to provide the client with a written piece, which did illuminate the ways in which she felt mistreated and discriminated against and how this is interrelated with larger structures of discrimination within the university and society at large. The client did assure Martha, that she would've not been able to enmesh her own experiences with such legitimate critiques of the more structural levels of racism, sexism and islamophobia, and therefore be able to convince her direct peers and professors, who were active perpetrators of this behaviour, of their wrongdoings.

I: I find this connects much to Black Feminist work, which has long critiqued the reproduction of hierarchy between everyday lived experience and academic knowledge, where the latter is regarded as more objectively true than the former, both in academic and non-academic circles[2]. In fact, Martha providing this service to the client exists in a tensional spasm between a re-colonization of marginalized voices and an investigation of (Martha's) whiteness and privilege. Don't you think so?

ME: Yes, definitely! Sure! Also, it felt very meaningful to Martha to grow so close with a client and engage with their personal (hi)stories. Knowing that providing this service was connected to more than just passing a course or getting a good grade, Martha still feels significantly connected to that client, even though they might never find out who exactly the other one is.

I: To shift the focus away from these seemingly rare instances of producing meaningful content as an academic ghostwriter to more common project requests: How does

Martha feel about writing scientific pieces, which must be rather low-quality compared to Martha's intellectual capacity and academic interests?

ME: Martha actually found that once again writing Bachelor and Master-level pieces was almost cathartic. It made Martha realize that while they were studying, they had no grasp yet of the whole, of the relation between the information conveyed to them and the interconnections between theories and methods applied by them. Looking back, Martha felt that their education taught them to successfully function in and navigate a room full of obscure and complex objects to be applied in research, while actually wearing a blindfold, which kept them from seeing how these objects interrelated with each other and with Martha themselves in that room.

Martha feels that this metaphor was further augmented by the experiences as a ghostwriter and the contact with clients. Often times the clients were lost in all the instructions and rules of how to do science properly, even though they knew them well. During Martha's doctoral research, Martha learnt to walk through the room, slowly removing the blindfold and thus being able to critically question all these theories, methods, tools and standards in science. For the first time Martha could experience, how – what is commonly referred to as – science interrelates with themselves by doing research. These emancipative experiences were enmeshed in pro-actively weaving out the historical embeddedness of today's academia, its colonial roots and capitalist-patriarchal heritage.

Ironically enough, it is this becoming a critical scholar, as Martha would refer to themselves, that enabled Martha to finally just write and do research in the way dominant paradigms define what science ought to be. Hence, Martha no longer jolted around with concepts, refused to use objective language to create the illusion of facts, or reflectively questioned the truths put forward by them: at least in their ghostwriting pieces, Martha finally just did what was asked of them.

I: What you are describing sounds quite cynical to me. For Martha to go through all that intellectual hardship and the enormous efforts of emancipating themselves from mechanistic, capitalist, masculinist and Cartesian science, to then end up not just catering to this knowledge production machine as it is, but doing so with their voice and name removed? This sounds awfully painful...

ME: Yes, when you put it like that, it does sound awful. But Martha took pleasure in the fact that they had mastered this cheap act of producing endless streams of nonsense data interpretation and objectively written facts, to the point where Martha would challenge themselves to do it ever faster and more efficiently. Martha's best time currently amounts to 33 hours for a 45-page empirical master's thesis in Business Administration. Also, Martha made sure, whenever possible, to take on projects which do interest them to some extent and which would grant leeway for the insertion of critical scholarship. Especially pieces on the care economy or feminist approaches to political economy were worthwhile playgrounds for Martha to insert some of their own critical thoughts into the work, while imagining that the respective professor might truly enjoy reading the piece – in case they even had enough time to actually read the requested papers.

More importantly though, Martha has wondered whether or not this work brought them closer to the essence of academia: To write and carry out intelligible scholarship for the sake of the research itself – not the career building, not the indices and impact factors, not the publication list... Whenever Martha writes pieces on topics that are meaningful to Martha, such as "a feminist view of friendship" or "a critical discussion of the #birthstrike movement", Martha feels that ghostwriting – writing without a name – possibly renders the pieces more honest in their pursuit for insight since they are less tainted by the thought-suffocating doings of neoliberal academia.

I: Well, it is nice to see that Martha nevertheless finds pleasure in particular aspects and moments of the profession. But I have to interfere once more by pointing out that this profession, even though – as we already learnt – it provides a rather widespread service and is publicly visible, at least digitally, it does exist in an obscuring mist, no? Not a lot of people talk about making use of this service (for obvious reasons) and not a lot of people talk about providing this service (at least not deanonymized). How does Martha feel about these truly ghosted aspects of the profession, about coming out into the open as a ghostwriter and about the sustainability of such a career?

ME: Well, call Martha naïve but during their work as a ghostwriter Martha has even openly discussed their profession in a job application for the position of a research assistant on the topic of higher education with a political party. Martha used the ghostwriting occupation as a prime example of all things wrong with current academia. The job application failed and it made Martha question whether or not this occupation is something that actually should be mentioned in a CV. Martha googled how other academic ghostwriters were handling this and concluded that its best to refer to themselves as a freelance scientific editor and author… In Martha's experience, no further questions were ever asked about the work as a freelance scientific editor and author during any of the following job interviews.

And yes, Martha has never actually considered this job a true, viable alternative to what one may want to refer to as a "real" job. It must be related to the precariousness of freelancing, which comes with a lot of insecurity in terms of securing future projects, at comparably high financial costs (such as taxes and health insurance) and a wealth of bureaucratic efforts, at least in Germany. Even though on average Martha received about 20 emails per day by the agency regarding new projects, demand fluctuated depending on the month. Of course, having been through an entire year of doing the job, Martha could to some extent foresee this and plan accordingly.

Maybe an even more pressing factor, which led Martha to continue to apply for other jobs during their occupation as a ghostwriter, was that Martha was scared that the longer they worked on a freelance basis the smaller their chances would become to score a permanent employment contract and thus be able to enhance their career within or outside academia. Furthermore, it started to bother Martha quite a bit that their skills, knowledge, and efforts remain fully invisibilized by working as a ghostwriter. The agency, of course, refers more and better-paid projects to those ghostwriters with whom clients are most satisfied. But to never be able to formally discuss the content of these projects with other scholars and to pretend that this work has never even come from Martha's mind and thoughts, just devastated Martha.

And lastly, I would like to mention here that Martha has indeed debated for quite a while whether or not to publish an academic piece on ghostwriting using their own name. The fear of being discredited as a professional academic by working as a ghostwriter is ongoing. At the same time, Martha sees a great contribution to be made by more openly talking about the work of an academic ghostwriter since it is a legitimate career within a growing industry that drastically improved Martha's project management skills, self-dependant work ethic, inter-disciplinary expertise, and proficiency in conducting as well as writing research.

I: I would like to dive into another meaningful aspect of the job of a ghostwriter. In how far do the clients belong to rich elites, who can actually afford someone else doing their studying for them? In other words, is there a class element playing into who becomes a client of Martha's and who doesn't?

ME: Well, Martha thought so too at the beginning. Martha thought only rich, spoiled brats are going to be requesting this service. Turns out, yes, they do make up quite a chunk of the clientele, but the majority of clients are actually between 30 and 40 and are working full- or part-time while obtaining their first or second university degree. Of course, this might also be due to the specific fields Martha is working in, such as Social Work and Business Administration, but the majority of Martha's clients were in the midst of obtaining the envisaged higher level of education to correspond with their already professional positions.

Nevertheless, ghostwriting is an expensive service to make use of and Martha is well aware that primarily middle- to upper-class people are able to afford it. I would like to point out here that Martha comes from a working-class background, the first in their nuclear family to obtain a university degree. In fact, Martha has witnessed first-hand the vast difference it makes whether or not one needs to take up loans and work part-time in order to finance one's studies. While course mates of Martha were able to focus solely on their studies, taking up unpaid internships and career-boosting opportunities often offered to them through their family's networks, Martha had to finish the degrees in the standard period of study, in order to not break the student loan regulations. Even though the hurdles for working-class kids to start studying were significantly reduced in the past 30-something years, fundamental hurdles remain for this marginalized group to successfully finish their studies or continue working in academia. And even if working-class children succeed in their academic and professional careers, they usually enter their professional life with substantial debts.

To be honest, I do think a big part of Martha's identity and (future) career is made up of the struggles they encountered by being a working-class child pushing through such an elitist environment. Certainly, they would not have worked as a freelance ghostwriter after finishing a PhD, if it weren't for their working-class background... Yet, I do not mean this by way of pitying Martha; I mention it because I know that Martha actually derives personal and professional grandeur from this fact. Martha's expertise in political economy, paired with a fierce pursuit of feminist and critical scholarship, is deeply rooted in their socialization and upbringing.

I: Thank you for elaborating on Martha's experiences as a ghostwriter and for substituting their stories with some of your own thoughts and feelings. We have nearly reached the allowed count of words for contributing to this edited book, but I would like to direct a final question towards you: What advice would Martha give to other academics considering taking this path?

ME: Well, I think people need to be aware that the freedom of this freelance work – like most others – comes at the cost of quite precarious working conditions, such as no paid vacation, no income guarantee and no paid sick leave. The efficiency level Martha was able to reach during the year of working as an academic ghostwriter, heavily relied on the fact that Martha only worked around 10 hours per week, thus having to pay a relatively small amount of taxes and health insurance. Martha would advise people to draw up an excel calculation chart, which shows the most efficient cut-off points for freelance income considering national tax and healthcare regulations. In Martha's case, this meant that they could earn anything up to 1800 Euros per month (before tax) and anything above 2800 Euros per month (before tax). Anything in between would decrease their net-income to less than below or above these margins.

Other than that, this career is definitely crisis proof since it is foreseeable that the market will keep growing with ever more people obtaining university degrees and ever more professions becoming "professionalized". The job as an academic ghostwriter is particularly suitable for people who enjoy doing academic research without the pressure of sticking to a specific discipline, of producing high-ranked publications, of networking for career building and of acquiring third-party funding for research projects. Furthermore, one can easily try this profession out by starting to work for a single agency. Building and cementing a career as an academic ghostwriter, on the other hand, could very well progress from working for a single agency, to working for multiple agencies, to building your very own web presence for attracting clients and thus cutting out the 50–60% margin, which the agencies earn for taking up the tasks of marketing, payment security and anonymized communication. In any case, Martha feels it is a very nice cushion to fall back on, especially in times of temporary working contracts both within and outside academia.

I: Thank you so much for all this valuable input. I hope that the above might intrigue the readership to think of our shared academic landscapes, our work as scholars, and our positions as always-already researcher and researched a little differently from now on.

Notes

1 For more information on the epistemological roots of this method see: Ettorre, E. (2019) *Autoethnography as Feminist Method*. New York: Taylor & Francis; Crawley, S.L. (2012). Autoethnography as Feminist Self-Interview. In J. F. Gubrium et al. (Eds.), *The Sage Handbook of Interview Research*. Thousand Oaks: Sage Publications, pp. 143–160.
2 For further reading in the field of Black Feminism see: McClaurin, I. (2001). *Black Feminist Anthropology: Theory, Politics, Practice, and Poetics*. New Brunswick: Rutgers University Press; Simmonds, F.N. (1999). My Body, Myself: How Does a Black Woman Do Sociology? In J. Price & M. Shildrick (Eds.), *Feminist Theory and the Body*. New York: Routledge, pp. 50–63.

References

Crawley, S.L. (2012). Autoethnography as Feminist Self-Interview. In J. F. Gubrium et al. (Eds.), *The Sage Handbook of Interview Research*. Thousand Oaks: Sage Publications, pp. 143–160.
Ettorre, E. (2019). *Autoethnography As Feminist Method*. New York: Routledge.
Honan, E. & Bright, D. (2016). Writing a Thesis Differently. *International Journal of Qualitative Studies in Education*, 29(5), 731–743.
Ingold, T. (2016). From Science to Art and Back Again: The Pendulum of an Anthropologist. *Anuac*, 5(1), 5–23.
Mazzei, L. A. (2013). A Voice without Organs: Interviewing in Posthumanist Research. *International Journal of Qualitative Studies in Education*, 26(6), 732–740.
McClaurin, I. (2001). *Black Feminist Anthropology: Theory, Politics, Practice, and Poetics*. New Brunswick: Rutgers University Press.

Phillips, M., Pullen, A., & Rhodes, C. (2014). Writing Organization as Gendered Practice: Interrupting the Libidinal Economy. *Organization Studies*, 353, 313–333.

Pierre, A. S. (2011). Post Qualitative Research: The Critique and the Coming After. In N. K. Denzin & Y. S. Lincoln (Eds.), *The Sage Handbook of Qualitative Research*. 4th ed. Thousand Oaks: Sage Publications, pp. 611–625.

Shiva, V. & Mies, M. (2014). *Ecofeminism*. 2nd ed. New York: Zed Books.

Simmonds, F.N. (1999). My Body, Myself: How Does a Black Woman Do Sociology? In J. Price & M. Shildrick (Eds.), *Feminist Theory and the Body*. New York: Routledge, pp. 50–63.

Środa, M., Rogowska-Stangret, M., & Cielemęcka, O. (2014). A Quest for Feminist Space and Time. *Women: A Cultural Review*, 25(1), 114–122.

UNWAGED AND REPURPOSED

Transitions from accidental to non-institutionalised academic

Ruth Elizabeth Slater

A career reflected 'through a glass (tower) darkly' – the reflected gallery

I see you, my visitor, peering into this gallery. I see you scanning the rough walls and wondering what you will find here. I see you taking in the pictures around the wall. I expect that you think that they are portrayals of significant and worthy people. Ah, yes, you can see that they are portrayals of a place and some people, and you are reading the legends: *The Glass Tower; The Colleague; The Student; The Supervisor.* You seem to be seeking answers to some barely formed questions and quite content to be here. I'll invite you inside.

You squint in the crepuscular half-light and your eyes alight on the cracked mirror at the end of the gallery. I am here but you cannot see me because the shadows envelop me. From the depth of the shadows, my disembodied voice urges you to come closer, step through.

You willingly cross the rift through the grimy glass. The gallery fades behind you and before you, a disordered scene appears of seats, books and papers. You do not see me.

"Well, hello, I'm glad you came and, yes, you are in the right place, especially if you are seeking answers!" I let that salutation drift on the troubling air and then add, "I am glad of the company. I know you want some answers, but I too need to reflect, to turn a mirror on my past working reality".

You step closer and notice the inscription behind me. I can see that you make little sense of it – neither do I; the letters and the statements are in confusion.

I see you fumbling in the half-light for your phone. I interrupt, "If you are going to look that up, then don't bother – it's mirror-writing". My intervention stops you in your tracks so I continue, "I expect it looks almost diabolical to you. I think that is the story of an unconventional academic career. But I am struggling to make sense of it myself".

You move closer to the inscription, then still struggling to make out the words and meanings, give up.

"'Ah!' You are thinking, 'Whoever wrote this is anxious and ill-at-ease; a mind seeking something unattainable and out of reach'".[1] You do not disagree and deafening silence descends again.

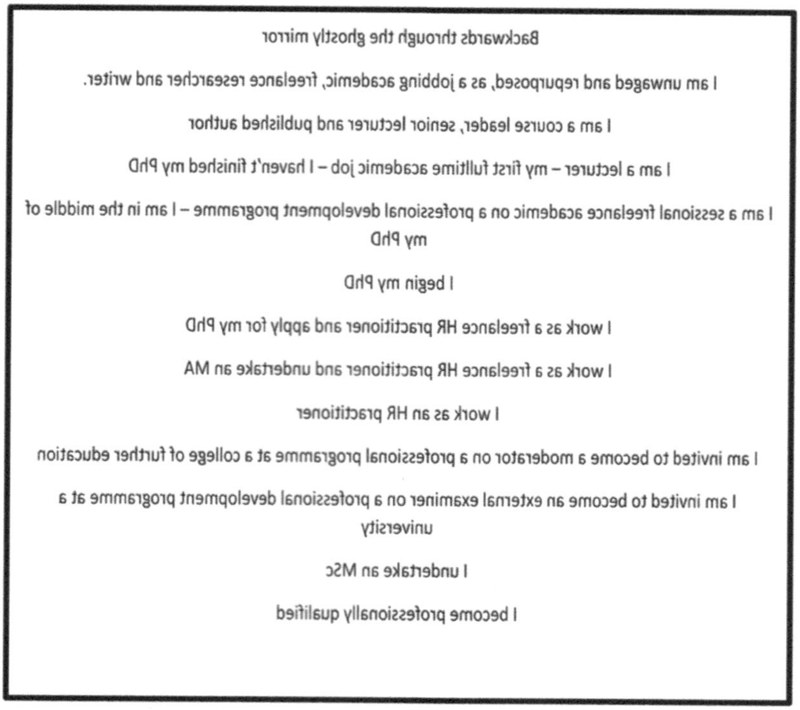

> Backwards through the ghostly mirror
>
> I am unwaged and repurposed, as a jobbing academic, freelance researcher and writer.
>
> I am a course leader, senior lecturer and published author
>
> I am a lecturer – my first fulltime academic job – I haven't finished my PhD
>
> I am a sessional freelance academic on a professional development programme – I am in the middle of my PhD
>
> I begin my PhD
>
> I work as a freelance HR practitioner and apply for my PhD
>
> I work as a freelance HR practitioner and undertake an MA
>
> I work as an HR practitioner
>
> I am invited to become a moderator on a professional programme at a college of further education
>
> I am invited to become an external examiner on a professional development programme at a university
>
> I undertake an MSc
>
> I become professionally qualified

FIGURE 54.1 Mirror writing.

I have the floor so I continue, "You see, I have always been haunted by feelings of inadequacy, never being in the right place or time – the spirit of something good just hangs there but is tantalisingly out of reach".

Time stretches into more painful silence, so I add, "I think I belong in some of the other galleries – not sure I belong here – and I think that is why you cannot see me". You shuffle uncomfortably – I have captured your curiosity; I have my podium! You clear your throat and ask me what I mean.

"Well", I say, "I had only just arrived at where I decided, rather late, I wanted to be and then, I left with slender ritual.[2] You see, over a working life, I've had such a diverse pocketful of jobs and now I'm wondering if I am a master of none. I think that those pictures tell something about my story. But they do not explain why things happened in the way they did. I was hoping being in this reflected gallery might help me make sense of it. Perhaps you can help me'.

The glass tower

In the deepening half-light, you walk over to the pictures on the walls. The first one is a glass tower set in an urban landscape arising from its industrial past; it rises from a collection of buildings of varying age and condition. The glass tower attends to aspiration and modernity. The glass is modern, cheap and available to everyone; it is sharp and upwardly mobile and reflects the goal of contemporary attitudes towards mass qualification.

I can see that you are curious and I say, "It's the place where I used to work. It's a factory for the production of qualifications for which there may be no purpose. In the age of the third-way, there was a goal of mass qualification. But it faltered because it overlooked the journey of curiosity towards citizenship of thinkers and the joy and emancipation of learning".

I pause and then you ask, "But what do you do now?". I think about all the things I have done with my precious time in the months since leaving the glass tower. It is difficult to explain but I try.

"I am unwaged and a repurposed academic who arrived in this glass tower from a career as an organisational professional".

There is awkward silence while I think. The year of leaving turned into a plague year but I have done many of the things I planned to do and I sit here wondering whether I would have achieved them but for the plague. But I digress. You do not need to know that, so I press on.

"You see, I am an accidental academic and I don't belong anywhere. I never did! I would never meet anyone's ideal as an academic".

You sense my despondency and probe a little further: perhaps you are trying to cheer me up.

'So, what *do* you do now?'

"Oh, you know, reading, researching, writing things: things that matter. I keep in touch with former students and colleagues. They use me as a mentor. You can see them keeping me company in this gallery".

I wave my hand but you cannot see it.

"Let's take a closer look because you can help me make sense of all this – my *res gestae*".[3]

We head off in the shadows towards the second picture where an earnest and diligent woman stares back apprehensively.

The colleague

You point and ask "Who is this?"

"That's the ex-colleague who keeps in touch, usually to ask a question. Barely a week passes when she contacts me and we keep acting out the same little play that always goes in the same direction – a back and forth – she seeks advice, I give it based on my supposed and putative experience and knowledge – ha!". I cannot help but laugh but continue, "The virtual dance usually concludes with an exchange of useful material and thanks, but it is a reminder of the collegiality that was missing in action in the glass tower".

"Do you enjoy what you do now, then?" you ask. I think to myself, "So, you are not going to ask me about the lack of collegiality, then?", so I answer, "Who wouldn't? I pick what I do and when I do it. I have *my* ivory tower, the ivory, not the glass, of a lost age where scholarship was slow and focused on research, teaching and pastoral care in orderly measure.[4] I no longer travel long distances to get to work, no longer have to struggle with a blisteringly busy timetable, or cope with rules which privilege the student as a customer at the expense of scholarship".

Still no questions.

The student

You move along and you point to another picture.

"That is a former student who recently asked me whether I missed the university work. I said I did miss the interactions with students like the one we were having at the time. I thought about how I missed the promise of collegiality… except there was not much time for that; there was no time to develop as colleagues. I said that I did not miss half-empty lecture halls, the spoon-feeding, the poor writing, the epidemic of mental health issues, no time, no academic freedom".

I sense I am beginning to sound irritated and tetchy but I press on.

"I knew I was inseparable from the world, bound by many ties to many people. So as I got older and more experienced, I did not want to get into arguments with students or younger colleagues about things which are part of the warp and weft of my history, things which I held dear and saw value in; this was because I suspected that others might not see the point – or worse still be offended! No, I do not miss it. My life is full of novel and interesting things. I now fill my days with writing, researching, and generally doing far more professional development than was ever required by my professional body or my former university … and there is time for my interests too!"

At last, a question!

"Isn't the academy like that now?"

"If you are asking that, I can only think that you are thinking of an academic career yourself. No, education in the academy has become commodified; cheap and undervalued".

I feel my eyes droop, sad for things lost. You cannot see it though as the murk and formless shadows render me still indistinct. I decide to put on a brave façade and brighten up.

"Still", I add, "I had an enjoyable time – for the most part".

You move on tracing the outline of the unsympathetic walls.

The supervisor

Seeing the next picture, a don identifiable by the professorial garb, you ask, as if you already knew, "What is the achievement you are most proud of?"

"Ah, that is the doctorate – the long-awaited opportunity for a scholarship to find answers to things that had long been bothering me".

"Tell me about that".

"I felt that I shouldn't be there – it was a deception; I was a fraud. I spent my time skulking in academic corridors of this very ivory tower. Older than my peers and with baggage to boot, it was a time of loneliness and personal anguish from life events, but the reward and satisfaction were great. I did not always feel supported or understood. And yet, in the library I felt most at home, content and almost joyful – it was like a sweetie shop with so many ideas to choose! Supervisors came and went and I still succeeded. It irks me that I never got the support to publication as a post-doc – I fell between two stools – neither an early career researcher nor someone of great scholarly experience. In the end, I did it all myself! I am sad I never achieved what I could have done, but I am too weary now to return to *any* academic tower'.

The torches on the unyielding stone walls in the dark side of the gallery start to flicker more brightly and unexpectedly you can see my indistinct form quivering this way and that in spectral surges.

Backwards through the ghostly mirror

We re-enter the reality of the gallery through the mirror. The mirror has lost its grime and casts a bright light. It throws the inscription out of its mystery. The phantasm is over and the spectre of the glass tower is gone. As the trappings of materiality reappear, so do I. I must look disarranged to you because that is how I feel.

I am a picture and this is my legend.

---

nearly but not quite

I am unwaged and repurposed, as a jobbing academic, freelance researcher and writer.

I am a course leader, senior lecturer and published author

I am a lecturer – my first full-time academic job – I haven't finished my PhD

I am a sessional freelance academic on a professional development programme – I am in the middle of my PhD

I begin my PhD

I work as a freelance HR practitioner and apply for my PhD

I work as a freelance HR practitioner and undertake an MA

I work as an HR practitioner

I am invited to become a moderator on a professional programme at a college of further education

I am invited to become an external examiner on a professional development programme at a university

I undertake an MSc

I become professionally qualified

This portrait concerns transitions in an academic career which was relatively short-lived, entered into late but with purpose and passion. It describes and illuminates the transitions from accidental to non-institutionalised academic. The life is set against the background of increasing surveillance, targets, micro-management, intensification of academic life.

The subject of this portrait is a white woman in late middle age, a member of the sandwich generation[1]; her lived experience has been dissonant between many identities requiring a type of performativity.

The title of the portrait signified the inner feelings that she always seemed to have been on the verge of something but never really made it. She remains haunted by the spectre of what she has missed and of what she could have been.

FIGURE 54.2 The legend.

You are leaving but ask for advice and I say that if I have learnt anything it concerns belief, purpose, curiosity and the need to have a pair of scissors to hand to rip up the canvas of the expectations imposed by others.

There is always time for some rethinking and some fitting in – some shapeshifting and that is what I have done.

You move towards the door, stop and stoop – you have found it! My scraps of wisdom:

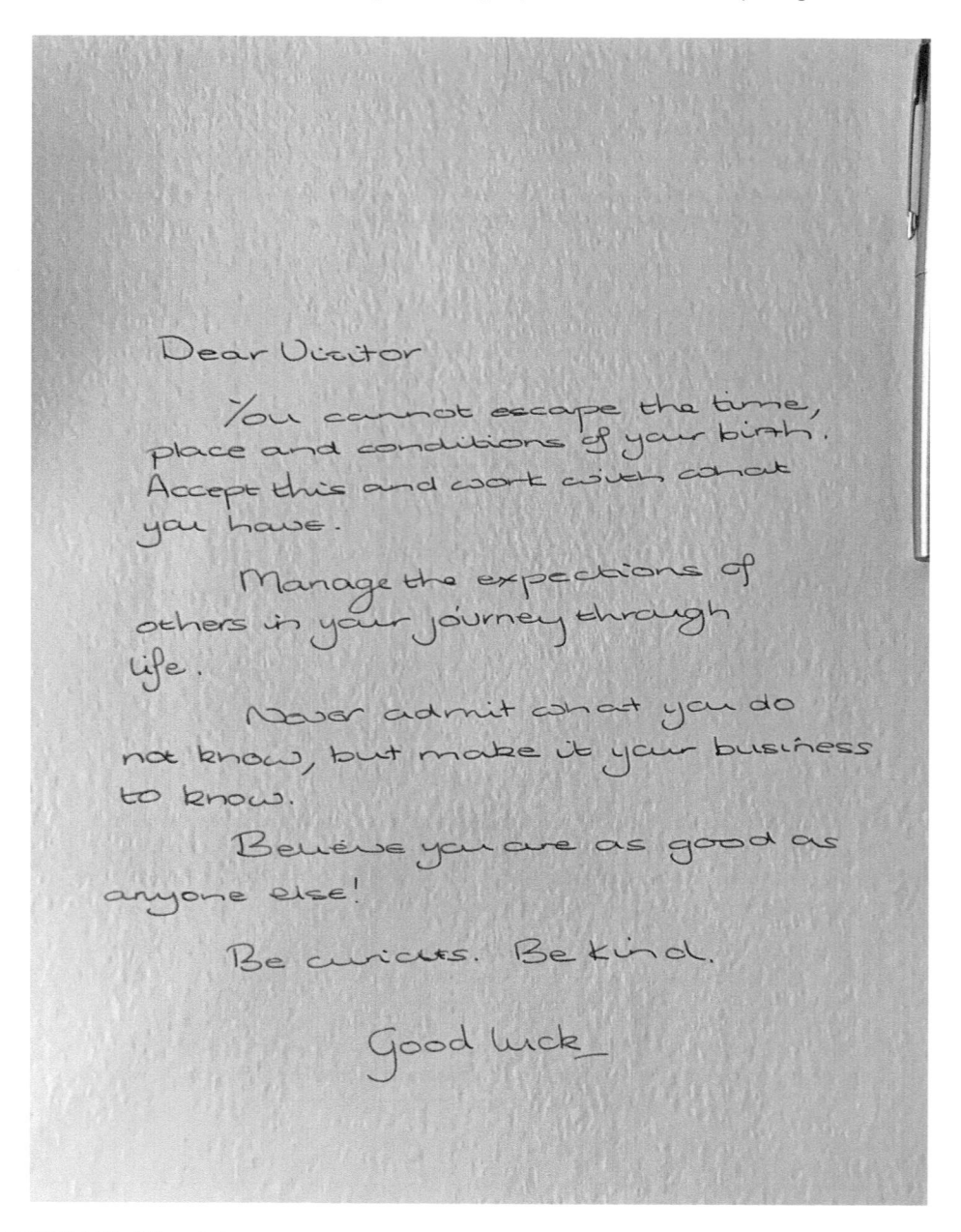

> Dear Visitor
>
> You cannot escape the time, place and conditions of your birth. Accept this and work with what you have.
>
> Manage the expectations of others in your journey through life.
>
> Never admit what you do not know, but make it your business to know.
>
> Believe you are as good as anyone else!
>
> Be curious. Be kind.
>
> Good luck

FIGURE 54.3 The advice.

Notes

1 Writing letters backward and in reverse order, sometimes called mirror writing, may be a sign of a deteriorating brain, but in one woman's case, researchers found that the unusual condition was actually caused by anxiety. https://www.livescience.com/48703-backward-mirror-writing-anxiety.html#:~:text=Writing%20letters%20backward%20and%20in%20reverse%20order%2C%20sometimes,the%20unusual%20condition%20was%20actually%20caused%20by%20anxiety.
2 I left the university under a voluntary redundancy programme – it was a cost-saving exercise – it seemed to favour the university rather than the staff or students; as a professional, I wanted to stay to see my students through the programme, but the university wanted everyone to leave within the first semester. My choice had been driven by personal reasons concerning the ill-health of a spouse, long travelling distances and bereavement.
3 Res gestae (Latin) The achievements. Emperor Augustus died in AD14 and he entrusted several documents to the Vestal Virgins in the Temple of Vesta in the Roman Forum. One of these documents detailed all the achievements of the Emperor which he wanted to be recorded in bronze tablets for his mausoleum. They are self-congratulatory and propaganda. P. A. Brunt and J. M. Moore (eds) 1967. *Res gestae Divi Augusti*, Oxford University Press.
4 Mountz, A., Bonds, A., Mansfield, B., Loyd, J., Hyndman, J., Walton-Roberts, M., ... & Curran, W. (2015). For slow scholarship: A feminist politics of resistance through collective action in the neoliberal university. *ACME: An International Journal for Critical Geographies*, 14(4), 1235–1259.

Reference

Mountz, A., Bonds, A., Mansfield, B., Loyd, J., Hyndman, J., Walton-Roberts, M.,... & Curran, W. (2015). For slow scholarship: A feminist politics of resistance through collective action in the neoliberal university. *ACME: An International Journal for Critical Geographies*, 14(4), 1235–1259.

THE REDUNDANT ACADEMIC

Am I academic, or am I still an academic?

Mark Hughes

Introductions

My name is Emily Play,[1] and I'm a Senior Research Fellow on the *Doing Academic Careers Differently* research council funded project. As one part of the larger project, I work with a small team of qualitative researchers exploring the lived experience of academics leaving academia. We have been conducting a series of in-depth research interviews over the past 18 months. One of my research subjects was Mark Hughes (referred to subsequently as MH). My research focusses on identity (see Play, 2014). The usual research anonymity has been impossible because our subjects' identities were often embedded in their publications and public activities. I do want to acknowledge that I have minimal interest/expertise in organizational change which is MH's academic passion.

We have papers based on the *Doing Academic Careers Differently* project under review with leading academic journals. So, when MH asked if I would write this chapter, I was very reticent. I knew that a chapter as a tangible output, might calm down my excitable *Head of School*, but that wasn't quite enough for me. It was when MH explained that I was the best person to capture my observations of his academic identity that he convinced me. He claimed to have been swimming around in a sea of social constructionism for a little too long. He said that even imagining the frame around the portrait he had found challenging. The lengthy semi-structured research interviews I had conducted, confirmed that his 'world view' had recently become increasingly unorthodox.

The awkward bit was that he wanted an informal, but most of all, candid portrait, not a flattering picture. I was very uneasy, he was a bloke twice my age and putting it politely, I did not share his 'world view'. In the research project, the safety net had been that I didn't have to share my impressions with him, just to listen and record non-judgementally. It was probably a mistake to turn for guidance to my Principal Investigator. It transpired she was also a big fan of 'tangible outputs', she lost me when she started going on about alternative creative research engagement metrics.

The breakthrough came when MH suggested that I was the artist, the portrait could be as partial as I wanted it to be. I appreciated that I could sidestep his obsessive and slightly boring interests in Arsenal FC and composting. The idea of telling a very particular story of the social identity threat of MH leaving academia, and the way he had responded seemed interesting. We agreed that I would write the chapter entirely independently. MH would have sight of it, but for information rather than his editing, before I sent it to the Editors. At times I was more honest than I would have liked to have been, but that was one of MH's pre-requisites. Upon completion, MH read the chapter and thanked me, sincerely I think, for my honesty. Subsequently, Faye and I were due to go with him to a Mogwai concert in Brighton, but Covid-19 stopped that little adventure and so much more.

MH volunteered for redundancy and departed the Business School at which he had worked for over three decades on the 31st July 2019. He initially worked with undergraduates and students on professional courses, but for most of his career, he worked with postgraduates on campus and with organizations off-campus. He specialized in organizational change and the theories and practices of managing and leading such changes. At our first research interview meeting, he showed me some of the books he had written. I was aware of these because we always request CVs before the research interviews. There was something about the physical artefacts which seemed essential to him, almost as if he needed to hold something real, and he wanted me to see something real. The other odd memory I have of our first meeting was when he introduced himself as having just turned 57 years old. I am not sure why it was important to him? I remembered my little niece making a big thing about nearly being seven years old. So, I guess, we grapple with time in different ways at different stages of our lives.

My experience of the interviews with him was similar to wading into a swimming pool, starting shallow and going deeper. While this is the norm in conducting this type of research interview, the final interviews went very deep. As my niece says, 'scary deep'. In painting a portrait, I want to major on these awkward deeper aspects as I feel these are the best ways to convey residual aspects of academic identity and how he had creatively responded to identity threat. At times I thought that he was transitioning into a life beyond academia; at other times, I felt he was unable to let go of his academic identity, I remain undecided. In what follows, we have my initial attempts to understand MH in terms of the identity literature. Our in-person interviews were then interrupted by the government-imposed lockdown, but the story of Zoom and the shielding adventure illustrates MH searching for meaning.

He increasingly appeared to inhabit another self-constructed world. I playfully labelled it Marky-World, a label he intensely disliked, unfortunate given that it features in the title of our forthcoming *Organization Studies* paper. If we think metaphorically, he seemed to have created this intellectual playground, which amused him, but as I will explain later, I am not sure how many others enjoyed the fairground rides. We are still relatively shallow, until he takes me to *The Graveyard of Disappointed Hope*, the place some of his unpublished papers go to rest in peace. As I delve deeper, I realize how this graveyard is another part of his alternative academic world. However, it is the notebooks he left behind, which best portray his increasingly liminal/dubious academic identity. These troubling notebooks were to make me question my own academic identity. I conclude with questions for myself about doing academic practice differently.

Am I academic, or am I still an academic?

My early interviews with MH had been about gathering background information and developing rapport. I enjoyed the train journeys down to Brighton, invariably visiting the quirky shops in the North Laines before or after the interviews. Thankfully on this project, the interviews did not have to be too structured. We wanted to understand the unique lived experiences of these end of career academics. However, we had agreed as a research team that we would initially explore academic identity issues with subjects using some standardized frameworks from the literature. I sensitively started with Alvesson's (2010) seven academic self-images. We both agreed that the storyteller identity was the best fit for MH. He even asked me to email him the reference, so that he could read the full paper.

I was very aware in the first interview of how he was crafting a personal narrative of his academic self and how real this self-image was to him. My unease was around how he would accommodate redundancy into this personal narrative, how would he maintain order as this personal narrative began to disappear? I didn't raise this concern at this early stage. I was sad that MH and some of the other research subjects had signed legally binding non-disclosure agreements in exchange for financial settlements. He did reveal that any criticism of institutional management was the main restriction placed on him. I felt that there was 'stuff' MH and other subjects wanted to talk through, but they were legally prohibited. It left me cold that universities could behave in such a way. MH and the other research subjects seemed to accept the instrumental nature of their exchange, but I wondered whatever happened to the belief in Socratic questioning?

Emboldened by the application of Alvesson (2010), I introduced the Knights and Clarke (2014) framework. I had a pre-text here, in that the research team were particularly interested in the insecurity issues around academic identities. MH dismissed the imposter form suggesting, I felt slightly cynically, that it might be more applicable to somebody working in an old university. We discussed the aspirant form, but he didn't seem convinced. He claimed to have been chuffed to have become a Reader but aspiring to that role had come to him relatively late in his academic career. He noted that at that time, all his peers aspired to be Professors, but that was not for him. He did become serious at this point, acknowledging that the Reader title was one of the few things he missed in his post-institutional life. However, he claimed to relish his self-defined Former Reader title.

I could feel him drifting back to the world of Alvesson (2010) as he crafted this very personal narrative. So, I interrupted and introduced the third of Knights and Clarke's (2014) forms – the existentialist. I had a suspicion that this might resonate, and it did. He conceded that he had recently been grappling with what was real and what was meaningless. Looking pointedly towards me, he had asked – 'am I academic or am I still an academic'? I reassured him that he was still an academic, yet I was mindful that the research project team wanted to understand the experiences of exiting academia. He walked me to the railway station from the centre of Brighton, which was sweet, although I had wanted to take in the North Laines, they would keep for another day.

Zoom and the shielding adventure

I had my train ticket from London to Brighton booked. However, when the Covid-19 pandemic lockdown was imposed, face to face interviews were no longer possible. Some of the research team were on fixed-term research contracts, so we would continue interviewing using Zoom. I was glad I had met MH a couple of times because some rapport had developed, which would have been difficult going straight into Zoom interviews.

During our only Zoom interview, MH explained that the immunosuppressant medication he was taking required him to shield (go into strict social isolation). He seemed more animated than previously and so I decided to ask some very open questions. He went on about the shielding, which I felt wasn't relevant to the research project. I decided to humour him, and as it transpired, I was glad that I did. The government had emphasized that they would target resources for the elderly and vulnerable through health practitioners identifying patients to go onto a list of approximately 2.5 million of the most at risk people. He hadn't been included, and seemed very philosophical, acknowledging that there were far needier cases than himself. He checked the health websites, discovering he was classed as a two. Only those classed as a three were high-risk and needed to shield. Acknowledging that he wasn't very quantitative, he had been reassured by this ranking system. He also joked that he hadn't been convinced by evidence-based management, but he was less inclined to question evidence-based medicine.

Hospital doctors had always impressed upon him that the medicine they prescribed, and he injected switched off his immune system. Explaining that doubts remained, he found himself wondering why he was not classified as high risk? Six weeks after the original shielding letters were sent out, he received a letter from the government telling him to shield as he was at high risk. He wondered what had changed. He had a suspicion that the timing of the shielding letter was close to his latest hospital medicine prescription, but what had changed? A high mortality rate, or a policy change?

He used his academic skills to search the internet. In particular, he went through papers accepted for publication, but not fully published, in respected medical journals. He found the answers to his questions in a journal called *Clinical Medicine*. It was a pre-publication paper authored by the clinical staff who had drawn up the criteria for the list of rheumatology patients included on the overall shielding list. They explained that initially, they wanted the patients on the immunosuppressant medicine for clinical reasons to be classified as high risk. However, there was a government-imposed limit on the numbers of people included on this list, so not all patients could be included. While the resource limitations were understandable, messaging to these patients that they were not at high-risk for MH was unforgivable.

I initially thought MH had been so isolated in lockdown that he just needed to talk, and I think he did. But I began to appreciate why MH had wanted to share this saga with me. It looped back to Alvesson (2010), and the paranoia Knights and Clarke (2014) highlighted. His shielding adventure was about being an academic once more and answering questions, which in this instance had real-life consequences. He also questioned the government rhetoric of following the evidence and how they framed knowledge. This questioning wasn't new to me, but I remember thinking that he seemed to be implying something else, something closer to academia, which he would reveal subsequently.

Thrills and adventures in Marky-World

The lockdown had ended, and it was good to be on the Brighton train once more. One of the standard questions we had been asking all research subjects was how they coped with the loss of their carefully cultivated 'research profiles' and digital presence. MH smiled and then asked me to go to woodlanddecay.com on my research laptop. Using WordPress, he had created a personal site. The site included the ingredients of a business school staff page, details of publications, contact details and social media links. There were many posts on organizational change, but he also appeared to include anything that took his fancy.

He explained that he had begun to develop this digital presence even when still working at the business school, smiling he said 'think Colditz'. He suggested he disliked institutional templates and edicts around what to say and how to say it. He went on a bit of a tangent telling me that apparently on early university sites they had prominent staff search engines on their home pages so that you could search for academics. He witnessed the decline of these facilities with 'traffic' directed towards student course registrations or purchasing academic services.

I have this stereotype of organizational change as excessive, shiny and sleazy, and drenched in discourses of excellence and performance. Consequently, I was genuinely curious when I asked – why woodland decay? Smiling, he explained, that he loved the simple natural metaphor of the interplay between the old and new. He also conceded that he loved nature and that nature currently made more sense to him than the organizational world. He liked the subversion of the label, being the antithesis of most people's stereotype of organizational change, ouch I thought to myself.

He claimed that woodlanddecay.com now reached way beyond this site and suggested that I visit one of the posts. The post title was Woodland Decay Broadcasting. Yes, you guessed it – he was broadcasting to the nation via YouTube. Hesitantly, I said could we have a look and there he was merrily reviewing academic books sat beneath a tree, in the middle of a wood. I couldn't help noticing the viewing figures were very low. It seemed indiscrete to comment on the viewing figures. Oddly, I had the feeling viewing figures were not his objective. He seemed to be parodying the impression management of large universities with these playful and very amateurish productions.

As we talked, he was smiling, and I tried to gauge how serious he was about this enterprise. He said, 'enterprise' was the wrong term; he neither expected to make money nor did making the videos cost him money. He conceded that they were resource-intensive in terms of time, but these days it was his choice how he spent his time. I still wasn't sure if this self-curated world he was revealing was serious or humorous? I am not sure if he knew.

He spotted that I was trying to process all of what he was sharing with me and ironically said 'and there is more, we have a publishing wing'. He suggested that we check out his Amazon author page, and again I found another of his self-curated worlds. Among the more familiar titles that I recognized from his CV, there were three self-published notebooks which had not been on his CV.

> No.1 How they framed organizational change failure.
> No.2 How they constructed change leadership.
> No.3 Did I really claim that organizational change tends to fail?

It was as I read the titles that I was glad we were doing this interview at a very public Brighton seafront café. These notebook titles hinted at academic paranoia. That film, *A Beautiful Mind,* flashed through my thoughts. I feared that what MH lacked in terms of the John Nash status he might be compensating for in this self-curated world.

I felt very uncomfortable with the academic wonderland that MH had created, but equally, I was mindful that we were meeting as a researcher and research subject. I regret the next question I asked, with hindsight I see now that he was sharing his world with me, however odd it was, it was his world. I asserted – 'what if all of this is nonsense, you seem to have taken on all the academically valuable editorial roles now in your self-editing, where are the reality and validity checks?' He went quiet, retreating into the existentialism (Knights and Clarke, 2014) we had discussed in an earlier interview.

We sat quietly for a few moments, and then he recomposed himself and delved into his small rucksack. He withdrew copies of the three notebooks and offered them to me as a gift. I explained that organizational change wasn't my thing, but they now seemed to have taken on the role of some kind of symbolic peace offering, and this was awkward. As I leafed through them, he suggested one of the joys of self-publishing books was that you could give them away at minimal cost, which I knew was very different from traditionally published books. The books had been carefully formatted and with arty covers featuring different illuminations of Brighton Pavilion. I did like the covers. He explained that one of his joys at the end of his career had been reclaiming his labour process. He found it fascinating learning first-hand the different skills required in publishing, formatting, editing and video production, and I believed him. When MH went to buy us more coffees, I wanted to check my phone, but I felt feigning interest in these notebooks might be a kinder act.

The graveyard of disappointed hope

When he returned, I even had a notebook related question for him 'so why do each of your notebooks end with an *Appendix* called '*The graveyard of disappointed hope?*' I wasn't feigning interest at this point, imagining this as an excellent title for that *Critical Management Studies* conference paper we were writing on the tyranny of writing for publication. Initially, he said in a resigned way, you know, those papers that never quite make it through the journal review process, it is the place they go to, to die. I told him that I knew that place and that I had suffered such painful bereavement more than once. He reached over and found a quotation in one of the notebooks:

> Even disappointed hope wanders around agonizing, a ghost that has lost its way back to the cemetery and clings to refuted images.
> *(Bloch, 1995: 195)*

He told me that he had turned to Bloch's (1995) famous *The Principle of Hope* at a moment of academic despair earlier in his career. Perversely, the three-volume encyclopaedia of human hoping had been one of the most depressing things he ever read. That said, the book had made a big impression on him.

He explained that in writing the notebooks, he wanted to offer a resting place for some of his papers that had not made it through journal review processes. He didn't need to remind me about the time, emotion, and hope that we invest in journal submissions. Papers intended to be revised and resubmitted, at some point, to another journal with better taste and better reviewers. But instead, these ghosts of writings wander around agonizing, clinging to that belief that they contain something worth publishing.

I asked about the purpose of the graveyard and how it worked? He explained that the Latin derivation of publication was 'publicare', which meant to make public. Through inclusion in the self-published notebooks, these papers were made public. The notebooks were a reflection/meditation on 30 years inhabiting academia, the idea for the graveyard had arisen out of these thought processes. He didn't expect or need any readers, just like some gravestones receive very few visitors. Choosing each paper to be included as an appendix for each notebook was enjoyable. He conceded that there were quite a few potential candidates for his graveyard. I did like the ritual and symbolism of this graveyard and thanked him for letting me use the title for our conference paper. That said, I left the interview feeling quite sad. A bit like the smell you get from a pub, if you pass it early the next day. A deflated sense of after the party, which never quite sparked and a smell of stale beer and urine. After the interview, I had planned to go to the North Laines; I was no longer in the mood.

The notebooks that he left behind

Our final interview took place in Kew Gardens. I didn't get to revisit the North Laines, but I was grateful for the significantly reduced commuting time. We needed to talk about the notebooks as they were something he had pointedly left behind (not just metaphorically). These notebooks didn't interest me, and he knew that, but they did play a role in framing his final narrative (Alvesson, 2010) and keeping his existential fears (Knights and Clarke, 2014) at bay. Would these notebooks be sufficient to alleviate his lost academic identity? I was doubtful, and the appropriate research question was to ask him what he was trying to say through these notebooks.

I had touched on his specialist subject, and I was glad we were doing the interview in a quiet part of Kew Gardens. He seemed to come to life in trying to persuade me about the unacknowledged misrepresentation of organizational change. Throughout the interviews, I had thought of him as a nice old bloke with some issues. Now, as he passionately talked, he seemed to become younger. It isn't easy to put into words, but his passion reassured me about my own academic identity. I don't have the recordings here at home, as I am writing this, but from memory, this is my best effort at summarizing the three notebooks.

No.1 *How they framed organizational change failure*

His academic moment had been questioning a 70 per cent organizational change failure rate (Hughes, 2011). Up until that point, most academics, including the professors, had cited this 'statistic', because it emanated from *Harvard Business School*. In his subsequent search for meaning, he wanted to know why Harvard and other business schools were claiming organizational change failed as it was big business for them. His epiphany had been that they were framing managing change as failing, to encourage belief in leading change. He hadn't been able to convince anyone else of this framing. I feared that we were back in his graveyard of disappointed hope. However, he seemed proud that in some small way, he had questioned the belief promoted by many respected academics that organizational change tended to fail.

No.2 *How they constructed change leadership*

In recent years he had been reviewing literature informing the shift towards change leadership and leading change. He had been unable to find the academic theories/research to support this shift. He believed that change leadership was an ideal type, which academics now erroneously perceived as an empirical reality. He felt there had been a discourse/

narrative shift as much as an empirical shift. Journal editors had suggested he look harder. There was a bit more, but I was reflecting on how objectionable the *Head of School* was after attending that leadership development course, and I missed it.

No.3 Did I really claim that organizational change tends to fail?

There was an odd twist in the story with the third notebook. He explained that he had submitted a paper to a Special Issue of *Human Relations* on framing organizational change failure. In his dreams, this was to be his capstone, and then he could retire into his gardening sunset. Sadly, his submission was desk rejected. It transpired that this was the catalyst for writing the two notebooks. They were his reflections on debates which had fascinated him for decades. He had thought he might do another notebook, perhaps on technological change, which increasingly frustrated him. I began to appreciate, these were free writing notebooks but made public.

The catalyst for writing the third notebook had been the *Human Relations* Special Issue editorial. His 2011 paper featured prominently in the editorial; the odd twist was that his 2011 paper was now cited as the primary evidence that organizational change tends to fail. He paused at this point to ensure that I appreciated the irony. In a special issue on framing change failure, he now believed that he had been framed for the failure of organizational change.

I did get the irony, though I was confident that the *Human Relations* Guest Editors wouldn't have gotten it wrong. More likely that MH had misunderstood the subtle nuances of the editorial. I perceived the third notebook as 'and another thing' type therapy, sad but harmless. It did oddly echo his belief that the organizational change failure debate was largely rhetorically informed and framed, rather than theory/research-informed as most academics believed.

I tried to move our conversation on from his specialist subject, asking what he valued most in his academic career. His response was swift – autonomy. Even at the bottom of the academic hierarchy back in the eighties, academics had had so much more independence. Gradually autonomy was eroded over the decades. He claimed to be loving his newfound freedom to write and film whatever he wanted, whenever he wanted and wherever he wanted, and I believed him. At this point, as it had started to rain, we decided to conclude the final interview and say our goodbyes.

About a month later, I was writing up the research project case study based on MH. I was very uneasy with his comments about the Special Issue. In instrumental terms, *Human Relations* was one of the target journals the *Head of School* highlighted at that very heavy 'performance metrics' staff seminar. I wanted to tread carefully and also to look at the evidence myself. There was a vast gulf in quality between Hughes (2011) and Schwarz et al. (2021). But he didn't claim that organizational change tends to fail; to me, he did seem to argue the opposite. I pragmatically fudged this perceived contradiction when I wrote up the case study.

Today, as I finish this portrait, something haunts me. As I write, I wish that I still didn't hear his excitable claims from our last meeting in Kew Gardens; he seemed so animated. All we know for sure is that he left behind those notebooks. Are they a postscript to an academic career of disappointed hope clinging to refuted images, or are they his legacy in critically questioning our sacred assumptions about knowledge?

Doing academic practice differently

We use word collages to convey research findings during the project seminar presentations succinctly. By way of conclusion, I want to share some of the words that I used when recently presenting an MH case study word collage. These concepts surfaced in our research interviews. I have added the questions that these concepts raised for myself about doing academic practice differently. I share these questions with a large caveat that many of MH's 'freedoms' were a by-product of escaping academia.

Orthodoxy – I challenge orthodoxy in my writing, but how often do I challenge academic orthodoxy?
Autonomy – Do I embrace my autonomy, or do I surrender my autonomy?
Passion – I have been very successful in writing for publication, but am I passionate about what I write?
Freewriting – Would a little freewriting enable me to write more creatively?
Bereavement – I invest time, hope and emotions into papers, but do I deal with rejection emotions?
Time – My lifespan is finite; am I making conscious choices about how I choose to use my time?

Acknowledgement

Thank you to Alexandra Bristow for a constructive, caring and collegiate review of the draft chapter. Emily (aka Mark) remains fully responsible for anything contentious.

Note

1 The submission to ASQ was desk rejected, the research project funding bid was unsuccessful, Emily does not exist. Everything else is real, or at least I think it is real.

References

Alvesson, M. (2010). Self-doubters, strugglers, storytellers, surfers and others: Images of self-identities in organization studies. *Human Relations*, 63(2): 193–217.
Bloch, E. (1995) *The Principle of Hope*. Translated by N. Plaice, S. Plaice, and P. Knight. Cambridge: The MIT Press.
Hughes, M. (2011). Do 70 per cent of all organizational change initiatives really fail? *Journal of Change Management*, 11(4): 451–464.
Knights, D. and Clarke, C.A. (2014). It's a bittersweet symphony, this life: Fragile academic selves and insecure identities at work. *Organization Studies*, 35(3): 335–357.
Play, C.E. (2014). Identity: It's a great big tragedy. *Administrative Science Quarterly*, 20(12): 423–454.
Schwarz, G.M., Bouckenooghe, D. and Vakola, M. (2021). Organizational change failure: Framing the process of failing. *Human Relations*, 74(2): 159–179.

EXIT VIA THE GIFT SHOP

Olivier Ratle, Sarah Robinson, and Alexandra Bristow

If you want to avoid the gift shop, you can escape via the fire exit. However, you may wish to read on before you make that decision. The gift shop is a collective endeavour by the editors and authors of this book. The initial idea came from Mark Stringer during one of our Zoom conversations with contributors, the purpose of which was to share thoughts for chapter and book development. The idea grew from there. The shelves in this shop have been stocked by our authors as well as editors. Fittingly, the gifts on offer are as eclectic as the rest of the exhibition. If you choose to stay and browse, you may well find something to further provoke or inspire you, or at least make you smile.

Looking around the gift shop is another opportunity to reflect on the portraits in the exhibition. What were you drawn to and why? What can you afford? What is a little bit out of your reach and why? What do you find distasteful? What are you going to take away? It is also another opportunity to consider the nature of academia and academic careers. Within the gift shop, tensions and contradictions abound. There is a tension between the shop and the gifts, consumerism, and the gift economy, the richness of academic life and its impoverishment through commercialisation. There is tension in the question mark over whether this gift shop does not in fact sell anything, or whether, conversely, everything inside it is for sale (and very expensive). And, in the meandering movement towards the exit, there is a tension between academic careers as a drive or flight towards *vacating* the premises vis-à-vis the lingering sense of *vocation*.

You might experience some familiarity on entering the gift shop, as the senses are assaulted by the sights, sounds, and smells common to gift shops everywhere. There is plenty of the usual fare on display, much of the merchandise featuring items related to the galleries and the exhibits: posters, canvases, signed copies, and originals, as well as mugs, coasters, mousepads, vases, scarves, tea towels, notebooks, pencils, pens, and so on. However, if you persevere through the aisles, you will also begin to encounter more unusual items and displays.

Starting from your left, the wall is lined with *bookshelves*, full of many offerings, including a book of portraits and paintings entitled 'An Academic Career Is…'. Each image within this book reflects different perspectives on an academic career (e.g., an academic career is a journey (featuring a map), an academic career is random (a cubist painting), an academic career is a pattern (geometric shapes), and an academic career is reflection (a mirror)). This book by Sama and colleagues is (at the point of writing) exclusive to this gift shop and populated with the authors' and readers' collective imagination.

Next, you spot an edited book by Rune Todnem By, Bernard Burnes, and Mark Hughes (2023) on 'Organizational Change, Leadership and Ethics'. This book is part of Mark Hughes' ghostly endeavours. It has a particularly poignant ending, concluding with a chapter entitled 'Towards intelligent disobedience: academics leading by example'. Also eye-catching are several books recommended by exhibitors, including one titled 'Art Matters: Because Your Imagination Can Change the World' (Gaiman, 2018) and another called Notes to Self (Fine, 2019), with the chapter entitled 'This is not on the exam' particularly endorsed.

Next to the bookshelves there is a *computer* where you can access relevant articles and websites. Currently the screen is showing an article by Jesus Rodriguez-Pomeda and Fernando Casani (2022) on 'The contemporary university: some ontological and empirical aspects'.

Opposite the bookshelves and the computer, you will find a display with *hobby, art and stationary supplies* labelled provocatively by Hoppe and colleagues: 'supplies for frivolous activities that have no space in the streamlined, neoliberal academia'. If you have been inspired by Russ Vince's reflexive journal practice, you may wish to pick up a moleskin sketchbook and some Winsor & Newton watercolour marker pens here. Knitting needles and gardening supplies are also available.

As you get deeper into the shop, you discover the *corner of curiosities*, jam-packed with oddball knick-knacks, and artefacts. There is Ruth Slater's cracked mirror and a parting note.

There is also a gold framed pocket mirror reflecting struggles and challenges (known all too well by you and others), and, signed by Stephen Linstead, an inflatable banana (which you can blow so big that you can hide behind it) that does not have a slippery skin. Next to the banana, you can pick up a (non-hairy) bag of boiled sweets (or two bags, if you fancy the 'buy one get one free' offer), and a gift voucher for a driving lesson. There is also a puzzle of linked chains that you must unlink to 'free' the order of things, and a magnetic collage where you can arrange the pieces in different ways to come up with different forms or pictures (these come recommended by Sama and colleagues). Close by, on a multi-hat stand, there is a collection of funny hats selected by Sarah Stookey. Her accompanying note explains that when we inhabit academic spaces, we need to resist the pressures and urges to conform. Instead, the note says, we should celebrate our differentness, and that there is liberation in being ourselves, inside or outside 'the house'. Above it all proudly hangs a protest banner contributed by Oscar Javier Montiel Méndez, Duncan Pelly, and Araceli Almaraz, accompanied in solidarity by a PhD hat and sword from the Finnish tradition symbolising the freedom of research and the fight for what is good, right, and true (donated by Ann Armstrong).

Deepest in the curiosities corner, there is a display of various escape devices – keys, parachutes, skateboards (another offering by Sarah Stookey). These are a reminder that you can *leave* academia, because sometimes our quirky heroism just does not work out. You might also consider picking up the key labelled *'to the back door'* and head towards the back of the gift shop. If you wish to unlock this door you will find yourself in a bar with a bunch of 'misfit' friends welcoming you to the family.

If instead you continue to browse the gift shop (or come back to it after the trip to the bar), you will find a *self-care display*, which includes a pile of self-care packages brought back from the bushland by Ahuja and colleagues. Hidden among the packages, 'resilience' is provided in the form of easily ingested liquid with a note round the neck of the bottle from Hoppe and colleagues: 'almost like liquid courage just not quite'. Alongside it (and from the same source), sits an array of lotions to be applied copiously to the entire body. Doing an academic career differently is ultimately an embodied experience, and the whole body needs to be inoculated against the harsh, homogenous academic reality.

Further along, there are wooden boxes separated into sections with dividers and filled with different kinds of pebbles. On closer inspection you find a note from Mark Saunders encouraging you to differentiate between gift shop junk and gift shop gems. Among the junk, he says, you will find perfectly formed pebbles to practise skimming with. While these are enticing (and expensive), if you purchased them, you could never get them to skip because they had been created by someone else and so do not fit with who you are. Also among the gift shop junk, he says, is time, because you cannot really buy it but have to make your own. On the other hand, among the gift shop gems there are 'vantage points from which to view the academic pond, skip pebbles and see the ripples and reflections along with the time to muse and meditate upon what they might or could mean'. Even more important are 'critical friends to comment constructively on the utility of the pebbles we choose to try and make skip and act as a sounding board on our own reflections and, crucially, to share our pebble skipping success and failures as we meander through academia'. The vantage points and critical friends are, of course, priceless. The pebble boxes share their display with other equipment for engaging with and appreciating the great outdoors, including native pot plants, a Sydney bush walking guide, gardening tools and seeds, and sunscreen.

The gardening display also marks the beginning of the place where the gift shop opens up into a *hands-on section*. Here you can reflect on and share your own gift of stories of marginalisation, trauma, delight, wonder, and love of academia and beyond, through poetry, song, dance, art, writing, and other means of expression. It is a meeting place and a restorative space in the style of Sama and colleagues, with comfortable chairs dotted around tables with essential oils diffusers, soft rugs, and a small staging area. It is a starting point for many individual and collective experiences: from reading and talking to walking, swimming, running, cycling, playing, building, and creating. To facilitate the above, set in its own secluded niche, there is also what looks like an airport-style security body scanner, except that this one is opaque and glowing dark purple, with faint sparks floating inside. Instructions pinned to the wall next to it announce it to be a time and space machine for academic transformation, and for finding your own exit and entrance to alternative academic careers. It can take you to multiple other places made up of human and non-human bodies, to contexts that are life affirming, and spaces that are mind-bogglingly different, including other gift shops that are empty and have no walls.

Just to the side there is a fortune teller's tent. Peep inside and on the table next to the crystal ball and tarot cards you will find a handwritten note:

> Whatever future is held by the cards, it looks bright. Your visit to the Hall of Mirrors today has shown you that there are more of you. One of you in every mirror, reflected back and forth into the thousands. Growing exponentially for every mirror added

and every new person who visits. You can leave this place feeling calm and reassured. We're heading for better times. Signed: The Misfits.

Past the hands-on section, you will find a rotating *postcard stand*, where you can choose a card featuring a design to your liking, whether it be poignant, humorous, or artistic. Next to the postcards, there is a magnetic board, where you can leave comments, reactions, updates, and even some *'suggestions on a postcard'*. Some notes are already displayed there. Among them, there are takeaways and policy suggestions for university deans, for recruitment, promotion, and evaluation committees, and for research funders. You spot a note from Adrián Zicari with a suggestion for a more balanced view when recruiting and evaluating faculty. Without compromising academic standards, he says, schools would do well in having faculty coming from different backgrounds, and sometimes with professional, entrepreneurial, and NGO experience. There are also more personal notes and photographs on the board, including one of a happy-looking Jaime Bayona, with an added note from Jaime that he 'is currently fine, doing road trips around the country with his son, doing meditation, and enjoying work and life'.

When you get to the *tills* (these seem to be Schrödinger's tills, simultaneously closed and operating), you can select a tote bag featuring exhibits and quotes from the galleries, so that you can carry all your souvenirs and ideas from the book.

On the way out of the shop, there is a door marked *'Lost Property'* with a mirrored window that lets you peer into the room. There is a note stuck to the door in Mark Hughes' writing, which reads as follows:

> This room contains assorted business consultants we found wandering around aimlessly in their shiny suits and incessantly playing with their smartphones. Please do not enter the room as it tends to provoke them into jabbering about B2B, CRM and KPI and going on about something they call their Kotter. They are taking up valuable space which we would like to repurpose as a creche or as a resource hub. If nobody claims them by the end of the month, we plan to humanely downsize all of them to free up this valuable space.

And finally, just before you leave, dear visitor, please stop at the *membership desk* located by the exit. Sign up to our *mailing list* to receive special offers (including free entrance if you bring a friend), discount codes, and exhibition updates on our companion website[1]. Please fill in our *visitor experience feedback form* for the opportunity to win a year's unrestricted visiting. We also invite you to become a 'critical friend' of the 'Doing Academic Careers Differently Gallery' whereby we will place your portrait in the friends' section of the entrance hall in return for an annual contribution of your ideas and experiences. We depend on your patronage and support for the ongoing maintenance and development of this gallery.

We hope you have enjoyed your visit and will return regularly for inspiration, courage, and hope.

Note

1 www.academiadifferently.org.

References

By, R.T., Burnes, B., and Hughes, M. (Eds.) (2023). Organizational Change, Leadership and Ethics. 2nd Edition. London: Routledge.

Gaiman, N. (2018). *Art Matters: Because Your Imagination Can Change the World*. Illustrations by Chris Riddell. London: Headline Publishing Group.

Pine, E. (2019). *Notes to Self*. London: Penguin Random House.

Rodriguez-Pomeda, J., and Casani, F. (2022). 'The contemporary university: Some ontological and empirical aspects'. *TRAMES, A Journal of the Humanities and Social Sciences*, 26(3): 251–272.

INDEX

absent presence 369
absurd 238, 242, 257, 258
absurdism 258
absurdist philosophy 257
abuse 371
academic belonging 93
academic capitalism 375
academic care work 184; *see also* care work
academic conventions, challenging 223; *see also* challenging orthodoxy
academic despair 413
academic ecosystem 75, 146
academic entrepreneur 226
academic freedom 372, 404; *see also* freedom
academic ghosts 4, 370
academic house 120
academic identity 75, 305
academic integrity 391, 393
academic lives 224
academic of colour 94, 96
academic management 239
academic precariat 321
academic publishing 239
academic 'quit lit' 364; *see also* leaving academia
academic service 9, 14–15, 30, 334, 363
academic silos 133, 191, 232, 301
academic subjectification 190, 205–206
academic trajectory 226
academic/practitioner divide 298
academic/praxis relationship 304
accidental academic 201, 403
acme 67
activism/activist 110, 238, 248
adjunct 371, 384
adversity 230

air 76
alienating 240
alternative: paths in academia 133; spaces 384
ambivalence 306
anticolonial 252
antiracism 254; *see also* anti-racist
anti-racist 251; *see also* antiracism
anxiety 2, 238, 242; of mothers 338
apartheid 107, 380
arbitrariness of the tenure process 297
Argentina 138
The Argumentative Indian 370
art 214, 374
Art History 117
art of reflection 191, 210
artist 214, 376
arts-based: journal 217; methods 75
Asperger's syndrome 277
Australia, academia in 76
automation of academic work 163
Autonomist 385
autonomy 372, 415, 416

the back-door academic 120
Bakhtin, M. 339
de Beauvoir, S. 388
belonging 4; not 372
bereavement 416
bitterness 361
black early career academic 108
Black feminism 395
blossom 78
body 247, 249; work 206
Boje, D.M. 224
boundaries, pushing the 276; transgression of 237

Brahmanical 380
breath 86
burnout 143, 325
bushfire 77
Bushland 75
business 137; practice 139; practitioner 140
business school 117, 125, 137

calling 17
Camus, A. 239, 257, 258, 259, 262, 263
capitalism 393
care work 145, 165; undervaluation of 168; *see also* academic care work
career change 31
career portraits 224
career success, norms of 1, 298; challenging norms of 327; *see also* ideal academic; traditional successful academic; typical academic
career trade-offs 329, 334
career trajectory 1, 94
careering 49, 52; *see also* careerism and careerist
careerism 4, 49; *see also* careering and careerist
careerist 70; norms 73; *see* also careering and careerism
caring 70, 239
caste 378, 379
casualisation 371, 384
catharsis 396
challenging orthodoxy 20, 416; *see also* academic conventions
childcare: as a research expense 174; seen as women's responsibility 331, 342–343
civil servant 64
class 94, 117, 379
classism 250
Coalition S 271
collaboration 61; calamitous 151
collaborative work 61
collective 247
the collective academic 62, 94; model 61
collective narrative 102
collegiality 403
colonial 379
colonial influences 108
coloniality 251
commercialisation of academic life 417
common good 62
communitarian 128
communities of colour 96
community 126, 247; -centred creative approaches 130; engaged scholarship 99
competing goals and priorities 300
competition 288
concealment 393
conferences 23, 26–27, 32, 36, 40, 84, 89, 128, 138, 144, 149, 151–152, 271, 281, 313, 340–341, 354, 363

confrontation 192
connected biographies 61
connection(s) 154, 191, 200–221, 248; between disciplines 392
consultancy 32, 280, 303, 350
consumerism 417
contestation 238, 240–241
contradiction 111
conventional and unconventional careers 139
cooperation 50, 61
corporeal experience of doctoral studies 308
COVID-19 2, 27, 73, 77, 129, 144, 147, 155, 158, 160–165, 175, 189–191, 202, 219–223, 264, 314, 322, 327, 345, 409–410; lockdown 88, 213; positive effects of 345
creativity 13, 237, 238, 239, 281, 371, 372
criminal law 391
critical: research 206; scholar 206; work 208
critical academic career studies 1, 224
critical arts-based narrative inquiry 96
critical becoming 207
critical career studies 1
critical friends 419–420
Critical Management Studies 54, 261, 268, 392, 413
critique 208
cultivating the shadows 190

daredevil 228
dean 50, 52; deputy 52; not becoming a 30, 35
death 258, 369–371
deception 404
decolonisation 94
defiance, practice of 363
delight 419
depression 173, 220, 261–262, 322, 351, 359
de-professionalisation of academic work 163
descolonial 238, 248
descolonisation 249
despondency 403
dialogic thinking 100, 322, 339
dialogue 16, 50–51, 65, 70, 75, 96–103, 162, 250, 322, 339, 378, 383
different pedagogies 139
digital presence 1, 412
dilemmas 189
dislocation 94, 199, 219
disobedience 151, 372
disruption 70
distortions 190
diverse 1; academic orientation 392
diversity 74, 389
divorce, graduate school as a generator of 170; *see also* marriage/relationship breakdown
doctoral: experience 23, 348; studies 331, 358
doctoral students as second-careerers 304
dogma 260, 262

domination 108
Douglas, F. 107
doxa 298
ducks 61
dystopia 146

ecosystem 79, 51, 90, 148
edge effect 147
ego-death 383–384
elitist 197, 207, 362, 376, 398
emancipation 109, 112, 383, 390, 403
ethical design principles 146
ethicality 372, 391, 393
ethics 375; of care 144, 159, 165, 208
excellence 1, 49, 70; re-thinking 72
exclusionary 197
existentialism and existentialist philosophy 257–258
exploitation 288
external funding 198

façade 11, 25, 404
failure 58, 238–239, 370
fake news 272, 389
family support 331
fathers' role in raising children 344
fear 292
feelings 239–240, 247, 289, 291
femininity 371, 388
feminism 249, 251
feminist 238, 248; philosophy 388; spaces 163; voice 344
First Nation People 76
first-generation scholar 130, 134
flexible 23
flourish 75
foreigner, being a 161
fostering children 173
the Fourth Estate 267
France 138
fraud 391, 404
freedom 13, 107, 238, 372, 374, 383, 392, 415; of freelance work 398; *see also* academic freedom
freelance 370, 376, 391, 398
freewriting 416
friends, support from 170
full professor 18, 29, 35–36, 52, 67, 134, 153, 167, 174, 181
fun 24, 29, 36, 372
funding cuts 386

gardening 80
gaslighting 251
gender 388; gap 338; inequalities 364; roles expectations differing 331
ghostwriter and ghostwriting 371, 390–391
gift economy 417
gig academy 324

global career paths 137
Global South 251, 374
globalisation 374
grassroot organising 243
graveyard of disappointed hope 372, 409, 413, 414

H index 1, 260, 269–270
hall of mirrors 189
handicap 330
happiness 263
head-hunters 53
heresy, risk of 298
heterodox path 64
Hindu/Hinduism 378
historical reflexivity 212
home, reconfiguration of 158
hope 238
humane 239
Hungary 329
hustling 324
hybrid careers 311
hypocrisy 194

ideal academic 70, 90, 326; *see also* career success; traditional successful academic; typical academic
identities, multiple 167
identity 277, 408; insecurity 410; threat 409; work 206
illegality 391
illness 70, 84, 170; mental 261; *see also* long-term, multiple sclerosis
impact 117, 266, 270–273
imported academic 137
imposter syndrome 199
inadequacy 401; feelings of 177
incidental academic 137
inclusive 1
independent: researcher 362, 370, 376, 383; scholar 323
indigenous 253
industry connections 308
ingenuous 128
injury 309
injustice 1, 251
innovation 13
insecurity 2, 197, 397
inspiration to others 191
institutional normality 196
institutional support, lack of 363
integrity 93
intellectual excellence 113
intellectual playground 409
intelligent disobedience 418
intrepidness 93
introversion 277
introvert 383
invisibility 397–399

invisible, longing to be 163
invisible labour 179
Islamophobia 395
isomorphism 137

Jefferson, T. 133
journal, impact factor 271; publishing 266, 384; ranking 385
joy 371
Junior Scholars of Color (JSOC) 96–97

Kierkegaard, S. 257, 258, 263, 387
kindness 173, 327, 359–360

labour of love 383
Lacanian 'Other' 314
Laclau, E. 268
later entry academic 95, 297, 300, 303, 313
Latin America 138
leadership 58; responsible 138
leaky pipeline phenomenon 333
learning 19, 29
leaving academia 239, 370, 408–409, 417–418; see also academic 'quit lit'
legality 371
Lewin, K. 268, 273
liberal arts college 125
light 76
liminal space 148, 306, 313
linearity 1
literature 374
loneliness 159, 238, 243, 404
long-term: condition 348; illness 322; see also illness; multiple sclerosis
love 419; of nature 412

making a difference 54
male-dominated campus 169; see also masculine university
managerialism 2, 10, 149, 327
manifold struggles (or writing) 191
marginalisation 99, 108–109, 253, 419
marketization 375
marriage/relationship breakdown 170, 330, 350; see also divorce
masculine university 163; see also male-dominated campus
masculinist norms 339
Maslow E. 270; pyramid of 270, 273
mass qualification 403
maternity leave 71
meandering 4, 10, 13, 38
meaning: of life 257–259; of work 385
media 239, 247–248; news 266, 270, 272; social 269–270
mental: breakdown 79; health 264, 358, 372, 404; illness 261
metaphors 2, 75, 146

metrics see performance
Mexico 224
micro-practices of writing and reflection 224–225
mid-career 50, 70
middle management 55
migrant 249; activism 249
migration 249
minoritization 99
mirror 189, 224
mirroring 190
the mirrored academic 192
misfit 196, 276, 277, 418
motherhood 135, 167, 322, 330, 338; penalty 331
mothers, societal disdain for 168
Mouffe, C. 268
multi-disciplinarity 392
multiple sclerosis 348; see also illness; long-term

naïve, being 358
narrow 23
Nature, benefits of 143
navigating 81; academia 93, 130
navigation 74, 93
negated bodies 308
negotiation of self 118
neoliberal 1; academia 393; academy 224; society 61; university 49, 61
neoliberalism 55, 374, 390
New Higher Education 1
new materialist methodologies 390
Nicaragua 122
niche 24, 40
Nietzsche, F. 257–259
nomad 10; -ic 376; -ism 20, 380
non-academic jobs 363
non-collaboration 371, 385
non-disclosure agreements 410
non-English speaking contexts 333
non-survival 370
non-tenure-track 362
normative pressures 50
normativity 1
nurturing 1, 51, 75

obsessiveness 351
online learning 385
open access 239, 266, 270, 271
openness 237, 283
oppression 108, 248
organisational change failure 414
orthodoxies 1
outsider(s) 20, 196, 374

pain 238, 246, 370
pandemic see COVID-19
parenthood 88, 144, 322, 341, 344, 370
parrhesia 50, 62, 66
partnerships 61

part-time work 74, 172, 345; benefits of doing 155
passion 40, 374, 389, 414, 416
passionate critical research 384
patriarchy 250, 393; and guilt 342; overcoming 322
paywalls 269, 271, 364
performance: measurement 1; metrics 57, 86, 149, 152, 165, 304, 308, 326, 335, 384, 408, 415
performance management 1; universalist approach to 330; unrecognised dimensions of 335
performing arts 23–40
permaculture 143
permanent lectureship 130; *see also* tenure
perpetuating dominant norms 192
personal challenge 55
plus zone challenge 232
Poetic academic 219
poetry 222, 241, 245
poetry as therapy 359
political activity 228
political statement, making a 144
politics 55
polyvocal narrative 98
postcolonial 251
postmodern 230
post-socialist context 329
poverty, stress of 167
power 112, 180, 248, 388; relations 1
precarious identity 190
precariousness of freelancing 397
precarity 4, 321, 370; of early career 324
productivity, obstacles to 331
profane illumination 194
professional development 372, 404
professional trajectories 61
promotion, turning down 153
protest 249, 252
psychoanalytic lens 34, 213, 314
public intellectuals 378
public value 267
publications, low count of 181
publish or perish 40, 69, 266, 385
publishing 266, 384, 412
putting the body 251

racial: discourse 97; hierarchy 96
racialisation 99
racism 395
racist 250
radical 237, 241, 371; collectives 384
radicalism 237, 384
real world experience 308
rebel 370, 375
redundancy 410
reflection 86, 189, 210
reflexive 4; academic 210; journal 191, 210; methodology 350

rejection 266, 276
relationship: -building 98; maintaining 144
research 9, 23, 29, 40, 239, 260, 266, 268, 270, 371, 385, 396, 404
Research Excellence Framework (REF) 117, 270
research profiles 1
research-intensive universities 327
resilience 69, 204, 419
resistance 49, 110, 233, 247, 384; studying as an act of 169
resurrection 370
revolt 247
rhythm 11, 20

sadness 372
Sartre, J.P. 257–258
saying 'no' 149
scatter-gun researcher 199
second careers/second careering/second careerers 4, 298, 303, 372
seduction 360; of academia 314
self-alienation 240
self-care 165, 419
self-deception 325
self-employment 391
self-made academic 95, 137
self-portrait 210
self-publishing 372, 412, 413
self-regulation 147
Seneca 262
senior manager 50
service *see* academic service
sexism 168, 388, 395; systemic 202
shadow economy 369
shapeshifting 406
shards 190, 197
single parenthood 167, 332
Sisyphus 259; happy 259, 262, 265
slavery 107
slow 9, 239, 372; journalism 272; scholarship 403
social activism 191; and academic activism 225
social change 238, 249
social commitment 225, 233
social interests 69
social justice 238, 248
social movement 249
social solidarity 225
sociology 71, 135, 169, 172, 371, 377, 383
soil 76
Spain 61
starting a new job 352
storytelling 97
stress 24, 52, 93, 143, 146, 149, 167, 196, 207, 239, 264, 355, 357
struggle 94
subtle hierarchies 297
success *see* career success
suffering 238, 262

suicide 258, 259, 261–264, 380
surprised academic 133
survival 370
surviving 361
Sussex Writes 129
sustainability, teaching and researching 335
sustainable: academic lives 159; lifestyles 146

teaching 9, 29, 40, 239, 261, 268, 289, 292, 371, 385, 389; as a burden 183
teaching-focussed universities 327
team action 61
teamwork 61
technology: invasion 161; possibilities offered by 345; as tool of surveillance 159
tenacious 225
tensions 80, 111, 189, 321; and contradictions 417
tenure 18, 50, 54, 61–64, 71, 120, 133, 147, 153, 170–172, 181–183, 230, 260, 271, 297, 305, 323, 362; clock 301–302; *see also* permanent lectureship
testimonios 99
thinking differently 211
third mission 66
time 10, 20, 416, 419
time rigidity 170
toxic: academia 323; masculinity of academia 163, 169; performance pressures 208; work environment 192
trade-offs 322
traditional family discourse 332
traditional successful academic 134; *see also* career success; ideal academic; typical academic
traitor 116
trauma 18, 105, 109, 144, 168, 173–174, 241, 250, 277, 280, 348, 354, 374, 390, 395, 419

Twitter 269; -verse 221
typical academic 330; *see also* career success; ideal academic; traditional successful academic

UK 70, 116
unemployment 371, 380, 384
university management 62
unpublished 372
unwaged 372; academic 403
unwritten rules 203
uprising 247
uprooting oneself 354
USA 224

Valenzuela, M. 224
value-driven 94
veil/unveil 194
violence 238, 248, 250, 376; of academia 96
virtues 113
vocation 51, 68, 374, 417
voluntary redundancy 372, 383, 409
vulnerability 134; to judgement 302

water 76
Western philosophy 388
whiteness 97
women: overburdened by care work 364; under-representation of 167, 333
wonder 419
working conditions 398
working mothers 338
working-class 398; academic 116
work-life balance 55, 79
writing 181–183, 404; advice 181; differently 221, 347; work 207

yield, obtaining a 147